THE 1986 BOSTON RED SOX

THERE WAS MORE THAN GAME SIX

Edited by Bill Nowlin and Leslie Heaphy

Associate editors—Greg Erion, James Forr, Len Levin, and Carl Riechers

Society for American Baseball Research, Inc.
Phoenix, AZ

The 1986 Boston Red Sox: There Was More Than Game Six
Edited by Bill Nowlin and Leslie Heaphy
Associate editors—Greg Erion, James Forr, Len Levin, and Carl Riechers

ISBN 978-1-943816-19-4
Ebook ISBN 978-1-943816-18-7

Cover and book design: Gilly Rosenthol
Cover photograph and materials courtesy of Bob Brady.

All photographs courtesy of the National Baseball Hall of Fame, with the exception of the following:

Courtesy of the Boston Red Sox: 63, 159, 206, 226, 263, 271, 278, 289, 311, 389.
Courtesy of Bob Brady: frontispiece, 322, 340, 361, 366, 367.

Society for American Baseball Research
Cronkite School at ASU
555 N. Central Ave. #416
Phoenix, AZ 85004
Phone: (602) 496-1460
Web: www.sabr.org
Facebook: Society for American Baseball Research
Twitter: @SABR

TABLE OF CONTENTS

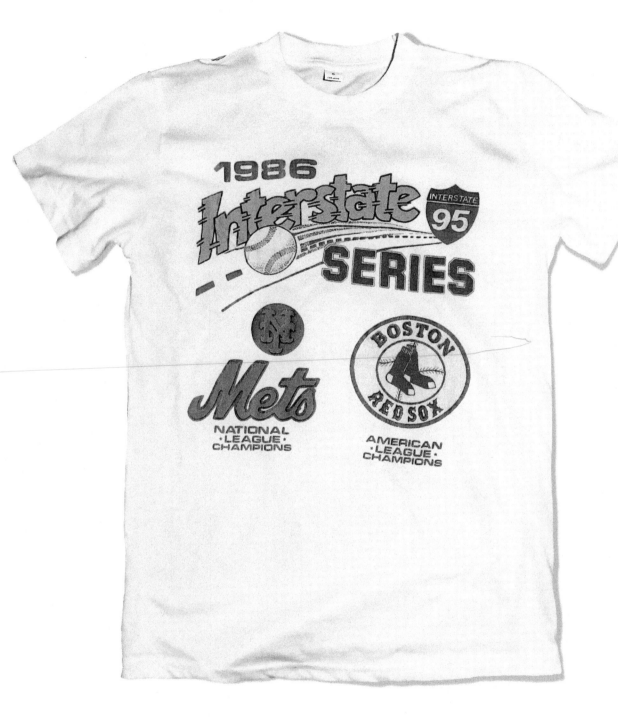

Courtesy of Bob Brady.

INTRODUCTION

A LIFELONG METS FAN AND A LIFELONG Red Sox fan were talking at a SABR board meeting. Leslie Heaphy (the Mets fan) mentioned to Bill Nowlin (the Sox fan) the idea of a book on the 1986 Mets. Bill responded that Mark Armour, the head of BioProject, had been pushing him to do a 1986 Red Sox book sometime. "But they lost!" Bill said to Mark. "And that's too recent." "Wait a minute," he said to Leslie. "It's been nearly 30 years. OK, let's do a combined book." Leslie responded, "That could be fun, putting the two teams together again." Thus, the germination of this book.

The goal was to create a book that would draw upon people's memories of that classic World Series but also challenge those recollections. When we think of 1986, Bill Buckner and Mookie Wilson first come to mind but there is so much more to that season than that. How did each respective team find their way into the Series? What were the various ups and downs each team faced to set up that final confrontation?

As with many of the books published by the Society of American Baseball Research, this was a true collaborative effort. We may have set a record with this one—there are 74 different SABR members who contributed to making this book a reality. In fact, we also had so much material that we ran past the page limit for one volume through the Print on Demand service we use – so we decided to print two companion books.

If you're reading the 1986 Mets book, be advised that there is a companion 1986 Red Sox book. If you're reading the 1986 Red Sox book, be advised that there is a companion 1986 Mets book.

Greg Erion, James Forr, and Russ Lake did all the fact-checking. Veteran copy editor Len Levin put the final touches on the more than 100 items which make up these two volumes.

It was quite a Series, with each team losing the first two games at home, first the Mets at Shea and then the Red Sox at Fenway. After four games, it was 2-2 and no team had won at home. Then the Red Sox won Game Five at Fenway, and were one game away from winning their first World Championship in 86 years. It came to the point they were one pitch away from baseball Nirvana.

And then....

Just about everyone knows what happened, but there are takes on it here you might not have read elsewhere. Mostly, this is the story of each of the players, coaches, managers, and broadcasters, their lives in baseball and the way the 1986 season fit into their lives.

As between the teams, things have balanced themselves out since 1986. The Mets returned twice more to the World Series, but came up short both times. The Red Sox have fared better. In baseball, things do sometimes seem to even out. But don't tell that to any Chicago Cubs or Cleveland Indians fan.

TONY ARMAS

By Augusto Cárdenas

IN THE 2015 SEASON, MIGUEL CABRERA SUR-passed Andres Galarraga as the Venezuelan with the most home runs in the major leagues. His 400th home run, on May 16 at St. Louis, gave to the Detroit Tigers first baseman a record that had been held by the "Big Cat" since 1997, when he eclipsed the record of the first great Venezuelan slugger, Antonio Rafael Armas Machado.

Tony Armas was born on July 2, 1953, in Puerto Piritu, Anzoátegui state, a town in eastern Venezuela, 235 kilometers (about 150 miles) from Caracas. His father, Jose Rafael Armas, was an electrician, while his mother, Julieta Machado de Armas, was engaged in house-hold chores, taking care at home Antonio and his 12 brothers.

"My parents were able to keep me on track," Armas said. "We were a very poor family, and lived on what was achieved. My dad was a farmer too."

In a place having beautiful beaches, the Armas family also had land that they worked. "We used to plant all kinds of beans, all kinds of fruits. We were poor and planted all kinds of fruit for the sustenance of the house," Armas said. "As the oldest I was the one who was in charge of that, to load sacks of corn, pumpkin, watermelon, everything that was harvested. I think my strength came from there."

There was no Little League or the Criollitos of Venezuela in those days, no organized movements that help children and young people today to start polishing their skills. Armas began to imitate his idols playing baseball in the street with older people in his neighborhood.

"There were no baseball schools, no little-league base-ball. You become a baseball player through hard work," he said. "I played *caimaneras* (baseball in the street) with adults, as everyone did in those days. I played since I was a boy, since I was in school. It is not like today, when children are born with a uniform. Right now they have coaches, all benefits that a little boy may have from birth until (he) reaches his youth. At that time, no, at that time you had to make yourself as a player."

At 17, Tony played for the first time on a team in an organized league, Deportivo Pachaquito, and began to develop his skills on defense.

"I ended up not playing the tournament," he recalled. "I started the championship, but didn't finish it, because there was a National Youth Championship, to be played in Cumaná city and as I was 17, I was called from the Double A to the youth team to go play."

Armas had an outstanding performance, starring as his team won the Anzoátegui state title. He was called to the national team to play for the World Youth Championship in Maracaibo. That was where he caught

the attention of the former major leaguer Pompeyo "Yo-Yo" Davalillo, a scout for the Pittsburgh Pirates.

Davalillo, brother of the former All-Star Vic Davalillo, played in the majors in 1953 with the Washington Senators, but a broken leg shortened his career and he devoted his life to trying to recruit players from Venezuela to play in the United States.

"Pompeyo Davalillo had checked me in both the national junior and youth world championships. I also went to a worldwide Double-A championship, in Cartagena, Colombia. I didn't have much chance to play, because I was very young and we had players who were better prepared than me at that time. I did not play, but I had a pretty good time. I kept playing and in 1971 Pompeyo Davalillo arrived at my house, talked to me, said he thought I could make it to the majors, that I could go far in baseball. He spoke with my parents and that's how I started my career."

On January 18, 1971, Armas signed as a free agent with the Pittsburgh Pirates for $5,000. At the same time he signed for 30,000 bolivars to play Venezuelan winter ball with the Caracas Lions, a club that had previously featured two of his idols, Vic Davalillo and Cesar Tovar. Tovar played in the majors from 1965 to 1976 with the Twins, A's, Rangers, Phillies, and Yankees, with a lifetime average of .278; Davalillo batted .279 between 1963 and 1980 with the Indians, Angels, Cardinals, Pirates, Dodgers, and Athletics.

"I was a fan of Caracas and my favorite players were Cesar Tovar and Vic Davalillo. I also admired Joe Ferguson, a power hitter who came as a foreign player." Ferguson, who played 14 seasons in the majors with Dodgers, Cardinals, Astros, and Angels, played with the Lions in Armas's rookie year in Venezuela and batted .294 with 15 homers and 51 RBIs, an inspiration for the young prospect.

"I think they signed me because I was a good outfielder. I was not a good hitter," he said. "You learn to hit with constant work."

Pittsburgh assigned Armas to play with Monroe and with Bradenton in 1971, dividing his time between rookie ball and Class A, where he combined for a .230 batting average; it was clear he had to work harder to improve his offense.

"I was a good outfielder and I realized I had to work twice (as hard as) the Americans to keep my job. That's the way it was at that time, not like now, when someone comes to the majors with a lot of money and have to call you up. Plus there are more teams now. That is the reality of my career."

In 1972 Armas batted .266 with 9 homers and 51 RBIs in Class-A Gastonia, and in 1973 he got the opportunity to play at Double A in an unusual way, after being a batboy for almost two weeks.

"Not that I was happy with what they were doing, but actually they had a lot of players in spring training. There were about 80 players in camp and on the field there were nine. I had no chance to play," he said. "The manager of Class A needed a batboy and from among those 80 players they called my name. So I spent a week doing that. It bothered me a little bit, because I didn't go up there to collect bats. I went to earn a spot. There was a Mexican named Mario Mendoza who helped me a lot; what I did was thanks to him, because I told him I wanted to go home, I was not up there to collect bats. He told me to stay calm, that I was being observed to see what kind of character I had, whether I was spoiled. I followed his advice and stayed. The next week was all the same. We arrived on Monday and started the game the same, 'Armas, you're the batboy.' It turns out that on Wednesday, in a game between Double A and Triple A, the Double-A center fielder got injured. The manager shouted that they needed an outfielder and then he said, 'Armas, get in there.' I went in, and I stayed."

His bat began to speak for him with Sherbrooke in the Double-A Eastern League; he hit .301 with 11 homers and 45 RBIs in 84 games, despite suffering a broken arm that had him away from action several days.

The young prospect continued his rise in the organization and, after another season in Double A in 1974, he was promoted to the Charleston (West Virginia)

Charlies (Triple A) in 1975. With Charleston again the next season he showed some power, hitting 21 homers, and earned a call-up to the Pirates. Armas debuted on September 6, 1976, against the Philadelphia Phillies at Three Rivers Stadium. He replaced Richie Zisk in left field in the ninth inning. He played in four games during his call-up. On October 3, in the last game of the season (the second game of a doubleheader), Armas got his first start, in the lineup as the center fielder and batting sixth. He got his first major-league hit off Pete Falcone of the St. Louis Cardinals, a single to center field to lead off the bottom of the fifth.

Falcone was locked in a pitching duel with Jerry Reuss, and the game went into the bottom of the ninth scoreless. Armas came up with a runner on second base and two outs in the bottom of the ninth and singled to right field to give the Pirates a 1-0 walk-off victory to end the season.

Still, Armas faced trying to break in to an outfield populated by Al Oliver, Omar Moreno, and Dave Parker.

"I had no chance to play, because the Pirates had many good players," he said. "At the time I was in that organization was (Roberto) Clemente, Al Oliver, Willie Stargell, Dave Parker, Richie Zisk, and I had no opportunity to climb. In 1977 (I was out of options), so they had to keep me on the roster or trade me. At the last minute, they traded me to the A's. It was there that I got the chance to show my full potential."

Armas was sent to Oakland on March 15, 1977, along with pitchers Dave Giusti, Doc Medich, Doug Bair, and Rick Langford, and outfielder Mitchell Page, for pitcher Chris Batton and infielders Tommy Helms and Phil Garner.

Oakland, a rebuilding team, relied on the talents of Armas, who hit 13 homers and drove in 53 runs in 118 games. The next two seasons, he played in only 171 games because of injuries.

"In Oakland I obviously had to work hard, because no Latin at that time had a safety spot in the big leagues," he said. "Thanks to Oakland I received the opportunity to play every day and I was able to prove myself."

In 1980 Armas was healthy and able to deploy his strength to become one of the most feared sluggers in the American League. That year he hit 35 homers and drove in 109 runs, with a respectable .279 average.

The following year, in a strike-shortened season, Armas tied three other players for the American League lead in home runs with 22. (The others were Dwight Evans, Eddie Murray, and Bobby Grich. Armas drove in 76 runs, took part in his first All-Star Game, and finished fourth in the voting for the MVP award. He was chosen by *The Sporting News* as the Player of the Year.

Thanks to Armas and Rickey Henderson, the Athletics advanced to the playoffs and swept the Kansas City Royals in the Division Series. Armas was 6-for-11 with two doubles and three RBIs. His bat cooled off in the ALCS against the New York Yankees (2-for-12 with five strikeouts); Oakland was eliminated in three games.

Armas's power caught the attention of the Boston Red Sox. He hit 28 homers for the A's in 1982 and set an AL record for the most putouts in a game by a right fielder (11, on June 12 against the Toronto Blue Jays). After the season the Red Sox acquired Armas and catcher Jeff Newman in exchange for third baseman Carney Lansford, outfielder Garry Hancock, and Jerry King.

"They wanted a player who would protect Jim Rice and they made the deal," said Armas, who was surprised by his departure from Oakland. For Boston, Armas played center field, although he wasn't a particularly fast fielder, but with Rice and Dwight Evans he helped form one of the most powerful outfields in Red Sox history.

"It was a good team," Armas said. He hit a career-high 36 homers, with 107 RBIs, topping 100 for the second time in his career, finishing with 107. Rice led the club with 39 homers and 126 RBIs, but Evans fell short with 22 homers and 58 RBIs, playing only 126 games in the final season of future Hall of Famer Carl Yastrzemski.

"It was a real experience to play with a superstar like Carl Yastrzemski was," Armas said. "I met Ted

Williams in spring training and it was a great experience to meet those two legends."

Despite his power, Armas heard some boos from Red Sox fans because of his anemic .218 average and 131 strikeouts in 145 games. "At that time, Latinos and black people were not beloved in Boston. I came to Boston and they started to boo me. I spoke with my lawyer and told him to get them to trade me. I didn't want to play in Boston anymore. There was a pressure in playing for that team. They talked with me and said, 'Hey, you came over here to help Jim Rice and Dwight Evans.' 'Yes, but I can't, this way. It is very difficult to play like this.' At that time it was different from the way it would be now—if I had been signed to a $120 million contract, I wouldn't have cared if they shouted at me and booed me. But at that time you had to earn your place and play hard."

A year later the Venezuelan, led by his power, changed those boos into ovations. Injury-free, Armas played 157 of the team's 162 games and home runs steadily found their way into the stands. He finished as the American League leader in both home runs and RBIs (43 and 123). He dominated the circuit with 77 extra-base hits and 339 total bases.

"You never have those goals. Your goal is having a good year, but I never thought I would be the home-run king or the RBI champion when there were many superstars in the majors—Reggie Jackson, Jim Rice, Dave Kingman, Lance Parrish, Dwight Evans, many good players. That I could compete with these superstars made me proud, and that year, thank God, I was able to play an almost full season."

Armas's remarkable season earned him his second All-Star Game and his only Silver Slugger Award, and he placed seventh in the MVP voting.

Injuries cropped up again in 1985 and Armas was limited to 103 games; his production declined sharply to 23 homers and 64 RBIs.

In 1986 Armas got into 121 games as the Red Sox advanced to their first World Series since 1975. And if the defeat in 1975 was painful, after the famous Carlton

Fisk homer in Game Six forced a deciding seventh game, the loss to the New York Mets was even worse.

"These were frustrating days for me," admitted Armas, who was the greatest home-run hitter in the American League from 1980 through 1985, with 187 round-trippers, but he hit only 11 in 1986. "In the ALCS I hurt and I couldn't play anymore, because my right ankle was swollen."

If Armas's home runs had seemed to become a constant in Boston, so had injuries. During his career he spent 12 stints on the disabled list, but no injury was as painful as the one in the fifth game of the ALCS against the California Angels at Anaheim Stadium.

In the second inning, Armas chased down a long fly ball hit by Doug DeCinces. "Many of my leg injuries were from running, but the one in the ankle was because I was hooked in the center-field fence," he recalled. "Now they are cushioned but back then, the walls were all concrete." Dave Henderson took over for Armas for the rest of the playoffs. Henderson had an immediate impact.

"I tried to play, but I couldn't anymore," Armas said. "And that's when Dave Henderson replaced me and he did a good job." Henderson's ninth-inning homer in Game Five against Anaheim spared the Red Sox a loss, and he drove in the winning run with a sacrifice fly in the 11th. Though Armas's ankle improved, Henderson made the most of his opportunity; Armas was sentenced to the bench.

In the World Series, Armas was limited to one pinch-hitting appearance in Game Seven, after 15 days without playing.

"The ankle still bothered me, but I could pinch-hit. I could not run at 100 percent," he recalled. "It was difficult, but I had a strong desire to appear in the World Series. Even if it was just an at-bat, it doesn't matter, and I appeared in the World Series, which is what anyone wants."

Armas pinch-hit for pitcher Bruce Hurst in the seventh inning with the game tied 3-3. The Venezuelan struck out swinging in what it was his last at-bat in a Red Sox uniform.

About Game Six, he was philosophical. "What happened is what happens so often in baseball. We were winning an easy game. At the end we felt champions but Bill Buckner's error left us without the victory. Then we lost the World Series," said Armas. "We lost by an error that cost us the Series. These are things that happen in baseball."

"The pitching also faltered. Roger Clemens couldn't do the job, Dennis Boyd couldn't do the job, many players didn't do the job," he said. "For me it was frustrating because I was playing every day, but then I couldn't help the team in the World Series because of an injured ankle. That's not easy for any baseball player."

After the season Armas became a free agent and, a likely victim of collusion, signed with the Angels but not until July 1, 1987. "The team owners got together and agreed to not sign free agents that year and I was one of those affected," he recalled. "I had offers from Mexico, but spent all that time practicing in Caracas with Pompeyo Davalillo, who was working with the Angels at the time. That's where I signed."

After so much downtime, Armas was sent to Triple A for the first time in more than a decade. He played in 29 games for Edmonton before returning to the majors for the last month and a half of the season. He batted .198 in 28 games.

Armas's days as a regular came to an end in California, where he was used primarily against left-handed pitchers by manager Cookie Rojas, with whom he had a difficult relationship in 1988. "I started to play against left-handed pitchers and that was hard," he said. "There was a time when I began to play every day and in a week I hit like five homers—but that's when I had the mishap with Cookie Rojas."

"One day we went to Oakland to play and Chili Davis, who was the regular, did not want to play; people were booing him, because he'd played the year before with San Francisco. Oakland was going to start Dave Stewart and they said I was not going to play because I was playing against lefties only. Then I got a chance to start playing against some righties, and I hit two home runs in that game (August 14). Rojas didn't put me to play anymore and there came all the controversy with the journalists, saying that if I was hitting well, why I did not play. He said it was because he was the manager, and I told them to talk to the manager, that if they did not play me, it was a matter of him."

From July 28 to August 14, Armas hit .440 with 4 homers and 12 RBIs over a 16-game stretch, including 11 starts, so some sportswriters suggested more playing time for the Venezuelan, even against righties.

"There was this controversy with journalists and Cookie Rojas blamed me because I spoke with the press. Once a newspaper did an article and it was sent to him in Boston and I was called to his office and he asked me why I had told the newspapers that I wasn't playing. 'Look, Cookie, I haven't talked to the press in a long time. They just are realizing what you're doing to me.' 'So you want to play?' And I got to play against Roger Clemens in Boston. I said, 'Cookie, if you think you're going to intimidate me because it is Roger Clemens, you're wrong. If he was going to give me four strikeouts, I'll get four strikeouts. If I'm going to hit him, I'll hit him.'"

And Armas homered against Clemens (two days earlier he had hit one off Bruce Hurst), and then he hit another the next day, on his return to California, against the Yankees. It was Armas's most explosive month of the year and his last major production in the majors: .386 with 8 homers and 19 RBIs in 24 games in August. Nevertheless, his differences with Rojas continued.

"It came out another article in California, after he took me out in a game for a pinch-hitter, even when I had a hit and a home run. I showered and went to the hotel. I did not talk to any journalist. When we got to California he called me to his office, and we hadn't an argument, because I'm not used to that, but he said why I had talked again to the press. 'No, no. I have not spoken to the press.' But they were already realizing who he was."

The relationship ended on September 24, when Rojas was fired as the manager of the Angels. Armas returned to the Angels the following year, his last in the major leagues.

"My third year in California was in the same role, as a pinch-hitter and playing against lefties, and because my knee was bothering me and I couldn't take it anymore, I retired. I could have played for three more years, but unfortunately the knees did not allow it."

Armas remained active in the Venezuelan Winter League, where he was already a legend for his power. He was the first Venezuelan to lead the majors in homers and RBIs, but his 251 career home runs led all Venezuelans. He was also the home-run king in Venezuelan winter ball, after hitting his 97th home run in the last at-bat of his career in the 1991-1992 season. (His mark was surpassed by Robert Perez in 2008.)

Armas played a few more seasons in Venezuela, but the knee hampered him badly and he'd have to take off a week now and again. "I thought it was better to retire than continue to suffer, but I thank God for giving me the opportunity to get where I got. Thanks to baseball I am who I am."

The home run was always Armas's calling card; it also happened to be his farewell letter. He was an investor in the Caribes de Oriente club and he was able to fulfill another dream there, playing with his brothers Marcos and Julio, all three taking up positions as outfielders.

"That was a great thing," Armas said. "It's never been written in any book. I was with the right team on the right day."

Both brothers followed in the footsteps of his older brother, but only Marcos managed to make the majors, with the Athletics for a brief period in 1993.

Tony and his wife, Luisa de Armas, had six children. The third was their son Tony Armas Jr., who played 10 major-league seasons with the Expos, Nationals, Pirates, and Mets, between 1999 and 2008.

"I have much to thank my dad for. Since my childhood he always took me to the stadiums. When you are a child you are like a sponge, absorbing all the information and always trying to imitate someone," said Armas Jr. "When I decided to play baseball, he said to me, 'I was a hitter, but if you don't want to be a hitter, don't do it.' He told me, 'Son, do what you want to do. I support you.' That was important. My parents, at that time, supported me the most."

After he stopped playing, Armas remained active in baseball, mainly in winter ball, as coach of the Caracas Lions. Tony Armas Jr. also played with the Lions. "That was special," said Armas Jr. "It was one of the most special times. I grew up in the Caracas stadium of Caracas, because he always took me there when he played. He felt the same way."

In 1998 Armas was inducted into the Caribbean Baseball Hall of Fame, thanks to his all-time home-run leadership in the Caribbean Series, with 11. In 2005 he was inducted into the Venezuelan Baseball Hall of Fame and in 2013 into the Latino Baseball Hall of Fame. In 2009 Armas was the hitting coach for the Venezuelan team in the World Baseball Classic, working next to Andres Galarraga, who eclipsed all his home-run records in the majors. (In 1996 Galarraga hit 47 homers and drove in 150 runs with the Colorado Rockies to set the single-season marks for a Venezuelan.)

"Tony was a role model for all the boys that had power," Galarraga said. "I was fortunate to sign with the Lions and privileged to play with him in Venezuela. He taught me many things, gave me some batting tips and that kind of thing."

"I always knew that many good players would follow, because in Venezuela we had many academies and we had many players out there," said Armas. "After Galarraga came Bob Abreu, who was a complete player, Magglio Ordonez, and now Miguel Cabrera, who is even more complete. There is always someone who opens the doors."

And Armas, 62 in 2015, continued to share his knowledge with the younger generation in Venezuela, as a coach of Leones del Caracas (the Caracas Lions) in winter ball. "He loves to teach, because baseball is his life," said Armas Jr. That's never going to change with him. He ends a winter season and during the break goes directly to become a manager in the Bolivarian League with Deportivo Anzoátegui. He is always working with the boys and never stops. He's always traveling; he is never in one place. That is what he likes to do."

"Baseball has given me a lot. Now I'm giving to baseball, trying to help young people," said Armas, who still lives in his native Puerto Píritu. "I am very proud of my career, proud of baseball, and proud of what I do right now, because in my time there were no hitting coaches and I'm proud to work with so many young boys to help them become better players."

SOURCES

Author interviews with Tony Armas on November 12, 2014, and August 5, 2015. All quotations attributed to Armas come from these interviews.

Author interview with Andrés Galarraga on July 30, 2015. All quotations attributed to Galarraga come from this interview.

Author interview with Tony Armas Jr. on July, 28, 2015. All quotations attributed to Armas Jr. come from this interview.

articles.latimes.com/1987-08-19/sports/sp-773_1_tony-armas

articles.latimes.com/1988-08-25/sports/sp-1345_1_tony-armas

articles.latimes.com/1988-09-01/sports/sp-4439_1_home-run

articles.latimes.com/1988-09-24/sports/sp-2381_1_interim-manager

el-nacional.com/deportes/lvbp/Antonio-Armas-puesto-acepte-recogebates_0_289171243.html

vidaydeportes.com/entrevista-exclusiva-antonio-armas

Cárdenas, Augusto. "El jonronero de Venezuela," *Diario Panorama,* December 18, 2005.

Cárdenas Lares, Carlos Daniel. *Venezolanos en las Grandes Ligas* (Fundación Cárdenas Lares, 1994).

MARTY BARRETT

By Mark Kanter

1986 – A SEASON THAT TUGS AT THE HEART-strings of every Boston Red Sox fan who watched and listened to the American League Championship Series and the World Series. The World Series was a classic seven-game affair. If the Red Sox had kept a two-run lead going with two outs in the bottom of the 10th inning against the Mets at Shea Stadium in Game Six, Marty Barrett would have been the MVP of that game as voted by the NBC announcers. In the Series he had a .433 batting average, in 30 at-bats, and an on-base percentage of .514. Now, as Paul Harvey would say: The Rest of the Story.

Marty Barrett was born on June 23, 1958, in Arcadia, California, a Los Angeles suburb, one of seven children of Charlotte and Randy Barrett. Of his five brothers, four played college or professional baseball: Charlie (born in 1955) played in the Los Angeles Dodgers farm system; Tommy (1960) played with the Phillies and Red Sox; Joe (1964) played at the University of Nevada Las Vegas; Andy (1966) played at Mesa (Arizona) Community College. John, born in 1954, did not play in college or the pros. Their sister, Susie (born in 1962) was a cheerleader.

Randy Barrett, who was a firefighter, moved the family to Las Vegas to find work when Marty was very young. Marty would play "ball" in the living room with his two older brothers and his brother Tommy. When Marty was 10 years old, he was playing on a 10-11-year-old team, and continued to play, often with boys a year or two older. By the time he was 15, he was playing on the Rancho High School varsity team, which won the state championship in 1974 and 1976. On the Rancho American Legion team, his coach was Manny Guerra, a longtime scout for the St. Louis Cardinals. Nine of his players made it to professional baseball, including Marty and Tommy, Mike Maddux, and Mike Morgan.[1]

Undrafted out of high school, Marty Barrett enrolled at Mesa Junior College, where he played baseball from 1976 to 1978. In 1979 he attended Arizona State University, where among his teammates was future major leaguer Hubie Brooks. During his college years, he played for Rod Dedeaux, the legendary coach of the University of Southern California, in a baseball tour of Japan. He also played summer ball in Anchorage, Alaska, with future major leaguers Tim Wallach and Mike Boddicker.

Barrett was selected by the Red Sox as the first pick of the first round of the now defunct secondary draft in June 1979. Red Sox scout Ray Boone is credited with the signing.[2] Barrett's first minor-league stop was at Winter Haven in the Class-A Florida State League in 1979, hitting .298 with a .719 OPS. The next season at Double-A Bristol, he batted .274 with a .677 OPS, and stole 22 bases.

In 1981 Barrett moved up to the Triple-A Pawtucket Red Sox, where he hit a home run in his first at-bat. The team, managed by Joe Morgan, included a number of players who went on to star in the majors — Wade Boggs, Rich Gedman, Bruce Hurst, and Bobby Ojeda.

Early in his time in Pawtucket, Barrett participated in the longest game in the annals of Organized Baseball. It began on April 18, 1981. The night was cold in Pawtucket, a 12-to-20-degree chill factor as the game wore on, and to keep warm players started fires in trash cans. Pawtucket trailed 1-0 in the bottom of the ninth inning, but tied the score on a sacrifice fly by Russ Laribee. Barrett remembered the Rochester relief pitcher throwing nine no-hit innings and the umpires having difficulty reaching the league president. (The Rochester pitcher, Jim Umbarger, actually pitched 10 no-run innings, the 23rd through the 32nd, giving up four hits.) Barrett had two hits in 12 at-bats.

Finally, at 4:00 A.M. the game was suspended. It was completed on June 23 while major-league baseball players were on strike. Media people were on hand in Pawtucket from as far away as Japan on the 23rd, as this was the "only interesting game in town." Barrett remembered this as a "neat atmosphere" with a "nice spread" of food.[3] Rich Gedman, Bruce Hurst, Luis Aponte, Mike Smithson, and Jose Valdez were other future major leaguers who played in the game. Rochester pitcher Steve Grilli hit Barrett with the first pitch in the bottom of the 33rd inning. Future major leaguer Chico Walker executed a hit-and-run play that moved Barrett to third base, and Dave Koza singled him in for the winning run,

In 1982 Barrett spent his first spring training with Boston but with Jerry Remy as the starting second baseman for the Red Sox, Barrett spent the season with the PawSox again. After batting a team-leading .300, he was called up to the Red Sox on September 6. He got into eight games, with his first major-league hit coming off Mike Caldwell on September 22, but it was his only hit that season, as he finished 1-for-18. In the season's final series, against the Yankees, he went 0-for-14.

In 1983 Barrett started the season in Boston, mostly playing as a defensive replacement, then was sent down to Pawtucket again. He was recalled near the end of June, ultimately appearing in 33 games and going 10-for-44 at the plate. He spent the entire 1984 season with Boston, taking over from Jerry Remy at second base and getting into 139 games for manager Ralph Houk. He batted .303 with 45 RBIs. His first career homer came on May 11, 1984, off Larry Gura of the Kansas City Royals.

Barrett was a right-hander, 5-feet-10 and listed at 175 pounds. The hidden-ball trick is one of his claims to fame. Joe Morgan, his manager at Pawtucket, taught him the trick. As an example: In 1981 he pulled off the hidden-ball trick on Bobby Bonner of the Rochester Red Wings. Barrett made the putout at first on a sacrifice bunt, and kept the ball. (This is where the ball is hidden.) The pitcher stood off the rubber with his back to first, and Barrett said to the runner, now at second, "Let me clean off the base."

Barrett said he executed the hidden-ball trick about five to seven times in the minor leagues.[4] He pulled it off three times in the major leagues with Red Sox, doing it twice in two weeks against the California Angels in 1985. In Anaheim on July 7, he tricked Bobby Grich, who was on first base, by pantomiming a throw to Glenn Hoffman, the Red Sox shortstop. On the 21st, in Boston, he pulled the same trick on Doug DeCinces, the Angels' third baseman. (DeCinces had been needling Bobby Grich on the plane ride to Boston about how Grich had fallen for the hidden-ball trick. Naturally, Grich took a little satisfaction when DeCinces himself became a victim.) After Barrett performed the trick one more time, the umpires started to call time outs after the play was considered to be finished. Barrett felt that if he attempted to pull off the trick, again, he would make the umpires "look bad."

By 1984 Barrett was already being favorably described as being an Eddie Stanky type of player, with more ability, by Detroit Tigers manager Sparky Anderson. Bill Buckner, who came to the Red Sox from the Chicago Cubs, in a May 1984 deal for Dennis Eckersley, gave Barrett the moniker of "Dekemaster" for his ability to pull off the hidden-ball trick, as well as fooling some baserunners into believing that a pitch had been fouled off.[5]

By 1985 Barrett was already receiving accolades as a player who got the most out of his physical and mental capabilities. Teammate and keystone partner Glenn Hoffman called him very smart and cagey.[6] Coach Tony Torchia said Barrett understood that in a hit-and-run situation, he had to manipulate the bat to somehow meet the ball to protect the runner.[7] In 1985 Barrett's batting average dipped to .266 but he had a .987 fielding percentage and 56 RBIs to his credit. His lifetime fielding percentage was .986.

Everything went right in 1986. Barrett batted .286, the Red Sox with a career-high 15 stolen bases, and led the American League with 18 sacrifice bunts. He was "hot" for two to three weeks during the American League Championship Series and the World Series, against the New York Mets. In Game Six of the World Series, with the Red Sox up three games to two, Barrett's single drove in a 10th-inning run that put the Red Sox ahead 5-3 and seemed to ice their Series triumph. But with two outs in the bottom of the 10th and the Series seemingly over, there came three or four bloop hits in a row. Future Hall of Famer Gary Carter flipped a hit into left field. Kevin Mitchell hit a bloop to center. Ray Knight fisted a pitch over Barrett's head. Then, of course, there came the sinker away and the Mookie Wilson groundball the skittered under Bill Buckner's glove. The Mets won the World Series in the next game.

In October 2014, Barrett reflected on Game Six of the 1986 World Series. He said it was manager John McNamara's call to remove pitcher Roger Clemens for a pinch-hitter in the top of the eighth with the Red Sox leading 3-2. Most Red Sox players were upset with the wild pitch that allowed Mitchell to score the tying run in the bottom of the 10th. Prior to Mookie Wilson's groundball, Barrett was trying to position himself to attempt a pickoff play on the runner at second base. Commenting on Mookie Wilson's grounder, Barrett said, "What goes around comes around, but I didn't think it would come around this quick." He was

referring to the fact that the Red Sox had advanced to the World Series on similar dramatics — Dave Henderson's home run that pulled the Red Sox back from defeat in the ALCS.

Interestingly, in 1986, Barrett had not hit well against the Angels, hitting .188 (9-for-48). What made him so valuable in the American Championship Series? He watched videotapes of the season before the ALCS. He indicated that he had learned a lot from those tapes.[8] Sure enough, with five RBIS and a .367 average, Barrett was named the MVP for that unforgettable series against the Angels. (He donated the Chevrolet Sportsvan he received as the MVP to the Childhood Cancer Association of Southern Nevada.)

Barrett hit a solid .293 in 1987, and then .283 with a career-high 65 RBIs in 1988. On June 16, 1988, he stole home in a game at Baltimore. In the fourth inning of a scoreless game, Barrett singled leading off the inning against Jeff Ballard. He was on third base with two outs. Mike Greenwell was the Red Sox batter. At an opportune moment Barrett dashed home. His steal of home gave the Red Sox the early lead, but Baltimore eventually won, 8-4. The Red Sox made the postseason again in 1988 but were swept in four games by Oakland; Barrett was just 1-for-15.

In 1989 Barrett signed a big contract with the Red Sox but suffered his first serious injury when he tore the anterior cruciate ligament in his right knee on June 4. He missed 55 games after the injury and, for the season, played in only 86 games. The next season, 1990, was his last with the Red Sox. He played in only 62 games, batting .226. He was ejected from Game Four of the American League Championship Series, against Oakland. Roger Clemens had been ejected in the bottom of the second by umpire Terry Cooney. After a pitch that Cooney called a ball, Clemens erupted and shouted expletives. Cooney promptly tossed him. Barrett was so incensed that he started to throw things on the field, so he was ejected as well.

After the season Barrett was released by the Red Sox. He signed on with the San Diego Padres, but played in only 12 games (3-for-16) before being released in

June 1991. His time in the majors was complete. He played 16 games for Las Vegas, batting .319, but then retired from the game.

In 1992 Barrett sued Dr. Arthur Pappas, the Red Sox' team physician and a limited partner in the Red Sox ownership, for malpractice. This stemmed from the torn ACL that he had endured in the summer of 1989. Dr. Pappas advised Barrett to do physical therapy and rehabilitation. This had allowed him to return to the field in six weeks, but in 1995, when the verdict was read, it was concluded that he should have had surgical reconstruction of the knee. He received $1.7 million in back salary.[9]

Barrett spent some time in 1995 managing Rancho Cucamonga in the Class-A California League, but despite opportunities to manage elsewhere, elected to stay at home with his family. Interestingly, in an interview in the spring of 1987 discussing his three-year, $2 million contract, he said he loved to spend time with his family. That may explain why he decided to get out of Organized Baseball in 1996 and help to coach Little League baseball back home in Las Vegas.[10]

In March 2014, in an appearance in West Hartford, Connecticut, Barrett opined on a number of subjects in an interview.

He told the interviewer, Alan Cohen, that he liked the idea of instant replay. It would keep the umpires focused and not allow game outcomes to be determined by "brutal calls." Replay may cut down on arguments, shortening the length of games. He also noted, "As you look back, you realize how dumb you were when you first got big money at a young age. Kids need more tutoring at handling money."

Barrett said his favorite ballparks to hit in were Anaheim Stadium and Baltimore's Memorial Stadium. On the subject of steroids, he said he felt that ownership turned a blind eye. Growing up, his favorite player was Pete Rose and he said Rose should be admitted to the Hall of Fame. His current favorites were Bryce Harper and Dustin Pedroia, who "dives for everything" and shows "unmatched drive and desire."

The toughest pitcher during Barrett's time in the majors was Jack Morris. Although he tipped his pitches, he had excellent control. Barrett spoke highly of his batting coach, Walter Hriniak, who stressed the importance of taking batting practice seriously, and stressed work ethic, even more than technique.[11]

Barrett and his wife, Robin, had three children: Eric, Katy, and Kyle. Katy, a fine athlete in her own right, is an assistant golf pro in the Las Vegas area. Robin Barrett sold real estate, and Marty owned rental properties. In 2014 he was still active with baseball in Las Vegas, where he coached a team of 14-year-olds. Barrett began coaching in 1996, when his son Kyle recognized him from his baseball cards more than in person. It was at that point that he decided to leave Organized Baseball; he had been with the Rancho Cucamonga Padres. There is still a Marty Barrett Little League in North Las Vegas. Marty had provided his name to the Little League, in the 1990s, because it was dying at the time in North Las Vegas.

Barrett said he played golf as much as possible, and at one time had a 3-handcap. He said he considered former teammate Jim Rice the best golfer among baseball players.[12]

SOURCES

Marty Barrett was a pleasure to talk with in October of 2014. He gave an hour and a half of his time to talk with me. He and I had never met before. My friend Kevin Hunt, an anthropology professor at Indiana University, helped arrange the interview. SABR member Alan Cohen provided much help, as well. His article "Marty Barrett at World Series Club" was a great help and is cited in this article.

NOTES

1   lasvegassun.com/news/2008/jan/24/rancho-high-alums/.

2   Nick Cafardo, *Lewiston* (Maine) *Daily Sun*, June 24, 1988.

3   Marty Barrett interview with author, October 14, 2014.

4   Barrett interview.

5   Associated Press, *Bangor Daily News*, March 4, 1985, 12.

6   Mike Fine, *Lewiston* (Maine) *Daily Sun*, June 26, 1985.

7   Ibid.

8   Associated Press, *Bangor* (Maine) *Daily News*, October 9, 1986, 17.

9   Associated Press, *Lewiston* (Maine) *Sun Journal*, October 26, 1995, 4C.

10 Nick Cafardo (Patriot Ledger Sports Service), "Barrett is cautious, conservative – and totally dependable," *The Telegraph*, Nashua, New Hampshire, March 24, 1987, 11. news.google.com/newspapers?nid=2209&dat=19870324&id=Uo9KAAAAIBAJ&sjid=zJMMAAAAIBAJ&pg=2824,8086749. Accessed February 10, 2015.

11 Alan Cohen, "Marty Barrett at World Series Club," December 11, 2014. linkedin.com/pulse/marty-barrett-world-series-club-alan-cohen.

12 Todd Dewey, "Marty Barrett remembers the Sox' last streak and talks Vegas golf," lasvegasgolf.com/departments/features/marty-barrett-profile.htm, October 12, 2003. Accessed January 12, 2015.

DON BAYLOR

By Malcolm Allen and Alfonso L. Tusa C.

DON BAYLOR WAS A HUSTLING PLAYER WHO ran the bases aggressively and stood fearlessly close to home plate as if he were daring the pitcher to hit him. Quite often they did, as Baylor was plunked by more pitches (267) than any other player in the 20th century, leading the American League eight times in that department and retiring as the category's modern record-holder (though he's since been passed by Craig Biggio). Notoriously tough, Baylor wouldn't even acknowledge the pain of being hit, refusing to rub his bruises when he took his base. "Getting hit is my way of saying I'm not going to back off," he explained. "My first goal when I go to the plate is to get a hit. My second goal is to get hit."[1]

Baylor played for seven first-place teams in his 19 seasons and was a respected clubhouse leader, earning Manager-of-the-Year recognition in his post-playing career. The powerfully built 6-foot-1, 195-pounder hit 338 home runs and drove in 1,276 runs, and clicked on all cylinders when he claimed the AL Most Valuable Player award in 1979. Not only did he lead the California Angels to their first-ever playoff appearance by pacing both leagues in both runs scored and RBIs, he proved unafraid to kick 30 or so reporters out of the clubhouse. After a critical loss in Kansas City late in that season's pennant race, the press corps made the mistake of asking losing pitcher Chris Knapp about a "choke" within earshot of Baylor, who promptly ordered them to leave.

Baylor broke into the majors with the Baltimore Orioles when the Birds were in the midst of winning three straight pennants. The Baltimore players policed their own clubhouse with a "kangaroo court" that handed down a stinging but good-natured brand of justice for a variety of on- and off-field infractions. Before he'd even played in the majors, a 20-year-old Baylor ran afoul of the court by predicting—even though the Orioles had a trio of All-Star outfielders

plus skilled reserve Merv Rettenmund—"If I get into my groove, I'm gonna play every day." Court leader Frank Robinson read the quote aloud in the Baltimore clubhouse, and shortstop Mark Belanger warned Baylor, "That's going to stick for a long time." Indeed, Baylor was known as Groove in baseball circles even after he retired.[2]

Don Edward Baylor was born on June 28, 1949, in the Clarksville section of Austin, Texas. His father, George Baylor, worked as a baggage handler for the Missouri Pacific Railroad for 25 years, and his mother, Lillian, was a pastry cook at a local white high school. Don had two siblings, Doug and Connie, and going to church on Sundays was a must in the Baylor family.

Baylor was one of just three African-American students enrolled at O. Henry Junior High School when Austin's public schools integrated in 1962. One of the friends he made was Sharon Connally, the daughter

of Governor John Connally, and Baylor would never forget hearing her screams from two classrooms away when Sharon learned over the school's public-address system that her father had been shot along with President John F. Kennedy on November 22, 1963.

At Stephen F. Austin High School, Baylor had to ask the football coach three times for a tryout, but by his senior year he had made honorable mention all-state and got a half-dozen scholarship offers, including ones from powerhouses like Texas and Oklahoma. Baylor also played baseball, as a sophomore becoming the first African-American to wear the school's uniform, and being named team captain for his senior season. After a tough first year under a coach who wasn't accustomed to dealing with blacks, Baylor benefited when a strict disciplinarian named Frank Seale, who believed in playing the game the right way, took over the program for his last two seasons. "Frank was not only my coach, but my friend," said Baylor. "He looked after me and made me feel like I was part of his family."[3] When Baylor finally got to the World Series two decades later, Frank Seale was there.

After suffering a shoulder injury serious enough to inhibit his throwing for the rest of his career, Baylor decided to spurn the gridiron scholarship offers and pursue a career in professional baseball. Some teams, like the Houston Astros (who opted to draft John Mayberry instead), were scared off by Baylor's bum shoulder, but the Baltimore Orioles selected him with their second choice in the 1967 amateur draft. Scout Dee Phillips signed Baylor for $7,500.

Baylor reported immediately to Bluefield, West Virginia, where he wasted no time earning Appalachian League player-of-the-year honors after leading the circuit in hitting (.346), runs, stolen bases, and triples under manager Joe Altobelli. "Alto taught me the importance of good work habits," Baylor recalled. "He was a tireless worker himself, serving as manager, batting-practice pitcher, third-base coach, and, when you got right down to it, a baby sitter."[4]

The 1968 season started with a lot of promise. In 68 games for the Class-A Stockton Ports, Baylor smashed California League pitching at a .346 clip to earn a promotion to the Double-A Elmira Pioneers of the Eastern League. He stayed there only six games, batting .333, before moving up to the Triple-A Rochester Red Wings. In 15 games against International League pitchers, Baylor batted only .217 and was benched for the first time in his life by manager Billy DeMars. "I felt frustration for the first time in my career," Baylor admitted. "Maybe DeMars hated young players, period. I also noticed that his favorite targets were blacks like Chet Trail, Mickey McGuire, and a guy from Puerto Rico named Rick Delgado. I felt that DeMars did not have my best interests at heart. I was trying very hard to learn, but I got nothing from him."[5]

Nonetheless, the Orioles invited Baylor to his first big-league spring training in 1969, and he got to meet his role model, Frank Robinson. Soon, Baylor was even using the same R161 bat (taking its model number from Robinson's first MVP season in 1961) that the Orioles right fielder did so much damage with. With it, Baylor began the season by hitting .375 in 17 games for the Class-A Florida Marlins of the Florida State League. He spent the bulk of the year with the Double-A Dallas-Fort Worth Spurs, hitting .300 in 109 games to earn a Texas League All-Star selection.

After a strong spring training with the Orioles in 1970, Baylor returned to Rochester to bat third and play center field every day. Midway through the season, he reluctantly moved to left field because manager Cal Ripken didn't believe Baylor's weak arm would allow him to play center in the big leagues. "Don's our triple threat," teammate Merv Rettenmund quipped. "He can hit, run, and lob." Pretty much everything else that happened that season, however, couldn't have been scripted more perfectly for Baylor. He was married before a summer doubleheader, and tore through the International League by leading all players in runs, doubles, triples, and total bases. *The Sporting News* recognized Baylor as its Minor League Player of the Year. He batted .327 with 22 home runs and 107 RBIs, and was called up to the Orioles on September 8. Ten days later, Baylor made his major-league debut at Memorial Stadium in Baltimore, batting fifth and playing center field against the Cleveland Indians. The bases were loaded for his first at-bat, against right-hander Steve Hargan, and Baylor admitted feeling "scared to death."[6] He didn't show it, though, driving the first pitch into right field for a two-run single. In 17 at-bats over eight games, Baylor batted .235.

After the 1970 season Baylor went to Puerto Rico to play for the Santurce Crabbers in the winter league. The manager was Frank Robinson. "There I would get to know Frank even better because he was my manager and hitting guru," Baylor remembered. "Mostly he taught me to think while hitting. He would say, 'A guy pitches inside, hit that ball right down the line. Look for certain pitches on certain counts.' Frank also wanted me to start using my strength more. Frank knew there was a pull hitter buried somewhere inside me and fought to develop that power. In Santurce, Frank worked with me to strengthen my defense and throwing. I wound up hitting .290."[7]

With nothing left to prove in Triple-A but no room on the star-studded Orioles roster, Baylor returned to Rochester in 1971 and made another International League All-Star team. He put up strong all-around numbers, hitting .313 with 31 doubles, 10 triples, 20 homers, 95 RBIs, 104 runs scored, 79 walks, and 25 steals as the Red Wings won the Little World Series. The Triple-A playoffs went on so long that Baylor got into just one major-league game after they finished.

He returned to Santurce with the island still celebrating Roberto Clemente's MVP performance in the 1971 World Series, in which he helped the Pittsburgh Pirates dethrone the Orioles. "When Roberto played in Puerto Rico that winter I got a chance to witness up close what a great player he was," Baylor recalled. "In a game against Roberto's San Juan team, I tried to score from second base on a hit to right. I know I had the play beat. I ran the bases the right way; made the proper turn, cut the corner well. But by the time I started my fadeaway slide catcher Manny Sanguillén had the ball. I couldn't believe it. I was out."[8]

Baylor wound up hitting .329 to win the Puerto Rican League batting title. He was confident that he'd be

on some team's major-league roster in 1972, but was shocked when the Orioles cleared a spot for him by dealing away Frank Robinson before Baylor returned from Latin America. The Orioles effectively had four regular outfielders in 1971 (Robinson, Merv Rettenmund, Paul Blair, and Don Buford), so Baylor still had some competition in front of him.

Baylor got into 102 games with an Orioles team that missed the playoffs for the first time in four years. By hitting .253 with 11 home runs and 24 steals, he was named to the Topps Rookie Major League All-Star Team. He became a father when Don, Jr. was born shortly after the season ended. Baylor came back from Puerto Rico to get his son, before the family returned to the island together to help him get ready for the next season.

Much like the Orioles, Baylor started slowly in 1973, but heated up when it mattered most. Baltimore was in third place in mid-July, and Baylor was batting just .219 with four homers in 219 at-bats. Starting on July 17, though, he mashed at a .366 clip the rest of the way, contributing seven home runs and 30 RBIs as the Orioles played .658 ball and won the American League East title going away. Baylor batted .273 in his first taste of playoff action before sitting out a shutout loss to Catfish Hunter in the Series' decisive Game Five.

He played enough to qualify for the batting title for the first time in 1974, batting a solid .272 when the average American Leaguer hit 14 points less. The Orioles were eight games out on August 28, in fourth place, when Baylor and the team caught fire again for another furious finish. Baylor batted .381 as the Birds went 28-6 to finish two games ahead of the Yankees before getting swept by the Oakland A's in the American League Championship Series.

Baylor joined the Venezuelan League Magallanes Navigators that winter, displaying good patience and power with seven homers, 32 RBIs, and 29 walks in 56 games while batting .271. When major-league action got underway in 1975, Baylor's talents continued to blossom. He hammered three home runs in a game at Detroit on July 2, and smacked 25 overall. That made the league's top 10, and his .489 slugging percentage was also among the leaders. With 32 stolen bases, Baylor cracked the AL leader board for the fourth of what would eventually be six consecutive seasons. Though the Orioles finished second to the Red Sox, Baylor's name appeared towards the bottom of some writers' MVP ballots. He was only 26 and going places, just not where he imagined.

Just a week before Opening Day in 1976, Orioles manager Earl Weaver pulled Baylor out of an exhibition game unexpectedly. "When he told me to sit beside him I knew something was wrong, Baylor recalled. 'I hate to tell you this,' Earl said quietly, 'but we just traded you to Oakland for Reggie Jackson.' I looked at Earl but he couldn't look at me. I was stunned. I started to cry right there on the bench. 'Earl,' I sobbed. 'I don't want to go anywhere'."[9] Weaver believed Groove would one day be an MVP, but the Orioles sent him packing in a six-player deal to land a guy who'd already won the trophy. Other than a career-high four stolen bases on May 17, and his best season overall for swipes with 52, the highlights were few and far between for Baylor in 1976. He didn't hit well at the Oakland Coliseum, and batted just .247 with 15 homers overall. On November 1, Baylor became part of the first class of free agents after the arbitrator's landmark decision invalidated baseball's reserve clause.

Just over two weeks later, Baylor signed a six-year, $1.6 million deal with the California Angels, but he struggled to justify his salary for the first half of 1977. When manager Norm Sherry got the axe midway through the season, Baylor was hitting a paltry .223 with nine home runs and 30 RBIs. Dave Garcia took over as skipper, and hired Baylor's ex-teammate Frank Robinson as his hitting instructor. Under the Hall of Famer's tutelage, Baylor broke out to bat .281 with 16 homers and 75 RBIs the rest of the way. He never looked back.

Baylor finished seventh in American League MVP voting in 1978 after a breakout season that saw him smash 34 home runs, drive in 99 runs, and score 103. The surprising Angels logged their first winning season in eight years and remained in the West Division hunt until the final week, but Baylor will always remember that September for one of his saddest days as a ballplayer. Teammate Lyman Bostock made the last out of a critical one-run loss on September 23 in Chicago, then stormed by Baylor ranting and raving before exiting the clubhouse after a fast shower. "Veterans know enough to leave other veterans alone," Baylor said. "So when Lyman walked by, I didn't say a thing. I didn't know there would be no next time for him."[10] Bostock was shot to death that night in Gary, Indiana. The career .311 hitter was only 27.

Baylor propelled the Angels to their first playoff appearance in franchise history in 1979, batting cleanup in all 162 games and earning 20 of a possible 28 first-place votes to claim MVP honors. His totals of 139 RBIs and 120 runs scored led the major leagues, and he added career bests in home runs (36), on-base percentage (.371), slugging percentage (.530), and walks (71) while striking out just 51 times. He batted .330 with runners in scoring position. Baylor struggled while battling tendinitis in his left wrist in June, but sandwiched that down spell with player-of-the-month performances in May and July. He earned his only All-Star selection, starting in left field, batting third, and getting two hits with a pair of runs scored. In his first at-bat, he pulled a run-scoring double off Phillies southpaw Steve Carlton. On August 25 at Toronto, Baylor logged a personal-best eight RBIs in one game as the Angels romped, 24-2.

In the 1979 playoffs, Baylor and the Angels met the same Baltimore Orioles club that developed him, but a storybook ending was not in the cards. Though Baylor went deep against Dennis Martinez in California's Game Three victory, he batted just .188 as the Angels lost three games to one.

As wonderful as 1979 played out, the 1980 season was a nightmare. The Angels started slowly, and were buried by a 12-28 stretch during which Baylor missed nearly seven weeks with an injured left wrist. He struggled mightily when he returned, batted just .250 with five homers in 90 games, and missed most of the last month with an injured right foot. The Angels went from division champions to losers of 95 games. The next season, 1981, Baylor became almost exclusively a designated hitter, and remained one for the balance of his career. Though he batted a career low (to that point) .239, his totals of 17 homers and 66 RBIs each cracked the American League's top 10 in the strike-shortened season.

In 1982 Baylor homered 24 times and drove in 93 runs as the Angels made their second postseason appearance in what proved to be his last season with California. After beating the Brewers in the first two games of the best-of-five Championship Series, the Angels dropped three straight and were eliminated. It certainly wasn't Baylor's fault; he batted .294 and knocked in 10 runs in the series.

Baylor became a free agent for the second time in November 1982, and signed a lucrative deal to join the New York Yankees. In three seasons with the Bronx Bombers, he was twice named the designated hitter on *The Sporting News'* Silver Slugger team (1983 and 1985), and averaged 24 home runs and 88 RBIs. His batting average declined from a career-best .303 to .262 to .231, however, and they were not particularly happy years as Baylor feuded with Yankees owner George Steinbrenner. In 1985 Baylor was selected as the winner of the prestigious Roberto Clemente Award, presented annually to a major leaguer of exceptional character who contributes a lot to his community. He was recognized for his work with the Cystic Fibrosis Foundation and the 65 Roses (so-named for the way one child pronounced Cystic Fibrosis) club.

The Yankees traded Baylor to the Boston Red Sox shortly before Opening Day in 1986 for left-handed-hitting designated hitter Mike Easler. Though Baylor struck out a career-high 111 times and managed to bat just .238 in '86, his 31 home runs and 94 RBIs were his best since his MVP year. He also established a single-season record by getting hit by pitches 35 times. The Red Sox won 95 games to beat out the New York for the American League East title, with Baylor operating a kangaroo court as his mentor Frank Robinson had done in Baltimore. On the night Roger Clemens set a major-league record by striking out 20

Seattle Mariners, Baylor fined him $5 for giving up a single to light-hitting Spike Owen on an 0-2 pitch. In the American League Championship Series, against the Angels, Boston was two outs from elimination in Game Five when Baylor smashed a game-tying, two-run home run off 18-game winner Mike Witt to spark an amazing comeback. Baylor batted .346 in the seven ALCS games, but started only three of seven World Series contests against the New York Mets as designated hitters were not used in the National League ballpark. This time the Red Sox let a Series clincher slip away, losing to New York in seven games.

Baylor turned 38 in 1987, and he posted the lowest power totals since his injury-plagued 1980 campaign, declining to 16 homers and 63 RBIs. He did reach a milestone on June 28, his 38th birthday, when he was hit by a pitch for a record 244th time. "Change-ups and slow curves feel like a butterfly, a light sting," he said. "Fastballs and sliders feel like piercing bullets, like they're going to come out the other side."[11] He added that getting hit in the wrist by a Nolan Ryan heater in 1973 was the worst feeling of all.

The Minnesota Twins, making a surprising playoff run, craved Baylor's right-handed bat and presence and acquired him from the Red Sox for the final month of the 1987 season. Baylor batted .286 to help Minnesota reach the postseason for the first time in 17 years, and his eighth-inning pinch-hit single drove in the go-ahead run in Game One of the ALCS against the Tigers. Baylor batted .385 in the World Series against the St. Louis Cardinals, including a game-tying two-run homer off John Tudor in Game Six, helping the Twins to a comeback victory en route to the title.

Baylor wrapped up his playing career with a return to the Oakland Athletics in 1988. Though he batted just .220 in 92 games, the club won 104 regular-season contests and became the third American League pennant winner in a row to feature Baylor on its roster. Oakland defeated the Red Sox in the ALCS but lost the World Series to the Los Angeles Dodgers in an upset, and Baylor struck out against National League Cy Young winner Orel Hershiser in his only at-bat. In the offseason Baylor called it a career after

2,135 hits with a .260 batting average, 338 home runs, and 1,276 RBIs. He stole 285 bases and was hit by a pitch 267 times.

Baylor returned to the big leagues for a two-year stint as the Milwaukee Brewers' hitting coach beginning in 1990, and spent 1992 in the same role with the Cardinals. In 1993 he was named the inaugural manager of the expansion Colorado Rockies, and earned Manager-of-the-Year honors in 1995 when he led the third-year club to a playoff berth faster than any previous expansion club. Pitching coach Larry Bearnarth observed, "He doesn't lose his cool very often. On the other hand, he can be intolerant sometimes of people who don't give their best. He is very direct and he never varies from that, so players are never surprised. If he has something to say, he just says it like he's still a player, like players used to do to each other."[12]

Baylor's Rockies played winning baseball for two more years, but he was fired after the club fell under .500 and slipped to fourth place in the five-team division in 1998. He turned down an offer to become a club vice president, instead opting to become a hitting coach again with the Atlanta Braves. After earning rave reviews for helping Chipper Jones develop into an MVP candidate, Baylor got another chance to manage in 2000 with the Chicago Cubs. Despite 88 wins and a surprising third-place finish in his second year in Chicago, Baylor was fired after a Fourth of July loss in 2002 with a disappointing, highly-paid club sputtering in fifth place. Overall, he went 627-689 as a major-league manager.

Baylor resurfaced with the Mets the next two seasons, serving as a bench coach and hitting instructor under Art Howe, while battling a diagnosis of multiple myeloma. When the Mets changed managers, Baylor moved to Seattle in 2005 to work with Mariners batters. In 2007 he worked part time as an analyst on Washington Nationals telecasts. After three years out of a major-league uniform, Baylor returned to the Rockies in 2009 as their hitting coach. In 2010, Baylor lived with his wife, Rebecca, a former flight attendant.

SOURCES

In addition to the sources cited in the notes, the author also relied on:

Gutiérrez, Daniel, Efraim Alvarez, and Daniel Gutiérrez hijo, *La Enciclopedia del Béisbol en Venezuela* (Caracas, 2006).

Neff, Craig. "His Honor, Dn Baylor," *Sports Illustrated*, June 16, 1986.

NOTES

1   Jack Friedman, "For Don Baylor, Baseball Is a Hit or Be Hit Proposition," *People*, August 24, 1987.

2   Don Baylor, *Nothing But The Truth: A Baseball Life* (New York: St. Martins Press, 1990), 47.

3   Baylor, *Nothing But The Truth*, 32.

4   Baylor, *Nothing But The Truth*, 38-39.

5   Baylor, *Nothing But The Truth*, 44-45.

6   Baylor, *Nothing But The Truth*, 52.

7   Baylor, *Nothing But The Truth*, 60.

8   Baylor, *Nothing But The Truth*, 68.

9   Baylor, *Nothing But The Truth*, 92.

10 Baylor, *Nothing But The Truth*, 125.

11 Friedman, "For Don Baylor."

12 Howard Blatt, "Ultimate Player's Manager Baylor is Tough But Fair With Rockies," *New York Daily News*, July 15, 1995.

WADE BOGGS

By Steve West

"**T**HAT KID'S GOT A HELL OF A STANCE! Everything's perfect! He ought to become a great hitter!" Legend has it that Ted Williams uttered these words while critiquing a photo of an 18-month-old boy.[1] He was absolutely right; that boy, Wade Boggs, went on to win several batting titles on his way to becoming one of the best hitters of all time in a Hall of Fame career.

Winfield "Win" Boggs was a Marine during World War II, and met Susan Graham, a mail-plane pilot, in 1945, marrying her just two weeks later. Win stayed in the military, serving as a pilot in the Air Force during the Korean War and moving his family around as military people often do. The couple had a son, Wayne, and daughter, Ann, and their third child, Wade Anthony Boggs, was born in Omaha, Nebraska, on June 15, 1958.

Wade loved the idea of being in a military family and having a regimented routine every day. This is something that would carry over to his entire baseball career, in which he would become known for doing set things at set times every day before a game.

Wade began playing baseball in Little League, receiving instruction from his father and several coaches. Win Boggs had retired from the military in 1967, and moved the family to Tampa, Florida, where he opened a fishing camp. At Henry B. Plant High School in Tampa, Wade played baseball and football. After he hit .522 as a junior, scouts began watching him play, and he switched from quarterback to kicker on the football team to avoid injury. He was good enough to become All-State in football and get a scholarship offer from the University of South Carolina.

In baseball Boggs had earned a reputation as a hitter, and pitchers wouldn't throw strikes to him. When he tried to hit balls out of the strike zone he struggled, until his father got him the book *The Science of Hitting*

by Ted Williams. After reading the book he realized he had lost some of his patience at the plate, and took Williams's advice about not swinging at pitches out of the strike zone.[2] When this forced pitchers to throw strikes he hit everything, finishing the season hitting .485.

Scouts had seen Boggs struggle, and even when he hit they weren't sure if he had the necessary talent to play professional baseball. He didn't have much speed or range, and was rated poorly in most areas. The Major League Scouting Bureau called him a nonprospect. One scout wrote, "needs a lot of help with bat," and thought it would take more money than he was worth to persuade him to turn down the football scholarship. But that scout hadn't seen the drive that Boggs had to play baseball. Boston Red Sox scout George Digby had seen him play, and persuaded the team to select Boggs in the seventh round of the 1976 amateur draft. When

the Red Sox offered $7,500, Boggs's father said "You're going to have to make a choice, son, college ball or pro ball."[3] An easy choice for the young baseball fan, Boggs signed and went to the minor leagues.

Boggs was assigned to Elmira (New York) of the Class-A (rookie season) New York-Penn League, where he hit .263 and was below team average in almost every category. But the Red Sox saw enough in him to promote him to Winston-Salem of the Class-A Carolina League in 1977. Boggs proceeded to hit .332 that year, and showed an excellent batting eye by walking much more often than he struck out, something he would do every year until he was 40 years old.

Boggs still moved slowly through the Red Sox system. He was slow and he didn't have much power; all he was showing was that batting average and the ability to earn bases on balls. "I was told in the minor leagues that I'll never play third in the big leagues. That I don't hit for power so I'm not going to play in the big leagues. I'm not fast enough. I was told so many different things."[4] What he did have was drive. "The only thing I ever wanted to do was play professional baseball and in the minors I was getting paid to play so I didn't get discouraged."[5]

He spent the 1978 and 1979 seasons at Bristol (Connecticut) of the Double-A Eastern League, followed by the 1980 and 1981 seasons at Pawtucket in the Triple-A International League. An event in baseball history that Boggs played in was the longest-ever professional baseball game, a 33-inning affair in 1981 between the Pawtucket Red Sox and the Rochester Red Wings that began on April 18 and, after being suspended in the wee hours of Easter morning, was finished on June 23. "When I doubled in the tying run in the 21st inning, I didn't know if the guys wanted to hug me or slug me," he said.[6] In 1981 he led the International League in hitting with a .335 average, and still didn't get called up in September. On the last day of the season, his manager, Joe Morgan, suggested that Boggs play first base in winter ball. He went to Puerto Rico to play, but because of injuries to others he ended up playing third base again. This time he hit

.374, and the Red Sox couldn't ignore him any longer, adding him to the 40-man roster.

Boggs knew Debbie Bertucelli in high school, and they began dating. Shortly after his debut in the minor leagues he proposed, and they were married in December 1976. Two years later they had a daughter, Meagann, and eight years later a son, Brett (named for George Brett).

In 1982 Boggs was trapped behind reigning American League batting champion Carney Lansford, the Red Sox third baseman, but he had a good spring and manager Ralph Houk kept him as a utility infielder. It took a couple of extra days due to rainouts, but he made his major-league debut in the second game of a doubleheader at Baltimore on April 10, 1982. Boggs played first base and hit ninth, and didn't show anything against Orioles starter Dennis Martinez or reliever Sammy Stewart. "I hit four dribblers in the infield, all off changeups," he said.[7] He had a pinch-hit flyout a few days later, then sat for almost two weeks before again playing first base and batting ninth in the first game of a twi-night doubleheader in Chicago. This time, after a couple more groundouts, he came up and led off the eighth inning with a single off White Sox starting pitcher Richard Dotson. Boggs eventually came round to score, on Jim Rice's single, what proved to be the winning run in a 3-2 game.

Before the June 23 night game versus Detroit, and hitting only .258, Boggs had played in just 15 of the team's first 66 games. During that evening, Lansford tried for an inside-the-park home run, and suffered a severe ankle sprain in a collision with Tigers catcher Lance Parrish. Coming off the bench to replace Lansford, Boggs was hitless in two at-bats. his batting average dropping to .242. Houk said, "We'll find out about Boggs,"[8] and Boggs took the opportunity with both hands, playing in 89 of the team's last 96 games, hitting .358 while filling in for Lansford and playing first base when Carney returned a month later. That was enough to convince the Red Sox that he could do the job, and they traded Lansford to the Oakland Athletics after the season, giving Boggs the third-base job full-time. He would keep the job for the next 10 years.

Boggs finished a distant third behind Cal Ripken Jr. and Kent Hrbek for the American League Rookie of the Year award. But he knew he would be starting in the major leagues, and he would take the opportunity he had been given.

The comfort of being set as the everyday third baseman in 1983 gave Boggs a great deal of confidence. He spent the first month primarily in the leadoff position for the Red Sox, moved to fifth in the order for a couple of months, and spent the second half of the year hitting second. These moves never fazed him; he hit wherever he was put. Boggs was 6-feet-2 and weighed 190 pounds. He threw right-handed, but was a left-handed batter. He hit .397 in Fenway Park, hitting to the opposite field and taking advantage of the Green Monster, and hit .321 everywhere else. Boggs was consistent no matter what happened, and he was rewarded by comfortably winning his first American League batting title with a .361 average, which was 22 points better than runner-up Rod Carew (.349) of the California Angels. Boggs's .444 on-base percentage led both leagues.

He followed up in 1984 by hitting .325, which placed him third in the American League, then began a streak of four batting titles in a row, 1985 through 1988. Consistency was again the watchword, as in those four seasons Boggs's highest average was .368 and lowest was .357. His 240 hits in 1985 were the most in a major-league season since 1930. He led all of baseball in on-base percentage for five years in a row, through 1989. In 1985 he got his first of 12 consecutive All-Star selections, as the league recognized his hitting talent.

Boggs hit 24 home runs in 1987, more than double his total of any other years, seeming to indicate that he had more power potential than he usually employed, focused as he was on getting base hits and getting on base.

For all his efforts, and before Boggs arrived in Boston, the Red Sox had meandered around the middle or bottom of the AL East Division since 1980, until it all came together in 1986. Pitcher Roger Clemens came into his own, starting 14-0 as the Red Sox climbed to the top of the division. On May 14 they moved into a tie for first place in the division, and two days later they had the lead by themselves and never relinquished it for the rest of the season.

But a terrible disruption to the season occurred for Boggs on June 17, when his mother was killed by the driver of a cement truck who ran a red light. That driver was on work release from jail, and wasn't supposed to be there, and got off with a charge of running a red light. Boggs was devastated. It took him years to let the incident go.[9]

Boggs returned to baseball six days after his mother's death, and baseball gave him a relief from it. He had his routines, embracing everything he did on game day, and that helped keep him from thinking about his mother. He resumed hitting, the Red Sox kept winning, and they ended up back in the postseason for the first time since losing the 1975 World Series. A tough best-of-seven American League Championship Series with the California Angels ensued, the Red Sox trailing three games to one before rallying to win three in a row. Boggs hit just .233 in the series.

In the 1986 World Series, the Red Sox faced the New York Mets. Boggs fared a little better, hitting .290, but was not much of a factor until the 10th inning in Game Six, when he doubled and later scored to give the Red Sox a 5-3 lead. But in perhaps the most famous ending to a World Series game ever, Boggs was playing third base when the ball was hit to Bill Buckner, and watched it travel through his legs to lose the game. Boggs said, "The ball could've easily been hit to me and gone through my legs. Nobody is blaming anybody. It's fate."[10]

In Game Seven Boggs singled with two outs in the second inning to push the Red Sox to a 3-0 lead. But they couldn't hold the lead and the Mets took over in the late innings and won the World Series. Boggs sat in the dugout and cried, the world thinking he was crying because his team had lost. But Boggs later said that wasn't the case, that he had buried himself in baseball to forget about his mother's death, and now that baseball was over his mother had come flooding back in. "When it was over, I was thinking, 'Now I've got to go home and when I walk in the house, she's not going to be there.'"[11]

Boggs went home and commiserated with his father. Wade had decided that he would retire from baseball, because he wanted to spend more time with his family. Win persuaded him to carry on in baseball. "I told him life goes on, that he had to face up to his loss," Win said.[12]

Boggs returned to baseball and the Red Sox, and resumed hitting. He hit over .300 every year from 1982 to 1991, and in 1988 and 1990 the Red Sox won the AL East again, but both times they were swept by Oakland in the ALCS. Boggs hit .385 and .438 in the two series, but that wasn't enough to get his team to a single win.

Scandal began for the Boggs family in 1988, when it was revealed that Wade had a four-year affair with a woman named Margo Adams. She had sued him for millions of dollars in a palimony lawsuit, and began telling her story to anyone who would listen, including *Penthouse* magazine and the Phil Donahue daytime television show. She said she had traveled with Boggs on Red Sox road trips, and that the whole team knew about her. Any time he would be away from home he would try to arrange for her to be there; even when he left spring training (with permission) for a couple of days to record his voice for an episode of the TV show *The Simpsons*, he took her with him to Los Angeles.

As the scandal broke around the team, Boggs told his wife, Debbie, everything. It was his honesty that made her want them to stay together. "I never had that feeling (of wanting to leave him) because of the way Wade handled it. We had an agreement that he would tell me everything." The lawsuit was settled out of court and Boggs moved on, but to this day his name is always entwined with that of Adams.

In 1992 everything changed for Boggs. It was the worst year of his career; he hit only .259. He later blamed the Red Sox front office, saying that they had betrayed him in contract negotiations. He had a promise from Jean Yawkey, the Red Sox owner, for a five-year contract, because she wanted him to follow in the footsteps of Ted Williams and Carl Yastrzemski as career-long Red Sox legends. But she died before the contract was signed, and when Boggs talked to the new management, all they were offering was a year and an option. Boggs felt slighted, lost his legendary focus, and struggled in his last season with the Red Sox before the team decided not to re-sign him and let him become a free agent.

Despite his carefully regimented lifestyle, Boggs managed to find himself in the headlines for odd reasons over the years. In 1988 he received a minor cut on the neck from a knife after an altercation outside a bar in Gainesville, Florida. Two men, possibly attempting to rob Boggs and his friends, threatened them with the knife and a gun. Boggs said that he "willed himself invisible" during the fight.[13] In another incident, Boggs fell out of the family Jeep and was run over by his wife, Debbie. Although he was not seriously injured, his arm had scrapes and bruises. Comedians across the country suggested that Debbie was getting payback for the Margo Adams situation.[14] Red Sox fans tended to love Boggs more for his many quirks.

The last line on Boggs's Hall of Fame plaque is "Legendary for his superstitions," and he was. Numerous stories tell of his different superstitions, whether it was wearing the same socks for every game, or fielding exactly 150 groundballs in practice each day. Every time he batted, he drew the Jewish word "chai," meaning good luck and life, in the dirt, to wish himself luck. Perhaps the best-known superstition Boggs had was eating chicken before each game every day, and he became known as "Chicken Man" because of it. Boggs even authored a book titled *Fowl Tips*, which presented various chicken recipes. He readily acknowledged his superstitions, saying in his Hall of Fame induction speech, "Believe me, I have a few superstitions, and they work."

In a surprising move, after so many years with the Red Sox, Boggs signed a three-year, $11-million contract to play for their archrivals, the New York Yankees. From being a Boston hero, he found himself returning to boos every game. His focus meant he was able to block it out, and resume his hitting. Again Boggs was back over .300 for his first four years with the Yankees.

The Yankees were on the rise, and Boggs wanted to be part of it. He enjoyed some good seasons with New York, and won a Gold Glove in both 1994 and 1995, but they missed the playoffs his first season, the entire 1994 postseason was wiped out by the players strike, and in 1995 they lost a classic best-of-five ALDS to the Seattle Mariners.

In 1996 the Yankees again made the playoffs, and Boggs struggled. He hit just .158 that postseason, losing playing time for hitting so poorly. His biggest moment was as a 10th-inning pinch-hitter in Game Four of the World Series, when he walked with two outs and the bases loaded to give the Yankees the go-ahead run. But the rest of the Yankees did well during the Series, coming back against the Atlanta Braves, and Boggs got his first World Series ring. In yet another iconic moment, he rode around Yankee Stadium on the back of a police horse as he celebrated.

In 1997 Boggs hit .292, split time, and ultimately lost his third-base job to Charlie Hayes. Boggs hit .429 in seven postseason at-bats, but New York again lost in the ALDS, this time to the Cleveland Indians, and his time with the Yankees was over.

Boggs returned home to Tampa, to play in his hometown for the expansion Tampa Bay Devil Rays. As a 40-year-old his time was over; he hit an anemic (for him) .280 in 1998 and finished out his career hitting .301 in 1999. He had been hanging on long enough to get his 3,000th hit, which came on August 7, and was ironically, given his lack of power throughout his career, a home run off Chris Haney of the Indians. A couple of weeks later he was done, ending his career with 3,010 hits and a career batting average of .328.

Boggs spent some time in the front office of the Devil Rays, acting as assistant general manager in 2000, then returning to the field as hitting instructor for the team in 2001. After that he took off the uniform for good.

Boggs was elected to the National Baseball Hall of Fame in 2005, his first year of eligibility, receiving 91.9 percent of the votes. Speaking about being elected, he said, "The only time the Hall of Fame ever came into my mind was probably the time I was rounding first going into second when I hit my home run for my 3,000th hit. I thought, 'Well, there's my ticket. If anybody wants to vote for me for Cooperstown then I've got the credentials to get in.'"[15]

There was controversy before Boggs's induction when it was reported that the Devil Rays had a part of his contract written so that when he went into the Hall of Fame his plaque would have a Devil Rays cap on it. Boggs denied that had happened, and noted that the Hall of Fame had the choice of what cap he would wear. As it happened, given his five batting titles with Boston, they put him in a Red Sox cap.

Boggs was widely known as a beer drinker, and in retirement undertook promotional tours for the Miller brewing company. His teammates have told stories about his drinking prowess, including stories of Boggs downing dozens of cans of beer on cross-country flights. Boggs did not downplay these stories, and it is fair to say that the stories of his consumption of beer have now reached legendary status.

After retiring from professional baseball, Boggs didn't stay unemployed for long. His son, Brett, was playing high-school baseball, and Wade became an assistant coach for the team while Brett was there. Brett moved on to play at the University of South Florida, where Wade would watch him play. As of 2015, Wade and Debbie lived in Tampa, where they both grew up.

SOURCES

Thanks to Dana Berry for getting this biography under way.

NOTES

1   Dan Shaughnessy, "Wade Boggs: 2005 Hall of Fame Inductee," *Boston Globe,* July 31, 2005.

2   Peter Gammons, "Pretty Fair for a Fowl Guy," *Sports Illustrated,* April 14, 1986.

3   Wade Boggs Hall of Fame Induction speech.

4   Shaughnessy.

5   Ibid.

6   Ira Berkow, "33 Innings, 882 Pitches and One Crazy Game," *New York Times,* June 24, 2006.

7   Shaughnessy.

8   Christopher L. Gasper, "Fact is, injuries can cost you a job in sports," *Boston Globe,* November 25, 2012.

9   Ian O'Connor, "Wade's World: Boggs, Dad bounce back after series of struggles," *New York Daily News,* October 16, 1996.

10 O'Connor.

11 Shaughnessy.

12 O'Connor.

13 Jack Curry, "Did someone say Boggs? Not in Boston," *New York Times,* March 18, 1993.

14 Dan Shaughnessy, "Leave it to Boggs to spice up spring," *Boston Globe,* March 31, 1991.

15 Ibid..

OIL CAN BOYD

By Bill Nowlin

DENNIS "OIL CAN" BOYD STARTS HIS AU-
tobiography recalling back in 1964 when
he was 5 years old, and his uncle Frank
Boyd brought three civil-rights workers
by the family home. Later that same year, James
Chaney, Andrew Goodman, and Michael Schwerner
were discovered murdered. Dennis believes they were
killed just after they left the Boyd home to head
for Memphis.[1]

The home was in Meridian, Mississippi, where he
had been born on October 6, 1959, to parents known
as Skeeter and Sweetie. Skeeter was Willie James
Boyd and Sweetie was his wife, Girtharee (McCoy)
Boyd. Willie Boyd worked in Meridian as a land-
scaper and Peter Gammons, in the speech he gave on
being honored with the J.G. Taylor Spink Award at
the Baseball Hall of Fame in 2005, recounted a 1985
meeting with Mr. Boyd, who himself said he was
literally "landscaping the yard of the grand dragon of
the Ku Klux Klan" when he saw the cars heading out
"to take care" of the three civil-rights workers. Then
Mr. Boyd looked at Gammons and talked about the
Klansman: "Today that man is destitute and crippled
with arthritis, and my boy, Dennis Boyd, is pitching
in the major leagues for the Boston Red Sox."[2]

That he was. Dennis won 15 games that year, and in
1986 pitched in the World Series. Willie Boyd himself
had been a baseball player, as had his father before him.
And Willie's work in Meridian included maintaining
the baseball field in town.

Dennis was African American, but he also had Choctaw
lineage on his father's side, and his great-grandfather
on his mother's side was "as white as snow."[3] It was
a complicated heritage, one great-grandfather Irish
and another a slave.

The Boyd family also had a baseball pedigree. As
Boyd himself said, "My father played just a little bit

of a while in Negro League baseball. My two uncles
played. K.T. Boyd, my dad's brother—Kansas City
Monarchs. And Robert Boyd—he played for the
Kansas City Athletics but he also came out of Negro
League baseball. He played for the Memphis Red Sox.

"And my great-great-uncle played, Benjamin Boyd.
He played for the Memphis Red Sox and the
Homestead Grays."[4]

Robert Boyd—Bob Boyd—was the first African
American to sign with the Chicago White Sox, in
1950, and broke in with them the following year. He
played for the Orioles, Kansas City, and Milwaukee
over parts of nine seasons.

With [at least] five older brothers, Dennis played a
lot of baseball and often with boys older than him.
Dennis even played in games himself with former
Negro Leaguer Early Moore. Three houses away

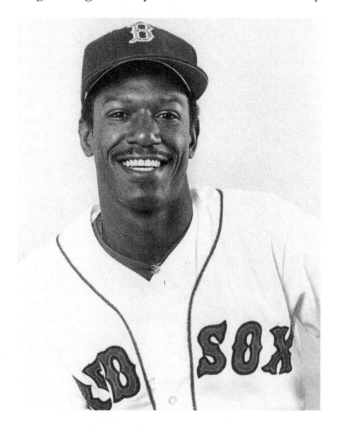

from the Boyds lived former Negro League pitcher Roy Dawson.[5]

Family ties didn't end there. "I've had a few cousins, too—Barry Larkin. My dad's first cousin. Troy Boyd played for the Chicago Cubs and San Diego Padres. And in minor-league baseball, Brian Cole and Popeye Cole—Robert Cole. Brian Cole is the one that *Sports Illustrated* did an article on two years ago. He got killed. He was in the Mets organization. Bob Stanley coached him in the minor leagues. He got killed in 2001 in a car accident coming from spring training. It was called 'The Best Player You Never Saw.'[6] Albert Pujols and a lot of them made comments about him. They saw him in the minor leagues and they didn't believe what they was seeing."[7]

Dennis played ball in Meridian; in 1972, he was named MVP of the little league all-star game held in Hattiesburg.[8] The next year—1973—two of his brothers were drafted, Mike by the Dodgers (he was a pitcher and his team had won the Mississippi state championship, but he was never offered a contract because of the negativity coming from his getting a white girl pregnant), and Don by the Cardinals. A 15th-round pick, he was a second baseman who played one season at rookie ball in the Gulf Coast League.

Dennis was fortunate to have a high-school coach, Bill Marchant, who taught him baseball strategy, the mental side of the game. As a white man coaching an integrated team in Mississippi at the time, Boyd wrote, Marchant "could have been killed … not harmed, not threatened, but literally *killed* for putting my brothers on the team."[9] It was Marchant who bought spikes for Dennis and his brother Neal. The Meridian team went on to the state playoffs, and Dennis got a scholarship to Jackson State University, where he was coached by Robert Braddy. He said his record at Jackson State was 20-5 and he's in the school's hall of fame. The Boston Red Sox drafted Dennis Boyd in the 16th round of the 1980 draft and he was signed by Red Sox scout Ed Scott.

Boyd was assigned to Elmira in the New York-Penn League and was 7-1 in 1980 with a 2.48 earned-run

average. In 1981 he pitched in Class A for the Winter Haven Red Sox of the Florida State League and was 14-8 (3.63). That winter he went to Colombia to play some winter ball and, he writes, was first introduced to cocaine.[10]

Boyd advanced to Double A in 1982, pitching in Connecticut for the Eastern League's Bristol Red Sox, and recorded an identical 14-8 mark, but with an improved 2.81 ERA even at the higher level of play. He was dubbed "the hottest pitching prospect in the Red Sox farm system."[11] An Associated Press story at the end of August explained his nickname, dating it back to high-school days when he would drink beer with his friends: "They called it 'oil' then, and Boyd sure could put away a few cans."[12] His 191 strikeouts (in 205 innings) led the Eastern League. At the very end of the 1982 season, Boyd was a September call-up and was given a look at the majors, debuting at Fenway Park with a start against the Cleveland Indians on September 13. He gave up one run in the first inning and one more in the fourth, but that was enough to cost him the game. He worked 5⅓ innings, giving up just the two runs, but the Red Sox offense scored only one run, in the bottom of the ninth, and lost the game, 3-1.

Manager Ralph Houk used Boyd twice more in relief, both times against the Yankees, and he gave up three more runs in three innings of work. But he'd gotten his feet wet. He'd made the big leagues.

The 1983 season was spent in Triple-A with Pawtucket, with a couple of call-ups to Boston, once in June and then again at the beginning of August. Boyd picked up his first major-league win, against Minnesota, on June 3 and worked a total of 98⅔ innings in 15 games, 13 of them starts. His best outing was a September 2 complete-game 5-1 win over the White Sox. His record for the season was 4-8, but he had a solid 3.28 ERA.

Part of 1984 was also spent in Pawtucket, after he'd begun the season 0-3 (with a 7.36 ERA) for Boston and had an argument with Houk that resulted in his being sent back down, though Houk was generous in his praise of Boyd at the time and the argument could be made that he'd been "much too easy" on the young pitcher.[13] After spending a month back in Triple-A, Boyd was summoned back to the Red Sox and won 12 games for a 12-12 season with an overall 4.37 ERA. He spent the full 1985 and 1986 seasons with the big-league club, working both seasons under new manager John McNamara. Boyd won a club-leading 15 games in '85 with 13 losses and won 16 games in '86, against 10 losses. He worked 13 complete games in 1985 and 10 in 1986. The game Oil Can thought was his best was the June 19, 1986, complete-game three-hit shutout he pitched against the Orioles at Memorial Stadium, working with Dave Sax behind the plate.[14]

The Red Sox won the pennant and went to the seventh game of the World Series in 1986. Boyd's 16 wins were second only to Roger Clemens, whose 24-4 record won him both the Cy Young Award and the American League MVP. Bruce Hurst was 13-8 (2.99).

Boyd was a right-hander, standing 6-feet-1 and listed at a lean and wiry 155 pounds. He pitched the pennant-clinching game, a 12-3 complete-game win over the Toronto Blue Jays on September 28. When it came to the postseason, Clemens was hammered by the Angels' offense in the first game of the ALCS, giving up eight runs (seven earned) in 7⅓ innings. The Red Sox lost, 9-1. Hurst won Game Two, a complete-game 9-2 win. Just one of California's runs was earned. Boyd pitched Game Three, in Anaheim, and the two teams were tied, 1-1, after six, the Angels having scored once that inning. After getting two outs in the bottom of the seventh, however, Boyd gave up a solo home run to Dick Schofield, a single to Bob Boone, and a two-run homer to Gary Pettis. McNamara pulled his pitcher, but the damage was done, and Boyd took a 5-3 loss. After Dave Henderson's heroics saved the Red Sox from elimination in Game Five, Boyd was the starting pitcher in Game Six back home in Boston. He worked seven full innings, giving up three runs, and left with a comfortable 10-3 lead that wound up a win.

After Boston won World Series Games One and Two at Shea Stadium, Oil Can Boyd was asked to start Game Three at Fenway. It didn't go well. Leadoff batter Lenny Dykstra homered. Two singles and a

Gary Carter double produced a second run and saw runners on second and third with still not an out. With one out, Danny Heep singled in two more. It was 4-0 Mets before the Red Sox came to bat. Boyd worked seven innings, giving up only two more runs over the next six, but Boston scored just one run all evening. The way it worked out, he wasn't called upon to pitch again at any point in the remaining four games. Naturally, like any competitive athlete, he wished he'd been given the opportunity. He didn't think the Mets would be able to beat him twice in a row. "We had an opportunity to win Game Seven. I pitched very well in Game Three; after the first inning, I pitched overly well. If I came out with that same momentum, knowing the hitters like I did, facing the same guys … no, no, no. I've got too good a stuff. I'm too good a pitcher. I can't see myself giving up more than two or three runs and getting into the seventh or eighth inning, no question."[15]

Though 1985 and 1986 were his best seasons, "Can" (as he was called) acknowledges he had a serious problem with cocaine. He was hospitalized before the '86 campaign began. "I had the whole cover story about hepatitis," he wrote, "but it was flat-out me smoking crack every damn day. I was smoking cocaine, freebasing, doing crack; they had all kind of names for it back then. But whatever you call it, that's what I was doing."[16] Helping counsel him through this was team physician and co-owner Dr. Arthur Pappas. "He was almost like a father figure to me at that time."[17]

Because he had pitched so well both in 1985 and 1986, Boyd felt he should have been selected for the All-Star Game. He took being passed over the first time, but in 1986 when he clearly was having an exceptional year and was second in the league in victories, he snapped at what he took as a snub (Mike Boddicker had the same number of wins as Boyd and was also passed over)—and Boyd bolted. He quit the team. It didn't go over well with him teammates; Don Baylor said, "No one player is bigger than the team."[18] It also wasn't the first time his volatile behavior had resulted in disciplinary action; he'd been fined a day's pay after an August 21 loss to the Texas Rangers and a locker-room run-in with Jim Rice.[19] In spring training 1987, he'd "exploded" at a writer who questioned him regarding videotapes he had not returned; that became known as "Can's Film Festival."[20]

This time Boyd was suspended for 21 days but eventually came back in early August. While he was out, though, he had gotten into a tussle with some police and his arm had gotten wrenched. He says he never fully recovered. Indeed, though one wouldn't know looking at his pitching record, he was pitching in pain and subpar for the rest of the season and into 1987. He said he didn't give up even one run in spring training 1987, but the pain remained. He was able to pitch in only seven games all year, until surgery in August when it was discovered he had a hairline fracture.

The problem finally fixed, Boyd was able to start 23 games in 1988 (9-7, with a 5.34 ERA) but though the Red Sox reached the postseason once more, Boyd had developed blood clots and wasn't able to pitch after August 26. He started the 1989 season with the Red Sox but had an even poorer start and from the beginning of May to the start of September, all he could manage was to get into three games in the minors for a total of 12 innings.

After becoming a free agent, Boyd signed with the Montreal Expos in early December 1989, and he enjoyed his time with the Expos: "It was the best time I ever had playing baseball."[21] And he had a very good year in 1990, 31 starts and a 2.93 earned-run average — the best of his career. His record was 10-6, reflecting the fact that many of the games were resolved in the late innings. He pitched most of the 1991 season with Montreal, his 3.52 ERA not reflected in his 6-8 record, but he was traded to the Texas Rangers on July 21, for three players. He took it personally that he'd been traded, an indication to him that the Expos didn't want him.[22] Texas didn't suit Boyd at all and it showed in his work, 2-7 with a 6.68 ERA the rest of the season.

As it happened, Oil Can never got back to the big leagues. His final stats show him 78-77 with a 4.04 ERA over 10 seasons in the majors.

The Pirates organization signed Boyd to a minor-league contract for 1992, but he came to understand that as somewhat of a difficult personality, "I knew I'd been blackballed out of the game."[23] When Indians manager Mike Hargrove gave him a look in the spring of 1994, Boyd quotes him as saying, "If it was my choice and I was in control of this, you would be in my rotation. You wouldn't just be on my pitching staff, you'd be in my five-man rotation. But your personality is bigger than your right arm."[24]

In 1993 Boyd played in the Mexican League for Industriales of Monterrey (at one point earning 11 consecutive saves in 11 consecutive days), and in the first part of 1994 he pitched for the Yucatan Leones. He finished the year with the Sioux City Explorers in the independent Northern League, where pitched again in 1995. There were occasional problems that cropped up off the field, but Boyd played some independent ball in Maine and Massachusetts, in 1996 and 1997.

He also tried to become a developer in Meridian that year, building homes on spec, but lost it all when none of the black families who were interested could get financing from local banks. When he moved back north to rejoin his wife and family, a woman he'd been seeing in Meridian was upset and said she was going to burn his things. He responded heatedly, and she recorded the conversations. "I threatened to beat her ass if she burned my stuff."[25] It was the kind of thing people might understandably say in what they thought was private. Boyd's words, uttered across state lines, led to his arrest by the FBI. After some twists and turns, he wound up in the Fort Dix Federal Penitentiary for 120 days.

At age 45, Can pitched again, in 2005, in the independent Canadian-American League for the Brockton Rox. He worked in 17 games and was 4-5 with a 3.83 ERA.

The year 2005 was, as Boyd puts it, "my last year of professional baseball." He's kept busy since then, living in East Providence, Rhode Island. "I've been doing a lot teaching up here. A lot of lessons from the beginning of January through May. I got a book out. I'm working on a minor-league baseball project down in Mississippi, to bring minor-league baseball to my hometown of Meridian, Mississippi. It's a project I started on years ago but it's finally in the last stages of actually materializing in the next year or so. And I'm getting ready to do a reality TV show. It's called *Second Chance*. They're going to do 12 episodes, over 24 months.

"I do a lot of charity things. I do a lot of stuff with the Red Sox over the summer. Some cameo appearances, motivating speaking, autograph signing."[26]

Boyd has two children—Dennis, and his daughter Tala—in their 20s as of this writing in 2015. "And I'm a granddad. Looking forward to that part of my life, too."

SOURCES

In addition to the sources noted in this biography, the author also consulted the *Encyclopedia of Minor League Baseball*, Retrosheet.org, Baseball-Reference.com, and the SABR Minor Leagues Database, accessed online at Baseball-Reference.com.

Notes

1   Dennis "Oil Can" Boyd with Mike Shalin, *They Call Me Oil Can* (Chicago: Triumph Books, 2012), 9-11. Chaney was a native of Meridian and a "close friend" of Frank Boyd. See p. 13.

2   Ibid., v.

3   Ibid., 16.

4   Author interview with Dennis Boyd, January 6, 2015.

5   *They Call Me Oil Can*, 27.

6   *Sports Illustrated*, April 1, 2013.

7   Author interview with Dennis Boyd, January 6, 2015.

8   Photograph and caption in the photo insert in *They Call Me Oil Can*.

9   Ibid., 46, 47.

10   In his autobiography, Boyd devotes a full chapter to cocaine and its effect on him. See Ibid., 59-74.

11   *Springfield* (Massachusetts) *Republican*, August 14, 1982.

12   *Boston Herald*, August 29, 1982.

13   *Boston Herald*, May 20, 1984. The assessment was Joe Giuliotti's.

14   Boyd, *They Call Me Oil Can*, 136.

15   Author interview with Dennis Boyd, January 6, 2015.

16   In the *Boston Globe*, March 13, 1986, Pappas explained Boyd's prolonged illness and six-day hospital stay as due to a noncontagious form of hepatitis." In *They Call Me Oil Can*, Boyd told about the time he was pitching in Oakland and had a few rocks of crack in his baseball cap, which scattered on the mound when his cap flew off of his head after one energetic pitch. See page 71.

17   Ibid., 70.

18   *Boston Globe*, July 11, 1986.

19   "Boyd, Rice in Clubhouse Tiff," *Boston Herald*, August 22, 1985.

20   *Boston Globe*, February 28, 1989.

21   Boyd, *They Call Me Oil Can*, 89.

22   Ibid., 90-91.

23   Ibid., 95.

24   Ibid., 97.

25   Ibid., 117. The story of his experiences as a developer is on pages 112ff.

26   Author interview with Dennis Boyd, January 6, 2015.

MIKE BROWN

By Nick Waddell

PROMISE UNFULFILLED DENOTES THE playing career of right-handed pitcher Mike Brown. When the Red Sox drafted the Clemson University star in the second round in the 1980 amateur draft, *Boston Globe* baseball writer Peter Gammons wrote that "two teams whose scouts I respect" considered Brown among the top 20 prospects in the country.[1] But after six seasons with the Red Sox and the Seattle Mariners and a less-than-mediocre 12-20 won-lost record, largely as a starter, Brown was done as a major-league pitcher.

Michael Gary Brown was born on March 24, 1959, in Camden County, New Jersey. In 1977, when he pitched for Marshall High School in Vienna, Virginia, he was drafted in the 20th round by the Atlanta Braves, but chose to attend Clemson University.

Pitching for Clemson, Brown had a 23-9 record with a 3.25 ERA, mostly as a starter. He was second-team All Atlantic Coast Conference in his first year (1978) and first-team All ACC his last year (1980). In the latter year he pitched a seven-inning perfect game in 1980 against UNC-Wilmington. Among his teammates was future major leaguer Jimmy Key. Brown led the Tigers in victories in 1978 and 1980 with nine wins each season. These high marks led the Red Sox to draft Brown in the second round in 1980, the 48th overall selection.

Brown got his feet wet in professional baseball by pitching in 17 games for the Winter Haven Red Sox of the Class-A Florida State League in 1980. He was 3-4 with a 4.31 ERA. Perhaps Brown's best year in professional baseball was 1981; in 21 starts he was 14-4 with a 1.49 ERA for the Winston-Salem Red Sox of the Carolina League. Brown led the team in wins, ERA, complete games, shutouts (6), innings pitched (145.0), strikeouts (144), WHIP (0.917), and strikeout/walk ratio (3.69). That earned him a promotion to Bristol of the Double-A Eastern League for 1982.

There, Brown made 15 starts, going 9-6 with a 2.45 ERA, and earned a September call-up (along with teammate Oil Can Boyd) to the third-place Red Sox.

Brown debuted on September 16, 1982, in Detroit, throwing the final inning in a 4-2 loss to the Tigers. He gave up a single but no runs. Eleven days later, on the 27th, he pitched the final inning against the New York Yankees at Fenway Park. Dave Winfield doubled to lead off the inning but tried to stretch it to a triple and was thrown out. Brown retired the next two batters. His third and final appearance came against the Yankees in New York. He came into a game tied 3-3. Brown worked four innings, allowed five hits and a base on balls, but no runs, and picked up the win when the Red Sox scored twice in the top of the 11th.

The Red Sox liked what they saw, and gave Brown a rotation spot in 1983 along with his Bristol teammate Boyd. Manager Ralph Houk believed Brown would

make the rotation based on his short stint in 1982. "I had him penciled in after the last day of last season. He knows how to pitch. … This kid is really a good pitcher," Houk said.[2] Brown was a bit more modest about his minor-league stats, including 307 strikeouts in 326 innings to that point. "The strikeouts are deceptive," he said. "I'm not going to be a big strikeout pitcher in the big leagues. I struck out all those in A and Double A with my slider, like the night I punched out 17 in Hagerstown in '81. Major-league hitters hit that slider."[3]

Brown's first major-league start came in the Red Sox' third game of the season, against the Texas Rangers. He pitched six innings, giving up two runs while striking out seven. He got a no-decision, as the Red Sox won 8-5. Brown ended April 1-2 with a 6.00 ERA. His strikeout-to-walk ratio was less than one. May was a bounce-back month, though. He was 3-1 with a 2.75 ERA in six starts (three complete games, including a shutout of the Seattle Mariners, his future team). Brown continued his hot pitching through mid-June, but cooled off at the very end. He was shut down for the entire month of September due to a sore arm, which was a lingering effect of a pulled groin muscle he suffered in Toronto on May 28. He ended the year 6-6 with a 4.67 ERA.

Houk went into the offseason with high hopes for Brown. "If Mike Brown can throw a lot during the winter and get his arm in good shape before we get to spring training, he can be a winner," the manager said.[4] Brown did rehab during the offseason,[5] and broke camp with the Red Sox after spring training in 1984. The rough end to the 1983 season continued.

In the last spring-training game, Brown was drilled in the shin by a Steve Garvey line drive. Initial reports indicated Brown would not be ready for his first start of the regular season.[6] Brown defied the odds and returned to action a week later. This return might have been premature, as he was roughed up in his first start, lasting only a third of an inning in Oakland and giving up six runs. May was once again his best month of the year, when he brought down his ERA by over a run to 5.40. Boston sent him to Pawtucket for some additional work. Brown started 12 games for Pawtucket, going 6-3 with a 3.40 ERA, but this success did not translate to the major leagues when he was recalled. Over his last four outings, Brown had an ERA of over 10.00, and wound up with a record of 1-8.

Brown did not make the Red Sox out of spring training in 1985, but was called up after three starts at Pawtucket. After two starts totaling 3⅓ innings, with eight runs given up. Brown was sent back to Pawtucket in mid-May to pitch mostly out of the bullpen. Brown's time with Pawtucket was not much better than with Boston, as he had a 2-5 record with a 5.60 ERA in 20 games.

Brown came to spring training in 1986 with a purpose. "It's time for me to either be in the big leagues or be with another team," he said. "I don't have any arm problems; I just need the chance to throw. Nothing against the Red Sox, but if I don't get a chance to pitch, I should move on. I know I can pitch. The thing I don't understand is why I got filed away last year."[7] He carried that attitude over to the regular season. His first start for Boston was a seven-inning two-run win over the White Sox. Brown was a mainstay in the rotation in May and June, but was replaced when the Red Sox traded for veteran Tom Seaver. Brown was moved to the bullpen, where he struggled. In four relief appearances, he gave up eight runs in 4⅓ innings, and he was sent back to Pawtucket in July.

In August Brown got his wish of being on another team when he was traded to Seattle on the 22nd in a five-player deal, a momentous one as it turned out. While Boston was gearing up for its eventual pennant, the Mariners were mired in last place. The trade netted the Red Sox Spike Owen and the star of the 1986 ALCS, Dave Henderson. It was a two-part trade; on the 19th, Rey Quinones and cash went to the Mariners with players to be named later. Three days later, the two players named were Mike Brown and Mike Trujillo.

Brown was given two starts by Seattle in August; his first was a disaster, while his second showed promise. The September call-ups again pushed Brown to the bullpen, where he continued to struggle in four relief appearances.

The last year Brown wore a major-league uniform as a player was 1987. He spent the entire season in Triple A except for one mid-August outing for Seattle at Minnesota. He lasted only a third of an inning, giving up three hits and two runs. He was returned to Triple-A Calgary, and sent to Baltimore in a trade for fellow minor leaguer Nelson Simmons a week later. Brown made one start for Triple-A Rochester.

Brown signed a minor-league deal with the Cleveland Indians in the offseason, and played the entire season at Triple-A Colorado Springs. As primarily a starter, he went 10-9 with a 6.12 ERA. That was his last season as a player in Organized Baseball.

For the next three seasons Brown managed Cleveland's Class-A affiliate in Columbus, Georgia. In 1992 he was named pitching coach for the Yankees' Triple-A affiliate, the Columbus (Ohio) Clippers. During those two years, Brown worked with many future major leaguers, including Sterling Hitchcock and Bob Wickman. Brown was promoted to the Yankees as a major-league bullpen coach in 1994.

Brown returned to the Indians organization in 1995 as the pitching coordinator. He also held the titles of assistant director of minor leagues and special assistant to the GM until he was named pitching coach in 2002. Brown helped the development of CC Sabathia, Jake Westbrook, and Cliff Lee. Brown

was let go at the end of the season, and moved on to Japan for four seasons, including a stint as the pitching coach for the 2006 Japan Series champion Hokkaido Nippon-Ham Fighters.

Brown returned to the United States and joined the Arizona Diamondbacks as a scout in 2007. In 2015 he completed his ninth year in the position. That same year his son MJ Brown was an infielder on the baseball team at Lee University in Cleveland, Tennessee.

SOURCES

In addition to the sources cited in the notes, the author also consulted:

2015 Arizona Diamondbacks Media Guide

Clemson University 2015 Baseball Media Guide

NOTES

1   Peter Gammons, "The Go-All-Out All-Star Team," *Boston Globe*, June 13, 1980.

2   Peter Gammons, "Head Start for Sox; Mike Brown Is Thinking Man's Pitcher," *Boston Globe*, March 31, 1983.

3   Ibid.

4   Peter Gammons, "Houk Makes His Pitch for the '84 Season," *Boston Globe*, October 4, 1983.

5   *Lewiston* (Maine) *Journal*, February 27, 1984: 11.

6   Peter Gammons, "Brown Hit in Leg, Will Miss At Least 1 Start with Bruise," *Boston Globe*, April 2, 1984.

7   Dan Shaughnessy, "Order Is Maintained," *Boston Globe*, March 06, 1986.

BILL BUCKNER

by Jeff English

"**GAMER** 1. A player who approaches the game with a tenacious, spirited attack and continues to play even when hurt; a competitor; a player who doesn't make excuses. The term is a compliment, most especially when it comes from another player."[1]

BILL BUCKNER WAS A GAMER. HE PLAYED the game of baseball as hard as any player of his generation. Los Angeles Dodgers manager Walter Alston once said of Buckner, "He gets the red neck a lot, but I sort of like that."[2] Alston was referring to the fiery temper and intensity that fueled Buckner's approach at the plate and in the field. Buckner detested strikeouts, which he considered failure. In nine different seasons he ranked either first or second in his league in at-bats per strikeout.

To say Buckner played hurt is an understatement. He suffered a severe ankle injury in 1975 and never fully recovered. For the remainder of his career, he was forced to rely on a series of elaborate pregame rituals in order to force his body onto the baseball field. Chicago Cubs manager Herman Franks once remarked, "You should see this guy getting ready for a game. He rides that bike in there and does all kind of exercises. Then he goes in, and Tony (trainer Garofalo) tapes him from here to here."[3]

A selfless player in an age of big salaries and bigger egos, Buckner was willing to switch positions when it meant improving the lineup and the club's chances of winning. Before the ankle injury, he was a speedy outfielder capable of making outstanding catches. After the injury he gradually evolved into a full-time first baseman, making his last appearance as an outfielder in 1984. Over the course of his career, he played well over 600 games in the outfield and more than

1,500 games at first base. At the plate he possessed a compact swing capable of generating extra-base power to all fields. He won the National League batting title in 1980 and twice led the league in doubles. That he managed to do so despite lingering effects from the ankle injury is a tribute to his toughness.

His hustle and determination on the field brought with it the admiration and respect of teammates, opponents and those who merely watched him play. Columnist Dick Young once called Buckner "one of the guttiest players around today. He plays with a bad ankle, takes an aspirin and steals a base."[4] Buckner once cited Pete Rose's style of play as an inspiration for his own and, like Rose, exuded immense confidence on the field. He set an example for his teammates to follow and sacrificed his body for the opportunity to play winning baseball. It is not an exaggeration to suggest that, were it not for the ankle injury, it might be easy

BILL BUCKNER

to imagine Buckner having fashioned a career worthy of enshrinement in Cooperstown. He was one of the purest hitters of his generation, topping the .300 mark in seven different seasons.

William Joseph Buckner was born on December 14, 1949, in Vallejo, California. He was raised by his parents, Leonard and Marie Katherine Buckner, in American Canyon, California. His father died when Bill was a teenager. His mother worked for more than 20 years as a captain's stenographer for the California Highway Patrol. In 1971 she remarried, to Harold Eugene McCall, a California Highway Patrol officer. Bill was raised with his three siblings, brothers Bob and Jim, and Jim's twin sister, Jan. It was Marie who saw to it that the Buckner kids found their way into organized baseball. While attending a Cub Scout mothers meeting, she signed her boys up for Little League. "I thought it would keep them busy and out of trouble," she recalled. "So they signed up. Their father was active in Little League with them, and they all used to practice in the living room. Even my daughter, Jan played softball in Napa and won a trophy to keep up with her brothers."5 Bill was a natural athlete, and advanced for his age. As a seven-year-old, Marie falsified Bill's birth certificate in order to get him into Little League a year early.6 He excelled from the beginning. His brother Bob, recalling Bill's days in Little League, has said, "Pretty soon he was telling everyone what to do. Nobody could play the sun field, so he told the coach to put him out there. Here was this little kid with freckles showing everyone how to do it."7 Even as a seven-year-old, Bill Buckner was intense. He probably got the "red neck" from time to time, back then, too.

Buckner was an A-minus student in high school who excelled on the gridiron as well as the baseball diamond. As a pass-catching end for the Napa High Indians, he compiled 963 receiving yards on 61 total catches, good enough to be named to the Coaches All-American team two years in a row. As a first baseman on the baseball team, he hit a whopping .667 in 1967 and .529 in '68. Recalling high school, Buckner stated, "I was very goal-oriented. I was going

to go to school and college, play sports, and go on to professional baseball. I didn't spend a lot of time doing nothing."8 He narrowed his college choices down to USC and Stanford. But his reputation as a hitter caught the attention of big-league scouts. Former New York Yankees second baseman and California Angels scout Joe Gordon recalled that Buckner "had the finest swing I saw anywhere on the West Coast, and probably is one of the best young hitters in baseball with his compact swing and power to all fields. He seems to have complete control of his bat and his body."9 For the goal-oriented Buckner, college would have to wait.

The Los Angeles Dodgers selected Buckner in the second round with the 25th overall pick of the June 1968 amateur draft. That was a historically great draft class for the Dodgers, who managed to acquire 15 future major leaguers from among the four draft phases that existed in 1968. Bobby Valentine, Davey Lopes, Tom Paciorek, Doyle Alexander, Steve Garvey, and Ron Cey were among the young players who joined Buckner as new members of the Dodgers organization.

Buckner was assigned to the Ogden Dodgers in the rookie-class Pioneer League. His manager was Tommy Lasorda. Buckner played every game at first base, and recorded a .344 average in 275 plate appearances while swiping 15 bases in 16 tries. Paciorek, Buckner, and Garvey finished 1-2-3 in the batting race, propelling Ogden to the best won-loss record in the league. After the season ended, Buckner attended the University of Southern California, where he roomed with his Ogden teammate and roommate, Bobby Valentine.

Buckner began the 1969 season at Double A Albuquerque, where he batted .307 in 70 games. On July 24 he was promoted to Triple-A Spokane to replace first baseman Tommy Hutton, who had been called up by the Dodgers to fill in for the injured Wes Parker. His .315 mark in 36 games led to a September promotion to Los Angeles. On September 21 Buckner pinch-hit for pitcher Jim Brewer and popped out to second base in a 4-3 loss to Gaylord Perry and the San Francisco Giants, his lone appearance for the Dodgers that season. After the season, Buckner batted .350 with 10 stolen bases in 46 games in the

Arizona Instructional League. He played 38 games in the outfield, improving his chances to gain more playing time with the big club the following season.

Buckner was expected to compete for a roster spot on the Dodgers in 1970. Dodgers manager Walter Alston suggested, "It's possible Bill could be our starting left fielder. He'll certainly get a good look in the spring."[10] Buckner, not lacking for confidence, responded by saying, "I think I can hit .300 in the majors. I know I'm a better hitter right now than some who have been playing there."[11] Some within the Dodgers organization were urging Alston to commit to playing Buckner. Scout Goldie Holt told club vice president Al Campanis, "Buckner has so much ability and is so far advanced that I would put him in left field and leave him there against all kinds of pitching."[12] Holt was not the only one who predicted big things for Buckner. When the Dodgers traveled to Pompano Beach to play the Washington Senators in a spring training match-up, the Dodgers' batting practice turned into a hitting clinic of sorts as players and coaches gathered around Washington manager Ted Williams, who discussed hitting techniques. After watching Buckner take some swings in the batting cage, Williams remarked, "You don't have to worry. You're going to be an excellent hitter one of these days."[13] He predicted Buckner would eventually win a batting title.

Buckner received the Dearie Mulvey Memorial Award as the Dodgers' outstanding rookie of the spring after batting .303 in 19 games with a club-leading five doubles and five stolen bases. He didn't commit an error in the field or strike out at the plate. His performance earned him a place on the big-league roster, and he opened the regular season as the starting left fielder. He recorded his first major-league hit on April 8 against the Cincinnati Reds, but struggled to a .121 average in 14 games. In early May he was optioned along with Steve Garvey to Spokane. Buckner opted not to immediately report to Spokane in order to complete his semester of college courses at Southern California. He was given permission by the Dodgers to remain in Los Angeles to complete the courses and reported roughly three weeks later to Spokane. Dodgers general manager

Al Campanis, who approved Buckner's request, said he didn't "understand what Billy was doing about his schooling when we were on the road. If he was making up the courses through correspondence, why can't he continue to do so from Spokane? He certainly has our permission to return for tests."[14] Once Buckner arrived at Spokane, he wasted little time. He recorded seven hits in nine at-bats before suffering a broken jaw in a collision with teammates Davey Lopes and Bobby Valentine. He played two games before x-rays revealed the fracture. Recalling the injury, Spokane manager Tommy Lasorda said, "Buck broke his jaw and the front office told me to sit him out for five weeks. Buckner missed only one game and wound up hitting .335 and learned to spit and swear with his jaw wired shut."[15] He strung together a 12-game hitting streak in July, and wound up as one of seven Spokane batters to hit at or above .300. The club's .299 team average established a modern Pacific Coast League record. Buckner, who played 65 games at first base and 57 in the outfield, was one of six Spokane players named to the PCL All-Star Team. He was recalled by the Dodgers in September and batted .257 in 14 games to raise his overall major-league season average to .191.

Buckner stuck with the Dodgers as an outfielder out of spring training in 1971. He liked playing for the Dodgers, confidently declaring, "I know I can play in the big leagues and hit .300, and I hope it's with the Dodgers because this club has a good chance to win, and that means a lot of money. In fact, it means more than my entire season's salary. This club gives you something to shoot for."[16] He hit his first big-league home run in the second game of the season and went on a tear in June and July. He hit his first career grand slam on July 27 in an 8-5 win over Pittsburgh, his second five-RBI game of the month. San Francisco Giants manager Charlie Fox observed of Buckner, "I think his position eventually will be first base, and I'd like to have him right now to fill in there when we needed him. He's going to be quite a hitter."[17] Buckner and some of the other young Dodgers batters faded late in the season. He finished at .277 in 108 games as the Dodgers placed second in the National League West behind the Giants. He was selected as an outfielder on the Topps

Rookie All-Star Team. Since the previous season, Buckner had been the subject of frequent trade rumors, as other teams coveted the Dodgers' young talent. While speaking at a banquet in Southern California, Buckner said of the trade rumors, "The Dodgers may now have Frank Robinson and Tommy John, but they won't have a chance at the pennant if they trade me."[18] He and the club expected big things in 1972.

Buckner caught fire at the plate in July 1972 to move into the top 10 among National League batting leaders (though lacking enough at-bats to qualify) while earning starting opportunities against righties and lefties. He hit in 13 of 16 games, going 25-for-57 with two home runs, three stolen bases, and 15 RBIs. In all, he played in 105 games, splitting time between first base and the outfield, while improving his batting average to .319. Many felt that Buckner was a good bet to replace the retiring Wes Parker at first base in 1973. After the season he enrolled for the fall semester at the University of Southern California as a junior in the School of Business Administration.

Buckner once again split time at first and in the outfield in 1973. He finished the season batting .275 with 12 stolen bases in 14 attempts, while scoring 68 runs. The Dodgers managed their fourth straight second-place finish in the division, this time 3½ games behind the Cincinnati Reds.

Before the 1974 season began, several Dodgers went Hollywood. Buckner, Tom Paciorek, and Tommy Lasorda agreed to shaves and haircuts for the opportunity to serve as extras in scenes filmed for *The Godfather Part II* in Santo Domingo, Dominican Republic, in January 1974. As Paciorek recalled it, "After we spent all day there getting fitted for uniforms and getting our hair cut, they called and told us that our parts had been canceled. Later, Tommy, Buck, and I were going deep-sea fishing. Buck wanted to get in the film and they were filming that night, so we went back. The scene they were filming is when Michael Corleone finds out it was Fredo. We are in that scene. We didn't actually get our faces in the scene, but my right arm is!"[19]

Buckner enjoyed his best season to date in 1974. He hit in 17 straight games before going hitless in the second game of a doubleheader on May 15 against Houston. He had four hits in his next game, against Atlanta. He also made play after play in the outfield, including several highlight-reel-quality catches, prompting *The Sporting News* to note, "Even more impressive than Buckner's hitting has been his fielding. The left fielder has made five brilliant catches."[20] Buckner finished the regular season batting .314, and with his stellar defensive play received some modest consideration for National League MVP. Dodgers pitcher Don Sutton said, "And Buckner. Wow! If he doesn't get some votes—I mean a lot of votes—it's an injustice. He's made so many unbelievable catches out in left field we're starting to take him for granted."[21] Buckner finished 25th in the voting.

The Dodgers won 102 games and the division, and beat the Pittsburgh Pirates three games to one to advance to the 1974 World Series against the two-time defending World Series champion Oakland A's. The clubs split the first two games, and Oakland took Game Three despite an eighth-inning home run by Buckner off ace Catfish Hunter. As motivation prior to the start of Game Four, A's owner Charlie Finley called a team meeting and read a *San Francisco Examiner* article that quoted Buckner as suggesting the A's were an inferior ballclub. The article quoted Buckner as saying, "I definitely think we have a better ballclub than they do. The A's have only a couple of players who could play on our club. Reggie Jackson is outstanding. Sal Bando and Joe Rudi are good and they have a good pitching staff. Other than that … I think if we played them 162 times, we could beat them 100."[22] Oakland won Game Four by a score of 5-2. In the top of the eighth inning of the decisive Game Five, Buckner laced a hit to center, but was thrown out trying to stretch it all the way to third base, ending any threat to mount a late-inning scoring opportunity. He made no apologies for the play, noting, "It was something I did all year and I'll do it again. I can't stop taking chances because I got caught once."[23] Dodgers manager Walter Alston agreed, calling it "one of those plays. If you make it, it's a great play. If you don't, it's a bad play. We let our players go all season. We want them to play aggressively. Bill just ran into two great throws, a perfect throw from the outfield and a perfect throw from the relay man."[24] The A's, the club with only "a couple of players" who could play on the Dodgers, clinched their third straight World Series title with a 3-2 victory.

Buckner hoped to build upon his successful 1974 campaign the following season. But it was not meant to be. The 1975 season proved trying for Buckner, who suffered a severely sprained left ankle sliding into second base against the Giants on April 18. Forced to wear a cast, he did not return to the playing field until May 16, and he went hitless in eight of his first nine games back. His ankle never healed. Suffering from a pulled thigh muscle as well, he remained in the lineup, saying, "Every game is critical now, so I've got to keep playing. Between that and the bad ankle, I must be carrying three pounds of tape around every night. I can't be as aggressive as I want to be. I can't bunt. If I hit grounders on the infield I can't beat 'em out. That's probably 35 or 40 hits over the whole season."[25] Managing a meager .243 batting average in just 92 games, Buckner was finally shelved in late August and had ankle surgery on September 1.

With his season over, Buckner believed himself to be a trade option for the Dodgers, offering, "I definitely think I'm available. It all depends on what the Dodgers decide that they need. I've been hurt and I think the Dodger management is the best in baseball. But you have to remember that there's no sentiment in baseball."[26] Nevertheless, he opened the 1976 season as the Dodgers' starting left fielder and rebounded to play 154 games, bat .301 and set a new career high with 60 runs driven in. He sat out three games in late April/early May with a sprained left ankle, but returned on May 2 to beat out a pinch-bunt single to beat the St. Louis Cardinals. "I figured I could hold my breath four seconds," Buckner said of the surprise bunt.[27] He once again underwent surgery on his left ankle at the conclusion of the season.

On January 11, 1977, The Dodgers traded Buckner, shortstop Ivan de Jesus, and minor-league pitcher Jeff Albert to the Chicago Cubs for outfielder Rick Monday and pitcher Mike Garman. Initially Buckner was furious and bitter, but eventually warmed to the idea. Of the trade, he said, "Sure, I'll miss the Dodgers. And I'll miss Tommy Lasorda. Lasorda raised me up. I even played for him when he was managing in the minors. I was looking forward to playing for him in his first year as the Dodger manager. At least I know this: The Cubs wanted me. The Dodgers didn't."[28] The Cubs intended to make Buckner their everyday first baseman.

Buckner's Cubs debut was placed on hold, as he began the season on the disabled list, still recovering from ankle surgery and a fractured left index finger suffered the first week of spring training. He delivered a pinch-hit single in his first game, on April 19, and proceeded to hit safely in eight of his first 10 games. He was relegated to pinch-hitting duties for most of May after re-injuring his left ankle while trying to go from first to third in a game on May 4. Buckner returned to the starting lineup on June 6, but struggled at the plate before catching fire in August. He exacted a sort of revenge on the Dodgers on August 19, recording four hits, including a pair of home runs, to go along with five RBIs in a 6-2 win in Chicago.

Years later Buckner fondly recalled, "I felt better than I had that game and my ankle didn't seem to bother me at all. The Dodgers were going good — they had something like a 12-game lead in their division — and we were struggling. I seldom had as good a stretch in my career. Altogether I had eight hits, eight runs batted in and three homers in three games. I don't think any other achievement in baseball has given me as much satisfaction. I'd shown the Dodgers I could still play."[29]

Buckner's August included one six-game stretch in which he went 14-for-28 with two home runs, two doubles, and seven RBIs. He was voted NL Player of the Week for the period ended August 21. He did so while playing hurt every day. Cubs manager Herman Franks lamented, "Lord knows where we'd be if we had him healthy all season. He's probably playing at no more than 50 percent. I'd just like to have him at 90 percent next year."[30] The Cubs played .500 ball in

1977 and finished fourth in the NL East Division, 20 games behind the Philadelphia Phillies. As the season drew to a close, Buckner was considered among the leading candidates for the annual Hutch award, given to a player "who best exemplifies the character, fighting spirit, and competitive desire" of Fred Hutchinson, who died of cancer. He finished the 1977 season with a .284 average and a career-high 11 home runs.

Despite his initial misgivings about the trade, Buckner embraced the city of Chicago. His gritty hustle on the field made him a fan favorite. With the acquisition of free-agent slugger Dave Kingman, optimism ran high going into the 1978 season. Buckner, often hobbling on his bad left ankle, turned in a .323 average and 74 runs batted in. But the Cubs finished in third place, four games under .500. In the offseason, Buckner utilized ballet techniques in an effort to stay fit and improve his legs and ankle. He decided to stay the winter in Chicago. No one on the club made more personal appearances. General manager Bob Kennedy remarked of Buckner, "He's the one guy we can count on to get out and represent us. He's our Steady Eddie, just like he is at the plate."³¹ In the winter, Buckner accepted the Player of the Year Award from Chicago's baseball writers at their annual Diamond Dinner.

The following spring, Buckner was one of 17 players under consideration for the annual Roberto Clemente Award, given to the man who "best exemplifies baseball on and off the field." He agreed to a contract extension through 1984 for an estimated $1.3 million. The deal was applauded by the fan base. Chicago baseball writer Dave Nightingale described Buckner's place in the hearts and minds of Cubs fans by writing, "He created an image that was totally foreign to the Cubs last year by running out grounders to second base with his leg dragging behind him. He didn't peel off to the dugout at the 45-foot mark."³² The 1979 Cubs were a disappointment, despite a career year from Kingman and a Cy Young season from reliever Bruce Sutter. In one of the season's strangest games, Buckner had four hits, including a grand slam, and seven RBIs in a 23-22 10-inning loss to the Phillies on May 17. He finished the season with a .284 average and 14 home

runs. The club finished a disappointing fifth place with an 80-82 record.

Cubs manager Herman Franks announced his retirement at season's end, but sparked controversy on his way out when an article by Bob Nightengale appeared in the *Chicago Tribune* headlined, "Franks Blasts Cubs 'Whiners.'" Franks criticized several players including Buckner, of whom he is quoted as saying, "I thought he was the All-American boy. I thought he was the kind of guy who'd dive in the dirt to save ballgames for you. What I found out after being around him for a while is that he's nuts. … He doesn't care about the team. All he cares about is Bill Buckner."³³ Upon reading the comments, Buckner was furious. In an interview with the *Tribune*, he said, "Have you ever seen a rip job like that? He'd better come down here and give me an apology before the whole team. I've been busting my tail for three years. I've played when I shouldn't be playing. The fans have appreciated me in the past. I don't know how many millions read that paper and it's really making me look like an idiot."³⁴ Franks ultimately refused to apologize for the comments, but stated that he wished they had not been printed.

Buckner married flight attendant Jody Schenck on Long Island on February 16, 1980. They planned to move to Chicago from a northwest suburb. Buckner found an old church that was being converted into condominiums and bought the tower apartment. As is the case every spring, the Cubs began the 1980 season hoping to compete. For his part, Buckner went to the plate 114 times before finally striking out against Joe Beckwith of the Dodgers on May 14. When the Cubs acquired slugging first baseman Cliff Johnson from the Cleveland Indians in June, Buckner volunteered to go the outfield to make room for Johnson's bat in the lineup. Asked about the move, he responded simply, "I'd rather not, but if it will help the club, I'll do it."³⁵ Despite a bad ankle, bad feet, and bad legs, a 10-game hitting streak that ended on September 14 saw him push to the lead in the batting race. He went 0-for-4 on the final day of the season, but finished ahead of the St. Louis Cardinals' Keith Hernandez, .324 to .321, for the batting title. As the end of the season neared, articles started appearing suggesting that Buckner wanted out of Chicago. Commenting on the club's season, he confessed, "I've never been this depressed ever in baseball."[36] After the season he asked general manager Bob Kennedy for a trade. "I feel maybe it's time to make a move," he said. "I'm in my prime, but it doesn't seem like they're going to put a winning club on the field. If I thought we had a chance to be competitive, I'd stay."[37] Buckner was once again honored as the Chicago Player of the Year by the Chicago chapter of the Baseball Writers Association of America.

With four seasons remaining on his contract, Buckner threatened to sit out the 1981 season on his cattle ranch in Idaho if the Cubs did not renegotiate his $310,000-a-year contract. He was the frequent subject of trade rumors, and was nearly dealt to the Yankees for pitcher Dave Righetti in the spring. For season he batted .311, led the league with 35 doubles, made his first All-Star Team, and finished 10th in MVP voting. But Buckner's dissatisfaction with losing and his desire to leave Chicago became a constant issue for the remainder of his time with the Cubs. Before the 1982 season, the Cubs renegotiated his contract and he responded by establishing new personal bests with 201 hits, 15 home runs, and 105 runs batted in. He again finished 10th in MVP voting. When offseason rumors swirled around the possibility of Steve Garvey becoming a Cub, Buckner was more than receptive if it improved the team. "I want to be on a winning club more than anyone. If that's the way they feel they can improve the most, I'll give it my best shot." said Buckner, who even volunteered to go back to playing left field.[38]

Though he batted .280 with a league-leading 38 doubles in 1983, Buckner's role on the club in 1984 was uncertain. He opened the season as the first baseman, with trade rumors swirling around him, but was quickly benched in favor of Leon Durham. Cubs fans gave Buckner a standing ovation during introductions at the home opener at Wrigley Field. Durham was booed. After the game Cubs manager Jim Frey praised Buckner, saying he "has handled this about as well

as a player as good as he is can. I'm proud he hasn't initiated any problems. … He's had the chance, with the media around, to go the other way. It would be easy for him to say a lot of negative things. But the only thing he has said is that he wants to play, and I can't fault him for that."[39] On May 25 Buckner was traded to the Boston Red Sox for pitcher Dennis Eckersley and outfielder Mike Brumley. Buckner was ecstatic, announcing, "It's a new league and a new park. I'm excited about the deal. You never know how good you have it in baseball until you're not playing. Trades are part of the game. I was treated very well in Chicago. I have no complaints. But now I'm in Boston, and I just want to get off to a good start and make a good impression."[40] He suited up and started at first base for the Red Sox on May 26 against the Kansas City Royals.

Buckner sparked his new club, batting .321 with nine runs batted in as the Red Sox won 12 of the first 15 games he started. He got his 2,000th hit against the Baltimore Orioles in June, as he quickly acclimated himself to his new surroundings with the Red Sox. Discussing Boston, Buckner declared, "I couldn't have picked a better place to go. I love the city. I love the ballpark and I like everybody on the team. It's something to motivate me to do as well as I can so I can play as long as I can."[41] The Red Sox finished the season in fourth place, as Buckner contributed a .278 average, 11 home runs, and 67 runs batted in in 114 games. At the conclusion of the season, he underwent surgery to remove bone fragments from his left elbow.

Boston dropped to fifth place in 1985 with an 81-81 record. Buckner batted .299 with a career-high 110 runs batted in. He finished the season strongly, getting 16 hits and three home runs while driving in 11 runs in his last six games. His 201 hits for the season broke Jimmie Foxx's 49-year-old franchise record for hits in a season by a first baseman. Reflecting on his performance, Buckner regretted the club's fortunes, noting, "Personally, it is a very satisfying season. But there is no substitute for winning, and we didn't win. I thought we were going to do something when we left spring training, but it wasn't to be. The injuries hurt, and we didn't play well."[42] The Red Sox and their fans were disappointed, but the pieces were in place for a more successful campaign in 1986.

The 1986 Boston Red Sox finished the season fifth in the American League in runs scored. But the team's real strength was its pitching staff. Starter Roger Clemens emerged to win 24 games and claim the title of the game's best pitcher. The entire staff finished second in the league in strikeouts and tied for the third-highest saves total in the league. Buckner recognized the staff's value and spoke highly of Clemens, saying, "I've never played behind a pitcher who I felt so confident behind, so sure that we would win."[43] In July Buckner announced his intention to address painful bone spurs in his left ankle with offseason surgery. Even in constant discomfort, he managed 18 home runs, a new season high, and his third and final 100-plus-RBI season. The Red Sox won the AL East by 5½ games over the Yankees. They beat the California Angels in dramatic fashion to advance to the World Series against the New York Mets. Buckner had batted a disappointing .214 against the Angels, but hobbled into the Series against the Mets confident in his team's chances.

The Mets won the 1986 World Series. Game Six is now legendary, and widely regarded as one of the greatest games ever played. The Mets won the game in 10 innings, by a score of 6-5. Bill Buckner's role in the loss is well-known. On the game's final play, a groundball off the bat of Mets outfielder Mookie Wilson rolled between his legs at first base, allowing Ray Knight to score the winning run and push the series to a decisive Game Seven. The headline in the *Boston Herald* the next morning read, "Buckner Boots Big Grounder." Boston went on to lose Game Seven, 8-5, failing to end the organization's 68-year championship drought known by some as "The Curse of the Bambino." For many Boston fans and observers, Buckner's error was the reason the curse remained intact. For Buckner, it marked the beginning of near-constant criticism, heckling, and abuse. His name became synonymous with the derisive term "goat," and the error was destined to be replayed on television ad nauseam. More than a decade later, Buckner remarked, "I'll be seeing clips

of this thing until the day I die. I accept that. On the other hand, I'll never understand why."[44] Most experts acknowledged that the error was only one of several mistakes and blunders that contributed to the loss to the Mets. But for many there was little question the bulk of the blame was placed on Buckner's shoulders. It would prove a heavy burden.

Buckner had offseason surgery on his feet and ankles, but faced a slow rehabilitation process. He started the 1987 season at first base, but after batting .273 with two home runs through 75 games, he was released. The decision, not made easily, prompted Red Sox manager John McNamara to say, "He has been one of the most competitive people I've ever been associated with. It wasn't easy for him to get ready to play, but he had a tolerance for pain and did a great job for us. It was a difficult decision. There was a lot of sentiment involved."[45] For his part, Buckner confidently declared, "I think I can help somebody. I just hope I get the chance to prove it."[46] On July 28 he signed with the California Angels. He batted .306 in 194 plate appearances, and was the club's top hitter after his signing.

Buckner was released by the Angels on May 9, 1988, while sporting a meager .209 batting average. Four days later he signed with the Kansas City Royals. He remained with the Royals through 1989, primarily serving as a pinch-hitter. He was granted free agency on November 13 and in February 1990 reached agreement to return to the Red Sox. But after batting just .186 in 48 plate appearances, he was released on June 5. Acknowledging that it was the end of the line, Buckner said, "I'm disappointed. I would have liked to finish the last year here. It's the end of the line and I wanted to be on a winning team. It would have been nice, but…"[47] He retired with a .289 career batting average, 2,715 hits, and 498 doubles.

In the summer of 1993, Bill and his wife moved their three children, daughters Brittany and Christen and a son, Bobby, to a ranch in Meridian, Idaho. Buckner's wife, Jody, described one of the primary benefits of the location, pointing out that Meridian "isn't a sports town. Nobody in this town would talk about Willie in a derogatory way."[48]

Buckner invested in real estate in the Boise area, and worked briefly in the Toronto Blue Jays organization as a hitting instructor. In 1996 he was hired as hitting coach by the Chicago White Sox, replacing his own former hitting tutor, Walt Hriniak. He was fired in August 1997, despite the fact that the club was batting .271, good enough for eighth in the league. Other coaching stops included serving as manager for the Brockton Rox of the independent Can-Am Association in 2011, and as hitting coach for the Boise Hawks, the Chicago Cubs' short-season affiliate, from 2012 until his announced retirement in March 2014. Stating his desire to spend more time with his family, Buckner said, "Just too much time away. My wife has put up with it for 30-something years. I know that Jody would want me to be home. It was just the right thing to do. I've been doing it a long time, and it's been great. I will miss it. I enjoyed it. I enjoyed working with the kids. Some of them I worked with the last couple years are getting at-bats in spring training now. That's fun to watch."[49] Buckner worked with several of the young players in the Cubs' organization who contributed to the club's appearance in the 2015 postseason.

On April 8, 2008, Bill Buckner returned to Fenway Park to throw out the first pitch at Boston's home opener. The club was celebrating its 2007 World Series title, and Buckner received a four-minute standing ovation. After the game, an emotional Buckner reflected on the day's events, saying "[It was] probably about as emotional as it could get. A lot of thoughts [were] going through my mind. I wish I didn't have to walk all the way from left field, too many things. But just good thoughts, which is a nice thing. I really had to forgive, not the fans of Boston, per se, but in my heart, I had to forgive the media for what they put me and my family through. I've done that, and I'm over that and I'm just happy."[50] The Boston fans not only forgave Buckner, but accepted him back with open arms.

On September 17, 2015, President Barack Obama spoke to a friendly crowd of supporters in Boston, where he criticized congressional Republicans for failing to pass a budget and risking a government shutdown.

Using sports analogies to make his point, he was quoted saying, "So a shutdown would be completely irresponsible. It'd be an unforced error. A fumble on the goal line. It'd be like a ground ball slippin' through somebody's legs."[51] The obvious reference to Bill Buckner and the 1986 World Series drew sharp boos and groans from the crowd. For Bostonians, Buckner was back to being family and that carries with it an allegiance that transcends everything, even politics.

NOTES

1   Paul Dickson. *The New Dickson Baseball Dictionary* (San Diego: Harcourt Brace & Company, 1989), 215.

2   *The Sporting News*, March 25, 1972: 29.

3   *The Sporting News*, August 27, 1977: 13.

4   *The Sporting News*, July 16, 1977: 15.

5   *Vallejo Times-Herald*, October 20, 1974.

6   Jim Kaplan, "He's Off in a Zone of His Own," *Sports Illustrated*, September 13, 1982.

7   Ibid.

8   Ibid.

9   *The Sporting News*, October 4, 1969: 10.

10 *The Sporting News*, January 10, 1970: 51.

11 Ibid.

12 *The Sporting News*, February 28, 1970: 21.

13 *The Sporting News*, April 4, 1970: 14.

14 *The Sporting News*, May 23, 1970: 47.

15 Peter Gammons, "The Hub Hails Its Hobbling Hero," *Sports Illustrated*, November 10, 1986.

16 *The Sporting News*, April 10, 1971: 28.

17 *The Sporting News*, July 31, 1971: 21.

18 *The Sporting News*, December 25, 1971: 28.

19 Colin Gunderson, *Tommy Lasorda: My Way* (Chicago: Triumph Books, 2015), 164.

20 *The Sporting News*, June 8, 1974: 7.

21 *The Sporting News*, October 12, 1974: 11.

22 *The Sporting News*, November 2, 1974: 10.

23 Ibid.

24 Ibid.

25 *The Sporting News*, August 9, 1975: 25.

26 *The Sporting News*, August 30, 1975: 5.

27 *The Sporting News*, May 22, 1976: 16.

28 *The Sporting News*, February 5, 1977: 36.

29 *Baseball Digest*, April 1981.

30 *The Sporting News*, August 27, 1977: 13.

31 *The Sporting News*, December 23, 1978: 46.

32 *Baseball Digest*, August, 1979.

33 *Chicago Tribune*, September 25, 1979.

34 *Chicago Tribune*, September 26, 1979.

35 *The Sporting News*, July 26, 1980: 25.

36 *The Sporting News*, September 20, 1980: 14.

37 *The Sporting News*, November 29, 1980: 45.

38 *The Sporting News*, November 22, 1982: 42.

39 *The Sporting News*, April 30, 1984: 12.

40 *The Sporting News*, June 4, 1984: 19, 20.

41 *The Sporting News*, July 16, 1984: 27.

42 *The Sporting News*, November 18, 1985: 48.

43 *The Sporting News*, October 13, 1986: 16.

44 *Wall Street Journal*, July 24, 1998.

45 *The Sporting News*, August 3, 1987: 18.

46 Ibid.

47 *The Sporting News*, June 18, 1990: 15.

48 *Wall Street Journal*, July 24, 1998.

49 baseballthinkfactory.org/newsstand/discussion/bill_buckner_
retires_from_baseball.

50 m.mlb.com/news/article/2504342/.

51 politico.com/story/2015/09/obama-boston-buckner-labor-
baseball-red-sox-213383.

ROGER CLEMENS

By Frederick C. Bush

ROGER CLEMENS' LAST MAJOR-LEAGUE start, on October 7, 2007—for the New York Yankees against the Cleveland Indians, the very team against which he had made his major-league debut in May 1984—ended with him limping off the mound after only 2⅓ innings with a hamstring injury. Clemens had already allowed the Indians one run in each of the first and second innings, and, after facing two batters in the top of the third, he could pitch no more. He was charged with a third run, though the Yankees came back to win the game 8-4 for their lone victory in this American League Division Series. Such an ending is not what a movie screenwriter would have scripted as the final chapter of "Rocket's" 24-year career, but at least one element of Clemens' last appearance was storybook in character: He struck out the final batter he faced, Indians catcher Victor Martinez.

In spite of the abrupt end to Clemens' evening and career, as he left the mound, it seemed a certainty that he would be inducted into the National Baseball Hall of Fame in Cooperstown, New York, as soon as he passed the five-year waiting period for eligibility. Few pitchers in the history of baseball could boast anything near to his accomplishments: a record seven Cy Young Awards, 354 victories, 4,672 strikeouts, seven-time ERA leader with a career 3.12 ERA, six-time 20-game winner, five-time strikeout leader, 46 shutouts in the era of relief specialists and closers, and two-time World Series champion. He was too much of a polarizing figure in his career to exceed Tom Seaver's then-record of being named on 98.8 percent of the Hall of Fame ballots, but he seemed certain to be a first-ballot selectee.

On December 13, 2007, little more than two months after Clemens' final Yankees start, doubt was cast over his future enshrinement among baseball's immortals when he was mentioned repeatedly in the Mitchell Report on the use of performance-enhancing drugs in baseball. In the years following the report, Clemens spent almost as much time in courtrooms as he spent on pitcher's mounds during his career. By the time his first year of eligibility for the Hall of Fame arrived in January 2013, he was named on only 37.6 percent of the ballots and, in his second year, that number declined to 35.4 percent while two of his contemporaries and fellow members of the 300-win club, Greg Maddux and Tom Glavine, were elected.

Clemens' life is the tale of a fanatically driven man who worked hard to achieve his dream of stardom and attained the pinnacle of success. Jorge Posada, Clemens' catcher with the Yankees, was complimentary when he said, "The only thing he wants to do is just win."[1] Cito Gaston, Clemens' manager with the Toronto Blue Jays until he was fired toward the end of the 1997 season, intended no such praise when he commented, "It's all about him, nobody else but him."[2] Clemens' ambition

gained him both fans and detractors, helped him to achieve massive success, and ultimately contributed to his fall from grace.

William Roger Clemens was born on August 4, 1962, in Dayton, Ohio, the fifth child of Bill and Bess Clemens. He was only 5 months old when his mother took her children and left his father, with whom he claims to have spoken only once in his life, when he was 10 years old. Less than two years later, Bess married Woody Booher, whom Roger looked up to as a real father. But he became fatherless again at the age of 8 when Booher died of a heart attack.

While his mother provided Roger with an example of the work ethic he would adopt by laboring at several jobs to support her children, he came under the tutelage of his older brother Randy, whom he idolized. In high school Randy was a shortstop on the baseball team, the star shooting guard for the basketball team, and the king of his senior prom, leading Clemens to admit, "While I was growing up, Randy was the star as far as I was concerned."[3] Though the two brothers have become estranged, Randy's influence was immense as he "instill[ed] in his brother a simple philosophy: Either you're a winner or you're a failure."[4] It was a mantra that caused Clemens to question at times whether he was good enough to become the star athlete that both of them wanted him to be.

While Clemens' baseball career dwarfs his brother Randy's high-school athletic exploits, his initial attempts to emulate his elder sibling were less than encouraging. He played baseball, basketball, and football, but distinguished himself in none of these sports. In fact, the only notable event from his youth baseball exploits was that he split starts for his 1977 squad with Kelly Krzan, who was the first girl in Ohio to play on a boys' Little League team.

By the time Clemens was 15 and a high-school sophomore, Randy had married and moved to Sugar Land, Texas, a suburb 20 miles southwest of downtown Houston. Randy had failed to achieve athletic stardom of his own largely due to the development of a substance-abuse problem, but he now wanted to guide his younger brother's athletic career. After the two brothers received their mother's permission, Ohio-born-and-raised Roger Clemens made the sojourn to Texas, the state with which he has become identified.

Clemens enjoyed initial success by amassing a 12-1 record and helping Sugar Land's Dulles High School win a district title, but Randy was plotting a move to more competitive fields. After watching a tournament game between two of the Houston area's premier high-school teams, Bellaire and Spring Woods, Clemens decided that he wanted to play for the latter team. Bess Clemens had moved to Houston now as well, and she made sure that her son's wish was granted.

The time spent at Spring Woods High School was a mixed blessing: Clemens played for a coach, Charlie Maiorana, whom he credits for much of his knowledge about mechanics and conditioning, but he spent his junior year seeing little action on a team with two of the state's best pitching prospects. His determination showed as he became known for his workout regimen, especially his running, and he had his turn as Spring Woods' number-one starting pitcher during his senior year. Still, at that point in his life, the player who came to sit at number three on the major-league strikeout list still threw too softly to draw any notice from either professional or college scouts.

As a favor to Clemens, Maiorana called a colleague, Wayne Graham, the new coach at San Jacinto Junior College, to ask if he could pull any strings to get Clemens to his desired destination, the University of Texas in Austin. Graham could not accomplish that feat, but he did offer Clemens a scholarship to San Jacinto, which is where Clemens' fortunes were reversed. The failure to achieve high-school stardom resulted in the season that launched Clemens on the path to professional greatness.

The year 1981 was Wayne Graham's first season to coach at any college level, but he has become a legend by guiding San Jacinto to five national junior-college championships in six years (1985-1990)—a feat that earned him *Collegiate Baseball Magazine*'s Junior College Coach of the Century Award—and leading

Houston's Rice University to the NCAA College World Series Championship in 2003. What Graham did with Clemens—turning a soft-tossing youth into a flamethrower—was an equally impressive accomplishment. He preached to Clemens that he needed to finish hard on his pitches or he would never have a chance to realize his dream of pitching in the major leagues, a message Clemens took to heart as he finished his sole season at San Jacinto with a 9-2 record while the college won the Texas Junior College Athletic Association championship. His coach's assessment was that "Roger began the year as one of the guys, and he ended it as an ace."[5]

Graham anticipated that Clemens would remain at San Jacinto for a second year, an expectation that was buoyed when Clemens turned down an offer from the New York Mets, who had selected him in the 12th round of the 1981 draft. Clemens went through the motions of throwing for Mets manager Joe Torre and pitching coach/legend Bob Gibson at Houston's Astrodome, but he had other plans in mind. He had been contacted by University of Texas Longhorns coach Cliff Gustafson, who was now interested in the improved pitcher. The opportunity to play at Texas had been Clemens' dream, and he pounced on it; however, he failed to contact Graham about his decision and alienated the man who had placed him on the road to stardom.

Clemens fulfilled expectations at Texas, although there were some hiccups along the way. The 1982 Longhorns began their season with a 33-game winning streak that was one win shy of tying the NCAA record. Clemens, who had begun the campaign 7-0, pitched in game number 34 but lost 4-3 to the University of Houston. It was later revealed that he had bursitis while pitching that game, and he missed the next two weeks of the season. He finished 12-2 with a 1.99 ERA, but Texas was eliminated from the College World Series by Wichita State.

The Longhorns suffered under the burden of high expectations in 1983 and plodded through an up-and-down season. At one point, the driven Clemens became so frustrated by his personal mound setbacks that he

was ready to quit the team, an example of the toll that the insecurity caused by Randy Clemens' "winner or failure" mentality took on him. While he was not yet a polished pitcher, he still demonstrated great potential. Houston Astros scout Gordon Lakey reported that Clemens' delivery was not compact enough, but he believed it could be helped and that Clemens would develop more leg drive and become a power pitcher.[6] Chicago White Sox scout Larry Monroe's report echoed that of Lakey as he wrote of Clemens: "Delivery is fluid but does not use body at all. Should be easily improved and no reason why he shouldn't be in low 90's. I'm surprised he doesn't have shoulder problems from standing up and just throwing. Some bend in legs and drive to plate would help velocity, life, and location."[7] Both scouts projected Clemens as a likely second-round draft pick. Owing to rare encouragement from the usually gruff Gustafson, Clemens persevered—he went 13-5 with a 3.04 ERA—and the Longhorns survived their inconsistency to make a return trip to the College World Series.

Before Clemens took the mound for his start against Oklahoma State in the College World Series on June 6, the Boston Red Sox selected him as the 19th player chosen in the major-league draft, a circumstance about which he said, "I was completely surprised. As far as I was concerned, Boston was a foreign country."[8] Five days after defeating Oklahoma State, Clemens capped his Texas career with a complete-game 4-3 victory over Alabama in the College World Series Championship Game to put himself and his team on top of the collegiate baseball world before he departed Austin for Boston, having now been signed by Red Sox scout Danny Doyle. Of course, Clemens did not make it to the parent club straight out of college, but he did take the fast track through the Red Sox' minor-league system where he already exhibited character traits that became hallmarks of his career.

His first stop was with the Winter Haven Red Sox of the Class-A Florida State League, for whom he went 3-1 with a 1.24 ERA in four starts and where he established his reputation for pitching inside to hitters. Two days before his final Winter Haven start, Clemens had taken umbrage at the Lakeland Tigers' Ronald Davis taking out his Red Sox (and ex-University of Texas) teammate Mike Brumley at second base, a play on which Brumley was injured. Clemens pitched a 15-strikeout shutout against Lakeland in which he also retaliated for Brumley's injury by hitting Davis in the head in his first at-bat. Clemens claimed—as most pitchers do—that he had only wanted to brush Davis back and that the pitch had gotten away from him; however, he also claimed that he was prepared to fight, something for which Davis was in no condition as he collapsed and was taken to a hospital.

The split opinion among baseball observers as to whether Clemens merely pitched inside or was a headhunter mirrors the split in opinion about his character in general. Few players thought poorly of Don Drysdale or Nolan Ryan for pitching close inside, but these two pitchers were held in high regard while Clemens was often considered arrogant. Clemens fanned the flames of this negative reputation by both his actions and his words, never more infamously so than after winning the 1986 American League MVP Award. When informed that no less a luminary than Hank Aaron had asserted that pitchers should not receive the MVP, he retorted, "I wish he was still playing. I'd probably crack his head open to show him how valuable I was."⁹

After his debacle-marred gem, Clemens was promoted to the New Britain (Connecticut) Red Sox of the Double-A Eastern League and amassed a 4-1 record with a 1.38 ERA in seven starts, but he also continued to draw controversy. In the team's first-round playoff series, Reading Phillies manager Bill Dancy protested that Clemens was using a glove that had writing all over it and claimed that it was distracting. The home-plate umpire ordered Clemens to use a different glove—an order the pitcher complied with—but he began to curse at Clemens due to the grief he was getting from New Britain's bench. Clemens charged the umpire but stopped short of any physical contact. Instead he calmed down, borrowed a teammate's glove, and proceeded to dominate Reading. Charging umpires became another Clemens trait as his career

progressed, but calming down did not. As he accumulated successes, his "winner or failure" mentality and its resultant insecurity morphed into hypercompetitive intensity on and off the mound.

New Britain dispatched the Phillies and faced the Lynn Sailors for the championship, which they won when Clemens pitched a 10-strikeout shutout in Game Four. After he had breezed through two levels of the minor leagues and won his second championship in three months, Clemens' baseball future looked bright. His personal life became equally so when he began to date Debra Lynn Godfrey, whom he had known in passing at Spring Woods High School, in the offseason. Godfrey was a fellow fitness fanatic who twice auditioned for the Dallas Cowboys cheerleaders squad, and the two of them worked out together regularly. They became engaged in May 1984 and were married in November of that year.

Before his engagement to Godfrey, Clemens made one final stop on his way to Boston. He took part in spring training with the parent club in the familiar surroundings of Winter Haven, Florida, but ended up being assigned to Pawtucket of the Triple-A International League to begin the season after posting a 6.60 ERA in Grapefruit League games. Clemens did not allow his disappointment to keep him from excelling at yet another level as he posted a 1.93 ERA in 46⅔ innings for Pawtucket. Enough was enough and, on May 11, 1984, Roger Clemens was officially called up by the Boston Red Sox.

On Tuesday, May 15, 1984, Clemens made his major-league debut against the Indians before a mere 4,004 fans at chilly Cleveland Stadium and learned that minor-league success does not always carry over instantly to the majors. He received no decision after surrendering 11 hits, three walks, and five runs (four earned) in 5⅔ innings, but what was alarming was that Indians baserunners had swiped six bases against him because, in the words of his catcher, Gary Allenson, "(a)t that point, he had no real concept of keeping opposing runners in check."¹⁰ In his next start, against the Minnesota Twins on May 20, he pitched seven strong innings to earn his first major-league victory.

The remainder of Clemens' rookie season was not as memorable as the one put together by his National League counterpart, Dwight Gooden of the New York Mets, who finished with a 17-9 record and easily won the NL Rookie of the Year award. Clemens was up and down from start to start and later conceded that some people were beginning to question whether he might fall into the same category as David Clyde, the 1970s poster boy for young pitchers who had been rushed to the major leagues too quickly. That fear was put to rest by a 15-strikeout performance against the Kansas City Royals on August 21, but soon a new specter—that of injury—arrived to haunt the Red Sox and their fans. In his final start of the season, on August 31 against the Indians, Clemens registered seven of 11 outs by strikeout and then exited the game with a strained tendon in his right forearm. Though the injury was minor, Clemens was shut down for the year and finished a solid but unspectacular rookie campaign at 9-4 with a 4.32 ERA.

Clemens endured nagging injuries on his way to a 7-5/3.29 sophomore campaign in 1985. The low point of his season came on July 7 when he could not make his scheduled start against the California Angels due to what he described as "[…] an intensely sharp pain, as if someone stuck a knife in the back of my shoulder."[11] Clemens' early-career insecurity came to the fore again as he engaged in a clubhouse meltdown in Anaheim that day, and his fear of failure caused him to break down in tears while repeatedly asking, "Why me?" The next day he was placed on the 15-day disabled list due to shoulder inflammation and, though he returned to the rotation, he never recovered fully that year. On August 30 surgeon James Andrews removed a small piece of cartilage from Clemens' right shoulder in a 20-minute procedure. Clemens spent the offseason learning new exercises to strengthen his shoulder and waited for the 1986 season to come around.

The Red Sox started out slowly in 1986, but Clemens overcame his spring-training fears about his rehabilitated shoulder and charged out to a 3-0 record with a 1.85 ERA. His fourth start provided the harbinger of things to come as April 29, 1986, became the night on which Roger Clemens vaulted himself to stardom. Facing a free-swinging Seattle Mariners team that had struck out 166 times in 19 games, he turned in a record-setting performance by striking out 20 batters in a nine-inning, complete-game effort at Fenway Park. Clemens began the game in form by brushing back his former college teammate and role model Spike Owen with his second and third pitches of the night. Afterward, he denied throwing at Owen, but a conflicting account exists in which former Longhorns teammate Mike Capel dared him to plunk Owen on the day before the game.

Whatever the truth about Clemens' intent, the tone for the game was set and the Mariners were baffled for all but one pitch. Gorman Thomas launched Clemens' lone mistake for a solo home run and a 1-0 Mariners lead in the top of the seventh inning and, for a moment, it looked as though Clemens' brilliance might be for naught. Fortunately for Clemens and the Red Sox, Dwight Evans hit a three-run homer in the bottom of the inning for the final 3-1 margin of victory. From that point on, Clemens struck out four more batters to reach the record-breaking total of 20. He became an instant superstar and fulfilled a dream he claimed to have had when he was 12 by making the cover of *Sports Illustrated*'s May 12, 1986 issue, which carried the headline "Lord of the K's."[12]

After an 11-strikeout victory at Baltimore on June 27, Clemens was only the fifth pitcher in major-league history to start a season 14-0. He suffered his first loss on July 2 against the Toronto Blue Jays, but his 15-2 first-half record led Kansas City manager Dick Howser to name him the American League's starter in the All-Star Game, which would be held in his adopted hometown of Houston. The Red Sox, meanwhile, were in first place in the AL East with a 56-31 record and a seven-game lead at the break.

There was, however, a downside that accompanied all of this success, and it involved his relationship with the media and its burgeoning demands on his time. According to Clemens, "The attention I enjoyed and appreciated at first after breaking the strikeout record soon became stressful." He claimed that the press did not realize "how I needed to stay on my program and work."[13] For their part, the reporters began to perceive Clemens as alternately aloof or difficult, depending upon whether or not they could get any worthwhile quotes from the new star. Clemens correctly conceded that this period was "the first time I experienced some problems with the media,"[14] but it would not be the last.

The media crush of an All-Star Game that matched Clemens and fellow fireballer Dwight Gooden as the starters did not deter him from turning the event into yet another showcase for his talents. While Gooden surrendered two runs in three innings of work, Clemens retired all nine NL batters he faced, struck out two, and did not allow a single baserunner, a performance that earned him the game's MVP award. His newfound stardom also birthed a new arrogance that surfaced in the second half of the 1986 season.

In his July 30 start against the Chicago White Sox at Comiskey Park, Clemens had a new manner of meltdown after first-base umpire Greg Kosc made a disputed call that went against him. With two outs in the fifth inning, Red Sox first baseman Bill Buckner had flipped a Harold Baines grounder to Clemens, who thought he had beaten the runner to the bag. Instead, Kosc ruled that Clemens had missed first base and called Baines safe, which allowed what ended up being the winning run to score for the White Sox. Clemens charged at Kosc to argue the call and made incidental contact with the umpire, which resulted in his automatic ejection. Now he came completely unglued—he claimed to have hyperventilated twice during his rampage—and eventually was carried off the field by teammates Jim Rice and Don Baylor. Clemens was suspended for two games and fined, but his outlook on his punishment was revealing: In his autobiography, he stated, "As it turned out, all I lost was a day's pay—little more than $1,000—and $250" [for paying his teammates' (Bruce Hurst and Al Nipper) minor fines].[15] A fine was no great consequence to Clemens and, from this point on, he often alternated feats with fits over the course of his career.

The 1986 Red Sox rolled into the playoffs, with Clemens winning his last seven decisions, but Clemens' own postseason hopes seemed jeopardized when John Stefero's line drive hit his pitching elbow in his final regular-season start, against Baltimore on October 1. X-rays were negative and the swelling went down in time for Clemens to make his Game One start in the ALCS against the California Angels at Fenway. Clemens made three starts in Boston's hard-fought seven-game series against the Angels: Game One was forgettable as he surrendered eight runs (seven earned) in 7⅓ innings and Game Four resulted in a no-decision in 8⅓ innings during Boston's extra-inning loss, but in the clinching Game Seven he dominated the Angels and allowed only one run in seven innings to help send the Red Sox to the World Series for the first time since 1975.

World Series Game Two was a Clemens-versus-Gooden rematch, but neither pitcher lasted longer than five innings; a flu-ridden Clemens gave up four walks and three runs in 4⅓ innings of a game that Boston won 9-3. His second start came in Game Six, with the Red Sox holding a 3-2 edge in games, and he struck out eight while surrendering only two runs (one earned) in seven innings. The Red Sox had a 3-2 lead when Clemens was lifted from the game for a pinch-hitter in the eighth inning, but there was controversy over the timing of his exit. Clemens had torn open a blister and had begun bleeding, and manager John McNamara later claimed that Clemens had asked out of the game as a result, a contention that Clemens and several of his teammates denied. Game Six went down in Red Sox infamy as Calvin Schiraldi combined with Bob Stanley, Bill Buckner, and fate to lose to the Mets 6-5 in 10 innings. The Mets' 8-5 victory in Game Seven kept Clemens from putting the ultimate jewel in the crown of his 1986 season, a campaign during which he went 24-4 with a league-leading 2.48 ERA and became the first player to win the Cy Young Award, American League MVP Award, and All-Star Game MVP Award in the same season.

In addition to all of his on-field success, Roger and Debbie Clemens welcomed their first son, Koby, into the world on December 4, 1986. In what became a theme, Clemens gave all four of his sons names that begin with the letter "K"—Kory, Kacy, and Kody followed Koby—since it is the baseball scoring abbreviation for a strikeout.

The relationship between Clemens and the Red Sox took a downturn when Clemens walked out in the middle of spring training over a contract dispute. Commissioner Peter Ueberroth eventually negotiated an agreement between the team and its star, but the incident did not bode well for the future. The Red Sox had a miserable 1987 season, finishing at 78-84, though Clemens won his second consecutive Cy Young Award with a 20-9 record, 2.97 ERA, and seven shutouts.

In 1988 Clemens created a minor stir by deciding to pitch against the Angels in Anaheim rather than return to Houston for the birth of his second son, Kory. He earned a complete-game victory in that May 30 game on his way to an 18-12, 2.93, eight-shutout season. The Red Sox rebounded to win the AL East in 1988 but were swept in the ALCS by the Oakland Athletics, though Clemens pitched adequately in his Game Two start.

The biggest firestorm Clemens ignited that year came on December 5 when he gave an interview to a Boston television station in which he attacked anyone and everyone associated with the Red Sox, from management to teammates to fans. His complaint, "Travel, road trips and carrying your own luggage around isn't all that fun and glory,"[16] propagated the stereotype of the spoiled, pampered athlete and cast him in a negative light to fans.

Clemens did play for the Red Sox through the 1996 season, winning his third Cy Young in 1991 and leading the AL in ERA from 1990 to 1992, but he continued to be antagonistic with the media and, in turn, both the media and fans emphasized his shortcomings—real and perceived—more than his accomplishments.

One highly scrutinized event was a tantrum in Game Four of the 1990 ALCS in which the Athletics again swept the Red Sox. Clemens had pitched six shutout innings in Game One, but Boston had lost, and things were not going well at the outset of Game Four. With

Oakland leading 1-0 and two outs in the second inning, Clemens began cursing from the mound at home-plate umpire Terry Cooney over balls and strikes and was ejected from the game. When Clemens realized that he had been tossed, he charged Cooney and pushed right-field umpire Jim Evans aside, an offense for which he was fined $10,000 and suspended for the first five games of the 1991 season.

Rather than lie low after such an ignominious end to the season, Clemens gained additional notoriety off the field when he and older brother Randy were arrested at a Houston nightclub on January 18, 1991. Randy had become involved in an altercation, and Roger was arrested for hindering the security guard—an off-duty police officer—who was attempting to arrest his brother. He was found "not guilty" of the charge, but his fame was now increasing for the wrong reasons.

In 1992 Clemens further strained his relationship with the Red Sox when he reported eight days late for spring training; however, he still registered another stellar campaign on the mound, finishing 18-11. After he posted his first losing record in 1993—11-14 with a 4.46 ERA—speculation renewed about how much longer Clemens would last. He pitched well in strike-shortened 1994, but in 1995 he had a bloated 4.18 ERA and again came up short in the postseason, though he received no decision in the Red Sox' ALDS Game One extra-inning loss to the Cleveland Indians.

While Clemens was in an up-and-down phase of his career on the mound and was in the process of alienating Boston fans and management, he was still popular enough with fans nationwide that he made several guest appearances as himself on different television shows. Clemens even showed a sense of humor by taking a role in the animated *The Simpsons* episode titled "Homer at the Bat." In the course of the story, Clemens—as himself—is hypnotized into thinking that he is a chicken and spends much of the episode squawking and clucking. His acting exploits also included the big screen, for which his most notable role was as an unnamed flamethrower who pitches to Ty Cobb in the 1994 film *Cobb*, based on Al Stump's biography of the Georgia Peach.

In 1996 Clemens posted his second losing record, 10-13, but had a more respectable 3.63 ERA and led the AL with 257 strikeouts. He momentarily turned back the clock 10 years by registering his second career 20-strikeout game, against Detroit at Tiger Stadium on September 18; it was also his 192nd victory, which tied him with Cy Young atop the Red Sox' all-time list. Nonetheless, Red Sox general manager Dan Duquette considered his 40-39 record for the team from 1993 through 1996 and questioned whether Clemens might be in the "twilight" of his career; he apparently did not see him as a player around whom to rebuild the team into a perennial contender. Clemens spurned Boston's contract offer and signed for three years and $24.75 million with the Toronto Blue Jays.

Toronto was far removed from its consecutive World Series victories of 1992-1993 and was not a contender during Clemens' stint with the team, but "Rocket" was not finished yet after all. Quite the contrary, the brief Blue Jays era of 1997-1998 was Clemens at his dominant best as he went a combined 41-13 with a 2.33 ERA and 563 strikeouts, winning the pitching Triple Crown—wins, ERA, strikeouts—in both years as well as his fourth and fifth Cy Young Awards. He also exacted revenge against the Red Sox in his first start as a Blue Jay at Fenway Park on July 12, 1997 when he pitched eight innings of one-run ball and struck out 16 batters.

In time, a cloud of suspicion gathered over this mid-30s pitching renaissance for two reasons: 1) The prevalence of performance-enhancing drugs (PEDs) in baseball by this time, and 2) the hiring of Brian McNamee as Toronto's strength and conditioning coach after the 1997 season. Baseball was in the midst of its PED era and—as was the case with most players—no public accusations were made against Clemens at the time; however, McNamee later claimed that he injected Clemens with the steroid Winstrol in 1998.

Clemens longed to pitch for a contender again and his trade request was granted on February 18, 1999, when Toronto traded him to the New York Yankees—an old adversary with whom he had engaged in numerous beanball wars—for starter David Wells, reliever Graeme Lloyd, and second baseman Homer Bush. As a Yankee, Clemens was back in the center of the baseball universe, but that was a mixed blessing as he turned in an inconsistent 14-10, 4.60 campaign.

The 1999 postseason began promisingly as Clemens pitched seven scoreless innings in the ALDS-clinching Game Three against the Texas Rangers, but the ALCS was another matter altogether as Clemens fizzled in his return to Fenway in a Game Three marquee matchup against Boston's new ace, Pedro Martinez. While Martinez pitched seven shutout innings and struck out 12, Clemens suffered the Yankees' only loss of the series and was battered for five runs in only two innings. As he left the mound in the bottom of the third, Boston fans taunted him by chanting "Where is Rog-er?" That game became a distant memory for Clemens after he won World Series Game Four against the Atlanta Braves with a 7⅔-inning, one-run performance that capped a Yankees sweep. The one prize, a World Series ring, that had eluded Clemens for his entire career was now his: "Tonight, I know what it's like to be a Yankee. I am blessed," he exulted.[17]

Prior to Game Two of the World Series at Atlanta's Turner Field, Clemens had been named—along with 29 other players—as a member of the All-Century Team. The 100 nominees for the team had been chosen by a panel of experts and had been presented at that year's All-Star Game, but it was the fans who had voted for the players. Clemens was the only active pitcher—and one of only four active players—voted onto the team, joining Cal Ripken Jr., Ken Griffey Jr., and Mark McGwire. This accolade and his first World Series championship appeared to validate Clemens' tunnel-vision tenacity in pursuit of his goals.

On the heels of reaching the pinnacle of professional success, Clemens experienced one of the lowest points in his personal life. In May 2000 his ex-sister-in-law Kathy, who had been married to his brother Randy and had been like a mother to him when he had first moved to Texas, was murdered in a home-invasion robbery in Houston. Kathy's son Marcus had adopted his father Randy's drug habit, and the robbery was tied to money and drugs. Roger blamed Randy's substance-abuse addiction for the couple's divorce, his nephew's drug addiction, and Kathy's murder, and he became alienated from the brother who had exerted such tremendous influence on his life, his outlook on the world, and his early career.

On the mound in 2000, Clemens posted a pedestrian 13-8 record and lost his two starts against Oakland in the ALDS, but he experienced a reversal of fortune from the previous year's ALCS in Boston in his Game Four start against the Seattle Mariners. In a game as dominant as any he had ever pitched, he set an ALCS record by striking out 15 batters in a one-hit shutout. It was an amazing performance for a 38-year old power pitcher that also served as an endorsement for Clemens' now-legendary workout regimen—one that players half his age were unwilling to attempt—which again fell under the auspices of Brian McNamee, who had joined the Yankees as an assistant strength coach in 2000.

Clemens turned in another eight shutout innings in World Series Game Two against the crosstown Mets, a Series the Yankees won in five games. The focus of the game, though, was a bizarre incident that occurred in the top of the first inning. Mets catcher Mike Piazza, whom Clemens had hit in the head with a pitch in a regular-season game on July 8, shattered his bat hitting a soft liner that squibbed foul into the Yankees dugout. Clemens picked up the barrel piece of the bat and threw it in Piazza's direction as he ran up the baseline. The shard almost hit Piazza, who was angered and exchanged words with Clemens as both benches emptied. Clemens was not ejected for his action and dominated the Mets with eight innings of shutout ball in which he allowed only two hits and no walks, and struck out nine. After the game, Clemens offered the implausible excuse that he had thought he had the ball, rather than the barrel of Piazza's bat, which still did not explain why he threw it toward Piazza rather than first baseman Tino Martinez. Nobody believed Clemens, and he was fined $50,000 for the incident.

In 2001, a season in which McNamee has claimed he injected Clemens with the steroids Sustanon 250 and Deca-Durabolin, Clemens raced out to a 12-1 record

that garnered him his second career All-Star Game start. He took his record to 19-1 before his first attempt at win number 20 was placed on hold by the terrorist attacks against the United States on September 11, 2001. After America regrouped, and MLB resumed play on September 17 at the behest of President George W. Bush, Clemens finished the season 20-3 with a 3.51 ERA and earned his sixth Cy Young Award. The Yankees again made it to the World Series, and Clemens registered a 1.35 ERA over 13⅓ innings in two starts against the Arizona Diamondbacks. He engaged in a Game Seven duel against Curt Schilling that the Yankees lost when Luis Gonzalez looped an RBI single off Mariano Rivera to win the game in the bottom of the ninth inning.

Clemens was solid, though no longer spectacular, with the Yankees in 2002-2003. He did reach both the 300-win and 4,000-strikeout milestones in a 5-2 victory over the St. Louis Cardinals at Yankee Stadium on June 13, 2003, becoming the first pitcher to hit both landmarks in the same game. He had said repeatedly that he was retiring after the 2003 season, so when he walked off the mound of Miami's Pro Player Stadium after pitching seven innings of three-run ball in World Series Game Four on October 22, 2003, everyone assumed it was his swan song. There was no fairytale ending to his story, though, as the Yankees fell to the Florida Marlins in six games.

Clemens' retirement lasted little more than 2½ months. Shortly after Yankees free agent, friend, and fellow Houstonian Andy Pettitte signed to play for the Houston Astros, Clemens joined him and the pair set Houston abuzz with the hope that they could help franchise icons Jeff Bagwell and Craig Biggio reach the promised land of the World Series before they too reached retirement age.

Although 2004 was his first year in the National League, Clemens registered the same results he had through most of his career: He posted an 18-4 record, 2.98 ERA, and 218 strikeouts for which he won his record-extending seventh Cy Young Award, joining Gaylord Perry, Randy Johnson, and Pedro Martinez as the only pitchers to win the award in both leagues.

He also started his third All-Star Game—this time for the NL—in his adopted hometown of Houston, where he had started his first All-Star Game for the AL 18 years earlier.

The Astros were the NL wild-card team in 2004, and Clemens started the franchise toward its first-ever postseason-series victory in 43 seasons of existence by winning NLDS Game One against the Atlanta Braves. Against the St. Louis Cardinals in the NLCS, he won Game Three but lost the decisive Game Seven; however, he received none of the criticism he had often endured in Boston and New York when he had fallen short in the postseason. He could do no wrong in his hometown and was becoming a Texas legend on a par with his boyhood idol Nolan Ryan.

Clemens returned to the Astros in 2005 and added to his increasingly larger-than-life exploits. At the age of 43, he led the majors with a 1.87 ERA and might have won an eighth Cy Young Award had he received more run support to improve his 13-8 record. On September 14, in a decision reminiscent of his choice to pitch on the day of his son Kory's birth, Clemens defeated the Florida Marlins after his mother, Bess, died that morning. In response to those who questioned his decision, Clemens replied that his mother had made him promise to pitch and that the game was important to the Astros' playoff hopes. It was clear that he was still as driven to win as he had always been.

The Astros were the NL wild-card entry again in 2005 and faced the Atlanta Braves once more. Clemens lost Game Two, but for Houston fans his status grew to mythological proportions three days later in Game Four. On October 9, after the Astros had exhausted their bullpen by the 15th inning of their marathon contest against the Braves, Clemens came to the rescue and pitched three scoreless innings. He earned the win when Chris Burke ended the game with a solo homer in the bottom of the 18th, and the Astros advanced to the NLCS. As if pitching on short rest were not enough, Clemens had also demonstrated a bit of batting acumen when he laid down a perfect sacrifice bunt in the bottom of the 15th.

In the NLCS, the Astros met another familiar opponent—the Cardinals—whom they defeated in six games to reach their first World Series, with Clemens contributing a victory in Game Three. The magic ran out in the World Series, though, as he exited Game One with a sore hamstring after allowing three runs in only two innings. The Chicago White Sox swept the Astros, and Clemens seemed likely to retire permanently.

Alas, he could not stay away from the game, and he lost much of the goodwill he had engendered in 2005 by appearing willing to sell himself to the highest bidder as he engaged in talks with numerous teams. The so-called "family-friendly" clause that had allowed Clemens to remain home for road trips during which he was not scheduled to pitch—and which he insisted upon to the end of his career—now had some people questioning whether his true motive was team success or money. In the end, he signed with the Astros on May 31 and still posted a 2.30 ERA in 113⅓ innings over 19 starts, but the team failed to make the playoffs.

Clemens played the same "Will he or won't he pitch?" game at the start of the 2007 season before announcing his return to the New York Yankees from owner George Steinbrenner's luxury box during the seventh-inning stretch of a Yankees-Mariners game on May 6. He posted a mediocre 6-6, 4.18 line over 99 innings before limping off the Yankee Stadium mound with yet another hamstring injury in the Yankees' October 7 ALDS game against Cleveland.

Once his career was finally over, the countdown to Clemens' Hall of Fame induction began. Whether media members and fans liked him or not—and there were plenty of people in both camps—his statistics pointed to him being one of the best pitchers ever to play the game. Even so, the voters who cast ballots for players to gain entry into the National Baseball Hall of Fame are told to take a player's character into account, and all sorts of skeletons fell out of Clemens' closet upon the release of the Mitchell Report.

First, there were Brian McNamee's allegations of steroid use. Clemens vehemently denied McNamee's accusations and, under the advice and guidance of his lawyer Rusty Hardin, went on the offensive. On January 6, 2008, Clemens filed a defamation suit against McNamee. Though Clemens eventually dropped his suit, McNamee filed his own defamation suit against Clemens in 2008, which dragged on for almost seven years before McNamee received an out-of-court settlement to be paid by Clemens' insurer—not Clemens himself—in March 2015.

The same day that Clemens filed his lawsuit in Houston, CBS-TV's investigative news show *60 Minutes* aired a Mike Wallace interview of Clemens. In the interview Clemens claimed that McNamee had only injected him with vitamin B12 and the painkiller Lidocaine, an assertion that was dubious to many viewers and which made him the butt of countless pain-in-the-butt jokes.

The next day Clemens and Hardin held a press conference in Houston and played a recording of a recent phone conversation between Clemens and McNamee that was to prove Clemens' innocence. The tape proved nothing as McNamee sounded both too desperate and too cautious to say anything that might incriminate him. Clemens fielded questions from the media, but grew increasingly aggravated and angry as the conference continued. When asked if he thought McNamee's allegations would affect his chances at being elected to the Hall of Fame, his retort, "I don't give a rat's ass about the Hall of Fame,"[18] was another statement no one believed, and he soon stormed out of his own press conference.

On February 13, 2008, Clemens was called to testify before a congressional committee in Washington, where he continued to profess his innocence. Some of his testimony contradicted a sworn statement made by Andy Pettitte, who claimed Clemens had told him that McNamee injected him with human growth hormone (HGH). Clemens responded that Pettitte had "misremembered" [sic] their conversation and that he had told Pettitte it was his wife, Debbie, whom McNamee had injected with HGH. There were enough inconsistencies in Clemens' testimony that a drawn-out legal process resulted in an August 19, 2010,

grand-jury indictment for making false statements to Congress. His first trial, in July 2011, quickly resulted in a mistrial, while his second trial ended with his acquittal on June 18, 2012.

Along with the steroid allegations and their attendant legal troubles, Clemens was also accused of having extramarital affairs with numerous women. The two most notable names were those of the late country singer Mindy McCready and pro golfer John Daly's ex-wife Paulette. Clemens denied these accusations as well, but McCready and Paulette Daly neither confirmed nor denied them, which gave them implicit affirmation in many people's minds.

All of this dirty laundry was aired in the media in the immediate aftermath of the Mitchell Report, but two books contributed further to the decline of Clemens' reputation: Jeff Pearlman's unauthorized biography *The Rocket That Fell to Earth*, and *New York Daily News'* Sports Investigative Team's *American Icon: The Fall of Roger Clemens and the Rise of Steroids in America's Pastime*. Pearlman's book portrays Clemens in such a consistently negative light that it is easy to dismiss it as one-sided, but the *Daily News* team's research into McNamee's claims casts serious doubt on Clemens' assertion of innocence. The facts remain, however, that Roger Clemens never tested positive for PEDs and that he was acquitted of all charges of lying to Congress.

Nonetheless, the repercussions of the allegations have resulted in a lack of support for Clemens' Hall of Fame candidacy. If he is ultimately enshrined, it is entirely possible that a Veterans Committee will have determined his fate after his initial 10-year period of eligibility has passed. His new road to baseball immortality involves rehabilitation of his former reputation as a hard-working star, which will be an arduous process since everything he does now is greeted with suspicion and cynicism, a circumstance that was in evidence when he pitched two games with the independent Atlantic League's Sugar Land Skeeters in 2012.

Sugar Land, where Clemens lived when he first moved to Texas, received a national publicity boost during the Skeeters' inaugural season when Clemens pitched in two games in August and September 2012. His motive for doing so was suspect, however, as he had just been acquitted of lying to Congress in June and needed positive publicity during his first time on the Hall of Fame ballot. Some media members believed that Clemens was attempting a late-season MLB comeback to push back his Hall of Fame eligibility by five years in the hope his legal troubles would blow over and that he would be a first-ballot selectee. Clemens denied such claims, but his comment—"I probably overextended myself a little bit. I wanted to see where I was at"[19]—after his August 25 start for the Skeeters was interpreted to mean that he was gauging his comeback status.

By his second start, on September 7, the Skeeters had signed Clemens' oldest son, Koby, a catcher, and father and son formed the battery against the Long Island Ducks. This time, the 50-year-old Clemens clearly left open the possibility of a major-league comeback attempt when he said, "I would have to get ready. It would be fun. There's no reason why I couldn't do it next year."[20] Though he had pitched well in both games—and no doubt enjoyed being the center of attention for his pitching rather than his court appearances—this was unaffiliated minor-league ball and his fastball had topped out at 88 MPH, which was hardly the dominant stuff he had once had in his prime.

In the end, Clemens chose to go out as a hometown hero and a winner after his appearances for the Skeeters rather than to risk going out as a failure in one last major-league stint. As of 2015, he and Debbie reside in Houston, where they work to benefit children through the Roger Clemens Foundation and where he also serves as a special assistant to the Astros' general manager.

Clemens' work with the Astros and his induction into the Red Sox Hall of Fame at Fenway Park on August 14, 2014, prior to Boston's game against the Astros, show that there is still a place for him in baseball. The March 2015 settlement in the McNamee case may eventually allow Clemens to move past

constant discussion of the steroid allegations against him, though the court of public opinion is unlikely to change its judgment. Clemens did not attend the McNamee settlement, saying, "I was not present, nor would have I participated in paying one dime. Everyone knows my stance on the subject."[21] The fact that he had been named on only 37.5 percent of the Hall of Fame ballots in January 2015 demonstrated that the Hall of Fame voters have not changed their stance in regard to Clemens either.

SOURCES

Baseballhall.org

Baseball-Reference.com

Boston Globe

CBC Sports

Chicago Tribune

Clemens, Roger, with Peter Gammons. *Rocket Man* (Lexington, Massachusetts: The Stephen Greene Press, 1987).

ESPN.com

Hartford Courant

Houston.astros.mlb.com

Houston Chronicle

Lexington (Kentucky) *Herald-Leader*

New York Daily News

New York Times

Pearlman, Jeff. *The Rocket That Fell to Earth* (New York: Harper, 2009).

Riceowls.com

The Sporting News

Sports Illustrated

Sugarlandskeeters.com

Texassports.com

Thompson, Teri, et al. *American Icon* (New York: Knopf, 2009).

Yankeeography: Pinstripe Legends, "Roger Clemens," (2011, A&E Home Video), DVD.

NOTES

1   Yankeeography: *Pinstripe Legends*: "Roger Clemens," (2011, A&E Home Video), DVD.

2   CBC Sports, "Clemens lambasted by Blue Jays' Gaston," http://www.cbc.ca/sports/baseball/clemens-lambasted-by-blue-jays-gaston-1.817361, accessed July 27, 2014.

3 Roger Clemens with Peter Gammons, *Rocket Man* (Lexington, Massachusetts: The Stephen Greene Press, 1987), 20.

4 Jeff Pearlman, *The Rocket That Fell to Earth* (New York: Harper, 2009), 13.

5 Pearlman, 39.

6 Gordon Lakey, "Houston Astros Free Agent Report – William Roger Clemens," scouts.baseballhall.org/report?reportid=01373& playerid=clemer002, accessed April 11, 2015.

7 Larry Monroe, "Chicago White Sox Free Agent Report – Roger Clemens," scouts.baseballhall.org/report?reportid=00948&player id=clemer002, accessed April 11, 2015.

8 Clemens with Gammons, 33.

9 Mark Story, "22 things you should know about 'Rocket,'" web. archive.org/web/20060615043527/http://www.kentucky.com/mld/ kentucky/sports/14749611.htm, accessed August 3, 2014.

10 Pearlman, 76.

11 Clemens with Gammons, 52.

12 si.com/vault/cover/1986/05/12, accessed April 11, 2015.

13 Clemens with Gammons, 75.

14 Ibid.

15 Clemens with Gammons, 110-111.

16 Pearlman, 132.

17 Jeff Jacobs, "From Ruth To Clemens, Monumental Dynasty," articles.courant.com/1999-10-28/sports/9910280137_1_yankee-stadium-25th-world-series-babe-ruth-s-monument, accessed July 30, 2014.

18 Mike Lupica, "Either Roger Clemens or Brian McNamee will tell lies on the Hill," nydailynews.com/sports/baseball/yankees/ roger-clemens-brian-mcnamee-lies-hill-article-1.311566, accessed December 12, 2014.

19 ESPN.com, "Roger Clemens shines in return," espn.go.com/ mlb/story/_/id/8303548/roger-clemens-impressive-comeback-sugar-land-skeeters, accessed December 15, 2014.

20 Associated Press, "Roger Clemens solid in outing," espn.go.com/ mlb/story/_/id/8350222/roger-clemens-solid-again-second-outing-sugar-land-skeeters, accessed December 15, 2014.

21 ESPN.com news services, "Defamation suit vs. Clemens settled," espn.go.com/mlb/story/_/id/12509911/roger-clemens-brian-mcnamee-reach-settlement-2008-defamation-lawsuit, accessed March 19, 2015.

STEVE CRAWFORD

By John DiFonzo

STEVE CRAWFORD WAS A PITCHER WHO spent most of his 10 major-league seasons fighting for a job on a major-league roster, the majority of them with the Boston Red Sox. He was a once-promising prospect, but became almost a forgotten man by 1986. He would have been left off the Red Sox' postseason roster that year had fate not intervened twice. Crawford went on to make a significant contribution to the Red Sox' postseason run and earned a victory in one of the most exciting games in baseball history with the Red Sox season hanging in the balance; he was credited with the win in one of the most highly anticipated pitching matchups in World Series history.

Steven Ray Crawford was born on April 29, 1958, in Pryor Oklahoma, the youngest of six children (three boys and three girls) of Lorraine (Emme) and Opie Crawford. Opie served in the Army during World War II in the Philippines. He was an undefeated boxer until he was wounded when caught in a bomb explosion that left his right side partially paralyzed. After the war, he was a Pentecostal preacher for 35 years and a pulpwood cutter. Lorraine, originally from Nebraska, ran the family farm, which included 300 to 400 head of cattle. Crawford remembered hauling a lot of hay in his younger days.

Crawford's father was an early influence. "My father was my number one influence. He was my first coach at the age of 5. He taught me how to approach and play the game," he told the author.[1] Early in his career he told a sportswriter, "I've been fortunate that I've had excellent help my entire life. My father was the biggest help early. He was a three-sport star in high school and used to help me throwing baseballs every day."[2]

Crawford was a three-sport high-school star in Salina, Oklahoma. After high school he had full-scholarship offers in three sports, with baseball being his third sport. He played fullback and defensive end on the football team. His older brothers talked him out of football and convinced him that he had a better chance to make it as a baseball player. Crawford was a pitcher-first baseman for Claremore Junior College (now called Rogers State University) from 1977-1978 Crawford drew interest from most of the major-league clubs as they believe he had first-round talent.

On May 6, 1978, the 20-year old Crawford chose to sign as an amateur free agent for less money with the Boston Red Sox by scout Danny Doyle "Carl Yastrzemski was my idol," Crawford said. "He always was. I used a Yaz bat. I signed with the Red Sox because Carl Yastrzemski was with the Red Sox. That was one of my reasons, and to play with Carl Yastrzemski, right over there. You never think it could happen. Now you're talking with him, talking pretty good."[3] Crawford didn't even know who Yastrzemski was but he liked his bat, then he found out what a great

player he was. "The first day I walked into Fenway Park, I was in total awe seeing Carl Yastrzemski and Fenway, a day I will never forget."[4] The Red Sox felt that signing Crawford partially made up for losing three draft picks that year by signing Mike Torrez, Jack Brohamer, and Dick Drago as free agents.

Crawford started his professional career with Winston-Salem in the Class-A Carolina League. He pitched in 19 games, started 14, and sported a 9-5 record with a 3.44 ERA. One of his teammates, Michael Moore, called Crawford "Shag" because of his bushy long hair and mustache, and the nickname stuck.[5] The next season, still at Winston-Salem, he started 28 games, compiled an 11-11 record, improved his ERA to 2.94, and walked only 67 batters in 211 innings.

In 1980 Crawford was promoted to the Bristol Red Sox of the Double-A Eastern League. He impressed with a 2.64 ERA in 177 innings and gave up only six home runs. Called up to the Red Sox in September, Crawford made his major-league debut on September 2 at Fenway Park against the California Angels with the Red Sox leading 10-2 in the eighth inning. Crawford pitched a perfect eighth and got out of a two-on, one-out jam in the ninth without surrendering a run, preserving the victory. On September 13 at Fenway Park he relieved Mike Torrez after Torrez gave up four runs to the New York Yankees in the fourth inning. Crawford pitched 4⅔ shutout innings in the 4-3 loss. The next day manager Don Zimmer announced that Crawford would replace Torrez (14 losses) in the starting rotation. With the Red Sox 13½ games out of first place, Zimmer, who was on the hot seat, said, "If I'm still the manager next year, I would like to know if the kid is capable of pitching in the big leagues before we get to spring training."[6]

Crawford pitched a complete-game 8-3 victory against the Cleveland Indians on September 18, winning manager Zimmer's praises again. Crawford said of his performance, "I proved to myself that I could pitch up here. I wasn't nervous at the start, but I did load the bases [in the first inning]. Then I got the double-play ball and I said to myself that I'm going to be all right."[7] He started four more times, earning a complete-game victory over Toronto, to go 2-0 with a 3.62 ERA. Crawford was one of the few bright spots the Red Sox had in September 1980. Zimmer was fired in the last week of the season.

During spring training in 1981 (Ralph Houk was the new manager), expectations were high for Crawford and he was rated ahead of top pitching prospects Bruce Hurst and Bobby Ojeda by the Red Sox. Crawford on his 1980 season, "I know all of this is in the past, and I will have to go out and prove myself all over again."[8] The 6-foot-5, 225-pound, 22-year-old Crawford, although not overpowering, possessed a 94-mile-per-hour fastball and a good break on his curve. Mild-mannered, he was termed too polite to be called "nasty."[9] Baltimore super-scout Jim Russo called him "one of the three best young pitchers in Florida,"[10] and Red Sox minor-league pitching coach Bill Slack said, "He has four good pitches and command of all of them. Not only does he have an idea how to pitch, but he does the little things that help you become a better pitcher."[11] Crawford made the Red Sox rotation.

On April 13, dueling Baltimore's Jim Palmer, Crawford lost 5-1 but didn't give up an earned run and four of the Orioles' runs tallied after he left the game. Red Sox pitching coach Lee Stange praised his fastball, saying "It really moved."[12]

Crawford's season and career took a downturn from this point. He started 10 more games, was 0-5, and his ERA rose to 4.96. Before starting against Oakland in June 6, he shaved his distinctive mustache in an effort to change his luck. "I did it in the minors when things were going bad and I won three in a row after that,"[13] No such luck in the majors: Crawford lasted only two inning in a 6-2 loss to Oakland and lost his spot in the starting rotation. The Red Sox planned to send him to Triple-A Pawtucket and call up Bobby Ojeda. But a players strike loomed, and the Red Sox decided not to call up Ojeda before the June 11 strike deadline and risk having him not pitch. Crawford stayed on the major-league roster and was inactive until play resume on August 10. The rest of the season, Crawford had one start and three relief appearances in mop-up roles.

The Red Sox were still high on Crawford, despite his 0-5 record, and hoped for a rebound in 1982. "There is no question he has a big league arm," Ralph Houk said.[14] Unfortunately for Crawford, he developed bone chips in his elbow from throwing the slider in winter ball. "I changed from being a fast ball pitcher to a breaking ball pitcher and that's how I hurt my arm," said Crawford.[15] The Red Sox team physician, Dr. Arthur Pappas, performed surgery and the timetable was for Crawford to be throwing by the end of spring training and be back on the field by the All-Star break.

When Crawford regained his health, he was on a rehabilitation program and started the 1982 season in Pawtucket. He started 10 games and compiled a 1-4 record with a 4.11 ERA, striking out only 21 batters in 46 innings. Crawford was called up in September and fared better in the majors. He pitched in five games in relief, winning one game with a 2.00 ERA.

Crawford came to spring training in 1983 fighting for a job on the Boston roster. He was on a strict diet and had lost 15 pounds to get back to his 1980 playing weight of 225 pounds. "The one goal I have right now," he said, "is to be on the plane to Boston. I've got a pretty good chance of making the club. But I've got to come in and show what I can do. That's what the Red Sox want to know, to see if my elbow is OK."[16]

Crawford didn't make the cut and spent the entire 1983 season in Pawtucket. He started 27 games, compiling a record of 8-11 with a 5.18 ERA striking out 104 batters in 154⅔ innings. Crawford was disappointed at not making the major-league roster and by his own admission went to Pawtucket with a bad attitude. "The only reason I wasn't called up last season was me. But I learned a lesson," he said.[17]

Crawford entered 1984 spring training again fighting for a job with the Red Sox. The starting rotation looked set with Oil Can Boyd, Bobby Ojeda, Bruce Hurst, and Mike Brown, with the rookie Roger Clemens impressing everyone. Crawford did not make the cut and started the season in Pawtucket. He moved to the bullpen to get another shot at the big leagues, and

was recalled on May 9. "Bob Stanley says I'm doing what he did coming back and changing lanes," said Crawford. "I'm a reliever now and I have to like it a lot. It got me back to the big leagues and that's where I wanted to be."[18] The important thing," Houk said, "is that he wanted to do it."[19] During the rest of the season he pitched in 35 games (62 innings) and posted a 5-0 record with a 3.34 ERA.

Still, Crawford was deemed expendable by the Red Sox. In the offseason they attempted to trade him to open up a spot in the bullpen for a left-handed reliever. General manager Lou Gorman had a deal in place at the winter meetings, but it fell through. Crawford said, "I got the feeling I wasn't wanted despite what I had done and went to spring training to win a job and show some people I could pitch."[20] This time he would have to impress new manager John McNamara. Crawford was impressive in spring training, pitching 11 shutout innings at the start and had this to say about his situation, "I'm happy about my spring thus far, but I'm not taking anything for granted."[21]

One difference this season — the once-promising prospect, now 27 years old, knew his role would be middle reliever. "I know what my role is," he said. "I'm a reliever, not a starter. I can work on growing in that role — going out every other day to get my arm used to that kind of pitching."[22]

Relief pitching, said Crawford, was something that suited him. "I can pitch 4-5 innings," he said, "and it doesn't bother my arm. I can bounce back in a couple of days. I'd survive for a little while as a short reliever. But the better job, and the place where I'll make my money, is as a long and a middle man."[23]

Using a newly developed four-seam fastball, Crawford was used as a long reliever and spot starter for the first three months of the 1985 season. When closer Bob Stanley needed surgery on his index finger, McNamara turned to Crawford, who responded by leading the club in saves with 12. He also posted a 6-5 record with a 3.76 ERA, pitching in 44 games despite two trips to the disabled list.

There was even speculation that Crawford could be in the mix as Boston's closer in 1986. Pitching coach Bill Fischer said, "I think he could develop into a fine short man. He's big, mean-looking on the mound, and can throw hard. Once he starts believing in himself, he's going to be good."[24]

But the Red Sox bullpen was thin and had only 29 saves in 49 opportunities. To shore up the bullpen, the Red Sox traded struggling left-handed starter Bobby Ojeda to the Mets for Wes Gardner and Calvin Schiraldi.[25] McNamara wanted another short reliever so he could move Crawford back to his long-reliever/spot-starter role. The Red Sox then traded utility infielder Jackie Gutierrez and acquired veteran long reliever Sammy Stewart from the Baltimore Orioles. During the regular season, Crawford went 0-2 with a 3.92 ERA. In July he went on the DL with a shoulder injury and then spent 20 days in Pawtucket on a rehab assignment. The Red Sox called up Schiraldi to take Crawford's spot on the roster and Schiraldi would eventually emerge as the closer. Crawford made it back to Boston in September and pitched in 10 games.

The Red Sox made the postseason for the first time since 1975 and faced the California Angels in the American League Championship Series. Crawford would have been left off the postseason roster, but a knee injury to Tom Seaver opened up a spot for him.

The Angels took a commanding three-games-to-one lead and were winning Game Five in the top of the ninth inning, 5-2, when Boston staged a dramatic comeback and scored four runs, capped off by Dave Henderson's two-run home run. In the bottom of the ninth inning, the Angels battled back to tie the score against Bob Stanley and Joe Sambito. Left-hander Sambito gave up a run scoring single to Rob Wilfong, and Crawford was called in to pitch to Dick Schofield. Sammy Stewart was unavailable as he was hit by a line drive during batting practice the day prior. There was one out and Wilfong, with better than average speed, on first base. With the count 2-and-1, Schofield swung at a fastball tailing in on him and hit a sharp groundball past the diving first baseman,

Dave Stapleton. Wilfong advanced to third base. Brian Downing was intentionally walked to load the bases.

The next batter was Doug DeCinces with the potential ALCS winning run 90 feet away. The infield and the outfield were both playing in. DeCinces was 4-for-9 lifetime against Crawford. DeCinces swung at the first pitch and hit a popup to shallow right field, not deep enough for Wilfong to try to score. The infield and outfielders went back to normal depth.

Up came Bobby Grich, fastball hitter against fastball pitcher. Crawford's first pitch was a fastball sailing inside to the right-hander for ball one. The second pitch was a fastball that was not close to a strike, outside and away. With the count 2-and-0, Crawford needed to throw a strike as Grich would probably be taking a pitch. Crawford's pitch was low and away for a strike, a borderline pitch, and he got the call. Crawford's nerves were apparent; he was taking heavy breaths between pitches. On Crawford's next pitch, Grich fouled the ball into the stands. With the count 2-and-2, Crawford threw a fastball tailing in on Grich, who hit a soft liner to Crawford who reached to his left to make the catch, ending the inning and extending the game and the Red Sox season. "That was the biggest thrill in my baseball life, getting out of that jam," Crawford said.[26]

In the bottom of the 10th, with the score still 6-6, Crawford came out to face Reggie Jackson. Jackson worked the count to 3-and-2 before grounding out. Devon White struck out swinging. Crawford then walked Jerry Narron on four pitches. Gary Pettis worked a 3-and-2 count and drove a ball to deep left field. Jim Rice took a bad turn, backed up against the wall, and reached over his head to catch the ball for the third out. The Red Sox went on to take the lead in the top of the 11th inning. Schiraldi came in to pick up the save and give Crawford the win. After the game, Crawford revealed the pressure he felt during the game, saying, "If there was a toilet on the mound I would have used it."[27] Summing up the moment, he said, "There is nothing like being in game like this, the atmosphere is just terrific. It was a dream come true and it was the game of my life."[28]

The Red Sox took the series in seven games and went on to play the New York Mets in the World Series. Boston won Game One and Game Two featured a pair of Cy Young Award winners, Roger Clemens and Dwight Gooden. Boston led 6-2 in the top of the fifth when Clemens faltered. With runners on first and third with one out, Crawford was called in. Gary Carter drove in a run with a single but Crawford struck out Darryl Strawberry and got Danny Heep to ground out to avoid further damage. In the top of the sixth inning, Crawford batted for the first time in the major leagues against Rick Aguilera. He popped out to Strawberry. In the bottom of the sixth, Crawford got the side in order. The Red Sox went on to win, 9-3, and Crawford picked up the win.

Crawford also pitched in Games Four and Seven. He did not fare well, giving up home runs to Lenny Dykstra and Gary Carter. In his three World Series games Crawford had a 1-0 record with a 6.23 ERA in 4⅓ innings of work, striking out four. The 1986 postseason would be the highlight of Crawford's career.

As had been the case in the prior seven years, Crawford came to spring training in 1987 having to prove himself and he was growing a bit tired of it. "I'm the Rodney Dangerfield of the team," he told a sportswriter. "No matter what I do the year before, I get no respect. Why is it every time I come to camp, I have to worry about winning a job or being traded? I've been coming here for seven years and it's always the same and I'm sick of it."[29] Crawford also wanted to know what his role was. "I'd like to know whether I'm a long man, middle man, short man or starter."[30] Crawford did not want to leave the Red Sox, but he was growing frustrated; he would be 29 years old in April and no longer the prized prospect with high potential.[31]

The season was not a good one for Crawford; he was 5-4 with a 5.33 ERA and no saves. He went on the disabled list and had bone chips removed from his elbow for a second time. He opted for free agency at the end of the season and signed with the Cleveland Indians but was released before the season began. He signed with the Los Angeles Dodgers and spent the entire year in the minor leagues, first with in Double

A with the San Antonio Missions of the Texas League and then in Triple A with the Albuquerque Dukes of the Pacific Coast League. The Dodgers released him at the end of the season.

The 30-year-old veteran worked hard during the offseason to save his career, working out with his friend, neighbor, and former Red Sox teammate Marty Barrett. Crawford called 20 teams in the offseason for a job and they all said they were all set. He went to Florida looking for a job. "I finally decided to just come down here to Florida and call these teams again," Crawford said. "A friend of mine, a cop from Duxbury, let me use his house in Winter Haven. I flew down here on my own and just started calling. I told these people, 'Look, I'm just asking for 20 minutes of your time.'"[32]

The Kansas City Royals were looking for middle-relief help. After throwing 20 minutes to the pitching coach, Crawford signed a minor-league contract. He was a long shot to make the club. "I'm really hoping he does well," Barrett said. "It has to have been humiliating for him, making all those calls, going from making $450,000 a year to just calling around and asking for a tryout. If he hadn't come down here, just asking, I don't think anyone would have called."[33]

Crawford started the 1989 season in Triple A, with Omaha. One of his teammates was Donnie Moore, the losing pitcher of the 1986 ALCS Game Five. The two became friends before Moore was released and took his life on July 18, 1989.

Crawford was recalled to the Royals and pitched in his first major-league game in more than a year on July 5. He had one of his better seasons, going 3-1 and posting a 2.83 ERA. Crawford pitched two more seasons with the Royals and was released at the end of the 1991 season. He attempted a comeback during the lockout in 1995 but decided to retire for good, because he did not want to be called a scab.

Crawford stayed with the Royals, doing pregame and postgame shows on Kansas City radio station WDAF. He enjoyed doing radio and, in his words, "raising cain with former teammates such as George Brett."[34] He moved back on the field as a minor-league pitching coach in the Royals organization from 1995 to 2001. He gave it up because, in his words, the game had changed. "Being a pitching coach became more of a business aspect with the computer than teaching," he said.[35] Also, Crawford was injured when he was struck by a truck and hurt his right arm limiting his ability to help.

Crawford and his first wife, Debbie, had a daughter, Ashley, and two sons, Blake, and Casey. Blake grew to 6-feet-8 and played forward for the University of Missouri-Kansas City. Casey was State of Kansas "Mr. Basketball" his senior year in high school and 2006 Kansas Gatorade Player of the Year. Casey played forward at Wake Forest, then transferred to the University of Colorado. After graduation he played professionally in England, Japan, and Canada. Crawford had a daughter, Jade, with his second wife, Ingrid.

Until 2014, Crawford owned Crawford Pro Sports in Pryor, Oklahoma. As of 2015, Crawford is living in Claremore, Oklahoma with his wife and high school love Becky (Phillips). The couple has six children between them including Lacey and Austin. He found satisfaction in teaching youngsters how to pitch, when coaches ask him how much he charges, Crawford said, he tells them, "Buy me a Coke and we'll be OK."[36]

NOTES

1   Author's interview with Steve Crawford on August 20, 2015 (Hereafter Crawford interview).

2   Larry Whiteside, "Crawford's Big Chance; Sox Rate Him as Top Prospect," *Boston Globe*, February 28, 1981.

3   Leigh Montville, "Salina's Rocket Is Taking Off," *Boston Globe*, March 26, 1981.

4   Crawford interview.

5   Crawford interview. Some think the nickname came from former National League umpire Shag Crawford (1956-1975).

6   Joe Giuliotti, "Torrez's Misery is Almost Over," *The Sporting News*, October 4, 1980: 21.

7   Larry Whiteside, "Crawford gets off to a Good Start", *Boston Globe*, September 19, 1980.

8   Larry Whiteside, "Crawford's Big Chance; Sox Rate Him as Top Prospect."

9   Larry Whiteside, "Crawford's Big Chance; Sox Rate Him as Top Prospect."

10 Peter Gammons, "The Forgotten Arm; Crawford, Once Phenom is Fighting Back," *Boston Globe*, March 3, 1984.

11 Larry Whiteside, "Crawford's Big Chance; Sox Rate Him as Top Prospect."

12 Larry Whiteside, "Sox Lose to Orioles, But Crawford Shows He's for Real," *Boston Globe*, April 14, 1981.

13 "American League Flashes," *The Sporting News*, June 27, 1981: 25.

14 Joe Giuliotti, "Experienced Houk Anxious for '82," *The Sporting News*, November 28, 1981: 57.

15 Peter Gamons, "The Forgotten Arm; Crawford Once Phenom is Fighting Back", *Boston Globe*, March 3, 1984.

16 Larry Whiteside, "He Ain't Heavy, He's Sox Sleeper; Crawford Loses to Win," *Boston Globe*, February 25, 1983.

17 Joe Giuliotti, "Crawford's Attitude Key to Return," *The Sporting News*, May 21, 1984: 25.

18 Larry Whiteside, "Crawford Earns Relief" *Boston Globe*, May 9, 1984.

19 "Crawford Earns Relief".

20 Joe Giuliotti, "A Crawford Trade Is Taken Off Hold," *The Sporting News*, May 6, 1985: 15.

21 Larry Whiteside, "Crawford Finds a Niche," *Boston Globe*, March 24, 1985.

22 Ibid.

23 Ibid.

24 Joe Giuliotti, "Crawford May Be Sox' Short Stopper," *The Sporting News*, October 7, 1985: 18.

25 The complete November 13, 1985, transaction had the New York Mets receiving Chris Bayer, Tom McCarthy, John Mitchell, and Bobby Ojeda and the Boston Red Sox receiving John Christensen, Wes Gardner, Calvin Schiraldi, and La Schelle Tarver.

26 Michael McKnight, "The Split," *Sports Illustrated*, October 4, 2014.

27 Ibid.

28 Mike Tully, United Press International, October 12, 1986.

29 Joe Giuliotti, "Crawford Seeks a Title," *The Sporting News*, March 30, 1987: 18.

30 Ibid.

31 Ibid.

32 Leigh Montville, "Hitting Home," *Boston Globe*, March 28, 1989.

33 Ibid.

34 Crawford interview.

35 Crawford interview.

36 Crawford interview.

PAT DODSON

By Bob LeMoine

"**N**OW, IF I CAN JUST GET THE CHANCE...**"** an optimistic Pat Dodson remarked during spring training with the Red Sox in 1988.[1] Dodson excelled at the Triple-A level, becoming the International League MVP, and was a top prospect in the Red Sox farm system. However, his chances were limited, and success didn't translate to the major-league level. Dodson either underperformed in key moments or became a victim of a numbers game. Still, he saw his first major-league action in September of 1986, during the wild pennant race in Boston, and was able to contribute to the Red Sox team bound for the World Series.

Patrick Neal Dodson was born on October 11, 1959, in Santa Monica, California, the son of Kenneth and Carole (Corrigan) Dodson. Kenneth was a computer programmer at Garrett AiResearch[2] and Carole worked as a dispatcher in the trucking industry. Pat had a brother, Kenneth Jr., and a sister, Kristy-Lee. Kenneth was also a baseball coach, so young Pat always knew of baseball from his very early days. "We always found ways to play," he said, including memories of "playing wiffle ball in the backyard."[3] Dodson attended Inglewood High School and had a .455 batting average in 1977, and was selected to the second team of the California Interscholastic Federation.[4]

Dodson attended UCLA from 1977 to 1980, playing on the baseball team in 1979-80 with future major leaguers Tim Leary, Mike Gallego, Dave Schmidt, Don Slaught, and Matt Young. "Playing for UCLA was a dream for me," said Dodson, a West Coast boy who admired the school. As a sophomore in 1979, he had a six-RBI game in a May 7 win over Cal Poly Pomona.[5] Dodson finished that year batting .327 with 15 home runs and 46 RBIs for the PAC-10 champions, who finished 21-9 and came within one victory of qualifying for the College World Series. Gary Adams called the team "the hardest working, most unspoiled, scrappy" team he ever coached and of

the combination of Dodson at first base and Gallego at second, said, "I don't think there's a better right side in the conference."[6]

Dodson helped the 1979 baseball Team USA win the Bronze Medal at the Intercontinental Cup, held December 15-26 in Havana. He had six doubles in the tournament on a team with future major leaguers Terry Francona and Joe Carter. "It was a great honor to go there for a young kid like me," he said. The team played before crowds of near 60,000. Team USA was the first US team to visit Cuba in 37 years.[7]

Dodson was drafted by the Boston Red Sox in the sixth round of the 1980 amateur draft. He spent three years at Class-A Winter Haven (Florida) of the Florida State League, batting .274 and then identical seasons of batting .252 in 1981-82. He started to hit for power in 1982, connecting on 15 home runs. In 1983 Dodson played for the Double-A New Britain (Connecticut)

Red Sox of the Eastern League, batting .261 with 12 home runs and 70 RBIs for the Governor's Cup champions. In 1984 he played for Triple-A Pawtucket (Rhode Island) club, batting .257 with 16 homers and 51 RBIs. Still, Dodson was not called up to Boston despite his consistent power numbers. The Red Sox felt Dave Stapleton was their future first baseman, and then during the 1984 season they acquired veteran Bill Buckner. Dodson had to wait for his chance, and later admitted, "I never felt like I was in their plans."[8]

In the 1985-86 offseason Dodson played for the La Guaira team in Venezuela, and drove in two runs in the clinching game over Aragua in the Venezuelan Winter League playoffs. He and future Red Sox teammate Wes Gardner were roommates.[9]

Dodson spent the 1985 season again at Pawtucket. On May 16 the Red Sox came to Pawtucket for an exhibition game and Dodson smacked four hits, including two home runs.[10] On June 7 he slugged three home runs against the Richmond Braves, each to a different area of the field. On June 21 Dodson was the second out in the bottom of the 27th inning, which was followed by an Ed Jurak walk-off single to defeat the Syracuse Chiefs and end the seven-hour game played over parts of three days.[11] Despite hitting 18 home runs, his .223 batting average and only 47 RBIs for the weak Pawtucket team (48-91) made 1985 a season to forget. "I stunk; the whole team stunk in '85," Dodson said. "It was my sixth year in the system and I looked like some guy who never played before."[12]

Dodson credited Rac Slider, his manager at Winter Haven, New Britain, and Pawtucket, with giving him the motivation through his difficult times. "He was a tough Texan," Dodson recalled, "and as the years went by I valued his lessons on how to carry myself. When you were down he was right there for you. This was during one of my first real experiences of tough times. This guy knows the people around him."[13] Dobson also tweaked his workout regimen over the winter, skipping a 17-pound rope as part of his routine.

When he arrived for spring training in 1986, Dodson was helped by a Red Sox legend. "Every morning at 8

I worked with Carl Yastrzemski. He helped me refine a few things and stressed discipline. Everything came together for me. I was stronger all season," Dodson recalled.[14] With the hobbling of Red Sox first baseman Bill Buckner, Dodson seemed destined for a Red Sox call-up. "His fielding is very dependable and if he keeps hitting, he'd help us," farm director Ed Kenney commented.[15]

The motivation paid dividends. In 1986 Dodson had his best season in Organized Baseball. The hope was that he was simply a late bloomer after six years in the minor leagues. "He worked awfully hard last winter," Kenney said. "Maybe he saw the handwriting on the wall, I don't know. But the hard work sure is paying off."[16] Dodson was a powerhouse at the plate for Pawtucket in 1986. He was named the International League MVP with stellar power numbers: a .269 batting average with 27 home runs and a league-leading 102 RBIs. On August 15 he broke Jim Rice's Pawtucket record of 93 RBIs set in 1974.[17] "This season was my last hurrah and I knew it," Dodson said. "I was going to be a free agent and I knew that I had to produce. It was now or never."[18]

In 1986 Dodson was finally on his way to Boston, called up on September 2 when the rosters were expanded. "So being here today, getting to the big leagues is a dream coming true," he said.[19] "Now that I'm here, I just want to contribute any way I can. The fact that I'm here in a pennant race makes it even more exciting. The Red Sox have been very patient with me. They waited for me to come along."[20]

Dodson saw his first action with the Red Sox in an exhibition game against the New York Mets on September 4. His first official major-league appearance came on September 5, when he entered the game to play first base in a 12-2 Red Sox win over the Minnesota Twins. His first major-league hit came the next night, September 6, against the Twins, and at a clutch moment. He entered the game to play first base in the ninth inning with the game tied 2-2. With two outs in the bottom of the ninth, Dodson had his first major-league at-bat, against pitcher George Frazier. Dodson grounded the ball between first and second for an infield single. Steve Lombardozzi made a diving stop on it but had no chance to throw Dodson out. Dave Henderson ran for Dodson and scored on a walk-off single by Marty Barrett, giving the Red Sox their seventh straight win.[21]

"I was lucky that I had an experimental at-bat against the Mets," said Dodson after the game. "It took the edge off. I was a little nervous, but I was trying to more or less downplay it, so I didn't swing at bad pitches. I had two strikes on me, so I was just trying to put the ball in play. I wanted to make sure I handled the pitches right."[22] Tom Seaver presented Dodson the ball, with "Joe Frazier" listed as the pitcher instead of George, and Dodson's name misspelled. Seaver apologized for messing up Dodson's memorable item, then gave him the real, properly labeled game ball.[23]

In Dodson's next at-bat, on September 14 at Yankee Stadium, he pinch-hit for Ed Romero in the eighth inning and slugged his first major-league home run, off Tim Stoddard in an 11-5 Red Sox loss.

On September 15, 1986, a Red Sox offday, Dodson and Lisa R. Dawson, an airline stewardess from California, traveled to Old Orchard Beach, Maine, and went before a justice of the peace to become husband and wife.[24]

The next night Dodson made his first big-league start, playing at first base and batting third in a 9-3 win over Milwaukee. Dodson went 2-for-4 with two RBIs, two runs scored, and a walk. He was 4-for-6 in his first six at-bats, and credited the Red Sox veterans for their mentorship. "I really didn't know what to expect," Dodson admitted. "But I'd heard from some guys who came up last year that the guys who played every day weren't all that friendly. I haven't found that to be the case at all. Both times before I got base hits last night, I went right up to Wade Boggs to ask him about a certain pitcher. Both times he told me some information that was helpful. ... I try to stay in the games even though I am not playing. I talk with Rice after every time he bats about what he's done or hasn't done.... It really helps to talk about hitting."[25] Dodson finished September batting .417 with one home run in

12 at-bats and received a one-sixth World Series share and a ring. "Me, I can't complain," he said. "When I arrived, the team was on a roll, and I hadn't done anything to get them there. I didn't contribute but I got to be a part of it."[26]

While the Red Sox went on to the postseason, Dodson returned to California to work his winter job as a health-club instructor in Manhattan Beach. "I'm not sure about my status," Dodson said. My age makes me a rookie in name only. But I'm not over the hill, either. I think I turned a few heads, though. I hope so."[27]

"It hasn't been easy for me," Dodson said during spring training in 1987. "I`ve had to work very hard to get better. It`s been discouraging at times, but I`ve never considered giving up. I always felt that if I kept working at it, I could make it one day. ... I came to spring training determined to do well because I knew Bill [Buckner] was having trouble with his ankle and that I would have a chance to prove myself. And I think I have proved myself."[28] Dodson played a lot at first base in spring training. "Right now my confidence is building because I know I can hit," said Dodson, who batted .364 in his first nine spring games. "I know I have come into my own, as people say. But just to be here playing with these guys gives you confidence, too. It means someone else thinks you can play."[29]

Overall Dodson batted .319 during spring training and displayed excellent defense at first base. He made the Red Sox roster and was living his dream being on a major-league team on Opening Day. "It's a dream come true," he said. "I've been waiting for this for a long time. Since I first picked up a baseball, since I was seven years old, I've always wanted to play in the big leagues. To have it come true. ... It's a hard feeling to explain."[30] Dodson would be used as a defensive replacement at first base and a pinch-hitter. "It'll be an adjustment being a player who has to be ready to come off the bench because I haven't done that before, but this is great," he said. "I just have to be ready when I'm called upon."[31]

However, April proved to be a nightmare for Dodson. He was 0-for-the-month, batting 11 times with no hits and six strikeouts, although he showed excellent defense and felt confident of his progress. The Red Sox were on a West Coast trip and the California native purchased tickets for family for all three games of a weekend series at Anaheim May 1-3. But the cruel realities of baseball as a business interfered with what could have been a highlight of Dodson's career and life. He never got to Anaheim, and was instead optioned back to Pawtucket on April 29. The Red Sox were in need of outfield help, and promising rookie Ellis Burks was coming up to the major leagues, where he would stay for the next 18 years. Dodson would be catching a red-eye flight back to Pawtucket. He had to call his family members to break the news to them. "I had 24 tickets for each game. … Everything hit me at the wrong time," Dodson remembered. "I had to face everybody and try to tell them what happened over and over without getting depressed. I didn't have any answers for them, really. It was like, 'Here we go again.' It was tough. I don't feel like I played myself out of the major leagues. … It doesn't seem that I got enough of a chance."[32]

Dodson's demotion was a huge letdown, and it showed in his .223 batting average in June. "I thought I had done what I had to do to get out of here. It's real tough right now. Real discouraging. You start wondering what you have to do to make it to the major leagues."[33]

Dodson found motivation from his wife, Lisa, who would catch up with him on road trips. She helped him talk out his frustrations, and he also gave himself pep talks. "I just kept seeing those 0-for-4's day after day, and that was enough to motivate me," Dodson said. "That was enough to kick me in the rear. I put the demotion in the back of my head and started to concentrate on what I had to do for the present and for the future."[34] The pep talks worked, as Dodson batted .335 in his final 49 games in Pawtucket and finished with a .275 batting average, 18 home runs, and 72 RBIs. "It finally kicked in," Dodson remembered. "It was more like I kicked myself, really."[35]

Dodson was recalled to Boston in September, but was arriving with a flat Red Sox team mired in fifth place in a season that couldn't end soon enough. Dave

Henderson and Don Baylor, heroes of the 1986 team, had been traded away to contending teams, opening a roster spot for Dodson. He batted only .226, however, with 2 home runs and 6 RBIs to finish the season.

When Dodson arrived for spring training in 1988, he was now 28 years old and seeing little opportunity on his horizon. He asked the Red Sox to trade him. "All I can do is the best I can," Dodson said. "I've requested a trade. I talked to (general manager Lou Gorman) about 2½ weeks ago and he said he'd try to accommodate me. I'd rather play here, but I know I don't have any more to prove at Triple-A."[36] Dodson had new competition as the Red Sox experimented with moving longtime right fielder Dwight Evans to first base, as well as Todd Benzinger and Sam Horn. "When I first got here, they had Dave Stapleton. And when I got to Triple A, it was Bill Buckner, and that kind of closed the door for a while," Dodson reflected. "Now I've got Evans."[37] Dodson was competing with Randy Kutcher, Jody Reed, and Kevin Romine for two open roster spots. "I don't know if my chances this time around are better or worse, to tell you the truth," he said. "I'm more relaxed, and Lou Gorman's told me he'd try to trade me if I didn't make it this time. … And I just think, with all that happened last year, that I've grown up some. I think I can handle the whole situation better."[38]

"The Rodney Dangerfield of the organization," wrote Dan Shaughnessy of the *Boston Globe*. "He's easily Boston's best-fielding first baseman, but manager John McNamara has never been a Dodson booster, and the Sox keep sending him to Pawtucket where he annually hits .275 with 100 RBIs. Dodson will be 29 before the end of the World Series."[39] It didn't help matters any when Dodson would watch Sam Horn be taken out of the lineup against a tough lefty pitcher. "I didn't get that grace," Dodson said. "That would've been nice."[40]

In a spring training game at Winter Haven, Florida, on March 4, 1988, the Red Sox played the Chunichi Dragons from Japan. Dodson commented, "I told my agent to talk to some Japanese teams. Imagine if I played there with a name like Dodson. They'd probably call me Nissan."[41] To make matters even worse, Dodson hit a line drive during batting practice that struck pitcher Oil Can Boyd in the right knee, reminiscent of a line drive he hit off Boyd's chest six years earlier. "The first thing he said to me was, 'You remember 1982,' " Dodson said.[42]

At the end of spring training, Dodson was batting only .226 and was returned to Pawtucket. Gorman found no interest in Dodson from other teams. "He deserves to go somewhere," Gorman said. "He's one of the best kids in the world."[43] Dodson batted .262 in 44 games for Pawtucket, with 5 home runs and 23 RBIs. Dodson got another chance with the Red Sox on June 4. Buckner had been released, Evans was moved back to right field, and Dodson was recalled.[44] "I didn't anticipate it," said Dodson. "I got off to a slow start in Pawtucket, got really hot, then leveled off."[45] He was bothered by a stiff neck, which he joked resulted from turning his head when he heard a phone ring. "It's a great opportunity to show them I can play. … As long as I can help with the bat or with the glove, we're gonna be a better team."[46]

Dodson homered on June 19 at Baltimore off Doug Sisk in a 15-7 Red Sox victory. But in 45 at-bats in June he hit.178 and was optioned back to Pawtucket. Dodson played in only 20 more games at Pawtucket, suffering a broken wrist on July 5.[47] Still, he had a .400 on-base percentage and the Red Sox could have used his quality defense at first base in later innings. Gorman claimed the injury prevented Dodson from throwing,[48] which Dodson heard while watching a Red Sox broadcast. "I'm sitting there looking at my wife," he said. "I've been lifting weights every day. I've been working out with Steve Ellsworth. … It was sore, but I could throw fine. I was playing catch every day. It gave me trouble swinging, but I was able to throw." Gorman later retracted his comments and said Dodson wasn't recalled because the Red Sox were settled with Todd Benzinger at first base. "I'm better off this way," Dodson said, concluding that his time in Boston was likely over. "We'll see what happens now."[49] The Dodsons packed up their Natick, Massachusetts, home and moved to Oklahoma to be with Lisa's relatives.

Before the 1989 season, Dodson signed a minor-league contract to play for the Milwaukee Brewers, but the Brewers then dealt his rights to the Kintetsu Buffaloes in Japan. He signed a $269,000 one-year contract, a huge raise from his $40,000 contract in the Boston organization the year before.[50] Dodson injured his right shoulder diving for a ball and was limited to very few games in Japan.[51]

After the 1989 season, Dodson signed a contract with the Texas Rangers and participated in spring training in 1990. On March 29 he was sent to the Triple-A Oklahoma City 89ers.[52] He injured his shoulder reaching for a high throw on May 6 in Omaha. Dodson had shoulder surgery and played in only 23 games at Oklahoma City.[53] "I was done, mentally," he recalled of his rehab days in Oklahoma City.

The Dodson family had settled in Grove, Oklahoma. Seeing his professional baseball career coming to an end, Dodson finished his degree from UCLA, and taught school for more than 20 years. From 1993 to 2003 at Grove High School, he taught government and Oklahoma history and coached the baseball and softball teams.[54] He led the baseball team to the Oklahoma state championship in 1997 and the girls softball team to the state title in 2000. Dodson attended Northeastern State University in 2000-2002 and received a bachelor of arts in social studies teacher education. He was the assistant principal at Grove Middle School from 2003 to 2007, and became the principal in 2007.[55] Lisa went to work in the library at the Grove Early Childhood Center.[56]

The Dodsons' three children, daughter Taylor and sons Ryan and Tyler, all played baseball or softball in college. Tyler played at Northern Oklahoma College, Ryan played at the University of Arkansas at Fort Smith, and Taylor received a softball scholarship to the University of Kansas.[57] Pat, along with other major-league alumni including former Red Sox teammate Steve Crawford, taught at youth baseball clinics in Tulsa, Oklahoma.[58]

Dodson found his playing days have helped him in coaching and working with youth. "When you can sit and tell stories about guys like (Ted Williams), your credibility is way up there," Dodson said. The Dodson family also remained Red Sox fans through the years. "I consider myself today a Red Sox fan," Dodson said. He has returned to Fenway Park over the years, taking part in the 100th anniversary of the ballpark in 2012, and praised the Red Sox ownership for showing great respect to former players. He said, "They have treated me like a Hall of Famer, which I am not."[59]

Despite a career that makes one wonder what might have been, Dodson said he was grateful for those years. "I have all those good memories," he emphasized.[60]

SOURCES

In addition to the sources listed in the notes, the author was assisted by the following:

"Obituary for Hazel Corrigan," retrieved February 4, 2015. honoringmemories.com/book-of-memories/1460565/Hazel-Corrigan/obituary.php?Printable=true.

"Pat Dodson, Impressive Spring- 437," The Greatest 21 Days. Retrieved February 3, 2015. greatest21days.com/2014/10/pat-dodson-impressive-spring-437.html.

Stroud Richard. "Grove Sun Athlete Of The Week: Grove Third Baseman Taylor Dodson," *Grove* (Oklahoma) *Sun,* September 15, 2011. Retrieved February 3, 2015. grandlakenews.com/sports/article_5e96d224-df98-11e0-b287-001cc4c03286.html?mode=jqm

NOTES

1   Kevin Paul Dupont, "Dodson Makes Bid in Roster Sweepstakes; First Baseman Delivers Winning Hit Against Twins," *Boston Globe,* March 17, 1988: 62.

2   The company was known by various names, but this was the one Dodson remembered most. Phone interview with Pat Dodson, August 20, 2015. (Hereafter Dodson interview).

3   Dodson interview.

4   *Valley News* (Van Nuys, California), June 22, 1977: 37.

5   "Dodson's 6 RBI Lead UCLA Victory," *Los Angeles Times,* May 8, 1979: D3.

6   Bob Cuomo, "Bruins Have Tough Act to Follow in '80," *Los Angeles Times,* March 9, 1980: D15.

7   Dodson interview; "1979 Intercontinental Cup," baseball-reference.com/bullpen/1979_Intercontinental_Cup, retrieved August 20, 2015.

8   Dodson interview.

9   Dodson interview.

10   Mike Shalin, "PawSox Rip Guests, 9-4," *Boston Herald,* May 17, 1985: 73.

11   "Pawtucket Breaks 27-Inning Marathon," *Greensboro* (North Carolina) *News And Record,* June 22, 1985: 18.

12   Gerry Finn, "Dodson Will Be Working in California But Not For Red Sox," *Springfield* (Massachusetts) *Union,* September 19, 1986: 7.

13   Dodson interview.

14   Joe Gordon, "Dodson Moves Up For Last Hurrah," *Boston Herald,* September 3, 1986: 11.

15   Ibid.

16   Tim Horgan, "Major Talents in the Minor Leagues," *Boston Herald,* May 14, 1986: 91.

17   Joe Giuliotti, "Crawford Goes South," *Boston Herald,* August 16, 1986: 12.

18   "Dodson Moves Up For Last Hurrah."

19   Ibid.

20   Larry Whiteside, "Dodson Gets Break," *Boston Globe,* September 3, 1986: 65.

21   Larry Whiteside, "Boyd Smokes Twins; Barrett's Hit In 9th Fires Up Sox, 3-2," *Boston Globe,* September 7, 1986: 57.

22   Larry Whiteside, "In The 9th, Rookie Dodson Proves to Be Most Valuable," *Boston Globe,* September 7, 1986: 61.

23   Dodson interview.

24   Dodson interview.

25   Larry Whiteside, "Dodson Credits His Quick Success to Veterans' Advice," *Boston Globe,* September 18, 1986: 38.

26   Michael Globetti, "Dodson Digging Into Position," *Boston Herald,* January 29, 1987: 81.

27   "Dodson Will Be Working in California."

28   Robbie Andreau, "Dodson's Future May Rest on Buckner's Gimpy Ankle," *Sun-Sentinel* (Fort Lauderdale, Florida), April 3, 1987. Retrieved February 3, 2015. articles.sun-sentinel.com/1987-04-03/sports/8701210773_1_ankle-pat-dodson-bill-buckner.

29   Larry Whiteside, "Dodson: Good First Impression," *Boston Globe,* March 18, 1987: 50.

30   David Cataneo, "Sox Rookies Can't Wait for First Pitch," *Boston Herald,* April 6, 1987: 78.

31   Dan Shaughnessy, "Demotion Hurts Hoffman After an Impressive Spring Training; Infielder Doesn't Understand Move," *Boston Globe,* April 4, 1987: 22.

32   David Cataneo, "Dodson's in the Doldrums," *Boston Herald,* May 22, 1987:108.

33   "Dodson's in the Doldrums."

34   David Cataneo, "Dodson Moves Back To Bigs," *Boston Herald,* September 2, 1987: 96.

35 Ibid.

36 Dan Shaughnessy, "Whither Dodson?" *Boston Globe*, February 22, 1988: 53.

37 "Dodson Makes Bid in Roster Sweepstakes."

38 Ibid.

39 Dan Shaughnessy, "Who's On First? Sox Don't Know," *Boston Globe*, February 24, 1988: 31.

40 Dodson interview.

41 Dan Shaughnessy, "Sox Bid Dragons Sayonara," *Boston Globe*, March 5, 1988: 33.

42 Mark Blaudschun, "Liner to Knee Puts Can on Shelf Again," *Boston Globe*, March 6, 1988: 57.

43 Ron Borges, "Dodson, Four Others Sent to Minors," *Boston Globe*, March 29, 1988: 70; Dan Shaughnessy, "For McNamara, The Heat Is on With Experts Picking Red Sox for First; The Manager Is Under the Gun," *Boston Globe*, April 3, 1988: 45.

44 Mark Blaudschun, "Horn, Anderson Go to Pawtucket; Dodson, Kutcher, Romine Recalled," *Boston Globe*, June 5, 1988: 76.

45 Marvin Pave, "He's on the Move: Romine Is Ready for Prime Time," *Boston Globe*, June 6, 1988: 47.

46 Mike Shalin, "Dodson's New Start at Fenway," *Boston Herald*, June 5, 1988: 4.

47 Dan Shaughnessy and Larry Whiteside, "Boyd May Get Call Tomorrow," *Boston Globe*, July 9, 1988: 33.

48 Bob Ryan, "A Rookie Mistake," *Boston Globe*, September 12, 1988: 45.

49 Mike Shalin, "Dodson Wanted to Get First Call," *Boston Herald*, September 14, 1988: 102.

50 Dan Shaughnessy, "Brewers Have Been Bruised, Battered," *Boston Globe*, April 16, 1989: 60.

51 Dodson interview.

52 Steve Fainaru and Nick Cafardo, "Expos Appear to be Serious About Boyd," *Boston Globe*, December 5, 1989: 81; "Rangers Send Six Players to 89ers," *Oklahoman* (Oklahoma City), March 30, 1990. Retrieved February 2, 2015. newsok.com/rangers-send-six-players-to-89ers/article/2312005.

53 "89ers Fall to Omaha," *Oklahoman*, May 7, 1990. Retrieved February 2, 2015. newsok.com/89ers-fall-to-omaha/article/2316559.

54 Dodson interview.

55 Pat Dodson's LinkedIn page, retrieved February 3, 2015. linkedin.com/pub/pat-dodson/55/721/a88; Grove Public Schools. Retrieved February 3, 2015; ridgerunners.net/schools/ms/ms_index.html retrieved February 3, 2015.

56 See the *American* (Fairland, Oklahoma), archived story from March 11, 2010 aft.stparchive.com/Archive/AFT/AFT03112010p17.php retrieved August 20, 2015.

57 "Taylor Dodson," Kansas University Athletics. Retrieved February 1, 2015. kuathletics.com/roster.aspx?rp_id=5931.

58 Barry Lewis, "MLB Alumni Instruct at Oklahoma's ONEOK Field," Major League Baseball Players Alumni Association. June 17, 2014. Retrieved February 2, 2015. mlbpaa.mlb.com/mlbpaa/news/article.jsp?ymd=20140617&content_id=80227240&vkey=mlbpaa2008&fext=.jsp.

59 Dodson interview.

60 Dodson interview.

DWIGHT EVANS

by Bill Nowlin

Dwight Evans was the best Red Sox right fielder I ever saw.

—Johnny Pesky

A MEMBER OF THE RED SOX HALL OF FAME, Dwight Evans was voted Red Sox MVP four times by the Boston Baseball Writers. It might not be a stretch at all to agree with Herb Crehan, who writes, "Dewey might be the most underrated player in the history of the Red Sox."[1]

A three-time All-Star, Evans won eight Gold Gloves in the stretch running from 1976 through 1985. At one time or another, he led the American League in on-base percentage, OPS, runs, runs created, total bases, home runs, extra base hits, bases on balls, and times on base. He had a rifle of an arm, patrolling Fenway's capacious right field for 18 years from 1972 through 1989 (serving another year as the team's DH), and three times led the league in assists - but runners quickly learned not to try to score on Dwight Evans.

Born Dwight Michael Evans on November 3, 1951, in Santa Monica, California, his family moved to Hawaii when he was still an infant and he spent his early years living in there, mostly before Hawaii was granted statehood on August 21, 1959. Hawaii was built on beach culture, and Dwight did not get involved with baseball until the family moved to the Los Angeles suburb of Northridge at the age of 9. He attributes his passion for baseball to a Dodgers game his father took him to soon after they arrived in the area. Dwight joined Little League, pitched and played third base, and became all-star both in Little League and Colt League. At Chatsworth High School, though, "I tried out for the junior varsity baseball team and I didn't even get a uniform."[2] He was determined, though, and not only made the team his junior year but made

All-Valley in the San Fernando Valley League. He won the league MVP award his senior year and found himself being scouted.

Boston Red Sox scout Joe Stephenson recommended Evans highly, and on June 5, 1969, the Red Sox selected Evans in the fifth round of the 1969 amateur draft. The 17-year-old Evans was assigned to the Jamestown, NY farm club. The Sox had so many people coming into Jamestown at one time that he had to wait a week to get a uniform and worked out in his sweatshirt and jeans. He got in 100 at-bats, though, and a .280 average, enough to be promoted to Greenville, South Carolina for the 1970 season. He kept advancing, spending 1971 with Winston-Salem, and making it to Triple-A Louisville for 1972. It was the classic trip up the ladder, one year at a time.

Evans told Herb Crehan that it was Louisville manager Darrell Johnson who made the difference when Dwight found himself outmatched at the Triple-A

level. "You are my right fielder whether you hit .100 or .300," Johnson told him, imbuing the 20-year-old with enough confidence to turn his season around.[3] He hit .300 — on the nose — with 17 HR and 95 RBIs. Evans was named International League MVP for his 1972 season - and got a ticket to Boston to join the big league club in the middle of a classic pennant race.

Dwight Evans played his first game for the Boston Red Sox on September 16, 1972, entering the game as a pinch runner for Reggie Smith in the bottom of the sixth in a game against the Indians at Fenway Park. He stayed in the game, playing right field. In his one at-bat, he popped out to the shortstop. It's an interesting tidbit that he batted out of order his first time up, but since he had made an out, the Indians chose not to make a point of it. He got his first major-league hit the very next day, pinch-hitting with two outs in the bottom of the ninth in a game the Indians were winning with ease, 9-2. Evans singled to left off Gaylord Perry. He added another hit the following day, starting in left field and going 1-for-3 with a single.

On September 20, Evans had himself a breakthrough day, playing left in both games of a doubleheader against the visiting Orioles. Dwight was 2-for-4 in the first game, with a couple of singles and two RBIs. He was 2-for-4 in the second game as well, but the two hits were a seventh-inning triple off Mike Cuellar and an eighth-inning home run off Eddie Watt. In 57 September at-bats, Evans batted .263 and helped keep the Red Sox in the pennant race; this was the year they fell just a half-game short of the Tigers.

The following year, Evans was the regular right fielder most of the season, playing 119 games, 94 of them in right. He was still finding himself in his first full season of major-league ball, batting just .223 and with only 32 RBIs, but he showed some power with 10 home runs, and made only one error all year long. 1974 featured another 10 homers, but a .281 average as Evans drove in 70 runs. His defense, and especially his throwing arm, was what kept him in the lineup.

In 1975, he had another good year playing a solid right field while Fred Lynn and Jim Rice joined him to form one of the all-time great outfields. Evans was involved in a league-leading eight double plays. Though he was sub-par in the League Championship Series, Evans batted a strong .292 in the World Series and drove in five runs. His dramatic ninth-inning two-run home run tied up Game Three, a contest the Red Sox lost in the 10th. As always, it was on defense where Evans excelled; his catch of Joe Morgan's long fly ball in the 11th inning of Game Six was one of the most spectacular in World Series play. After tracking down what looked like an extra-base hit and snaring the ball, he fired to first base and doubled off Ken Griffey to retire the side.

Evans told Jennifer Latchford and Rod Oreste, "I think all great plays are always anticipated… I was actually, before that pitch thinking if the ball is hit in the gap…I've got to go into the stands. Of course, I didn't end up doing that, but that's what went through my mind, and then when the ball was hit, I was actually prepared for it. It wasn't the best catch I ever made, but it was the most important catch I ever made."[4]

Looking back on that Series, Evans said, "We had a team that we thought, 'We're going to be back in the next five years three or four times.'"[5]

The next season, Dewey hit .242 with 17 home runs in 146 games, and won his first Gold Glove award for his defensive play. In 1977 he battled a knee injury all year, spending much of the season on the disabled list. It was a shame, since he hit better than he ever had, finishing with 14 home runs and a .287 average in just 73 games.

The 1978 season saw the Red Sox leap out to a commanding lead, and then give it all away in September. They fought back to tie the Yankees and force a single-game playoff for the pennant. Boston might have done better, but Dewey was a little woozy for the final month of the season following an August 28 beaning. Even in the playoff game, he rode the bench, only coming in for a last-ditch ninth-inning pinch-hit role, in which he flied out to left field. It was his first appearance in a week. One wonders if a playoff game would have been necessary had Evans been better able to contribute that final month. He hit .247 with a (thus far) career-high 24 home runs on the season, but hit just .164 with one home run in September.

After two more fairly typical seasons (.274 BA, 21 HR, 58 RBIs in 1979, and .266, 18 HR, 60 RBIs in 1980), Dwight Evans reached his 29th birthday with eight seasons under his belt. He was part of a great outfield, but clearly the third wheel amongst two of the better players in the game. His reputation was as a good hitter and a great right fielder. Beginning with the 1981 season, though, Evans underwent a remarkable offensive transformation, and was one of the best all-around players in the league for the next several years.

His first great season, 1981, unfortunately was marred by a seven-week player strike. Besides his fourth Gold Glove award, Dewey hit a new career high .296, and paced the league in home runs (22), walks, total bases, runs created, and OPS. Whereas he had typically hit seventh or eighth under Don Zimmer, new manager Ralph Houk recognized Evans' great on-base skills and hit him second in the order for all four years he managed him. He finished third in the balloting for Most Valuable Player. After playing in the shadow of his more famous teammates for several years, Evans was now the team's best player. Lynn and Carlton Fisk were gone, Carl Yastrzemski was nearing the end of the line, and Jim Rice would never again be the hitter he was in the late 1970s.

In 1982, Evans proved his resurgence was no fluke, hitting .292 with 32 home runs and 98 RBIs, leading the league with a .402 on-base-percentage. After an off year in 1983 (.238, 22, 58), he had another big year in 1984, slugging 32 home runs, driving in 104 runs (remarkable for someone hitting second in the batting order), and leading the league in runs, runs created, extra base hits, and OPS. On June 28, 1984, Evans doubled, tripled, made three outs, then singled in the 10th, and finally completed the cycle in style with a three-run walkoff homer in the bottom of the 11th off Edwin Nunez, for a 9-6 win over the Mariners.

The next two seasons were more of the same for Evans, as he hit 29 and 26 home runs, and generally was among the league leaders in walks and on-base-percentage, and got more than his share of extra-base hits. New manager John McNamara moved Evans to leadoff in 1985, though he eventually started hitting him sixth in 1986. Leading off the game for the Red Sox on Opening Day 1986, on April 7 at Tiger Stadium, Evans hit a home run on the first pitch of the entire major league season. The Red Sox got back to the World Series in '86. Again, Evans' bat was quiet in the Division Series (.214), but just as in 1975, he ratcheted it up in the World Series, batting .308 with two homers and a team-best nine RBIs. In Game Seven, Evans led off the top of the second with a solo home run, for the first run of the game.

Although the team struggled in 1987, it was another great season personally for Evans, with a .305 average (and a league-leading 106 walks), 34 HR, and 123 RBIs. Despite a big drop-off from the team, Evans finished fourth in the MVP voting. Turning 36 after the season, Evans had two more fine years in 1988 and 1989. In 1987, he began playing first base quite a bit as the team had come up with a few young outfielders, and by 1989 he was often the designated hitter.

After the 1990 season, in which he suffered serious back problems, limiting his playing time, the Red Sox declined to re-sign Evans and granted him his release on October 24. The Baltimore Orioles snapped him up on December 6 and he played in 101 games for Baltimore, batting .270 and acquitting himself well. Dewey received a tremendous ovation the first time the O's visited Fenway. Evans played his final year in the majors in 1991. The Orioles re-signed him for 1992, but he was released at the end of spring training 1992.

With the exception of 1977 and 1980, Evans won the Gold Glove Award every year from 1976 through 1985.

Steady in the field, steady at the plate, Evans played 20 seasons in all, ending with a .272 average, with 385 home runs, and 1,384 runs batted in. Evans was, interestingly, a better hitter in the second half of his career than in the first half. A commonly-asked trivia question poses the query: Who hit more home runs in the American League than any other player during the 1980s? From 1980 through 1989, the answer was: Dwight Evans, with 256 homers in the decade-long stretch. He also led the AL in extra-base hits over the same period of time.

Playing 19 years with the Red Sox (only Yaz played in more games) enabled Dwight Evans to rank among team leaders in a number of batting categories. No Red Sox fielder approaches Evans in the number of Gold Gloves. The only major-league outfielders with more are Willie Mays, Roberto Clemente, Al Kaline, and Ken Griffey, Jr.—pretty good company.

After baseball, Evans worked for the White Sox in their minor-league system for a few years, then hooked on with Colorado as major-league hitting instructor in 1994. He was welcomed back to Boston in 2001, serving first as a roving instructor and then, in 2002, as hitting coach for the Red Sox. Dewey is a frequent visitor to Red Sox functions and for many years—into 2014—serves as a player development consultant for the team.

It has often been said that Evans' career statistics are similar to many in the Baseball Hall of Fame. Bill James has written, "Dwight Evans is one of the most underrated players in baseball history." He did so making the case for Evans to be brought into the Hall in a lengthy piece from Grantland in 2012.[6]

Others have suggested that Dwight Evans is already in another very special hall of fame for fathers. He and his wife Susan (Severson) met at Chatsworth High School and married at age 18. They have a daughter, Kirsten, and two sons—Tim and Justin—both of whom have suffered from neurofibromatosis, a condition described as "a sometimes disfiguring genetic disorder character-ized by soft tumors, usually benign, that grow on the nerves."[7] Tim, their first-born, had already undergone 16 surgeries by the age of 16. He lost one eye. The pain throughout is said to be excruciating. Their lives have been a struggle, but Susan Evans said the family is a strong one: "The No. 1 thing, Dwight and I have always had each other."[8] The couple bore the burden privately.

Jim Rice, who played in the same outfield with Evans for so many years, hadn't learned about their children's condition until around 2008. Evans had gone public, to help fund efforts for research and treatment. He said he "would have traded his talent and fame in a heartbeat to have spared his boys."[9]

"It was the eleventh inning, and Ken Griffey was on first base. At the time, he was probably the fastest guy in the game. Joe Morgan is batting, and I'm thinking all kinds of scenarios: 'What if he hits it over my head? What if he hits it in the gap?' I'm thinking that I have to go into the stands to catch it if I have to, because if we lose, there's no tomorrow. All of these scenarios are going through my head.

"All great plays are actually made in your mind before they're made in real time. You have to anticipate. A player like Ozzie Smith, with all the great plays that he made, was thinking about making them before they even happened. That's what I would do in right field.

"When Morgan hit the ball, it came right at me, but over my head. Normally a ball like that will start curving toward the right-field line, going from my right to my left, so I would always go toward the line a little bit when I was running back. This ball did not curve…

"I'm going back — the ball is behind me — and I actually lose sight of it. I lost the ball. I jumped up and threw my glove behind my head. That's why I looked so awkward. I lost it for a split second. That's a scary moment in any player's mind. Somehow, the ball landed in my glove. I was surprised." The full interview is available at: http://www.fangraphs.com/blogs/dwight-evans-hall-of-fame-individual/

Note: Thanks for James Forr for several suggestions which made this a better biography.

NOTES

1   Herb Crehan, *Red Sox Heroes of Yesteryear* (Cambridge, Massachusetts: Rounder Books, 2005), 250.

2   Ibid., 252.

3   Ibid., 253.

4   Jennifer Latchford and Rod Oreste, *Red Sox Legends* (Charleston, South Carolina: Arcadia, 2007), 122. Evans expanded on the catch at some length in an interview with David Laurila.

5   *New York Post*, October 29, 2013.

6   http://grantland.com/features/an-open-letter-mlb-hall-fame-dwight-evans-rightful-place-cooperstown/

7   Randi Henderson, "Dwight Evans' family fights uncertainties of disease," *Baltimore Sun*, September 1, 1991.

8   Ibid.

9   Laurel Sweet, *Boston Herald*, June 21, 2010. "If he had a bad day, he didn't want (NF) to be an excuse," explained Susan Evans. When Jim Rice began to learn what the Evans family had gone through, Dwight Evans told the *Herald*, "He looked right at me and said, 'You never told me about this.' Then, he broke down."

WES GARDNER

By Joanne Hulbert

THE SCORE STOOD AT 11-1 WHEN TIM LOLLAR left the mound and Wes Gardner took over in the seventh inning in the sixth game of the season at Chicago. With Boston's comfortable lead, Gardner could relax a little for this, his first game in a Red Sox uniform and his debut in the American League. The team's lack of early-season luck was reflected in the 2-3 record they now held before this Sunday-afternoon game on April 13, 1986.

First up against Gardner, shortstop Ozzie Guillen hit a triple to center. Outfielder John Cangelosi struck out; Wayne Tolleson hit a sacrifice fly to right—Guillen scored—and Bobby Bonilla, pinch-hitting for Reid Nichols, popped a fly to shortstop Ed Romero. One run, one hit, none left. The lead still secure, the Red Sox went on to win 12-2, and returned to Boston no better or worse than at the beginning of the season. What Gardner did not know then was that the box score that day would tell all about him for the 1986 season:

1986	G	W	L	ERA	IP	H	R	SO
	1	0	0	9.00	1	1	1	1

Gardner left after the seventh inning with a sore shoulder. At the home opener the next day, he looked forward to his first encounter with the Boston fans. He noticed a "cloud of doom".[1] "It seems to be a sore spot on this team. There's been so much emphasis on it, but we've only played six ballgames. If I can do what Wes Gardner can do, the Boston fans will have a lot to cheer about."[2] He soon found out that there was as much for him to learn about the Boston fans as the fans needed to learn about him. "I have to think I'm the best individual for the job," said Gardner. "Pitching in the opener would make it more fun. I want to do that. It's more fun when all the marbles are on the table."[3] Two days later, he was placed on the disabled list with what team physician Arthur Pappas described as "a muscle separation in his throwing shoulder."[4]

Wesley Brian Gardner was born in Benton, Arkansas, on April 29, 1961. He never said much about his childhood other than that he had it rough. His life before baseball was not a part of conversations with teammates or others who asked. He steered conversations away from the subject, and in the lengthy interview for this biography, he expressed simply that baseball provided the happiest years of all. His life before baseball is a story only he can relate. His entrance into major-league baseball began in the 22nd round of the 1982 draft, a promising right-handed pitcher out of the University of Central Arkansas. He compiled 20 saves in 40 games with the 1984 Tidewater Tides. He tied for the league lead with 18 saves in 1985 and was named International League Fireman of the Year. But the Mets had a lot of relief pitchers.

Gardner made his major-league debut with the Mets on July 29, 1984, and he stuck with the team the rest

WES GARDNER

of the season, working in 21 games of relief with a 1-1 record and a 6.39 ERA.

Gardner credited Mets minor-league pitching coach John Cumberland with teaching him the no-windup delivery and helping him perfect the split-finger fastball, which he intended to use as a change of pace off his slider and regular fastball.[5] He had been a reliever since 1983, but had occasionally worked as a starting pitcher, posting a 3-6 record and 3.71 ERA for the Little Falls Mets in 1982. He also recorded six saves, reflecting his ability in challenging situations, and the Mets sent him to the Instructional League to work on improving as a reliever.

Coming to the Red Sox, Gardner had just 105 days of major-league experience, but he did not lack confidence, another quality the team could use. "I want the ball every day," he told a Boston sportswriter. "I have pitched as many as 14 days in a row. It doesn't matter if I have good stuff or bad stuff. I'll go out there and do what I can do."[6] And Gardner realized, "I just wasn't going to get the opportunity (with the Mets) that I will get (with the Red Sox), especially with Jesse Orosco and Doug Sisk ahead of me. They had two or three years on me and had done very well."[7] Gardner looked durable, a quality that attracted the Red Sox along with his compact, smooth, no-windup delivery and his split-fingered fastball.

Gardner arrived in Boston along with Calvin Schiraldi, John Christensen, and a minor leaguer as part of a trade that sent Bobby Ojeda and three minor leaguers to the Mets. Red Sox general manager Lou Gorman, who was in the Mets organization when Gardner and Schiraldi were signed, said, "We see Gardner as a stopper out of the bullpen. We feel he's the guy to come in in the eighth or ninth and get the last four or five hitters out. He's going to be an impact pitcher."[8]

Gardner first saw Fenway Park in December 1985. "It kind of reminded me of Wrigley Field a little," he said. Gardner wore uniform number 44. His first-year salary in Boston was $70,000. He was confident. "I look at it with the idea that if anybody can do it, I can. I've never had any problems. And I pitch more effectively the more times I have the ball. I have a hard time if I sit five or six days at once."[9]

That sore shoulder in his Red Sox debut was something new. "Nothing like this has ever happened to me and it's very upsetting."[10] One inning, a sore shoulder, 15 days on the disabled list on April 16, and a roster replacement marked the beginning of Gardner's baseball experience in Boston. He now contributed to the woeful outcome of the Sox-Mets trade. Three of the players the Red Sox acquired in the trade — Schiraldi, Christensen, and Tarver — were biding their time in Pawtucket. Despite his misfortune Wes had spent one inning more in a Red Sox uniform than they had so far. "It's about to kill my soul that I can't pitch right now," Gardner said after being placed on the DL. "It's hard to come to the ballpark, do exercises and know you're not going to pitch the rest of the day. And that's what I've got to look forward to for the next 15 days. What's done is done."[11]

Dr. Pappas blamed the slight muscle separation on pitching batting practice in the bitter cold at Tiger Stadium. Rest and exercise were prescribed and after a one-inning rehab stint Gardner felt better but the next day it swelled up again. "I can't get on top of the ball and throw a breaking ball. When I do, it bleeds and swells up," he said.[12] With replacements lining up, with little improvement from rest and exercise, and despite another good day of throwing batting practice, once he was completely healthy he'd likely return to the bullpen. But then the Sox would have a roster problem, and to relieve that, considered sending Gardner to Pawtucket for a 20-day rehab program until the dilemma was sorted out. All Gardner got from all of that was more uncertainty. "He simply needs to get in the time on the mound and pitch," said one Red Sox official.[13] On July 2, 1986, the Red Sox announced that Gardner, still on the disabled list, was lost for the rest of the season. He underwent arthroscopic surgery to repair the damage.

What did he do the rest of the season and during the World Series with Boston playing against the team he once was a part of? "I didn't leave Boston. I was at Fenway every day, shagging balls in the outfield, throwing some batting practice. As much as they'd let me. It was a great time, even if I couldn't pitch a game. We kept winning because we had fun."[14] Gardner gave credit to John McNamara, praising him as the best manager he ever had, because McNamara didn't give up on him.

Gardner felt ready to get back to pitching when spring training began in February 1987. As Kevin Paul Dupont of the *Boston Globe* reported from Winter Haven in March, "Gardner's slow return has progressed this spring at glacial speed. After six outings he owned the highest ERA on the staff (10.13) and without a decision in six appearances."[15] The post-surgery phase had been frustrating. "I thought after the surgery, 'Heck, they'll poke two holes in the shoulder and in a couple of weeks I'll be good.' Well, in a couple of weeks I was doin' good just to lift up my arm."[16]

At least the pain was gone, but now Gardner struggled with control. He was convinced that the only way he could improve was to just keep throwing. He that he had been hit hard, and had been wild. These days, in his mind, he was throwing "underneath the ball."[17] He wanted one of the five relief jobs, and apparently only Wes Gardner—and John McNamara—thought there was still hope, while sportswriters predicted nothing more for him than a Triple-A club.

To all the beat writers who had Gardner banished to the minor leagues searching for control of his slider, fastball, and splitter, he answered their grim assessment in a game against the Texas Rangers on April 15, 1987. Larry Whiteside, in a poetic tribute wrote, "On a lazy day in April, he rose like the ghost of Dick Radatz. His name is Wes Gardner, and he hardly had been an imposing figure. But yesterday he brought the Fenway faithful to their feet with a dazzling exhibition of speed and confidence."[18] With help from Dwight Evans's sixth-inning grand slam, the score stood at 5-4 when Gardner came in during the seventh inning to preserve the precarious lead. What Bruce Hurst had left on the bases for Gardner to contend with—runners on second and third and nobody out—gave pause to the Fenway crowd of 16,870. The rest was up to Gardner, and he most definitely was up to the challenge. He

struck out the side with 14 pitches, protected a one-run lead "as if it were the Royal Crown of England."[19] Gardner's spring-training record was still a concern, but in this 40-pitch, 28-strike performance, the concern could be set aside for now. Gardner struck out two more in the eighth, another two in the ninth, and brought the howling crowd to their feet in celebration of a memorable performance that raised the Red Sox to the .500 level with their third straight victory. Lou Gorman, who drafted Gardner for the Mets in 1982 and sent him to the minor leagues to develop as a relief pitcher. Gorman, general manager of the Red Sox in 1984, was still impressed by Gardner's pitching, saying, "That's the Wes Gardner I knew when he was in the Mets organization."[20] The skeptics still wondered if Gardner's performance was just a fluke.

In July Gardner went 8⅓ innings in a relief appearance against the California Angels and six days later was handed his first major-league start in a game in Toronto. "The long relief and that start gave me the chance to face guys over and over. It reminded me, I think, that you have to keep the ball over the plate. Sitting for a year, the way I did, maybe I forgot that."[21] As Kevin Paul Dupont of the *Globe* believed, the Red Sox had kept Gardner for no other reason than that they couldn't turn to anyone else. "I didn't have consistency. I'd pitch well in one game, then awful in the next. I had highs and lows. What I finally decided was to start over, I told myself to forget all the numbers, to just throw 'em away because there weren't any worth saving, anyway. That's the way I went for the rest of the year. I told myself to relax."[22]

By August 1987 he had made 60 major-league appearances without recording a victory since August 5, 1984, in a Mets game in Pittsburgh. On August 15, 1987, in a game against the Texas Rangers at Fenway Park, Gardner was handed the ball in the seventh inning with his 1987 record of 0-5 in 33 appearances hanging on his back. This time he held the Rangers off, allowing the Red Sox to eke out a lead and hold it for the win. Somewhere between the mound and the clubhouse, someone asked Gardner the obvious question: "Hey, Wes. Did you get the ball?"

"What would I want the ball for?" he said.[23] What might have been a better memento for Gardner's first victory in a Red Sox uniform, wrote Dupont, would have been a picture of the final out of the game. With runners at first and second and Larry Parrish at the plate, Gardner turned around and threw the ball to Marty Barrett who picked Jerry Browne off second base for the final out. With a dramatic gesture and a well-timed toss, he finished off his second career victory flashing an "out!" sign as Mary Barrett raised his glove in celebration. "A straight daylight play," said Gardner, with a little daylight back in his life.[24]

Training for the 1988 season began on January 1, when Wes recruited Rich Gedman to help him work on pitching. "We went to Fenway Park. Never missed a day. Then we came down here [Winter Haven] and kept working."[25] He followed Roger Clemens's exercise regimen, ran two miles farther than Clemens did, and was able to throw freely and loosely, better than he had been able to do in two years. With all that was going on during spring training, no one was paying much attention to Gardner. But Leigh Montville noticed that Gardner, very quietly, had pitched 10 closeout innings allowing only one run, and very quietly, struck out nine batters. There had been a grand hoopla about all the things Lee Smith was doing, but very quietly, Wes Gardner was developing into the closer others thought Smith was going to be. John McNamara pointed out that he couldn't realistically use Smith as closer in every game, that there was enough room in the bullpen for another.

On June 28, 1988, Gardner made his first start of the year and the second of his major-league career when he was pressed into service after Jeff Sellers suffered a broken hand.

Gardner remembered that day, in an interview in 2011: "John McNamara said, 'I've got to have a starter, and he came up to me one night and said I'm going to start you in a ballgame. I just want you to go as far as you can go.'"[26] Giving up one run and three hits in seven innings and striking out four, Gardner won 6-1 in his 99th appearance in the major leagues, and he lowered his ERA to 1.49.

At the All-Star break the Sox were nine games out of first place, but Gardner seemed to be writing a new chapter in his pitching career. Then everything changed. Red Sox president John Harrington had warned that John McNamara would be fired if the team was not in the pennant race by Memorial Day. Despite the recent encouraging turnaround, McNamara was out, and third-base coach Joe Morgan was in. Gardner spent the All-Star break back home in Benton and didn't know about the firing. When he arrived in Boston a few days later, he found a message on his answering machine. "He said, 'Have the clubhouse guys put all of my stuff out of my office into your truck and bring it by here when you come home. 'Uh-huh, they did it,' he said."[27]

Disappointed by McNamara's firing, Gardner recalled that the manager had always treated him fairly, and credited the ex-skipper for his recent winning streak. "We won because we had fun," he said, and he didn't appreciate the way the firing was handled. He found Mac easy to talk to and was comfortable with his different approach to the game.[28] "We already knew where Mac stood and what he expected out of each and every one of us. We didn't know how Joe (Morgan) was going to be because he had never been a manager before. He made some guys mad to start with and after everybody got on the same page, we started playing. He was all right."[29]

At first, Morgan was named the interim manager until it was clear that under his direction the Red Sox made an immediate turnaround, giving birth to the term "Morgan Magic." The team won its first 12 games and 19 of 20 under his management. The bullpen endured a rash of injuries, affording Gardner more time on the mound, and by August, though normally utilized as a reliever, he made his seventh start. Paul Harber of the *Boston Globe* asked him if he wanted to return to the bullpen. "I'd rather not answer that," said Gardner.[30] After enduring three hard-luck losses in August, on September 6 Gardner pitched the first complete game of his career to lead the Red Sox to a 6-1 victory over the Baltimore Orioles, throwing 130 pitches, giving up one run in nine innings to put Boston two games ahead of Detroit as the Red Sox held on to the division lead until the end of the season.

Morgan Magic did not transport the Red Sox deep into the postseason. On October 9 the Oakland Athletics completed a four-game sweep of the ALCS with Dennis Eckersley saving all four games for the A's. Gardner pitched in relief of Mike Boddicker in Game Three, the only playoff appearance of his career. Gardner had come into the game with two outs in the bottom of the third inning after Ron Hassey hit a two-run homer that put the Athletics up 6-5. He gave up three runs, six hits, and two walks while striking out eight. Bob Stanley replaced Gardner in the eighth inning, gave up another run, and Boston went down to defeat, 10-6.

Despite the rough start to the 1988 season, the fistfights, scandals, a manager fired, the adjustments to a new leader, the antics on and off the field, more than 25 years later Wes Gardner recalled, "1988 was a fun year, and 1989, too. We just couldn't get past Oakland. Don Baylor used to say we were the only team that could hit four singles and score only one run, so we had to hit home runs or doubles. … We had a chemistry and we all got along."[31] Despite the negative publicity that haunted the 1988 team, something had to click, Gardner said, in order for the team to have gone to the ALCS.

On January 16, 1989, Gardner filed for salary arbitration and then signed for one year at $285,000, more than double his 1988 salary of $117,000. With the departure of Bruce Hurst, it seemed Gardner was set to assume a full-time starting role, as he had been a starter in 18 of his 36 appearances in 1988. Pitching coach Bill Fischer was cautious, saying, "I like his stuff. He's got a good fastball and better-than-average control. He's been working with a forkball, and that has helped him. But one of the things we're going to talk about this spring is coming up with a curveball. If you throw everything hard like he does, the hitter has a pretty good idea of what to look for the second or third time he faces a pitcher. He's going to have to work on that."[32]

On March 4, 1989, Gardner threw his first curveball since he pitched at the University of Central Arkansas where, he recalled, the ball went foul into the seats. He decided then to leave it out of his pitching repertoire. His father had discouraged throwing curveballs until Wes was older than 18, concerned about damage it might do to his arm. Besides the crash course in curves, Gardner, as the Red Sox player representative, was involved with the threatened 1990 strike. He figured he had more time to devote to the job, since he was a starting pitcher. "While everybody else is fishing, I'll be working on this."[33] Rich Gedman, whom Gardner succeeded, said he felt no pressure from management while he was the player representative and didn't think his place on the roster was in jeopardy: "If I'm still around after all that's happened the last three years, it can't be true."[34] One week later, the Red Sox reportedly talked with the Kansas City Royals about a possible deal that would bring Danny Tartabull and Floyd Bannister to Boston for Wade Boggs and Gardner.[35]

There was confidence that Gardner could contribute significantly in 1989 now that he was a full-time starter and had made some adjustments to his fastball and breaking ball while adding a curve. But he didn't pitch well in his first 1989 start, against Kansas City; his velocity was down and his control was off. He redeemed himself in 3⅓ innings of relief against Cleveland. At the end of April he would turn 28, and he was learning valuable lessons: Nothing comes easy, and a starting pitcher is constantly adjusting.[36]

By early May elbow soreness returned and worsened. Joe Morgan had predicted that Gardner would be a significant part of the bullpen, but so far his pitching had been a concern. He exhibited brief flashes of success and future promise, then was neutralized by problems with control and inconsistency. Steve Fainaru of the *Boston Globe* wrote that when he was ahead in the count, Gardner could be devastating, that he could throw a slider, the key to his success, while setting up his fastball.[37] He had won just 12 games since he came to the Red Sox, and he had been on and off the disabled list, pitching in relief, as a closer, and now a starter. He was the player representative, had endured trade rumors, and earned a modicum of fame for his handsome features that appeared in magazines as well as that popular clothing advertisement on the wall of the Copley T station.

The rift grew wider between Morgan and Gardner, who learned about his removal from the rotation by way of the media, not from Morgan himself. Morgan complained about Gardner's inconsistency, about the poor performance in 1⅓ innings against Oakland on May 20, when he was removed from the game by Morgan and tossed the ball to Joe Price instead of handing it to Morgan. The manager acknowledged that Gardner was a victim of bad luck but that he also had nothing good—no breaking ball, no slider, only his fastball was effective and that wouldn't last long. Morgan added to Gardner's frustration when he publicly mused that he couldn't understand how a guy "pitching professionally for a long time … ought to know how to make things happen."[38]

Neither the relationship with Morgan, the curveball, the day-to-day pitching rotation, his private life, nor the right elbow were working well for Gardner, and a July 17 game in Texas was no help. With two outs and runners on second and third in the first inning, he was ordered to walk Julio Franco, the American League RBI leader at the time, and he then pitched a fastball to the slumping Pete Incaviglia, who proceeded to hit a grand slam. Said Gardner afterward, "I take full responsibility for everything that happened tonight. If I don't give up two home runs, we win the ballgame. Incaviglia hit a homer off me and if you check the books, you'll see it was his first hit off me. I just threw him a bad pitch." "We got trounced," said Joe Morgan.[39]

On August 28 Gardner collapsed on the mound after he was struck by Mike Brumley's smash in the fifth inning of the Red Sox win over Detroit and suffered a fractured cheekbone that put him on the 21-day disabled list. The hit was the first time his head had met with a batted ball, and the injury cut short a frustrating and painful season.

On April 12, 1990, in the third inning in Detroit, Gardner walked off the mound to the disabled list when his right elbow again failed him. According to Dr. Arthur Pappas, Gardner's injury was common to pitchers who threw sliders. Steve Fainaru of the *Globe* mused, "One has to wonder what will become of Gardner, a fixture in Boston despite a long run of mediocrity. The team's player representative, he will turn 29 on April 29. He has a 14-19 record with the Red Sox and a 4.75 ERA. This is the fifth time on the disabled list, leading him to mutter an expletive yesterday while croaking, 'So what's new?' when talking about his elbow."[40]

As he was coming back from the latest DL stint, rumors circulated that the Red Sox were interested in working out a trade, offering Gardner and Marty Barrett to the Kansas City Royals, "to deal either or both for a humble return."[41] Trade talks all year long would become the bane of Gardner's existence, not that he hadn't seen the writing on the wall. But he hoped for the best. Gardner recalled that though the Boston fans were great, sometimes the writers were not. He remembered that the curly red-haired one often irritated him, and recalled the tall blond sports reporter who waited patiently outside the Fenway Park clubhouse door, politely asking for some comments from him—words he returned as cordially as she had asked of him. While some of those writers were beginning to write his pitching obituary, Gardner carried on, pitching a good game alternating with another disaster. Morgan pulled him out of a 1-0 game in the sixth inning on June 10, 1990, conceding that he was "very good," that he had pitched a nice game, but he had given up three walks and they all scored, didn't they? (Only two of them scored.) The game was Gardner's first start since August 27, 1989, the one in which he had been injured by Mike Brumley's hit to his face.

"Everybody would like to be Roger and win 20 games. But certain people have to fill a role and pick up the slack here and there. I got on a roll in 1988 and I'd like to get on another one of those rolls. And I think I will, sooner or later, if they don't give up on me."[42]

But the 1990 season was the best of times and the worst of times for Wes Gardner. A great game here, a blowout there, no run support, a start, a short relief, a perfect game spoiled in the fifth inning, stints on the disabled list. "I just have buzzard's luck," said Gardner. "What can I do?"[43]

The Red Sox somehow found a way to win the division title on the last day of the season and again faced the Athletics, who had swept them in the 1988 ALCS. Gardner was cut from the postseason roster. He declined when invited to travel with the team. The Athletics repeated that four-game postseason sweep. Trade talks heated up as Boston looked to improve the bullpen and considered the available free agents and many promising young players. Gardner was on the auction block, although previous offers had not been successful and he hadn't gathered much interest as a reliever. Lou Gorman declined to comment on the possibility that Gardner might be released, hoping he might be at least useful for that once sought-after "humble return." On December 15 the deal was made. Gardner was traded to San Diego for two minor-league prospects, outfielder Steve Hendricks and pitcher Brad Hoyer. Boston also acquired the high-priced Astros free agent Danny Darwin, who was next to wear Red Sox number 44. Gardner left Boston behind, declared "a bust" by *Boston Globe* writers Peter Gammons and Nick Cafardo.[44]

1990	G	W	L	ERA	IP	H	R	SO
	34	3	7	4.89	77.1	77	43	58

When Gardner landed in San Diego in 1991, several former teammates were already there. Calvin Schiraldi had arrived the year before at what became a refugee camp for Red Sox players who also included Bruce Hurst, Marty Barrett, and Tony Torchia, once a Red Sox coach who had a lawsuit pending against his former employer. Gardner avoided placing blame for his problems on Boston's management of him or the team. He thought most of his problems stemmed from an abundance of talent that led to being shuffled from relief to closer to starter. "I feel good about being over here," Gardner said. "At least I know what my role is

going to be."[45] But the sore right elbow continued to cause trouble. He pitched in relief in 14 games with San Diego before being handed his unconditional release on May 31. He was picked up by Kansas City but pitched in only three games for the Royals and spent most of his time with their Omaha affiliate.

A telephone interview with Gardner was a 2½-hour riot through baseball anecdotes, nostalgia, reflections on life as a pitcher, and life after the career he had that was filled with fun, challenges, and the inevitable regret of a retired major-league pitcher. He recalled that Boston had been trying to improve the bullpen, and he was part of a project that would give him more opportunity to pitch. He didn't care if he was a starter, closer, or reliever, the position he thought he was best suited for. "I like the challenge of coming in for a tight situation and trying to get out of it," he said. "You gotta have a thick skin for that stuff. I didn't only come in a game a reliever, I did sometimes start—and close a few times. Rich Gedman caught me a lot."

Gardner's pleasant memories of playing in Boston, he said, have never faded. "Tony Peña! What a great guy! He caught me the last two years I was in Boston. He knew how to get me going and calm me down. I remember one time Tony walked out to the mound when I was having a bad time of it, and he said: 'Wes, now or never, ball up.' Great memories," he laughed. "It was a great time for me."

Leaving baseball behind was difficult. Back in Benton, Arkansas, he was far from a major-league team to watch up close. He enjoyed watching young players coming up like Torii Hunter, Travis Wood, and Bo Jackson. He especially was interested in the second talented pitcher to graduate from Benton High School, Cliff Lee, who has accomplished much that he admires.

In 2001, Gardner was inducted into the University of Central Arkansas Bears Hall of Fame. Beyond baseball, he worked as a master electrician, lived with his family in his hometown, but still thought back about his years playing baseball. Former catcher Ed Hearn, a teammate of Gardner's on the Mets who kept in touch with him, said he thought Gardner had the perfect mentality as a reliever, and that he still has a big heart, one that remains full of baseball.[47] After all that he experienced in Boston, one might presume Gardner would be contrite about the time spent with the Red Sox, that he might have wished he'd been somewhere else, but he said, "If I went back to baseball now, I'd go back there. My heart is in Boston."[48]

NOTES

1 Dan Shaughnessy, "The Opening Act Is a Show," *Boston Globe*, April 14, 1986: 33.

2 Ibid.

3 Ibid.

4 Larry Whiteside, "Gardner Placed on Disabled List," *Boston Globe*, April 17, 1986: 55.

5 Ibid.

6 Larry Whiteside, "Gardner Longs for Short Relief," *Boston Globe*, February 27, 1986.

7 Ibid.

8 "Sox Acquire Schiraldi, Gardner," *Boston Herald*, November 14, 1985.

9 Ibid.

10 Whiteside, "Gardner Placed on Disabled List."

11 Ibid.

12 Ibid.

13 Larry Whiteside, "KC's Park is a Royal Pain," *Boston Globe*, April 25, 1986: 45.

14 Ibid.

15 Kevin Paul Dupont, "Gardner Is Trying to Get Back in Control," *Boston Globe*, March 28, 1987: 25.

16 Ibid.

17 Ibid.

18 Larry Whiteside, "Gardner Gives Sox Shot in Arm, 5-4," *Boston Globe*, April 16, 1987: 35.

19 Ibid.

20 Associated Press, "Gardner's Relief, Evans' Grand Shot Floors Texas," *Paris* (Texas) *News*, April 16, 1987: 15.

21 Kevin Paul Dupont, "His Sun Shines—At Last Three Years After the First One, Gardner Notches Another Win," *Boston Globe*, August 16, 1987: 58.

22 Leigh Montville, "Relief At Last Gardner Finds Belated Success," *Boston Globe*, March 31, 1988: 33.

23 Kevin Paul Dupont, "His Sun Shines."

24 Ibid.

25 Leigh Montville, "Relief At Last—Gardner Finds Belated Success."

26 Tony Lenahan, "Former Major League Pitcher Wes Gardner Talks Baseball, Playoffs," *Saline Courier*, Saline County, Arkansas, December 16, 2011.

27 Ibid.

28 Telephone conversation with Wes Gardner, May 1, 2015.

29 Lenahan, "Former Major League Pitcher Wes Gardner Talks Baseball, Playoffs."

30 Paul Harber, "Gardner Refused to Give the Rangers a Break," *Boston Globe*, August 3, 1988: 25.

31 Lenahan, "Former Major League Pitcher Wes Gardner Talks Baseball, Playoffs."

32 Larry Whiteside, "Gardner Signs One-Year Pact," *Boston Globe*, January 19, 1989: 55.

33 Dan Shaughnessy, "Gardner Takes Over As Player Rep," *Boston Globe*, March 21, 1989: 83.

34 Ibid.

35 Jim Brown, "The Clipboard," *Macon* (Missouri) *Chronicle-Herald*, March 28, 1989: 2.

36 Larry Whiteside, "Sox Show Confidence in Gardner," *Boston Globe*, April 17, 1989: 37.

37 Steve Fainaru, "Still On Hold Injuries, Lapses Stalling Gardner," *Boston Globe*, May 13, 1989.

38 Steve Fainaru, "Demotion Irks Gardner," *Boston Globe*, May 21, 1986: 21.

39 "Rangers Rout Red Sox, 12-6," *Kerrville* (Texas) *Times*, July 18, 1989: 9.

40 Steve Fainaru, "Pitching Staff Shows Signs of Deep Trouble," *Boston Globe*, April 13, 1990: 73.

41 Nick Cafardo, "No Takers on These Two, Gorman Unsuccessful in Dealing Gardner, Barrett," *Boston Globe*, May 15, 1990: 68.

42 Dan Shaughnessy, "Gardner Remains Confident That His Luck Will Change," *Boston Globe*, June 11, 1990: 41.

43 Nick Cafardo, "Red Sox Keep Skidding on the Road," *Boston Globe*, July 7, 1990: 29.

44 John Snyder, *Red Sox Journal* (Cincinnati: Emmis Books, 2006), 567.

45 Larry Whiteside, "The San Diego Red Sox," *Boston Globe*, March 19, 1991.

46 Ibid.

47 Telephone conversation with Ed Hearn, April 26, 2015.

48 Telephone conversation with Wes Gardner, May 1, 2015.

RICH GEDMAN

By Tyler Ash

RICHARD LEO GEDMAN FULFILLED HIS childhood dream in his tenure in the major leagues, suiting up for over a decade for the team he grew up rooting for. Gedman, a native of Worcester, Massachusetts, spent parts of 11 seasons (1980-1990) as a catcher for the Boston Red Sox. The two-time All-Star also played for the Houston Astros and St. Louis Cardinals in his 13-year career.

Born on September 26, 1959, Gedman was the middle of five children. He grew up with two brothers and two sisters—the children of Martha Gedman, a homemaker, and Richard Gedman Sr., a truck driver for the Atlas Distributing Company before an injury forced him into early retirement. He also spent time as a semiprofessional bowler. Rich's father died in 1986 at the age of 55. Martha Gedman died in 2005.

Losing his father at the start of the 1986 season was crushing for Gedman, who told Stan Grossfeld of the *Boston Globe* that he cried before every World Series game against the New York Mets. "… (B)efore every game I wanted to make sure I thought of him," Gedman told Grossfeld. "So as the national anthem was playing, tears would be welling up. It's a pretty emotional time, that separation of thought there that he was there with me even though he wasn't there. He was watching me play."[1]

Playing as a first baseman and pitcher, Gedman led St. Peter-Marian, a Catholic high school in Worcester, to a state baseball championship in 1977. He met his future wife, Sherry Aselton, at St. Peter-Marian that year. (They were married in 1982, and have lived in Framingham, Massachusetts, ever since.)[2] Sherry was an athlete herself, dominating on the mound in softball and earning a full scholarship to the University of Connecticut. Rich went undrafted in the June 1977 major-league draft, but the 17-year-old was signed by the Red Sox on August 5.

The father of three gifted athletes, Gedman attributed much of his baseball success to the late Bill Enos, a scout for the Red Sox, who in 1977 recognized the teenage slugger's talent. Enos liked Gedman's batting, but was concerned about his defense.[3] Gedman's lackluster speed made him a liability as an outfielder and he was subpar at first base. Enos recommended that Gedman make a permanent transition to catcher, a position he mastered playing in Boston's farm system.

Gedman's journey through the minors began in 1978 for the Class-A Winter Haven Red Sox of the Florida State League. In 98 games Gedman batted a team-best .300. In the offseason he worked two jobs, in a newspaper mailroom and on a brewery loading dock. He maintained these jobs during the offseason until he got the eventual call-up to the majors.

After an impressive showing for Winter Haven, Gedman was promoted in 1979 to the Double-A

Rich Gedman

Bristol Red Sox (Eastern League). There he showed some power, hitting .274 with 12 home runs, 25 doubles, and 63 RBIs in 130 games.

The next year Gedman was moved up to Triple-A Pawtucket. He led all International League catchers in assists and double plays. In 111 games played, he clubbed 11 homers, though his batting average fell to .236. A September call-up, the 20-year-old Gedman made his major-league debut on September 7 at Fenway Park against the Seattle Mariners. He pinch-hit for Carl Yastrzemski in the third inning, flied out to center field against Byron McLaughlin, and replaced Yastrzemski as the designated hitter. In the fifth Gedman singled to right field off McLaughlin for his first major-league hit. He singled again in the seventh and scored his first major-league run on Garry Hancock's three-run homer. Gedman popped out to third base in his final at-bat of the Red Sox' 12-6 loss, finishing 2-for-4 in his major-league debut.

On September 17 Gedman made his first major-league start, at home against Cleveland. The DH that day, he went 1-for-5 in Boston's 6-5 loss. His first start as a catcher, on the 26th, was auspicious: Gedman was behind the plate for a one-hitter pitched by Dennis Eckersley, a 3-1 victory over the Toronto Blue Jays in Toronto, and drove in a run with a single. For the abbreviated season, Gedman hit .208 in 24 at-bats.

Red Sox catcher Carlton Fisk signed with the Chicago White Sox in the offseason. Eventually Gedman would replace him, but he started the 1981 season at Pawtucket and played in one of the minor leagues' most fabled games, the 33-inning contest between Pawtucket and Rochester that began on April 18. The starting catcher, Gedman caught the first nine innings, going for 1-for-3, before being lifted for a pinch-hitter. The game was suspended after the 32nd inning. When it resumed on June 23, the Red Sox won it in the 33rd.[4]

Gedman was called up to the Red Sox in mid-May after catcher Gary Allenson went on the disabled list. Seizing the opportunity, Gedman batted .288 with 5 homers and 26 RBIs in 62 games of the strike-shortened season. He finished second in the baseball

writers' American League Rookie of the Year voting, but was named AL Rookie Player of the Year by *The Sporting News*.

As he shared the catching duties with Allenson in 1982, Gedman's batting average dipped to .249. In 1983 he got only 53 starts as he continued to split time with Allenson. He lifted his batting average to .294, though he collected just 19 extra-base hits (two homers). After the season Gedman played winter ball in Venezuela, appearing in 60 contests.

The inclusion of winter ball, along with the strong relationship he built with new hitting coach Walt Hriniak, laid the foundation for a career year for Gedman in 1984. Not only did he belt a career-best 24 home runs that season, he also established himself as the everyday catcher for the Red Sox. He batted .269 with 72 RBIs. Gedman sustained his success in 1985, registering career highs in batting average (.295), hits (147), doubles (30), triples (5), runs scored (66), walks (50), and RBIs (80). He was named to the American League All-Star team for the first time (he struck out in his only at-bat), led all catchers in assists, and threw out 53 of 122 would-be basestealers (43 percent). On September 18, in a 13-1 victory over Toronto at Fenway Park, he hit for the cycle and drove in a career-high seven runs.

In the pennant-winning 1986 season Gedman set an American League record for putouts by a catcher with 20, as Roger Clemens set a record with 20 strikeouts in a game against the Seattle Mariners. The next day Gedman collected 16 putouts (eight strikeouts from starter Bruce Hurst) for a total of 36 in two games — the most ever by a catcher in consecutive days. He finished the season with a league-high 866 putouts. Gedman earned his second straight All-Star selection (he caught the last two innings of the American League's 3-2 victory).

The 1986 American League Championship Series between the Red Sox and the California Angels was arguably the pinnacle of Gedman's career. The Red Sox fell behind in the best-of-seven series, three games to one. Hosting Game Five, the Angels were an inning away from a trip to the first World Series in their history. Gedman had batted the Red Sox to an early lead with a two-run homer off Angels ace Mike Witt in the second inning. But the Red Sox trailed 5-2 entering the ninth. Witt was two outs away from a complete game before the Red Sox engineered a dramatic rally. Don Baylor pulled Boston to within a run, 5-4, with a two-run home run. With Gedman coming up, Angels manager Gene Mauch lifted Witt. Gedman had been 3-for-3 off Witt. Reliever Gary Lucas was unable to close out the game. He hit Gedman with his first pitch of the at-bat and then surrendered a towering two-run homer to Dave Henderson.

The Red Sox could not sustain their 6-5 lead, however, and needed extra innings to capture the road victory. Boston scored the eventual winning run in the top of the 11th, and Gedman played a role in getting the run home. With runners on first and second, he laid down a perfectly placed bunt to third for a single. Baylor, who advanced to third on Gedman's bunt, came around to score on Henderson's sacrifice fly. Gedman finished the win 4-for-4 at the plate with a homer, two runs scored, and two runs batted in. He also threw out two runners on the basepaths.

With the series now tied, three games to three, and shifting back to Boston, the Red Sox captured Games Six and Seven to advance to the World Series against the New York Mets.

The Series brought great frustration to Gedman and Red Sox Nation. Gedman became a scapegoat in perhaps the most devastating loss in franchise history. The Red Sox led the Mets, three games to two and, in the 10th inning of Game Six, led by two runs and were within an out of capturing their first World Series title in 68 years. But the Mets got consecutive singles by Gary Carter, Kevin Mitchell, and Ray Knight to come to within a run. With Kevin Mitchell on third and Mookie Wilson at bat, Red Sox reliever Bob Stanley threw a pitch that Gedman failed to corral. The official scorer called it a wild pitch, but much of Red Sox Nation viewed it as a passed ball, and felt that while the pitch was uncatchable, Gedman could have at least blocked the ball.

Mitchell scored on the wild pitch, tying the game, and the Mets won when Wilson's grounder went betweem Bill Buckner's legs. The Mets then won Game Seven to secure the second World Series championship.

Gedman's career spiraled downward after Boston's crushing defeat. After the World Series ended, he was set to join other major leaguers in a seven-game exhibition series in Tokyo. Gedman, though, was unable to participate in the series after fracturing his cheekbone while warming up Detroit Tigers pitcher Willie Hernandez.[5]

As the calendar flipped to 1987, a banged-up Gedman had a bigger issue to worry about—he was a free agent. Despite his All-Star Game appearances in each of the prior two seasons, the Red Sox were leery of giving Gedman the lengthy contract extension he desired. The Red Sox had concerns, in part because of Gedman's injury. His mental strength was also a new concern, as Boston's brass knew he would field incessant questions from the media as to whether Stanley's wild pitch was actually a passed ball. The two sides eventually agreed to terms, but Gedman could not return to the Red Sox until May 1 because of a free agency rule in the Collective Bargaining Agreement.[6]

Behind the eight-ball for the season, Gedman suffered a dismal year in 1987. He hit just .205 with one home run in 151 at-bats. Gedman tore a ligament at the base of his left thumb in a home-plate collision with Jesse Barfield of the Toronto Blue Jays on July 27, ending his season prematurely.[7]

After rehabbing in the offseason, Gedman returned to the Red Sox—now sharing the catching duties with Rick Cerone. The two split time behind the plate in each of the next two seasons with Gedman hitting .231 and .212 in 1988 and 1989, respectively. The Red Sox, in need of hitting help at catcher, signed All-Star Tony Peña before the 1990 season. The writing was on the wall for Gedman, and he was traded on June 7 to the Houston Astros in a conditional deal after playing in just 10 games for the Red Sox that season.

In 40 games for the Astros in 1990, Gedman hit .202 with one homer and 10 RBIs. The Astros declined to re-sign him in the offseason. Gedman signed a two-year deal with St. Louis, for whom he served as the backup to Tony Pagnozzi. A shell of his former All-Star talent, Gedman batted a woeful .101 in 46 games in 1991. The 1992 season turned out to be his last in the major leagues. He batted .219 in 105 at-bats spanning 41 games. Gedman got the starting nod in the Cardinals' season finale, against the Philadelphia Phillies at Busch Stadium. In his last major-league contest, he went 2-for-4 with an RBI and a run scored in the Cardinals' 6-3 triumph over the Phillies.

The Oakland Athletics signed Gedman in January 1993. He spent most of spring training with the A's, but was released before Opening Day. Gedman signed a minor-league contract with the New York Yankees in hopes of eventually being called up. But he never got a call-up and spent the entire year with Triple-A Columbus, batting .262 with 12 home runs and 35 RBIs in 89 games.

Gedman made one last attempt at returning to the majors the next year, signing with the Baltimore Orioles. He failed to make the major-league roster and was assigned to Triple-A Rochester. Rather than play a second straight year in the minors with little chance of being called up, Gedman retired.

In 13 major-league seasons, Gedman batted .252 with 88 home runs and 382 RBIs. He tasted playoff action in 1986 and 1988 with the Red Sox. In 18 postseason games, he hit .292 with 3 home runs and 8 RBIs.

Gedman coached in the independent leagues, and in 2005 he became the manager of the Worcester Tornadoes of the Canadian American Association.[8] He managed the Tornadoes for six seasons (2005-2010), before rejoining the Red Sox organization in 2011 as the hitting coach for the Lowell Spinners. He got a chance to coach his son Matthew that year, before moving up the coaching ladder to Class A in 2012 as the hitting coach for the Salem Red Sox.[9] Gedman was promoted to Double-A the next season as the hitting coach for the Portland Sea Dogs.[10] In 2015 he was the hitting coach for the Triple-A Pawtucket Red Sox.

The Gedmans' three children, sons Michael and Matt and daughter Marissa, all enjoyed success in athletics. Michael played college baseball at Le Moyne College in his freshman year, before transferring to the University of Massachusetts at Amherst, where he spent the final three years of his collegiate career.[11] The first baseman batted .312 in three seasons with the Minutemen, graduating in 2010. Marissa was a defender on the women's ice hockey squad at Harvard, where in 2015 she was a senior.[12] Matt went to UMass, where he played shortstop for the Minutemen from 2008 to 2011. After a stellar senior season, in which he led the Atlantic-10 with a .402 batting average, he was drafted by the Red Sox in the 45th round of the 2011 MLB Draft.[13]

NOTES

1   *Boston Globe,* March 3, 2014.

2   *Boston.com,* July 4, 2010.

3   Chaz Scoggins, *Game of My Life; Memorable Stories of Red Sox Baseball* (New York: Sports Publishing, 2006), 180.

4   *New York Times,* June 24, 2006. See also Dan Barry, *Bottom of the 33rd: Hope, Redemption, and Baseball's Longest Game* (New York: Harper, 2012).

5   *Reading* (Pennsylvania) *Eagle,* November 3, 1986.

6   Associated Press, April 18, 1987.

7   *New York Times,* August 4, 1987.

8   *Portland* (Maine) *Press Herald,* January 27, 2013.

9   MassLive.com, August 25, 2012.

10 *Bangor* (Maine) *Daily News,* March 25, 2013.

11 Umassathletics.com, April 1, 2010.

12 gocrimson.com/sports/wice/2013-14/bios/gedman_marissa.

13 ESPNBoston.com, June 9, 2011.

MIKE GREENWELL

By Joseph Wancho

I N MID-SEPTEMBER OF 1988, THE BOSTON RED Sox were closing in on an American League East Division title. With 18 games left on its schedule, Boston held a 4½-game lead over New York and Detroit. The Red Sox were in the midst of a nine-game homestand, having thus far taken four of five games from Cleveland and Baltimore. They would close the homestand with three more games against the Yankees. Not only were these games with Boston's biggest rivals, but there was a lot riding on the series.

So as they prepared to take on the Orioles on September 14, looking for a sweep in the series, it may have been easy to be caught peering ahead. The Orioles, after all, had set an American League record in futility, as they lost 21 straight games to begin the season. Boston had already taken 8 of 12 games from Baltimore thus far. But the Red Sox had once been floundering, too. At the All-Star break their record stood at 43-42 and they were nine games behind first-place Detroit. John McNamara was replaced as manager by third-base coach Joe Morgan. After the break, Boston won 19 of 20 games to close to a tie with the Tigers on August 3. Was it a shrewd move by the front office, or perhaps happenstance? The one constant throughout the whole season was the consistent play of Mike Greenwell.

Greenwell was putting up some heady offensive numbers. He was hitting .334 with 20 homers, 109 RBIs, and 36 doubles heading into the game with Baltimore. With Boston trailing 2-0 in the second inning, Greenwell deposited a fastball over the Baltimore bullpen for his 21st home run of the season to slice the lead in half. In the fourth inning Greenwell doubled and eventually scored on Jim Rice's fly ball. The Red Sox scored two runs in the frame to seize a 3-2 lead.

Greenwell led off the bottom of the sixth inning with a triple to left field. Left fielder Larry Sheets appeared to have a bead on the baseball, but it dropped behind him near the scoreboard. Greenwell legged it to third base. Baltimore manager Frank Robinson, perhaps showing his frustration over an already long season, was not pleased with the official scorer's ruling of a triple. "What is this?" said Robby. "Christmas? They giving away triples around here?"[1] Greenwell scored on a sacrifice fly by Ellis Burks, and the Red Sox now led 4-3.

"I knew I needed a single for the cycle," said Greenwell. "Somebody jokingly asked me what I would do if I hit one in the gap. In a one-run game? I'd get as many bases as I could."[2] Greenwell singled to right field in the eighth inning, to cap his 4-for-4 day. All his hits came off Baltimore starter Jose Bautista. Greenwell was excited about his accomplishment. "You all saw

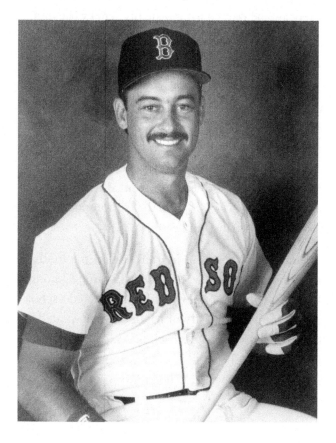

how I felt," he said afterward. "I had my fist clenched before I reached first base. When I was on the radio after the game, Ken Coleman and Joe Castiglione told me that hitting for the cycle is rarer than pitching a no-hitter. This is definitely one of my biggest thrills in baseball."[3]

On his triple, Greenwell said, "When I first hit it I thought it might be caught. Then I saw he was having trouble with it so I put my head down and kept running hard. Once I saw it on the ground, I put my head down and just kept running."[4] That is Mike Greenwell in a nutshell; he was always hustling and never gave up on a play.

Michael Lewis Greenwell was born on July 18, 1963, in Louisville, Kentucky. He was one of seven children (two boys, five girls) born to Leonard and Martha Greenwell. When Mike was 5 years old, the family relocated to Fort Myers, Florida, where Leonard was a contractor for United Telephone. As a boy Greenwell spent many days hanging around Terry Park in Fort Myers, the spring-training home of the Kansas City Royals. His favorite player was George Brett, and he wanted to emulate his hero by becoming a third baseman.

His baseball coach at North Fort Myers High School, Ted Ferreira, was impressed with Greenwell's ability as early as his sophomore season. "The thing I remember best about him is his eye-hand coordination," he told the *Boston Globe*. "In three years he must have struck out only 10 or 12 times. When it came to being a leader, he was it. He would lead our team workouts, and if anybody tried to beat him on the lap around the park, Mike would sprint and beat him."[5]

Greenwell was also the quarterback on the football team, and had great speed and a terrific arm. Although he did not play his senior year, he was offered a scholarship to the University of Miami. "They wanted to give me a shot at quarterback or wide receiver," said Greenwell. "Who would have I competed against at QB? Vinny Testaverde. Who knows what would have happened?"[6]

Boston chose Greenwell in the third round of the amateur draft on June 7, 1982. He was signed by scout George Digby. Instead of heading to Miami, Greenwell joined the Elmira Pioneers of the New York-Penn League. The Pioneers positioned Greenwell at third base (48 games) and second base (24 games), but as he escalated through the Red Sox farm system, he was tried at both his natural position of third base and the outfield. In 1985 and 1986 Greenwell began the season at Pawtucket of the Triple-A International League. At the end of both years, he found himself in Boston.

Greenwell made his major-league debut as a pinch-runner for Jim Rice in the second game of a September 5, 1985, doubleheader against Cleveland. However, his capable work at the plate was not that far away. Greenwell's first hit in the big leagues was a two-run homer on September 25 at Toronto. The 13th-inning round-tripper won the game for Boston, 4-2. He hit another two-run blast the next night, and a solo shot on October 1 at Baltimore. His first three hits were all homers. "I remember I was driving to the park about a week ago with Marc Sullivan and I kept saying that I wanted at least one hit, that's all, just one hit," said Greenwell. "I couldn't dream this would happen. It's unbelievable."[7]

Perhaps because of Greenwell's power surge, the Red Sox didn't wait as long to call him up in 1986. He knocked out 18 home runs for Pawtucket before being recalled in late July. He showed plenty of promise, batting .314 for the Red Sox. Boston captured the AL East Division for the first time since 1975. Greenwell was added to the postseason roster, serving as a left-handed bat off the bench. The Red Sox defeated California in the ALCS in seven games. The Angels had a 3-games-to-1 lead, but Boston came roaring back, winning three straight games to claim the pennant. The turning point was Game Five, when the Red Sox scored four times in the top of the ninth inning on two-run homers by Don Baylor and Dave Henderson.

As dramatic as the ALCS was, it paled in comparison to the World Series. The Red Sox' opponent was the New York Mets. Boston won the first two games at the Mets' Shea Stadium, but then lost two of three at Fenway Park. They headed back to New York with a 3-games-to-2 lead, and seemingly had a firm grasp on the world championship after scoring two runs in the 10th inning of Game Six. But New York bettered them with three runs in the bottom of the frame to win and forced a Game Seven, which the Mets also won.

There was no stopping in Pawtucket in 1987 as Greenwell, who was also known as Gator for wrestling alligators in Florida, came north with the Red Sox after spring training. The Red Sox outfield was in makeover mode as Dave Henderson moved to right field to make room for Ellis Burks in center field. Henderson was later traded to San Francisco and Todd Benzinger took over in right. Greenwell became the fourth outfielder, and platooned at DH with Don Baylor. By the end of the season, he was the starting left fielder; Jim Rice was in and out of the lineup with hand and knee injuries. "My goal was to show people I can play, and I think I did," said Greenwell. "I was brought along slowly, like I should have, showed I could hit right-handed pitching, and now my goal is to be an everyday player."[8] In what was his official rookie season, Greenwell hit 19 home runs, drove in 89 runs, and batted .328. "He can hit. There was never a doubt in anybody's mind,"[9] said McNamara.

Greenwell became the starting left fielder in 1988 as Jim Rice assumed the role of designated hitter. Gator had a lot to live up to, as he was following a long lineage of great left fielders, all of whow would one day be enshrined at Cooperstown. From Ted Williams to Carl Yastrzemski to Jim Rice, they combined for 48 straight years of stellar left-field play. Greenwell, who was being dubbed the New Green Monster, gave credence to that moniker with a big year in 1988. He was third in the league in hits (192), RBIs (119), and batting average (.325), and second in OBP (.416). The truth was that Greenwell trailed teammate Wade Boggs in all of these categories, except for RBIs. Boggs also led the circuit in walks, runs, and doubles. If there was an MVP candidate from Boston, it probably should have been Boggs. Nonetheless, Greenwell was touted as a strong candidate for the award, but finished second in the voting to Jose Canseco. The power

hitter of the Oakland A's became the first 40/40 man in major-league history, smacking 40 home runs and stealing 40 bases. Years later, when it was uncovered that Canseco was a steroid user and his play on the field was affected by them, Greenwell railed against the vote. "Nobody remembers who finishes second," said Greenwell. "It cost me my legacy. There's only so many guys who can walk around saying 'I'm an American League MVP.' It bothered me to lose to a guy who was using steroids."[10]

The Sporting News named Greenwell to its All-Star and Silver Slugger teams in 1988. He was also recognized by the Boston Chapter of the Baseball Writers' Association of America as the Red Sox MVP.

After winning the division title in 1988, the Red Sox finished third in 1989, then won the title again in 1990. Both division-winning years, they were swept by Canseco's Oakland team.

In 1988 and 1989 Greenwell was named as a bench player on the American League All-Star team. After the All-Star break in 1989, he posted the longest hitting streak of his career, 21 games from July 15 to August 20. He batted .361 during the streak, going 30-for-83. On September 1, 1990, Greenwell hit an inside-the-park grand slam off Greg Cadaret of New York. With the bases loaded and no outs in the fifth inning, Greenwell smashed a groundball just inside the first-base bag. Right fielder Jesse Barfield, trying to cut it off, lunged for the baseball, but missed it and it rolled away. Barfield fell and knocked his knee against the wall. Greenwell just kept motoring around the bases. "When's the last time you saw that on a grounder?" said manager Morgan. "That may be a first in the history of the game. Call up Willie Wilson. If he hasn't done it, nobody has."[11] Greenwell was one of only 11 Red Sox players to hit an inside-the park grand slam.[12]

After a .300 season in 1991, Greenwell's 1992 season was cut short after multiple stops to the disabled list. He was placed on the DL in May with strained muscles in his right forearm, and again on June 22. On July 2 he had surgery on his right elbow to repair ligament damage and also had arthroscopic surgery on his right knee. He bounced back in 1993 to have another outstanding offensive year, batting .315, smacking 13 home runs and 38 doubles, and he drove in 72 runs.

In 1994 the four major league divisions were realigned into six. (Central Divisions were added to go with the East and West Divisions.) A wild-card team was added, creating another level of playoffs. But the players strike on August 11 washed out the rest of the season and the postseason. It also carried over to 1995, as that season was reduced to a 144-game schedule.

Boston had little trouble winning the AL East Division in '95. Entering September, they held a 14-game lead over New York, and coasted through the final month to win by seven games. But they were swept by Cleveland in three games in the Division Series.

Greenwell injured the ring finger on his left hand in 1996, and missed all of May and June and the first half of July. He also battled a sore back and a bruised right foot. On September 2 at Seattle, Greenwell set a career high with nine RBIs, setting a record by driving in all the Boston runs as the Red Sox topped the Mariners in 10 innings, 9-8. "It was a career night for him," said Mariners manager Lou Piniella. "It was a week's work. Two weeks' work."[13]

The Red Sox offered Greenwell a one-year contract for the 1997 season, but he rejected it. "My time is done here," he said. "It's time to move on and I'm not coming back. It's unfortunate, it's sad, it doesn't break my heart, but it sure makes it awful heavy."[14] Greenwell batted .303 in his 12 years with the Red Sox, and had 130 home runs, 726 RBIs, 1,400 hits, and 275 doubles. He led AL left fielders in assists in 1989 (11) and 1990 (12).

In 1997 Greenwell joined the Hanshin Tigers in Japan. But a foul ball off his right instep on May 10 resulted in a broken foot. After seven games, he retired for good. "After having the back issues and then turning right around and, after only six games, breaking my foot, I kind of felt that was a sign to move on, he said.[15]

And move on is precisely what Greenwell did. He served as a coach on Bob Boone's staff in Cincinnati in 2001. A racing enthusiast, Greenwell joined the NASCAR Truck Series, and did some racing on his own. Todd Bodine, a Truck Series racer, mentored Greenwell. "Mike's real good. He's a racer who understands about driving," said Bodine. "He's won a lot of races and championships. He's not a Jerry Glanville, a guy who came in here and wanted to be a racer and didn't know what he was doing."[16]

Closer to home in Cape Coral, Florida, Greenwell opened Mike Greenwell's Bat-A-Ball and Family Fun Park since 1992. Cape Coral residents, he and his wife, Tracy, had two sons, Bo and Garrett. Bo was drafted in 2007 by Cleveland and also spent time in the Boston minor-league chain.

When Mike Greenwell was selected to his first All-Star Game in 1988, it was also George Brett's final appearance in the midsummer classic. Brett referred to Greenwell as a "Wade Boggs clone" for his hitting ability. From his perch among the trees at Terry Park, Greenwell would study Brett. As they were both left-handed hitters, Mike would take note of Brett's swing. Once, as Brett was doing his sprints in the outfield, Greenwell yelled to him. Brett tossed him a can of his chewing tobacco. "I've still got the can," says Greenwell. "I'm just going to save it. Nobody knows what it is but me."[17]

Some might argue that Mike Greenwell was a "George Brett clone."

NOTES

1   *Boston Globe*, September 15, 1988: 94.

2   Ibid.

3   Ibid.

4   *Boston Herald*, September 15, 1988: 98.

5   *Boston Globe*, December 15, 1988: 84.

6   Ibid.

7   *Providence Journal-Bulletin*, October 3, 1985.

8   *The Sporting News*, August 31, 1987: 14.

9   *Baseball Digest*, October 1988: 82.

10 *New York Daily News*, February 17, 2005.

11 *Boston Herald*, September 2, 1990: B1.

12 *1995 Boston Red Sox Media Guide*: 52.

13 *Miami Herald*, September 6, 1996.

14 *Cape Cod Times*, September 27, 1996: B-3.

15 *USA Today Baseball Weekly*, May 21-27, 1997: 49.

16 ESPN.Com, May 23, 2006.

17 *Baseball Digest*, October 1988: 83.

earlier. Henderson saw limited action in the season's final month, but with his hamstring afflicted yet again, he was a nonfactor as the Athletics shuffled various outfielders—including Reuben Sierra, brought in from Texas in the Canseco trade—to finish a year in which they surpassed Minnesota to win the AL West. The bleak 1992 totals for Henderson were only 20 games played, a batting average of .143 (9 hits in 63 at-bats), no home runs, and a mere two runs batted in. LaRussa is due all credit for keeping his team victorious through the onslaught of injuries, a remarkable achievement when one considers that the envisioned Oakland outfield of Rickey Henderson, Dave Henderson, and Jose Canseco—a heady combination of power and speed—never played together in the same contest the entire year.

By 1993—and now in the final year of his con-tract—Dave Henderson had to prove that his nagging leg injuries were in the past, yet LaRussa was prepared to make alternate arrangements as spring training opened. "I don't know if he's absolutely certain in his mind he's going to hold up. But he's working," said the Athletics manager. But he also conceded that Henderson could not be expected to perform as often as he had in his heyday: "I know that he's not going to be a 162-game player."[21]

Henderson met LaRussa's lowered expectations, playing 76 games in the outfield, most of them in his accustomed place in center, but he clearly felt the effects of troubled legs, spending more time (28 games) as a designated hitter in 1993 than he had as a DH in the previous five years combined. Another unwelcome trip to the disabled list with a groin injury took place from June 5 to June 29. To that point, he was batting only .203 with 8 home runs and 15 RBIs, and he had struck out in 40 of 133 at-bats. In the second half of the season, Henderson raised his average marginally to finish at .220, and ended with 20 homers and 53 RBIs. Nothing that most Athletics players did could rescue the club from sinking to last place in the AL West. And just as Jose Canseco had been swapped the previous year, so too was Dave Henderson's other outfield partner, Rickey, traded at the end of July to the Toronto Blue Jays. When Dave was granted free agency after the completion of the 1993 World Series, he became a former Athletic in search of a job.

Injuries having rendered Henderson as a liability, only the Kansas City Royals were willing to take a chance on an oft-hurt player in his mid-30s. They signed him in late January 1994 at a drastic pay cut, $750,000, and relegated the former All-Star to the corners of the outfield and to the DH slot, which he shared with rookie Bob Hamelin. At the end of July and shortly before the players followed through on their threat to go on strike, miseries with Henderson's upper hip took a toll once more and forced him onto the disabled list. When the major leagues effectively ceased operations with the stoppage of play in early August, Henderson's career also came to an end to all intents and purposes. The Royals extended an offer of assistance to the rehabilitating Henderson and several other injured players, but this proved to be the final curtain for the man with an infectious smile. The tally for Henderson's last year in baseball shows a .247 average with 5 home runs and 31 RBIs in 56 games.

The trajectory of Dave Henderson's baseball career began at a relatively high level considering that he was a top draft pick. Making excellent use of his talent to rapidly ascend through the minor leagues, he became a good player on a bad team who moved on to play a vital role with teams that reached the World Series four times in a five-year stretch. His admission to being "kind of weird" emphasized the fact that he was "just a big kid playing baseball."[22] While Henderson's appearances in five different major-league uniforms may lead some to label him a journeyman, it is doubtful that if given a chance to be spend 14 years in his shoes and travel the same road that he did, few players would turn down the offer.

In his retirement, Henderson served in the Seattle Mariners' broadcast booth and was a participant at Mariners' and A's fantasy camps. He also supported the cause to combat Angelman Syndrome, a genetic condition that affected one of his sons. In October 2015, Henderson underwent kidney transplant surgery, but quite sadly he succumbed to a heart attack in Seattle on December 27, 2015 at the age of 57. He was survived by his wife, Nancy, two sons, Chase and Trent, and his first wife, Loni.

SOURCES

1984 *On Deck*, Official Program and Souvenir Magazine of the Seattle Mariners.

1986 Boston Red Sox American League Championship Series Program.

1978 Official Baseball Guide, The Sporting News—1978 through 1992.

Sporting News Baseball Yearbook—1988-1993.

1988 Sporting News American League Box Score Book, 1988-1992.

The Sporting News.

Sports Illustrated.

1984 Seattle Mariners Media Guide.

1985 Elias Baseball Analyst—1985, 1987-1992.

Williams, Dick, with Bill Plaschke. *No More Mr. Nice Guy: A Life of Hardball* (New York: Harcourt Brace Jovanovich, 1990).

Gillette, Gary, and Pete Palmer. *The ESPN Baseball Encyclopedia,* Fourth Edition (New York: Sterling Publishing Company, 2007).

Mercurynews.com

Baseball-reference.com.

YouTube video of 1986 ALCS Game Five (1:45 into the video shows Henderson tipping Grich's ball over the fence).

NOTES

1   *The Sporting News,* April 18, 1981, 26.

2   *Sports Illustrated,* May 6, 1991.

3   *The Sporting News,* April 18, 1981, 26.

4   Tracy Ringolsby, "Young Henderson Wins an 'A' From M's," *The Sporting News,* April 18, 1981, 26.

5   *The Sporting News,* August 25, 1986, 16.

6   Dick Williams with Bill Plaschke, *No More Mr. Nice Guy: A Life of Hardball* (New York: Harcourt Brace Jovanovich, 1990), 298.

7   *Sports Illustrated,* May 6, 1991.

8   Ibid.

9   1987 *Sporting News Guide,* 204.

10 *1987 Elias Baseball Analyst,* 23.

11 *The Sporting News,* October 20, 1986, 20.

12 *The Sporting News,* September 14, 1987, 15.

13 1989 *Official Baseball Guide,* 105.

14 *The Sporting News,* August 22, 1988, 20.

15 *The Sporting News,* November 7, 1988, 55.

16 *The Sporting News,* September 3, 1990, 15.

17 *1991 Sporting News Yearbook,* 124.

18 Williams/Plaschke, *No More Mr. Nice Guy,* 298.

19 *1992 Elias Baseball Analyst,* 110.

20 *The Sporting News,* April 20, 1992, 31.

21 *The Sporting News 1993 Yearbook,* 84.

22 *Sports Illustrated,* May 6, 1991.

GLENN HOFFMAN

By Clayton Trutor

GLENN EDWARD HOFFMAN PLAYED NINE seasons of major-league baseball (1980-1987, 1989). He spent the vast majority of his career with the Boston Red Sox (1980-1987) and much briefer stints with the Los Angeles Dodgers (1987) and California Angels (1989). He was a member of the Red Sox' 1986 American League championship-winning team. The right-handed hitting and throwing Hoffman played primarily at shortstop and third base but he played occasionally at first base and second base as well. Though only a .242 career hitter, Hoffman distinguished himself at the plate in several seasons, including his rookie year of 1980, when he hit .285 in 114 games. After his playing career, Hoffman has served as a coach and a manager at both the minor- and major-league levels. In 1998 he was the interim manager of the Los Angeles Dodgers for 88 games after the dismissal of Bill Russell. Hoffman is the older brother of former San Diego Padres closer Trevor Hoffman, a seven-time All-Star whose 601 saves are the second most in the major leagues (as of 2014).

Glenn Edward Hoffman was born on July 7, 1958, in Orange, California, the son of Edward and Mikki Hoffman and the middle of three brothers. (Greg, the oldest, was born four years before Glenn, and Trevor nine years after.) Edward Hoffman was a veteran of World War II who was a professional singer for a time but spent most of his working life with the US Postal Service and working as an usher for the California Angels after they moved to Anaheim in 1966.[1] Edward came to be known to Angels fans as the "Singing Usher." He led the Anaheim crowd in the singing of "Take Me Out to the Ball Game" during the seventh-inning stretch and often sang the National Anthem as well.[2] Mikki Hoffman received the George and Barbara Bush Little League Parent of the Year award in 2002 for her involvement in the Northwest Anaheim Little League program during her sons' tenures in the league.[3]

Like his father and younger brother, Glenn Hoffman grew to be tall, 6-feet-1-inch. He graduated from Savanna High School in Anaheim, after starring on the Savanna Rebels baseball team, a perennial Orange County power. (Savanna High School has produced a number of prominent major-league players, including Glenn's brother Trevor, Al Hrabosky, Greg Mathews, Marty Castillo, and Don Aase.) Hoffman was named to the All-County and All-League teams and broke the school records for hits and doubles. He also starred on the Savanna Rebels basketball team, earning All-League honors as a guard.[4]

The Red Sox selected Hoffman in the second round of the 1976 amateur draft. Boston sent the highly-touted young prospect to Elmira of the Class-A New York Penn League. The 17-year-old Hoffman played

shortstop next to 18-year-old Wade Boggs at third base. Hoffman's .272 batting average bested Boggs' .263 on the 1976 NYPL champion Elmira Pioneers. The next season, Hoffman moved up to Winter Haven in the Class-A Florida State League. He excelled on the Rac Slider-managed 1977 Winter Haven Red Sox, posting a team-leading .289 batting average with 61 RBIs in 126 games. After Winter Haven's season ended, he played in four games for the Pawtucket Red Sox. In 1978 Hoffman was with Triple-A Pawtucket for the full season and again excelled. He hit .282 as the PawSox' everyday shortstop. Despite his strong numbers in 1978, Hoffman remained in Triple-A since the left side of the Boston infield, Rick Burleson at shortstop and Butch Hobson at third base, was strong. In 1979 Hoffman continued his excellent production at the Triple-A level, batting .285 for the PawSox and splitting his time between shortstop and third base.

After a strong performance in 1980 spring training, Hoffman made the Red Sox Opening Day roster as a third baseman. Initially, Red Sox manager Don Zimmer used him primarily as a late-inning defensive replacement for Hobson at third base and an occasional starter against left-handed pitchers. Hobson's nagging shoulder injury during June 1980 helped Hoffman break into the starting lineup.[5] He played well, posting a .285 batting average with 4 home runs, 42 RBIs, and 37 runs scored. Hoffman's production at the plate helped him keep the starting job at third base for the remainder of the season. Hoffman was named to the Topps and Baseball America 1980 All-Rookie teams.[6]

The Red Sox revamped the left side of their infield after the 1980 season with the idea that Hoffman would become a fixture on that side of the diamond. In December 1980 Boston traded Hobson and shortstop Burleson to the California Angels for third baseman Carney Lansford, right-handed pitcher Mark Clear, and outfielder Rick Miller. With standout third baseman Lansford on the team, Boston moved Hoffman from third base to shortstop in 1981. Despite questions about his range at shortstop due to his large frame, general manager Haywood Sullivan expressed his confidence in Hoffman's ability to excel at the posi-

tion defensively.[7] Hoffman opened the 1981 season as the Red Sox' starting shortstop. Glenn's father, Ed, sang the National Anthem at the Red Sox' home opener at Fenway Park. (Years later, Glenn described that moment as the most memorable of his major-league career.[8]) Hoffman played a solid defense at shortstop in the strike-shortened 1981 season, but he struggled at the plate, hitting .231 with 20 RBIs and 28 runs scored.

Hoffman was the Red Sox' everyday shortstop again in 1982. Questions persisted about his lack of range at shortstop, but he fielded the position well again that season. Hoffman struggled at the plate though, hitting a mere .209 but enjoying an uptick in his power with 7 home runs and 49 RBIs. He displayed a marked improvement in his hitting for the 1983 season, batting .260 in 143 games as the everyday shortstop. But the trajectory of Hoffman's career changed considerably on September 24, 1983, when he dislocated his left knee in a collision at second base with Lance Parrish of the Detroit Tigers on a force play. Hoffman had surgery and tried to make a comeback the following spring, but he struggled at the plate and in the field early in the 1984 season. A cumbersome brace on his left knee limited his mobility in the field and his power at the plate considerably. He lost his starting job to rookie Jackie Gutierrez in mid-May.[9] Hoffman batted .189 in 64 games, and played the entire season in excruciating pain.[10]

Hoffman made a major comeback in 1985. Despite continuing knee problems, he had his best season in the major leagues since his rookie year. He hit .276 in 96 games, sharing the shortstop position with Gutierrez. Defensively, Hoffman played his best season at shortstop, with a .975 fielding percentage and 10 errors in 93 games. The Red Sox went 50-30 when Hoffman played shortstop and 31-51 when Jackie Gutierrez played the position.[11] "I worked at my hitting last winter," Hoffman said of his preparations for the 1985 season, "I lifted weights every day, strengthened my knee and I took extra batting practice whenever I could."[12]

Hoffman opened the 1986 season as the starting shortstop, but his season was derailed when he suffered a severely sprained ankle as a baserunner in the second game of the season. Compounding his new leg injury was a bout of severe headaches, characterized by blurriness in his vision, that he suffered beginning in spring training. Hoffman was diagnosed as having a defective micro-valve in his heart, a condition his doctors said was curable. He spent most of the season rehabilitating his body, working out with a doctor in Worcester to improve his overall physical health.[13] Hoffman played in only 12 games: eight games in April and May and then four games in September and October. He also played in four games for the Double-A New Britain Red Sox. Hoffman was not a member of the Red Sox postseason roster in either the American League Championship Series or the World Series. Because Jackie Gutierrez had been traded to the Orioles in December 1985, the Red Sox were forced into a shortstop-by-committee situation during the 1986 season: Ed Romero (who got most of the starts), Rey Quinones, and Spike Owen.

Owen asserted himself as the Red Sox starting short-stop during the 1987 season, relegating Hoffman to the bench. In 21 games, Hoffman hit .200 for the Red Sox before being demoted to Triple-A Pawtucket in June. He played in 46 games for Pawtucket before being traded to the Los Angeles Dodgers in August 1987 for a player to be named later, who turned out to be minor-league pitcher Billy Bartels. Hoffman became the Dodgers' everyday shortstop for the remainder of the 1987 season, playing in 40 games and hitting .220 in 132 at-bats, but was released after the season. Boston re-signed him in March 1988 to a minor-league contract. He spent the 1988 season with Pawtucket, hitting .240 in 109 games.

After the 1988 season, the Red Sox released Hoffman. In January 1989 the California Angels signed him as a free agent. Again plagued by nagging knee and leg injuries, Hoffman played in only 48 games for the Angels, batting .212 in 112 plate appearances. After the season, the Angels released the 31-year-old Hoffman.[14] The Dodgers signed him to a minor-league deal and assigned him to Triple-A Albuquerque (Pacific Coast League). Hoffman played in 24 games for Albuquerque

in 1990 before retiring as a player. As a major leaguer he batted .242 in 766 games with 247 runs scored, 524 hits, 23 home runs, 210 RBIs, and 106 doubles. He posted a .966 career fielding percentage.

In 1991 Hoffman began a long coaching career in the Dodgers organization. He coached for three farm teams in the early 1990s: the rookie league Great Falls Dodgers (1991), the Class-A Vero Beach Dodgers (1992), and the Double-A San Antonio Missions (1993). From 1994 to 1996 Hoffman was the Dodgers' minor-league field coordinator. In 1997 and 1998 he coached for Albuquerque. Over five seasons as a manager in the Dodgers' minor-league system, Hoffman compiled a 246-302 (.449) record.[15]

Hoffman became the interim manager of the Dodgers when Bill Russell was fired on June 21, 1998, after the club's 36-38 start. Hoffman guided the Dodgers to a 47-41 (.534) finish in 88 games. The team finished in third place in the National League West with an 83-79 record, 15 games behind the division and eventual National League champion San Diego Padres.[16] Hoffman was not considered for the managerial position in 1999;[17] Davey Johnson got the job and Hoffman was named the bullpen coach. In late May he was named the third-base coach, and held the job through the 2005 season. The Red Sox considered hiring Hoffman as manager in both 2002 and 2003, but he declined their overtures, preferring instead to stay on the West Coast and not disrupt his family's life in California.[18] Hoffman left the Dodgers when Grady Little became manager in 2006 and joined the San Diego Padres as third-base coach. As of the 2015 season he still held the position.[19] His brother Trevor played for the team from 2006 to 2008.

Hoffman and his wife, Cheryl, settled in the San Diego area. They have three daughters, Sarah, Stacy, and Sabrina, and twin boys, Drake and Dylan.[20]

SOURCES

Newspapers and magazines:

Hartford Courant

Las Vegas Sun

Los Angeles Times

New London (Connecticut) *Day*

Ocala (Florida) *Star-Banner*

Sports Illustrated

The Sporting News

Websites:

ESPN.com

SanDiegoPadres.com

Utsandiego.com

NOTES

1   Buster Olney, "Change Artist: How Did Trevor Hoffman Go From a Scrawny Minor League Shortstop with One Kidney to a Hall of Fame Closer?" ESPN.com, July 10, 2012: sports.espn. go.com/espn/magazine/archives/news/story?page=magazine-20060911-article33, accessed November 20, 2014; Tom Verducci, "Case Closed," *Sports Illustrated*, May 13, 2002: si.com/vault/2002/05/13/323394/case-closed-with-his-intimidating-entrance-and-a-changeup-from-hell-trevor-hoffman-of-the-padres-nails-down-wins-better-than-anyone. Accessed November 20, 2014.

2   Steve Wulf, "The Team of Your Dreams," *Sports Illustrated*, April 15, 1985: sportsillustrated.ca/vault/article/magazine/MAG1119352/7/index.htm. Accessed November 20, 2014.

3   "Glenn Hoffman #30," SanDiegoPadres.com. sandiego.padres.mlb.com/team/coach_staff_bio.jsp?c_id=sd&coachorstaffid=116027. Accessed November 20, 2014.

4   "Glenn Hoffman #30," SanDiegoPadres.com.

5   "The Rookie Spotlight," *The Sporting News*, March 8, 1980, 11; Joe Giuliotti, "Hoffman Escapes Bosox Shadows," *The Sporting News*, August 23, 1980, 31.

6   "Glenn Hoffman #30," SanDiegoPadres.com.

7   Joe Giuliotti, "BoSox Gamble on Budding Star Hoffman," *The Sporting News*, January 17, 1981, 43.

8   Dan Norcross, "Ten Questions with Third Base Coach Glenn Hoffman," utsandiego.com, July 9, 2011: utsandiego.com/news/2011/jul/09/ten-questions-third-base-coach-glenn-hoffman/. Accessed November 20, 2014.

9   Dave O'Hara (Associated Press), "Hoffman is Healthy, Confident," *New London Day*, March 4, 1986, B1: news.google.com/newspapers?id=8pVGAAAAIBAJ&sjid=afgMAAAAIBAJ&dq=glenn-hoffman%20hoffman-said&pg=5205%2C591655. Accessed November 20, 2014.

10 Tommy Hine, "Glenn Hoffman is Happy to be Contributing," *Hartford Courant*, June 29, 1985: articles.latimes.com/1985-06-29/sports/sp-9882_1_glenn-hoffman. Accessed November 20, 2014.

11 Peter Gammons, "16: Boston Red Sox," *Sports Illustrated*: si.com/vault/1986/04/14/633799/16-boston-red-sox. Accessed November 20, 2014.

12 "Hoffman Works Out in Double-A," *Ocala Star-Banner*, July 12, 1986: news.google.com/newspapers?id=KMFPAAAAIBAJ&sjid=BQcEAAAAIBAJ&dq=glenn-hoffman%20hoffman-said&pg=4574%2C5633395. Accessed November 20, 2014.

13 "Hoffman Works Out in Double-A."

14 "Angels Ask Waivers on Hoffman," *Los Angeles Times*, November 2, 1989: articles.latimes.com/1989-11-02/sports/sp-373_1_glenn-hoffman. Accessed November 20, 2014.

15 "Glenn Hoffman #30," SanDiegoPadres.com.

16 Beth Harris, "Dodgers Fire Manager Bill Russell and GM Fred Claire," *Las Vegas Sun*, June 22, 1998: lasvegassun.com/news/1998/jun/22/dodgers-fire-manager-bill-russell-and-gm-fred-clai/. Accessed November 20, 2014; Jerry Crowe, "Hoffman Move Means Malone has 'I' on Team," *Los Angeles Times*, October 1, 1998: articles.latimes.com/1998/oct/01/sports/sp-28197. Accessed November 20, 2014; Mike DiGiovanna, "Hoffman Says No to Boston," *Los Angeles Times*, March 10, 2002: articles.latimes.com/2002/mar/10/sports/sp-dodgers10. Accessed November 20, 2014.

17 Jerry Crowe, "Hoffman Move Means Malone has 'I' on Team."

18 Mike DiGiovanna, "Hoffman Says No to Boston," *Los Angeles Times*, March 10, 2002.

19 "Padres Hire Glenn Hoffman as Third Base Coach," ESPN.com: sports.espn.go.com/mlb/news/story?id=2213137. Accessed November 20, 2014; "Glenn Hoffman #30," SanDiegoPadres.com.

20 "Glenn Hoffman #30," SanDiegoPadres.com.

BRUCE HURST

By Gregory H. Wolf

"I LOVED FENWAY. I LOVED PLAYING THERE," SAID southpaw Bruce Hurst, who hurled for the Boston Red Sox from 1980 to 1988 before signing as a free agent with the San Diego Padres.[1] Best known for his command performance in the 1986 World Series against the New York Mets, which included two impressive victories and a Game Seven start on three days' rest, Hurst was one of the most consistent and underrated pitchers of his era. During a 10-year stretch from 1983 to 1992, he was the only big leaguer to notch at least 10 wins in each season, averaging almost 14 victories and 220 innings per campaign.

To understand Bruce Hurst, one needs to know his roots, and they begin in St. George, Utah, a small Mojave Desert town of about 4,000 people in the southwest corner of the state, 120 miles from Las Vegas. Called Dixie by the locals, St. George was founded by Mormon missionaries in the nineteenth century to develop a cotton-farming industry. Mormon culture still permeates the picturesque town, enveloped by jagged rock formations. Bruce Vee Hurst was born there on March 24, 1958, the fifth and final child of John and Beth (Bruhn) Hurst, who divorced when he was 5 years old. Raised in a tight-knit Mormon community, Bruce had plenty of father figures, including his two other brothers, Ross and Buck, and uncles, and a nurturing family. His mother owned and operated the Hurst Variety department store, which provided the family a solid middle-class lifestyle.

Bruce's adolescent years were filled with sports, fishing, and a fondness for music, but were also marked by an early challenge. By the time he was 2, his legs were so badly bowed that doctors put on plaster casts that eventually corrected the malady. A tall, gangly kid, Bruce played Little League baseball, learned how to throw a curveball, and enjoyed opportunities to travel, but didn't take the sport too seriously. His favorite pastime was basketball, and as he matured he fancied

himself as a future NBA star. Athletics enabled Bruce, a shy, sensitive, and self-conscious youngster, to get out of his shell.

By his teenage years, Bruce began to take baseball more seriously, owing to the tireless and selfless mentoring of Kent Garrett, a former baseball player at Brigham Young University who coached a local team. "For some reason Garrett saw something in me," Hurst told the author. "He was a stickler for fundamentals and detail. We'd get baseball magazines and cut out pictures of pitchers … and look at the positions they were in. I'd get in front of the three-way mirror and practice my windup. He gave me confidence." Garrett spent countless hours teaching Bruce the mechanics of pitching. "[Bruce] had the uncanny ability to interpret what you were saying and convert it into what he was doing," said Garrett.[2] Nonetheless, Bruce, who stood 6-foot-3 as a 16-year-old, still dreamed of a basketball career. Called "Rooster" by his teammates at Dixie

High School, Bruce led his team to the state tournament in his junior and senior seasons, and overcame a scare—a cracked vertebra—his senior year.

Hurst's first serious encounter with big-league scouts was after his junior year while participating in an American Legion state tournament. "It all happened really fast, in a year," said Hurst with an air of incredulity about his rapid and unexpected rise as a serious prospect. "It went from seeing if I was good enough to make a college team to the major-league draft. We weren't even thinking about the big leagues." By the end of his prep career he owned a 24-2 record and averaged 14 strikeouts per game as a senior. Hurst admitted that he felt overwhelmed at times by the attention of baseball scouts, scholarships to play college basketball, and a two-year religious mission, a requirement of all Mormons. The Boston Red Sox, on the advice of scout Don Lee, made Hurst the first Utah native chosen in the first round of the baseball draft when they selected him with the 22nd overall pick on June 8, 1976. Several days later Hurst, just weeks removed from graduation, accepted a $50,000 bonus and signed with Boston.

Hurst's transition to professional baseball was anything but easy. "My insecurities," he said when asked about his biggest challenge. "I was a small-town boy who had never seen high-caliber baseball before. Now I'm playing against them. I'm a Mormon guy, so the baseball lifestyle was different. The fear of what I'd do in certain situations. That was the way I was raised in the church." As an 18-year-old with the Elmira Pioneers in the short-season Class-A New York-Pennsylvania League in 1976, he went 3-2 in nine starts and participated in the Florida Instructional League that fall. "Most of the guys couldn't understand why I didn't go out and drink with them after games," said Hurst, who was homesick and concerned about his mother, who lived alone. "That was the first time in my life I had been outside the sheltered Mormon environment."[3] Injuries ended his next two seasons prematurely. He suffered a torn elbow muscle with Winter Haven (Class-A Florida State League) after an impressive start (5-4, 2.08 ERA in 91 innings). Promoted to Bristol in the Double-A Eastern League in 1978, Hurst logged only 33 innings before succumbing to shoulder pain. "I was so worried about hurting my elbow again that I altered my pitching motion."[4] When he left the team to get medical treatment back home in Utah, teammates and the organization wondered if he had quit. In fact, Hurst openly questioned whether a career in baseball was the right career choice for him.

In 1979 Hurst enjoyed a breakout season, going 17-6, splitting his time between Winter Haven and Bristol. More importantly, wrote Boston sportswriter Peter Gammons, "[He] grew out of the head case classification and became the best prospect in the Red Sox organization."[5]

"I am amazed that I'm even on the big league roster," Hurst told Gammons prior to his first spring training, in 1980. "Last spring they had serious reservations about my future."[6] Described as an "early sensation" in camp and touted for his live arm and good control, Hurst jumped from Double-A to prime time, but was rocked in his debut, giving up four hits and five runs in an inning of relief on April 12 against the Brewers in Milwaukee.[7] After two rough starts (surrendering nine runs in 3⅔ innings), Hurst was shaky again in his third start (two hits and three runs in the first inning) before firing five no-hit innings to earn his first win on April 26, against the Detroit Tigers.[8] With 27 earned runs in 23 innings, it was no surprise when Hurst was optioned to Triple-A Pawtucket on May 14.

Recalled in September, Hurst had a confidence-destroying encounter with his gruff manager, Don Zimmer, notoriously hard on pitchers, "Go home and grow up," said Zimmer, when he grabbed the ball from Hurst in a first-inning meltdown in a relief outing against Baltimore on September 23. "I was lost and confused," recounted Hurst in his 1986 biography, *Flood Street to Fenway. The Bruce Hurst Story*, written by Lyman Hafen.[9] The headline-grabbing episode contributed to the perception that Boston had wasted its first-round pick on Hurst.

"I honestly didn't know if my stuff was good enough to play in the big leagues and the episode with Zim didn't help," said Hurst candidly. Assigned to Pawtucket to start the 1981 season, Hurst abruptly jumped the team on May 2. "I wasn't enjoying the game anymore," he said. "I couldn't see any reason to stay."[10] Three days later, he returned, tied lefty Bob Ojeda for the team lead with 12 wins, and posted a robust 2.87 ERA in 157 innings.[11] Called up to Boston in September, Hurst made five starts, winning two of them.

In 1982 Hurst overcame a seriously sprained rib-cage muscle in spring training to earn a spot on Boston's staff and remained with the team the entire season. He made 19 starts, but was plagued by elbow pain most of the season and underwent surgery in the offseason to remove bone chips. Though Hurst's numbers were unimpressive (3-7, 5.77 ERA in 117 innings), Peter Gammons recognized the southpaw's potential: "[Hurst's] curveball, fastball and change-up constitute the best combination of pitches on the staff."[12]

Described by Red Sox beat writer Joe Giuliotti as "the best pitcher on the staff most of the year" in 1983, Hurst enjoyed a breakout season, going 12-12, logging 211⅓ innings and posting a 4.09 ERA for a sixth-place club.[13] Pain-free, he made 32 starts (completing six of them) and tossed his first two big-league shutouts. Asked what contributed to his success, Hurst replied unequivocally, "Houk and Roarke." Hurst credited Ralph Houk, Boston's skipper from 1981 to 1984, for giving him confidence and a chance to learn to pitch. "Mike Roarke, my pitching coach in Pawtucket, had a profound impact on my career and helped with my delivery," said Hurst. "[Hurst] was more compact with his delivery and seemed to have much better command with his pitches," said Houk. "He used to pitch with his arms flailing and his high leg kick."[14]

Fenway Park can be a nightmare for left-handed pitchers. With the Green Monster looming just about 315 feet away in left field, right-handed batters salivate when a southpaw is on the mound. "I'll be honest with you, Fenway was intimidating, the size, the history, the fans and their intensity," responded Hurst when asked about pitching in the historic park. A cerebral and reflective player, Hurst learned to adjust. "It didn't take me long to realize that Fenway giveth and taketh

away," he continued. "There were cheap balls that went out, but there were some rockets that were singles. I knew I was going to give up a lot of hits in that ballpark, but I also knew that I had places to pitch to—a big right-center field, a big right field. I had to use that to my advantage. I had to learn to make guys hit the other way." During his nine years as a member of the Red Sox, Hurst won 57 games at Fenway Park, a total that trails only Mel Parnell's 71 (1947-1956), and exceeds Lefty Grove's 55 (1934-1941) and Jon Lester's 51 (2006-2014). With a chuckle, Hurst was quick to point out he enjoyed an advantage Lester didn't. "Back then, they didn't block out the center-field bleachers [at Fenway Park]. My curve came out of those white shirts and a lot of guys complained."

Named Opening Day starter in 1984, Hurst got off to a strong start, completing eight of his first 13 starts with a sparkling 1.98 ERA in 95⅔ innings. Gammons opined that Hurst might "have the best curveball in the American League."[15] After tossing 382 pitches over a three-start stretch in June, he missed 12 days with tightness in his arm. Eventually he developed back spasms which worsened as the season progressed, and landed in traction.[16] Hurst improved his record to 10-5 with a complete-game victory over the California Angels on July 21, but was running on fumes. He struggled in his last 13 starts (6.50 ERA in 72 innings) to finish a once-promising campaign with another 12-12 record, while pacing the team in starts (33) and innings (218).

Hurst's season-ending struggles from the previous campaign continued in 1985. By the end of May he was 1-4 with a 6.36 ERA and soon lost his spot in the rotation. The Boston media and fans, as well as the Red Sox front office, vented their frustration over an underachieving club at Hurst. "[Hurst's] actions off the field have contributed to the milque toast image," wrote Dan Shaughnessy.[17] He was described as an enigma, mystery, different, fragile, and not tough enough to be a front-end starter.[18] "The press labeled me as too shy, too timid, too Mormon," said Hurst matter-of-factly. "There's a competitive part of me and I've always had an edge. I knew I was insecure and unsure, but I was not timid." He demanded a trade, and Boston openly shopped him. Defying expectations, Hurst tuned his season around. From June 28 through the end of the season, he was a completely different pitcher. He won 9 of 15 decisions and suddenly transformed into a strikeout pitcher, whiffing 10 or more batters for the first five times of his career. He established a new Red Sox record for lefties with 189 strikeouts to go along with his 11 wins (13 losses) and logged 229⅓ innings.

Hurst had a clear explanation for his success. "I had learned a straight change from Johnny Podres, one of my pitching coaches in the minor leagues, but I lost my feel for it in the big leagues," he explained to the author. "I knew I needed another pitch, something soft. Everybody was talking about the forkball at that time." Roger Craig, pitching coach for the Detroit Tigers (1980-1984), helped revive the pitch, most often associated with relievers Elroy Face and Lindy McDaniel of the 1950s and 1960s. Starters Jack Morris of the Tigers and Mike Boddicker of the Baltimore Orioles were successful practitioners of the pitch in the early 1980s. "Craig showed me the grip one day at Fenway in '84 and I also talked to Bods about it," said Hurst. "I started to throw it '85, but I didn't want to give up on my changeup. I was stuck between the two. About halfway through the year I decided to go for it."

Hurst explained that a new mental approach to the game accompanied his trust in his forkball. He recalled a game against the Brewers (July 3, 1985), when leadoff hitter Paul Molitor nonchalantly reached out over the plate and casually fouled off a pitch. "That guy had no fear of me. I thought he could do whatever he wants. I said, 'No more. That's it.' And I threw a fastball up and in [and struck him out]. That was the point that turned me from a 12-12, really unsure pitcher to a much better big-league pitcher." Hurst shut out the Brewers on five hits and registered 10 strikeouts in that career-altering game.

With a new-found sense of self-confidence, Hurst got off to a strong start in 1986. He whiffed at least 10 in four of his first nine starts, including 11 in a career-long 10-inning complete-game victory, and a career-high 14 in a complete-game loss in consecutive starts. On May 31 he heard something pop while pushing off the

mound and landed awkwardly. Carried off the field, Hurst, who was leading the AL in strikeouts at the time (89), was diagnosed with a severely pulled groin muscle and missed seven weeks. Sportswriter Moss Klein's prediction that Hurst "can't be expected to be at top form" once he returned appeared accurate as the southpaw was pummeled in his two starts in July while Boston's eight-game lead in the AL East had dwindled to just three.[19] Proving his critics wrong and that he was a big-game hurler, Hurst won a team-high eight times in August-September, and posted a 2.66 ERA in his final 12 starts of the season. Hurst (13-8, 2.99 ERA in 174⅓ innings), Roger Clemens (24-4, 2.48 ERA), and Dennis "Oil Can" Boyd (16-10, 3.78 ERA) propelled Boston to its first division crown since 1975.

The ever modest Hurst was quick to give credit to his teammates for his success and maturity. "Clemens was the epitome of teammate. We talked a lot about pitching. And Oil Can Boyd, too," he said. "In 1986 we had Tom Seaver, and it was like the University of Seaver. [Pitching coach] Bill Fischer kept me on task." Mentioning players—catcher Rich Gedman, second baseman Marty Barrett, and outfielder Dwight Evans, among others, Hurst said, "I saw what it looked like to be a pro and tried to emulate them on the pitching side."

The Red Sox march to the World Series appeared derailed in the ALCS against the California Angels. Down three games to one (Hurst tossed a complete game to win Game Two), Boston won three consecutive games to advance to the fall classic to face the seemingly invincible and heavily favored New York Mets, winners of 108 games. Given that Clemens had started the final game against the Angels, skipper John McNamara chose Hurst to start Game One. "I prepared the same way, but I was keenly aware that it was the World Series," said Hurst. "It was crazy at Shea. I knew what to expect from the fans and how they react. Once I took my first warm-up toss, I looked around at my infield. 'Hey, these are my boys. Let's go to work.' It felt so comfortable. You just create the environment in your mind." Hurstie, as his teammates called him, tossed eight scoreless innings, yielding just four hits to win the game. In Game Five he outdueled Dwight Gooden, hurling a complete-game 10-hitter to push the Red Sox to within one game of their first championship since 1918. "We were not overly excited," said Hurst about the mood in the clubhouse after his victory. "We knew that things could change on a dime after our experiences in the playoffs against California. After we lost Game Six, we all said we now know how the Angels felt."

"I wasn't surprised about getting the start in Game Seven," said Hurst. "Actually, I was ready for it." His teammate, Oil Can Boyd, who had been pummeled in Game Three, was livid and charged his skipper and the entire Red Sox organization with racism for skipping him. "Dennis's reaction still bothers me today," said Hurst honestly. "In a roundabout way, it didn't show a lot of confidence in me." Hurst tossed five scoreless innings, before yielding three runs in the sixth and leaving with the game tied, 3-3. The Mets tacked on three more runs in the seventh off reliever Calvin Schiraldi en route to the championship. Years later McNamara, widely panned for going to Schiraldi, who picked up a record-setting third loss in the series, confirmed reports that Boyd was too drunk to pitch in relief in Game Seven.[20]

While Boston slumped to a fifth-place finish in 1987, Hurst picked up where he left off in the postseason. Named to his first and only All-Star squad (he did not play), Hurst possessed a stellar record (14-6) in mid-August before a severe virus (typically reported as mononucleosis) sapped his energy. He lost seven of his last eight starts to finish with a 15-13 record and set career highs with 15 complete games and 190 strikeouts.

With his free agency looming in the offseason, Hurst celebrated his 30th birthday in March 1988 by winning a career-best 18 games and finishing fifth in the Cy Young Award balloting. He was named AL pitcher of the month in August when he won five consecutive starts (and extended his personal winning streak to a career-best seven). Included were a 10-inning shutout and an 11-strikeout performance which pushed him over the 1,000 mark in career whiffs, only the third Red Sox player to reach the milestone.[21]

Despite personal milestones or accolades (he was named the Red Sox player of the year by Boston chapter of the Baseball Writers Association of America), Hurst's season was anything but enjoyable. "I was an emotional wreck during free agency," he explained. "I didn't want to negotiate publicly. I told my agent [Nick Lampros], 'Let's go and hammer this out quickly during the season.' But collusion was going on. It turned into a media circus in Boston and became everything I didn't want it to become." When the two sides could not agree on terms early in the season, Boston GM Lou Gorman played hardball and suggested that Hurst test the market. "I felt challenged [by Boston] and never felt their [negotiations] were authentic."

One of the most sought-after free-agent pitchers, Hurst was wooed by a dozen teams. He ultimately signed a three-year deal with the San Diego Padres, crediting team president Dick Freeman's honestly and integrity as a deciding factor. More than 25 years after that decision, Hurst took a serious tone when talking about the fateful night when he accepted the Padres' offer. "I remember hanging up the phone and just sobbing," he said solemnly. "I thought, 'What have I done to all the people I care about, that I'd been in the trenches with, and that had been so important to me?' And now I'm going to a new place. It was a weird feeling. It was not what I had intended to do."

Hurst made a seamless transition to the National League and San Diego, where the sports media and the fans were much less rabid. "I'm not a savior," he said in words typical of his team-first attitude. "I just want to be a cog in the machine."[22] In his first four seasons (1989-1992) with the Padres, Hurst continued his solid, consistent performances, posting records of 15-11, 11-9, 15-8, and 14-9 while averaging 227 innings for middle-of-pack teams (save for the second-place finish in 1989). En route to a career-high 244⅔ innings in 1989, Hurst enjoyed revenge of sorts when he tossed one of his NL-high 10 complete games to defeat the Mets on August 17 at Shea Stadium to notch his 100th career victory. "Back in the early '80s," he said, "there weren't many people in Boston who expected me to do it. Maybe in slow-pitch softball."[23] The following season he tied for the NL lead with four shutouts and tossed a career-best 27⅓ consecutive scoreless innings.

After battling a number of injuries in 17 years in professional baseball, Hurst saw his career derailed by a torn rotator cuff suffered near the end of the 1992 season. "I started to feel the injury after a start in St. Louis," he said. "The next day we were in Chicago and I could not even pull out my golf clubs from my bag." He underwent surgery in the offseason, but made only 13 more starts in his career. He had a brief stint with the Colorado Rockies in 1993 and signed with the Texas Rangers as a free agent in 1994. "I had a few good games [with Texas], but I knew I was never going to be what I was before, said Hurst. "Maybe a fourth or fifth starter and squeeze out a few more years. But quite honestly, I didn't know what I was going through." On June 19, 1994, he announced his retirement, bringing an end to a 15-year big-league career during which he compiled a 145-113 record and posted a 3.92 ERA in 2,417⅓ innings.

Called "crafty" by Vin Scully, "marvelous" by Sparky Anderson, and a "deceptively good pitcher" by Lou Piniella, Hurst developed into a master tactician during his career.[24] "I think pitching is a lost art. In today's world we only see things in relation to the radar gun," he said. "Young guys never learn pitch sequencing, separation of speeds, and location. I wasn't overpowering, but wasn't soft either. In hindsight, I probably would use my fastball more often. I had a really good hook, then my split-finger change became a really good pitch. Learning how to command those pitches and add and subtract speed and [alter] location helped me. I also learned how to expand the strike zone." Hurst also transformed into an unlikely strikeout pitcher, whiffing 10 or more in a game 17 times and twice ranking second in the AL in strikeouts per nine innings (1985-1986). "Pitching is a lot of psychology," he said. "I learned how to create doubt in the batters."

After retiring from baseball, the 36-year-old Hurst settled in Utah with his wife, Holly (née Barton), whom he had met in 1979 while studying at Dixie College in St. George. They married in 1981 and raised four children. Hurst wanted to remain connected to baseball; however, experiences coaching at the college level and with an independent team left him unfulfilled. "I wasn't interested in going to an organization and climbing through the minor leagues," he explained. In the late 1990s Hurst found the perfect fit when he accepted an offer to coach at a Major League Baseball Academy in Italy, as part of MLB's attempt to grow the sport internationally. His involvement in the Major League Academies throughout Europe for a dozen years led to additional opportunities to coach internationally, and serve as a tireless advocate of the sport. He served as pitching coach for the Chinese national baseball team in 2005-2006 and again in 2012-13. Praised for his keen evaluation of talent, Hurst also maintained a close connection to big-league ball in the US. Inducted into the Boston Red Sox Hall of Fame in 2004, Hurst served as special assistant for player development for the Red Sox in 2008. In 2015 he worked in the international office for the Los Angeles Dodgers evaluating talent in Latin and South America. When he along with approximately 40 others were let go in the club's massive reorganization of its baseball operations in August of that same year, Hurst seemed fed up. "I think I'm kind of done with baseball," he told Dan Shaughnessy of the *Boston Globe*.[25] As of 2015 Hurst resided with his wife in Phoenix.

SOURCES

In addition to the sources cited in the notes, the author consulted:

BaseballReference.com

Retrosheet.org

SABR.org

Author's interview with Bruce Hurst on January 29, 2015.

NOTES

1   The author expresses his sincere appreciate to Bruce Hurst, whom he interviewed on January 29, 2015. All quotations from Hurst are from this interview unless otherwise noted.

2   Lyman Hafen, *Flood Street to Fenway. The Bruce Hurst Story*. (St. George, Utah: Publishers Palace, 1987), 26.

3   Hafen, 48.

4   Hafen, 56.

5   Peter Gammons, "On Baseball. A lefthanded longshot comes of age," *Boston Globe*, December 21, 1979.

6   Ibid.

7   *The Sporting News*, March 29, 1980, 40.

8   "Pudge (catcher Carlton Fisk), I can't say enough about him. He came to the mound and kept on me, especially after that rough first inning," AP, "Rookie Bruce Hurst wins first game for Red Sox," *Tuscaloosa* (Alabama) *News*, April 27, 1980, 4B.

9   Hafen, 64

10 Hafen, 98

11 On April 18, 1981, Hurst was involved in the longest professional baseball game. The Pawtucket Red Sox battled the Rochester Red Wings for 32 innings when the game was suspended with the score tied, 2-2. The seventh of eighth Pawtucket pitchers, Hurst tossed five scoreless innings. The game was resumed on June 23, and the Red Sox scored a run in the 33rd inning to win, 3-2.

12 *The Sporting News*, December 12, 1982, 44.

13 *The Sporting News*, September 12, 1983, 16.

14 *The Sporting News*, April 18, 1983, 23.

15 *The Sporting News*, May 21, 1984, 16.

16 *The Sporting News*, July 2, 1984, 16.

17 Dan Shaughnessy, "On Baseball. Bad Raps on a Good Guy," *Boston Globe*, March 4, 1986, 65.

18 Alan Greenwood, "Fans See Worst in Sox Hurst," *The Telegraph* (Nashua, New Hampshire), June 26, 1985, 15; Bill Reynolds, "A great enigma, a mystery—and, now a winner," *Providence* (Rhode Island) *Journal*, July 5, 1985.

19 *The Sporting News*, July 28, 1986, 26.

20 Tyler Kepner, "For McNamara, A Final Out That Wasn't Meant To Be," *New York Times*, November 7, 2011.

21 The other two are Cy Young (1,341) and Luis Tiant (1,075).

22 *The Sporting News*, December 19, 1988, 51.

23 *The Sporting News*, September 4, 1989, 23.

24 Lee Benson, "Bruce Hurst. The seesaw road from St. George to Boston," *The Deseret News* (Salt Lake City, Utah), October 21, 1986.

25 Dan Shaughnessy, "Catching up with Bruce Hurst, the Series MVP who wasn't," *Boston Globe*, December 1, 2015.

TIM LOLLAR

By Gregory H. Wolf

AFTER AN ALL-AMERICAN CAREER AS A DH, and pitcher, at the University of Arkansas, Tim Lollar broke in to the big leagues as a reliever with the New York Yankees in 1980. Traded to the San Diego Padres the following season, Lollar emerged as one of the senior circuit's most promising starters, winning 16 games in 1982. Battling injuries and struggling with control, Lollar did not achieve his success his breakout season portended, finishing with a 47-52 record in seven big-league seasons, including pennant-winning campaigns with the Padres (1984) and Boston Red Sox (1986).

William Timothy Lollar was born on March 17, 1956, in Poplar Bluff, a town of about 15,000 inhabitants located in the southeast corner of Missouri. His parents were Homer Fredrick and Betty Jo (McHenry) Lollar, both native Missourians who married in 1948. Despite claims otherwise, Tim is not related to longtime Chicago White Sox catcher Sherm Lollar. When Tim completed second grade, his family relocated to Farmington, a mining town situated in the Ozarks, almost equidistant between Poplar Bluff and St. Louis. The elder Lollar owned a wholesale meat business. He was tragically killed in a hunting accident when Tim was about 13. His mother worked as a teacher's aide to provide for him and his sister, Janis. An athletic youngster and unabashed St. Louis Cardinals fan, Tim started playing baseball on local sandlots and youth leagues, graduating to Babe Ruth and then American Legion by the time he was 16. He starred in baseball and football at Farmington High School, but his school did not field a baseball team. Upon graduation in 1974, Lollar accepted an athletic scholarship to attend nearby Mineral Area College.

Lollar's baseball career seemed to reach its end when he completed his second and final year of junior college in 1976. But like so many players before and since, he had a stroke of luck. Longtime St. Louis Cardinals

scout Fred Hawn, based in Fayetteville, Arkansas, had seen the youngster pitch and hit. Upon his recommendation, Norm DeBriyn, head baseball coach at the University of Arkansas, recruited Lollar. "Lollar has a lively arm, and his fastball has good velocity," said DeBriyn. "He played very little baseball until he was a freshman but has developed rapidly."[1] Lollar majored in forestry, anticipating a career as a game warden, but those plans were put on hold. Over the course of the next two seasons with the Razorbacks, Lollar emerged as a formidable hitter and hurler. Additionally, he showcased his talent in two collegiate summer leagues — the Texas College League (1976) and with the (Fairbanks) Alaska Goldpanners (1977). The Cleveland Indians chose Lollar in the fifth round of the 1977 amateur draft, but the 21-year-old decided to return to Fayetteville for his final season. It was a wise move. He led the Razorbacks with a 7-1 record and sub-2.00 ERA; however, he was even better as a

slugger. Serving primarily as designated hitter, but also playing first base, Lollar led the Southwest Conference with a .423 batting average.[2] He was named SWC player of the year and a national All-American at DH, becoming the school's first player to achieve All-American distinction. The New York Yankees chose him in the fourth round of the 1978 amateur draft. The University of Arkansas honored Lollar in 2005 by naming him to their Hall of Honor.

Lollar spent his first two years in the Yankees farm system with West Haven (Double-A Eastern League) not knowing if the club expected him to be a pitcher, first baseman, or designated hitter. At 6-feet-3 and about 195 pounds, Lollar cut an impressive figure on the mound and in the batter's box. After logging 31 mostly ineffective innings (5.81 ERA), but batting .255 in 1978, Lollar posted a steady 3.18 ERA in 119 innings while hitting just .230 the following season, suggesting that his future was on the mound. "It was obvious to me that he was a pitcher even if he didn't know it," said West Haven and future Padre teammate Chris Welsh.[3]

After participating in his first spring training with the Yankees, as a nonroster invitee in 1980, Lollar was optioned to the Columbus (Ohio) Clippers in the Triple-A International League. With teammates and prospects Dave Righetti and Welsh projected as future starters, Lollar was moved to the bullpen and set the circuit on fire. He surrendered only 13 hits and posted a 1.09 ERA in his first 33 innings, earning a promotion to the Yankees' 40-man roster and a call-up to New York on June 24. To make room, the club moved aging utilityman Paul Blair into the role of team scout and minor-league instructor. New York's starting rotation was lefty-heavy (Tommy John, Ron Guidry, Tom Underwood, and swingman Rudy May), but lacked a portside relief specialist to complement hard-throwing Goose Gossage. In his debut, on June 28, Lollar gave up two hits and one run in two innings of relief at Yankee Stadium. Lollar pitched well (3.86 ERA in 25⅔ innings), but was sent back to Columbus in mid-August. He returned on September 13. With the Yankees' AL East crown already clinched, Lollar

was given his first start on the last day of the season. He tossed two-hit ball over six innings to pick up his maiden win in a game that saw New York establish a new home attendance record.

In the 1980-1981 offseason, Lollar played winter ball in Ponce, Puerto Rico, for manager Stan Williams. He reported to spring training in 1981 in strong form, yet did not pitch very much. "I didn't know what was going on," said Lollar. "I thought I'd get sent down to the minors."[4] On March 31 Lollar was shipped along with Welsh, center fielder Ruppert Jones, and utilityman Joe Lefebvre to the Padres in exchange for flychaser Jerry Mumphrey and right-hander John Pacella. Lollar struggled with his new team during the strike-shortened season, posting miserable numbers (2-8, 6.10 ERA, and 51 walks in 76⅔ innings). The highlight of his season was probably connecting off Cincinnati's Tom Seaver on April 28 for his first major-league hit, a solo blast in an otherwise forgettable performance yielding seven runs (five earned) in two innings of relief to pick up his first big-league loss.

Lollar went from being called a failure by San Diego beat writer Phil Collier after the 1981 season to being honored as the club's most improved player during spring training in 1982, posting a 1.87 ERA and walking just five in 24 frames.[5] Collier suggested that Lollar's unexpected turnaround could be traced to a shouting match the southpaw had with manager Vern Benson while playing winter ball with the Barquisimento Cardinales in the Venezuelan winter league.[6] No longer trying to shave the corners, Lollar reared back and let his natural stuff take over. "Tim has been one of our nicest surprises in spring training," said first-year skipper Dick Williams, who had taken over for Frank Howard after the team's last-place finish in the NL West. "Last year was frustrating," said Lollar as the '81 season commenced. "I was mentally prepared to pitch in the major leagues, but physically I wasn't," while acknowledging that he didn't pitch regularly enough to establish consistency.[7]

Lollar began the 1982 season by reeling off five straight victories, earning praise from GM Jack McKeon as "the best deal I've made."[8] On April 29 he tossed a five-hitter to record his first of four career shutouts, and belted a home run to defeat the New York Mets at Jack Murphy Stadium. "He's much more aggressive with his fastball and slider this year," said catcher Terry Kennedy. "He's challenging the hitters, not nibbling and missing. He's giving them his best stuff."[9] Lollar, 10-2 with a 2.71 ERA at the All-Star break, was the topic of a mini-controversy when Tommy Lasorda, skipper of the NL squad, snubbed him. League President Chub Feeney subsequently issued a public apology. Lollar struggled after the midsummer classic, losing five of six decisions, suffering from both a "dead arm"[10] and a circulation problem in his index finger, which physicians diagnosed as Reynaud's Phenomenon.[11] Returning to his first-half form, the 26-year-old Missourian finished with a bang, going 5-2 and posting a stellar 1.98 ERA over his last eight starts of the season to help the Padres jump to a fourth-place finish (81-81) and record just their second nonlosing season in their 14-year history. Syndicated columnist Furman Bisher described Lollar as a "throwback to the age of baggy britches and sleeper jumpers" with his exuberant approach to all aspects of the game.[12] Lollar finished with career bests in practically every category, including wins (16), starts (34), innings (232⅔), and ERA (3.13); he also batted .247 (21-for-85), hit three homers and drove in 11 runs. He joined Clay Kirby, Randy Jones, and Gaylord Perry as the only hurlers in Padres history to win at least 15 games in a season.

Looking to capitalize on his success, Lollar refused the Padres' 1983 salary offer of $200,000 and became the first player in team history to file for arbitration. He was awarded a dramatic increase to $300,000, six times his '82 salary. Notwithstanding his new financial status, Lollar struggled in spring training after having pitched in excess of 350 innings the previous year in winter ball and the regular season. "My arm was so tired I felt like I was floating the ball to the plate. … Baseball is a series of adjustment," Lollar said. "You have to make adjustments with your teammates, with the hitters, the umpires, with yourself. I learned a lot about the hitters last year. I learned a lot about myself. A pitching arm has only a certain amount of elasticity and I pitched some games where I didn't have anything

except good location"[13] After just three ineffective starts, Lollar was sidelined for three weeks with elbow pain and inflammation in his ulnar nerve. He returned in early May, but failed to find the groove that made him one of the most promising young hurlers in the NL the previous year. He dropped to 7-12 and completed only one of 30 starts, while struggling with his control (85 walks in 175⅔ innings). His ERA (4.61) was the NL's third worst among qualifiers. When he did pitch well, he seemed to be beset by bad luck and poor run support (the Padres scored two runs or fewer in nine of his losses). Twice he carried no-hitters into the seventh inning, only to lose each game.

If anything, Lollar was confident as the Padres broke camp in 1984 as a dark-horse selection to capture the NL West crown after two consecutive .500 finishes. "I would be really disappointed if we didn't win the division," said the lefty.[14] The pitching rotation was led by a core of five under-30 hurlers — Lollar, Eric Show, Ed Whitson, Mark Thurmond, and Andy Hawkins, with swingman Dave Dravecky and offseason acquisition Goose Gossage in the bullpen. The Padres got off to a hot start (14-5) and were in sole possession of first place from June 9 to the end of the season. Lollar praised Williams's tough, no-nonsense approach en route to the skipper's first postseason berth since he guided the Oakland A's to their second consecutive World Series title in 1972. "Sometimes a little chewing out doesn't hurt a player," said Lollar. "I don't think I could ask for a better manager."[15] Although Lollar struggled with his control all season, finishing with the second most walks in the NL (105 free passes and 10 wild pitches in 195⅔ innings), he limited the opposition to just 7.7 hits per nine innings. On June 8 he blanked the Cincinnati Reds on four hits, tied his career high with 12 punchouts (the fifth and final time he recorded at least 10 strikeouts in a game), and knocked in two runs. Though not at his best, Lollar recorded the hitherto biggest victory in franchise history when he tossed eight-hit ball over 5⅓ innings, yielding three runs, in the division-clinching 5-3 victory over the San Francisco Giants in San Diego on September 20. Lollar supplied offensive fireworks, too, belting a three-run homer off Mike Krukow.

The Padres lost the first two games to the Chicago Cubs in the NLCS before waging one of the most storied comebacks in championship history by taking the next three games, and stabbing a dagger in the hearts of Cubs fans who had hoped that their team's first postseason appearance since 1945 might end a World Series championship drought that extended back to 1908. In Game Four, Lollar lasted just 4⅓ innings, and was charged with three runs and four walks. San Diego's luck and timely hitting did not continue against the Detroit Tigers, overwhelming favorites in the World Series. Crushed in five games, the Padres' starting pitchers lasted only a combined 10⅓ innings, yielding 25 hits and 17 runs (16 earned) for a 13.94 ERA. Lollar recorded only five outs in Game Three, victimized for four runs on four hits and four walks.

During the 1984 baseball winter meetings, Lollar was involved in a blockbuster trade when the Padres sent him, highly touted shortstop prospect Ozzie Guillen, third baseman Luis Salazar, and minor-league pitcher Bill Long to the Chicago White Sox in exchange for right-hander LaMarr Hoyt and two minor-league throw-ins (Kevin Kristan and Todd Simmons) who never made it to the majors. The trade was widely panned by the Chicago press and fans. A South Side favorite, Hoyt had led the AL in victories in 1982 and 1983, capturing the Cy Young Award in the latter year on the basis of a 24-10 record for the AL West champs; weight problems limited him to 13 wins and an AL-high 18 losses in '84. Lollar had a good spring for the White Sox (2.10 ERA in 26 innings), drawing praise from skipper Tony LaRussa: "He has a real idea how to pitch."[16] However, Lollar's success did not translate into the regular season. After making it through seven innings just once in 13 starts, Lollar was traded to the Boston Red Sox for reserve outfielder Reid Nichols, who was batting a paltry .188 at the time. "Lollar will add depth to our pitching staff and that is something we badly need," said GM Lou Gorman optimistically.[17] Slotted as the fifth starter, Lollar went 4-5 in his first 10 starts for the Red Sox, but the final one, on September 13, was disastrous (five runs in 1⅔ innings). He was shunted to the bullpen for the

rest of the season and finished with a combined 8-10 record and 4.62 ERA in 150 innings, while the Red Sox finished with a disappointing 81-81 record, good for only fifth place in the tough AL East.

While the Red Sox captured the pennant in 1986, their first in 11 years, the season was a long and agonizingly frustrating one for Lollar. He logged only 43 innings over 32 appearances (one start) and posted a team-worst 6.91 ERA. "They didn't know what my number was toward the end of last year," said Lollar who pitched only six times after July 30. "It wasn't fun for me —even winning."[18] Boston sportswriter Larry Whiteside reported that Boston had tried to trade Lollar after the '85 season, but his high salary (reported at $625,000) drew no takers, while skipper John McNamara had lost confidence in the hurler because of his wildness (34 walks).[19] "I am a better starting pitcher than I am a reliever," said Lollar. "I'm at the point in my career where I need to pitch. It doesn't do me any good to sit around."[20]

After the Red Sox' unsuccessful attempts at unloading Lollar yet again in the offseason, the club released him during spring training in 1987. He caught on with the Detroit Tigers, and split the season with the Triple-A Toledo Mudhens of the International League and subsequently with the Louisville Redbirds, the St. Louis Cardinals' affiliate in the American Association. "The game was no longer fun," said Lollar, who posted a 3-4 record and 5.87 ERA in 76⅔ innings. "It came off to me as more business than game, and as such I just felt like it wasn't worth it."[21] Just 31 years old, Lollar retired. In parts of seven big-league season he posted a 47-52 record, carved out a 4.27 ERA in 908 innings, and made 131 starts among his 199 appearances. Always a threat with the bat, Lollar also collected 54 hits, good for a .234 average, clouted 8 home runs, and drove in 38 runs.

After his playing days, Lollar and his wife, Robyn (Schaub) Lollar, a former San Diego sportscaster intern whom he married in 1983, moved to Breckenridge, Colorado, on the recommendation of good friend Goose Gossage. He was involved in homebuilding industry, but was unsatisfied. During his active playing days, Lollar had started golfing and began to take the sport more seriously as a member of the local country club. Eventually he attended the San Diego Golf Academy and was hired by Breckenridge Golf Club in 1992. "He's one of the best athletes that I've ever met," said Gossage. "Nothing Tim does would shock me."[22] In 1996 Lollar was named the head golf professional at the Lakewood (Colorado) Country Club, and held the position as of 2015. In 2010 he was named the Colorado PGA golf professional of the year. "I feel like I had a great career in baseball," said Lollar in 2009, "But the things I have done after baseball, getting in the golf business, are more rewarding. This was more brain power and effort and attitude, along with personality and sacrifice. Baseball was all of that too. But throwing a baseball was also God-given talent."[23] As of 2015, Lollar resided in Colorado.

SOURCES

Tim Lollar player file at the National Baseball Hall of Fame, Cooperstown, New York.

Ancestry.com.

BaseballLibrary.com.

Baseball-Reference.com.

Retrosheet.com.

SABR.org.

NOTES

1 "Porkers Sign Lefty Hurler, Tim Lollar," *Northwest Arkansas Times* (Fayetteville, Arkansas), May 23, 1976: 20.

2 Lollar's college statistics are from UPI: "Razorbacks, Bears Pace All-SWC BB," *Galveston* (Texas) *Daily News*, June 30, 1978: 2-B.

3 Alexander Wolff, "They were playing his song," *Sports Illustrated*, May 31, 1982. si.com/vault/1982/05/31/627601/nfl.

4 Suzanne Seixas, "When a Young Pitcher Strikes It Rich," *Money*, June 1983: 110.

5 *The Sporting News*, November 14, 1981: 53; April 17, 1982: 29.

6 *The Sporting News*, April 17, 1982, 29.

7 Ibid.

8 *The Sporting News*, June 7, 1982: 7.

9 Wolff.

10 *The Sporting News*, August 9, 1982: 17.

11 *The Sporting News*, July 12, 1982: 29.

12 *The Sporting News*, August 9, 1982: 9.

13 *The Sporting News*, March 21, 1983: 34.

14 *The Sporting News*, January 23, 1984: 35.

15 *The Sporting News*, January 2, 1984: 40.

16 *The Sporting News*, April 15, 1985: 24.

17 "Red Sox acquire Lollar," *New York Post*, July 12, 1986: 95.

18 Larry Whiteside, "For Lollar, It's Life in Limbo," *Boston Globe*, February 25, 1987: 25.

19 Ibid.

20 Ibid.

21 Robert Moreno, "Where are they now?—Tim Lollar," *Friars On Base*. friarsonbase.com/2013/02/05/where-are-they-now-tim-lollar/.

22 Tom Kensler, "Lollar Went From Diamonds to Clubs," *Denver Post*, June 9, 2009. denverpost.com/headlines/ci_12789838

23 Ibid.

STEVE LYONS

By Donna L. Halper

STEVE LYONS WAS A UTILITY PLAYER WHO spent nine years in the major leagues, including four stints with the Red Sox; a left-handed hitter, he batted.252. But while that number might not seem impressive, it doesn't tell the whole story. In fact, throughout his major-league career, Lyons frequently got people talking. Fans, sports reporters, and even his own managers never knew what to expect from Lyons, whose nickname was "Psycho." He could be brash, emotional, and capable of boneheaded mistakes; or he could be a reliable clutch player whose versatility enabled him to step in at just about any position (during one exhibition game, he played all nine of them). Lyons acknowledged that he was probably an overachiever: "I was never a great athlete or a great hitter," he said. "I was never supposed to make the big leagues."[1] But he did, and during the nine seasons that he played for the Red Sox, Chicago White Sox, Atlanta Braves, and Montreal Expos, there were a number of memorable moments.

Stephen John Lyons was born on June 3, 1960, in Tacoma, Washington. He was strongly influenced by his father, Richard, who had been a three-sport star athlete (Class of 1953) at Hudson (Massachusetts) High School.[2] Richard did not play college ball, but he never lost his love of sports, especially baseball. After relocating to the West Coast while in the US Army, Richard Lyons coached Little League; he also continued to follow the team he loved as a boy, the Boston Red Sox. "We would always watch the Red Sox [on television] when they were on the Game of the Week," Steve recalled. His father's favorite player was Carl Yastrzemski, while Steve's was Fred Lynn.[3]

Steve's interest in baseball developed early. He told a college newspaper reporter that he'd dreamed of a big-league career since he was 5.[4] Like his father, he played several sports: When he attended Marist High School in Eugene, Oregon, he became known for basketball. But when he transferred to Beaverton High School for his senior year, he turned his focus to baseball, playing the outfield and distinguishing himself as a fielder. Although his batting average in his senior year was only .239, his enthusiasm and how hard he played the game earned him some attention. So did the trouble he had controlling his emotions: He would sometimes throw his helmet or bat in frustration when a call didn't go his way.[5]

Despite the low batting average, at least one area coach saw Lyons' potential and he was able to get a partial athletic scholarship to Oregon State University in Corvallis. He majored in business administration, and when not in the classroom, he was winning praise for his skill on the diamond, especially as a fielder for the Oregon State Beavers: He won two Gold Gloves, one in 1979 as an outfielder, and the other in 1980 as a third baseman. He also played some games at

shortstop, and did well there too. But Lyons' hitting skills needed improvement: his average hovered around the .250 range throughout his three years at Oregon State. His coach, Jack Riley, believed that the 6-foot-3 utility player had "all the tools" to become a success, noting his skill at fielding and running the bases. But Riley also noted the flaw in Lyons' hitting. Pitchers had quickly learned that he couldn't hit a breaking ball. His coach predicted a bright future for Lyons if he worked hard, but said he would first have to "mature mentally and learn how to hit."[6]

Lyons did show some flashes of hitting ability. He played summer ball in Dodge City, Kansas, in 1980; as the shortstop for the Dodge City Athletics,[7] he hit .377, with 20 home runs.[8] Despite his low batting average for his college team, that success in summer ball got Lyons noticed. When the 1981 amateur draft took place, he was chosen by the Red Sox in the first round, as the 19th overall pick. The Boston newspapers described Lyons as someone with "above average speed, and a very fiery and intense approach to the game."[9] Reporters immediately noticed that he was very talkative (and quotable), and he seemed confident in his own ability. As soon as he signed his contract, he decided to drop out of college to pursue his dream of playing pro ball,[10] and his first stop was at Class-A Winston-Salem, in the Carolina League. Lyons made a good first impression: He alternated between playing shortstop and the outfield, impressing Buddy Hunter, his manager, with his fielding. He also started off well at the plate, with 9 hits in his first 20 at-bats.[11] But by season's end, his average was similar to what it had been in college: In 64 games, he hit .242.

In 1982 Lyons was assigned to Double-A Bristol (Connecticut) of the Eastern League, where he mainly played outfield. While he stole 35 bases, he struck out 119 times and batted .243. In 1983 he was back in Double-A, playing the outfield for New Britain (Bristol's successor). The team decided to try the versatile Lyons at third base. He played 87 games at third, along with 47 in the outfield. He even pitched in three games, and in one of them, he was the winning pitcher. And he continued to be a force on the base-

paths, stealing 47 bases. But although he struck out far fewer times than the previous year, his average was just .246. On the other hand, Lyons did have some noteworthy moments while playing for New Britain. One of them involved his teammate, pitcher Roger Clemens, who made headlines by striking out 15 as New Britain defeated the Reading Phillies, 11-3. Lyons made headlines of his own, going 4-for-5, scoring four of his team's runs, and stealing five bases.[12] Boston sportswriters who watched Lyons play believed his batting average didn't tell the whole story. One noted that even when not getting hits, he knew how to get on base, having walked 77 times, and because of all the positions he played and his speed and fielding ability, he was named New Britain's MVP that year.[13]

In 1984 Lyons was promoted to Triple-A, spending the season with Pawtucket as the third baseman. It turned out to be an amazing year for the PawSox. The team was not expected to do much, but at year's end not only were the PawSox in first place, they then won the International League championship in dramatic come-from-behind fashion.[14] Lyons was a major contributor, and this time not just with his speed or his fielding ability. In the first half of the season he was one of Pawtucket's best hitters, with big games like one against Rochester when he hit two homers and drove in six runs.[15] And even though his average tailed off during the second half, he still finished the season at .268. He was named to the International League's final all-star team, the only member of the PawSox to win that honor.[16]

By spring training of 1985, baseball writers were wondering what the Red Sox planned to do with Lyons. He was praised for his work ethic and his desire to improve, but he still had problems hitting the curveball.[17] He spent many hours working with Red Sox hitting coach Walt Hriniak, who believed Lyons had major-league talent. Hriniak advised the young man to be more patient, saying Lyons was "a hyper, aggressive kid who naturally jumps at everything. ... He's got to learn to wait on the ball." But Hriniak had no doubt Lyons would become an asset to the Red Sox, even if he never became a power hitter. "[Steve] is someone you want on base. You want him to get as many hits and walks as he can because … when he gets on the bases, he makes things happen."[18] Hriniak's tutelage seemed to help: By late March, Lyons was hitting .342 and finally showing the potential to handle major-league pitching.[19]

But although Hriniak and others defended Lyons, pointing out that not every successful major leaguer had put up big numbers in the minors, there was one other problem facing him: There seemed to be no place for him in the regular lineup. Third base was not the answer, since the Red Sox had Wade Boggs at that position, and the team needed his bat in the lineup. The other positions also seemed set, and Lyons' best chance for making the team seemed to be as a utility player. Manager John McNamara believed that would be the right decision.[20] In early April Lyons got the good news that he had made the team, even though he was not likely to play every day.

Lyons' first major-league appearance was uneventful. He came in as a pinch-runner in a game against the Chicago White Sox on April 15. It would not be until five days later that he played in the field and got his first at-bat, and that was due to a knee injury that center fielder Tony Armas suffered. Lyons came in late in the game; in his first at-bat, he walked and then stole second, went to third on an error, and slid home safely when White Sox catcher Carlton Fisk failed to block the plate. The Red Sox went on to win, 12-8, thanks in large part to Marty Barrett's first career grand slam. But Lyons' speed and hustle did not go unnoticed. Peter Gammons wrote that Lyons "showed why it's important he's here instead of Pawtucket. … No one else on this team could have come in and created that sort of run."[21]

But as versatile as Lyons was, that didn't guarantee regular playing time. There was occasional pinch-hitting or pinch-running, but it wasn't until May 27 that he got his first start, once again as a result of an injury to Tony Armas, who had sprained his wrist. Steve made the most of that opportunity, hitting two home runs and driving in four runs in a 9-2 win over the Minnesota Twins.[22] But he was well aware that

as soon as Armas was feeling healthy again, it would be back to the bench for him. Meanwhile, he was winning over Red Sox fans, who loved his aggressive and enthusiastic style of play. It even earned him the nickname "Psycho," referring to his at times eccentric behavior, and his willingness to call attention to himself. "Maybe I go overboard sometimes … but I have so much fun playing the game," he told a Boston reporter. "I'm the kind of player who … entertains people."[23]

As it turned out, that would be a mixed blessing. While fans loved to watch Lyons, there were rumors that John McNamara, his manager, felt the rookie was too much of a showboat, once referring to him as "my self-proclaimed star"; but when questioned by the press, both Lyons and McNamara denied there was any problem.[24] (Lyons later acknowledged that McNamara was tough on him, perhaps because he was one of the few rookies on the team. "He wanted to make an example out of me."[25]) Several teammates, notably Rich Gedman and Bill Buckner, tried to help and mentor Lyons as he adjusted to the major leagues.[26] Meanwhile, the fact that Tony Armas had not fully recovered and Lyons was playing well kept him in the lineup for more than two months.

After Armas returned to the lineup in August, Lyons went back to occasionally pinch-hitting, and waiting for his next opportunity. But if the rumors of friction between Lyons and McNamara hadn't been true before, Lyons managed to get on his manager's bad side with a baserunning blunder against the Twins in late August. Lyons was on second and Dwight Evans was at bat. Without waiting for permission, Lyons tried to steal third; Evans struck out, and Lyons was easily thrown out, ending the inning in a very close game. McNamara was furious, and it would not be the last time the two would clash.[27]

On the other hand, even with occasional errors in the field or displays of poor judgment, Lyons had become a fan favorite. Despite not playing regularly (he appeared in 133 games), he hit .264, with 5 home runs and 30 RBIs. And although he mostly played center field, he showed his versatility by playing some innings at third, short, right field, and left field. After the season the Boston Baseball Writers Association named him the Red Sox Rookie of the Year,[28] and he was also given the Tenth Player Award by Boston's WSBK-TV.[29]

During spring training in 1986, Lyons was excited to capitalize on what he felt he had achieved in his rookie year. He played an exhibition game at second base, adding another position to his repertoire.[30] The always quotable Lyons told a reporter that "I'm most comfortable [playing] in the outfield, but I like the infield better. It suits my personality because there's more people to talk to."[31] Meanwhile, there were signs that Lyons might get more playing time. Tony Armas spent much of April struggling at the plate. As the month ended, Lyons finally found himself back in the regular lineup. But once again he got on his manager's bad side: For one thing, Lyons was in a slump of his own, swinging at bad pitches, and going 0-for-22 before finally getting a hit. For another, in a game against the Oakland A's, he ignored a hit-and-run sign, and also got thrown out of the game for arguing a third-strike call. McNamara was very vocal about how upset he was with Lyons' inability to stay focused and control his emotions.[32]

Sportswriters had often suggested that Lyons was not a good fit for the Red Sox. He was a nonconformist, someone who had his own unique style.[33] That could have been ignored had he not also made careless mistakes, some of which cost his team a win. In early June against Milwaukee, Lyons tried to steal third with two out in the ninth inning and the tying runs on base (and, no, his manager had not given him permission to go). He was thrown out, ending the Sox rally. McNamara said it was the "stupidest [expletive] thing" he had ever seen, and also said he was tired of Lyons making stupid moves that hurt the team. McNamara announced that Lyons would be benched.[34] As one writer remarked, Lyons had made an amazing transformation, and not in a good way: He had gone from being a bright young prospect to being a permanent resident of his manager's doghouse.[35] In late June the

26-year-old Lyons was traded to the Chicago White Sox for 41-year-old pitcher Tom Seaver.

Lyons joined his new team eager to play every day and determined not to be known for his mistakes. But with the White Sox, he struggled at the plate, and had few extra-base hits; in less than a month, he found himself back on the bench, frustrated at his missed opportunity.[36] While manager Jim Fregosi did not openly criticize Lyons, there were rumors that he had never wanted Lyons on the team.[37] At one point Fregosi hinted that he was not impressed with Lyons' playing skills. When a reporter asked what Lyons's strong points were, Fregosi replied, "He gives good TV interviews."[38] By mid-August the White Sox had optioned him to Triple-A Buffalo; Lyons wasn't recalled till early September, when major-league rosters expanded. But his average remained low. He hit .203 in the 42 games he played for Chicago. Combined with the .250 he had hit before being traded, he finished the year batting .227.

In 1987 Lyons again alternated between the White Sox and the minor leagues. He began the season by being sent to the Pacific Coast League to play for the Hawaii Islanders, a decision he was bitterly unhappy about. But as luck would have it, he was recalled several days later when Chicago outfielder Harold Baines was injured.[39] He was sent down again in May. In all, he played 47 games for Hawaii. With the White Sox, he played 76 games, and he finally showed some improvement at the plate. In fact, in another disappointing season for Chicago (fifth again in the AL West, this time with a 77-85 record), Lyons was one of the bright spots. He was platooned against right-handed pitchers and despite not playing regularly, he hit .280 and got some clutch hits later in the season. With the 1986 White Sox, Lyons had mainly played in the outfield, but in 1987 he was playing a majority of games at third base.

But at the end of the season, manager Jim Fregosi was still trying to decide how best to utilize Lyons. The White Sox were grooming Kenny Williams to be their everyday third baseman, and Lyons was on the verge of once again being the odd man out.[40] Fregosi suggested that Lyons learn to be a catcher, so he went to the Instructional League to learn the position, even though he expressed some doubt about whether he was cut out for it.[41] Fregosi wanted to give Lyons some time behind the plate during spring training, but there was also a plan to showcase his versatility in an unusual way. Several days before an April 1, 1988, exhibition contest against Cincinnati, Fregosi told the media that Lyons would attempt to play every position in the game. While two major-league players (Bert Campaneris of the Oakland A's in 1965 and Cesar Tovar of the Minnesota Twins in 1968) had already done it, this attempt would be unique, as Fregosi explained: "Lyons is going to do it in order of positions on the scorecard, one through nine. He'll start as a pitcher, and finish as the right fielder. Don't think that's ever been done before."[42] But we will never know whether this was said as an April Fool's Day joke, or if Lyons would actually have accomplished it. The game was rained out.

During the 1988 season, Lyons got into 146 games (the most he'd played in a major-league season). He hit .269, with 5 homers and 45 RBIs; he also got the most hits he had ever gotten—127. However, he had a surprisingly poor year in the field. Normally reliable, Lyons took over at third base in July, but he made 25 errors in 128 games. Overall, he led the American League with a total of 29 errors. (The other four came when he was playing other positions.) But Lyons wasn't alone. During 1988, the White Sox had the worst defense in the AL, committing 152 errors in 159 games.[43]

The White Sox had a new manager in 1989, Jeff Torborg. Lyons wanted to make a good impression, so he got his normally long hair cut to conform to Torborg's dress code.[44] But it was on the field that Lyons hoped to impress, and he seemed to get along with his new manager. He even told reporters he was having fun playing again.[45] Lyons ended up batting .264 for the White Sox, with 2 homers and 50 RBIs. He also turned his fielding troubles around somewhat: Playing nearly every position except pitcher, he finished the season with a total of 15 errors, not as good as he wanted, but certainly better than he did in 1988.

But if there was a year when Lyons lived up to his nickname of "Psycho," it was in 1990. On July 16, against Detroit, he slid into first base, beating out the throw in a close play. The front of his uniform was covered with dirt, and there was also dirt inside his uniform. And that was the problem. Lyons dusted off the front of his uniform, but then, on live TV, as shocked viewers (and equally shocked fans in the stands) watched, he pulled down his pants to shake out some of the dirt. I just kind of got my business done right out there on the field and then … uh-oh, after three or four seconds, I realized I wasn't wearing any pants so I yanked them right back up as fast as I could."[46] But it was too late. The jokes and snide comments began almost instantly, as did offers to pose for *Playgirl* magazine.

There were other noteworthy moments for him in 1990, not all of them as outrageous. He finally achieved a goal that he nearly reached in 1988: He played all nine positions in one game. It was on April 23, 1990, during an exhibition game known as the Windy City Classic, between the White Sox and the Cubs at Wrigley Field. The White Sox won, 6-5, as Lyons gave the ultimate demonstration of his versatility.[47] (Since it was an exhibition game, it didn't go into the major-league record books, but it was still quite an accomplishment.)

Lyons also made his major-league debut as a pitcher, the one position he had not yet played in a regular-season game. On June 16, 1990, he came in during a blowout game against Oakland. He pitched two innings in Chicago's 12-3 loss. While not making the world forget Cy Young, he also didn't do a terrible job. He gave up one run, two hits, and four walks. More importantly, he gave the other relief pitchers some needed rest.[48] Still, despite a season with some unique moments, he played in only 94 games and batted .192. And by now, he had gotten his manager upset by complaining about his lack of playing time.[49] Lyons was fairly certain he would not be in Chicago's plans for 1991.[50]

The White Sox did invite Lyons back to spring training, but on April 13, they put him on waivers. What happened next was a surprise. After Red Sox general manager Lou Gorman first denied that the team had any interest in him,[51] on April 18 the Red Sox signed Lyons as a free agent. It turned out that Red Sox manager Joe Morgan was one of Lyons' biggest supporters. As Morgan explained, "What I like is his attitude about the game and the fact he can play anywhere. … He's played all nine positions and I know he could play seven of them [not catcher or pitcher] pretty decently."[52] The fans were delighted to have Lyons back, although several of the players were not as enthusiastic. (They believed the club should have kept utility player Randy Kutcher, who was waived to make room for Lyons.[53]) Joe Morgan's assessment of Lyons' abilities proved accurate. During the 1991 season, he played every position for the Red Sox except catcher. He even took another turn as a pitcher, hurling the ninth inning in a 14-1 loss to the Twins and giving up two hits and no runs.[54]) And while Lyons' batting average was higher than in 1990, he ended the year at .241. Several months later, when Lyons and the Red Sox management were unable to agree on his salary, the team let him go, ending what some reporters had called the "Psycho II" era.[55]

But Lyons' major-league career was far from over. The Atlanta Braves signed him in early January 1992, and things seemed to be looking up. But he didn't hit, going 1-for-14. The Braves quickly soured on their new acquisition and wanted to demote him to Triple-A. When he refused, the team released him. He was briefly picked up by the Montreal Expos, but didn't hit well for them either, going only 3-for-13. And then … in late June, he was purchased by the Boston Red Sox, becoming the first player in the team's history to be hired three times.[56] After only six plate appearances, Lyons was sent to Triple-A Pawtucket, with the promise that he would be brought back in September. He had now played for four teams (Atlanta, Montreal, Boston, and Pawtucket), and the season wasn't even halfway over. "It's been a disastrous season, really," Lyons said, "because I want to play and I haven't been able to play all that much." Lyons played 37 games for the PawSox in 1992, batting .259; with Boston, he played a total of 21 games, hitting .250. But his hitting

totals for the Red Sox were deceptive: He was able to get some clutch hits on a number of occasions.[57] However, when the Red Sox cleaned house at the end of their disastrous 1992 season, Lyons once again was released.

He briefly latched on with the Chicago Cubs in February 1993, but was released at the end of March. In May, the Red Sox announced they had signed Lyons yet again, this time to a minor-league contract. And by mid-June, when the Red Sox needed someone to fill in at second base, Lyons was called up. A month later, he was on his way back to Pawtucket, where once again he tried to make the best of the situation. He even told reporters he was working on a book about his experiences.[58] (That book, *PSYCHOanalysis*, was released in 1995, published by Sports Publishing LLC, with a foreword by Stephen King.[59] Lyons wrote a second book, *The Psycho 100: Baseball's Most Outrageous Moments*," in 2009, published by Triumph Books.)

In 1993 Lyons hit just .213 for Pawtucket, and .130 for Boston. At the end of the season he filed for free agency, but was not picked up by anyone. It was not entirely surprising. "I knew [by then] my skills were declining," he said.[60] The former first-round draft pick, who had at one time been so highly touted, decided to retire as a player. Looking back on his nine years in the majors, Lyons said, "I know I was an average major-league player. I got tabbed as a utility player right away and didn't play all the time, but I do believe I lived up to my potential. I never hit for average, but I was always an impact player."[61]

Lyons returned to something he had begun doing in 1985: sportscasting. He had first done baseball reports for an AM station, WSRO in Marlboro, Massachusetts.[62] Now he was able to get hired as an analyst by ESPN and ESPN2, and beginning in 1996, he spent 11 years working for Fox Sports, and also did color commentary for the Los Angeles Dodgers games. He was fired from Fox in October 2006, after being accused of making a racially insensitive remark about Lou Piniella.[63] And when Lyons' nine-year association with the Dodgers ended in 2013, he was hired by New England Sports Network (NESN) in 2014 as a

Red Sox studio analyst.[64] Although at times he has been criticized as too talkative, or has said something politically incorrect, Lyons has carved out a successful niche as a sports broadcaster. And he didn't find the transition from player to announcer difficult: "I talk about the game better than I played it," he said. [65]

One of the best assessments of Steve Lyons' career comes from the foreword that Stephen King wrote for *PSYCHOanalysis:* "Lyons epitomizes what may be best in sport: a player who is not great, but who was at times elevated (crazed, some might believe) by his love of the game and his determination to play it well."[66]

NOTES

1   Personal interview with Steve Lyons, conducted by telephone, July 24, 2015.

2   Peter Gammons, "Snow Puts Rangers, White Sox in Hole," *Boston Globe,* April 11, 1982: 52.

3   Lyons interview.

4   Larry Peterson, "Lyons, Hunsinger Turn to Pros," (Oregon State) *Daily Barometer,* June 30, 1981: 15.

5   Dwight Jaynes. "Red Sox Rookie's Tale of Trail to Big Time like Fable Come True," *The Oregonian* (Portland), June 4, 1985: D1-2

6   Larry Peterson.

7   "A's Take Low Scoring Twin Bill," *Dodge City* (Kansas) *Daily Globe,* July 3, 1980: 10.

8   "Bosox Tab Beavers' Lyons," *The Oregonian,* June 9, 1981: D3.

9   Steve Harris, "On the Road With the Sox," *Boston Herald-American,* June 9, 1981: B3.

10 "Bosox Tab Beavers' Lyons."

11 Peter Gammons, "Winston-Salem Has Some Winners," *Boston Globe,* July 4, 1981: 24.

12 "Clemens Fans 15," *Boston Herald,* August 25, 1983: 53.

13 Michael Madden. "No Chance of a Lifetime," *Boston Globe,* March 11, 1984: 52.

14 Joe Gordon, "The Man Behind the PawSox," *Boston Herald,* September 23, 1984: 59.

15 "Lyons Belts 2 HRs in PawSox Romp," *Boston Herald,* April 23, 1984: 54.

16 Joe Giulotti, "Clemens to Miss Start," *Boston Herald,* September 6, 1984: 70.

17 Bob Ryan, "Of Red Sox Third Basemen, Present and Future," *Boston Globe,* August 5, 1984: 59.

18 Quoted by Peter Gammons in "Lyons a Bit Player with Star Potential," *Boston Globe,* March 11, 1985: 34.

19 Tim Horgan, "The Lyons of Winter Haven a Real Smash," *Boston Herald,* March 28, 1985: 77.

20 Peter Gammons, "Lyons Has Been a Tiger, Burning Bright," *Boston Globe* August 2, 1985: 42.

21 Peter Gammons, "Lyons an Able Replacement after Armas Injures Knee," *Boston Globe,* April 21, 1985: 50.

22 Ben Walker, "Rookie Lifts Red Sox Over Twins," *Centre* (Pennsylvania) *Daily Times,* May 28, 1985: D-2.

23 Joe Gordon, "Lyons' Act Big Hit at Fenway Park," *Boston Herald,* June 4, 1985: 70.

24 Dwight Jaynes, "Red Sox Rookie's Tale of Trail to Big Time Like Fable Come True," *The Oregonian,* June 4, 1985: D1-D2.

25 Lyons interview.

26 Lyons interview.

27 Joe Gordon, "Smithson Silences Sox 1-0," *Boston Herald,* August 25, 1985: 43.

28 "Sox Honor Lyons," *Boston Herald,* November 17, 1985: 8.

29 Larry Whiteside, "Lyons Voted Tenth Player," *Boston Globe,* September 23, 1985: 38.

30 Larry Whiteside, "Lyons Can't Wait for Second Chance," *Boston Globe,* March 23, 1986: 99.

31 Dan Shaughnessy, "Trade Should Bolster the Sagging Sox," *Boston Globe,* March 30, 1986: 80.

32 Joe Giuliotti, "Rice Surprised by 2,000th Hit," *Boston Herald,* May 11, 1986: 43.

33 Dan Shaughnessy, "Lyons on the Loose," *Boston Globe,* July 29, 1986: 57.

34 Joe Giuliotti, "Lyons Benched for Ninth-Inning Gaffe," *Boston Herald,* June 7, 1986: 68, 72.

35 George Kimball, "Hawk Lends Helping Hand," *Boston Herald,* June 30, 1986: 59.

36 Gerry Finn, "Steve Lyons Still Sittin', but It's Not on Top of the World," *Springfield* (Massachusetts) *Union,* August 5, 1986: 8.

37 Carrie Muskat, "(No) April Fooling," *Rockford* (Illinois) *Register Star,* April 1, 1988: 1D.

38 Joe Giuliotti, "Baseball Notebook," *Boston Herald,* August 24, 1986: 68.

39 Jeff Baker, "Few See Beavers Blast Hawaii," *The Oregonian,* April 10, 1987: E1, E4.

40 Carrie Muskat, "Sox Catcher Lyons a Seedy Character," *Rockford* (Illinois) *Register Star,* March 3, 1988: 4C.

41 Bob Verdi, "Sox Put Lyons in Odd Position," *Chicago Tribune,* March 29, 1988: C1.

42 Ibid.

43 Carrie Muskat, "Where the Cubs, Sox Stand in '89," *Rockford* (Illinois) *Register Star*, December 11, 1988: 1-2E. Lyons made one error at second base, one in center field, and two in right field.

44 Carrie Muskat, "Image Now Biggest Concern in Baseball," *Rockford* (Illinois) *Register Star*, April 3, 1989: 3C.

45 Marvin Pave, A Good Break for Lyons, *Boston Globe*, July 22, 1989: 31.

46 Michael Madden, "Lyons' Popularity is Peeking," *Boston Globe*. August 1, 1990: 25.

47 "Baseball: White Sox Edge Cubs," *Aberdeen* (South Dakota) *Daily News*, April 24, 1990: 2B.

48 Mark Curnutte, "Pitching Performance Not Significant to Lyons," *Rockford* (Illinois) *Register Star*, June 18, 1990: 14.

49 "Lyons Surprised to Be Back," *Rockford* (Illinois) *Register Star*, March 1, 1991: 2C.

50 Mike Shalin, "Greenie Effect Worries Sox," *Boston Herald*, December 16, 1990: B21.

51 Mike Shalin, "Joe: Ump too Quick on Draw," *Boston Herald*, April 15, 1991: 66.

52 Nick Cafardo, "Lyons Isn't Any Tamer," *Boston Globe*, April 20, 1991: 37.

53 Steve Fainaru, "Lyons Back With Boston, Kutcher Is Given His Release," *Boston Globe*, April 19, 1991: 30.

54 Joe Giuliotti, "Psycho Bails as Sox Sink," *Boston Herald*, July 22, 1991: 68.

55 Nick Cafardo, "Braves' 2-Year Offer Guarantees Lyons' Exit from Boston," *Boston Globe*, January 9, 1992: 29.

56 Nick Cafardo, "Lyons returns—But What's Next?" *Boston Globe*, June 30, 1992: 55.

57 Nick Cafardo, "Sox Clean House in Big Way," *Boston Globe*, December 26, 1992: 34.

58 Nick Cafardo, "Lyons Up to His Old Tricks and Throws in New Stuff," *Boston Globe*, August 22, 1993: 59.

59 Jim Greenidge, "Lyons Shares Some Laughs," *Boston Globe*, July 2, 1995: 52.

60 Lyons interview.

61 Lyons interview.

62 Jim Baker, "Short Takes," *Boston Herald*, February 9, 1986: 52.

63 Nick Cafardo and Gordon Edes, "Lyons Fired by Fox; Hispanic Remarks Called Insensitive," *Boston Globe*, October 15, 2006: D7.

64 Chad Finn, "Dell is officially done at NESN," *Boston Globe*, May 13, 2014: C8.

65 Lyons interview.

66 Steve Lyons, *PSYCHOanalysis* (Champaign, Illinois: Sagamore Publishing, 1995), xi.

AL NIPPER

By Gregory H. Wolf

F ANYONE KNEW THE DEFINITION OF PAIN, IT was right-hander Al Nipper, who toiled for parts of seven seasons in the big leagues (1983-1988, 1990), most notably for the Boston Red Sox. His list of injuries and maladies seems hard to fathom: nerve problems in his neck and elbow, chronic elbow inflammation, a blood disorder eventually diagnosed as stomach ulcers and anemia, a serious injury to his right knee during a collision at home plate that almost severed a muscle, back spasms requiring traction, toe pain, and bone chips in his left knee. Somehow, he found time to win 46 games and log almost 800 innings. "I didn't have the best God-given ability and was fortunate enough to hang around as long as I did," said Nipper, who relied primarily on breaking balls and a knuckler for his success. "I had to work to know the hitters. I had to be a student of the game to maximize my ability."[1]

Boston sportswriter Peter Gammons once called Nipper a pitcher and not a thrower, and suggested that he was the personification of the "Baltimore Orioles pitching manual" with his cerebral and fundamentally sound approach to the game.[2] Not blessed with the natural talent of teammates Roger Clemens, Bruce Hurst, or Oil Can Boyd, Nipper was known for his large array of pitches, including a screwball, slider, curve, knuckleball, sinker, forkball, fastball, and changeup, all of which he could throw at different release points, from overhand to three-quarters, and at varying speeds. His nickname, "the man with a thousand pitches," needs no clarification. Baseball lifer Don Zimmer, Nipper's manager with the Chicago Cubs in 1988, once claimed that only his former teammate with the Brooklyn Dodgers, Russ Meyer, threw more kinds of pitches.[3]

Albert Samuel Nipper was born on April 2, 1959, in San Diego, California, the second and final child of Frederick and Gertrude (Schmid) Nipper, both of German heritage. In the mid-1960s the Nippers relo-

cated to Hazelwood, a northwest suburb of St. Louis, Missouri, where Al became an unabashed Cardinals fan. "I always wanted to be a big leaguer," said Al, who claimed he went to 30 to 40 games a season at Busch Stadium.[4] "I'd go sit down by the bullpen before every game so I could watch the pitchers warm up," he continued. "I learned from watching."[5] He idolized Tom Seaver of the New York Mets, and collected books on pitching to teach himself proper mechanics and delivery. In his teenage years, Al played baseball from spring to late autumn, progressing through the area's youth leagues, and then starring as a pitcher at Hazelwood West High School. In 2011 he was in the school's inaugural class for its hall of fame.[6]

Upon graduating in 1977, Nipper enrolled at Northeast Missouri State University (renamed Truman State University in 1996), located in Kirksville, about 200 miles northwest of St. Louis. During his three years

with the Bulldogs, Nipper posted a misleading 10-18 record, and 2.65 ERA; he completed 18 of 23 starts and struck out 152 in 160 innings for teams that had a combined 26-46 record.[7] Nipper began to attract the attention of baseball scouts in 1979 when he carved out an impressive 0.98 ERA in 55⅓ innings and was named to the Missouri Intercollegiate Athletic Association All-Star squad. That same year he led his St. Louis-based amateur team to the national tournament of the National Baseball Congress in Wichita, Kansas.[8]

The Boston Red Sox chose Nipper in the eighth round (205th overall pick) in the 1980 amateur draft. Assigned to Winter Haven in the Class-A Florida State League, Nipper surprised the Red Sox by going 6-4 and posting a 2.54 ERA in 85 innings, while their first-round draft choice, lefty Mike Brown, struggled (3-4, 4.31). Back with Winter Haven in 1981, Nipper tossed 28 consecutive scoreless innings early in the season, and was named to the league's all-star team. He won 14 games for the last-place club and paced the circuit in ERA (1.70), complete games (15), and innings (212, a career best).

Promoted to Double-A Bristol in the Eastern League in 1982, Nipper suffered the first of what seemed to be annual injuries that limited his effectiveness. Early in the campaign he hurt his neck (diagnosed as thoracic outlet syndrome), causing a nerve problem in his right elbow, and he limped to a disappointing 6-7 record and 3.68 ERA. He attempted to pitch through the pain, but in doing so aggravated the injury, which bothered him for the next two years. "An injury like mine takes time to come back and rebuild all of the strength," said Nipper in 1984. Not only was the injury a red flag for Boston; his Bristol teammates Mike Brown (9-6, 2.45 ERA) and Oil Can Boyd (14-8, 2.81) seemed primed for the big leagues.

The 24-year-old Nipper started the 1983 season with Bristol and was promoted in midseason to Triple-A Pawtucket in the International League when Boyd was called up to the Red Sox. Nipper won a club-high nine games and posted a 4.45 ERA in 109⅓ innings for the league's cellar-dwellers.

En route to its worst season since 1966, Boston called up Nipper when the rosters expanded in September. In his debut, on September 6, he hurled one inning of relief and walked one in a loss to the eventual World Series champion Baltimore Orioles; they also handed Nipper a loss in his first start, a week later. Elbow inflammation kept Nipper sidelined until the final game of the season, one which marked an end of an era in Red Sox history as Carl Yastrzemski retired after 23 seasons. Somewhat lost in the day's emotional festivities was Nipper's complete-game nine-hitter to defeat the Cleveland Indians, 4-1, at Fenway Park.

As spring training opened at the Red Sox camp in Winter Haven in 1984, the media's attention focused on 21-year-old rookie Roger Clemens. Nipper was given little chance of making the squad given that five starters from the previous year were back (Hurst, Bob Ojeda, Boyd, Brown, and 29-year-old Dennis Eckersley; John Tudor had been traded in the off-season); however, Nipper surprised skipper Ralph Houk, who unexpectedly chose him as his long reliever instead of veteran Rich Gale. "I'm elated the pressure is off," said Nipper.[9] The key to his success in spring training was a screwball. "[It] helps me tremendously against left-handed hitters," said the pitcher. "I can get them looking outside and then bust a fastball inside."[10] Little used through May and still bothered by elbow tenderness, Nipper moved into the starting rotation in June after Eckersley was shipped to the Chicago Cubs for Bill Buckner and Mike Brumley, and Brown was optioned to Pawtucket. Hit hard in his first two starts, Nipper transformed into the "surprise of the staff," according to beat reporter Gary Santaniello.[11] During a stretch of eight starts, Nipper won three of five decisions and carved out an impressive 2.71 ERA in 63 innings while batters hit at just a .218 clip against him. "I've had to go out and challenge hitters," said the 25-year-old, "and that's what I've done."[12] While the Red Sox trailed the Detroit Tigers by double digits in the AL East, Nipper emerged as the team's most consistent hurler. Over a seven-start stretch from August 14 to September 15, he won a career-best six straight decisions and posted a 2.33 ERA in 58 innings. "Gradually this year I've been able to build my arm back," said Nipper. "[N]ow I'm throwing every bit as well as I did three years ago. Every start I've gotten a little more confidence."[13] While sportswriter Peter Gammons claimed that Nipper was one of the best at changing speeds in the AL, pitching coach Lee Stange liked his control and the way he mixed up his pitches, saying, "He's not an overpowering pitcher, but he gets his curve and the slider over and can spot the fastball."[14] For the fourth-place Red Sox, Nipper finished with an 11-6 record and a 3.89 ERA (best among starters), and logged 182⅔ innings. The Boston chapter of the Baseball Writers Association of America named him co-rookie of the year with Roger Clemens (9-4, 4.32). Nipper finished seventh in voting for the AL Rookie of the Year Award.

During his tenure with Boston (1983-1987), Nipper had a reputation as a fun-loving prankster and master of the pie-in-the-face-routine when teammates were being interviewed. He roomed with Clemens, seemingly got along with everyone, and helped forge a team identity by defusing tensions with his humor. "I guess I was one of the few people who understood Oil Can," said Nipper of his relationship to the controversial pitcher. "I always knew where he was coming from."[15] Boston sportswriter Nick Cafardo described Nipper as "the media's go-to guy" who was always willing to give the inside scoop on the team and explain the inner workings of the club, as well as to defend his teammates.[16] He also had peculiarities, such as one he copied from Steve Carlton. He buried his right hand in a barrel of rice and pushed his fingers down as far as they could go in order to build strength.[17] But Nipper was not a flake; rather, he took a studious approach to the game. He was an early advocate of studying films to gain a competitive advantage, and pored over films of himself and his opponents in the offseason to look for ways to improve.[18]

Nipper had the scare of his life in 1985. He reported to spring training early for new manager John McNamara and pitching coach Bill Fischer, but soon noticed that he was quickly fatigued from working out. An examination by the team physician, Dr. Arthur Pappas, revealed a low blood count and fears rose that the pitcher might have leukemia. Nipper was eventually diagnosed with a serious stomach ulcer and anemia, and missed almost all of spring training. "One thing this did was change my perspective on life," said Nipper, who came off the disabled list on April 15. "I appreciate having my health back. You hear a lot of griping, especially among ballplayers. We make a lot of money, and we're pampered and babied, and we get bent out of shape about a lot of the little things."[19]

Physically weak, Nipper struggled as the 1985 season got under way, losing five of his first six decisions with a 5.40 ERA through May. He seemed to reach his stride in June, winning three straight starts (two of which were complete games), but then developed serious back spasms. As they worsened in July, Nipper was hospitalized and placed in traction. "[It] was just a weird year for me. I was always waiting for something next to happen. I was fighting everything," said Nipper, who battled shoulder and toe pain in August and September.[20] Through it all, Nipper maintained an even keel, and his humor. "I was actually waiting for (the elbow) to blow out, but it never did."[21] The season was a disappointment for the Red Sox, as well as Nipper. The third-highest-scoring offense in the AL was offset by the league's most porous defense and Boston slipped to fifth place. "I wasn't consistent in my mechanics," said the 26-year-old Nipper, who finished with a 9-12 record and a 4.06 ERA, and surrendered 82 walks in just 162 innings.[22] Rumors of Nipper's trade in the offseason to the Chicago White Sox for boyhood hero Tom Seaver proved to be false; however, the Red Sox acquired the aging right-hander in June 1986 for utilityman Steve Lyons.

"I feel better mentally, because I know I'm fine physically," said Nipper during spring training in 1986.[23] He added a knuckleball to his arsenal of breaking balls, changeups, and an occasional fast one. Nipper had played around with the knuckler since college, and was encouraged to master the pitch by pitching coach Bill Fischer, a former knuckleball thrower.[24] *The Sporting News* tabbed Nipper, along with Cleveland's Tom Candiotti, as the "best bet" to carry on the knuckling tradition of Phil and Joe Niekro and Charlie

Hough.[25] Nipper unveiled the knuckler in his fourth start of the season, a masterful four-hit complete-game victory against reigning Cy Young Award winner Bret Saberhagen and the Kansas City Royals. "I might not have that good stuff, but at least I'll feel confident enough I'll trick 'em or find a way to get by," said Nipper, who compared himself to Charlie Liebrandt and Frank Tanana. "I've got to pitch inside to be effective. I've got an average fastball, but with all the other breaking stuff I throw, it makes my fastball look a little quicker."[26]

Just when Nipper seemed to have some momentum, he suffered what Boston sportswriter Joe Giuliotti called a "career threatening" injury against the Texas Rangers on May 18 at Fenway Park. "I was [ticked off] about throwing one to the backstop with Toby Harrah up and I convinced myself I wasn't going to let [Larry Parrish on third] score," explained Nipper. "So I blocked the plate and he came and got me in the [right] knee. I made the tag and held up the ball to show the umpire. Then, my leg just collapsed."[27] Nipper suffered a deep, four-inch gash in his vastus medialis (one of the three major muscles in the kneecap) and was bleeding profusely. "It was a terrible sight," said McNamara.[28] Carried by teammates off the field, Nipper was taken to the hospital and underwent emergency surgery that evening. Widely expected to miss as much as two months, Nipper returned five weeks later and defeated the Yankees in his first start, on June 25, to give the Red Sox a five-game lead in the Al East. The fourth starter, behind Clemens (24-4, 2.48), Boyd (16-10, 3.78), and Hurst (13-8, 2.99), Nipper posted a 10-12 record with an inflated 5.38 ERA as Boston captured its first division crown since 1975.

"It was a good club and no one really expected us to do anything in '86," said Nipper, who did not see action in the ALCS as Boston overcame a three-games-to-one deficit to defeat the California Angels. "We had a nucleus of good players and good team chemistry."[29] A prohibitive underdog against the New York Mets, winners of 108 games, in the World Series, Boston won the first two games, at Shea Stadium in New York. Described by syndicated sportswriter Moss

Klein as the staff's "weak link," Nipper started Game Four, at Fenway Park, and held the high-powered Mets to three runs over six innings but was collared with the loss in a 6-2 defeat to even the series at two games each.[30] After the game, McNamara was widely criticized and second-guessed for starting Nipper, who had struggled in his final 10 starts of the season (6.97 ERA).[31] His next appearance came in the deciding seventh game. After the Mets took the lead in dramatic fashion against Calvin Schiraldi in the seventh inning (and collared him with the loss in the final two games of the series), Nipper suffered through a forgettable relief appearance in the eighth inning. He yielded a home run to Darryl Strawberry, the first batter he faced, and was charged with three hits and two runs, and issued an intentional walk while retiring just one batter as the Mets won, 8-5, to capture their first title since the "Miracle Mets" of 1969. "I sat at my locker for an hour after that game with my head staring down at the ground," said Nipper. "That's how bad I felt."[32]

At 6-feet-1 and about 185 pounds, Nipper did not have a commanding presence on the mound like Clemens and Hurst, both of whom stood 6-feet-4 and weighed in excess of 200 pounds; however, Nipper had a no-nonsense, combative approach to pitching, and never backed down from a hitter. He was peeved in Game Seven of the World Series by what he considered Strawberry's slow trot around the bases after his home run in the eighth inning and the way Red Sox players were treated. "I don't care if I ever see New York again. The fans there are animals," he said, referring to an incident when traveling secretary Jack Rogers was hit by a flying beer bottle. "They don't have any class whatsoever."[33] When the Red Sox and Mets faced off in an exhibition game the following spring, on March 14, Nipper took "old school" revenge by plunking Strawberry, and benches cleared, though no brawl ensued. Commissioner Peter Ueberroth fined Nipper, who denied throwing at Strawberry. "I tried to come up and in with a fastball and it got away," he said. "I think he overreacted."[34]

In 1987 Nipper began relying on his knuckleball more often. At times he "baffled" opponents, such as the

Yankees, against whom he tossed consecutive complete-game five-hit victories in June;[35] at other times, he was clobbered. (In 11 of his career-high 30 starts he failed to go five innings.) He suffered a severely pulled rib cage muscle in June, landed on the DL, and missed almost four weeks. Other than Clemens, who captured his second consecutive Cy Young Award, the rest of the Red Sox hurlers seemed to be in a collective funk as the staff finished 12th out of 14 teams in ERA, contributing to the club's disappointing 78-84 record and fifth-place finish. Nipper finished with an 11-12 record and 5.43 ERA in 174 innings; he surrendered 30 homers. "[He's] a No. 5-type starter, a gutsy pitcher who gets by on guile," wrote *The Sporting News*, "but he doesn't get by enough."[36] On December 8 Nipper and Schiraldi were shipped to the Chicago Cubs in exchange for closer Lee Smith.

Nipper's short, injury-filled tenure with the Cubs was an unmitigated disaster. Hobbled by a hamstring injury in spring training, he began the season in the bullpen before moving into the rotation. After a promising six-start stretch (2.43 ERA in 37 innings), he landed on the DL with elbow soreness in late May. Limited to occasional relief duty when he returned a month later, he made five starts before the pain ended his season prematurely in mid-August, after he logged just 80 innings, but posted a promising 3.04 ERA. Nipper suffered yet another injury the following spring training when physicians diagnosed bone chips in his left knee. "I can't win a job," said a frustrated Nipper, "but there's nothing I can do. I can't land on [my left leg] in my follow-through. They can't do an arthroscopy because the bone chips are on the tendon. If I pitch too soon, I can hurt my elbow again, so I'm in a Catch-22."[37] The Cubs released him on March 28, 1989, after which he filed a grievance with the players' union. Nipper argued that he was entitled to his full salary, while the team claimed he had been injured prior to camp and was eligible for only a fraction of it. According to the *Chicago Tribune*, the two sides reached an agreement in June under which the Cubs paid Nipper half of his estimated $350,000 salary.[38]

After operations on his knee and elbow, Nipper missed the entire 1989 season. He accepted the Cleveland Indians' invitation to join them in spring training in 1990 and made the team as a free agent. After four mainly ineffective relief appearances, he was optioned to Colorado Springs in the Pacific Coast League. He was recalled in June and made his final five starts in the big leagues (winning two of them) before being sent back to Colorado Springs. Released in the offseason, he had a brief stint with the St. Louis Cardinals' affiliate in the American Association, the Louisville Redbirds, in 1991, before retiring.

A courageous competitor, Nipper finished with a 46-50 record, started 124 of 144 games, completed 21, and posted a 4.52 ERA in 797⅔ innings. He whiffed 381 and walked 303.

Nipper made a smooth transition to his post-playing days. In 1992 he inaugurated his coaching career that (as of 2015) is in its fourth decade by accepting the Red Sox' invitation to serve as a minor-league pitching coach. "[I] knew I always wanted to get into coaching even when I played," he said.[39] His former manager, Ralph Houk, was not surprised. "He's the type of guy who would be a good pitching coach because he got the most out of his abilities. He didn't throw very hard, but he knows how to pitch. He asked a lot of questions."[40] In July 1995 Nipper returned to the big leagues when he was named Boston's pitching coach for the remainder of the season. As he did during his playing days, Nipper had a pragmatic approach to coaching. "As coaches, we wear lots of different hats. We're psychiatrists, confidants, leaders, and many other things," he said, asserting also that the most important aspect was earning the players' trust.[41] He also served as pitching coach for the Texas Rangers (1998-2000) and Kansas City Royals (2001-2002). After working in the Boston and Detroit organizations, Nipper was the pitching coach the Triple-A Toledo Mud Hens in 2014. Coincidentally, the manager of that team was Larry Parrish, whose collision with Nipper at home plate in 1985 left a visible reminder on the pitcher's knee. In 2015 Nipper was named pitching coach for the Kansas City Royals' affiliate in the Pacific Coast League, the Omaha Storm Chasers.

As of 2015, Nipper lived with his wife, Leslie (Schweppe) Nipper, in Chesterfield, a suburb of St. Louis.

SOURCES

In addition to the sources listed in the notes, the author consulted:

Baseball-Reference.com.

Retrosheet.org.

SABR.org.

Al Nipper player file, National Baseball Hall of Fame, Cooperstown, New York.

NOTES

1   Jon Goode, "Catching up with … Al Nipper," SouthCoastToday (New Bedford, Massachusetts), July 3, 2005. southcoasttoday.com/article/20050703/News/307039964.

2   Peter Gammons, "Learned Experience," *Boston Globe*, July 14, 1984.

3   Jerome Holtzman, "Cubs' jack of all pitchers but master of none must search for his niche," *Chicago Tribune*, March 1, 1989, B3.

4   Gammons.

5   Ibid.

6   "Inaugural Class at Hazelwood West High School to induct six honorees," Hazelwood School District. hazelwoodschools.org/News/Pages/InauguralHallofFameatHazelwoodWestHigh Schooltoinductsixhonorees.aspx.

7   Nipper's college statistics are from 2005 Truman State Baseball Media Guide: gobulldogs.truman.edu/mediaguide/men/baseball/05baseballmg4.pdf.

8   "Liberal Wins at NBC," *Garden City* (Kansas) *Telegraph*, August 16, 1979, 6.

9   Hugh McGovern, "Al Nipper Earns Spot in Sox Pen," *Evening Gazette* (Worcester, Massachusetts), March 27, 1984.

10 McGovern.

11 Gary Santaniello, "Nipper becomes Stopper For Sox," *Telegram* (Worcester, Massachusetts), 1984 article (no further date) from player's Hall of Fame file.

12 *The Sporting News*, August 6, 1984, 16.

13 Gammons.

14 *The Sporting News*, September 17, 1984, 14. According to Gammons, Nipper joined Scott McGregor, Doyle Alexander, Frank Tanana, and Mike Boddicker as the best at changing speeds; Rich Thompson, "Nipper gets major league lesson in win," *Boston Herald*, July 7, 1984.

15 Nick Cafardo, "Groomed to be a coach," *Boston Globe*, July 23, 1995.

16 Cafardo, "Groomed to be a coach."

17 *The Sporting News*, January 21, 1985, 38.

18 Ibid.

19 Bill Richardson, "Nipper glad to be battling hitters again," *Kansas City Times*, April 15, 1985.

20 Jim Lazar, "New Year, a new attitude for a determined Nipper," *Salem* (Massachusetts) *Evening News*, March 19, 1986.

21 Nick Cafardo, "Everything OK for Nipper except score," *The Telegraph* (Nashua, New Hampshire), August 13, 1985, 11.

22 Win Bates, "Nipper's '86 spring: 'Viva la difference,'" *The Enterprise* (Brockton, Massachusetts), March 19, 1986.

23 Bates.

24 "Nipper Goes to Knuckleball, Pitches Red Sox Past Yankees," *Schenectady* (New York) *Gazette*, June 29, 1987, 27.

25 *The Sporting News*, March 31, 1986, 32.

26 Larry Whiteside, "Nipper knuckles down," *Boston Globe*, April 28, 1986.

27 Cafardo, "Groomed to be a coach."

28 Joe Giuliotti, "Nipper won't be ready until July," *Boston Herald*, May 19, 1986,

29 Goode.

30 *The Sporting News*, October 27, 1986, 18.

31 *The Sporting News*, November 3, 1986, 11.

32 Cafardo, "Groomed to be a coach."

33 Ibid.

34 "Nipper fined for Mets incident, Red Sox for a lack of control," March 28, 1987. Unattributed article in player's Hall of Fame file.

35 *The Sporting News*, July 22, 1987, 19.

36 *The Sporting News*, December 21, 1987.

37 *The Sporting News*, March 27, 1989, 35.

38 Fred Mitchell, "Bit and Pieces," *Chicago Tribune*, June 27, 1989, B7.

39 Goode.

40 Cafardo, "Groomed to be a coach."

41 Nick Cafardo, "Thinking man's coach is Nipper," *Boston Globe*, March 1, 1996.

SPIKE OWEN

By Norm King

THE LIST OF MAJOR-LEAGUE RECORD-HOLD-ers contains names familiar to all baseball fans—Hank Aaron, Babe Ruth, Nolan Ryan, Spike Owen … wait a minute! Spike Owen?

Yep. While his name won't roll as easily off the casual fan's tongue as some others would, Spike Owen was indeed a record-setter during a steady 13-year career, primarily as a switch-hitting shortstop, with the Mariners, Red Sox, Expos, Yankees, and Angels.

Spike Dee Owens was born in Cleburne, Texas, on April 19, 1961 to Don Owen, who owned a used car dealership, and Margie (nee Spikes, and yes, that's how he got his name) Owen, a homemaker. He and his older brother, Dave, who had a brief career with the Cubs and Royals, were always playing sports with the strong support of his mom and dad.

"I don't recall (his parents) ever missing a Little League game we played in," Owen recalled. "And Dad was always out in the backyard throwing balls to me and Dave, whatever season it was."[1]

Owen developed his skills first at Cleburne High School, where he was voted to the Class 3A All-State tournament team at shortstop in 1979. After graduating, he began a decorated career with the University of Texas, where he played for a powerhouse team that went to the College World Series in 1981 and 1982.[2] Although the Longhorns didn't win the championship in either season, Owen distinguished himself in the field and at the plate. He had 10 assists in a 1981 CWS game and tied a career record, which still stood as of 2015, for most triples, with three. He also led the 1982 tournament with a .529 batting average. Owen's accomplishments were honored in 2010 when he was named shortstop on the NCAA CWS Legends Team chosen to commemorate the closing of Johnny Rosenblatt Stadium, home of the College World Series since 1950.

Owen's junior year at Texas in 1982 was one for the ages. He hit .336 with a .478 on-base percentage and 39 stolen bases. The honors rolled in that year; he was a first team All-American (after being a third team All-American in 1981), was voted to the All Southwest Conference All-Star Team by the Associated Press, and was named the Longhorns' team captain.

That combination of skill and leadership made Owen an attractive commodity to major-league teams. After finishing his junior year, Owen decided to make himself available for the 1982 amateur draft. The Seattle Mariners chose him in the first round and sent him to the Lynn Sailors of the Double-A Eastern League, where he batted .266 with one home run and 27 RBIs in 78 games. The Mariners were impressed enough with Owen's performance at Lynn to promote him to Triple A with the Pacific Coast League's Salt Lake City Gulls for 1983.

Even before he reported to the Gulls, Owen took a big step forward in his life when he married Gail Lockhart on New Year's Day 1983. The couple have four children.

Owen was showing similar numbers in Salt Lake City (.266, one home run, 32 RBIs in 72 games) when he became the beneficiary of a major shakeup by the parent team. After winning no more than 67 games in any season during their first five years of existence, the Mariners showed some promise in 1982 when they finished with a 76-86 record, good enough for fourth place in the American League West Division. The 1983 edition wasn't living up to expectations and on June 25 manager Rene Lachemann was fired and replaced by Del Crandall. The Mariners also designated incumbent shortstop Todd Cruz (as well as pitcher Gaylord Perry) for assignment and brought Owen up to replace Cruz. He got a hit in his first at-bat as the Mariners ended an eight-game losing skid with a 5-2 victory over the Toronto Blue Jays. Owens was thrilled to finally arrive in the majors, but it is fair to say that the circumstances and his timing on arriving in a big-league locker room could have been better because he showed up just after the team found out about the changes.

"I was in the room for five minutes and was so happy at being here," he said. "I didn't realize I was the only one acting happy."[3]

That awkward moment aside, player development director Hal Keller, the man who picked him in the draft, saw qualities in Owen's play that he felt could help the Mariners. "I don't expect him to hit .350," Keller said, "but he's doing everything the way we expected. We looked at his lifestyle, his enthusiasm, and his hard-nosed approach to the game and we liked what we saw."[4]

As it seldom does, changing managers didn't improve the team, and Seattle went on to a 60-102 record. But Owen made the shortstop position his own, despite hitting only .196 in 80 games. The Mariners were a young team, with 11 players 25 or younger on their 25-man roster, and growing pains were to be expected.

The Mariners began the 1984 season with a scorched-opponent policy, winning six of their first seven games, including a walk-off 3-2 victory over Toronto in the home opener in which Owen scored the deciding run. They even swept the eventual World Series champion Detroit Tigers in a three-game Memorial Day weekend series in Seattle. Owen's season also started well; he had an 11-game hitting streak between May 5 and 16 that pushed his batting average up to .309.

"It's just one of those things," Owen said at the time. "I worked hard on my swing during the offseason, and I'm really feeling good up there now."[5]

As well as Owens was playing—Keller, who became the general manager in 1984, put the brakes on a deal that would have brought U.L. Washington over from Kansas City—both he and the team cooled off. By August 31 the Mariners had a 59-76 record and Crandall got the boot because he wasn't getting the most from his players. Chuck Cottier was named interim manager despite never having managed above Class A, and his relaxed managing style propelled the Mariners to a 15-12 record the rest of the way. It's hard to tell whether Crandall's more authoritarian style affected Owen's play. His batting average fell to .245 for the year, but he did have career highs with 16 stolen bases, 130 hits, and 67 runs scored. He also finished third among American League shortstops with a .977 fielding percentage.

As the 1985 season approached, it was clear that the Mariners were counting on young, home-grown players like Owen, because they didn't make any significant moves in the offseason. "We think one of the problems the Mariners have had in the past is not having continuity," said club president Chuck Armstrong. "We have striven hard to maintain continuity and not trade away our stars. I'd rather go with Alvin Davis, Mark Langston, Jim Beattie, Spike Owen—what I think are going to be big names for us—as opposed to guys on the decline, which is what this franchise has done time and time again."[6]

In "the best laid plans …" department, the 1985 season was full of highs and lows for Owen and the Mariners.

Again the team was hot out of the gate, winning its first six. But 12 losses in the next 13 games killed any momentum the Mariners might have had, and they ended up duplicating their 74-88 record. For his part, Owen started off poorly at the plate; on May 29 he was hitting .193. He went through some highs and lows after that. He enjoyed the high of being named American League Player of the Week for the week of June 23-30, when he hit .500 with two triples and two home runs. He then missed the last two weeks of July with a pulled hamstring, an injury that recurred throughout his career. He was back for one game on August 2, then didn't play until August 10, missing 19 games in that stretch. Owen managed to haul his average over the Mendoza Line for the season to a respectable .259, with 6 home runs and 37 RBIs. His .975 fielding percentage was third in the league.

Owen's 1986 season could have been made into an Andrew Lloyd Webber musical because it began with disappointment, rose to a euphoric crescendo, then came crashing down like a chandelier in an opera house. Prior to the season, *The Sporting News* said that the 1986 edition of the Mariners was the best in team history—on paper. Maybe if the team's grounds crew replaced the Astroturf in the Kingdome with papyrus, the Mariners would have had a better season; instead they were a disaster from the get-go. They didn't even bother teasing their fans with a hot start, going 7-14 in April and continuing downhill from there. Talented young players like Owen, Harold Reynolds, Alvin Davis (1984 Rookie of the Year), and Mark Langston (1984 Rookie of the Year runner-up) were not jelling as a team, even after the nomadic Dick Williams became manager on May 9.

Owen did his part as a team leader right from spring training, welcoming new teammate Steve Yeager by giving him his number 7, which Yeager wore with the Dodgers. He was also at his shortstop position on Opening Day despite having missed 10 Cactus League games due to his chronic hamstring problem. But just as the rest of the team wasn't performing, Owen's main strength, his defense, was also falling off. After committing 14 errors in all of 1985, he made

his 15th miscue of 1986 on July 4, and ended up with a career-high 21 for the season. Owen typified how the Mariners' season went when he became the answer to a baseball trivia question on April 29. On that night former Texas teammate Roger Clemens, now pitching for Boston, struck out 20 Mariners to set a new single-game record, breaking the old mark of 19 shared by several pitchers. Owen was the record-tying whiff in the top of the ninth.

As optimism turned into the calamity that ended up as a 67-95 season, Mariners management opted to unload some players. On August 19, Owen and Dave Henderson were traded to the Red Sox for rookie shortstop Rey Quinones and three players to be named later.[7] After that year's World Series, this is how Phil Elderkin of the *Christian Science Monitor* assessed the acquisition of Owen:

"What Boston saw in Owen was a steadying influence at shortstop, a guy with soft hands who could consistently make the routine plays every team needs to become a contender. Even if his throwing arm wasn't registered with the National Rifle Association, it was plenty good enough."[8]

For his part, Dick Williams thought that Owen's leg problems had diminished his ability. "I'm not taking anything away from Spike, Spike's legs are gone," he said in spring training 1987. "He's very, very shaky as a shortstop. He's a great competitor, but his legs were going on him before I joined the ballclub."[9]

Owens' legs were just fine, thank you, in his third game with Boston. In a 24-5 pasting of the Cleveland Indians on August 21, he went 4-for-5 with a home run and a major-league record-tying six runs scored. His tootsies were a little tender after it was over. "My feet are a little sore," he said. "I did a whole lot of running, but it was well worth it."[10]

The Red Sox won the American League pennant by 5½ games over the Yankees in a tough division in which five of the seven teams finished above .500. Owen's hitting stats for the regular season were typical (.231 batting average, one home run, 45 RBIs), but he batted

.429 in the American League Championship Series against the California Angels and scored five runs in seven games—although his defensive prowess disappeared as he committed five errors—to help propel the Red Sox to their first World Series since 1975.

Owen's first—and only—taste of World Series play was like the Bizarro world of the old Superman comics, where everything happened in reverse. The normally light-hitting shortstop batted .300 in the fall classic. As well, he, along with his teammates and all of Red Sox Nation, had to endure a crushing Series loss to the New York Mets; Boston was one out away from winning it all in the infamous (from the Red Sox' point of view) Game Six, before blowing a two-run lead in the 10th inning. Owen went 3-for-4 in that game with a run scored. The Mets won Game Seven to become world champions.

A tough postseason series loss can affect a team the next season, and such was the case with the 1987 Red Sox. They never really got on track and finished 78-84 for the year. After winning the starting job in spring training, Owen started horrendously, getting only five hits in his first 35 at-bats, and was benched for more than a month. He came back on May 24 and hit more consistently upon his return, finishing with a .259 batting average—despite an 0-for-29 slump in late August—with 2 homers and a career high 48 RBIs. He got more than half of those RBIs in a total of 11 games; he had six games with three RBIs and another five games in which he drove in two.

Owen must have felt like the old gunslinger from the Wild West forced to contend with a young hotshot when he arrived at spring training in 1988. Jody Reed, who hit .296 at Triple-A Pawtucket, was the latest threat to his job. If this had been a movie gunfight, it would have looked more like Laurel against Hardy than John Wayne against Gary Cooper. Manager John McNamara penciled Owen in the Opening Day lineup, then benched him after he started 3-for-27, in favor of Reed. Reed went 1-for-17, so Owen went back in.

"Both played excellent defensive shortstop, and I'm waiting for one to get hot at the plate," said McNamara.[11]

The plate was actually cold for the entire team early in the season, as the Red Sox faced such a total lack of home-run power that their total of nine home runs after 24 games was one more than the number hit by Oakland's Jose Canseco. Owen was tied for the team lead in home runs, with two, which was amazing for a roster that included Jim Rice, Dwight Evans, and Wade Boggs. It was only a matter of time before the front office made some changes.

Those changes began during the All-Star break, when McNamara was fired and replaced by baseball lifer Joe Morgan. The Red Sox went on a tear, winning 19 of their next 20 games, and Owen watched 16 of those games from the bench. He was also the cause of a dugout shoving match between Morgan and team captain Rice, after Morgan sent Owen in to pinch-hit for Rice during a July 20 game, which, let's face it, was like replacing Michelangelo with a house painter. Rice was suspended for three games, Morgan's authority was asserted, and Owen's fate with the Red Sox was sealed. Owen played sporadically as Captain Morgan led the Red Sox to the American League East title. Oakland swept the Red Sox in four straight in the ALCS—there must have been something in the juice—with Owen having only one plate appearance, in the top of the ninth in Game Four, as the Red Sox desperately and unsuccessfully tried to extend the series. That was Owen's last game in a Red Sox uniform. He had wanted to be traded after Reed got the starting job, and got his wish on December 8, 1988, when he was sent to the Montreal Expos along with minor leaguer Dan Gakeler for pitcher John Dopson and infielder Luis Rivera.

In his prognostications for the 1989 National League season, Peter Pascarelli of *The Sporting News* predicted that the Mets would win 100 games, the San Francisco Giants would finish fifth in the NL West and the Expos would do likewise in the NL East, citing Owen as "an average filler for the Expos' gap at shortstop…"[12] Pascarelli was wrong on all counts; the Mets finished second to the Cubs, the Giants went to the World Series and Owen provided solid fielding and leadership as the Expos finished fourth with an 81-81 record. He led the National League in fielding percentage (.979) and committed 13 errors in 633 chances. His offensive numbers were typical for him, a .233 average, 6 home runs, and 41 RBIs. The Expos were pleased enough with Owen's performance to give him a three-year contract extension during the season.

For a player relied on more for his defense than his offensive contribution, Owen's 1990 season couldn't have gotten off to a better start, as he set a National League record for consecutive errorless games with 63, breaking the previous mark of 60 set by the Mets' Kevin Elster in 1988. Game 61 was a piece of cake—he didn't have any groundballs hit to him, no putouts, and only one assist in a 2-1 loss to the Cubs on June 19. That record propelled him to a career-high .989 fielding percentage (again tops in the league) and a career-best six errors. Owen's defense contributed to a competitive 85-77 season for Montreal; the team was 4½ games out on September 20, but a 1-9 stretch knocked them out of the race.

The 1991 season collapsed on the Expos—literally. A 55-ton slab of Olympic Stadium concrete fell in early September, forcing the team to play its last 13 home games on the road. And while no one was hurt as a result, the event only added insult to the injury of a 71-90 season. Owen's numbers were typical—.255 batting average, 3 home runs, and 26 RBIs, along with a .986 fielding percentage (second in the league)—but the media were already talking about Owen being on the way out. Montreal had a rising star shortstop named Wilfredo Cordero playing at Triple A and projected to take the starting job at shortstop in 1992.

To borrow an old cliché, if Owen had a nickel every time someone was taking his job, blah, blah, blah, and 1992 was no different. Once the season started, Owen was at shortstop and Cordero was back in the minors. There was a bit of a difference this time, as Owen was 31, and again had problems with his hamstring; he was on the 15-day disabled list in July. He was also

in the $1 million salary range, which was a lot for a cash-strapped team like the Expos at the time. Even though he had a career high seven home runs and the highest batting average of his career to date at .269, the Expos wanted to get younger and cheaper.

Owen became a free agent after the season, and signed a three-year, $7 million contract with the Yankees. He loved playing in New York, and he knew that playing in the 1993 home opener wearing pinstripes was a special memory. "The atmosphere in parks like Yankee Stadium is so unique and hard to beat with the history and all the great players and all the ghosts," he said. To see the stadium jam-packed for a beautiful day game, even when I talk about it now it still gives me goosebumps to think I was out there and part of that game."[13]

The feeling, however, was not mutual. Owen started off very well, hitting .419 in his first 12 games. The adrenaline rush of playing in Yankee Stadium soon went away, as did Owen's starting job. He was benched in favor of Mike Gallego after the All-Star Game, and had only nine starts in the last two months of the season. He played in 103 games and had only two home runs and 20 RBIs along with 14 errors. After the season, New York traded him to the California Angels, and assumed a substantial part of the remaining $4.25 million of his contract.[14]

Owen spent the final two years of his major-league career as a part-time player with the Angels. He played 82 games in each of the 1994 and 1995 seasons. For the two seasons combined, he batted .274 with 4 home runs and 65 RBIs. He called it a career in April 1996, 2½ weeks after signing a minor-league contract with the Texas Rangers.

After his playing career ended, Owen went back to his alma mater at age 37 to obtain his degree in applied learning and development with an emphasis on sports management. In 2002 he started the first of two stints as a coach with the Round Rock Express, the Houston Astros' affiliate in the Double-A Texas League, and had two stints with them. The first lasted until 2006; he then returned from 2011-2014. As of 2015, he was manager of the High Desert Mavericks, the Rangers' affiliate in the Class-A California League.

SOURCES

In addition to the sources listed in the Notes, the author also used the following:

Thebaseballcube.com.

Baseballpilgrimages.com.

Galveston (Texas) *Daily News.*

Index Journal (Greenwood, South Carolina).

Ludington (Michigan) *Daily News.*

Mocavo.ca.

New York Times.

Omaha.net.

Oursportscentral.com.

Orlando Sentinel.

Paris (Texas) *News.*

San Bernardino County (California) *Sun.*

NCAA.org.

Special thanks to Shane Phillips of the High Desert Mavericks for his assistance.

NOTES

1 Kurt Kragthorpe, "Owen-Reynolds Combination Clicks," *Deseret News* (Salt Lake City, Utah), June 15, 1983.

2 The 1981 team included pitcher Calvin Schiraldi while the 1982 team included Schiraldi and Roger Clemens. Both later played with Owen on the Red Sox.

3 "Mariners' Owen adds lift to troubled team," *Evening Journal* (Lubbock, Texas), July 5, 1983.

4 Ibid.

5 Bill Plaschke, "Thomas Accepts Shoulder Surgery," *The Sporting News*, May 28, 1984: 20.

6 "Mariners Stood Pat During Off-Season," *Los Angeles Times*, February 24, 1985.

7 The players to be named were Mike Brown, Mike Trujillo, and John Christensen.

8 Phil Elderkin, "Seattle-to-Boston trade definitely agreed with two Sox stars," *Christian Science Monitor*, October 28, 1986.

9 Dan Weaver, "Mariners' manager has mellowed … just a little bit," *Spokane Chronicle*, January 29, 1987.

10 "Swindell's debut includes 24-5 shellacking," *Baytown* (Texas) *Sun*, August 22, 1986.

11 "A.L. East," *The Sporting News*, May 2, 1988: 21.

12 Peter Pascarelli, "Best Bets: Phils and Braves as Cellar Dwellars," *The Sporting News*, March 6, 1989: 14.

13 Ed Randall, *More Tales From the Yankee Dugout* (New York: Sports Publishing LLC, 2002), 84.

14 The *New York Times* on December 10, 1993, said it was unlikely the Angels would have agreed to the trade if the Yankees did not assume at least $2 million of Owen's salary.

REY QUIÑONES

By John Gregory

SOME BASEBALL PLAYERS HAVE THE LUCK of being in the right place at the right time. Many others never do. A few, however, momentarily have this kind of good fortune in their grasp, then see it taken away. Shortstop Rey Quiñones was a May call-up for the 1986 Boston Red Sox, a team destined to finish a single strike away from winning it all; but a celebrated midseason trade sent him away to last-place Seattle, and he missed out on being part of the postseason thrill (and ultimately the heartbreak) of being on this AL pennant winner.

Rey Francisco (Santiago) Quiñones, born on November 11, 1963, was raised in the Rio Piedras area of San Juan, which is home to the main campus of the University of Puerto Rico. Despite that distinction, Seattle Mariners scout Roger Jongewaard later called the neighborhood Rey lived in, "a very, very bad part of Puerto Rico."[1]

He was signed by local Red Sox scout Felix Maldonado in 1982 as an amateur free agent, at a time when the Commonwealth of Puerto Rico was not yet subject to the annual amateur draft. A right-hander, he was of about average height for a professional shortstop, reaching an eventual 5-feet-11, and was of slender build, topping out at around 160 pounds. These are not vital statistics that suggest a power hitter; nonetheless, power turned out to be one of his tools.

Quiñones began his professional career at Elmira in the short-season New York-Penn League. Teammate Dana Kiecker later was quoted as saying of the 19-year-old Quiñones, along with two other Latin teammates on the Pioneers, that "[n]one of them spoke a word of English."[2] Command of the English language did not come up as an issue for Quiñones during the rest of his career, however. He acquitted himself very well in his first taste of minor-league ball, not only batting .295 but showing very good power with 11 doubles and 12 home runs in only 261 plate appearances. Not

surprisingly for a young shortstop, he was error-prone and ended up with a .925 fielding percentage on 27 errors in 360 chances. He certainly was gaining the attention of others outside the Red Sox organization as well; *Baseball America* named him Boston's number 2 prospect during the following offseason.[3]

Rewarded with a promotion to Winston-Salem in the full-season Carolina League in 1984, Quiñones continued showing good results. He batted .279, and again showed unusual power for a middle infielder, chipping in with 30 doubles, 6 triples, and 11 home runs. His fielding percentage while playing for the Spirits was marginally better than the year before, at .930.

Quiñones continued his climb toward the American League, with 1985 spent on the Double-A New Britain Red Sox squad in the Eastern League. Anointed by *Baseball America* as the top Red Sox prospect[4] that previous offseason, he posted satisfactory numbers at

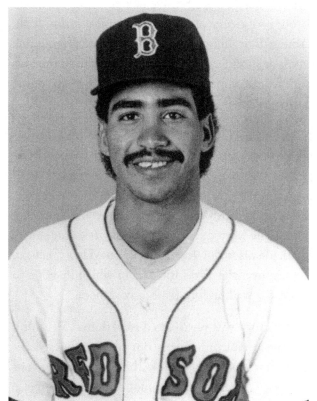

the plate, batting .257 with 19 doubles, 5 triples and 9 homers against this tougher level of competition. His fielding percentage showed some further improvement, ending at .947.

Retaining his number-1 *BA* prospect ranking, Quiñones in 1986 had reached the brink of the majors, as he started in Pawtucket of the International League. During spring training, his swing had impressed Ted Williams, who dubbed him "a pup out of Frank Robinson."[5] (It is hard to guess exactly what Williams may have meant by the analogy, since physically it would be hard to match up the slightly built short-stop and the muscular outfielder. But Williams likely saw something reminiscent in the swing, and the youngster certainly sported home-run power, rare in a legitimate shortstop prospect.) Veteran *Boston Globe* sportswriter Peter Gammons perhaps heard this remark and phrased it this way: "The prize apparently is 18-year-old Puerto Rican shortstop Rey Quiñones, a 6-foot-1 Frank Robinson lookalike, who is leading the club in homers (4) and has exceptional defensive tools."[6] Sports cartoonist Eddie Germano recorded his spring-training thoughts that year, and in a cartoon titled "Winter Haven Sketchbook" he captioned under a rough drawing of a fielder taking a groundball: "Young Rey Quinonez *[sic]* … still learning, quick hands at short … good release."[7] Apparently this was not an uncommon rendering of the player's name during his early career.[8]

In 24 games for the Triple-A PawSox, Quiñones batted .267 with two doubles and four homers in 98 plate appearances. His fielding percentage was up to .962, and the parent club deemed him ready. He was called up to Boston and was assigned uniform 51, a number he wore throughout his major-league career. He made his major-league debut on May 17, 1986, an 8-2 win over the Texas Rangers in which he got two hits and a walk in four plate appearances.

That victory was no isolated experience. Winning became a welcome habit during the first weeks Quiñones was in the majors. The Red Sox won 15 of the first 17 games after his promotion, May 17 to June 4. In that span he contributed greatly, with a .275 batting

average in 65 plate appearances, with three doubles and a homer plus an impressive 12 walks.

But defense remained a bugaboo. No one doubted Quiñones' talent and potential with the glove, but a .940 fielding percentage for his total time with the Red Sox attests to what were considered lapses in concentration. His hitting also came back to earth after that early success, with a batting average of .228, few walks, and only modest power. He was basically benched after being lifted for a pinch-hitter in the bottom of the eighth on August 5, in favor of Ed Romero, and played in only two more games for Boston. The team as a whole had also run into a bad slump (5-13) immediately after the All-Star break, coinciding partly with the July 10 suspension of pitcher Dennis "Oil Can" Boyd. Quiñones came in for a large share of the blame for the slide. Reviewing the 1986 season, *Boston Globe* journalist Dan Shaughnessy wrote, "[t]he Sox were a mess. Baylor had only 2 homers in 6 weeks, Quiñones was erroring *[sic]* all over the place. …"[9]

Quiñones was traded to the Seattle Mariners on August 19, 1986. The Red Sox received shortstop Spike Owen and outfielder Dave Henderson in return for Quiñones, starting pitchers Mike Brown and Mike Trujillo, and outfielder John Christensen. However, it was actually a little more complicated than that. On Sunday, August 17, Red Sox general manager Lou Gorman had agreed to the trade with his Seattle counterpart Dick Balderson, and it was announced to the public.[10] But, as Shaughnessy revealed, "[l]eague officials had discovered a problem with the trade Monday afternoon. Gorman had failed to ask for waivers on Brown and Trujillo. Though only a technicality, the Sox GM had illegally traded two players and the deal was put on hold until it could be restructured."[11] The trade was finally closed on the 19th, with Quiñones going to Seattle immediately, Brown and Trujillo being sent on the 22nd after clearing waivers, and Christensen not going to the Mariners until late September as a player to be named later. The swap was generally well received by Boston fans. The trade was portrayed as giving up youth for experience in order to make a pennant push, although only Quiñones could be considered a young prospect among the players Boston gave up, while both of the Seattle players, even though established as major leaguers, were still in their mid-20s. Gorman later remembered, "It was a good ballclub when I took over. The nucleus was there, and I knew there were only a few things I needed to do to make the club a contender. ... I decided that we could use another bat or two, with some pop, and a steadier shortstop."[12] This explanation left the implication that the team, going all-out for the pennant, wasn't willing to ride out some growing pains at this critical infield position.

It turned out that there were underlying reasons for the trade. Quiñones had somehow become tainted by his association with Boyd.[13] He had been renting a room in the Chelsea condominium owned and occupied by Boyd,[14] and the relationship was apparently close enough that Boyd had lent Quiñones his Chevrolet Monte Carlo.[15] When Boyd got into his July scuffle with police, both Quiñones and Boyd's wife were nearby and were questioned about the incident by the police. No charges were filed against either of them, and charges were eventually dropped against Boyd too.[16] But apparently Quiñones was in the wrong place at the wrong time, and it cost him in his professional life, or at least that is the interpretation offered by some.[17]

Moreover, the on-field staff and even the players had become less than enamored with the shortstop's work habits, a view that was to follow him for the rest of his baseball career. Sportswriter Shaughnessy quoted manager John McNamara immediately after the trade was announced: " 'Spike Owen is the type of ballplayer that fits right into a ballclub. He fits into the chemistry of this ballclub. He and Barrett are going to work well together. They complement each other,' McNamara said. McNamara had started to say that Owen fit into the Sox system better than Quiñones, but stopped himself short."[18] Even if he didn't say it, the implication was clear, and the core of the team seemed to agree with McNamara. Teammate Don Baylor was later quoted as saying, "You never know all there is to know about hitting. But Rey, he told Walter [Hriniak, the batting coach], 'I'll let you know when I

need you.' "[19] Shaughnessy also noted, "There was some fear in the Sox camp that Quiñones might develop into the next Dave Conception [sic], but [Baltimore manager] Earl Weaver shook his head and said, 'In five years, he'll be the same player he is now.' "[20]

In fairness, Quiñones' teammates found him generally likeable. Shaughnessy found it worth remarking that when Quiñones was informed of the potential for a trade a day or so beforehand, he "was unfazed. He was joshing with his teammates as they readied for the flight to Minnesota."[21] Decades later, catcher Rich Gedman could recall no negative issues with him during the short time they played together.[22]

So Rey Quiñones' short career with the Boston Red Sox was over, but he moved on to the Mariners with high expectations by his new team. "He could stand at home plate in the Kingdome and throw the ball into the second deck in center field," [Seattle trainer Rick] Griffin said. "He had the best arm of an infielder that I've ever seen."[23] Sports Illustrated apparently revived the Ted Williams observation, by saying Quiñones "has a classic hitting style and might be a Frank Robinson at shortstop."[24] His arrival in Seattle paid immediate dividends, not only for his new team but for the Red Sox as well, as he batted leadoff in Yankee Stadium and went 2-for-4, knocking in two runs plus making a sparkling defensive play, in Seattle's victory over Boston's chief rival, New York.

But just as with his multi-hit debut for Boston, this strong start did not signal lasting success at the plate or in the field. Indeed, Quiñones' batting statistics for Seattle during the rest of 1986 were even worse than they had been for Boston. His batting average was only .189, with few walks and little power. And his glove work remained erratic, as he compiled a fielding percentage of only .945, which is not made better by looking at modern fielding statistics.[25] In short, Quiñones was costing his team runs both with his bat and with his glove. Still, the Mariners stuck with him through the rest of their dreary 95-loss season, likely from an absence of better alternatives, and possibly also from an aversion to benching so quickly the centerpiece of their big trade.

Spring 1987 rolled around, and Quiñones again found himself at the center of controversy, this time entirely of his own making. Sportswriter Kirby Arnold chronicled some of the troubles in his book *Tales from the Mariners Dugout*: "He showed up late for spring training, telling the Mariners he had visa problems. 'Uh, Rey,' team president Chuck Armstrong told him, 'you're from Puerto Rico. You don't need a visa.'"[26] The Mariners press had reason to remember the day Quiñones finally arrived. "'Rey was lying on his back, flat on the floor the whole time,' [Larry] LaRue [of the *News Tribune* of Tacoma] said. 'We conducted the interview that way, the three of us and [PR director Dave] Aust standing above him. Among other things, Quiñones told the writers that he didn't need baseball, saying he owned a liquor store in Puerto Rico and could live off that.'"[27] This attitude toward money would show up again with the player.

But when Opening Day 1976 arrived, Quiñones began to exhibit signs of becoming the hitter that observers had always been saying he could be. He started a little slowly, with just one hit in his first three games, but quickly brought his batting average above .300. Even though he tailed off a bit, his month of April was robust, with a .296 batting average and enough power to accumulate an OPS of .725, a highly acceptable rate of production from a starting shortstop, especially one who was still only 23 years old. His month of May was also good, with a slightly lower batting average compensated by four home runs and more walks. The team was also playing better, posting (barely) winning records in both April and May. Quiñones missed 11 games in early June due to an injury, but when he came back he went on an absolute tear for almost a month, batting .356 from June 17 to July 10, with three more home runs. On July 7, skipper Dick Williams trotted out the year-old scouting report yet again: "Ted Williams said, don't mess with his stroke, and we haven't."[28] Of course, in light of the remark made later by Don Baylor regarding an unwillingness to be coached, it is possible there was a veiled message behind the crusty manager's comment.

Mariners trainer Rick Griffin was struck by Quiñones' competitive spirit. As Kirby Arnold related it, "Griffin remembers two games, one in Detroit and one in New York, when Quiñones announced in the dugout, 'This game is over, I'm going to hit a home run.' Then he went to the plate and did it."[29] Griffin probably was referring to the May 5, 1987, game in Detroit, which was won 7-5 on the strength of a two-run blast by Quiñones in the top of the ninth off Willie Hernandez. In his career Quiñones never hit a home run against the Yankees, so it is unclear what other game Griffin may have been thinking of. But the anecdote speaks to Quiñones' presence as a teammate.

The remainder of Quiñones' season at bat, mid-July through September, was more pedestrian, with only three home runs in 243 plate appearances, and a batting average of .257. Still, a seasonal batting average of .276 with an OPS of .715 seemed to mark his arrival as a major-league shortstop.

Consistency on defense continued to be the visible weak spot in Quiñones' game. His league-average range was partially undone by the 25 errors he committed during the course of the season for a lackluster .959 fielding percentage.

Less visible, at least to the public at large, was the continuing dismay by the front office and manager at Quiñones' approach to the game. There was an often-repeated story about the time in 1987 he angered his manager by making himself unavailable late in a game for pinch-hitting duty, because he was already in the clubhouse, busy reaching the seventh level of Super Mario Brothers on his Nintendo.[30]

Kirby Arnold documented an exchange as told by club president Chuck Armstrong before one game, among Quiñones, manager Williams, and general manager Dick Balderson. "'I'm a good shortstop, right?' Quiñones said. 'You're a very good shortstop, Rey,' Armstrong told him. 'I could be the best shortstop in the American League,' Quiñones said. 'Yes you could,' Armstrong replied. 'I'm so good,' Quiñones continued, 'that I don't need to play every day.' Armstrong was stunned as Quiñones continued. 'I don't need to play every day, and you have other guys who should play so they can get better,' Quiñones said. 'So I don't need to play tonight.' Williams reworked the lineup, replacing Quiñones at shortstop with Domingo Ramos. ... Other players on the team began calling Quiñones "Wally Pipp," and he had only one question. 'Who's Wally Pipp?' he asked."[31] Of course, Domingo Ramos was no Lou Gehrig, either.

The next year, 1988, Quiñones arguably had his finest season, even while his team sank back into 90-loss territory. He set a personal best in games played and increased his doubles production while matching his 1987 total of 12 home runs. Although his batting average declined to .248, the league as a whole had a lower offensive level. And his defense, while never airtight, was markedly more consistent, with fewer errors and good range, resulting in a slightly above average zone rating as a shortstop. By the numbers, Quiñones was a demonstrable plus for his team.

And yet the odd stories regarding the personal side of the player accumulated. He had been late to spring training again and had remained uncommunicative; "(T)here are telephones in Puerto Rico,"[32] GM Balderson observed. He was "the subject of controversy when he left the Mariners without consulting the team to attend the funeral of a relative in Puerto Rico. He also demonstrated an unwillingness to play with a series of minor injuries that failed to reveal anything in X-ray examinations."[33] Tacoma sportswriter Larry LaRue wrote humorously in 1997, "Long before the Mariners had winning seasons, they had characters. Rey Quiñones once threatened to kill me until a teammate pointed out that the story that had so enraged him had been written by another writer for another newspaper. 'They all look alike,' Rey said."[34]

Indeed, that 1988 spring holdout left lasting hard feelings with the front office. Notwithstanding his dryly humorous comment about telephones, Balderson did have a conversation with Quiñones before the latter came to camp, and it did not go well. "He alluded to his contract when I asked why he wasn't here," said Balderson, "and at one point he said he didn't like my tone of voice. I told him I didn't like the attitude,

the tone this sets."[35] Quiñones did receive a pay raise, playing for either $120,000 or $150,000 that season, according to varying sources, up from the $85,000 he received in 1987 and the $60,000 he had been paid as a rookie.[36] Balderson himself was replaced as general manager by Woody Woodward in July of that year, which may have earned Quiñones somewhat of a clean slate with the front office, coupled with the fact that Dick Williams had been succeeded as manager in June by Jim Snyder. Snyder in turn was replaced by Jim Lefebvre during the offseason.

But if Quiñones had been handed a chance for a fresh start in 1989 with the new management crew, he seemingly took little advantage of it. He again delayed his arrival at spring camp, despite the prospect of receiving another pay raise. The local press seemed to take the side of management, with, for example, one writer leading a day's story, "The Seattle Mariners are missing a key player, but it's (hardly) been noticeable,"[37] after a spring win brought the team to a 5-0 record. The article went on to provide some background: "The Mariners announced they have sent top scout Roger Jongewaard and instructor Marty Martinez to Puerto Rico to search for Quiñones, who was unhappy with his contract last season. The club said it hoped Jongewaard and Martinez would return with Quiñones to their Tempe, Arizona, training camp by the end of the week. Meanwhile, General Manager Woody Woodward renewed Quiñones' contract. Though terms weren't announced, Quiñones probably won't be happy with them. He made $150,000 last season, wanted $300,000 this year, and now faces the prospect of coming to camp to pay a healthy fine—$1,000 a day since March 1—and a base salary the same as in 1988."[38] Sources later stated that Quiñones earned $215,000 that year, but the fines for arriving late may have eaten into that figure.[39]

The story of tracking Quiñones down became even stranger as further details came out. He was literally hiding, in a house across the street from his home, when Jongewaard reached his neighborhood, but Quiñones' girlfriend helped get the parties together. Jongewaard later related, "We finally got to talk to

Rey for a just a couple of minutes. I told him that if he reported to camp and played this one year, he could very well earn himself a million-dollar contract the next year. Rey said he didn't need the money because he had $30,000 in the bank. A week or so later, he finally showed up at spring training."[40]

If Quiñones thought he could redeem his season with good play after a rough spring, the way he had done the previous two years, he was mistaken this time. He missed the first eight games of the regular season, then played in only seven, batting a measly .105 and making three errors at short. Rookie manager Lefebvre had already seen enough. GM Woodward later remembered, "He told me, 'Woody, you gotta get this guy out of here, he's driving me crazy.' I told him I had one shot and I'd give it a try."[41] The Mariners abruptly traded him to the Pittsburgh Pirates along with pitcher Bill Wilkinson, for outfielder Mark Merchant (a first-round draft pick in 1987), starting pitcher Mike Dunne, and starting pitching prospect Mike Walker. (As an irrelevant side note, this brought to four the number of players named Mike included in trades involving Rey Quiñones.)

The Pirates clearly were hoping to succeed with a reclamation project, but it didn't go that way. Quiñones remained in the same batting funk as with the Mariners that season, hitting just .209, and with only a little power and a few walks. His defense was judged to be subpar as well. After 71 games in a Pirates uniform, at age 25, Quiñones was released outright on July 22, 1989.

Quiñones never played in the major leagues again. There was a report that after the 1989 season he "was playing well in winter ball, had a number of teams interested in him and then started being late for games. Finally, he stopped showing up altogether."[42] Very likely he has played afterward, here and there, in leagues where official records do not reach the major media sources. Unexpectedly, after a long hiatus from the US spotlight, he showed up in 1999 in the independent Atlantic League, playing shortstop for the Atlantic City Surf, with a low batting average, a few extra-base hits, and unimpressive fielding statistics.

In 2012 the name Rey Quiñones showed up again in the news, once more in a way that was just a little off-kilter. According to *Sports Collectors Digest*, "An aggressive bidder from New York stepped up to the plate and slammed one out of the park by purchasing an actual 1996 New York Yankees World Series ring once owned by former ballplayer Rey Quiñones for $15,600. The sale took place during the 20th annual Cabin Fever Auction held March 25, 2012, by Tim's, Inc. Quiñones was a shortstop who played for three teams from 1986-1989 (the Boston Red Sox, Seattle Mariners and Pittsburgh Pirates). He held an administrative position with the Yankees in the 1996 season, entitling him to a ring. It was a beauty, featuring 1.5 ounces of gold, 23 brilliant round cut diamonds (one for each Yankee championship team) plus a faux sapphire."[43]

When contacted in 2015, the Yankees media relations office was unable to confirm either that Quiñones had ever worked for the team, or that he had received a World Series ring from them.[44]

What Quiñones has been doing to earn a living in recent years might not bear close scrutiny. A former ballplayer from Puerto Rico confided in December 2015 that Quiñones was operating in a "dangerous area," and said further, "Hopefully, one day we don't see him in jail."[45]

In the career of Rey Quiñones there is an element of classic tragic drama—where the factors of both success and failure are contained within the nature of one character and cannot be separated. The ingredients for a successful baseball career were apparent to many knowledgeable people in the game during his rise. But the comments of other knowledgeable people after the fact are tinged with great regret. Mariners trainer Rick Griffin, who was mentioned earlier from Kirby Arnold's book as attesting to the strength of Quiñones' arm, said further of the player, "[t]o this day, I think he is one of the most talented guys I've ever seen. But he didn't really care about playing the game. He enjoyed being there, but he didn't want to play."[46] He also remarked, "[i]t's a sad deal. You always wondered what kind of a player he could have been, but he just didn't have his priorities in order."[47]

" 'Oh, Quinones,' [Seattle GM] Balderson said in 1991. 'He broke my heart. He had the potential to be the best in the game, but what a strange guy.' "[48]

Jim Leyland, Quiñones' last major-league manager, was even more pointed in a 1989 interview with *New York Times* writer Murray Chass, and his up-close view, as summarized by Chass, deserves to be quoted at length. "I thought we were getting someone who wasn't the best of guys but had talent," the Pittsburgh manager said. "[Instead, we] got a guy who was a good guy but didn't show talent. I can put up with errors, but not errors with no effort. It was performance No. 1, approach to performance No. 2. He wasn't getting balls and he wasn't making an effort to get balls. He has a good arm, but he was lollipopping the ball over to first. I tried everything with him; I encouraged him. One day I said something to him about throwing the ball and that night he went out and flipped it underhand to first. He and his wife have a baby, and my wife is going to have a baby for the first time, and we'd kid about that. Then the game would start and he'd nonchalant the ball. I don't know why. I'd like to be inside his mind three games in a row to understand the way he thinks. He was not a problem off the field, only on the field. He's a personable guy, a good kid. He jokes around. He never caused any problems. From what we had heard, we thought maybe he'd get to the park late. But we never saw any of that. He was always on time. We traded three guys for him. That should've told him something. We rolled out the red carpet for him. He had a reputation with Boston and Seattle of being a lackadaisical player. I went to bat for him. I defended him. But he kept playing lackadaisically. We evidently made a mistake getting him. He had problems in Boston, Seattle and here. That was why we decided not even to make the attempt to send him down. We just wanted to cut the cord."[49]

Mariners teammate and fellow Puerto Rican Henry Cotto expressed his view more simply. "Rey Quiñones is hard to understand."[50]

SOURCES

In preparing this biography the author relied greatly on the biographical and career information provided online at baseball-reference.com and is very grateful for the existence of this resource. Additional sources are referenced in the text and the Notes.

NOTES

1   Bart Wright, *Remember Rey Quiñones? Those Were the Days* (web. kitsapsun.com/archive/1998/03-31/0002_bart_wright__remember_rey_quinone.html, 1998).

2   David Laurila, *Interviews From Red Sox Nation* (Hanover, Massachusetts: Maple Street Press, 2006), 98.

3   Baseball America, "1983-2000 Top 10 Prospect Rankings Archives." baseballamerica.com/majors/top-10-prospect-rankings-archives/.

4   Ibid.

5   Dan Shaughnessy, *One Strike Away* (New York: Beaufort Books, 1987), 141.

6   Chad Finn, *Top 50 Red Sox Prospects of Past 50 Years,* (boston.com/sports/touching_all_the_bases/2014/04/20-11.html, 2014).

7   Eddie Germano, *Red Sox drawing board: 25 years of cartoons* (Lexington, Massachusetts: The Stephen Greene Press, 1989), 119.

8   Finn; Baseball America, "1983-2000 Top 10 Prospect Rankings Archives."

9   Shaughnessy, 117.

10   Glenn Stout and Richard A. Johnson, *Red Sox Century—the Definitive History of Baseball's Most Storied Franchise* (Boston: Houghton Mifflin, 2000), 400.

11   Shaughnessy, 117.

12   Laurila, 242.

13   Stout and Johnson, 400.

14   Michael Madden, *Boston Globe*, July 12, 1986.

15   Shaughnessy, 108.

16   Kevin Cullen, *Boston Globe*, July 17, 1986.

17   Finn.

18   Shaughnessy, 141.

19   Ibid.

20   Shaughnessy, 142.

21   Shaughnessy, 137.

22   Rich Gedman, personal interview with author, November 28, 2015.

23   Kirby Arnold, *Tales From the Mariners Dugout* (Champaign, Illinois: Sports Publishing, 2007), Chapter Eight.

24   *Sports Illustrated*, September 1, 1986.

25 fangraphs.com/statss.aspx?playerid=1010615&position=SS#fielding.

26 Arnold, 63.

27 Ibid.

28 Associated Press "With Ted's Advice, Quinones May Gain Clout of 'Sugar Rey,'" *Spokane Chronicle*, July 7, 1987.

29 Arnold, 62.

30 Art Thiel, *Out of Left Field* (Seattle: Sasquatch Books, 2003), 21.

31 Arnold, 63-64.

32 Larry Larue, "Quiñones Missing From Seattle Camp," *Tacoma News-Tribune*, February 29, 1988.

33 Mike Shatzkin, ed., *The Ballplayers* (New York: William Morrow and Company, 1990), 888.

34 *Tacoma News-Tribune*, July 8, 1997.

35 Larue, *Tacoma News-Tribune*, February 29, 1988.

36 baseball-reference.com/players/q/quinore01.shtml.

37 Associated Press, "Marines Don't Miss Holdout Quinones, March 8, 1989.

38 Ibid.

39 baseball-reference.com/players/q/quinore01.shtml.

40 Wright, *Remember Rey Quiñones? Those were the days.*

41 Ibid.

42 Bob Finnigan, "Reynolds Looks Like a Million; Presley Looks Like a Red Sock," *Seattle Times*, January 14, 1990.

43 Tom Bartsch, "1996 N.Y. Yankees Ring Tips Scales at $15,600," *Sports Collectors Digest*, May 29, 2012.

44 Yankees Media Relations office, telephone interview with author, December 1, 2015.

45 Bill Nowlin interview with former Puerto Rican ballplayer. December 20, 2015.

46 Arnold, 61.

47 Arnold, 63.

48 Bob Finnigan, "Argyros' Discards Shine Elsewhere," *Seattle Times*, July 9, 1991.

49 Murray Chass, "Release of Quiñones Explained by Leyland," *New York Times*, July 27, 1989.

50 pitchersandpoets.com/2012/04/24/rey-quinones-a-hard-man-to-understand/.

JIM RICE

By Alexander Edelman

JAMES EDWARD RICE WAS BORN ON SUNDAY, March 8, 1953, in Anderson, South Carolina, to Roger and Julia Rice. Residents of the town say that even as a lanky teenager, "Ed," as he was — and remains — known to his friends, showed promise. He led his 1969 American Legion team to the state finals. However, it was still a time of segregation in the South, and Rice, despite his promise, had to attend Westside High School, as opposed to the all-white T.L Hanna High. Sometime before Rice's senior year, when integration was mandated, Anderson's district board drew lines to decide who would attend what school. The resulting line was drawn so that the Rice household was included in the Hanna district. His engaging personality and gentle charm won over most of Hanna, he was elected co-class president, and helped ease the racial tension that accompanied integration.

Rice's childhood hero was Westside alumnus and American Football League star George Webster, and Rice played football and basketball as well as baseball. In his senior year, Rice starred on Hanna's football team as an all-state kick returner, defensive back, and wide receiver, and played in the North Carolina-South Carolina Shrine Bowl, leading South Carolina to victory. After some time spent deciding between the Red Sox, who had taken him in the first round of the 1971 amateur entry draft (15th overall), and football scholarship offers from Clemson, North Carolina, and the University of Nebraska, Rice eventually settled on baseball — a $45,000 offer from Mace Brown and Sam Mele of the Red Sox helped.[1]

After being drafted by the Red Sox, Rice played 60 games in 1971 for Williamsport in the Class-A New York-Penn League at the tender age of 18. He hit .256 with five home runs and hated it. He wasn't used to curveballs, people calling him "Jim" instead of "Jim Ed," and being so far from home. But things would get better. In 1972 he was sent to Winter Haven in the Florida State League, where he continued to improve his skills, hitting 17 homers in 130 games. In 1973 the Red Sox promoted Rice to Bristol in the Double-A Eastern League, where he quickly flourished, winning the league batting title with a .317 batting average. He hit 27 homers and drove in 93 runs. Later that year, he joined the Triple-A Pawtucket Red Sox for the International League playoffs, and helped lead them to a Junior World Series championship over the American Association Tulsa team; in 10 playoff games, he hit .378 with four homers. The next year, 1974, Rice played with the PawSox for almost the whole year, and won the International League's Triple Crown, Rookie of the Year, MVP, and the honor of *The Sporting News'* Minor League Player of the Year (.337, 25 HR, 93 RBIs).[2]

The highly prized prospect joined the parent Red Sox for 24 games late in 1974, debuting on August 19.

He hit his first major-league homer on October 1, off Cleveland's Steve Kline. Rice batted .269 in 67 at-bats.

It took Rice a while to get settled in with the 1975 team. While fellow rookie Fred Lynn secured the center-field job, the comebacking Tony Conigliaro was the Opening Day designated hitter, a role earmarked for Rice. Furthermore, Rice was convinced that his difficulty fitting into the lineup wasn't all logistics-related. It wouldn't become public knowledge for a few years, but at the time, Rice believed that his progression with the Red Sox was being arrested by race. In an interview he'd give to *Sport Magazine* in 1978, Rice would cause a stir when he complained: "Race has to be a factor when Fred Lynn can hit .240 in the minors and I can hit .340 and he gets a starting job before I do."

Whatever arrested his rise to the majors, and however unsettled he may have felt, when Conigliaro's season fizzled a few weeks in, Rice had the job to himself. By July he took over left field and held it the rest of the season. He hit .309 with 22 home runs and 102 RBIs, ending up second to Lynn for the Rookie of the Year award. The two rookies Rice and Lynn were dubbed the "Gold Dust Twins" and formed what may have been the most productive rookie tandem of all time.

Hank Aaron was most impressed with the potential of the young slugger, and even speculated that Rice would go on to break his home-run record.[3] But Rice's season came to a premature end on September 21, in a 6-5 win over Detroit, when Tigers pitcher Vern Ruhle broke his left hand with a pitch, sidelining him for the rest of the season and forcing him to watch the Red Sox lose a grueling, seven-game World Series to Cincinnati from the bench.

Recovering from his injury, Rice regressed a bit in 1976, hitting .282 with 25 home runs. In 1977 he became a full-fledged star, leading the league in total bases (382), home runs (39), and slugging percentage (.593). On August 13, 1978, he became the first Red Sox player since Ted Williams in 1939-40 to total 20 homers, 20 doubles, and 10 triples in consecutive seasons. On August 29, 1977, in an 8-7 loss to Oakland, he had his

first three-homer game (his second—and last came exactly six years later, on August 29, 1983).

Jim Rice played his entire professional career with the Red Sox, but none of his seasons equaled the magic of 1978. He started the season off on the right foot, hitting a game-winning single in the 10th inning of the April 14 home opener, and continued his torrid pace into October, when the Red Sox lost to the New York Yankees in a devastating one-game playoff. It was a shame that one of the finest seasons in Red Sox history was overshadowed by the feeble swing of a weedy infielder. but Rice's accomplishments were rewarded.[4] He was voted the MVP award he so richly deserved, leading the majors in slugging percentage (.600), games (163), at-bats (677), hits (213), total bases (406), triples (15), home runs (46, the most for a Red Sox player since Jimmie Foxx hit 50 in 1938), and RBIs (139). He was the first American Leaguer to accumulate 400 total bases in a season since Joe DiMaggio in 1937.

In 1979 Rice had another big year, becoming the first player to have 35 homers (he had 39) and 200 hits (he had 201) for three consecutive seasons. Fans elected him, along with teammates Carl Yastrzemski and Fred Lynn, to start the All-Star Game.[5] It was an all-Red Sox outfield. Rice in particular was recognized as perhaps the best hitter in the game.

Rice had another hand injury in 1980, and suffered subpar seasons in 1981 and 1982 at least partially as a result. Nevertheless, in 1982, Rice had a day at Fenway Park worth remembering. He had a difficult relationship with the press, who presented him as a surly, unfriendly player. Jonathan Keane, from Greenland, New Hampshire, was a 4-year old boy in 1982, and he would probably disagree with this assessment. On August 7 Jonathan was attending one of his first Fenway games, sitting along the first-base line in the field boxes, and watched as his favorite player, Red Sox infielder Dave Stapleton, stepped into the batter's box against Richard Dotson of the Chicago White Sox.

Stapleton fouled a pitch sharply to the right, and the hard-hit ball cracked Jonathan in the head, cutting open his left temple and fracturing his skull. In a 1997 article, Arthur Pappas, the Red Sox team doctor in 1982, claimed he had never seen so much blood at Fenway. Rick Miller, who was near the on-deck circle, cried for Red Sox trainer Charlie Moss, but instead Jim Rice, who didn't see anyone moving, instinctively leaped into the stands and picked up the unconscious toddler. Cradling Jonathan, Rice ran into the clubhouse, where he brought him to Arthur Pappas in the trainer's room.

In a 1997 article describing the incident, Pappas was quoted as saying, "Time is very much a factor once you have that kind of a head injury and the subsequent swelling of the brain. That's why it's so important to get him to care so it can be dealt with. [Rice] certainly helped him very considerably."[6] The supposedly unfriendly outfielder did something that many other Hall of Famers surely haven't. He saved a young boy's life.

Jonathan Keane returned for Opening Day in 1983 to throw the ceremonial first pitch, and Rice's game returned as well, as he went on to lead the league in RBIs (126) and home runs (39). He won the Silver Slugger award and played spectacularly in his best year since 1979. And though the 1983 season was not Rice's best, it provided more weight in the argument of whether he should be a Hall of Famer. SABR member Paul White of Shawnee, Kansas, who was one of Rice's most vocal supporters for election to the Hall of Fame, wrote in 2001 that there were a few reasons offered by sportswriters for Rice not to be admitted to the Hall. Chief among them is that Rice was one-dimensional.[7] In his article, White quoted Jayson Stark of ESPN.com, explaining why he did not vote for Rice in 2000. Stark's main argument was that Rice was one-dimensional, citing his lack of Gold Gloves.[8] To counter Stark's claim, White offered baseball writer Peter Gammons, who wrote in his book *Beyond the Sixth Game*: "... [In 1983, Rice] probably should have won a Gold Glove for fielding excellence. Dwight Evans, who had the worst defensive year of his career, won one instead, proving clearly the value of a reputation."[9]

Rice had typically fine years in 1984 (28 HR, 122 RBIs, .280) and 1985 (27, 103, .291), garnering All-Star honors

each year. In 1986 the Red Sox returned to the postseason, and Rice was their primary weapon in the middle of the lineup. He hit .324, with 20 home runs and 110 RBIs, his last big season.

After missing the postseason in 1975, Rice was healthy this time. He hit just .161 with two home runs in the Red Sox League Championship Series victory over the California Angels, but one of the homers was a key three-run wallop in Game Seven. He hit .333 in the World Series loss to the New York Mets, in what was to be his only fall classic.

Bothered by an injured elbow, Rice fell off in 1987 (13 home runs, 62 RBIs, .277), and he had to have offseason knee surgery. These injuries and eyesight problems plagued Rice for the next two seasons, and hastened the rather sudden end to his career after the 1989 season. The last few unhappy at-bats of the season's difficult twilight dropped Rice's career average from .300 to .298, a drop that provide ammunition for critics in the Hall of Fame-eligibility years that followed.

Rice spent all 16 years of his big-league career with the Red Sox, playing his final game on August 3, 1989. He returned to serve the organization when he was appointed hitting coach in 1995, and young hitters from Nomar Garciaparra to Trot Nixon to Mo Vaughn benefited from his tutelage. Rice continued as Red Sox hitting coach until 2000.

Rice and his wife, Corine, settled in 1975 in Andover, Massachusetts, where they raised their children, Carissa and Chancey. Rice would prefer to be in a warmer climate, being from South Carolina, but his family preferred New England.[10]

Ironically, Rice joined the ranks of the Boston sports media as a baseball analyst for the New England Sports Network (NESN), and became a colleague of some of those he used to war with.

Honors followed the slugger out of baseball. On November 1, 1995, he was inducted into the Red Sox Hall of Fame in its inaugural class. His plaque can be viewed in the Red Sox Hall of Fame at Fenway Park. The Red Sox also put on display a row of silver bats, replicas of all the Silver Slugger awards won by Red Sox players. Two of those belong to Jim Rice. In 1999 *Sports Illustrated* rated him South Carolina's ninth best athlete of the 20th century. On February 18, 2001, Rice was inducted into the Ted Williams Hitters Hall of Fame. A community center in his hometown of Anderson is named in his honor, the Jim Ed Rice Center.

But despite all of the accolades, for years an argument like no other postcareer argument raged about whether Rice's statistics merited him Hall of Fame recognition. The late Dick Bresciani, the Red Sox' avuncular historian, was one of his fiercest advocates, and kept Rice's superior statistics available and showcased to anyone interested. His case for Rice's inclusion in Cooperstown focused on the fact that in his 16 seasons Rice led the AL in homers and RBIs, and that the only players with career averages and home run totals as high as his were baseball Olympians Jimmie Foxx, Lou Gehrig, Mickey Mantle, Hank Aaron, Willie Mays, Ted Williams, Mel Ott, Stan Musial, and Babe Ruth. In 2005 Bresciani started sending a report — a case for Rice's inclusion in the Hall of Fame — to voters, and the voting percentages started a steady climb. On January 12, 2009, the day the vote of his final year of eligibility was announced, Rice was sitting at home watching soap operas when he received a call from Jack O'Connell of the Baseball Writers Association of America. With 76.4 percent of the ballots naming him, he was finally in.[11]

In his Cooperstown speech in July of that year, Rice was in a reflective mood. He thanked Bresciani, "who kept my stats in the public eye," Mitch Brown and Sam Mele for signing him, and mentors ranging from his seventh-grade Westside High coach John Moore through Johnny Pesky and Don Zimmer. And he said, in a voice that grew husky with emotion:

"I am a husband, called Rice. I am a father, called Dad. I am a brother, called Ed. I am an uncle, called Uncle Ed. I am a grandfather, called Papa. I am a friend that doesn't call — some of my friends know that — and sometimes best not call at all. Finally, I do mean finally, I am Jim Rice, called a Baseball Hall of Famer."

Note

A version of this biography was originally published in *'75: The Red Sox Team That Saved Baseball*, edited by Bill Nowlin and Cecilia Tan, and published by Rounder Books in 2005.

NOTES

1   Baseball-Reference (baseball-reference.com/r/ricejio1.shtml).

2   BaseballLibrary (baseballlibrary.com/baseballlibrary/ ballplayers/R/Rice_Jim.stm).

3   Jeff Goldberg, "The Day Rice Made Contact: One of His Memorable Moves Was to Aid an Injured Young Fan, *Hartford Courant*, August 7, 1997.

4   The infielder was, of course, Bucky Dent.

5   Yastrzemski was injured, however, and unable to make a start in the outfield; he was moved to first base instead, replacing also-injured Rod Carew. He was replaced in the outfield by Don Baylor.

6   Goldberg.

7   Paul White, "My 2002 Hall of Fame Ballot: Slot #4, Jim Rice," posted on Baseballlibrary.com on December 11, 2001.

8   White quotes Stark as saying, "He was a one-dimensional player whose career thundered to a halt just as he was on the verge of cementing his sure place in the Hall (only 31 homers, 162 RBIs after age 34). And you essentially have to vote on him as a hitter only, because he DH-ed extensively. He gave you no speed, no Gold Gloves, no off-field 'character-and-integrity' points." This is from Stark's (reposted) November 19, 2003 ESPN.com article "Stark: My Hall of Fame Ballot."

9   Peter Gammons, *Beyond the Sixth Game* (Boston: Houghton Mifflin, 1985).

10 Andrew Neff, "Rice Enjoys TV Analyst Stint," *Bangor Daily News*, April 1, 2005.

11 Adam Kilgore, "Rice Elected to Hall of Fame," *New York Times*, January 12, 2009.

ED ROMERO

By Bill Nowlin

MILWAUKEE BREWERS SCOUT FELIX Delgado "found [Ed Romero] playing in the mountains of Puerto Rico two years ago." Romero was 17 at the time. "After one workout, the Brewers signed … Romero, along with four others."[1]

Edgardo Ralph (Rivera) Romero, born on December 9, 1957, in Santurce, Puerto Rico, was indeed signed at 17, in 1975 as an amateur free agent. His family was a supportive one. Father Rafael A. Romero was a civil engineer who worked mostly on housing construction projects. "He loved the game of baseball and had played semipro baseball himself. He was with me all the way in my career, and a very proud father to have his son playing in the big leagues. My mother Flor Maria was very supportive as well; she was a housewife who took care of us, all the school stuff, etc. They attended every game I played at every level until I was signed as a pro. Even after that, they visited me in the States when I was in the minor leagues, and traveled to see me in the big leagues after that."[2]

Ed had an older brother, Rafael, who also played some baseball. He is a civil engineer in Puerto Rico who had worked with Chevron and Texaco. His sister Alexis, also older, worked as a secretary with a number of companies, later marring and opening up a resort on Puerto Rico's west coast.

Ed's first assignment was to Class-A, the 1976 Burlington (Iowa) Bees in the Midwest League, and he was a rough talent. He played in 129 games, but hit for only a .219 batting average, though his .304 on-base percentage showed some plate discipline. He committed 41 errors in the field, in 647 changes, a .937 fielding percentage.

Romero started 1977 with Holyoke (Eastern League) and, in late July, got an unexpected break. Both Robin

Yount (pulled thigh muscle) and Don Money (back spasms) were unable to play effectively and utility infielder Tim Johnson went on the DL with a groin pull.

The Brewers called up Romero. He was asleep in his room in Holyoke when manager Matt Galante awoke him, saying, "Pack your suitcase. You're going to the big leagues."[3] He couldn't believe it, but he was on his way.

Romero was a right-handed infielder listed at 5-feet-11 and 165 pounds. His debut game, on July 16, saw him go 0-for-2 against the Baltimore Orioles, but he worked two bases on balls in the game. The next day, he singled three times in four at-bats and the third single (in the bottom of the eighth) drove in pinch-runner Jim Wohlford with what proved the winning run in a 3-2 win for the Brewers at County Stadium. All three singles had been off O's starter Dennis Martinez, who bore the loss.

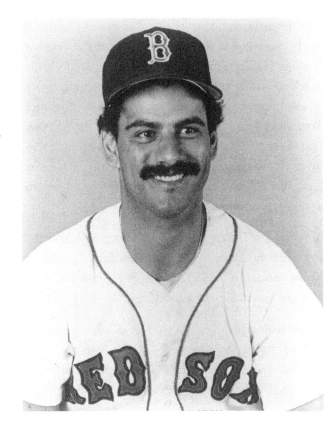

Romero played in eight more games in July, and then—with enough Brewers back in playing condition—was returned to Holyoke. He had hit 7-for-25, and walked four times (.280 BA, .379 OBP.) He felt it was easier to hit pitching in the majors than in the minor leagues. "Down there you don't know where the next pitch is going to be, up here or down there, way wide. But here every pitch they throw is in the strike zone. You can hit it better."[4] He hit .258 for the season with Holyoke, and matched his 41 errors from the year before.

In 1978 Romero played in the Pacific Coast League at Triple-A Spokane, mostly at shortstop. He hit better (.280, with 52 RBIs) and picked up his fielding percentage just a bit. It was Vancouver in 1979 (the Brewers had switched PCL affiliations), with his fielding definitely improved (.960), though his batting tailed off a bit to .260.

Romero returned to the majors in 1980, when he got another opportunity after Larry Hisle was placed on the 15-day disabled list. He got to the Brewers in time to play in the June 6 game (and was 2-for-3 with three RBIs his first game back, with a two-run double and a bases-loaded walk). That June 6 game was an emotional one because it was also the first game of the year for manager George Bamberger, who had suffered a heart attack in spring training and undergone quintuple-bypass surgery. The Brewers won the game, 8-4, and Bamberger said, "You always want to win the first one because you know you're on the board then. Romero did great. That's what makes this ballclub great—its depth. We got a lot of guys hurt, but a guy like Romero comes in tonight and picks us up."[5]

Romero got into 50 games in Vancouver and hit .273 while he appeared in 42 games for Milwaukee, hitting .260. He made 12 errors in 174 chances with the Brewers, mostly at second base.

Eddie Romero forged a very successful career as a utility infielder for the next decade, into the 1990 season, playing shortstop (288 games), second base (192), and third base (176), with 32 games in the outfield, 13 at first base, and 14 as a designated hitter. He was

with the Brewers in eight seasons and the Boston Red Sox in four, and played a number of games for both Detroit and Atlanta.

Romero made the postseason three times, the first time being in 1981 with Milwaukee. He had played in 44 games, driven in 10 runs, and scored 6. He hit .198. The Brewers played the New York Yankees in a best-of-five American League Division Series, and lost in five. Romero played in only the fifth and deciding game. He singled to left field with one out in the top of the third and came around to score, giving Milwaukee a 2-0 lead. The Yankees came from behind and won the game. Romero struck out his next time up and then was removed for pinch-hitter Don Money, who flied out.

Romero played in 52 games in 1982, batting .250, but driving in only seven runs (he scored 18), and then 59 games in 1983, with a .317 batting average (the best of his career), with 18 RBIs. A 1982 column by Tom Flaherty quoted Romero on the difficulty of utility work: "It can be tough. I've always been used to playing every day. In the minor leagues, everywhere I played, I played every day. It's a hard adjustment. There's no way you can afford to get down when you're not playing. If you do that, then when you get the chance, you might not do the job."[6] Manager Harvey Kuenn said, "I think he's one of the best utility players in the league. Anybody who can play three positions as well as he can is a big asset. And he's not an out at the player, either."[7]

In 1984, with Paul Molitor out for the season, Romero was effectively Milwaukee's first-string third baseman, playing in 116 games and batting .252 with a career-high 31 RBIs. Nonetheless, he still thought of himself as primarily a shortstop. Manager Rene Lachemann thought Romero could be a regular for a number of teams, but prized his versatility for the Brewers. He too believed Romero the best utilityman in the majors. Romero put in about 15 minutes of infield work at each base, to be ready for wherever he might be needed. GM Harry Dalton said, "I can't say he's untouchable because he's a utility player," but made it pretty clear how very much he valued Romero.[8]

In 1985, with Molitor back at third base, Romero was back to his utility role, but he got into 88 games. He hit .251 and drove in 21 runs.

After the season was over, the Brewers traded Romero to the Boston Red Sox on December 11 for pitcher Mark Clear, primed to be popular, according to acerbic *Boston Globe* columnist Dan Shaughnessy, if for no other reason than that the Sox had replaced the "universally loathed Mark Clear." Rene Lachemann was with the Red Sox, too, as their third-base coach in 1986. Romero knew he was penciled in for the same utility role, saying, "I do the best I can, but if nobody gives you a chance to play every day, you've got to be a good utility player. If I ever get a chance to play, I feel I could play every day. My lifetime average is .257, and that's not bad when you realize that you can go three weeks or a month without playing. That's tough. Just one year I'd like the chance to play every day."[9]

Romero committed three errors in eight games, and knew he was pressing. "I'm hurting myself and the team by trying too hard to prove myself," he said in the early going. Manager John McNamara said, "He'll settle down. I'm not worried about him. He's been a pretty steady player in this league for six years."[10] Anyone who plays in 100 ballgames for a pennant-winning team during the course of one season is making a real contribution. Romero played in an even 100 games for the 1986 Boston Red Sox, mostly at shortstop, 75 games, with another 18 at third base. He made only 12 errors, but hit just .210. He pinch-ran a number of times, scoring 41 runs and driving in 23.

The Red Sox made it all the way to Game Seven of the 1986 World Series before folding to the Mets. Romero played in four postseason games, but only briefly—the first three times as a pinch-runner, though he stayed in the game each time as a defensive replacement. In Game Seven of the World Series, he came in to play shortstop in the bottom of the eighth, with the Mets ahead, 6-5. They scored twice more, the one ball hit to him converted to an out. Romero was the first batter for Boston in the top of the ninth and fouled out to first baseman Keith Hernandez. He'd had two

previous plate appearances in the postseason, making an out both times as well.

Romero played only two innings in 1987 spring training, but Marty Barrett hurt his wrist the first week of the regular season, and Romero got more of a chance to play on a regular basis. Then Glenn Hoffman got hurt. Playing more regularly, Romero even put together a 15-game hitting streak from April into May, and in mid-May he was told the shortstop position was his.[11] He was batting over .300 much of the season, and even after cooling off in August (where he lost a few weeks of playing time) and September, he still finished batting .272. He'd played in 88 games, though remarkably he drove in only 14 runs all season long. He'd played almost the same number of games at third base, second, and short, and even eight at first base. He started to become reconciled to the role of utility infielder: "I really don't want to be jumping around. I just want to play four or five more years. After eight years in the big leagues, it's going to be difficult to become a starter. If I didn't get it this year, I'm not going to get it."[12] When he wasn't in the lineup, he often volunteered to throw batting practice.

After the 1987 season, a few days before he could have declared free agency, Romero got some extra security—a two-year contract with the Red Sox guaranteeing him $900,000.[13] Romero wasn't getting a starting role out of it, though. Fair or not, manager McNamara already had him pigeonholed: "He can't play every day."[14]

Romero's playing time was sharply reduced in 1988, in part due to a right knee problem that led to a lengthy stint on the DL in June and July, but the team got to the postseason again. There was the annual lament again about not getting the chance to prove himself as a regular. He didn't understand why he kept hearing he wasn't an everyday player. "I'm a utility player because that's the only thing I've gotten a chance to be. You can't say someone can't do something until they get the chance."[15] He played in only two June games and three in July, and just 31 games in all. Many of the appearances were late in games, on defense. Romero hit .240 and drove in five runs. The Red Sox faced off against Oakland in the ALCS. In Game One Boston went into the bottom of the ninth down by one run, 2-1. With two outs, Jody Reed doubled and Rich Gedman drew a walk. Manager Joe Morgan (who had taken over for John McNamara in midseason) put in the faster Romero as a pinch-runner for Gedman in hopes that Wade Boggs could drive in both the tying and the winning runs, but Boggs struck out. It was Romero's only appearance in the 1988 postseason.

Romero had more playing time in 1989, but chafed a bit under Joe Morgan, and his frustration at being consigned to the utility role boiled over when he was removed in the middle of an at-bat in a June 11 game against the Yankees. The Red Sox had just come from behind and scored five runs in the top of the eighth to tie the score, 7-7. There was a runner on first base with two outs. Romero ran the count to 3-and-0, when Yankees skipper Dallas Green decided to change pitchers. Once he did, Morgan decided to change batters and send up Rich Gedman. Romero exploded, throwing a Gatorade cooler onto the field. "I don't want to play for that man," Romero said of Morgan. He shows me no respect. I just want to go somewhere else and play."[16] Asked what was wrong with their relationship, Romero said, "Everything."[17] GM Lou Gorman said he wasn't going to be fined, but that Romero had it explained to him that no other teams had been asking about him, that no one had brought his name up.[18]

Morgan did, however, keep using Romero for the next couple of months, though Romero had been batting just .233 at the time. Finally, on August 5, after Marty Barrett was reactivated, the Red Sox released Romero. He was hitting .212 in 46 games, with six RBIs and only three errors in 161 chances. "I wasn't treated fairly here at all," Romero said after cleaning out his locker. "It's a relief to be getting away from here."[19] Seven days later, after clearing waivers, he signed as a free agent with the Atlanta Braves.

Romero was, of course, speaking out of frustration. "I just wanted a chance to play every day," he said many years later. "When the media asked me about it, I was very honest, never disrespecting anyone."[20]

Romero was 5-for-19 with a solo homer in seven games with the Braves when his old team—the Milwaukee Brewers—suddenly suffered a spate of injuries that cost them several infielders and caused them to seek out the veteran Romero. On August 23 the Braves agreed to trade him for a player to be named later; Jay Aldrich was that player. In 52 chances, Romero made just one error; he hit .200 with three RBIs. The Brewers granted him free agency in mid-November.

On January 15 Romero signed with the Detroit Tigers. He played with them until the Tigers released him on July 15. He'd gotten into 32 games and batted .229. He made just one error in 57 chances.

Romero's final major-league stats show a career fielding percentage of .967 and a .247 batting average. He had driven in 155 runs and scored 218. And he had plugged a number of holes for his various teams in the course of the 730 games over the 12 years he'd played in the big leagues.

There was a brief return to minor-league ball in 1991, with the Las Vegas Stars (Pacific Coast League), and Romero hit .284 in 28 games. Las Vegas was a Padres affiliate, and the Padres kept him on for five years as manager of their Class-A teams (a different team each year—Spokane, Waterloo, Springfield, Clinton, and Memphis) and one year working as infield coordinator. He also worked managing seven seasons in winter ball in Puerto Rico. The Brewers then hired Romero as a minor-league manager and instructor, working in El Paso, Huntsville (where his team won the Southern League championship in 2001), and Indianapolis. In 2007 he became their minor-league infield coordinator, and in 2008 manager Cecil Cooper hired him to become the third-base coach for the Houston Astros. He served as the bench coach for the Astros in 2009.

It was back to managing in the minors in 2010, in Greeneville, Tennessee, with assignments in 2011 and 2012 as manager of the Gulf Coast League Astros. Romero managed the New York-Penn League's Tri-City Valley Cats, of Troy, New York, an Astros affiliate, from 2013 through 2015.

"I'm happily married to a wonderful woman," he wrote on the last day of 2015. "Ivonne Romero, my high school sweetheart."[21] The two met at the Colegio Bautista de Carolina high school. The married on Christmas Day in 1977 and celebrated their 38th anniversary on Christmas 2015.

Ivonne and Ed Romero have two children. Ariana Kay Romero is a registered nurse working for an orthopedic doctor in West Palm Beach, Florida. Son Eddie Romero Jr. has also forged a life in baseball. In 2006 Eddie Jr. was named as an assistant in international and professional scouting for the Red Sox.[22] Within a few years, he was the team's Latin American coordinator, and by 2012 he had become the team's director of international scouting. In October 2015 he was promoted to vice president, international scouting.

Asked at the start of 2016 how he feels looking back on his first 40-plus years in baseball, Ed Senior said, "After 40 yrs in professional baseball I thank the Lord for a wonderful and successful career as a player and as an instructor."[23]

SOURCES

In addition to the sources noted in this biography, the author also accessed Romero's player file from the National Baseball Hall of Fame, the *Encyclopedia of Minor League Baseball*, Retrosheet.org, Baseball-Reference.com, and the SABR Minor Leagues Database, accessed online at Baseball-Reference.com. Thanks to Ed Romero for assistance in completing this biography.

NOTES

1 Lou Chapman, "Teen-Age Romero Eases Brewer Infield Woe," *The Sporting News*, August 6, 1977: 29. Ed Romero said of Delgado, "Felix had a good reputation as one of the best scouts in Latin America. A high number of players he signed made it to the major leagues." Ed Romero email to author on December 31, 2015.

2 Ed Romero email to author on December 31, 2015.

3 Chapman.

4 Chapman.

5 Associated Press, June 8, 1980.

6 Tom Flaherty, "Romero a Handy Sub for Brewers," *The Sporting News*, July 12, 1982: 38.

7 Ibid.

8 Tom Flaherty, "Romero May Be Top A.L. Utility Player," *The Sporting News*, July 16, 1984: 41.

9 Dan Shaughnessy, "No Substitute for Romero," *Boston Globe*, April 5, 1986.

10 Pete Farley, "Romero Pressing in New Role," *Brockton Enterprise*, April 19, 1985.

11 Steve Fainaru, "Longshot Romero Wins at Shortstop," *Hartford Courant*, May 12, 1987: D4.

12 Paul Jarvey, "Romero's Utility a Futility," *Worcester Telegram*, July 24, 1987: 17B.

13 Joe Giuliotti, "Romero Signs Two-Year, $900,000 Pact with Sox," *Boston Herald*, November 10, 1987: 99.

14 Stave Fainaru, "Romero's Role Is Clear: He's a Utility Player," *Hartford Courant*, May 5, 1988: B7.

15 David Cataneo, "Romero Reserved About Backup Role," *Boston Herald*, May 19, 1988: 103.

16 Joe Giuliotti, "Romero Blasts Morgan," *Boston Herald*, June 12, 1989: 74.

17 Steve Fainaru, "Romero Throws Tantrum, Asks to Be Dealt," *Boston Globe*, June 12, 1989: 38.

18 Joe Giuliotti, "No Fine, No Trade, No Interest," *Boston Herald*, June 13, 1989: 36. The *Globe*'s Larry Whiteside wrote a little later that Gorman left it up to Morgan to impose any fine, that there was one, but the amount was not specified.

19 Pete Farley, "Bitter Romero Is Released," *Brockton Enterprise*, August 6, 1989: D1.

20 Ed Romero email to author, January 2, 2016.

21 Ed Romero email to author on December 31, 2015.

22 Nick Cafardo, "Wallace Sidelined With Hip Infection," *Boston Globe*, February 9, 2006: C1.

23 Ed Romero email to author, January 2, 2016.

KEVIN ROMINE

By Thomas Ayers

ALTHOUGH HE WAS NEVER PROVIDED THE steady playing time he felt he needed to establish himself as a regular outfielder, Kevin Romine forged a career as a utility outfielder for the Boston Red Sox for six seasons. However, Romine's lasting legacy in professional baseball may not be as a player, but as a father; both of his sons have played major-league baseball.

Kevin Romine was born on May 23, 1961, in Exeter, New Hampshire. The Romines moved to California early in Kevin's childhood when his father, Willis, an airline pilot, changed his base to the West Coast.[1]

Romine was raised in the Huntington Beach area, south of Los Angeles, and attended Fountain Valley High School, where he was an accomplished baseball player, track and field athlete, and football running back.[2] In December 1978 Romine led Fountain Valley to the California Interscholastic Section Big Five Championship, rushing rushed for 218 yards and a touchdown in the title game.[3]

Romine received Division I football scholarship offers from Cal State Fullerton and Long Beach State.[4] He chose to play baseball at Orange Coast College. In 1980 Romine hit .389 and helped Orange Coast College win the California community college championship.[5] He was selected in the third round of the 1980 draft by the California Angels, but decided to transfer to Arizona State University instead of signing.

Romine hit .406 with 12 home runs and 28 stolen bases in the regular season and helped lead Arizona State to a 26-4 record in the Pac-10 Conference and a spot in the 1981 College World Series.[6] In the double-elimination tournament, Arizona State lost to Oklahoma State in 13 innings, then defeated South Carolina, Texas, and Oklahoma State to win the tournament. The American Baseball Coaches Association named him an All-American.

In his senior season, Romine hit over .400 and stole 60 bases.[7] He was a third-team All-American in 1982 and was scouted heavily in advance of the draft.[8] The Red Sox selected Romine 29th overall with a supplemental second-round selection.

Breaking in with the Winter Haven Red Sox in the Class-A Florida State League, Romine hit .254 with four doubles, four triples, and three homers in 55 games. The next season, with the New Britain Red Sox in the Double-A Eastern League. Romine hit .261, led the team with 26 doubles, and was second with 11 home runs.

In 1984 Romine was promoted to Triple-A Pawtucket, where he batted .253 but had 12 home runs and identical .396 on-base and slugging percentages. A nagging injury caused when he was hit by a pitch in July affected his production. At the time of his injury, Romine was hitting .280 and was second in the International

League with 59 RBIs. Although he returned from injury after a few weeks, he needed several cortisone shots to get through the season.

As a result of his injury, Romine didn't engage in strenuous offseason training. "I didn't do anything over the winter," he said. "The first time I picked up a bat was in spring training."[9] Likely because of the lack of winter conditioning, Romine started slowly at Pawtucket in 1985 and finished with a .243 batting average with only 5 home runs. He stole 19 bases, and might have stolen more, but hadn't been allowed to steal as often as he liked because Pawtucket fell behind early in the game so often.[10]

Romine's .300-plus batting average in the second half of the season caught the attention of the Red Sox and he was called up in September when rosters expanded. He made his major-league debut on September 5 in the first game of a doubleheader against the Cleveland Indians. With the Red Sox leading 12-4 in the bottom of the eighth, Romine pinch-hit for Tony Armas. Facing Ramon Romero, Romine hit a run-scoring single. In the second game of the doubleheader, Romine made his first major-league start, in right field. Batting leadoff, he doubled in the bottom of the first inning, off Jamie Easterly, and hit a single later in the game. By season's end he was 6-for-28 with a pair of doubles.

The following season Romine failed to break camp with the Red Sox. At Pawtucket he batted .292 and was recalled to Boston in late June. For the rest of the season he was mostly a defensive replacement, and accumulated only 35 at-bats. Although his infrequent playing time was a source of frustration, Romine enjoyed life in the major leagues. He reflected, "The meal money is better, the travel is better, you get first-class accommodations. Anything you need, they get for you."[11]

Given his lack of playing time in 1986, it was no surprise that Romine began 1987 with Pawtucket. It was perhaps his best season for the PawSox, as he played in 129 games and batted .267 with 24 doubles, 11 homers, 21 stolen bases, and 52 RBIs. In nine games

with the Red Sox in September and October, he hit .292. On September 18 he had one of the best games of his career against the Baltimore Orioles in the second game of a doubleheader. Romine had three hits, including two doubles, and scored two runs to lead Boston to victory.

Romine did well in 1988 spring training. Asked about the possibility of returning to the International League again, he said, "You get stagnant playing in the minors. It's hard to perform there year after year. ..."[12] The infrequent playing time he was provided in the majors was also a source of frustration, as he felt he couldn't get into a routine. He made the Opening Day roster, but he was demoted to Pawtucket in early April. Leading the International League in batting with a .358 average, Romine was called up by the Red Sox on June 4.[13] Romine got only 70 at-bats the rest of the season and hit just .192, but had several of his best games as a major leaguer this season and also hit his first major-league home run. On July 16 Romine was hitting .154 and wasn't in Boston's starting lineup for the nationally televised game at Fenway Park.[14] The Red Sox trailed the Kansas City Royals, 6-0, in the bottom of the sixth inning.

Romine pinch-ran for Mike Greenwell in the sixth inning and scored a run as the Red Sox scored four runs. He stayed in the game and the Red Sox tied the score in the eighth. Romine led off the bottom of the ninth inning with a walk-off home run to left field on a Steve Farr slider. Romine explained he just wanted to reach base for the hitters behind him. The comeback victory was part of a stretch during which the Red Sox won 19 of 20 games.

Romine generally saw more playing time down the stretch after Joe Morgan replaced John McNamara as the Red Sox manager. He explained, "Mac used to put me in for defense. Joe's getting me in a little earlier, so I can get that one at-bat per game."[15]

On July 27, against the Texas Rangers, Romine's single in the top of the eighth inning of a tie game drove in the go-ahead run in a 10-7 Red Sox victory.[16] On September 20 against Toronto he reached base four times in five plate appearances with two singles and a pair of walks. He scored twice and stole a base.

Romine got off to a bad start in 1989 when he reported to spring training overweight. In 1990 spring training he told a reporter that essentially the weight had snuck up on him without his noticing. "It's hard to explain what happened," Romine said. "There had been times when I'd done even less in the offseason and not put on weight, but your body when you're 22 isn't like your body when you're 28."[17]

The weight gain appeared to lead to the impression that the outfielder was lazy and wasn't dedicated enough to make it to the major leagues as an everyday player.[18] Romine defended himself: "I've worked hard to get here."[19] He saw it as an attack on his reserved nature, telling a sportswriter, "I'm just quiet and people can misinterpret that. I don't say much. I don't jump up and down and rah-rah all over the place. I'm quiet, but I'm intense on the field. Off the field I'm quiet and people interpret that and say that I'm lazy, that I don't want to be here. They get the impression that I don't care. That certainly isn't the case."[20]

Assigned to Pawtucket at the end of spring training, Romine batted .300 in 27 games and soon rejoined the Red Sox. He was given regular starts against left-handers as the right fielder or designated hitter.[21] Regular playing time helped Romine find offensive stability and he had the only five-hit game of his career on July 2 to lead the Red Sox to a 4-1 victory over Toronto. After 44 at-bats, Romine was hitting .364 and said that with regular playing time, he was more relaxed at the plate.[22]

Romine's five-hit performance started a stretch of 14 games where he went a combined 22-for-55 and reached base in every game but one. Filling in for the injured Ellis Burks, Romine had the best fortnight of his career and he reflected on the opportunity. "A week from now, two weeks from now, when guys start coming back, I might not have a place to play. But at least I know I got the chance and I showed them I can play. … I always thought I was capable of playing in the big leagues. It was just a matter of getting a

chance to play every day. If you don't get a chance, it's hard to show what you can do."[23]

Kevin also credited his wife, June, who had given birth to the couple's third child that offseason, for helping him keep his career in perspective. He said, "The biggest thing I figured out, with the help of my family, is there are other things in life. It's not going to hurt me when I leave. At least when I walk away, I'll know I did the best I could."[24] He added, "[My] family gave me a strong foundation and a perspective on what really matters in the overall picture. They grounded me and provided incentive to succeed."[25]

On July 27, 1989, Romine went 2-for-4 with a double, a home run, a walk, and two runs scored. At the end of the game Romine had a .339 batting average, having hit safely in 19 of his first 21 starts.[26] However, his playing time was reduced after Burks returned.

Romine had a pair of three-hit performances on September 10 and 28 and he batted .274, finishing 1989 with 75 hits, more than twice as many as he had in any other season. Romine was quick to credit hitting coach Richie Hebner for his success. "Richie has really helped me a lot this year," he said. "I was much more upright at the plate before, and he has coached me to get lower."[27]

Offseason conditioning was a much higher priority for Romine in the offseason and he reported to spring training in 1990 weighing 22 pounds less than the previous spring training. During spring training Dwight Evans was injured and Romine went north with the Red Sox as the starting right fielder. He helped his case by leading the team in runs batted in during spring training and hitting a grand slam on April 1, in one of the final exhibition games.

On April 9 Romine got his only Opening Day start, batting ninth. Romine doubled off Detroit's Jack Morris in his first two at-bats as the Red Sox won 5-2. However, once Evans returned from the disabled list, Romine played far less often, and almost exclusively as a defensive replacement. He had a few memorable games during the season, including reaching base five times in a doubleheader, including a double and a home run.

Another career highlight came on July 2, with the Red Sox trailing Nolan Ryan and the Texas Rangers 2-1 in the bottom of the seventh. Romine singled and scored on a double by Billy Jo Robidoux. In the bottom of the ninth off Kenny Rogers, Romine drove a pitch to deep left field for his second career walk-off homer.

That season Romine was hampered by shoulder problems and made only 39 starts.[28] He hit .272 with seven doubles and a pair of home runs.

Romine worked intensely over the offseason to rehabilitate his shoulder, but it did not fully heal. While he looked to have secured his status on the club as a utility outfielder for the 1991 season, the prospects of Romine, who turned 30 in May, becoming an everyday player looked slim.

Despite spending the entire season with the Red Sox, Romine was seldom used in what was to be his last season in the major leagues. His last major-league homer was a two-out grand slam on May 5 against Alex Fernandez of the Chicago White Sox. Any thoughts that this would lead to a bigger role on the club were extinguished when manager Morgan answered a question about whether Romine would get a start in the team's next game by simply replying, "He'll sit. That's his job."[29]

On July 29 Romine entered a game against the Texas Rangers in the first inning, replacing Greenwell in left field. He went 1-for-4, with a single off Jose Guzman. This was his last major-league hit. His last major-league appearance came on August 4 at Fenway Park against the Blue Jays, when he played as a defensive replacement for Tom Brunansky. Romine made only nine starts and played a full game only six times. With such infrequent playing time and an ongoing shoulder issue, it wasn't a surprise he struggled and hit only .164.

Romine retired after the season, citing nagging shoulder and knee problems.[30] He commented, "My knee was blown out at the time. … I wish I had played

longer, but things happen. You deal with injuries and it gets time to move on."[31] He also felt the pull of his young family, as Kevin and June had an 8-year-old daughter, Janelle, and two sons, Andrew, 5, and Austin, 2. Eight year later, the Romines had a second daughter, Rebecca.

Romine was grateful for the perspective his wife and children always provided "when I would come out of the locker room after a game and my wife and kids would be there to meet me with a smile on their faces. … It didn't matter whether or not we won or lost or if I had a good or bad day. There they were (with) unconditional love."[32]

The Romines raised their children in Lake Forest, California, After retirement, Romine went into law enforcement and eventually was a detective in the Los Angeles Police Department.[33] June worked as a special-education teacher. Kevin also played the role of devoted baseball father and built a batting cage with a pitching machine and 40-foot net. Of his sons, Andrew and Austin, Kevin recalled, "They were baseball rats even very young. Andrew would hide in my locker while Austin was hanging on my leg."[34]

As Austin and Andrew pursued the sport more seriously, Kevin helped each of them find a position where they excelled. At the age of 7, both were pitchers because they threw hard, but Andrew primarily played infield and Austin was a catcher.[35] Kevin coached his sons through childhood, beginning with tee-ball. He was careful never to push them into baseball or suggest they needed to play the game for his approval; he simply encouraged their love of the sport.

After the Philadelphia Phillies selected Andrew in the 36th round of the 2004 draft, Andrew chose to attend his father's alma mater, Arizona State University. He became the starting shortstop for the Sun Devils as a freshman, replacing Dustin Pedroia.[36] Austin signed a letter of intent to Arizona State, but he chose not to attend and was drafted by the Yankees in the second round of the 2007 draft. In the same draft, the Angels selected Andrew in the fifth round.

Andrew made his major-league debut on September 24, 2010. Austin made his on September 11, 2011. With Austin's debut, the Romines became the 14th family to have a father and two sons in the major leagues, joining such families as the Stottlemyres, the Alomars, and the Boones.

When Austin made his major-league debut, June wore an Angels jersey and a Yankees cap to the game, as a tribute to both of her sons. However, when it came to divided loyalties, Kevin chose differently and didn't wear any paraphernalia to the game. He said that he didn't have any issue with Austin playing for the Yankees, but added, "I do miss my Sox fans though. I am still a little Red, though."[37] The career Red Sox noted that he still can't bring himself to put on a Yankees or Angels cap.[38]

NOTES

1   Jon Goode, "Romine protects and serves," Boston.com, May 10, 2005, boston.com/sports/baseball/redsox/articles/2005/05/10/romine_protects_and_serves, accessed: August 15, 2015.

2   George Kimball, "Romine aims to stick around," *Boston Herald*, April 2, 1990: 78.

3   Mike DiGiovanna, "Romine Enjoys Life in Big Leagues," *Los Angeles Times*, July 26, 1986, articles.latimes.com/1986-07-26/sports/sp-208_1_minor-leagues, accessed August 1, 2015.

4   Earl Bloom, "Second time for third Romine," Orange County Register, June 19, 2013, http://www.ocregister.com/articles/romine-513583-high-third.html, accessed August 1, 2015.

5   DiGiovanna, "Romine Enjoys Life in Big Leagues."

6   Ibid.

7   Chaz Scoggins, "Around the Bases: Little things make Romine impressive," *New England Newsclip* (Lowell, Massachusetts), September 10, 1985: 17.

8   Goode, "Romine protects and serves."

9   Scoggins, "Around the Bases: Little things make Romine impressive," 18.

10 Ibid.

11 DiGiovanna, "Romine Enjoys Life in Big Leagues."

12 Joe Giuliotti, "Romine could miss salad days." *Boston Herald*, March 22, 1988.

13 Marvin Pave, "He's on the move," *Boston Globe*, June 6, 1988.

14 David Cataneo, "Romine's busy day sparks Fenway hope," *Boston Herald*, DATE: 11.

15 Stephen Harris, "Swinging the pine, not just riding it," *Boston Herald*, July 28, 1988: 87.

16 Harris, "Swinging the pine, not just riding it."

17 Kimball, "Romine aims to stick around."

18 Mike Shalin, "Romine stands critics, delivers," *Boston Herald*, July 19, 1989: 92.

19 Shalin, "Romine stands critics, delivers."

20 Joe Giuliotti, " 'Lazy' Isn't Word to Describe Romine," August 7, 1989.

21 Mike Shalin, "Romine's big day deserves high-five," *Boston Herald*, July 3, 1989: 59.

22 Shalin, "Romine's big day deserves high-five."

23 Giuliotti, " 'Lazy' Isn't Word to Describe Romine."

24 Shalin, "Romine stands critics, delivers."

25 Sarah Thomas, "Family Affair: Bees infielder Andrew Romine, brother Austin have followed in their father's footsteps," *Deseret News* (Salt Lake City), July 8, 2013, deseretnews.com/article/865582812/Family-affair-Bees-infielder-Andrew-Romine-brother-Austin-have-followed-in-their-fathers.html?pg=all accessed July 30, 2015.

26 Shalin, "Romine stands critics, delivers."

27 Mark Murphy, "Romine's been oh so fine," *Boston Herald*, July 28, 1989: 92.

28 Seth Livingstone, "Romine has Sox home," *Patriot Ledger* (Quincy, Massachusetts), March 13, 1991: 27.

29 Mel Antonen, "Red Sox's Romine: Ready and waiting," *USA Today*, May 8, 1991.

30 Jack Curry, "Family, Angels with Austin Romine on special day," My YES Network, September 15, 2011, myyesnetwork.com/16197/blog/2011/09/15/family,_angels_with_austin_romine_on_a_special_day, accessed August 15, 2015.

31 Goode, "Romine protects and serves."

32 Thomas, "Family Affair."

33 Anthony McCarron, "Family Guy: Yanks' Romine trying to follow in father's (and brother's) footsteps", *New York Daily News*, December 11, 2010, nydailynews.com/sports/baseball/yankees/new-york-yankees-prospect-austin-romine-follow-father-brother-footsteps-article-1.472806, accessed July 30, 2015.

34 McCarron, "Family Guy."

35 Ibid.

36 Goode, "Romine protects and serves."

37 McCarron, "Family Guy."

38 Thomas, "Family Affair."

JOE SAMBITO

By Gene Gumbs

CONSIDERING THAT HIS PROFESSIONAL career almost ended before it started, Joe Sambito made the most of his opportunity. His future in the game teetered several times, but for a period of five years, 1977-1981, the left-hander from Long Island, New York, with a good fastball and a nasty slider was arguably one of the best relievers in the National League. An elbow injury in 1982 changed the trajectory of his career, but Sambito, the grandson of Italian immigrants, still managed to get to the pinnacle of the baseball world by pitching in the All-Star Game in 1979 and the World Series in 1986.

Joseph Charles Sambito was born on June 28, 1952, in Brooklyn, New York, the first child for Anthony and Jennie (Olivieri) Sambito. All four of his grandparents came to the United States from Italy and settled in Brooklyn. (His parents grew up about 150 feet from each other.[1]) A sister, Annette, was born in 1954, followed by a brother, Robert, in 1957. Anthony Sambito worked as a foreman in the textile industry, and transferred his love of baseball to his firstborn.

"I do recall when I first started following major-league baseball," Sambito said. "It was the World Series in 1958, and the Yankees came from three to one down to beat the Braves. I got caught up in that, and I started understanding what my father was talking about. That was when I first understood what baseball was." He said he still vividly remembered his first trip to a major-league baseball game when he and his father made the car trip from Brooklyn to Yankee Stadium. "I remember parking about a mile away under the elevated trains and walking. I recall that walk taking forever. Finally we get there, and we go into the stadium and head up the ramp. Now I'm 7 years old, and all I see are people's bellies, because that's about how high I came up.

"We get to the top of the ramp—we're on field level in right field—and I dropped my father's hand, ran to the seats and looked up over the top and said, 'Holy cow, the grass is green!' Because the only thing I had seen to that point was black and white television. I was stunned by the colors. That made such a lasting impression on me."

Growing up, Sambito began to think he might have a chance to play professional baseball when scouts started showing up to the games he pitched for Bethpage High School. "I think it was my senior year when I first saw scouts and started to understand what they were all about. I would see these guys behind the backstop in their folding chairs with the notebook and the stopwatch, because that was back before radar guns. So I had to hope the guy had a quick-twitch thumb so my fastball would be a little bit quicker. I don't know how they ever did that."

After high school, Sambito was offered a scholarship to Adelphi University on Long Island. He helped the Panthers to a 20-7-1 record in 1972, and a 19-7 mark in 1973. He was named an All-American by the American Baseball Coaches Association in 1973, a first for the school. He threw a pair of shutouts that season, and his 1.27 ERA was, as of 2015, the third lowest single-season mark in Adelphi's history.[2]

Despite that, Sambito wasn't selected until the 17th round by the Houston Astros, something that surprised the lefty. "I expected to go earlier; I really did. I had people in my ear telling me I should go in the top five rounds. I said to myself, 'Well, that would be nice.' Again, not knowing much about it." This was the first time Sambito's potential career sat on a razor's edge. Word had circulated in the scouting world that he had a sore arm. The Astros' regional scouting director, Earl Rapp, called Sambito after the draft and indicated he would have to see him throw before offering him a contract, just to be certain there were no issues with Sambito's arm.

"So now I'm thinking to myself, 'What am I going to do?' because my arm was killing me," Sambito recalled, laughing. "The year before my elbow was sore as well, and I missed a lot of time in my sophomore year. So I thought to myself, 'If they find out I have a sore arm again, I'll never get a chance to play.' So I just kind of gritted my teeth. So I went out and threw—and it hurt. And I threw and it hurt, and I threw and it hurt. He took me through the paces for I'd say 10 or 15 minutes."

Sambito threw well enough to convince Rapp his arm was fine, and they went back to Sambito's house and hammered out a contract, with his father and mother in attendance. "And it wasn't much, believe me," Sambito said, chuckling.

It was the Vietnam War era, and because several of the Astros' minor leaguers had to leave the team to fulfill National Guard duty, the Astros assigned Sambito to their Double-A team in Columbus, Georgia. He was there for one game. He started a game a few days after being assigned, lasting just two innings.

"I gave up four runs in the first two innings because my arm was sore. I remember hanging a slider to a big left-handed hitter, who hit it forever. I came out after the second inning and went immediately to the trainer and said, 'I think I hurt my arm.' It was still part of my plan there," he recalled, laughing.

"So he said, 'We'll put ice on it; don't worry about it.' So I'm thinking he's a pro trainer. He must know I'm going to be okay. It was encouraging. Well, it turned out I was down for something like five weeks. And in that five weeks, with the treatment I was getting, the arm got better."

After the inauspicious debut, Sambito was assigned to Covington, Virginia, in the Rookie-level Appalachian League. He got in 11 games after rehabbing the arm, starting six. In his first game back, he took a no-hitter into the final frame of the seven-inning opener of a doubleheader. He threw a pair of shutouts that year, finishing with a 1.47 ERA and 57 strikeouts in 55 innings.

Sambito was assigned to Cedar Rapids of the Class-A Midwest League in 1974. The future reliever again showed excellent form as a starter. In 23 starts, he finished with an 11-8 record and a 3.00 ERA. He completed 12 games and fanned an impressive 182 batters in 156 innings.

While with Cedar Rapids, Sambito met another left-handed pitcher, Bob Cluck, who was to become a close friend. Cluck was a player-manager for a time that season in Cedar Rapids after manager Leo Posada was hit in the head by a line drive during batting practice. Cluck told Sambito, "'Joe, there was talk after your first year. There were some people in the organization that figured let's get rid of this guy; he's not going to make it.' But I guess there were more people who felt I showed them something and that they should bring me back and see what I can do."

Sambito moved to St. Petersburg, Florida, in 1974 after attending instructional league there in the offseason. There he met Denise Durocher, and the two were married in February of 1976. Joe became stepfather to Denise's 4-year-old son, Michael Lathrop, and the couple later had a daughter, Marisa.

Sambito was back in Double-A Columbus for the 1975 season, this time with better results. He pitched in 30 games, starting 28, and finished with a 12-9 record, a 3.01 ERA, and a league-leading 140 strikeouts. However, another scary moment arrived during an Instructional League game in the offseason when he suddenly felt some discomfort in his pitching shoulder. After 10 days of rest and ice failed to achieve the desired results, the Astros flew Sambito to Houston, where he received a cortisone shot.[3] A few shots later, Sambito was still in pain — but then he noticed something.

"This pain seemed to move," Sambito recalled. "Sometimes it was in front, sometimes in the back, and sometimes right on top. The night before I was to see the doctor, it was almost like it came to the surface. So I just drew an X around the pain. When I went in to see the doc the next day, I said, 'That's where it hurts, right there.'

"So he gave me a shot that was some cortisone and celestone, which is a pain reliever. It was a short needle and when he put it in there I felt like he pierced the pain. He said I should be fine in a couple of days. And the pain never came back."

The now pain-free newlywed returned to Columbus to start the 1976 campaign, starting 12 games and pitching to a 1.80 ERA in 100 innings. Then it was on to Triple-A, Memphis of the International League, for five games. He had a 3-0 record, but was roughed up, giving up 37 hits and 19 earned runs in 27 innings. Despite that, Sambito got the call from the Astros after the All-Star break, making his major-league debut on July 20, 1976, at Pittsburgh in the first game of a doubleheader.

His first appearance came just six batters into the game. Astros starter Tom Griffin was lifted after recording just one out, giving up three hits and a pair of runs, walking one, and hitting a batter.

"My major-league debut was with the bases loaded. Come on in, Joe!" he said with a laugh. "Well, I went

out there, and literally my knees are shaking. The first guy I am going to face is first baseman Richie Hebner. Lefty on lefty, just throw the ball over the plate; I should have a pretty good chance here. I walked Richie on four pitches and forced in a run."

The next batter was catcher Manny Sanguillen, who knocked a 3-and-2 pitch off the wall for a triple to clear the bases. "I think (Bill) Virdon knew it was a good time to see what I could do because we were so far behind," he said, laughing. "I ended up pitching another four innings in that game and did pretty well after that."

Sambito pitched in 19 more games that season, making four starts. Except for one start in 1977, they were the last of his major-league career. He earned his first save on September 24 at San Francisco, pitching the final three innings in relief of J.R. Richard in a 14-5 blowout.

The transition to the bullpen came easily for Sambito. "I was in the big leagues, and I didn't care how they used me as long as I could stay. That was my attitude. I am where I always wanted to be, so I was okay with it. And really, I didn't think I'd like it, but obviously it turned out that my stuff was better suited to the bullpen, and it worked.

"I learned to love it because I went to the stadium every day with a chance to get in there. I felt I could play a role in the outcome of today's game. It was an adrenaline flow for me."

Sambito really came into his own starting in 1977. He pitched in 54 games that season, throwing 89 innings with a 2.33 ERA, and finishing with a 5-5 record and seven saves. In 62 games in 1978, his ERA was higher at 3.07, but he struck out 96 batters in 88 innings. His 11 saves led the team.

The 1979 season saw Sambito make the All-Star team, though he didn't seem anywhere close to that when he took the mound in relief against the St. Louis Cardinals on May 1. J.R. Richard started the game and went the first seven, leaving with the score tied when the Astros scored twice in the top the eighth. Joaquin Andujar threw scoreless innings in the eighth and ninth, and Sambito came in to start the bottom of the 10th. He gave up a single and walked a pair of batters, but wiggled out of trouble, leaving the bases loaded when he got George Hendrick to fly out to center.

The Astros scored a pair of runs in the top of the 11th, and Sambito came up to bat with Rafael Landestoy on second and two outs. He doubled to right to give his team a three-run lead going into the bottom of the inning.

"I remember getting to the top step of the dugout, putting my hand in my glove and saying, 'Three outs before three runs.' Ya know? Just win the game," Sambito recalled.

Tony Scott led off the bottom of the 11th with a single for the Cards. Sambito struck out Ken Reitz, but then walked Ken Oberkfell and Steve Swisher to load the bases. He followed that with a strikeout of Garry Templeton for the second out.

"And then they send up a pinch-hitter named Roger Freed. Roger was an all-or-nothing guy. He was kind of a journeyman with good power," Sambito remembered. "Well, he works me to a full count, and I throw him a fastball a little higher than I wanted and he hits it out. He hits a grand slam to beat me. I mean, I was crushed. I couldn't believe it—neither could the Cardinal fans. In fact, I became a fan favorite in St. Louis for a while."

After that game, Sambito didn't give up another earned run in 27 straight appearances leading into the All-Star break, a total of 40⅔ innings, which lowered his ERA to 0.95. Perhaps the two most impressive performances were consecutive appearances against the New York Mets on June 10 and June 18, when he threw nine scoreless innings.

It's the selection to the All-Star team that Sambito recalled as the likely pinnacle of his career, especially considering that five years earlier he was on the razor's edge of having his career ending in its infancy.

"That's how quickly it happened, and that's why I scratch my head," Sambito said. "I wondered, 'How did this all happen, and why me?' I mean I played with guys that were better, but some had health issues, some couldn't handle the baseball life, whatever it was. It all just kind of worked for me."

The most surreal moment for him, he said, was just going into the locker room and sitting down. "I looked around the room at guys like Pete Rose, Joe Morgan, Steve Carlton, Gary Carter, Gaylord Perry—all guys that ended up being Hall of Famers—except for Pete, of course. I asked myself, 'What am I doing here?' I didn't say it out loud, of course, but I looked around and wondered, 'Do I even belong here?'

"Tom Lasorda was talking to us. … Chub Feeney was the National League president, and he came in and gave us a pep talk like it was the seventh game of the World Series. I'm telling you, that was when it was the real rivalry, the American League and National League. We went out of there pumped."

Sambito got into the game in the sixth after Gaylord Perry got into a jam, giving up a run on three hits without recording an out. Sambito got Reggie Jackson to ground into a fielder's choice to second, intentionally walked Roy Smalley, and got George Brett on a fly to center. He was then lifted in favor of righty Mike LaCoss to face right-hander Don Baylor. The National League won the game 7-6 with a run in the top of the ninth.

Sambito's string of scoreless appearances ended the first time out after the break when he gave up homers to Bill Robinson and Phil Garner in a 6-5 loss to Pittsburgh on July 21. He finished the season with 63 appearances, 91⅓ innings, a stingy 1.77 ERA, and a career-best 22 saves for an Astros team that finished a game and a half behind the Cincinnati Reds in the NL West.

He followed up his All-Star season with another impressive year in 1980. Sambito made a career-high 64 appearances and allowed just 65 hits and 22 walks in 90⅓ innings, striking out 75. His final ERA of 2.19 was a little skewed from one appearance when he gave up four runs without recording an out against the Cardinals.

The Astros family was struck with tragedy during the season, something that could have derailed the team's success. Thirty-year-old flamethrower J.R. Richard suffered a stroke on July 30 after posting a 10-4 record and a 1.90 ERA.

"We were on the road (when it happened)," Sambito recalled. "J.R. did not make the trip. He was on the disabled list. He had been complaining of a tired arm. It was really interesting. He'd go out, and for the first three innings he was untouchable. It seemed like around the fourth inning he'd take himself out of the game and say his arm was tired, and then five days later he's able to go out and do it again. So there were a lot of questions about what was going on."

He recalled that no one really understood exactly what had happened. "Like most people our age, unless they're hit with it from a family member, we don't really know what that is. I don't know if I understood what it was until we got the explanation."

Sambito's performance helped the Astros tie the Los Angeles Dodgers in the NL West and force a one-game playoff. Joe Niekro dominated the Dodgers, 7-1, in the showdown, sending Houston to the NL Championship Series against the Philadelphia Phillies.

"That game came on the heels of us losing three straight games to the Dodgers, setting up the one-game playoff," Sambito said. "With Niekro pitching, I felt we had our most consistent guy going and the guy who I felt would pose the most problems for the Dodger lineup."[4]

In Game Two of the NLCS, Sambito faced two batters, walking one, and striking out one, as the Astros won 7-4.

He got the call again in Game Four with runners at first and third and no outs in the eighth and the game tied, 2-2. He struck out Bake McBride and then gave up a sacrifice fly to Manny Trillo that gave the Phillies a 3-2 lead. Mike Schmidt tried to tag from first on the play and was thrown out to retire the side. The Astros tied it in the bottom of the ninth and Sambito took the mound for the 10th. He gave up a one-out single to Rose. After he got Schmidt to line to left for the second out, Greg Luzinski and Trillo followed with doubles to give the Phillies a 5-3 win.

Sambito retired the only batter he faced in Game Five, which the Phillies won 8-7 in 10 innings, dashing the Astros' World Series hopes.

"Having lost the three games leading up to the playoff put us at a disadvantage in that we no longer had our number-one pitcher going in Game One, plus the fact we had to travel from LA to Philadelphia immediately following the playoff game, arriving in the early-morning hours and having to play later that day," Sambito said.[5]

During the strike-shortened 1981 season, Sambito made 49 appearances and finished with a 1.84 ERA in 63⅔ innings. The Astros won the second half of the season in the NL West and made it to the playoffs for the second straight year, this time against the Dodgers.

After the Astros took Game One, 3-1, Game Two went into the 11th inning in a scoreless tie. Sambito pitched a scoreless top of the 11th and earned the victory when pinch-hitter Denny Walling drove home Phil Garner in the bottom of the frame for the 1-0 victory and a 2-0 series lead. LA came back to win Game Three, 6-1. Sambito came on in the eighth and gave up three runs in two-thirds of an inning. He would not get in Games Four or Five, and the Dodgers came back to win the series, three games to two.

The 1982 season started well for Sambito. He made nine appearances, giving up just one earned run in 12⅔ innings and earning four saves before an elbow injury ended his season. He wouldn't step back onto the mound until the 1984 campaign. It was the early days of Tommy John surgery, and neither Sambito nor his doctor knew exactly what his recovery would look like. They took a tendon from his right leg to repair his injured left elbow.

"Nine months out I developed problems with excessive scarring in the area and it restricted my ulnar nerve," Sambito said. "My fingers in my hand were getting numb. They had to go back and clean out the scar tissue, and that meant that I missed the entire 1983 season."

When he returned in 1984, the one thing Sambito knew was that his normal fastball velocity was not there. He started the season in Triple-A Tucson, making eight appearances there before being recalled by the Astros.

Another adjustment Sambito had to make when getting back to Houston was the fact that Frank DiPino had taken over the closer role in his absence. He put up respectable numbers, finishing with a 3.02 ERA in 32 games, but it was the first time in his career he'd failed to record a save during a season.

At the end of the spring training in 1985, the Astros told Sambito they wanted him to start the year in Tucson again. Because he had enough service time to refuse an assignment to the minors, he asked Houston for his release, which they granted.

"It was difficult," Sambito said. "Houston was where I grew up. The nucleus of the team was pretty much the same, and I always felt a part of that. It was not an easy decision. I really respected Al Rosen, but it was time for me to go, I felt."

The New York Mets signed Sambito on April 26, and it looked as though Sambito would have a chance to pitch in his native state. "At the time, my mother was still living there, and our home was only about 20 miles from Shea Stadium, so I just stayed with her until I felt I could get things back the way they should be."

Unfortunately for Sambito, his stay there was short. After just two months the Mets asked him to accept an assignment to Tidewater of the International League. In just eight appearances with the Mets, Sambito had a 12.66 ERA and had walked eight while striking out just three in 10⅔ innings.

Manager Davey Johnson asked Sambito to considering accepting the demotion to get his skills sharp, and

promising to get him back up as soon as he could. This time Sambito accepted the assignment, knowing his stuff was not where it should be, but the call never came. In fact, he struggled in Tidewater as well. He gave up 31 hits in 20⅔. He asked the Mets for his release, which they granted on August 23.

Still convinced he had something left in the tank, Sambito headed home to St. Petersburg and began working out at the Cardinals' complex with six other major leaguers who lived in the area. He also had some help from Billy Connors, who at the time was the pitching coach for the Chicago Cubs.

"One day I was out there, and Lee Thomas, who at the time was the farm director for the Cardinals, just happened to be in town," Sambito said. "He asked me if I would be willing to go down to Venezuela to play in the winter. His Triple-A manager was down there, and he said he wanted to see if it would work for me."

Sambito decided to go and pitched fairly well. A scout for the Boston Red Sox saw him throw and several weeks later he got a call from them, offering him a chance to come to camp in 1986 as a nonroster invitee.

Sambito made the Red Sox out of camp, thanks in large part to a heavy dose of the Detroit Tigers. "The Tigers were in our division back then, and we played them an awful lot in the spring because Lakeland and Winter Haven are very close together," Sambito said. "It seemed like we were playing them almost every other day, and they were loaded with lefties. I had no problem getting those lefties out, and that's how I made the team."

While he wasn't exactly a lefty specialist, Sambito was effective against them. During the 1986 season left-handed hitters batted just .200 against him, while righties hit a robust .368. "I didn't have the same fastball after surgery," Sambito said. "So I was working from a disadvantage there, but I was still able to throw the breaking ball over the plate. Although it wasn't as hard and sharp, I was getting lefties out. I threw with a low three-quarter arm angle, and I could keep lefties on their heels and still hit the outside part of the plate."

Sambito finished the year with 53 appearances, a 2-0 record with 12 saves, and a 4.84 ERA. More importantly, he helped the Red Sox win the American League East by 5½ games over the Yankees.

The Red Sox won the ALCS in seven games over the California Angels. Sambito got into three games, throwing just two-thirds of an inning and allowing one hit. For the first time in his career, the now 34-year-old left-hander was headed to the World Series.

The Red Sox lost the World Series in seven games to the New York Mets. Sambito pitched in two games. He gave up two hits and a run without recording an out in Game Three, a 7-1 loss. He got into Game Seven with one out in the seventh inning after Calvin Schiraldi had yielded two runs. He walked two, one intentionally, and surrendered a sacrifice fly. The Mets scored twice more off Al Nipper in the eighth to win the Series.

"I think there were many times I could have hung it up and walked away," Sambito said. "We should have won it, but I don't dwell on that. Again, I pinch myself still and wonder how I got that far. I found myself in a World Series in a year that maybe I shouldn't have been in baseball."

One of the other great things for Sambito in 1986 was the opportunity to play with Tom Seaver, a pitcher he idolized growing up in New York. It meant so much to him that when he saved Seaver's first win with the Red Sox, on July 1, 1986, in Fenway Park, Sambito went out of his way to retrieve the ball he'd thrown for the final out.[6]

"I think that Tom Seaver is the guy that I am most glad I got a chance to play with a little bit and get to know. It was really interesting how he would sit in the clubhouse and start talking about pitching, and those guys would crowd around hoping to get an earful.

"Nolan (Ryan) was that way in Houston too. Nolan didn't say much, but when he did, people stopped doing what they were doing."

Sambito was back with the Red Sox for the 1987 season. The team, which had won 95 games in '86, fell to 78-84 and finished 20 games behind the Detroit Tigers. Likewise, Sambito's numbers declined. Pitching in 47 games, he finished with an inflated 6.93 ERA and tied a career high by giving up eight home runs. He was still effective against lefties, holding them to a .241 average. His final appearance with Boston was a scoreless inning against the Milwaukee Brewers on October 3, 1987.

At the end of the year, Sambito had reached a crossroads. "It was just a bad year," Sambito said. "I still wanted to pitch, but I knew it's not good when you get into your mid-30s and you start aching. That's when mortality starts kicking you a little bit."[7]

Sambito decided to give it one more try, and when the Astros invited him to spring training a week after it started, he decided to accept. "The deal was, allow me to come into camp; my arm's feeling good," Sambito said. "If I make the team, great; that's what I want. If I don't, I'll call it a career and go home quietly."

The Astros cut Sambito on the final weekend of the spring, but because he'd thrown well, they asked him to take an assignment to Triple-A. He decided to report to Tucson, with the understanding that he didn't plan to stay there all year if he didn't see they had room for him.

He pitched well enough in Tucson that other teams took notice. "My agent at the time had nosed around, and the Texas Rangers made an offer for me that would have taken me from Tucson to Arlington, but the Astros wouldn't trade me because I was pitching well and they had only one lefty in the bullpen up in the big leagues. When I got wind of that I was not happy. I'm not Triple-A insurance. I think I'd earned the right, and if I've got a chance for an upward move, please let me move. I guess I could have walked away then, but I didn't."

Sambito continued to pitch in Tucson, but he could feel trouble on the horizon. "It's interesting that from that point — about mid-May to mid-July — I could feel that my shoulder was aching and my hand was starting to hurt me. So I called the Astros two weeks before the All-Star break. I didn't tell them I was hurting, but I said, 'I'll go up to the All-Star break. I'm just letting you know so you can find a replacement. I'm not just going to not show up one day. If I'm not in the big leagues with you or someone else at the All-Star break I am just going to go home and it'll be the end of the road."

The Astros never made a move to promote him, so Joe walked away at the end of July 1988. He wasn't unemployed for long.

He had been represented by agents Randy and Alan Hendricks while he was a player. They had indicated that they would like the personable Sambito to work for Hendricks Sports Management when his career ended. By September, he was in the Instructional League looking over young players.

"I knew I wanted to stay in baseball, but I didn't want to go on the field," Sambito said. "I got some calls to be a pitching coach, but I just needed more control over my life. I need to make plans to be where I want to be, as opposed to where the itinerary says I have to be. It was time to get off the field. I felt I was still in baseball—and I still feel that way."

One final baseball honor came to Sambito in 2013 when he was inducted into the Bethpage High School Athletic Walk of Fame.

After Sambito and his first wife divorced in 1997, his new profession led him to a next chapter in his life. While at spring-training game in Tampa to meet some clients, he met the woman who would become his second wife, Jennifer. A practicing attorney, five months after they met, Jennifer was offered a position in Houston, where Joe was based with Hendricks. Five months after they met, Jennifer was offered a position in Houston, where Joe was based with Hendricks. They started dating and later moved to Southern California, where they were married. They have a daughter, Sophia, and a son, Giovanni Antonio.

As of 2015 Sambito continued his work as an agent, now working for Relativity Baseball, after 23 years with the Hendricks brothers.

"After all the dreams I've lived, and all the great things I got to do because of baseball, I met her, and my post-baseball life has been the family. I couldn't be happier."

NOTES

1   Author interview with Joe Sambito, May 22, 2015. All quotations attributed to Sambito are from this interview unless otherwise indicated.

2   Adelphi University 2015 Baseball Media Guide

3   *The Evening Independent* (St. Petersburg, Florida), January 11, 1980.

4   *The Astros Daily*, September 4, 2001.

5   Ibid.

6   *New York Times*, July 3, 1986.

7   Ibid.

DAVE SAX

By Richard Bogovich

"**B**ASEBALL'S CLICHÉS REMAIN LARGELY unchanged through the years," observed the writer Mordecai Richler in a 1986 essay for *GQ*.[1] His first examples were the types of gripes from marginal pitchers and backup fielders: "If only they give me a chance to start, I know I can help this team," and "I know I'm a .300 hitter, but they've got to play me every day." Any such protestation from Dave Sax was more legitimate than most, validated while with the Red Sox in 1986 when he was the first player recognized with a tongue-in-cheek award for little-used major leaguers.

Dave Sax, who ultimately played in 37 major-league games spread across five seasons, is about 16 months older than 1982 NL Rookie of the Year Steve Sax. If you told their high-school teammates in 1976 that only one brother would become a five-time All-Star in the majors, by all accounts they would've found it difficult to predict which.

David John Sax was born in Sacramento, California, on September 22, 1958, to John Thomas Sax and the former Nancy Jane Colombani. John and Nancy, who knew one another before high school, also raised three daughters, Cheryl, Dana, and Tamara. In the mid-1960s the family moved to a farm outside the city, though John Sax also worked as a truck driver. Their father had reportedly been good enough at baseball as a high schooler in Sacramento to take their team's starting shortstop job from eventual major leaguer Woodie Held, who was three years older.[2]

Dave remembered that as a kid he and Steve "always seemed to be on the same team, from Little League, through Babe Ruth and high school and all that."[3] According to *Sacramento Bee* sportswriter Don Bosley, before Steve joined Dave on the varsity squad at Yolo County's James Marshall High School in 1976, Dave had already drawn attention from pro scouts and developed his own fandom. Nevertheless, Marshall

coach Norm Marks remembered Dave as "quiet and reserved," unlike Steve.[4] After the end of that season Dave was a co-player of the year in the interscholastic Golden Empire League[5] and was named as a third baseman to the Citizens Savings all-Northern California high-school team.[6] Dave was also named the Sacramento area's player of the year by virtue of the third highest average among local batters, at .460, along with a 1.20 earned-run average and a 7-2 won-lost record as a pitcher. By the end of 1976 he received additional recognition as the *East Yolo Record*'s Athlete of the Year.[7]

During the summer of 1977 Dave and Steve were starring together in American Legion baseball for the East Yolo team.[8] Separately from Steve, who was still in high school, Dave was also starring in baseball for nearby Cosumnes River College. In 1978 Dave was

Dave Sax, in his Dodgers uniform

named Northern California's junior-college Player of the Year. But a dream came true for only one of the Sax brothers on June 6, when Steve was selected by the Los Angeles Dodgers in that year's amateur draft, and Dave was ignored. "I saw all these guys with lesser numbers than me that were being drafted, and I was just wondering what was going on," Dave said.[9]

"We couldn't figure out why my brother wasn't drafted," Steve told an MLB.com blogger in 2014. "He was setting records up and down the state in junior college, and he certainly had all the tools to be a major leaguer. He was more highly touted than I was."

"When the scout came, my mom asked why he wasn't drafted," Steve said.[10] While Steve was signing his contract, Nancy Sax spoke up for her older son because her husband was recovering from a heart attack, his second in seven years. Scout Ron King apparently didn't have a satisfactory answer, so the next day he put Dave to the test at the high school's diamond, with fielding assistance from the youngest Sax, Tammy. Another day later, King took Dave to a tryout camp in Santa Rosa, and then signed him.[11]

As a result, both Dave and Steve soon found themselves on the Dodgers' rookie-league team in Lethbridge, Alberta. In the Lethbridge paper on June 22, manager Jim Lefebvre commented on players assigned to him. He said that Dave "shows lots of poise. He adjusts well, has a good bat and I am very pleased with him."[12] Dave played in 44 games, mostly at second base, and hit .269. Steve played in 39 games, exclusively at shortstop, and hit .328.

The brothers spent the 1979 season with the Dodgers' A-level affiliate in Clinton, Iowa, though both played different positions. Dave hit .270 in 97 games, mostly as a catcher. Steve played mostly outfield and second base while hitting .290 in 115 games. Dave also pitched in a game for two innings, both scoreless, and earned the victory. Dave played in the Midwest League All-Star Game that year but Steve wasn't selected.

The brothers also spent 1980 at the Single-A level, except that they spent about half of the season apart.

Steve played all year with Vero Beach in the Florida State League. Dave's other assignment that year was with Lodi in the California League. Without Steve around, Dave hit a mere .171 in 43 games, in stark contrast to his sparkling .352 average in 58 games for Vero Beach. Overall he caught in as many games as he had in 1979 but saw almost as much action as an outfielder.

The brothers were reunited with Double-A San Antonio in 1981, and both were Texas League All-Stars. Steve was named the league's Player of the Year after winning the batting title. Dave's average was also above .300, though he got into only 62 games. He again played almost as much in the outfield as behind the plate. Steve was called up to the Dodgers to sub for the injured Davey Lopes at second base and made his major-league debut on August 18. He then saw a little bit of action in the NL playoffs, logged his first World Series at-bat, and was in the majors to stay.

Dave Sax was at least promoted again for 1982, to the Albuquerque Dukes. He would never play another minor-league game below the Triple-A level. He displayed his most versatility to date, with 47 games as a catcher but just as many combined at third, first, and in the outfield. He hit .317 with career highs in games (117), home runs (12), runs scored (71), and RBIs (75). Dave had impressed enough by midseason for there to be open speculation about a promotion to join Steve with the Dodgers.

"It would be real nice to keep playing together on the Dodgers," Dave said. "But everyone wants to get to the big leagues like Steve has, and if I have to get there with another team, I'd want that opportunity."[13] Dave was indeed called up, and on September 1 he made his major-league debut with an at-bat against the St. Louis Cardinals. He had only one other plate appearance, also hitless, before the season's end.

A milestone of a different kind occurred the following month. On October 23 Dave married Patsy Gustafson Inderkum, another James Marshall graduate who was a young widow. In 1980 Patsy had married George Inderkum Jr., and their daughter, Summer, was born later that year. However, two days after Christmas, George was killed when his motorcycle crashed on a remote California road.

During spring training of 1983 Dave made an impression on at least one prominent sportswriter. In previewing the Dodgers' season, Roger Angell, writing for the *New Yorker*, drew attention to "their homegrown 1983 batch of pre-certified rookie stars like Greg Brock, Dave Sax, and Candy Maldonado, the new line of Cadillacs off the Los Angeles production line."[14] Brock would start 129 games at first base for the Dodgers that season and in 1984 Maldonado would play 102 games in the Dodgers outfield.

Dave Sax spent part of 1983 back with Albuquerque, but only made it into 75 games because of some stints with Steve and Los Angeles. He had an even better average of .343, accompanied by a career-best .529 slugging percentage for Albuquerque. Dave was summoned by Los Angeles in mid-May after catcher Mike Scioscia suffered a torn rotator cuff.

Dave and Steve made history on June 3 as the first brothers to ever start together for the Dodgers. Dave subbed for longtime catcher Steve Yeager, who was recovering from a bruised right shoulder. Alas, it did not go well from the beginning. On a steal attempt by the New York Mets' Hubie Brooks in the first inning, Dave threw inaccurately past Steve, and the Mets stole three more bases off him on the way to a 5-2 win.

Any dejection that Dave may have felt was supplanted one week later. It fell to Dodgers manager Tommy Lasorda to inform the Sax brothers that their father had suffered another heart attack (his fifth) and died, just a few days after Lasorda had delivered similar news to shortstop Bill Russell. John Sax was only 47 years old. Dave and Steve immediately left for home.

"It was really sad," Lasorda said. "If you could have seen the reaction of those two youngsters. We all cried." It was a doubly awful day for Dave in particular, as he was also demoted to Albuquerque in favor of catcher Gilberto Reyes. A reporter said that Lasorda wouldn't comment on when or if Dave Sax would return.[15]

Yeager went on the disabled list at the beginning of August and Dave was called up again, for about two weeks. All told, Dave didn't actually see much more action for LA during 1983 and went hitless in eight plate appearances across seven games. Instead, Los Angeles tried rookie catcher Jack Fimple in 54 games and Reyes behind the plate 19 times.

Through 1983 Dave had a .301 average in the minor leagues, but for 1984 it was back to Albuquerque again. Mike Scioscia returned to the Dodgers in fine shape and caught in 112 games, and Yeager caught in 65, so Dave didn't play for LA at all that season. He played in 106 games for the Dukes, roughly 30 percent more than in 1983, but he scored and drove in fewer runs while his average plunged to .259. On October 15 he was released.

On January 23, 1985, Dave Sax changed direction in his pro career by signing with the Red Sox. During spring training it was reported that he was in competition with veteran Jeff Newman for the second backup to starting catcher Rich Gedman. Boston played the Dodgers toward the end of March, and Dodgers players tried to help Dave while Newman was catching.[16] However, Dave "was reportedly unhappy when [brother] Steve stole second and third base … with the Dodgers already leading, 8-3, and already having stolen 5 of 7 against Newman," according to one reporter. Steve's late steals were interpreted as an attempt to additionally embarrass Newman and enhance Dave's bid to stick with the Red Sox as a backup catcher/first baseman, which he was already likely to do."[17] In fact, Jeff Newman never played in a regular-season major-league game again.

Within days the Red Sox announced their Opening Day roster, and Dave Sax was on it. "I can't believe I've actually made it," he said. "When the Red Sox picked me up, they told me I had a chance, but I assumed I'd get a Triple-A chance."[18]

During April, at least, it wasn't much of a chance. He waited until April 21 to make his first official appearance for Boston, as a ninth-inning pinch-runner. Not quite a week later, the Red Sox decided to call up pitcher Mike Brown from Pawtucket, and Dave was sent down.

In early June Boston put backup catcher Marc Sullivan on the disabled list, and Dave Sax was recalled. Rich Gedman soon injured his ankle so on June 8 Dave found himself starting, as catcher for Bruce Kison against the Baltimore Orioles. Boston won, 2-1, and in the fourth inning Dave's first major-league hit advanced the winning run from second to third.

The next day Dave caught Oil Can Boyd's three-hit shutout in Baltimore. "Sax deserves double credit, having caught a fine game for Kison and an even better one for Boyd," observed Larry Whiteside of the *Boston Globe*. "Sax thought the credit should go to Boyd and not him."

"I just sat there," Dave said. "And he threw strikes. The rest was easy."[19]

"The best game I ever threw was to a catcher named Dave Sax," Boyd recalled in 2012. Boyd agreed that he had made it easy for Dave, by being very decisive on the mound after Gedman told him how nervous Dave seemed before the game. Between innings, Boyd said Dave "would come back to the dugout and sit next to me and he would just turn—he had a big, pretty smile—he would just sit and smile and say, 'That's amazing.'"[20]

The next day Dave caught Bob Ojeda's 4-2 win over the Brewers, though Gedman came in to catch the ninth. He made a fourth straight start, in a 5-3 loss, after which Gedman returned to the starting lineup. Around that time Marc Sullivan agreed to a 20-day rehab assignment with Pawtucket, and Dave Sax still found himself with the team after the All-Star break because Gedman wasn't at 100 percent. As a result, he played a key role in an unusual event in Red Sox history. In lousy weather against the White Sox on July 31, his sacrifice fly in the seventh inning tied the game at 1-1, after which it was called due to a soaked field at Fenway. The tie broke a streak for Boston that dated back to June 8, 1961, and had been the longest stretch for a team without a tie in the majors at that time.

Dave was also in a position to chime in during September when Peter Gammons asked a few Red Sox about voluntary drug testing. "To me, the only people who should have any real problem with the tests are those who are using drugs," Dave said. "So get them out."[21]

In the end, Dave played only 20 games with Pawtucket, though only two more than that with the Red Sox. Still, that would represent the most action he'd see in any major-league season. He had 43 plate appearances for Boston scattered across those 22 games but hit an admirable .306.

The offseason began on a very nice note, when Dave and wife Patsy celebrated the birth of their second daughter, Lindsey, on November 5, and Dave would have his only Topps baseball card in the set for the 1986 season. Dave made the Opening Day roster again, but by mid-May he was the only player still around from then who hadn't played, and he was sent to Pawtucket. Marty Noble of *Newsday* playfully announced that Dave had thus won the first "a-Trophy," intended to evoke the noun "atrophy," a distinction he would also proclaim in subsequent seasons, though Jayson Stark of the *Philadelphia Inquirer* also took a leadership role in drawing attention to whoever was unfortunate enough to be the last player to get into a game after Opening Day.[22]

Dave hit .289 in Pawtucket in 99 games, and did play a little for the Red Sox from mid-September until the end of the 1986 season. Actually, he was preparing to catch the 10th inning of a game on September 3 but the Red Sox ended up scoring the winning run in the ninth. Though he didn't play much that month, the day before his birthday he filled in for an achy Bill Buckner at first base and even batted third. He rose to the occasion by going 2-for-3 and hitting his only major-league home run, the game-winning RBI, in a 3-2 game against Toronto. He made it into only four games but hit .455.

The Red Sox received permission to have four ineligible players in uniform for the ALCS, including Tom Seaver, Jeff Sellers, and Glenn Hoffman in addition to

Dave, and at least into mid-October Dave and Glenn were still taking batting practice. "They have remained as part of the postseason Red Sox picture because that's the way manager John McNamara wanted it," Neil Singelais of the *Boston Globe* wrote during the World Series. "He felt that each had something to offer, even if their value was confined to the dugout."

"Mac asked if I wanted to stay here and help out in the bullpen," Dave Sax said. "He said I should keep myself ready just in case. He figured he'd need two catchers, Marc Sullivan and myself, in the event that two pitchers were warming up at the same time in the bullpen."[23]

During 1987 spring training Steve Sax reflected on his brother's career. "It's tough because I know David could do the job. He was always a better hitter than me and he still is," Steve said. "I think he might hit .350 in time. And that's not a brother talking. It's the truth. I hit .322 last year and he can hit better than me."

"It's frustrating," Steve continued. "I just happened to be in the right place at the right time and David never has been. They've just got to give him a chance. Maybe this year."[24]

On Opening Day 1987 Dave found himself on the Boston roster for the third straight season, and that year he saw action much earlier than in the other two. On April 19 it was reported that his salary was $85,000 (after an erroneous report that it was $740,000).[25] However, he wasn't around much after that. He had a third hitless at-bat on the 26th and before the end of the month he was heading to Pawtucket to make room for Marty Barrett, who was coming off the disabled list. Dave Sax would never play in another major-league game.

On October 15 Dave was granted free agency, and on Halloween he signed with the Texas Rangers. After spring training in 1988 he was assigned to their Triple-A farm team, the Oklahoma City 89ers. As a result, he flew from spring training in Florida to Sacramento and then spent three days driving to

Oklahoma with Patsy and their daughters, who were 2 and 7 years old at the time.

"Sax rented an apartment and his wife was unpacking when he reported to All Sports Stadium … and was told he'd been traded to Buffalo," wrote *Oklahoman* sportswriter Volney Meece sympathetically. "So it was repack, get back in the car and make a non-leisurely drive to Buffalo. While his wife is unpacking again today, Sax will fly to Nashville to join the Bison."[26]

On April 6 Texas had traded Dave to the Pittsburgh Pirates for minor leaguer Billie Merrifield. Dave spent just one season with Buffalo. Steve signed with the Yankees on November 23, 1988, and it was reported that Dave joined that organization in mid-December, just in time for the Christmas birth of his son, David, Jr. He didn't play much for Buffalo in 1988, nor in 1989 with the Yankees' top farm club, Columbus, but his playing time would grow with Columbus in 1990 and 1991; during the latter season he got into 99 games. After a fourth year with Columbus, he called it quits at the start of 1993. He hit .278 in nearly 800 games during 11 Triple-A seasons. All told, in the minors he caught in 452 games, played third base in 153, in the outfield in 101, and at first base in 99.

Shortly after Dave announced his retirement, two commentators echoed sentiments offered by Steve Sax shortly before Dave's final game in the majors. "It seems like Dave wasn't ever in the right place at the right time," said Norm Marks, his old coach in high school.

"I thought he was a much better catcher than some people thought in the Red Sox organization," said Walt Hriniak, Boston's batting and first-base coach during 1986 and 1987. "Sometimes it's a matter of being in the right place at the right time. Sometimes that line is very thin."[27]

Twenty years later, Dave Sax was spending his time as a dairy distributor. He and Patsy were living near Sacramento, across the street from brother Steve, close as always. Sadly, on August 9, 2015, the Sax family had to endure an episode of the A&E documentary series

Intervention focusing on the plight of David Sax, Jr., who was struggling with a crystal meth addiction.

NOTES

1 Mordecai Richler, "You Know Me, Ring," *Dispatches from the Sporting Life* (Guilford, Connecticut: Lyons Press, 2002), 87.

2 The primary source for details about John Sax's youth and Dave's life before high school is Sara Solovitch, *Playing Scared: A History and Memoir of Stage Fright* (New York: Bloomsbury Publishing USA, 2015).

3 Michael Madden, "Sax' Number Isn't Up," *Boston Globe*, March 21, 1987: 25.

4 Don Bosley, "Sax Lessons: Baseball Has Been Kind, Cruel to Steve, Dave," *Sacramento Bee*, March 9, 1993: C1.

5 "All-League Teams Are Announced," *Mountain Democrat* (Placerville, California), June 3, 1976: A6.

6 "Ferroni, Ohrenschall Are Selected," *Independent Journal* (San Rafael, California), June 17, 1976: 17.

7 "More 1976 Newsmakers," *East Yolo Record* (Fair Oaks, California), January 5, 1977: 4.

8 For example, see "Legion team sweeps weekend series," *East Yolo Record* (Fair Oaks, California), July 13, 1977: 9. In a weekend series sweep by the Post 440 team against Fort Sutter, Dave Sax went 3-for-4 and had the winning hit in a 10-inning victory, while Steve went 2-for-4 to help them win another game that was decided by one run.

9 Bosley.

10 Cary Osborne, "Reminiscing with Steve Sax," April 19, 2014, dodgers.mlblogs.com/2014/04/19/reminiscing-with-steve-sax/.

11 Bosley.

12 Garry Allison, "Manager Lefebvre Assesses His Dodger Lineup," *Lethbridge* (Alberta) *Herald*, June 22, 1978: 20.

13 Earl Bloom, "Dave Sax in Position for Promotion," *Orange County Register* (Anaheim, California), June 27, 1982: D2.

14 Roger Angell, "The Sporting Scene (Baseball)," the *New Yorker*, April 25, 1983: 56.

15 Peter Schmuck, "Saxes Leave Team After Father Dies," *Orange County Register* (Anaheim, California), June 11, 1983: D3.

16 Gordon Edes, "Dodgers Close Call: Line Drive Hits Howe's Left Arm," *Los Angeles Times*, March 29, 1985: 7.

17 Ross Newhan, "Whitaker Has Second Thoughts About Third," *Los Angeles Times*, March 31, 1985: 5.

18 Nick Cafardo, "Red Sox make final cuts," *Lewiston* (Maine) *Daily Sun*, April 5, 1985: 23.

19 Larry Whiteside, "Sox Bury Orioles Behind Boyd, 12-0," *Boston Globe*, June 10, 1985: 33.

20 Dennis Boyd and Mike Shalin, *They Call Me Oil Can: Drugs, and Life on the Edge* (Chicago: Triumph Books, 2012), 136.

21 Peter Gammons, "Will Players Play Ball? Red Sox Have Mixed Reaction to Voluntary Testing," *Boston Globe*, September 25, 1985: 69.

22 For a history of this "award," see Marty Noble, "Hughes wins (not-so) coveted a-Trophy," April 16, 2010, at m.mlb.com/news/article/9341364/.

23 Neil Singelais, "Not Just Sitting Around," *Boston Globe*, October 24, 1986: 60.

24 Jim Van Vliet, " 'Other' Sax Waits, Wishes," *Sacramento Bee*, February 19, 1987: C1.

25 Dan Shaughnessy, "Timing Was Right for Nieves' No-Hitter," *Boston Globe*, April 19, 1987: 64.

26 Volney Meece, "Passing Thoughts for OSU," *The Oklahoman* (Oklahoma City), April 9, 1988.

27 Bosley.

CALVIN SCHIRALDI

By David Forrester

IF CALVIN SCHIRALDI HAD NEVER BEEN CALLED upon to pitch in the sixth game of the 1986 World Series, we might think of his career in baseball as a story of encountering and overcoming adversity—a series of comebacks. But Red Sox manager John McNamara *did* call Schiraldi in from the bullpen in the bottom of the eighth. And his name became synonymous with crumbling under pressure.

A hard-throwing right-handed pitcher since high school, Schiraldi spent eight years in the majors with six different teams between 1984 and 1991. He never again reached the level of performance he had in 1986, when he emerged from Triple-A Pawtucket to become the Red Sox' closer. His combined won-lost record for the two teams was 8-5 as he earned 21 saves and 114 strikeouts in 95 innings with a 2.08 ERA.

Calvin Drew Schiraldi was born on June 16, 1962, in Houston, Texas, and grew up playing baseball in and around Austin—establishing himself early as a strong pitcher. "He always threw hard," his father, Joe, told a reporter when recounting the story of Calvin's path from the backyard to the big league.[1] Joe had been a talented college athlete himself—attending Texas A&M in the early 1950s on a basketball and track scholarship before the army and working in the office products business for Remington Rand and G&LVBJ Co. Calvin's mother, Ramona (Powell), attended Baylor University and was a secretary and a teacher aide while raising Calvin and his sister, Rhonda. Both parents watched as Calvin helped pitch his Babe Ruth team into the state championship. Starting in his junior year at Austin's Westlake High School, Schiraldi was being watched and followed by major-league scouts.

In June of his senior year, the 6-foot-4 Schiraldi was drafted by the Chicago White Sox in the 17th round of the 1980 amateur draft. Two days later, he pitched the game that earned Westlake the AAA state championship, defeating the defending champion DeSoto

in a three-hour game. Schiraldi ended the game with a gutsy called strike on a 0-and-2 count to win 11-10. He was named to the All-State AAA team and chose to attend the University of Texas instead of signing with the White Sox.

At Texas Schiraldi joined future Red Sox teammates Roger Clemens and Spike Owen as the Longhorns won the 1981 Southwest Conference title and made it to the College World Series, only to be eliminated by top-ranked Arizona State. Schiraldi pitched in several games that freshman year, as did Clemens, but neither pitched during the College World Series.

The following season, Schiraldi saw much more action, amassing a 13-2 record with a 3.23 ERA as the Longhorns returned to Omaha for the 1982 CWS. This time the team's 57 wins and 4 losses earned its place as the top-ranked entrant. Schiraldi took the mound in the semifinal against Wichita State on June

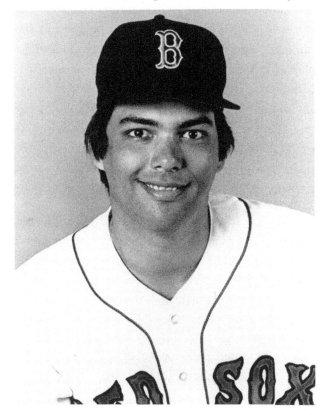

11, 1982. After gaining a 2-1 lead in the first inning, the Longhorns looked as though they might repeat the two wins they'd had over Wichita State during the regular season. But in the top of the second inning, Schiraldi accidentally hit Wichita State outfielder Kevin Penner just below the left eye with a 90-mph fastball, fracturing four bones and knocking him unconscious. Some accounts of the game noted that Penner lay in the batter's box for 10 minutes while awaiting an ambulance.

After Penner was taken to St. Joseph's Hospital, where he was reportedly in a coma for two days, Wichita scored six runs in the next inning as Schiraldi alternated between walking batters and giving up hits. Wichita eventually eliminated Texas in an 8-4 victory that Longhorns coach Cliff Gustafson attributed in large measure to Penner's injury.

"It's very difficult for you to see something like that happen—be afraid a guy is seriously injured, and go on the mound and concentrate like you need to. I think it was a big factor," Gustafson told reporters.[2]

In later interviews Schiraldi revealed how much it had rattled him. He told Michael Kelly of the *Omaha World Herald*, "It bothered me the whole rest of the summer. Just thinking that you might have injured a player like that…I was terrible over the summer: 4-6 with a 7.00 ERA. I didn't feel like I wanted to throw any more. Mentally, it affected me."[3] The following year, there was much talk about whether Schiraldi would rebound and whether Penner would ever play again. The tone was nearly identical to discussions after the 1986 World Series.

But in 1983 both men overcame the setback in dramatic fashion. After multiple surgeries and a long recovery, and with the aid of a special face mask on his batting helmet, Penner led Wichita State in hitting with a .437 average. He was named to the US Pan-American Games baseball team. Schiraldi came back stronger than ever, with a 12-2 record, 1.86 ERA, and 101 strikeouts going into the 1983 CWS. Schiraldi stopped James Madison 12-0 on five hits in the tournament opener, then led the team to a 10-inning victory over Alabama,

striking out 11 Alabama batters in 5⅓ innings of relief. Clemens won the final game, but Schiraldi's 2-0, 0.63 ERA performance earned him a place on the All-Tournament Team and the series' Most Outstanding Player title. More than 30 years later, with years in the major and minor leagues behind him, Schiraldi still pointed to the 1983 College World Series victory as his favorite moment as a player.

A few days after the victory, the New York Mets' director of player personnel, Lou Gorman, signed Schiraldi, whom he'd picked in the first round of the free-agent draft earlier that month. Gorman, for whom Schiraldi would later play in Boston, left for the Mets at the start of the season and Schiraldi was assigned to the Mets' Lynchburg team in the Carolina League, where he had six starts before being promoted to the Double-A Texas League team in Jackson, Mississippi, where he went 3-3 in seven games, with a 5.82 ERA.

In 1984, his first full professional year, Schiraldi was once again an all-star pitcher. Again with Jackson, he went 14-3 and was voted the league's most valuable pitcher. Promoted to the Tidewater Tides of the Triple-A International League, he went 3-1 before being called up to the Mets in late August.

On September 1, 1984, Schiraldi made his major-league debut as the starting pitcher in the second game of a Saturday doubleheader against the San Diego Padres. He lasted just 10 outs, allowing eight hits and five runs. He pitched 14 more innings in four games that month, earning two losses and a 5.71 ERA.

After 1985 spring training, the Mets sent Schiraldi to Tidewater, only to call him back two weeks later to start against the Cardinals in St. Louis. He pitched a six-hitter through six innings until being relieved by Roger McDowell and earned his first major-league victory. Then he pitched 7⅔ innings in three games before an infield hit by the Atlanta Braves' Claudell Washington broke his toe. Schiraldi went on the disabled list, came back in June and pitched in five games, including a hammering at the hands of the Philadelphia Phillies in which he Schiraldi gave up 10 hits and 10 runs in an inning and a third. He was sent back to Tidewater and recalled again in September. He pitched part of an inning against the Expos to finish the year 2-1 with an 8.89 ERA in 10 games (four starts) with the Mets. He posted a 4-5 record, 3.50 ERA in 17 starts with Tidewater.

"I didn't throw the ball that badly or pitch as poorly as it looked," Schiraldi later told Peter Gammons of the *Boston Globe*. "It was a combination of a lot of things, some of it bad luck; that can happen in four starts. Then when I started to throw the ball well, I got sent down, got down on myself and had what I consider a poor year."[4]

While on his honeymoon in Bermuda with his wife, Debra, in November, Schiraldi heard of his trade to Boston. Schiraldi, relief pitcher Wes Gardner, and outfielders John Christensen and La Schelle Tarver were traded for Boston's veteran pitcher Bobby Ojeda and three minor-league prospects. Everyone had high hopes for Schiraldi, including Roger Clemens, manager John McNamara, and general manager Lou Gorman. Alan Simpson, editor of *Baseball America*, saw the possibility that Schiraldi could become a dominant pitcher in the American League. Comparing him to Clemens, Simpson said, "When both came out of University of Texas, I thought Calvin was the better prospect."[5]

But at the end of 1986 spring training, there was talk of a lack of confidence. Maybe a change of scenery wasn't doing him any good. He had a 14.54 ERA. He was switched to relief. His father told a reporter later that Calvin had called him upset about the change. His arm was sore. In mid-March, in a particularly bad outing against the Mets in St. Petersburg, he'd allowed six hits and six runs in two innings of relief. And yet he'd struck out three batters. Manager McNamara said. "Schiraldi had good stuff, threw hard, but did not make good pitches and that's the second time that's happened."[6]

Schiraldi was sent to the team's International League outpost in Pawtucket. He soon settled into the relief role and earned 12 saves in 31 games with a 2.86 ERA. "Mainly, I was trying to get people out any way I could," Schiraldi told a reporter. "It just so happens my fastball came around, and that's what was doing it."[7]

When middle reliever Sammy Stewart went on the Red Sox injured list in late July, the team brought Schiraldi up. In his first outing, on July 20 in Seattle, he worked 2⅓ innings, giving up one run on three hits, with a walk and three strikeouts. Then on August 3, Schiraldi was sent out to face the Royals in a two-on, none-out jam in the ninth with the Red Sox leading, 5-3. Schiraldi ended in the game in 13 pitches—striking out Frank White and Steve Balboni and getting Mike Kingery to ground out on one pitch. It was his first save and, as the next eight weeks unfolded, the name "savior" was thrown around. In the next two months, Schiraldi earned a win or a save in 12 of 13 save opportunities. He finished the season with a 1.41 ERA and 55 strikeouts in 51 innings.

"He certainly came in here like someone who knew what he had to do," Red Sox catcher Rich Gedman told Dan Shaughnessy of the *Boston Globe*. "But the key to getting any type of confidence up here is to have some kind of success. By now, any questions or doubts Calvin may have had have obviously been relinquished."[8]

Schiraldi's oscillations between setback and recovery shifted closer together when Boston entered the playoffs. Game Three on October 10 found the Angels and Red Sox tied with a victory each in the American League Championship Series. Oil Can Boyd had started the game and in the bottom of the eighth, when Schiraldi was called in to make his first postseason appearance, the Angels led 4-3. A walk, an error by Wade Boggs, and Ruppert Jones's sacrifice fly helped Reggie Jackson add another run and the Red Sox lost the game, 5-3.

The next day McNamara put in Schiraldi to relieve Clemens in the bottom of the ninth after a leadoff homer by Doug DeCinces and a pair of one-out singles by Dick Schofield and Bob Boone. The Red Sox led, 3-1. Gary Pettis hit a double into left field, sending Schofield home. He then walked Jones, struck out Bobby Grich, and hit Brian Downing with a

1-and-2 curveball to force in the tying run. The game went into extra innings and Schiraldi lost the game in the 11th on two singles, an intentional walk, and a sacrifice bunt. Schiraldi cried in the dugout, shielded by a towel and his teammates.

Schiraldi was called upon again in the bottom of the 11th inning of Game Five. He was pitching for the third straight day, something he hadn't done during the regular season, and facing the top of the Angels' batting order. He struck out Rob Wilfong and Dick Schofield, then Downing went out on a foul caught by first baseman Dave Stapleton. The Red Sox won 7-6 and Schiraldi got the save. The *Boston Globe*'s Shaughnessy wrote the next day: "Imagine. Eighteen hours after he'd been enshrined in the Jim Burton/ Bucky Dent Red Sox Hall of Shame, Schiraldi was in the middle of a postgame celebration. They never had time to get Schiraldi's hat size. The goat horns didn't fit."[9]

Schiraldi avoided the metaphorical haberdashers again as he made his next playoff appearance. In Game One of the World Series, he replaced Bruce Hurst in the bottom of the ninth. After a walk to Darryl Strawberry, a groundout, and a flyout, Schiraldi sealed the 1-0 victory (and earned a save) by striking out pinch-hitter Danny Heep. "Right now it feels great," he told reporters. "I don't know what would have happened if we hadn't won the AL championship. I would have kinda felt it was my fault if we hadn't. Now we're in the Series and I've got a job to do—I just want to do the job."[10]

Schiraldi wasn't called on again to do his job until the now infamous Game Six at Shea Stadium on October 25. He entered in the bottom of the eighth after Roger Clemens was pulled for pinch-hitter Mike Greenwell. The Red Sox were leading 3-2. A single, two bunts, and an intentional walk later, Gary Carter's sacrifice fly sent Lee Mazzilli home. Darryl Strawberry flied out to end the inning, but the score was now tied, 3-3. Schiraldi held the Mets in the ninth and in the top of the 10th the Sox got two runs. In the bottom of the 10th Schiraldi took the mound. Leadoff hitter Wally Backman flied out to left, and Keith Hernandez flied

out to center. Schiraldi was one out away from what would have been the first World Series title for the Red Sox since 1918. Then he allowed three straight singles to Carter, Kevin Mitchell, and Ray Knight. He was replaced by Bob Stanley, who threw a wild pitch, which allowed Mitchell to score the tying run. Mookie Wilson followed by hitting a groundball that rolled between the legs of Bill Buckner, scoring Knight and giving the Mets the win and forcing a seventh game.

Game Six has been the subject of so much attention and consternation, it is almost easy to forget that the Red Sox also lost the next game. And Schiraldi had a hand in that, too. After a rainout on Sunday, the teams met at Shea Stadium on Monday, October 27. Bruce Hurst, who was 2-0 in the Series, was the starter. In the bottom of the seventh inning, with the game tied, 3-3, Schiraldi took to the mound and again faced Knight, one of the heroes of Game Six. Knight hit a home run on a 2-and-1 pitch. Schiraldi then allowed Lenny Dykstra a single and threw a wild pitch to Rafael Santana before Santana singled and Dykstra scored. Mets pitcher McDowell bunted Santana to second and Schiraldi was pulled from the game. The Sox went on to lose 8-5 and Schiraldi was again charged with the loss.

Schiraldi was understandably crestfallen. "I feel responsible for what happened," he told reporters. "I *am* responsible for what happened. I ought to feel like this."[11]

Schiraldi returned as the short reliever on the 1987 roster. At spring training in Winter Haven, Florida, he told reporters the same thing he has been saying for three decades since. "I was probably more relaxed in the seventh game than in any other game. I didn't feel nervous. I was ready to pitch. Things just didn't work out."[12] He was, more or less, getting on with his life. The press had a harder time letting go than Schiraldi seemed to.

After an injury in May Schiraldi had an inconsistent season as he tried to bring some variety to accompany his still-strong fastball. His performance was 8-5 with six saves and a 4.41 earned-run average. He gave up

15 home runs in 83⅔ innings. In December 1987 he was traded to the Chicago Cubs along with starter Al Nipper for Cubs closer Lee Smith. At the time (and later) Schiraldi said he was a little surprised at the change, but happy to have an opportunity to be a starter again.

Cubs manager Don Zimmer knew the transition back to starter would be tough for Schiraldi, but he and pitching coach Dick Pole gave him time in 1988 to develop additional pitches, including a forkball he had picked up in a brief stint in the Instructional League at the end of the season. Schiraldi had a 9-13 record with a 4.38 earned-run average and finished only two of 27 starts. But during spring training in 1989, both the Cubs and Schiraldi expected improvement as he returned to the bullpen as a short reliever.

By mid-June the Cubs were in first place in the NL East, but Schiraldi's performance was plagued by tendinitis in the shoulder and a sore elbow, for which he received cortisone shots. Zimmer seemed to be growing impatient—after a 10-7 loss to St Louis in mid-June he told reporters, "All I wanted was six outs from Calvin Schiraldi, but I didn't get 'em."[13] It was tendinitis again—this time his triceps—and Schiraldi was forced to sit out several games.

In July Donnie Moore, the Angels reliever who couldn't get the final out in Game Five of the 1986 ALCS, shot and seriously wounded his wife, then committed suicide in front of his children. At the time, pundits—and even other players—attributed Moore's actions to never having gotten over that failure in the ALCS. There was ample evidence of Moore's long-standing history of alcohol abuse and domestic violence predating 1986. But a myth was born. It had to have been frustrating to Schiraldi to have his name raised in news accounts of Moore's death, not just because he got the save in that game, but because of the growing belief that Schiraldi was doomed to struggle with his own loss to "get over." Some journalists almost seemed to be insinuating that perhaps he too should be on a watch list.

At the end of August, Schiraldi was 3-6 with four saves and a 3.78 ERA in 54 relief appearances. The Cubs were headed toward the playoffs, but minutes before the postseason deadline, the Cubs traded Schiraldi to the Padres along with outfielder Darrin Jackson and a minor-league player to be named later for outfielder Marvell Wynne and Luis Salazar. (The Cubs finished first in the NL East, and lost to San Francisco in the NLCS.)

Schiraldi's arm continued to give him trouble in San Diego—a strained forearm forced him to leave a late-September game against the San Francisco Giants. But a few days later, on September 23, Schiraldi hit a three-run homer off Fernando Valenzuela of the Los Angeles Dodgers. It was Schiraldi's first major-league home run (one of two in his career). Schiraldi made four starts with the Padres in 1989, going 3-1 with a 2.53 ERA.

In February 1990 Schiraldi signed a one year, $600,000 deal with Padres—the most he'd made in a season. That same month Lou Gorman was asked if he'd trade Lee Smith for Schiraldi and he paused and said he'd have to "consider it."[14]

Schiraldi was the steady middle reliever until Andy Benes went out with a sore should in late July. Starting the second game of a doubleheader against the Cincinnati Reds on July 25, he gave up two runs on five hits in six innings. But out of the bullpen, by August 6 he had let his last 16 inherited runners score. A rumor again circulated that the Sox were interested in getting Schiraldi back in Boston, but Gorman put it to rest, telling reporters, "We have absolutely no interest in Schiraldi."[15]

Schiraldi ended the year with a 3-8 record, one save, and a 4.41 ERA. In January 1991 he signed again for one year with the Padres. The new general manager was Schiraldi's old booster Joe McIlvaine, the Mets' former assistant GM. McIlvaine had been the scouting director in 1983 and had persuaded Gorman to sign him. Former Red Sox teammate Marty Barrett was also new to the team, having been released by Boston during the offseason. The reunion would be short-lived. Schiraldi blew a 6-1 lead in preseason play against San Francisco, and McIlvaine told reporters, "A major-league pitcher just doesn't blow five-run leads."[16]

The team waived Schiraldi before the season began. He would have been paid $740,000, but instead got $185,000 for not playing. He signed with the Houston Astros and was sent to their Triple-A team, the Tucson Toros of the Pacific Coast League, with whom he went 3-2 with a 4.47 ERA in 15 games before being dealt to Texas Rangers just after his 29th birthday in June, for a player to be named later. He pitched 4⅔ innings in three games for the Rangers and in 18 games for their Oklahoma City 89ers, before being released on waivers on July 8.

Schiraldi spent 1992 trying to get his arm back in shape, but when he threw for a scout and struggled, he knew it wasn't to be. He went back to University of Texas to study and prepare for a coaching career. His mother told a reporter, "He always said, even when he was younger, that what he really wanted to do was coach."[17] Schiraldi started as a volunteer assistant at St. Michael's Catholic School in Austin and as of 2015 had been the head coach there since 1997. His teams as of 2015 had earned two state championships, seven district championships, and 14 consecutive regional finals appearances.

In 2006 Lou Gorman and Bob Stanley were asked to compare another strong young Red Sox rookie reliever, Jonathan Papelbon, to Calvin Schiraldi and Roger Clemens. Both saw him as more reminiscent of Clemens. Stanley said that Schiraldi "went down the tubes" after the 1986 World Series loss. "I don't think he was ever the same," he said. "You've got to be able to roll with the punches."[18]

Gorman did not pin the gradual decline to that one game. He echoed his own assessment from his own 2005 memoir. Of Schiraldi he'd written: "[T]he one factor that kept coming to mind was his lack of intensity." He said of Clemens: "You had the feeling he would knock down his mother if it was necessary to win. With Schiraldi, I never had that feeling."[19]

On the 25th anniversary of the 1986 World Series, Keith Olbermann wrote of Schiraldi's graceful demeanor and of his work with young players: "Schiraldi has had an impact that merely getting the last out could never have afforded him."[20]

Calvin and Debra had two children, a daughter, Samantha, and a son, Lukas, whom he coached at St. Michael's. Lukas was a star high-school pitcher, like his father. He was an All-American at Navarro College and was drafted by the Washington Nationals, but also decided to go to the University of Texas instead. In 2015 he was with the Seattle Mariners' Double-A team in Clinton, Iowa.

SOURCES

In writing this biography I made extensive use of the archives of the *New York Times*, *Boston Globe*, *Boston Herald*, *Omaha World Herald*, *Richmond Times Dispatch*, *Rockford Register Star*, *San Diego Union-Tribune*, and *Dallas Morning News*. I also consulted Mike Sowell's 1995 book *One Pitch Away* and Lou Gorman's 2005 book *One Pitch from Glory*.

NOTES

1   Leigh Montville, "A Constant Vigil for Stopper's Father," *Boston Globe*, September 3, 1986.

2   Steve Sinclair, "Shockers Eliminate Top-Rated Longhorns," *Omaha World Herald*, June 12, 1982.

3   Michael Kelly, "Penner Injury Bothered Team," *Omaha World-Herald*, June 9, 1983: 38.

4   Peter Gammons, "Schiraldi and Clemens Reunited," *Boston Globe*, November 14, 1985.

5   Tom Shea, "Schiraldi Gets High Maarks From Insider," *Springfield Union*, November 14, 1985.

6   Joe Giuliotti, "Stanley Puts Finger on '85 Woes," *Boston Herald*, March 20, 1986.

7   Larry Whiteside, "Trade Said to Be Near," *Boston Globe*, July 22, 1986.

8   John Powers, "To the (Schiraldi) Finish," *Boston Globe*, October 7, 1986.

9   Dan Shaughnessy, "Schiraldi Gets His Turn—And Turns It Around," *Boston Globe*, October 13, 1986.

10   Kevin Paul Dupont, "They Both Pitched In for Win," *Boston Globe*, October 19, 1986.

11   John Powers, "Schiraldi Shoulders the Blame," *Boston Globe*, October 28, 1986.

12 Dan Shaughnessy, "Schiraldi Carries Unwanted Burden," *Boston Globe*, March 3, 1987.

13 Associated Press, "Smith Gets Five Hits in Cardinals' Fifth Straight Win," *Times of Trenton* (Trenton, New Jersey), June 12, 1989.

14 Nick Cafardo, "Red Sox' Mo Vaughn Has Work to Do on Defense," *Stamford Advocate*, February 11, 1990

15 Joe Giuliotti, "Clemens Feeling No Pain," *Boston Herald*, August 11, 1990.

16 Joe Giuliotti, "Brumley Surges in Utility Role," *Boston Herald*, March 24, 1991.

17 Tom Buckley, "Win Some…" *The Alcalde* (University of Texas alumni magazine), July-August 2006.

18 Gordon Edes, "Shades of Schiraldi?" *Boston Globe*, April 23, 2006.

19 Lou Gorman, *One Pitch From Glory: A Decade of Running the Red Sox* (Champaign, Illinois: Sports Publishing, 2005), 58.

20 keitholbermann.mlblogs.com/2011/11/10/calvin-schiraldi-sportsman/.

TOM SEAVER

by Maxwell Kates

4,256
755
5,714
511
.366.

AS BASEBALL HAS OFTEN BEEN described as a game of numbers, fans, reporters, and students of the game would most certainly recognize the preceding list of significant digits. They are career accomplishments forever linked to the respective immortals Pete Rose, Hank Aaron, Nolan Ryan, Cy Young, and Ty Cobb. To that list, another number should be added to commemorate a feat of equal important to longevity in base hits, home runs, strikeouts, wins, and batting average.

98.8.

On January 7, 1992, that was the percentage by which Tom Seaver was elected to the Baseball Hall of Fame. As of 2015, no player has ever received a higher approval rating by the Baseball Writers Association of America, not even Ty Cobb. Few players were ever more connected as a "franchise" player than Tom Terrific with the New York Mets. No member of the team was as intricately associated with their meteoric rise from cellar dwellers to world champions. Seaver was an immediate success upon arriving in New York in 1967. His miracle season of 1969 was highlighted by the game of his career against the divisional rival Chicago Cubs. He continued to pitch brilliantly in the 1970s, fanning 10 consecutive Padres in a game, collecting 200 strikeouts for nine straight seasons, and becoming the first right-hander win three Cy Young Awards. In 1977 an ugly contract squabble led to what became known as the Midnight Massacre, a trade to the Cincinnati Reds that devastated the Mets and drove countless fans away from Shea Stadium. After

five years of exile in the Queen City, Seaver returned to Queens in 1983. Although he wore socks of a different color scheme toward the end of his career, he saved his final crowning achievement for the New York fans to enjoy.

George Thomas Seaver was born on November 17, 1944, in Fresno, California. His mother, Betty, was a homemaker and his father, Charles, was an executive with the Bonner Packing Company, which harvested and shipped raisins to all corners of the country. The Seavers were an athletically minded family. Charles had been a Walker Cup golfer in his youth, while swimming, volleyball, and surfing were also represented in the family.

Seaver joined the North Rotary team in the Fresno Little League at the age of 9 as a pitcher and outfielder.

Tom Seaver on the mound, 1986.

Within three years, he had pitched a perfect game while batting a robust .540. Later, Seaver pitched for Fresno High, a school that had already graduated pitching luminaries Jim Maloney, Dick Ellsworth, and Dick Selma.

"Even … in high school, Tom was a thinking pitcher," remembered Selma, later a teammate of Seaver's on the Mets. "He knew how to set up a hitter by working the corners of the plate and the batter would usually pop the ball … for an easy out."[1]

After graduating from high school in 1962, Seaver registered at Fresno City College while working in the raisin trade. (While a student, he also put in training time in the Marines.) Scouts had begun to notice his pitching repertoire after his second year, when he won 11 consecutive games while setting numerous school strikeout records. So did Rod Dedeaux, the legendary baseball coach who led the University of Southern California to 11 College World Series titles. Dedeaux asked Seaver to join the Trojans for his junior year. To prove his reputation and earn his scholarship, Seaver went to Alaska to pitch for the semiprofessional Goldpanners.

At USC in 1965, Seaver went 10-2, striking out 100 batters in 100 innings. Although only one organization scouted Seaver in 1965, the Atlanta Braves wasted no time the following year, drafting him in January and signing him a month later. The Braves had been Seaver's team of choice growing up in Fresno. Hank Aaron was his hero, and as he told interviewer Marty Appel, "I loved their uniforms, and I loved their hitters … Aaron, Mathews, Adcock."[2]

But as much as he loved the tomahawk, Seaver never wore it for an inning of his professional career. Major-league rules prevented any organization from signing a college player while his season was in progress. Although Seaver had yet to pitch in 1966, the USC season was under way when the Braves signed their right-handed prospect. Commissioner William Eckert voided Seaver's contract with the Braves on March 2. If other teams matched Atlanta's offer of $51,500, they would participate in a lottery for Seaver's ser-

vices. Three teams — the Indians, the Phillies, and the Mets — stepped forward with contractual offers. The lottery was conducted on April 3 as each organization had its name thrown into a hat. Would Seaver join Sam McDowell and Sonny Siebert in Cleveland's rotation? Would he emerge as Philadelphia's third starter behind Jim Bunning and Chris Short? Neither. The winning paper selected belonged to the losingest team in baseball, the Mets.

Seaver earned a bonus contract worth $10,000 more than the Braves' offer, and began his professional career with Jacksonville. Pitching for the Mets' top farm club, Seaver went 12-12, throwing four shutouts and fanning 188 International League hitters. He married his high-school sweetheart, the former Nancy Lynn McIntyre, on June 6. Jacksonville manager Solly Hemus was overwhelmed by his pupil's talent and poise, insisting that his "35-year-old head attached to a 21-year-old body" was ready for prime time.[3] Earl Weaver, then managing the Orioles' affiliate at Rochester, agreed with Hemus from the visiting dugout: "It was apparent in Tom Seaver's pro debut that he was ready for the majors. He had an excellent fastball and slider and he put them precisely where he wanted to, in and out on the black of the plate, mostly knee-high. After Jacksonville beat us, I phoned [general manager] Harry Dalton and said that Seaver was going to be sensational and the Orioles could give up a piece of the franchise and do well to get him."[4]

Having never won more than 66 games or finished higher than in ninth place since coming into existence in 1962, the New York Mets underwent a 19-player overhaul under new general manager Bing Devine. One of the new faces in New York in 1967, true to Hemus's prediction, was Tom Seaver. His baptism into the major leagues for manager Wes Westrum occurred on the second day of the season, April 13, as he yielded six hits to the Pittsburgh Pirates in 5⅓ innings with eight strikeouts and four walks. Seaver gave up just two runs as the Mets won, 3-2, but Chuck Estrada was the winning pitcher. By July Seaver had amassed a record of 6-4 with a 2.60 ERA, commanding sufficient respect to merit a spot on the National

League All-Star team. This midsummer classic, played at Anaheim Stadium, was deadlocked after 14 innings. After Tony Perez homered to give the senior circuit a 2-1 lead, manager Walter Alston summoned Seaver to face the American League in the bottom of the 15th. On that night, a nationally televised audience was introduced to a rookie with a 35-year-old head; Seaver got Tony Conigliaro to fly out before walking eventual Triple Crown winner Carl Yastrzemski. After Bill Freehan flied out, Seaver ended the game by striking out Ken Berry on a high fastball. Tom Terrific was bound for greatness.

Seaver rewrote the Mets' pitching record book in 1967. It wasn't hard given the team he was on (10th and last in the National League with 60 victories and 101 defeats), but as of 48 years since, he had held his grip in most categories. His 16 victories, 18 complete games, 170 strikeouts, and 2.76 ERA in 1967 set new marks for the club. He also became the first Met in history to earn the National League Rookie of the Year Award. Even the normally reticent Hank Aaron expressed his admiration for Seaver. "You've got a nice pitch, kid," he told Seaver. "Good fastball, nice curve."[5] As for Bill Bartholomay, whose Braves were 0-4 against Seaver in 1967, all he could muster in light of the contract nullification was "I get sick every time I watch him pitch."[6]

As Mets broadcaster Howie Rose later reminisced to author Bruce Markusen, Seaver brought a sense of hope that was absent from previous Mets teams. Before he joined the Mets, Rose said, "There was this inescapable culture of losing, and at least among their fans, a growing sense of losing was going to be something permanent." He added, "People who watched [Seaver] as a rookie got the sense that they had finally developed a player who was capable of doing special things, and therefore capable of helping the Mets achieve some pretty good thing of their own along the way."[7]

Seaver did not fall prey to the sophomore jinx in 1968, winning 14, fanning 205, and committing only one error all season. He could sense that greatness was around the corner for the Mets:

"We pass over 1968 too quickly," Rose said. "That was the season the executives were getting the pieces together … getting Agee to play center field, getting Grote along as the catcher, getting the pitching staff together. They could see there was a Seaver, Ryan, Koosman, Grote, Harrelson, and getting Gil Hodges."[8]

If the Mets were destined for immortality in 1969, it was certainly not evident from their Opening Day performance on April 8. Broadcaster Ralph Kiner remembered Seaver "getting knocked out of the box" by the expansion Montreal Expos, who defeated the Mets, 11-10. The ensuing weeks were no kinder to the Mets. Injuries, slumps, erratic defensive play, and a lack of experience all prevented them from advancing beyond the second division of the National League East. In May, Hodges even told reporter Jack Lang that his hitters "looked like wooden soldiers."[9]

On May 21 in Atlanta, Seaver shut out the Braves to improve his record to 6-2. The Mets, meanwhile, evened their record at 18-18. To Seaver the milestone was no cause for celebration. He defined the .500 mark as "neither here nor there" and said that his teammates' embrace of mediocrity "isn't going to get us very close to a pennant."[10] As Ralph Kiner chronicled in his 2005 memoir, Seaver's role as a motivator was crucial for the Mets' renaissance in 1969.

"Tom Seaver was the driving force behind the players, always pushing the team to be better than they were, never letting them settle," Kiner reminisced.[11] He might not have remembered the legacy he imprinted on Seaver at a far younger age. At the Bing Crosby Pro-Am Golf Tournament, Charles Seaver approached Kiner and said he would appreciate an autograph for his son, who aspired to become a baseball player. The retired Pirates outfielder gladly signed a school photograph: "To Tom, work hard and good luck, Ralph Kiner."

Diligence and luck, along with talent, were essential ingredients in the Mets' 11-game winning streak in late May and early June. For every player, there was a different highlight that augmented their confidence, but for Seaver, it was an extra-inning clutch hit to win the contest on June 4 in Los Angeles.

"We were in a scoreless game until the 15th inning. Then [Wayne] Garrett hit a ball up the middle with [Agee] on second. There was going to be a close play at the plate. Willie Davis came charging in and the ball was under his glove. The winning run scored. There was real electricity. I remember going into the clubhouse and making eye contact with Grote," Seaver said. He described the experience as "the last ounce that tipped me over into believing we could win."[12]

By now, the Mets were in second place behind the Chicago Cubs. When he defeated the Padres on June 14, Seaver improved his record to 10-3. The Mets' mound excellence behind Seaver, Jerry Koosman, Don Cardwell, and rookie Gary Gentry was renowned throughout the league. Seaver claimed that a renewed collective excellence in the field was equally important, "especially up the middle with Grote, Harrelson, and Boswell, and Agee in center field."[13] The Mets upgraded their offense on June 15 when they acquired Donn Clendenon in a trade from Montreal. A veteran first baseman who studied law in the offseason, the sardonic Clendenon complemented the more cheerful Ed Charles across the diamond. In a tense racial period the year after the assassination of Martin Luther King, both clubhouse leaders on the Mets were African Americans. In Seaver's estimation, that hardly seemed to matter to his teammates, black or white. With sterling pitching and defense, solid offense, a hardnosed manager, clubhouse chemistry, and confident players, the Mets had no reason to look back. Only the Cubs stood in their way of a division title.

All of these factors set the stage for what was arguably the strongest game Seaver ever pitched. It certainly is the best-remembered Seaver game, even more than his no-hitter pitched for Cincinnati in 1978.

The Cubs, leading the division by four games, were visiting the Mets at Shea Stadium on July 8, 1969. Among the 59,083 exuberant spectators packed into the stands was Charles Seaver, who had flown from California on business. The younger Seaver had not even been certain he could pitch that evening due to a sore shoulder, but his pitches early on surpassed even his own perfectionist standards. While the Mets amassed a 3-0 lead in the third inning, no Chicago batsman even reached base. At this point, pitching coach Rube Walker broke one of baseball's cardinal rules, turning to Hodges and confiding, "Gil, I see something special out there. He's razor sharp. He's going to throw a no-hitter tonight."[14]

"Emotionally, I was fully aware of what was going on," remembered Seaver. "I came to bat and got this incredible standing ovation [in the sixth inning]. I felt as if I was almost levitating."[15] It mattered not that Seaver struck out. Eighteen Cubs batters had strode to the plate. Eighteen returned disappointed to the dugout. The Flushing faithful were glued to the edges of their seats both at Shea and on WOR-TV as Seaver continued to baffle the Cubs. Don Kessinger led off the seventh inning by flying out to left. Glenn Beckert flied out the opposite way before Billy Williams ended the inning with a groundout to third base. Seaver was equally masterful in the eighth inning. After Ron Santo flied out to center field, Tom Terrific fanned Ernie Banks and Al Spangler for his 10th and 11th strikeouts of the night. Twenty-four up, 24 down.

Shea Stadium, courtesy of Jim Bunning in 1964, had been the site of the first National League perfect game since 1888. Now it seemed like the perfect place for a repeat as Seaver took the mound for the top of the ninth. The inning began with a gasp as Randy Hundley led off with a line drive to the pitcher's mound. Seaver trapped it and tossed Hundley out at first base.

Enter Jim Qualls.

Of any Cubs hitter, Qualls had hit "the only hard-hit balls of the night." Seaver had already yielded two sharply hit balls to the obscure rookie outfielder. The pitcher mused that "if anybody gets a hit off me tonight, it would be this guy."[16] Seaver was right. He pitched the left-handed hitter away, and Qualls unleashed a clean base hit to shallow left field. The perfect game was over. The "imperfect game" became a part of the Mets lexicon.

A consummate professional, Seaver retired the last two batters and threw the first of his club-record five one-hitters. The Mets won, 4-0, defeating the front-running Cubs in the most crucial game of the season to that point. The baseball universe knew that the Mets were for real.

Although the Mets and Seaver faded in late July, the third-place Cardinals could not capitalize on their errors to overtake them in the standings. Then, in August, the Mets were dealt a grueling test of endurance: 20 games in 20 days, including four doubleheaders against three California teams. While some teams would have capitulated to the exhausting schedule and the transcontinental flights, the Mets went 15-5. As the winner of three games during the Golden State marathon, Seaver had improved his record to 19-7. He had not lost since August 5, when he dropped a decision to Cincinnati's Gary Nolan, and would be perfect in his final six decisions. The Mets took sole position of first place on September 19, and captured the division title five days later.

As the staff leader with 25 wins, Seaver was given the starting assignment for Game One of the National League Championship Series against the Atlanta Braves. But had the miracle run its course? The Braves, behind their ace Phil Niekro, jumped Seaver for five runs on eight hits in seven innings. Trailing by one in the eighth, the Mets rallied for five runs to preserve the victory for Seaver. The Mets easily disposed of the heavily favored Braves by winning the next two games, claiming a spot in the World Series against Baltimore.

Despite the best overall record in the National League, the Mets remained the heavy underdog in the World Series against the 109-win Orioles. The O's were an older, more experienced club with most of the same personnel who had won a world championship in 1966, when the Mets were still giddy over not losing 100 games for the first time. In the minds of many, the success of the Miracle Mets could not erase the image of Jimmy Piersall running backward around the bases or Marv Throneberry's disqualified triple on the grounds that he failed to touch first *or* second base. Earl Weaver, the first-year manager of the Orioles, was

not convinced that this would be another four-game sweep for the Birds. "I didn't think for a minute that the so-called 'Miracle' Mets would be easy opponents in the Series," he said in his autobiography. "Their pitching was too good, particularly that of Tom Seaver and Jerry Koosman, whom I managed in the minors."[17]

Yet after one batter in Game One, the skeptics appeared correct, as Baltimore's Don Buford unleashed a home run to lead off the bottom of the first against Seaver. The Mets found themselves in worse trouble by the fourth inning, when Seaver allowed four hits, including a double to Buford, to bring in three additional runs. The Mets, meanwhile, managed to produce only one run against Baltimore starter Mike Cuellar. Compounding matters, a journalistic rumor began to circulate that if the Mets won the World Series, Seaver would purchase a full-page advertisement in the *New York Times* urging the United States to withdraw from Vietnam. Though the statement was without an ounce of truth, the baseball establishment was shocked that one of its brightest stars could lend his name to a controversial and divisive cause. Although Seaver could not dodge the bats of Cuellar and his teammates, he circumvented the Vietnam issue by stating that he "did not want to be used for political purposes."[18]

As it happened, Seaver's next turn to pitch was Moratorium Day, a nationwide day of protest against the conflict in Indochina. Seaver, like countless others entering Shea Stadium, was asked to don a black armband as part of the demonstration. True to his word, he refused. Game Four was a rematch of the opener, with Cuellar and Seaver facing off again. Only now, the Mets had won two straight and Seaver looked almost as good as he had against the Cubs in June. He threw eight shutout innings and held a one-run lead on Clendenon's second-inning home run. The ninth inning was more cumbersome, particularly as Seaver faced Baltimore opponents named Robinson. A Boog Powell single advanced Frank from first to third, and Brooks hit a wicked liner to right that only a stupendous catch by right fielder Ron Swoboda kept as a game-tying sacrifice fly instead of a go-ahead triple. Despite losing the lead, Gil Hodges left Seaver in to pitch the 10th inning. In the bottom half of the frame, Grote led off with a double against 39-year-old accountant Dick Hall. Rod Gaspar pinch-ran. Pete Richert was called from the bullpen to face the left-handed J.C. Martin, who batted for Seaver. Martin bunted to the right of the mound, and Richert's throw glanced off Martin's wrist, then bounced into the outfield, allowing Gaspar to score from second base. Seaver got his only career World Series win and the next day the Mets completed one of the most stunning world championships in history.

One month shy of his 25th birthday, Tom Seaver was at the height of his game. He was a leader and motivator on a talented Mets team which, in its eighth National League season, defied all expectations. He led the league with 208 strikeouts while limiting opposing batters to a 2.21 ERA. He won the National League Cy Young Award and the *Sports Illustrated* Sportsman of the Year title, the only Met ever so honored. He finished a close second to Willie McCovey in the MVP voting (265 to 243), after no previous Met had even got near the top 10. Seaver took part in a ticker-tape parade described by the *Wall Street Journal* as a more colossal celebration than V-E Day, Charles Lindbergh's flight, and the return of the Apollo astronauts, all rolled into one.[19] He appeared on the *Ed Sullivan Show*, performed at a Las Vegas supper club, and purchased a Victorian farmhouse in Greenwich, Connecticut. However, if Seaver himself read this list of accomplishments, he probably would have added, "But you forgot one thing. I'm the only Mets pitcher who's lost a ballgame in the World Series."[20]

Seaver would not rest on his laurels. The next season, he led the league with a 2.81 ERA and 283 strikeouts. Nineteen of those whiffs were recorded on April 22 against the Padres, including the last 10 San Diego batters he faced, a feat still unmatched. In 1971 he had as good a year as he ever enjoyed in baseball statistically, setting personal marks with 289 strikeouts and a radiant 1.76 ERA to lead the NL in both categories. His 20 wins were four behind Ferguson Jenkins's total and the Cubs hurler took the Cy Young Award by 36 votes.

Tragedy overshadowed New York's 1972 season in spring training when Gil Hodges died of a heart attack after a round of golf. Seaver paid an eloquent tribute to his late manager, affirming that "Gil is here inside each man, and he will be here all season. The man made a terrific impact on this ballclub."[21] Under new skipper Yogi Berra, Seaver led the club with 21 wins and 249 strikeouts. In his first six seasons 1967-72, Seaver led all National League pitchers with 116 wins and 1,404 strikeouts. Only Bob Gibson's 2.42 ERA was better than Seaver's 2.44.

In 1973 Seaver became the first pitcher to win the National League Cy Young Award without winning 20 games. As was the case with his first Cy Young, it was evident to anyone associated with the Mets that he was indeed their franchise player. Off to a promising start, the Mets ended April atop their division with a record of 12-8. However, mediocrity soon prevailed, after injuries to key players Jerry Grote, Cleon Jones, Bud Harrelson, and even Willie Mays. By June 25 the Mets languished in the divisional basement, 8½ games behind the Cubs. Still, the second-place Montreal Expos were only two games ahead of the Mets. "It was the kind of year that nobody seemed to want to win," Seaver later remarked.[22]

The Mets entered July with a losing record, but so did four of their opponents in the "NL Least." Gloom prevailed in Flushing as the Mets posted a 32-49 record from May through July. When rumors circulated that Berra would be fired, chairman M. Donald Grant rushed to the manager's rescue, affirming that Berra would not be fired "unless public opinion demands it."[23] The *New York Post* capitalized on the remark, conducting a poll to ask which Mets executive should be fired, Berra, Grant, or general manager Bob Scheffing. Only 611 of the more than 3,000 ballots cast found Berra culpable for the Mets' futility.

Amid the despair there was one bright hope, embodied in a blue and orange pinstriped uniform emblazoned with the number 41. After defeating the Phillies on Opening Day, Seaver's consistency outshone that of his teammates. When the Mets were 30-35, Seaver was 7-3. In a three-week stretch of late May and early

June, Tom Terrific was responsible for the only four wins registered by the Mets. In one of those games, on May 29, he struck out 16 San Francisco Giants and was named National League Player of the Week. When Berra rhetorically asked sportswriter Terry Shore where the Mets would be without Seaver, the writer replied, "In last place with a 17-game losing streak and certainly out of any division race."[24] Seaver was particularly effective after Grote returned from the disabled list in late July.

Although the Mets remained in last place through late August, Grant ignited confidence in a clubhouse meeting in which he reminded his players that they could win their division if they believed in themselves. Tug McGraw's repeated exclamation of "Ya gotta believe!" drove Grant from the locker room and a rallying cry was born. Berra echoed Grant's sentiments in observing the divisional race. He remarked that every team had a hot streak except the Mets, adding, "It ain't over 'til it's over."[25]

Berra, Grant, McGraw, and company were right. The Mets surged in September, winning 21 of their last 29. On September 21 Seaver defeated the Pirates to even the club's record at 77-77, which in their mediocre division was good enough for first place. Seaver took the mound again on October 1 and defeated the Cubs, 6-4, to win his 19th and final victory of the regular season and clinch the division title. Until the San Diego Padres won their division in 2005, no National League team finished first with a worse record than the 1973 Mets' 82-79. For his part, Seaver led the league with 251 strikeouts and a 2.08 ERA. He completed 18 games, tying Steve Carlton for the league lead.

Yet there was some concern about Seaver's shoulder and it took a workout at Shea Stadium two days after the clinching for him to be pronounced as fit to start the NLCS opener against the powerhouse Reds, winners of 17 more games than the Mets and with an 8-4 mark against New York during the season. Cincinnati, which had represented the National League in two of the previous three World Series, had a lineup that was a veritable Murderers Row: Even if the Mets succeeded against Pete Rose, Joe

Morgan, and rookie Dan Driessen in one inning, they still had Tony Perez, Johnny Bench, and Ken Griffey due up the next inning. Facing Jack Billingham, a distant relative of Christy Mathewson, Seaver fanned 13 and walked none in the NLCS opener; he also benefited his own cause by doubling in a run in the second inning. Nevertheless, the ghost of Big Six smiled upon his cousin and the Big Red Machine in the latter frames of the game. Rose tied it in the eighth with a home run and Bench's ninth-inning blast won the game, 2-1. The Mets came right back from the disappointment and won the next day on Jon Matlack's two-hit shutout. The Mets took Game Three at Shea despite a nasty brouhaha between Rose and Bud Harrelson. Seaver, along with Mays, Berra, Cleon Jones, and Rusty Staub, went out to left field to restore order after fans at Shea pelted Rose in left field with everything from paper cups to a whiskey bottle. The Mets won the game, but Rose exacted some revenge by homering to win Game Four in 12 innings. The stage was set for a Seaver-Billingham rematch in the finale.

In the first inning of Game Five, Ed Kranepool drove in two runs with a bases-loaded double. The Reds struck back as Driessen brought in Morgan in the third inning, while Rose crossed home plate to tie the game on a single by Perez in the fifth. Then the Mets blew it open with four runs in the home fifth to chase Billingham, and who better to drive in the go-ahead run than the Say-Hey Kid. Having already said "goodbye to America" at his retirement game, the 42-year-old Willie Mays, batting for Kranepool, collected a bases-loaded single to score Felix Millan. Seaver led off the sixth inning with a double and scored on a Cleon Jones single to give the Mets a 7-2 lead. McGraw relieved Seaver and got the last two outs and then ran for his life as fans stormed the field.

Amid banners that proclaimed "Rose is a Weed" and "This Rose Smells," the series marked an acrimonious victory over the otherwise superior Reds. Charley Hustle compared the Mets and their fans to a flock of zoo animals, while manager Sparky Anderson expressed his dismay at their riotous celebration: "I can't believe this could happen in this country, but then I'm not sure New York is part of this country."[26] In spite of geography, and against all probability, the Mets were returning to the World Series for the second time in five years.

To paraphrase Yogi Berra's rhetoric, the 1973 World Series was indeed "déjà vu all over again" for the Mets. After winning an unexpected division title and then pulling off a stunning upset for the pennant, the underdog Mets faced a proven winner in the World Series: the Oakland A's. The defending world champion A's upset the baseball establishment by uniforming their long-haired, bearded players in green and gold haberdashery while experimenting with orange baseballs, designated runners, and ballgirls. Even their manager, Dick Williams, otherwise a traditionalist, sported long hair and a mustache. The Swingin' A's boasted a rotation featuring Catfish Hunter, Vida Blue, and Ken Holtzman, with Rollie Fingers in the bullpen, while their lineup was punctuated by Bert Campaneris, Joe Rudi, Sal Bando, Reggie Jackson, and Gene Tenace. After the teams split their first two games amid more controversy — Oakland owner Charles O. Finley forced infielder Mike Andrews to sign a waiver that he was unfit to play after he bungled two routine grounders in New York's 12-inning victory in Game Two — Seaver faced Hunter in Game Three. Night games in the World Series were still a novelty and didn't seem like such a great idea when the temperature hovered near 40 degrees for the three games at Shea. The Mets still started out hot, taking a 2-0 lead before Hunter could gain his composure. Bando doubled in the sixth inning and scored on another double by Tenace. Campaneris led off the eighth inning with a single, stole second, and tied the game on a single by Rudi. Seaver exited after eight innings. McGraw, who threw 10 innings in relief in the first three games, left after the 10th. Harry Parker allowed the go-ahead run the following inning. But the Mets managed to win the next two and jetted back to warm, sunny Oakland a win away from a world championship. Berra could have handed the ball in Game Six to George Stone, who became the favorite among second-guessers, but

Yogi went with his best and brought back Seaver to face Hunter again.

Seaver later admitted that he lacked his "good hard stuff" as Oakland scored twice early and held on for the 3-1 win that tied the Series. Remarkably, the A's had yet to hit a home run in the Series entering Game Seven, but two third-inning blasts by Campy and Reggie sank the Mets and Matlack, 5-2. A decade would pass before the Mets even competed again to play October baseball.

Despite a bittersweet 1973 season, Seaver converted his stellar performance and second Cy Young into a $172,000 contract. At the time, he was the highest-paid pitcher in baseball. However, the pain in Seaver's shoulder and hip that impeded his performance down the stretch continued to plague him in 1974. Facing Steve Carlton and the Phillies on Opening Day for the second consecutive year, Seaver twice failed to hold leads before Tug McGraw surrendered a winning home run to rising star Mike Schmidt. Seaver's fastball was even less effective in his second start, prompting pitching coach Rube Walker to ask if he was injured. Only after five starts did Seaver finally register a win; by Memorial Day, he was 2-5. Atlanta's Johnny Oates called his fastball "a lame duck."[27] Meanwhile, Seaver was being described as surly in the clubhouse and in dealings with the media. In his column in the *New York Daily News*, Dick Young wrote that Seaver was an agent of discontent among his teammates. In a summer of headlines dominated by Watergate, this curmudgeonly Dick made it perfectly clear that Seaver had made an enemy in him; it would not be the final war of words between the two.[28]

For the first time in his star-studded career, Seaver had an ERA above 3.00 and failed to make the All-Star team. But 1974 was not a complete washout. Through September, he managed to strike out 187 batters while pitching through pain. Late in the month, he attended two osteopathic sessions with Dr. Kenneth Riland. The doctor diagnosed him with a sciatic nerve problem and a dislocated pelvic structure, both legacies from years of hard throwing. Seaver later estimated that Riland worked on him for less than 10 minutes. After previously announcing that his season was over, he requested one final start. Facing Philadelphia in the next to last game of the 1974 campaign, Seaver still had a remote chance of becoming the first National League pitcher to strike out 200 batters in seven consecutive seasons. Despite an early two-run double by Willie Montanez that proved to be the deciding hit in an inevitable 2-1 loss, Seaver was masterful. He fanned eight Phillies through six innings and struck out the side in the seventh. The Phillies put the ball in play in the eighth and he entered the final inning still two strikeouts shy of the elusive 200 mark. After punching out Mike Schmidt with fastballs to lead off the ninth inning, Seaver fanned Montanez to achieve 200 strikeouts in seven seasons. The Mets had the cover image ready for their 1975 yearbook, a photo of Seaver posed with baseballs forming the number 7. Then, for good measure, Seaver ended his season by striking out Mike Anderson. The Mets went down meekly to ensure his first nonwinning season at 11-11.

With a rejuvenated arm and a new pelvic structure, the Seaver of old re-emerged at Shea in 1975. The pinnacle of his season occurred on September 1 when he reached two statistical milestones in midst of a shutout against Pittsburgh. When Seaver struck out Manny Sanguillen in the seventh inning, he reached a plateau that even Walter Johnson and Rube Waddell never attained. He became the first pitcher to strike out 200 batters in eight consecutive seasons. Earlier in the season, Dan Driessen became his 2,000th career strikeout victim. The victory for interim manager Roy McMillan—Yogi had been fired in August—would be Seaver's 20th of the season, and he added add two more to finish at 22-9 and earn his third Cy Young Award. He was denied another victory despite taking a no-hitter two outs into the ninth inning at Wrigley Field on September 24. Joe Wallis singled to break up the bid, but even if he'd gotten Wallis, it wouldn't have been a no-hitter because the Mets did not score. Seaver left after 10 shutout innings and the Mets lost on a bases-loaded walk in the 11th inning, 1-0.

Seaver edged out San Diego's Randy Jones to earn his third Cy Young, becoming the second pitcher, after

Sandy Koufax, to win the award three times. Contract negotiations, on the other hand, would prove to be a whole different ballgame.

Two National League pitchers, Los Angeles' Andy Messersmith and Montreal's Dave McNally, had played the entire 1975 season without contracts. On December 23 arbitrator Peter Seitz ruled that both players were free to negotiate new contracts to the highest bidding team on the open market. The reserve clause, which had bound a player to his employer for life, was obsolete, and the replacing system that granted free agency to players with six years' experience was met with vociferous opposition by the baseball establishment. As the Mets' union representative, Seaver worked to create an equitable negotiating environment for his fellow players. Now he wanted to experience the rewards.

Seaver demanded a three-year, $825,000 contract. Team president M. Donald Grant grew incensed and threatened to trade him to the Dodgers for Don Sutton. One pitch into the 1976 season, Seaver would become a "10-for-5 man." In another coup for the players in a previous round of labor negotiations, any player with 10 years' experience, five with the same team, could reject any prospective trade, leaving the Mets only a few months to arrange a deal for Sutton. Rather than risk a public-relations nightmare from trading their franchise player, the Mets agreed to renegotiate with Seaver, offering an incentive-based contract with a base annual salary of $225,000 through 1978. Though Seaver reluctantly agreed, it cost him any professional rapport he had with Grant.

Though Seaver's record in 1976 was a disappointing 14-11, his offensive support produced only 15 runs in his aggregate losses. Registering seven consecutive fruitless starts (0-4 with three no-decisions) between July 13 and August 24, he still managed to limit the opposition to a 2.13 ERA. Seaver's ERA for the year was 2.59 (third in the league), and his 235 strikeouts earned him his fifth NL strikeout crown. He also extended his record to 200 whiffs in nine consecutive seasons. As impressive as Seaver's 1976 numbers might have been, they represented his last hurrah in a Mets uniform.

The Mets reacted to baseball's new economic reality by failing to initiate any intention to sign any of the 24 potential free agents. After they had finished a pedestrian third place in each of the previous two seasons, the environment was ideal for the Mets to improve their offense by signing a free agent. In sportswriter Bill Madden's eyes, Gary Matthews would have been "a perfect fit" to play center field. Yet, as Seaver decried to a barrage of reporters in spring training, he was dismayed by his club's refusal to adapt to changing economic times.[29] The contract squabble of the year before still fresh in his mind, Seaver watched as other teams signed players of star caliber. Across town in the Bronx, the six-year, $2 million contract the Yankees gave Don Gullett to sign him away from Cincinnati suddenly rendered Seaver's contract outmoded. Observant of the ordeal teammate Dave Kingman endured in his own negotiations, Seaver wondered if he would have been better off not signing a 1976 contract and filing for free agency. Grant's reaction was predictable, deprecating Seaver as "an ingrate" and blasting the economic system his union had brought forth.[30]

"We will try to run our business in a sensible way," Grant said. "Nobody is going to plan to spend a lot of money for players and lose money at the park."[31] He understood the economics of the game, that free-agent contracts would inflate ticket prices, thereby pricing his product out of the reach of thousands of Mets fans. An acrimonious relationship between Seaver and Grant became even more pronounced. Most of the New York writers sided with Tom Terrific, including Maury Allen of the *New York Post*.

"When you have the best pitcher in the world, you sign him," Allen wrote. "You don't humiliate him. Grant can't stand opposition from Seaver or anybody." In assessing Grant's stance on contract negotiations, Allen charged that "he'd sooner lose a pennant" than accede to the demands of his players and their agents.[32]

There was one notable holdout in the press. On the Seaver front, Grant soon formed an axis with one of the city's most powerful voices, Dick Young of the *Daily News*. A maverick Republican in a city of Democrats, Young reacted to Seaver's free agency regret by labeling him "a troublemaker," insistent that no team would be interested in signing him.[33] The sports section at the *Daily News* was rendered into "the battle page," as Young and the pro-Seaver Jack Lang sparred using pens rather than foils. Seaver appeared unfazed by the diversions off the field, posting a record of 4-0 by the end of April and tossing his fifth one-hitter as a Met, against the Cubs. Seaver's performance did not prevent Young, however, from continuing his offensive:

"Tom Tewwific," he wrote, "[is] a pouting, griping, morale-breaking clubhouse lawyer poisoning the team."[34] This curmudgeonly Dick had made it perfectly clear that Seaver had topped his enemies' list. Young was correct about the Mets' position in the standings. By the end of May, the team was already 13 games out of first place. The Mets had hired their fourth manager in two years, replacing Joe Frazier with the untested Joe Torre. Meanwhile, the trading deadline was only two weeks away.

Rumors began to circulate that general manager Joe McDonald was arranging a deal with Bob Howsam, his counterpart in Cincinnati, to send Seaver to the Reds. On June 7 Seaver struck out 13 Reds in an 8-0 shutout at Shea to improve his record to 6-3. Sparky Anderson remembered the game: "For years, I had been naming Tom, whenever I was asked, as baseball's best pitcher. I never saw him better than he was [that night] when he whipped us. It was an artistic effort. I drooled when I thought of what a pitcher of Seaver's class could do for us."[35]

After Seaver won in Houston on June 12, the Mets offered to extend his contract so that it would be comparable to a free-agent offering elsewhere. He would receive a three-year extension which included a pay raise to $300,000 in 1979 and then to $400,000 in 1980 and 1981. On June 14, one day before the trading deadline, Seaver contacted McDonald to halt trade negotiations with the Reds. He planned to remain a Met.

Conventional wisdom suggests that if something sounds too good to be true, it often is. After he agreed in principle to a three-year contract extension with the Mets, the ordeal appeared over for Seaver. However, as he read the *Daily News* on the road in Atlanta, he became appalled by the latest offensive launched from Dick Young's typewriter:

"Nolan Ryan is getting more now than Seaver, and that galls Tom because Nancy Seaver and Ruth Ryan are very friendly and Tom Seaver long has treated Nolan Ryan like a little brother."[36] As Seaver told Bruce Markusen years later, his welcome mat with M. Donald Grant had finally run out. Incensed that Young would pull a false punch aimed at his family, Seaver bolted in search of public-relations director Arthur Richman. "Get me out of here!" he ordered Richman, "and tell Joe McDonald everything I said last night is forgotten." [37]

McDonald had no leverage to pull the trigger on a deal he regretted making. On June 15 Tom Seaver was traded to the Cincinnati Reds for a package of players, none older than 26: pitcher Pat Zachry, infielder Doug Flynn, and outfielders Steve Henderson and Dan Norman. Not only would New Yorkers endure the turbulence of the .44-caliber killer, a crippling blackout followed by massive looting and rioting, and a bitter four-candidate campaign for mayor of a near-bankrupt city—for Mets fans, the summer of 1977 would also live in infamy for a trade known as the Midnight Massacre.

After an emotional press conference in the Shea Stadium clubhouse, Seaver was ready to move on, joining his new teammates in Montreal. Disappointed by the situation he was leaving in New York, at least he would no longer have Johnny Bench, Pete Rose, or Joe Morgan to face. Though victorious in the previous two World Series, the Reds trailed Los Angeles in the 1977 National League West standings. Tony Perez was gone, but George Foster emerged as a power source; his 52 home runs were the most by any major-league slugger in a dozen years. Despite a 14-3 mark with a 2.34 ERA for Cincinnati—including a victory over old pal Jerry Koosman at Shea Stadium

in August—Seaver did not re-ignite his teammates to overtake the Dodgers in the standings. While he earned his fifth and final 20-win season, he fell short of his ninth straight 200-K season by four strikeouts.

He brought out scores of fans to Riverfront on days he pitched, and he also conveyed a presence to the locker room that was felt even among the two-time world champions. "Seaver was a joy to have around. He is such a bright young guy that his weird sense of humor almost seems out of character," recalled Sparky Anderson on Tom Terrific's immediate impact. "His personality fit right in with the veterans. They accepted him and he accepted them. Moreover, Tom was of tremendous help to our young pitchers who frequently sought his advice."[38]

Seaver, who hadn't really bonded with a manager since the death of Gil Hodges, worked well with one of the game's top dugout minds. "Sparky communicates well. He's intelligent. He has the 'smarts.' He believes in his convictions. He'll argue to the death when he thinks he's right. And he often is right."[39] Expectations were high for the 1978 Reds to re-establish themselves as the pre-eminent club in their division. Seaver did his part, posting a record of 16-14 with 226 strikeouts and a 2.88 ERA. On June 16 he reached an achievement never accomplished as a Met: He pitched a no-hitter, against the St. Louis Cardinals. The Reds, however, fell short in the standings to the Dodgers and with Dick Wagner now operating as the Reds' general manager, he wanted his own man in the dugout. Anderson was let go.

Although injuries impeded Seaver's performance early in the 1979 season, he recovered to win 14 of his last 15 games. After two bridesmaid finishes, the Reds won their division once again under new manager John McNamara. The Pittsburgh Pirates, clad in their stovepipe hats emblazoned with stars from Willie "Pops" Stargell, emerged victorious from a white-knuckle divisional race with the Expos. It would be the fourth League Championship Series of the decade between Pittsburgh and Cincinnati, with the first three won by the Reds. This time, however, Cincinnati was without Rose, who'd signed as a free agent with Philadelphia the year before. Though Seaver limited the Pirates to two runs and five hits in Game One, Pittsburgh starter John Candelaria was equally effective. Tom Terrific had long since exited the game when Stargell snapped the tie in dramatic fashion, hitting a three-run homer off reliever Tom Hume in the top of the 11th inning. The Pirates went on to sweep the Reds before defeating the Baltimore Orioles in the 1979 World Series.

Seaver's 10-8 season in 1980 was marred by disappointment. The Reds finished third and he suffered from arm trouble for the first time in his career. The following season was equally disappointing, but for vastly different reasons.

Although the Reds posted the best record in baseball, a midseason players strike resulted in a unique split-season format. As the Reds finished second in both halves, they had little recourse in the postseason besides watching the Dodgers' divisional playoff against the Astros on television. Moreover, Seaver's record of 14-2 represented the highest winning percentage in either league. Unfortunately, his comeback season coincided with Fernandomania, the pandemonium that surrounded the Dodgers' unhittable rookie phenom Fernando Valenzuela. Seaver lost the Cy Young Award to Valenzuela by one vote. The 1981 season was not without personal acclaim for Seaver. He reached the 3,000-strikeout plateau when he fanned Cardinal Keith Hernandez on April 8.

As the decade of the 1980s progressed, so did the frustration for Seaver. Defections continued as Ken Griffey and George Foster were traded, while Dave Collins was lost to free agency. Consequently, the Reds plunged to the division cellar in 1982, recording an abysmal record of 61-101 (even worse than the last-place Mets). Not even Seaver was immune; he went just 5-13 with an unsightly ERA of 5.50. Emerging from the worst record in franchise history, the Reds were eager to part with their 38-year-old pitcher with the suspect shoulder. At least one team was equally enthusiastic in trading for Seaver.

In 1980 the New York Mets had been sold to a consortium led by publisher Nelson Doubleday and de-

veloper Fred Wilpon. Rebranding the Mets as "the People's Team," Doubleday and Wilpon vowed to field a winning team at Shea Stadium, and allowed general manager Frank Cashen the pursestrings to field a contender. The resurrection of the Mets was a struggle at first. Not even George Foster, brought to the Mets with great fanfare, and new manager George Bamberger could lift the Mets in 1982. Cashen turned his sights to a third George, trading pitcher Charlie Puleo and two minor-league players to reacquire Seaver from the Reds on December 16. As M. Donald Grant had retired and Dick Young was reduced to journalistic obscurity, the coast was clear for Seaver's return to New York.

Over 48,000 fans flocked to Shea Stadium for Mets nostalgia on April 5, watching Tom Terrific throw six shutout innings against the Phillies in his return. Rookie Doug Sisk, who got the win in relief against Steve Carlton, observed that he "didn't know [Seaver] could still throw that hard."[40] It was his 14th Opening Day assignment, tying another Walter Johnson pitching record. Seaver was the most durable pitcher on the 1983 Mets, tying Mike Torrez with 34 starts and leading the staff with 135 strikeouts in 231 innings. However, not even Seaver, rookie Darryl Strawberry, or midseason acquisition Keith Hernandez could save the Mets. Seaver went 9-14 in New York's seventh consecutive losing season. Though that long streak was about to end, Seaver would not experience it.

The resolution of the 1981 players strike established an annual pool of players from which teams could select players as compensation for free-agent losses. With several young prospects they were anxious to keep, the Mets did not envision that any team would want Seaver, now 39, whose value was higher in New York because of his appeal as an attendance draw. The 68-94 Mets kept their young players but lost their Franchise. Again.

The Chicago White Sox lost pitcher Dennis Lamp to the Toronto Blue Jays as a free agent and were eligible to take an unprotected player from any other club as compensation. On January 20, 1984, they selected Seaver. On the heels of winning 99 games before losing the American League Championship Series to the Orioles, the White Sox were excited to bring in a pitcher of Seaver's craft and experience.

"Tom's a competitor. I think he's going to be happy here," said White Sox president Eddie Einhorn. "This is the best place for him for the rest of his career. It's an excellent way to end it. It's possible he'll get back into the World Series. He'll certainly reach 300 wins with us. And the atmosphere is great."[41]

Einhorn's predictions were not entirely wrong. Seaver did achieve his 300th win with the White Sox, on August 4, 1985, crashing Phil Rizzuto Day at Yankee Stadium to defeat the Bronx Bombers at home. (Tom Terrific joined the Scooter in the Yankees' broadcast booth after retiring as a player.) Though he ended his career with a World Series entrant, it would not be in a Chicago White Sox uniform.

The White Sox had capitalized on weak American League West opponents in 1983, winning the division by 20 games over second-place Kansas City. However, their style of "winning ugly" proved to be a one-year wonder. Though he won a respectable 15 games in 1984 and 16 in 1985, the White Sox had returned to mediocrity. Seaver did enter the record books by being the pitcher of record on May 9, 1984. When Harold Baines won the game with a home run in the 25th inning, Seaver won the first eight-hour game in major-league history. It had been stopped after 17 innings and resumed the next afternoon. As the scheduled starter later that day, he became the first White Sox pitcher since Wilbur Wood to win two games played in the same day. In 1968 Seaver had started and thrown 10 shutout innings in what turned into a 24-inning game at the Astrodome. Now he entered a game after 24 innings and picked up the win in his first relief appearance since 1976.

As the 1986 season approached, Seaver could see the terminus of his professional baseball career. After his mother died that spring, he wanted to spend more time with his family, which now included two young daughters. Seaver asked to be traded to a New York team or to Boston to be closer to his Connecticut home. On June 29 the White Sox granted him his wish, dealing him to the Red Sox for utilityman Steve Lyons. A change of Sox reunited Seaver with manager John McNamara in Boston. Led by perennial batting champion Wade Boggs, dependable outfielders Jim Rice and Dwight Evans, and pitching sensation Roger Clemens, these Sox were poised for their first World Series appearance since 1975. After a tight pennant race with the Yankees and an exciting Championship Series victory over the Angels, the Red Sox did indeed return to the October classic. As for Seaver, after posting a 7-13 record in an injury-plagued season, he was left off the postseason roster. He was unavailable in Game Six when Johnny Mac required a right-hander in the 10th inning, a frame that ended when a groundball passed between Bill Buckner's weathered ankles. The Red Sox went on to lose Game Seven and the World Series. The winners? The New York Mets.

Seaver did try to put on uniform number 41 for the Mets one last time. His attempted comeback with the 1987 Mets proved fruitless and Seaver announced his retirement on June 22. A year later he joined Casey Stengel and Gil Hodges on the short list of Mets notables to have their numbers retired. Two decades later, he remained the only Met to have his number retired for his achievements as a player. And they were many. Most of his Mets records may never be broken, including wins (198), complete games (171), shutouts (44), starts (395), innings (3,045), strikeouts (2,541), and ERA (2.57).

Besides broadcasting Yankees games for five seasons, Seaver worked as a public-relations representative for the Chase Manhattan Bank. He spent seven years as a Mets broadcaster before leaving after the 2005 season. Inducted into the Baseball Hall of Fame in 1992 by an unprecedented margin, Seaver attracted a then-record 10,000 pilgrims to witness his induction speech. Among them, Rudy Gafur, who chronicled the milestone in his baseball diary entitled *Cooperstown Is My Mecca*:

"Seaver finished his career with 311 wins and 205 losses. Among his numerous awards and honors are Rookie of the Year, National League Pitcher of the Year, and Cy

Young Award. He also shares or holds many National League records such as the lowest earned run average (2.73) for a pitcher with 200 or more wins and most consecutive seasons with 200 or more strikeouts. In a speech filled with emotion, Tom Terrific spoke of his deep love and respect for the game which meant so much to him. He thanked his family and friends for support."[42]

Now, after living most of his adult life in Connecticut, Seaver returned to his native California, establishing a winery with his wife, Nancy, near Calistoga. Seaver always has been a man of his times. Born into a middle-class family and raised during America's period of postwar prosperity, Seaver represented a new breed of player: independent, cerebral, educated. As the New York Mets' "franchise player," he was the spokesman for thousands of suburbanites, blue-collar workers, and immigrants united by their team's emergence as World Series champions in 1969. A man of profound opinions, he preferred not to disclose his personal opinions. Though he worked tirelessly on behalf of the Major League Baseball Players' Association, he never filed for free agency. Decades from now, fans will continue to visit his Cooperstown plaque, the only one in the Hall of Fame as of 2015 bearing a Mets insignia. In spite of Seaver's many complexities, to them, he will always be Tom Terrific.

SOURCES

baseball-reference.com.

IMDB.com.

retrosheet.org.

Allen, Maury. *After the Miracle: The Amazin' Mets — Two Decades Later* (New York: St. Martin's Press, 1989).

Anderson, Sparky, and Si Burick. *The Main Spark: Sparky Anderson and the Cincinnati Reds* (Garden City, New York: Doubleday & Company, 1978).

Appel, Martin. *Yesterday's Heroes: Revisiting the Old-Time Baseball Stars* (New York:

Wm. Morrow & Co., 1988).

Aron, Eric. "Dick Williams," in *The 1967 Impossible Dream Red Sox: Pandemonium on the Field*, Bill Nowlin and Dan Desrochers, eds. (Burlington, Massachusetts: Rounder Books, 2007).

Bock, Duncan, and John Jordan. *The Complete Year-By-Year N.Y. Mets Fan's Almanac* (New York: Crown Publishers Inc., 1992).

Gafur, Rudy A.S. *Cooperstown Is My Mecca* (Toronto: Rudy A.S. Gafur, 1995).

Hamilton, Tim, ed. "That Championship Season 1973," in *Now the Fun Starts! The New York Mets Official 1983 Yearbook* (Flushing, New York: Doubleday Sports Inc., 1983).

Jensen, Paul, and Ken Valdiserri, eds. *Chicago White Sox 1984 Yearbook* (Chicago: White Sox Public Relations Department, 1984).

Kiner, Ralph, and Danny Peary. *Baseball Forever* (Chicago: Triumph Books, 2004).

Lang, Jack, and Peter Simon, *The New York Mets: Twenty-Five Years of Baseball Magic* (New York: Henry Holt and Company, Inc., 1986).

Lyons, Douglas B. *The Baseball Geek's Bible: All The Facts and Stats You'll Ever Need* (London: MQ Publications Ltd., 2006).

Madden, Bill. "The True Story of the Midnight Massacre: How Tom Seaver Was Run

Out of Town 30 Years Ago," on the *New York Daily News* (June 17, 2007): 35 pars. [Journal Online]. Available from dailynews.com. Internet. Accessed October 5, 2007.

Manuel, John. "Coaching Legend Dedeaux Dies at 91," on *Baseball America* (January 6, 2006): 13 pars. [Journal Online]. Available from baseballamerica.com/today/news/060106dedeaux.html. Accessed February 2, 2008.

Markusen, Bruce. *Tales From the Mets Dugout* (Champaign, Illinois: Sports Publishing LLC, 2005).

Miller, Marvin. *A Whole Different Ballgame: The Sport and Business of Baseball* (New York: Carol Publishing Group, 1991).

Ranier, Bill, and David Finoli. *The 1979 World Champion Pittsburgh Pirates: When the Bucs Won It All* (Jefferson, North Carolina: McFarland & Company Inc., 2005).

Schoor, Gene. *Seaver* (Chicago: Contemporary Books Inc., 1986).

Weaver, Earl, and Berry Stainback. *It's What You Learn After You Know It All That Counts: The Autobiography of Earl Weaver* (Garden City, New York: Doubleday & Co. Inc., 1982).

Weissman, Harold, ed. *New York Mets Official 1975 Yearbook* (Flushing, New York: The New York Mets, 1975).

NOTES

1   Gene Schoor. *Seaver* (Chicago: Contemporary Books Inc., 1986), 32.

2   Schoor, 58.

3   Ibid.

4   Earl Weaver and Berry Stainback. *It's What You Learn After You Know It All That Counts: The Autobiography of Earl Weaver* (Garden City, New York: Doubleday & Co. Inc., 1982), 171.

5   Duncan Bock and John Jordan. *The Complete Year-By-Year N.Y. Mets Fan's Almanac* (New York: Crown Publishers Inc., 1992), 50.

6   Bock, 110.

7   Jack Lang and Peter Simon. *The New York Mets: Twenty-Five Years of Baseball Magic* (New York: Henry Holt and Company, Inc., 1986). 133.

8   Maury Allen. *After the Miracle: The Amazin' Mets — Two Decades Later* (New York: St. Martin's Press, 1989), 233.

9   Bruce Markusen. *Tales from the Mets Dugout* (Champaign, Illinois: Sports Publishing LLC, 2005), 22.

10   Ralph Kiner and Danny Peary. *Baseball Forever* (Chicago: Triumph Books, 2004), 198.

11   Ibid.

12   Allen, 236.

13   Allen, 235.

14   Schoor, 125.

15   Allen, 237.

16   Ibid.

17   Weaver and Stainback, 171.

18   Bock, 75.

19   Schoor, 162.

20   imdb.com.

21   Bock, 94.

22   Tim Hamilton, ed. "That Championship Season 1973," in *Now The Fun Starts! The New York Mets Official 1983 Yearbook* (Flushing, New York: Doubleday Sports Inc., 1983), 6S.

23   Bock, 106.

24   Schoor, 194.

25   Schoor, 195.

26   Bock, 111.

27   Bock, 120.

28   Bock, 117.

29   Bill Madden. "The True Story of the Midnight Massacre: How Tom Seaver Was Run Out of Town 30 Years ago." *New York Daily News*, June 17, 2007: par 9; [journal online]; Available from dailynews.com; accessed October 5, 2007.

30   Schoor, 235.

31   Bock, 138.

32   Schoor, 238.

33   Ibid.

34   Ibid.

35   Sparky Anderson and Si Burick. *The Main Spark: Sparky Anderson and the Cincinnati Reds* (Garden City, New York: Doubleday & Company, 1978), 224.

36   Madden, par 24.

37   Madden; Markusen, 88.

38   Anderson, 226.

39   Anderson, 281

40   Bock, 175.

41   Paul Jensen and Ken Valdiserri, eds. *Chicago White Sox 1984 Yearbook* (Chicago: White Sox Public Relations Department, 1984).

42   Rudy A.S. Gafur. *Cooperstown Is My Mecca* (Toronto: Rudy A.S. Gafur, 1995), 100-101.

JEFF SELLERS

By Niall Adler

MAY 11, 1964, WAS A GOOD DAY FOR pitchers to be born to the majors. On that day, Red Sox hurler Jeff Sellers, 16-year veteran Bobby Witt and Expos staffer Floyd Youmans were all delivered into the world. It was the world at the height of the Cold War. Nuclear tests being performed in Nevada and ordinary citizens huddled around their TVs watching the British Invasion and a witty television show about a team of comedy writers. The Beatles had just debuted on *The Ed Sullivan Show* in February and three weeks after that trio of arms were born, *The Dick Van Dyke Show* won five Emmy Awards. Television was an escape from everyday life, especially for Sellers, who for the next 18 years came face-to-face with the inner city, especially where he grew up in Paramount, California.

It was a city in Southern California landlocked by freeways, the 91 to its southern border, the 105 to the north, and 710 to the west. Neighboring cities include Compton, Lynwood, Downey, Bellflower, and Long Beach. The city's most famous resident? Frank Zamboni Jr., he of the eponymous ice resurfacer.

If Sellers wanted to go to the beach, he took the city bus. In a heavily black neighborhood, Sellers described it to the *Boston Globe* in 1988 as "a tough neighborhood, even dangerous." But Sellers was surrounded by friends, ignored the gangs and its temptations, and instead chose hoops and the diamonds because he had "confidence in myself."[1]

Sellers first caught the attention of scouts in high school, in a league then known as the Suburban League. Scouts were there to watch Cerritos High School's Rob Parkins (the 18th overall pick in the 1982 draft, also to the Red Sox). There in the bleachers that day was longtime Red Sox scout Joe Stephenson, who played in 29 major-league games during and just after World War II, and who signed Brady Anderson

(UC Irvine), Dwight Evans (Santa Monica), and Fred Lynn (USC), among others.[2] Stephenson told Nick Cafardo of the *Quincy Patriot Ledger* half a dozen years later, "There were several scouts there to watch Parkins, but Sellers outdueled him. I made it a point to see him again and kept impressing me with his competitiveness."[3]

The Red Sox took a flyer on Sellers and selected him in the eighth round in 1982, a round that also yielded major leaguers Mitch Williams and Rafael Palmeiro. That draft also included first overall selection Shawon Dunston to the Cubs and fellow first-rounder Dwight Gooden (Mets). Spike Owen, whom Red Sox fans would remember as their shortstop in the mid-'80s, was the sixth overall pick, selected by the Mariners. The Red Sox draft produced future major leaguers Sellers, Sam Horn (their first pick via the Rangers), Kevin Romine, and Mike Greenwell. The Red Sox

had three first-round picks in 1982: Horn, Parkins, and Jeff Ledbetter.

Sellers started his pro career with Greenwell and Horn in short-season Elmira later in 1982, pitching in 17 games with eight starts, and producing a 3.06 ERA. Greenwell hit .269 and Horn .300 on a team filled with 18-year-olds.

His first full season came in Class-A Winter Haven, where Sellers in 1983 was joined by Todd Benzinger and future ace Roger Clemens on his rapid ascent upward. (Clemens made four starts with a 1.24 ERA.) Sellers' second full season, in 1984, was even better, when he went 12-10 with a 3.41 ERA, as the 20-year-old tossed 182 innings, using finesse to strike out 94 and control to walk only 80. Sellers was joined by outfielder Ellis Burks and infielder Jody Reed on the team of up-and-comers.

On a talented 1985 Double-A New Britain club, Sellers was one of six Eastern League All-Stars that season, joining top prospect and shortstop Rey Quinones, Burks, Horn, Chris Cannizzaro, and John Mitchell. By September, Sellers was 14-7 with a 2.78 ERA, at one point winning 13 of 16. He would get the call.

The scouting report on Sellers in 1985 was that he had "good velocity, ball movement, and control" and "attacks the hitters well." Pawtucket manager Ed Nottle noted at the time that Sellers was "too wound up" and overthrowing and simply wasn't in "control of himself." In Triple-A the thought was that once a tighter breaking pitch developed, the slider would be his out pitch.[4]

The 1985 big-league club, under new skipper John McNamara, 13 years younger than the retired Ralph Houk, was beginning to make a run for the East Division title. The Red Sox traded away starter Dennis Eckersley, along with Mike Brumley to the Cubs for veteran first baseman Bill Buckner. Clemens was in his second year in the majors. The lineup featured Rich Gedman behind the plate, and fellow 20-somethings Marty Barrett at second and Wade Boggs at third. Veteran outfielders Jim Rice and Dwight Evans

defended the corners. The starting rotation featured a 22-year-old Clemens, Oil Can Boyd, who won 15 games, Bruce Hurst, Al Nipper, and Bobby Ojeda, who would face off against the Red Sox with the Mets a year later in the 1986 World Series. The team, though, was in the midst of an 81-81 season when Sellers was called up.

In a 4-2 win on September 15, before a quiet 11,124 at County Stadium in Milwaukee, Sellers struck out his first major-league batter, Mike Felder, and won his debut with 6⅓ innings of two-run (one earned), eight-hit ball. Glenn Hoffman pushed across the go-ahead single in the sixth.

"He threw groundballs and I was very impressed with him especially with his poise. We decided to get a look at him right away rather than wait until spring training," said McNamara.[5] "He was not over-awed by anything."[6]

Sellers finished the season with two no-decisions against Baltimore and Detroit (giving up a combined four runs) and a complete-game win on September 26 over 16-game-winner Doyle Alexander and the Toronto Blue Jays. Sellers gave up one run on three hits in a 4-1 win. He finished the year 2-0 with a respectable 3.63 ERA.

For fellow starter Bruce Hurst, Sellers showed something late in the year. "He pitched great ball against teams that were still in the race. He has outstanding control and he keeps the ball down," said Hurst a year later.[7]

In 1986 spring training, Sellers was the "talk of the Boston camp" early after his first three starts before his Grapefruit League ERA "swelled to 5.29."[8] Sellers had been battling for one of the final spots on the staff.[9]

Sellers was sent to Triple-A Pawtucket to start the season, and the Red Sox fell to as many as four games back as of April 25. With an 8-5 victory at California, the Red Sox caught the Yankees in the AL East. They would play at a .578 clip the rest of the season and never relinquish the lead, despite a number of injuries.

Buckner battled bone spurs in his left ankle, Rice had a deep thigh bruise, Tony Armas battled with a hamstring, and Wade Boggs with back problems. Sellers was called up in June, leaving behind his wife and two sons, still in Rhode Island.[10]

Again at Milwaukee's County Stadium, the site of his 1985 debut, Sellers gave up five unearned runs over 6⅓ innings in a 7-5 loss on June 5. He was wearing No. 19, which Dan Shaughnessy dubbed the "unofficial Southern California digit" worn by the last two Southern Californian natives, Lynn and Ojeda. The Red Sox pitchers were also battling injuries as both Nipper and Hurst were on the disabled list and Sellers was the third member of the Pawtucket pitching staff to get the call-up, following Mike Brown and Rob Woodward.

"He's a gutty little competitor," said Red Sox general manager Lou Gorman. "We rushed him a little (last year) but I figured it would be good to give him some experience in the big leagues."[11]

Five days later, in Toronto, Sellers again reached the seventh, as he gave up three early runs in another 6⅓ innings; the Red Sox won in extra innings. The team, however, lost three of his first four starts (as Sellers was 0-3). In fact, Sellers reached the seventh in each of his first seven starts of 1986 (as the Red Sox went 4-3).

Sellers' first win of 1986 came on June 29, when he threw a complete game at Baltimore, giving up three runs (two earned) on nine hits. He pitched into the eighth against Seattle and Oakland, both wins, as his ERA lowered to 3.20, and he was 3-3 over his six weeks in the majors. He did not win another game that season. Over his last four games in July, Sellers gave up 16 runs in 15⅓ innings. By August he was back in Pawtucket for the rest of the Triple-A season.

With September call-ups, Sellers made three starts in mid- and late September, tossing a combined 16 innings and giving up 11 runs. He was a question mark for the postseason, as it was between him and fellow rookie Rob Woodward as to who would take Tom Seaver's spot (sore right knee). Seaver had come to

the Red Sox in late June for Steve Lyons and was 5-7 with a 3.80 ERA in what would turn out to be his 20th and final major-league season. Seaver's last start lasted four innings on September 19 to open a three-game series in Toronto. Sellers gave up nine earned runs over 10⅔ innings in two starts, Woodward came out of the bullpen as the starting staff for the final two weeks for the Red Sox remained Nipper, Clemens, Boyd, and Hurst.

After the Red Sox lost to the New York Mets in the World Series, questions remained about both Sellers and Woodward. Sellers had surgery to clear bone chips in his foot. He pitched in Venezuela for four weeks of winter ball and battled to be the fifth starter in 1987 behind Clemens, Hurst, Boyd, and Nipper. He started the season with the club, going 2-1 before heading back to Triple-A in late May. He returned in June for the rest of the season. The overall numbers, 7-8 and a 5.28 ERA, do not look pretty for the 23-year-old Sellers and fifth-place Red Sox, but he made an impression in the rotation during the season's second half. Starting in July, he tossed four complete games, including shutouts of Oakland and World Series-bound Minnesota. Five of his losses came when the Red Sox managed just one run or none.

Never a strikeout pitcher, Sellers struck out 10 against Minnesota on August 23 (Detroit was 13½ games ahead by that point) and on October 2 he gutted out 11 innings and struck out nine as the Red Sox won in the 12th over Milwaukee, 3-2.

"Geez, that kid can pitch," said Dwight Evans at the time, as the *Salem News* proclaimed that he "went 11 STRONG innings against the second-best hitting team in the American League."[12] The Red Sox brass was auditioning candidates for their 1988 rotation behind Clemens, Hurst, and Boyd. (Nipper had been traded to the Chicago Cubs.)

During the latter half of 1987, Sellers' fastball was hitting 90 and his slider and breaking ball were baffling batters. He credited adding weight, to a high of 200 pounds, and working with pitching coach Bill Fischer. Most importantly, it was about staying consistent. All of that helped toward 1988, when the Red Sox were focused on the health of Boyd and Hurst.[13]

The accolades continued into spring training in 1988, as Clemens, whose locker was next to Sellers', told *The Sporting News* in February, "He's got great stuff, a very good fastball and has the makings of a very good pitcher."[14] A month later Clemens continued the praise: "Jeff Sellers has more natural ability than I do. He also has a better slider. The sky's the limit as far as he's concerned."[15]

With the chance to get the ball every fifth day, Sellers was slated to be the fourth man in the rotation for John McNamara. Again, he suffered from a lack of run support. The Red Sox managed just three runs in his first three starts; Sellers was 0-2 with a 2.35 ERA. He tossed into the sixth inning in each of his first five starts, but the Red Sox lost them all as Sellers' record was pushed to 0-4. He kept his team in the game despite three rainouts to start the year and, at one point, 15days of rest between starts. The offense sputtered with Sellers on the mound, scoring one run or fewer on average in seven of his 12 starts; he was 0-6.

When Sellers was struck by a line drive off the bat of Cleveland's Joe Carter on June 21, the Red Sox were seven games back and just 34-32. He was expected to miss two months. By the All-Star break, McNamara was out as manager and Joe Morgan was in. The Red Sox recovered, going 46-31 after the break (.597), finally taking over first in September and taking the AL East.

Sellers spent six weeks on the disabled list and after a rehab assignment in Pawtucket in August, he returned to the majors. In what would be his final major-league win, he tossed three shutout innings against AL champion Oakland on August 20. He again landed on the disabled list with bone chips in his right ankle and returned for the stretch drive on September 11, appearing just two times.

On October 1, 1988, a day after Boston clinched the division, Sellers came within five outs of a no-hitter at Cleveland. It was broken up by Luis Medina's eighth-inning homer. The final score? 1-0, dropping Sellers' record to 1-7 on the next-to-last day of the season.

After the Red Sox' division loss to the Oakland Athletics, Sellers, Todd Benzinger and Luis Vasquez were traded to the Cincinnati Reds in mid-December for first baseman Nick Esasky and pitcher Rob Murphy. The trade offered a new start for Sellers, who was 13-22 with a 4.97 ERA over 61 games for Boston.

He was to join a young staff of Jack Armstrong and Norm Charlton along with John Franco and Rob Dibble coming out of the bullpen. There were two openings on the 1989 staff for manager Pete Rose. Instead, Sellers tore his rotator cuff and missed 1989 and 1990. When he was ready to play again, he was released by the Reds.

Over the span of four seasons and six years following his near no-hitter, Sellers appeared in 18 minor-league games with four clubs, hanging up the spikes in 1994 with Colorado's Class-A affiliate after a combined five shutout innings.

In August 2011, he saw his son, Justin, debut at Dodger Stadium. An infielder who was born two months before the start of the 1986 season, Justin credited his father with his all-out fearlessness on the diamond. "My dad guided me in the right direction, with just enough pressure and just enough push."[16] In 2012 Justin was one of the six sons of big leaguers on the Dodgers, telling Jim Caple, "My dad helped me with what I can expect down the road. Travel. Interacting with the media. What to say and what not to say. Anything. Everything. He played a big role in this. He's given me an edge in every way."[17]

Jeff Sellers' travels from rough-and-tumble Paramount to Fenway Park traversed many directions. He may not have pitched in a World Series, but he accomplished many of the dreams that a boy playing catch in the street always dreams of.

NOTES

1 Mark Blaudschun, "Sox Seem Sold on Sellers," *Boston Globe*, February 29, 1988.

2 Baseballcube.com on Joe Stephenson thebaseballcube.com/players/profile.asp?P=Joe-Stephenson&Page=Jobs.

3 Nick Cafardo, "Smith's ready to achieve some fame," *Sunday Telegraph* (Nashua, New Hampshire), February 21, 1988.

4 Larry Dorman, "Laid Back Sellers Aims for the Strike Zone," *Hartford Sports Extra*, June 13, 1985.

5 Joe Giuliotti, "Red Sox Pitchers Blamed for Plunge," *The Sporting News*, September 30, 1985.

6 Dan Shaughnessy, "Cool Kid Hopes Boston Is a Sellers' Market," *Boston Globe*, June 5, 1986.

7 Ibid.

8 Ibid.

9 Larry Whiteside, "Sellers Thrives on Pressure," *Boston Globe*, March 20, 1986.

10 Shaughnessy.

11 Ibid.

12 Mike Grenier, "Sellers Makes Pitch for '88," *Salem* (Massachusetts) *Evening News*, October 3, 1987.

13 Nick Cafardo.

14 *The Sporting News*, February 22, 1988.

15 Joe Giuliotti, "A Market for Sellers," *The Sporting News*, March 21, 1988.

16 Baxter Holmes, "Justin Sellers Gets a Lot of Ink With the Dodgers," *Los Angeles Times*, May 30, 2012.

17 Jim Caple, "The Next Generation," ESPN.com, March 14, 2012, espn.go.com/mlb/story/_/id/7684649/los-angeles-dodgers-camp-features-seven-sons-former-major-leaguers.

BOB STANLEY

By Will Anderson

THE WINNINGEST PITCHER TO EVER COME out of Maine did not, alas, reside in his native state for very long. "The Steamer"—Bob Stanley—was 2 years old when his family packed up and moved from East Kidder Street in Portland to Kearny, New Jersey, Stanley's mother's hometown. And it's where job prospects appeared brighter for Stanley's father. Stanley, in later years, would label the move "break number one" in the series of events that landed him on the hill for the Boston Red Sox.

As he stated in a 1977 *Quincy* (Massachusetts) *Patriot-Ledger* interview: "You can play more baseball in New Jersey than Maine, so I got more opportunity to develop." Break number two was being left back a year in the second grade. As Bob related it: "By the time I got to high school, we had such a fine pitching staff that I couldn't break into it." He had to play the infield and outfield for his first three years. In his senior year, however, things changed: "If I hadn't been held back, I would have graduated with all those fine pitchers and wouldn't have gotten the opportunity to pitch as a senior." But he did get the opportunity, and he responded with a masterful 10-1 record.

The right-handed Robert William Stanley was born on November 10, 1954, in Portland. Although the Steamer moved from Maine at the tender age of 2, he did come back to his native state to visit almost every summer. His father's family all lived there and, Bob said, "I spent almost every summer of my growing years living with relatives and friends. My father and I would make a trip to Maine at the beginning of every summer. My mother knew to pack enough clothing because I always wanted to stay and lobster with my Uncle Jimmy."

On the strength of his senior year's performance at Kearny High School, Stanley was offered a contract by the Los Angeles Dodgers in the summer of 1973.

But he was a ninth-round pick and the Dodgers' offer fell short of what he had in mind. He turned it down. Six months later, in January of 1974, Stanley was the first-round pick of the Red Sox and this time he accepted the team's offer.

Stanley's first assignment was with Elmira in the New York-Penn League in the summer of 1974. His record was hardly earth-shattering. He was 6-6 with a 4.60 ERA. The next season saw him with Winter Haven in the Florida State League. At first glance his record there appears a disaster: He lost 17 games while winning but five. But the won-lost mark is deceiving. Winter Haven hitters couldn't hit. "I was 0-6 before that team even got a run for me," Stanley recalled. His earned-run average was what did impress. It was 2.93 and it was obvious to anyone who actually saw him pitch that Stanley's sinking fastball was a pitch to be reckoned with. It caused batters to hit the ball

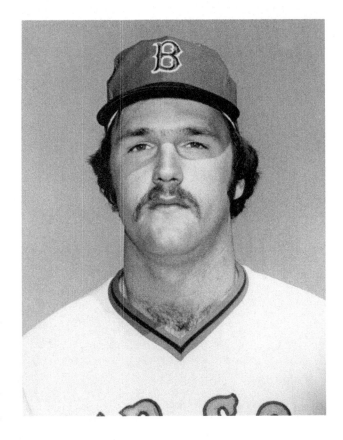

on the ground, easy pickings for a team with a good defensive infield.

The next stop in Stanley's professional career was Bristol, Connecticut, in the Double-A Eastern League in 1976. There he really strutted his stuff for the Bristol Red Sox: he was 15-9 in 27 games—all as a starter—and had a spiffy 2.66 ERA.

Between Double-A and the majors there's traditionally a year or so of seasoning at the Triple-A level. With the Red Sox that meant Pawtucket. Stanley, however, went directly to Boston. His work during the spring training of 1977 was so outstanding that Red Sox manager Don Zimmer decided to carry a 10-man pitching staff back to Fenway Park instead of his planned nine. Stanley was number 10.

In his first year in a Red Sox uniform, Stanley set the pattern that would forever make him such an asset to the team. He was, as the *Kansas City Star* later crowned him, the league's MVP—Most Versatile Pitcher. He was a starter. He was a long reliever. He was a short reliever. And he did it all well. His 1977 numbers include 13 starts, 28 relief appearances, and an 8-7 record, with a sub-4.00 ERA (3.99). His first game was in long relief, four innings on April 16 against the Indians in Cleveland, allowing just one earned run, earning him a save in the fifth game of the season, an 8-4 Boston win.

It was in 1978—the year of the ill-fated Bucky Dent playoff homer—that Bob Stanley really came into his own. Appearing in 52 games, all but three in relief, he posted a sterling 15-2 mark. He was second in the league in won-lost percentage (his .882 was bettered only by Ron Guidry's remarkable 25-3/.893) and tops in relief appearance wins (with an even dozen). Toss in 10 saves and just five home runs allowed in 141⅔ innings and you have one mighty fine season.

The next year, 1979, saw Stanley go almost full tilt. His relief appearances dropped to 10, but his starts numbered a career-high 30. He also won a career-high 16 games, four of them—just one behind league leaders Nolan Ryan, Mike Flanagan, and Dennis Leonard—coming via shutouts. He was selected for the American League All-Star team and hurled two innings of scoreless ball against the star-studded senior-circuit lineup, giving up one hit and one earned run.

Stanley had identical 10-8 records the next two seasons, 1980 and 1981. They came via very different routes, though: In 1980 he split his time between starting assignments (17) and the bullpen (35 appearances), while in 1981 he was used almost exclusively in relief, making but one start.

In 1982 Stanley enjoyed another banner season. He set an American League record for most innings pitched by a relief pitcher (168⅓), notched a 12-7 record, and recorded 14 saves.

In 1983 Stanley's 33 saves ranked him behind only Dan Quisenberry of Kansas City (who had 45). It was a Red Sox single-season record until broken by Jeff Reardon in 1991. As Boston manager Ralph Houk noted in a *USA Today* interview: "I can't recall ever managing anybody I could use either long or short as much as I use him." Stanley was once more named to the American League All-Star squad. He did, though, post his first major-league losing season (8-10). More would follow. In fact, he would not see a winning season again until 1988. Fenway Park fans started to get on Stanley along the way. His spare tire made him an easy target. So did his $1 million salary. As he joked to his teammates at one point: "Maybe I should change to Lou Stanley." That way, he reasoned, when the fans began to boo he could just say they were calling his name ... Lou.

In 1986 Stanley enjoyed his first trip to the postseason. He struggled a bit in the American League Championship Series against the California Angels (4.76 ERA), but in 6⅓ innings in the World Series while closing four of the games against the Mets, he didn't allow a run—though it was his wild pitch in Game Six, in relief of Calvin Schiraldi, that allowed Kevin Mitchell to score from third base in the bottom of the 10th with the run that tied the score.

In 1987 the bottom really fell out. Stanley took up work again as a starting pitcher but was 4-15, with a dismal 5.01 ERA. To his credit, though, the "Stanley Steamer" hung in there. As he reflected on more than one occasion, when asked about the catcall treatment he received at Fenway: "I love the Boston fans and I understand them."

Two more seasons of "understanding," though, were enough. Stanley resumed relief work exclusively in 1988 and was 6-4 with a 3.19 ERA, helping the Red Sox reach the postseason, though he faltered against Oakland in the one inning he pitched, giving up one run. He never had a decision in postseason play, but an overall 2.77 earned-run average.

In September of 1989—after a number of run-ins with manager Joe Morgan—the Steamer packed it in, announcing his retirement. He was officially released by the team in late December. Stanley held the Red Sox record for most saves (132) until Jonathan Papelbon passed him in 2009. He compiled a 115-97 career record with a 3.64 ERA, including 21 complete games. As of 2014, he ranked eighth in career wins for the Red Sox.

Stanley, his wife, Joan, and their three children had settled in Wenham, Massachusetts, about 25 miles northeast of Fenway Park. He owned a landscaping company. Bob began to play a little semipro ball. His fondest times, however, were very definitely family times. He was especially thankful for his son Kyle's victory over cancer, and a goodly share of Bob's time was spent participating in golf tournaments to benefit the Jimmy Fund, a charity supported by the Red Sox that raises money to fight cancer in children.

On April 4, 2011, Stanley was named president of the Seacoast Mavericks, a New Hampshire-based team in the Futures Collegiate Baseball League. In 2012 he was serving in the Pacific Coast League as pitching coach for the Las Vegas 51s, the Triple-A affiliate of the Toronto Blue Jays. When the Blue Jays switched their Triple-A affiliation to the Buffalo Bisons in 2013, Stanley continued as pitching coach. In 2014 he was the Blue Jays' bullpen coach, but was not brought back for the 2015 season.

The man who went from Portland to Boston—via Kearny, New Jersey—may be forever remembered as the pitcher who allowed the run that tied the sixth game of the 1986 World Series. He might better be remembered as the man who pitched in more Red Sox games—637—than any other player in the club's century-plus history. That's something really worth remembering!

SOURCES

This biography originally appeared in Will Anderson's book *Was Baseball Really Invented in Maine?* (Portland, Maine: Will Anderson, Publisher, 1991) and appears here with permission. This version has been slightly modified, and was updated by Bill Nowlin in May 2012 and by Len Levin in 2014.

DAVE STAPLETON

By Tyler Ash

DAVID LESLIE STAPLETON PLAYED HIS entire seven-year major-league career with the Boston Red Sox. An infielder and renowned utilityman, Stapleton made his lone World Series appearance as a member of the 1986 American League Champion Red Sox.

Stapleton was born on January 16, 1954, in Fairhope, Alabama. He grew up in Loxley, Alabama with his brothers, Jim, Larry, and John, and sisters Judy and Sandy. His father, Jim Stapleton, was a farmer who worked in the timber business, while his mother, Hazel, ran the household.[1]

A 6-foot-1, 180-pound second baseman, Stapleton smacked 39 doubles in his collegiate days for the University of South Alabama Jaguars.[2] Before starring for the Jaguars, he played two years at Faulkner Union, a junior college. He attended Robertsdale High School, a private institution. Stapleton led the Jaguars in RBIs (69) during the 1975 NCAA Division I season and was named to the university's athletic Hall of Fame in 1993. The Red Sox drafted right-hander Stapleton in the 10th round of the 1975 amateur draft.

Playing for the Winter Haven Red Sox in the Single-A Florida State League in 1975, Stapleton hit .241 with just 10 extra-base hits in 56 games played. He batted .288 the following year in Winter Haven, meriting a promotion to Double-A Bristol for the start of the 1977 season. Stapleton led the Bristol Red Sox with a .306 batting average in 86 games before his elevation near the end of the season to Pawtucket, where he hit .243 in 25 contests. He spent two seasons in Pawtucket, improving his average from .259 in 1978 to .306 with 15 homes and 64 RBIs in 1979, figures that earned him the International League MVP award. After Stapleton's torrid start to the 1980 season—a .340 batting average with three home runs and 19 RBIs in 37 contests—he was promoted to the Red Sox at the end of May.

Appearing in his first major-league game on May 30, 1980, at Fenway Park, Stapleton went 1-for-4 against the Milwaukee Brewers. He recorded his first career hit in his third at-bat, doubling off Lary Sorensen to begin the bottom of the fifth inning. John Flinn entered the game for the Brewers and Stapleton advanced to third on a groundout by Carl Yastrzemski, then scored his first career run on a sacrifice fly hit by teammate Tony Perez. The Red Sox won the contest 5-3.

A season-ending knee injury to Jerry Remy—who underwent the first of five operations on his knee in 1980—opened the door for Stapleton to be a full-time starter with the Red Sox.[3] Stapleton took advantage of the opportunity, and had the best season of his career in his rookie year. He registered a .321/.338/.463 batting line and bashed 33 doubles in 106 games. Stapleton finished second in the American League Rookie of

the Year voting behind Cleveland Indians outfielder Joe Charboneau.

Unable to replicate his rookie success in 1981, Stapleton lost the starting second baseman duties to Remy, who hit .307 in his return to action in 1981. Stapleton batted .285—the start of a trend that saw his batting average drop each season for the remainder of his career. No longer the everyday second baseman, Stapleton began his role as a utility player, starting at various infield positions. As of 2015, he was one of 19 major leaguers to start at least 12 games in a season at first base, second base, third base, and shortstop—a feat he accomplished in 1981.

Stapleton overtook Tony Perez for the starting first-baseman job in 1982. His numbers continued to dip, as he posted a .264/.305/.398 slash line. He kept the starting duties the following season, hitting .247 with 31 doubles in 151 games played. That season proved to be Stapleton's final as a starter. He appeared in just 82 games in the last three seasons (1984-86) of his career. The final regular-season game of Stapleton's career came on October 5, 1986, at Fenway Park against the New York Yankees. Stapleton entered the contest in the top of the eighth inning as a defensive replacement at second base for Marty Barrett. His lone at-bat came in the bottom of the ninth against the Yankees' Scott Nielsen, who pitched a 7-0 shutout and retired Stapleton on a groundout to third base.

In the final season of his career, Stapleton was primarily used as a defensive replacement. In particular, he often relieved first baseman Bill Buckner, who endured constant pain in his legs (particularly chronic ankle issues) throughout the 1986 season.[4] Red Sox manager John McNamara used Stapleton at the end of all seven of Boston's postseason victories in 1986.[5] Yet with the Red Sox leading the New York Mets, 5-3 (and holding a 3-2 series advantage) in Game Six of the World Series, McNamara opted not to sub in Stapleton for Buckner in the bottom of the 10th inning. This error in judgment saw the Mets complete their improbable three-run rally with a Mookie Wilson groundball through the legs of Buckner. Buckner's error completed the comeback for the Mets, who

went on to win Game Seven and capture their second World Series title.

Rumors swirled that McNamara kept Buckner in the game because he felt his first baseman deserved to be on the field when the Red Sox got the final out to clinch the championship. McNamara disputed that claim in a 2011 interview on MLB Network, which was celebrating the 25-year anniversary of the classic Mets-Red Sox World Series.

"Buckner was the best first baseman I had," McNamara said. "And Dave Stapleton has taken enough shots at me since that he didn't get in that ballgame, but Dave Stapleton's nickname was Shakey. And you know what that implies. I didn't want him playing first base to end that game, and it was not any sentimental thing that I had for Billy Buck."[6]

McNamara said he didn't trust Stapleton in the field (hence the "Shakey" reference), but used the infielder at the end of every previous playoff victory. Furthermore, Stapleton played terrific defensively in 1986, recording a perfect 1.000 fielding percentage during the regular season and in the playoffs. Stapleton (who posted a .993 career fielding percentage) told Steve Buckley for his book *Boston Red Sox: Where Have You Gone?* that McNamara was "afraid" to upset the veteran players (e.g., Buckner) and said that was the main reason he did not get the call to play first base in the potential championship-closing inning.[7]

Stapleton final major-league action came in Boston's 4-2 triumph in Game Five on October 23 at Fenway Park, as a defensive replacement for none other than Bill Buckner in the top of the ninth inning.

Stapleton's career had seemed destined to last a decade-plus, but he was finished after seven seasons. He was released by the Red Sox after the 1986 season. He signed with the Seattle Mariners on December 23, but was cut by the team just before the 1987 season.

Stapleton batted .271 for his career with 41 homers, 8 triples, and 118 doubles. He registered 224 RBIs, scored 238 runs, stole 6 bases, walked 114 times, slugged .398, and posted a .310 on-base percentage.

Among major leaguers who played for at least seven seasons, Stapleton is the only hitter in history whose batting average declined in each sequential season over his career.[8]

After being released by the Mariners, Stapleton started David Stapleton Builders, a house-building company, in Alabama in 1989. Stapleton, a member of the Baldwin County Home Builders Association, also spent his post-baseball years coaching his children in baseball from the time they were 4 years old until their completion of Little League.[9]

Stapleton fathered three children (Shaun, Joshua, Cara) with his wife, Cheryl, a former New England Patriots cheerleader and a lifelong Red Sox fan.[10] Shaun, the oldest child, graduated from Auburn University and as of 2015 worked as a project manager for a road-building company. The middle child, Joshua, played college baseball at his father's alma mater in his freshman year before transferring to Auburn University, where he started games from 2006 to 2008 at designated hitter, third base, and right field.[11] In 2015 he owned the Josh Stapleton State Farm Agency, in Cartersville, Georgia. Cara, a graduate of the University of Mississippi, was an event planner in Washington, D.C.

NOTES

1   Author interview with Dave Stapleton, July 21, 2015.

2   al.com/sports/index.ssf/2013/12/south_alabama_all-time_teams_s.html

3   "Evans Has Surgery," *Victoria Advocate*, November 1, 1984. Retrieved from news.google.com/newspapers?nid=861&dat=1984 1101&id=XiiJAAAAIBAJ&sjid=ln8MAAAAIBAJ&pg=4732,411 010&safe=strict&hl=en.

4   boston.redsox.mlb.com/bos/fan_forum/all_fenway_team_bios.jsp?bio=BENCH_Stapleton.

5   nytimes.com/2011/11/08/sports/baseball/former-red-sox-manager-john-mcnamara-recalls-final-out-that-wasnt-to-be.html?_r=0.

6   Ibid.

7   Steve Buckley, *Boston Red Sox: Where Have You Gone?* (Champaign, Illinois: Sports Publishing, 2005), 43.

8   soshwiki.com/index.php?title=Dave_Stapleton.

9   Author interview with Dave Stapleton.

10 Buckley.

11 auburntigers.com/sports/m-basebl/mtt/josh_stapleton_236269.html.

MIKE STENHOUSE

By Mark S. Sternman

THE SON OF AN ALL-STAR, A TWO-TIME ALL-American at Harvard University, and a first-round draft pick, Mike Stenhouse seemed destined to thrive in the majors. But in a five-year career with three teams that never saw him play in more than half the schedule, Stenhouse never hit. While he did not make the postseason roster for the 1986 Boston Red Sox, the best and last major-league squad he played for, Stenhouse did have one important plate appearance that season that sparked the Red Sox to an extra-inning win over a division rival.

Mike's father, Dave, began his minor-league career in 1955. In 1958 he began the season with the Pueblo (Colorado) Bruins, an affiliate of the Chicago Cubs. In Pueblo, Dave's wife, Phyllis (DeBiasio) Stenhouse, gave birth to Mike on May 29, 1958. As of August 2015, Dave and Phyllis had been married for more than 58 years.

Dave went just 16-28 as a Washington Senators pitcher for three years, but improbably started the second 1962 All-Star Game as a 28-year-old rookie. After baseball, Dave worked in the insurance business and co-founded the Insurance Center, a financial planning company. In 1968 he was named baseball coach at Rhode Island College, winning more than 200 games in 12 years. In 1980 he was named baseball coach at Brown University and held that post for 10 years.[1]

Mike's mother, Phyllis, a fellow student of Dave's at the University of Rhode Island, earned a master's in teaching and worked as a librarian at a junior high school in Cranston, Rhode Island.

Mike grew up in Cranston although he first played on a team in Honolulu when Dave pitched for the Hawaii Islanders of the Pacific Coast League. Mike's "ascent toward professional baseball began early. Mike was 9 … when Dave Stenhouse left professional baseball

and built a batting cage in the backyard of the family home. … [Dave] was always willing to throw—at full speed, he said—from the distance at which they would face their peers."[2]

Mike wanted to be like Dave. "My father told me just about all there is about baseball," he said.[3] "He loved it when he was up there, so it's always been one of my dreams to play in the majors."[4]

After carefully considering Brown University and Harvard University, Mike entered Harvard, an incubator of more Cabinet members than cleanup hitters.[5] He put up staggering offensive numbers that would help him realize his dream. As a freshman facing Northeastern University, Stenhouse "a) went five for six at the plate, b) hit for the cycle and added an extra single and sacrifice fly to boot, c) scored four runs and drove in six, and d) popped up in the ninth. That last one was simply to show that nobody's perfect."[6]

Stenhouse "hit .475 and knocked in 40 runs … as a freshman. Both are Harvard records, but believe it or not, underscore the fact that [he] is unconquerable by anything short of a frontal lobotomy once he stands in at the plate. Another couple of seasons like the one past for the big guy and he can forget about graduate school."[7]

At Harvard, Stenhouse set school records that still stood long after the conclusion of his Crimson career, for homers in a season (10 in 1978), batting average in a season (.475 in 1977), career triples (12), and lifetime batting average (.422). As of 2015 he ranked second in homers with 19, behind someone who played four years for Harvard as opposed to Stenhouse's three.[8]

Not only did Stenhouse make All-American twice, but he also, like his dad, played college basketball. Mike played key roles in two close games that went down to the final seconds. Against the University of Connecticut, Harvard trailed by one with seven seconds left but had a one-and-one situation at the foul line. The player who drew the foul got hurt, so Stenhouse had to shoot instead. He missed, and Harvard lost by one.[9]

Stenhouse redeemed himself against an Ivy rival as Harvard edged Dartmouth College thanks to "supersub Mike Stenhouse's 17-foot jumper with two seconds left. Stenhouse capped a hustling Crimson rally by snaring a loose ball … taking two quick dribbles and sticking a jump shot over two falling Dartmouth defenders … to give Harvard its first lead of the game."[10]

Stenhouse averaged 4.1 points per game for the 1977-78 Crimson. His teammate Charlie Baker averaged only 1.7 points before going onto political prominence as the governor of Massachusetts.[11]

Stenhouse, after again earning All-American honors as a sophomore, started to receive attention from "[s]everal scouts, [who] say that [he] is such a good hitter [that] he could go in the top five picks in the country next June."[12] The rest of Stenhouse's game proved more problematic. "There is, however, much doubt about Stenhouse's foot speed and also about whether he can be a major league fielder. 'Terrible' was one scout's assessment of Stenhouse's running ability. 'He's strictly an American League prospect, because that's where the DH is.'"[13]

After breaking his hand in a Cape Cod League game between his sophomore and junior seasons, Stenhouse chose not to play basketball before his junior year, a decision he later saw as "a mistake," adding, "I lost some rhythm, and the Seattle Mariners had considered drafting me with the first overall pick before taking some guy named [Al] Chambers instead. The only teams I did not want to draft me were Cleveland and Oakland, and Oakland picked me with the last pick of the first round, just before Seattle would have taken me with the first pick of the second round."[14] Said Stenhouse after the selection, "My father and I have to do some talking with the A's to see if we can reach a reasonable agreement."[15]

Oakland Athletics owner Charlie Finley did not always act in a conventionally reasonable fashion. Baseball writer Peter Gammons, who liked to tout New England baseball players generally and spent years hyping Stenhouse specifically, wrote, "The kid I feel sorry for is … Mike Stenhouse. … His father gets one call within the necessary 15 days from … Finley, and … [eventually] they come to terms for $12,000 and a guarantee to be brought up in September, but when it comes to signing, Finley reneged and wouldn't put his September offer in writing. …"[16]

Stenhouse characterized the discussions as "really ridiculous." He said, "I knew what I was looking for was not that unreasonable, moneywise and everything-wise. I wasn't looking for six figures. What they were offering was barely two figures."[17]

A little more than seven months after the A's picked and failed to sign Stenhouse, the Montreal Expos drafted him fourth overall in a secondary draft for previously picked players.[18] Jim Fanning, Montreal's vice president and director of player development, was enthusiastic about Stenhouse's prospects, saying, "We'll develop his skills, and hopefully we'll make a major-league player out of him."[19]

Although the Expos signed him for more than the A's had offered him, Stenhouse saw his decision to reject Oakland as a second mistake since "the A's had been unloading talent, and Montreal had Hall of Famers or All-Stars at every position I played."

Stenhouse began his pro career in 1980 with the Single-A West Palm Beach Expos. Early in the season Stenhouse went all Babe Herman and singled into a triple play: "Wayne Simmons singled to open the top of the fifth and Wally Johnson drew a walk. … Stenhouse ripped a hit to right field, scoring Simmons. Johnson was tagged out between third and home, and Stenhouse was caught and run down between first and second."[20] An appeal resulted in the umpire calling out Simmons for missing third base.

Montreal promoted Stenhouse to the Memphis Chicks of the Double-A Southern League, where he played in one game in 1980. He spent the entire 1981 season in Memphis after getting hit on the forearm with the Expos during spring training.[21]

In 1982 Stenhouse made the jump to the Triple-A Wichita Aeros, where he debuted with a hit, two walks, a stolen base, and two runs scored.[22] After a banner season in which he smashed 25 homers and drew more than 100 walks, Stenhouse got the call to the majors and played in the final game of the 1982 season, the last one in Willie Stargell's Hall of Fame career. "After not swinging a bat for weeks," Stenhouse struck out as a pinch-hitter against Pittsburgh's Don Robinson. Stenhouse had good company in becoming the second of four batters in a row fanned by Robinson, as he followed Andre Dawson and preceded Gary Carter and Tim Wallach.

Back at Wichita, Stenhouse got off to a sizzling start in 1983, batting a league-leading .393 through May 27 and finishing with a .355 average, 25 homers for the second straight year, and a 1.172 OPS (on-base percentage plus slugging average). Numbers like these caused the Expos to recall Stenhouse in July, but Montreal had no real spot for him even though manager Bill Virdon had said he would play regularly if called up."[23] First baseman Al Oliver would hit .300, and the Expos

had a regular outfield of Tim Raines, Dawson, and Warren Cromartie, none of whom had yet turned 30.

On July 28, 1983, Stenhouse made his season debut batting for the light-hitting Doug Flynn in game one of a doubleheader against the Cardinals. With one out and runners on first and second in a tie game, he pinch-hit against closer Bruce Sutter. "I had never really seen a forkball," recalled Stenhouse, "but I knew I should swing if it was up. Sutter's first pitch was a mistake right down the middle of the plate but slower in velocity than I imagined it would be. I was early on it and cued it off of the rounded end of the bat, something that happens only every few years. I fouled it off and knew I would never get another pitch like that. Then he threw another high forkball, and I did the exact same thing, except this time the ball stayed fair, but I barely got out of the batter's box because I did not know where the ball was." St. Louis turned a 5-4-3 double play on what Stenhouse eventually characterized as "the most embarrassing play of my career."

In the nightcap, Stenhouse had his first major-league hit, a double off Bob Forsch.

On August 4 Stenhouse got his first major-league RBI with a single off Ed Lynch of the Mets. But overall he struggled, batting .160 in his first 11 games with the Expos, and went back to Wichita, where he was voted the American Association's Most Valuable Player.[24]

Peter Gammons continued to promote Stenhouse, listing him 24th among the top nonpitching rookies of 1984. Gammons enthused about Stenhouse that "the former Harvard star can swing the bat … he works hard … and he hustles. No matter what the reports say, this guy is probably going to hit and end up the left fielder."[25]

Stenhouse had a monster spring training that seemed to justify Gammons's glorifications. Making Gammons look reserved, a Florida sportswriter wrote, "If Mike Stenhouse continues to hit the way he has this spring, he'll set records that Babe Ruth, Roger Maris and Hank Aaron never dreamed about."[26]

Stenhouse had his opening in 1984 with the free agent Cromartie having gone to Japan and Oliver playing in San Francisco after a trade. Montreal had signed Pete Rose as a free agent, star-struck by his historic career rather than his dismal 1983 season when at the age of 42 he had slugged a sickening .286 with a dismal OPS of .602. Gammons thought the lineup had room for both players, reporting that "the Expos are beginning to change their thinking and are pondering having Pete Rose move to first to make room for Harvardian Mike Stenhouse, who is hitting nearly .450 [in spring training] and fills their vital need for a lefthanded bat."[27]

With his hot spring start, Stenhouse certainly had self-confidence: "I have nothing left to prove in Triple A. I can play in the major leagues. I can help this team."[28]

Indeed, a young left-handed 1B/OF who had a sparkling college career with a father who starred in the American League would help the 1984 Expos. Unfortunately for Stenhouse, Terry Francona filled that role and batted .346 in 58 games. Montreal unwisely still gave Rose more than 300 plate appearances. At the age of 43, he improved his numbers slightly but insufficiently, slugging .295 with a .629 OPS.

Stenhouse did not even make the team at first following "an 0-for-22 drought"[29] and "temporarily quit … when the Expos optioned him to Indianapolis,"[30] which had replaced Wichita as the top minor-league affiliate of Montreal.

Stenhouse would play just 27 games for Indianapolis and continued to destroy Triple-A pitching, highlighted by a May 10 game in which he homered three times and drove in eight runs.[31]

Back with the Expos, Stenhouse hit his first major-league homers in 1984. His first came on May 23 on a "fastball from Andy Hawkins. Pete Rose was the first guy to congratulate me. He was a really good friend back then."

His second home run represented his fondest baseball memory because it reminded him of the camaraderie of his teammates. On July 14 Montreal faced Cincinnati's

Mario Soto, who came into the game with a 9-2 record. Stenhouse recalled, "Soto had the nastiest changeup. You couldn't tell the difference between that and his fastball. But Rose said Soto had a tell when pitching from the stretch. If he brings his glove down facing you, he'll throw a fastball. If the back of the glove is facing you, then he'll throw a changeup." With two runners on in the bottom of the first, Stenhouse forgot about the tell but managed to single and drive in a run. Expecting congratulations back in the dugout after the inning, Stenhouse instead got a hard time for missing the tell. In the third inning with a runner on and two out, Stenhouse remembered to look, got a fastball from Soto, and homered, sparking the Expos to a 6-2 win.

The homers notwithstanding, in 80 games at Montreal, Stenhouse put up Rose-like numbers, slugging .297 with a .586 OPS. The Expos in 1984 had a losing record for the first time since 1978. Virdon was fired on August 30. After the season, Montreal fan Stan Michne contributed a commentary to *The Bill James Baseball Abstract 1985* alleging "Virdon deserved to get fired on the basis of his handling of Stenhouse alone."[32]

To replace Virdon, Montreal reportedly considered Tim McCarver, Chuck Tanner, and Earl Weaver. Pittsburgh still had Tanner under contract so could require compensation to allow him to go to a division rival, and the *Pittsburgh Press* reported that Stenhouse might go to the Pirates.[33] Stenhouse's future in Montreal seemed short. He decided to play winter ball in the Dominican Republic "so someone could see me, and I could get traded."[34]

On January 9, 1985, the Expos granted Stenhouse his wish, trading him to the Twins for pitcher Jack O'Connor. According to the hyperbolic Gammons, "Few players have ever been happier about being traded than Harvardian Stenhouse, of Rhode Island's first family of baseball. 'I'd been hoping for a deal just to get some chance to play. … I'd really gotten to the point where I had to move on.'"[35]

On promise alone, Stenhouse should have played more than Rose did in 1984, but Stenhouse failed to produce for a struggling team. He made excuses: "The way I was used in Montreal—very much part-time—you find yourself going to the plate and trying to hit a six-run home run so they will keep you in the lineup. It was impossible for me to play that way. … Admittedly, the Montreal park was a little big for me. I left a lot of long fly balls on the warning track."[36]

The record shows, however, that the Expos gave Stenhouse more than 200 plate appearances at positions than demanded offense that season, and he hit just .183. Olympic Stadium may have hurt his extra-base power, but he hit all four of his National League homers there and twice as many as he ever hit in any other park. In three Montreal seasons, Stenhouse had an ugly .273/.269/.542 slash line that neither argued for more at-bats nor augured well for his future.

Minnesota offered a fresh start thanks to "Manager Billy Gardner … who pushed for the acquisition of the lefthanded-hitting Stenhouse. … Gardner thinks Stenhouse can provide lefthanded power to a Twins' lineup that—beyond Kent Hrbek—is severely lacking in lefties."[37]

In 1985 Stenhouse struggled but still had his best offensive season with career highs in every major offensive category except for doubles and OBP. The Twins had lost 10 straight coming into a June 2 game against the Milwaukee Brewers and trailed 4-3 with one on and two out in the bottom of the eighth. Milwaukee pitcher Bob Gibson threw Stenhouse "a slider, probably down out of the strike zone, but I was a lowball hitter." Stenhouse's two-run homer gave Minnesota a streak-busting 5-4 win.

On July 9 against Baltimore, Stenhouse smashed one through the box against rookie Nate Snell, breaking his rib, sending him to the hospital for an overnight stay, and putting him on the disabled list.[38] In the first game of a doubleheader on August 31 against future Red Sox teammate Steve Crawford in the ninth inning with two on, two out, and Minnesota trailing Boston 5-4, "Crawford was only one strike away from sealing the victory with … a 2-2 count on Mike Stenhouse, who hadn't driven in a run since Aug.

8."[39] Stenhouse went the other way with a single to tie the game, which the Twins won two batters later on a Ron Washington single.

Stenhouse said he had fond memories of his year in Minneapolis, where he met his first wife, but regretted that he did not play more with Minnesota unexpectedly using Greg Gagne at shortstop and Roy Smalley at designated hitter more than originally anticipated. "For all intents and purposes, that was the end of my career right there," Stenhouse concluded 30 years later. "I was feeling good and then my chance to play again went away. I never felt comfortable at the plate again."

On December 12, 1985, Minnesota traded Stenhouse to his hometown Red Sox. "General manager Lou Gorman, a Rhode Island guy who knew my dad well, got me to replace the retired Rick Miller as a left-handed-hitting outfielder/designated hitter," Stenhouse said. In exchange, the Twins received pitcher Charlie Mitchell, who never returned to the majors. "Every kid who grows up in New England dreams of playing in Fenway," Stenhouse said. "I'm happy to get that opportunity."[40]

By this point, however, even Gammons, Stenhouse's biggest media fan for more than seven years, seemed underwhelmed, concluding that the deal, "if nothing else, makes [Boston] better read."[41]

Somewhat more optimistically, Bill James wrote that Boston "picked up Mike Stenhouse cheap, and you know I like Stenhouse, while of course his chance of making it in the big leagues now isn't half of what it was a couple of years ago."[42]

Stenhouse started the 1986 season as he had in 1984. Again, he had a superb spring ("Ted Williams worked with me in spring training, which did not make [Red Sox hitting coach Walt] Hriniak happy"), failed to make the team, and balked at reporting to the minors. After initially refusing to speak to the media following his demotion, Stenhouse unloaded the following day: "I certainly earned a position and I didn't get it. When you don't get something you earned, you think maybe it wasn't there to get in the first place.

… I'm not criticizing anything. I'm just wondering why they got me in the first place. … The thing that bothers me is thinking whether the whole thing was a sham or not."[43]

As injudicious as his words seem on paper, Stenhouse probably did not feel better after the player Boston kept over Stenhouse—catcher Dave Sax—spent more than one month with the team without appearing in a single game. Ominously, the Sox recalled Stenhouse because "Bill Buckner says his sore elbow isn't improving."[44]

Stenhouse had the biggest moment of his Boston career on June 10, 1986. Facing Toronto's Mark Eichorn (Stenhouse remembered that "he threw side-arm slop, changeups and sliders") in the top of the 10th inning with two outs and the bases loaded in a 3-3 tie, Stenhouse drew a pinch-hit walk to drive in the winning run in a 4-3 final. "To go in for [Marty] Barrett … is amazing," Stenhouse said. "But to tell you the truth, it relaxed me."[45]

Stenhouse claimed that Barrett "walked halfway to the plate, turned around, and said to [manager John] McNamara, 'I can't hit Eichorn, Mac, hit Stenny for me.' It was a close 3-and-2 pitch, but I knew it was down and away."

The plate discipline of Stenhouse earned him an odd nickname in the Red Sox clubhouse when "his team-mates … started calling him 'Sony.' That's Sony as in Walkman. Stenhouse has walked six times in 12 pinch-hit appearances."[46]

The major-league career of Mike Stenhouse ended a little more than six weeks later on July 23, 1986. Facing Jay Howell, Stenhouse grounded out to end a 9-2 loss against Oakland, Boston's fourth straight defeat. The Red Sox decided to replace him with Mike Greenwell. Dan Shaughnessy wrote, "Stenhouse, another lefty hitter, had a disappointing stint in Boston."[47]

Boston tried to re-sign Stenhouse, but he chose to ink a minor-league contract with Detroit on February 4, 1987. Lou Gorman conceded that "he didn't get a lot of chances," but added, "with players like him, you've got to produce when you get the chance, and he didn't.

We think he had major-league ability and offered him another contract, but he chose to go elsewhere."[48]

Nate Snell, whose career Stenhouse had inadvertently derailed, had signed a similar deal with the Tigers two days earlier. Snell did play for Detroit in 1987, but Stenhouse did not after suffering "the worst injury of my career in spring training. On a cool morning BP session I strained a side muscle and then ripped it taking a swing in a game later that day."

At the end of his pro career, Stenhouse had a more realistic self-assessment as a classic Four-A player: one who could excel in the minors but could not stay in the majors. "You can play well in Triple-A ball over and over. That doesn't necessarily prove anything."[49]

Stenhouse played exceptionally well in Triple A from 1982 through 1984 with his low OPS a robust .949. With Pawtucket in 1986 and Toledo in 1987, however, Stenhouse posted consecutive OPS marks of .820. Having turned 29 in May 1987, Stenhouse turned down minor-league offers and ended his professional career after the 1987 season, returning to Rhode Island with his pregnant wife.

At first, he became an executive search consultant. "I went from the dugout to the corporate board room," quipped Stenhouse. Still, at first he dabbled in the game, "developing a fascinating statistical service called Stenstats, which show graphically a player or pitcher's performance over a season, several years and in comparison with other players."[50] Stenhouse also served as a commentator on radio and television for the Expos, and on cable television for Pawtucket.[51] He greatly enjoyed his broadcasting career: "It was really great—I did it for 12 years. Hardly anything I did I enjoyed more."

Stenhouse has had an unusually intellectual post-baseball career. According to his LinkedIn profile as of 2015, where he deemed himself "Defender of the free-enterprise-system!"[52] Stenhouse has since 2010 led two public-policy organizations in Rhode Island, the Ocean State Policy Research Institute and the Rhode Island Center for Freedom & Prosperity. He advocates for traditionally conservative economic approaches that would relax public-sector involvement with private businesses.

Stenhouse's two sons, Garrett and Kevin, played baseball at Bentley University and the University of Rhode Island, respectively, before getting jobs in accounting and capital budgeting. Stenhouse has married twice, first to Sue, the mother of his two children, who has worked in Rhode Island city government, and to Wendy in 2003. On the staff of the library at Bryant University, Wendy first impressed Mike with virulent pro-Red Sox and anti-Yankee views that she expressed even after the September 11 attacks in New York when many New Englanders briefly stopped loathing their archrivals. Mike is stepfather to Wendy's son, Neil.

While disappointed with his performance in the majors, Stenhouse still had a remarkable career overall considering his considerable collegiate and minor-league records. Nearly a generation after his playing days ended, Stenhouse expressed gratitude for the support of his family ("you cannot tell my story without their story") and seemed contentedly engaged in his advocacy of free-market policies in his home state.

NOTES

1   riheritagehalloffame.org/inductees_detail.cfm?iid=588 (accessed July 31, 2015).

2   Howard Sinker, "Stenhouse, Twins Turned Their Mutual Interest Into Reality," *Minneapolis Star and Tribune*, March 14, 1985: D4.

3   Bob Monahan, "Stenhouse Picked in 1st Round by A's," *Boston Globe*, June 6, 1979: 67.

4   Robert Sidorsky, "A Couple of Classy Guys," *Harvard Crimson*, April 22, 1978.

5   The 1986 Red Sox family would have at least one other Harvard connection. Rich Gedman's daughter Marissa captained the Harvard women's hockey team in 2013-2014 and played a prominent role on the Crimson's national runner-up squad in 2014-2015. See uscho.com/stats/player/wid,8117/marissa-gedman/ (accessed June 30, 2015). After Rich's father died in 1986, Stenhouse prepared to catch in case Boston needed an emergency backup. "'I caught two innings in a simulated game in the Instructional League,' said Stenhouse. 'And I caught some bullpen in Montreal. … Hey, my brother's a catcher [Dave Stenhouse was in the Blue Jays' minor-league system]. It's in the genes.'" Dan Shaughnessy, "There's Just One Catch," *Boston*

Globe, May 27, 1986: 29. Stenhouse never caught in professional baseball.

6   Michael K. Savit, "Batsmen Edge Northeastern; Stenhouse Gets Five Hits in 19-2 Thriller," *Harvard Crimson*, April 20, 1977.

7   Bill Scheft, "Harvard Baseball '78: This May Be 'Next Year,'" *Harvard Crimson*, March 22, 1978.

8   See gocrimson.com/sports/bsb/Record_Book/Records.pdf (accessed June 30, 2015).

9   Lesley Visser, "Harvard Stumbles, UConn Steals, 73-72," *Boston Globe*, January 15, 1978: 86.

10 John Donley, "Cagers Can Dartmouth, 71-69; Stenhouse Sticks Jumper at :02 to Win It," *Harvard Crimson*, March 1, 1978.

11 Statistics from sports-reference.com/cbb/schools/harvard/1978. html (accessed August 1, 2015).

12 Peter Gammons, "Why Sox Can Afford to Stall Rice signing," *Boston Globe*, August 6, 1978: 81.

13 Ray Fitzgerald, "Stenhouse Is Still Waiting," *Boston Globe*, July 31, 1979: 29.

14 Unless otherwise indicated, all quotations attributed to Stenhouse come from a telephone interview conducted August 1, 2015.

15 Nancy F. Bauer, "Oakland A's Draft Fielder Mike Stenhouse," *Harvard Crimson*, June 7, 1979.

16 Peter Gammons, "NL East Takes Turn for Better," *Boston Globe*, July 22, 1979: 39.

17 Jeffrey R. Toobin, "Mike Stenhouse Meets Charles O. Finley," *Harvard Crimson*, November 6, 1979. Toobin later gained renown for his legal commentaries for the *New Yorker* and various TV stations.

18 The Cubs picked Tom Henke 24th in this draft. Fans of the late, lamented Montreal Expos like the author of this profile wonder how history might have changed had the Expos picked (and signed) Henke instead of Stenhouse in 1980. If only Montreal could have rushed him to the majors the next year to face Rick Monday in Game Five of the 1981 National League Championship Series!

19 Mark H. Doctoroff, "Expos Pick Stenhouse Fourth in Draft," *Harvard Crimson*, January 9, 1980.

20 "Class A Leagues," *The Sporting News*, June 21, 1980: 45.

21 "Stenhouse Out Six Weeks; Felske Set to Go," *Harvard Crimson*, April 4, 1981.

22 Jaki Schllsinger, "Majoring In The Minors," *Harvard Crimson*, April 17, 1982.

23 Brian Kappler, "Will Stenhouse Find Lineup Spot?" *The Gazette* (Montreal), July 29, 1983: D-2.

24 "Class AAA Notes," *The Sporting News*, September 12, 1983: 27.

25 Peter Gammons, "The Rookies of '84," *Boston Globe*, January 15, 1984.

26 Chuck Otterson, "Expos' Stenhouse Slugging It Out in Fight for Job," *Palm Beach Post*, March 14, 1984.

27 Peter Gammons, "Jury Still Out on Yankee Doodlings," *Boston Globe*, March 18, 1984.

28 Ian MacDonald, "Stenhouse Making Noise With His Bat," *The Sporting News*, March 26, 1984: 26.

29 Peter Gammons, "Sox Cut Clemens; No Big Surprises in Houk's Moves," *Boston Globe*, March 27, 1984.

30 Peter Gammons, "Time for Birds to Molt?" *Boston Globe*, April 22, 1984.

31 "Class AAA Notes," *The Sporting News*, May 28, 1984: 39.

32 Bill James, *The Bill James Baseball Abstract 1985* (New York: Ballantine Books, 1985), 211.

33 Thomas Rogers, "Expos May Seek McCarver," *New York Times*, October 6, 1984. "Tanner has been traded once before during his managing career. The Pirates obtained him from the Oakland A's in November 1976 in exchange for Manny Sanguillen, the catcher."

34 Peter Gammons, "The Winter Game: The Dominican Republic Has Made Baseball a Game for All Seasons," *Boston Globe*, January 25, 1985.

35 Peter Gammons, "The Winter's Green for Dodger Blues," *Boston Globe*, January 13, 1985.

36 Patrick Reusse, "Metrodome May Suit Stenhouse," *The Sporting News*, February 18, 1985: 29.

37 Patrick Reusse, "Stenhouse Expected to Add Punch," *The Sporting News*, January 21, 1985: 40.

38 Jim Henneman, "Thundering Drive Hospitalizes Snell," *The Sporting News*, July 22, 1985: 14.

39 Larry Whiteside, "Red Sox Drop Pair to Twins," *Boston Globe*, September 1, 1985: 53.

40 Joel Rippel, "Twins Trade Stenhouse to Red Sox," *Minneapolis Star and Tribune*, December 13, 1985: D3.

41 Peter Gammons, "Stenhouse Joins Red Sox Bench," *Boston Globe*, December 13, 1985: 39.

42 Bill James, *The Bill James Baseball Abstract 1986* (New York: Ballantine Books, 1985), 143.

43 Dan Shaughnessy, "Baylor Feels at Home After Homer," *Boston Globe*, April 4, 1986: 65.

44 Ian Thomsen, "Sax Sent down; Stenhouse Up," *Boston Globe*, May 17, 1986: 26.

45 Larry Whiteside, "Red Sox Pinch Blue Jays in 10th," *Boston Globe*, June 11, 1986: 53.

46 Dan Shaughnessy, "Time to Reach for the Stars," *Boston Globe*, July 6, 1986: 54. In the 2015 interview, Stenhouse said Gammons gave him the nickname. Actually, he walked seven times in 16 plate appearances.

47 Dan Shaughnessy, "Burden on Clemens to Stop Downslide," *Boston Globe*, July 25, 1986: 45.

48 Sam Smith, "Now a Mud Hen, He Has to Know if Rocky Path Leads Nowhere," *Chicago Tribune*, August 3, 1987: B3.

49 Tom Loomis, "Stenhouse Still Has Big-League Hopes," *The Blade* (Toledo, Ohio), March 25, 1987: 25.

50 Nick Cafardo, "Hobson: No Room for Error," *Boston Globe*, December 20, 1992: 92.

51 Jim Greenidge, "A New Station in Life," *Boston Globe*, June 14, 1996: 100; Jim Greenidge, "Ch. 68 Taking Its Best Shots," *Boston Globe*, March 28, 1997: D10.

52 See linkedin.com/pub/mike-stenhouse/8/b73/813 (accessed June 18, 2015).

SAMMY STEWART

By Bill Nowlin

WHEN SAMMY STEWART WAS ASKED by the National Baseball Hall of Fame what he considered to be his most outstanding achievement in baseball, he quite justly answered that it was the rookie record he set in 1978 when he threw seven consecutive strikeouts in his major-league debut. No rookie has matched Stewart's totals. It was September 1, 1978, at Baltimore's Memorial Stadium, facing the Chicago White Sox. He got through the first inning, despite a leadoff single, his own error, and a wild pitch. The O's scored four times in the bottom of the first. Then Stewart struck out the side in the second, struck out the side in the third, and whiffed the first batter in the fourth. Mike Squires spoiled the streak by popping up to left field. Stewart and the Orioles won the game, 9-3. It's a record he still holds.

In his only other 1978 appearance, four weeks later to the day, he lost a tough 3-2 game to the Detroit Tigers. Stewart had allowed two earned runs, but an error by his center fielder cost the game.

Over the course of 10 seasons and 359 big-league games, the first eight with Baltimore, Stewart won 59 games and lost 48, with an earned-run average of 3.59. He sometimes suffered some pretty bad luck—in 1981, his 2.32 ERA was second in the American League[1] but his record was 4-8 (and that for an Orioles team that finished second in the AL East, just two games out of first place.)

He was a junior, born to Samuel Lee Stewart Sr. and the former Mary Faye Wardrup on October 28, 1954, in Asheville, North Carolina. The boy who became known as "The Throwin' Swannanoan" grew up in that North Carolina community, attending eight years of elementary school and Charles D. Owen High School. He completed two years at Montreat Anderson Junior College.

Stewart was selected by the Kansas City Royals in the June 1974 free-agent draft, but not until the 28th round. He elected not to sign that year, but did so as a nondrafted free agent when approached by Baltimore scout Rip Tutor, signing on June 15, 1975. The Orioles assigned him to the Bluefield Orioles in Bluefield, West Virginia, in the Appalachian League, a rookie league. He appeared in 18 games, starting in four, and compiled a 3-3 record with an ERA of 6.07 while getting his feet wet for the first time. He was still only 20 years old.

Stewart took full advantage of his first full season in Organized Baseball, pitching in Class A for the Miami Orioles (Florida State League). Throwing 182 innings, he put up a 12-8 record with an earned-run average of 2.42. Climbing two rungs on the ladder in 1977, Stewart was promoted to the Triple-A Rochester Red Wings. He was 0-5, then positioned a bit lower, moved to

Double-A and the Southern League's Charlotte O's (9-6, 2.08 ERA.) He finished 0-5 (6.33) with Rochester, but that's where he was reassigned in 1978, and this time he made good, winning 13 and losing 10 with a 3.80 ERA. And at the end of the year, he was given that first start and struck out those seven White Sox one after the other. He wouldn't see the minor leagues again other than for eight innings with Hagerstown in 1982 and 11⅔ innings in 1987 for Buffalo at the end of his career.

Stewart was a right-hander standing 6-feet-3 and listed with a playing weight of an even 200 pounds. He had married his high-school sweetheart, Peggy Jean Logan, in January 1977. The couple had two children, Colin and Alicia, both born with cystic fibrosis. It was important for him to remain as close as he could to hospitals of quality.

In 1979, Stewart was used primarily in relief—though he won each of the three starts he was given, pitching seven, nine, and eight innings and never giving up more than two earned runs. It was hard to crack manager Earl Weaver's five-man rotation featuring Mike Flanagan, Jim Palmer, Scott McGregor, Dennis Martinez, and Steve Stone. There were only five starts all season by anyone other than the main five, and Sammy had three of the five.

That rotation carried the Orioles to a division championship, eight games ahead of second-place Milwaukee, and to a pennant, winning the best-of-five American League Championship Series over the California Angels, three games to one. Sammy played no role in the ALCS. He did see action in the World Series, coming on in early relief of Dennis Martinez in Game Four at Pittsburgh's Three Rivers Stadium. The Pirates already had three runs in. He gave up one hit, allowing an inherited runner to score from second, but in 2⅔ innings of World Series work was not charged with a run, earned or unearned. The Pirates prevailed in seven games. Stewart came into baseball after the AL adopted the designated-hitter rule, and finished before interleague play. Accordingly, he never had a regular-season at-bat at any point, but he did bat once in the World Series. Jim Bibby struck him out.

The 1980 Orioles had not just one, but two 20-game winners (Steve Stone actually won 25), but they finished second to the Yankees. Stewart posted nearly identical stats to 1979—again, he started three times, but this time he lost the first of them. His ERA for the year was 3.56 instead of 3.52, negligibly different. He threw one more inning—118⅔ instead of 117⅔. The only significant difference was that Weaver had him close 20 games, double the year before.

And 1981 wasn't that much different in some regards. Again, three starts, 112⅓ innings, and the team finishing second to the Yankees. This time all the first three starts were losses, and all in the first half of the year which had been split into two halves due to a midseason players' strike. The Orioles finished two games behind the division leader in each half and weren't involved in the postseason at all. This was the year that Stewart finished second in ERA only to Dave Righetti's 2.05 among all AL pitchers, with his 2.32 mark—by far the best of his career—but suffered the 4-8 W-L record.[2] It was also a year when he almost threw left-handed in a game against the Yankees. "I've always been able to throw left-handed pretty good," Stewart told *Albany Times-Union* writer Bob Matthews. "Flanny [Mike Flanagan] bet me I'd never try it in a real game, but I came real close." It was May 26, and the Orioles had a 6-4 lead in the top of the ninth with nobody on. Left-handed hitter Dave Revering was up for the Yankees and the count was 0 and 2. "I turned my back to the plate, bent over, and shifted my glove to my right hand. Then I turned around real quick, and started to gear up for a left-handed pitch. Revering looked stunned and asked for time just as I was at the top of my windup." Jim Palmer recalled that Orioles pitching coach "Stu Miller had to run out there and stop him." Glove back on his left hand, Stewart got Revering to foul out to the catcher.[3]

The following year, Stewart still faced the challenge of cracking the rotation. One of his problems may have been that, despite such a stellar ERA in 1981, he was "too good for his own good … too good at what he does."[4] He was "Mr. Everything" for Weaver—a long reliever, a spot starter, a closer in the days before that was a specialty. Teammate Mike Flanagan really appreciated what Stewart brought to the bullpen: "He comes to the park prepared to pitch seven innings every night. It can be a thankless job," he added, thinking of the times that Stewart would come into a game with the Orioles already trailing and keep them in the game, eating up innings.[5] Miller saw Stewart as offering the team the luxury of having two starting pitchers on most nights—the man chosen to start, and then Stewart himself, who was always ready. "He'd be a starting pitching for at least 24 teams in baseball right now—all except ours and maybe Houston." Miller told Peter Gammons, "On a good staff, a guy in that role can hold everything and everyone together."[6]

"I like long relief," Stewart told Ken Nigro, "but I never know what's ahead. You look at the starters and you see it in their eyes. They know what's ahead, they know when they're going to pitch and in what town and to what batters. Me? I don't have anything to look forward to, no plan. They just tell me, 'Sammy, you might be in there tonight.'" A pitcher who can thrive in those circumstances is indeed invaluable to a manager. "I'd like to have the chance to pitch 250 innings and get 40 starts a year. … I think '83 is the year."[7]

In 1982 Stewart did get 12 starts, mostly in May, but the rest were spot starts, and as the year wore on he became more disappointed that he never had more opportunities to start on a regular basis. He did let it be known, but there wasn't a lot Weaver felt he could do. Stewart won 10 games (against nine losses), but saw his ERA climb to 4.14, in part because of problems due to bone chips in both knees which occasioned a 21-day disabled-list stint and a very brief two-game rehab stay in Hagerstown. The Orioles finished second, by just one game, to the Brewers for tops in the AL East. Sammy had pitched in the next-to-last game of the season, against the Brewers. Milwaukee had a one-game lead. Scott McGregor had given up three early runs to the Brewers, but Stewart came into a game tied 3-3 and allowed just two hits and no runs in the final 5⅔ innings, while watching his teammates build an 11-3 game and pull into a dead heat for first place with one game to play. Jim Palmer was outpitched

by Don Sutton in the final game, turning a 4-1 deficit over to the Orioles bullpen after five-plus innings. The final was Milwaukee 10, Baltimore 2. It was another year watching the postseason from home.

The 1983 season was dominated by a major accomplishment: a return to the World Series. Stewart got just one start, but he closed 21 games for new manager Joe Altobelli and put up a 9-4 record (3.62 ERA). The O's won the division, six games ahead of the Tigers, and took three out of four games in the ALCS. Stewart pitched a third of an inning in Game One, a 2-1 loss to Chicago and the only loss for Baltimore. He'd been brought on in the bottom of the seventh with runners on second and third, two outs, and catcher Carlton Fisk at the plate. He struck out Fisk, keeping it a one-run game. Touched in the eighth for a single and a walk, he was then replaced by Tippy Martinez. He entered the game in the sixth inning of Game Three with his team leading 6-1, and pitched one-hit ball over the final four innings as the Orioles took an insurmountable 3-0 lead in the ALCS.

It was the Orioles over the Phillies in five during the World Series, and Stewart pitched five innings of relief, appearing in Games One, Three, and Four. He faced 18 batters and struck out six, allowing two hits and walking two, and held Philadelphia scoreless throughout, ultimately leaving baseball with an earned-run average of 0.00 in six postseason games. At the plate, he had two more at-bats, striking out once and grounding into a double play. His career batting average was all zeroes as well. But no one cared. The Orioles had won the World Series. Rick Dempsey was selected as Series MVP, but Sammy Stewart was the runner-up.[8] It was Dempsey who had called Stewart "the unsung hero of the staff" even two years earlier.[9]

Mentioning Dempsey triggers a story from the August 22, 1980, game in Oakland. Baltimore led 3-2 heading into the bottom of the ninth. Pinch-hitter Mike Davis tripled to lead off, and Stewart starting shouting at Dempsey regarding the pitch he'd called. "I wouldn't mind if he got upset inside," Dempsey said, "but not prancing around on the mound. I told him the run hadn't scored so let's battle our way out of it." Two strikeouts and a groundout, and the battery embraced and walked off the field.[10]

It might also have been a year (1983) when Stewart overcame a problem with alcoholism. He was arrested on July 8, only driving 40 miles per hour but driving erratically. He was given a small fine and sentenced to 18 months' probation. Both Earl Weaver (who'd been arrested three times himself for drunken driving) and Joe Altobelli said they would work with him, and apparently they did. July 8 — "that's the date of my last scotch and water. I'm glad it happened. ... I needed help," Stewart said in October.[11] The episode was not the last problem he would have with substance abuse.

Things fell apart for the team in 1984. The Orioles finished 19 games out of first place. Stewart led the staff again, this time appearing in 60 games and became a defined closer, finishing 39 games and with a career-high 13 saves. He was 7-4, with an improved 3.29 ERA. It wasn't much better in 1985, and Stewart finished almost as many games (36), while pitching quite a few more innings and seeing significant increases in the number of hits, walks, and more than double the number of home runs allowed. His ERA at 3.61 was still superior to the team's 4.38. On December 17, 1985, Stewart was traded to the Boston Red Sox for infielder Jackie Gutierrez. Boston was anxious to build a better bullpen.

Other than the experience of leaving the only organization for which he'd ever played, in one way the year may have turned out better: the Orioles sank to last place, and the Red Sox went to the World Series. Stewart, however, missed a big chunk in the middle of the season, after a May 31 arm injury, not pitching at all from June 8 to July 27. He pitched 63⅔ innings, by far his lowest total, and, though he was 4-1, it was despite a 4.38 ERA. Worse, he'd lost the confidence of manager John McNamara. "If they let me pitch, we would've won that Series," he told the *Globe's* Stan Grossfeld. McNamara may not have cottoned to some of his clowning in the clubhouse, but Grossfeld says Stewart told him that he wound up in the doghouse due to a time the team bus pulled out and left him behind at Fenway Park. Stewart said he'd been visit-

ing his son Colin in the hospital, but had arrived at the ballpark on time, thrown his bag on the bus, and was parking his car when the bus pulled out without waiting. He got into bitter arguments with traveling secretary Jack Rogers and with McNamara, and may have burned a bridge or two. During the World Series, Stewart said of McNamara, "He lay down on me and it cost us the World Series. I hated to see Al Nipper come out of the bullpen when I've never been scored on in the postseason and my arm was feeling good."[12]

On November 12 Stewart was granted free agency — in other words, the Red Sox let him go.

Opening Day 1987 came and went, and Sammy Stewart still didn't have a job. On June 4 he was signed by the Cleveland Indians, shuffled to Buffalo for six innings of work in six appearances (0-1, with a poor 9.26 ERA) but still brought up to the big leagues for what proved to be his swan song: Beginning on July 2, he appeared in 25 games, throwing 27 innings. His first appearance helped the Indians win a game; he came in during the top of the ninth of a 1-1 tie in Chicago with one out and a man on. He retired five White Sox in a row, carrying the game through the 10th. Cleveland ultimately won it in the 11th.

Called upon again in the top of the ninth the next day, Stewart was hammered mercilessly by the same White Sox. This time he'd been asked to hold a 9-8 lead, but he gave up two hits and three walks, threw a wild pitch, and saw all five runs score. By season's end he had whittled that ERA down to 3.32 in mid-September, then seen it climb back to a final 5.67. He wasn't asked back, released on October 29, at which point he'd reached the end of the string in Organized Baseball. He retired the following year. His final totals were 59-48, 3.59, with 45 saves.

In his life after baseball, Stewart struggled. His son, Colin, died in 1991. His daughter, Alicia, had a double lung transplant. *Baltimore Sun* sportswriter Dan Connolly explained more: "Most Orioles fans know the dark side of Stewart's story, too. He became addicted to crack cocaine following his playing career, and was charged 46 times with more than 60 offenses over a decade-plus, primarily stemming from his drug use. At one point he was homeless and penniless." He'd thrown it all away. Connolly wrote, "In 2006, he began serving a sentence of at least six years for a felony drug charge and is currently incarcerated at the Buncombe Correctional Center in Asheville, N.C."[13]

In October 2006 Stan Grossfeld wrote a lengthy profile of Stewart in the *Boston Globe*, after visiting him at North Carolina's Piedmont Correctional Institution. Stewart wrote, "'There's a lot of times I wished I would have died because I was pathetic,' he says matter of factly. 'I guess I started digging a hole for myself and it got so bad I got homeless, moneyless, friendless. I just started covering myself up instead of climbing out of the hole.'" He told of sleeping under bridges, of shooting up and getting shot at. He untruthfully told people his daughter had died, so he could get some sympathy and ask for a little money to help out. Unsurprisingly, his wife, Peggy, and Stewart separated.

This author tried several times to correspond with Stewart at the facility he'd moved to after Piedmont, the Buncombe Correctional Center in Asheville—but never heard back until after his release.. However, following the August 2011 suicide of Mike Flanagan, Stewart did send an open letter to fans in care of Dan Connolly in which he said, in part, "These last five years have definitely altered my reality; prison is not the place to be. I'm glad I have learned humility, and I work hard to stay teachable. We all must.

"Thank you guys for all the good times and wonderful memories. I am a richer man for them. Hopefully, when I get out of prison on the 10th of January, 2013, there will be a 30th anniversary reunion for the '83 champs of this world; I will be there with clear and focused—and potentially dampening—eyes."[14]

Stewart was released from prison in January 2013 and settled in Hendersonville, North Carolina, hoping to rebuild a happier life.[15]

SOURCES

In addition to the sources cited within this biography, the author consulted the subject's player file and questionnaire at the National Baseball Hall of Fame, the online SABR Encyclopedia, Retrosheet.org, and Baseball-Reference.com.

Thanks to Sammy Stewart and his friend Cherie Linquist for reading over the biography for accuracy in September 2013.

NOTES

1 See Bill Nowlin and Lyle Spatz, "Choosing Among Winners of the 1981 AL ERA Title," *Baseball Research Journal*, Spring 2011.

2 Ibid. Righetti did not qualify for the American League title, however.

3 *Albany Times-Union*, June 2, 1981. The Palmer quote comes from the *Boston Globe* of October 25, 2006. Revering felt he'd been disrespected. A week later, on June 2, he hit an 11th-inning homer off Stewart to win a game.

4 *The Sporting News*, April 3, 1982.

5 *Albany Times-Union*, June 2, 1981.

6 *Albany Times-Union*, June 2, 1981. Gammons wrote in *The Sporting News*, March 28, 1981.

7 *Boston Globe*, October 25, 2006.

8 *Boston Globe*, October 25, 2006.

9 *Albany Times-Union*, June 2, 1981.

10 Unattributed September 13, 1980, clipping in Stewart's Hall of Fame player file.

11 Unattributed October 17, 1983, clipping by Mike McAlary in Stewart's Hall of Fame player file.

12 *Boston Globe*, October 25, 2006.

13 *Baltimore Sun*, October 10, 2011.

14 *Baltimore Sun*, October 10, 2011.

15 Dean Hensley, *Hendersonville Times-News* at BlueRidgeNow.com, April 22, 2013.

MARC SULLIVAN

By Armand Peterson

MARC SULLIVAN STARTED 35 GAMES IN 1986 as backup to All-Star catcher Rich Gedman. He made the squad in spring training because of his defensive skills, but many critical Red Sox fans and beat writers would not overlook his offensive shortcomings. He hit only .193, with 23 hits in 119 at-bats, and seemed to be booed more rabidly than other Red Sox players when he struck out or failed to advance a baserunner. A common assumption was that Sullivan was on the team only because his father, Haywood Sullivan, was the team's general manager and part owner. Toward the end of spring training the *Boston Globe's* Dan Shaughnessy expressed the view of many when he wrote that "Marc Sullivan is hitting .167 and is assumed to have the backup catcher's job because of his defensive ability (he's also the owner's son and makes $110,000.)"[1]

Sullivan started only two games in April, but manager John McNamara came to his defense. "He's not here because he's the owner's son," McNamara said. "He comes in with a shadow cast over him because of who he is, but he's a good catcher. We had a lot of interest in him [from other teams] in the offseason."[2]

The Red Sox surprised a lot of baseball fans and experts when they drafted Marc Sullivan in the second round (52nd overall) of the 1979 June amateur draft. (Boston lost its first-round pick to Oakland when it signed free-agent pitcher Steve Renko in January.) Although Sullivan grew up playing catch with Red Sox players like Carlton Fisk and Carl Yastrzemski, and had Fenway Park and the team's spring-training camp in Winter Haven, Florida, as playgrounds, his own baseball credentials had not been impressive.

He played on youth baseball teams, regularly attended the prestigious Ted Williams Camp in Lakeville, Massachusetts, and was a two-sport star—basketball and baseball—at Canton (Massachusetts) High School. Marc Cooper Sullivan had been born in Quincy, Massachusetts, just south of Boston, on July 25, 1958, when his father was a catcher for the Red Sox. Haywood had been a top catching prospect and signed an estimated $40,000 to 50,000 bonus contract with the Red Sox after the 1952 season. The Canton High baseball team played only 15 or 20 games a year, and Marc was listed as an infielder when he signed a grant-in-aid to play baseball at the University of Florida in July 1976.[3] He was following his father to Florida, where Haywood had starred in football and baseball.

Catching wasn't even Marc's favorite position. "But when it came time for me to go to college," he told Larry Whiteside in a 1982 interview, "I had to make a decision as to which position would get me the best shot of playing professional ball. I finally chose catching because a lot of young guys don't stick with

it because of the difficulty of the position. … I did pretty well as a catcher even though I didn't like it."[4]

Marc made the Florida varsity team as a freshman in 1977, but played in only nine games. He was the starting catcher in 1978, hitting .207 in 145 at-bats in 45 games. He missed half the season in 1979 with injuries, hitting .244 in 25 games. Sullivan's batting statistics while playing two summers in the Cape Cod Baseball League were not impressive, either. He hit .270 for Orleans in 1977, with two home runs in 89 at-bats, and .245 for Chatham in 1978, with four home runs in 110 at-bats. (Most colleges and the Cape Cod League used aluminum bats, which tended to inflate hitting statistics compared with wood bats used in professional baseball.) Nonetheless, professional scouts liked Sullivan's 6-foot-4 size, strong arm, and power-hitting potential. His playing weight is listed by baseball-reference.com as 205 pounds.

Marc decided to test the waters by declaring for the amateur draft after his junior season in 1979. "Dad and I talked about it a lot before I was drafted," he later told Peter Gammons. "We went over everything: that I would stay in school if I weren't drafted in the first three rounds. … We discussed the possibilities of being drafted by Boston. I knew there would be bad or negative aspects, but no matter where I went or whom I played for, I'd always hear stuff about my dad. If I couldn't take that, then how could I take the hard part of the game?"[5]

Predictably, many were quick to charge that the Red Sox drafted Sullivan only because he was the general manager's son. Haywood tried to deflect the criticisms. "Actually, I had nothing to do with the drafting, evaluating or selecting. That was done by [farm director] Eddie Kenney and [scouting director] Eddie Kasko. But I'll still be the one who gets knocked for it."[6]

Kenney defended the choice: "He's a kid who looks like he can throw and hit. First-class catchers are hard to find."[7] Marc was perhaps the most realistic. "I realize there are plusses [sic] and minuses," he said. "No one in his right mind would believe they'd waste a high draft pick on the father-son thing. But it's something I'll have to get used to and play my way out of."[8]

The Red Sox' choice was somewhat vindicated in August when Marc was selected to *The Sporting News* All-American team. This team was selected by professional scouting directors, whereas the "official" All-American team was selected by the American Baseball Coaches Association. Cal State Fullerton's Tim Wallach was the only player to appear on both teams. What team was the better predictor of professional success? It wasn't close — seven of 11 members of *The Sporting News* team played five or more years in the major leagues, only two from the coaches' team. Lou Pavlovich, editor of *Collegiate Baseball* magazine, said the professionals overlooked the fact that Sullivan had missed half the season. He "still was considered one of the fine catchers in college baseball. The scouts selected him on his known ability."[9]

Sullivan recovered from his injuries in time to play 31 games in 1979 with Winter Haven in the Class-A Florida State League, where he hit only .207. But he impressed players and coaches with his defensive skills in his first spring training in 1980. Peter Gammons wrote that "Marc Sullivan will probably only be in [Double-A] Bristol, but ask any of the minor league pitchers, and they'll tell you he is far away the best defensive catcher — receiving and throwing the ball."[10]

Sullivan returned to Winter Haven in 1980 and struggled with a .225 batting average, but he made significant improvement at Winston-Salem in the Class-A Carolina League in 1981. He hit a so-so .268, but showed power with 21 doubles, 14 home runs, and an .807 OPS. Sullivan was also the league's All-Star catcher, and was being compared to 6-foot-3 Carlton Fisk. "Marc's going to hear it increasingly because he reminds me more of Carlton Fisk every day," said Winston-Salem manager Buddy Hunter, who'd been Fisk's teammate three years in the minor leagues.[11] At least the focus was now on Sullivan the player, not on Sullivan the general manager's son. At the beginning of the season he had refused interviews about anything other than the Winston-Salem Red Sox. "What I don't like is when people want me to constantly comment on my father and the Red Sox. Who am I to do that? I'm a catcher in A ball."[12]

Sullivan moved up to Bristol in the Double-A Eastern League in 1982, but went backward at the plate, hitting .203 with one home run. Nevertheless, Boston called him up on September 18 after Rich Gedman had broken his collarbone and manager Ralph Houk wanted a defensive catcher to help out. Sullivan made his first major-league appearance on October 1 at Yankee Stadium, replacing Gary Allenson in the seventh inning of a 12-inning 3-2 victory. He hit an infield single in his first at-bat against Yankees ace Ron Guidry, threw out a would-be basestealer, and drew a compliment from Houk, who said, "I'm not sure I've ever seen an arm like this. Maybe Lance Parrish, but Sullivan's release is quicker."[13]

Sullivan's chances to make the major-league roster in 1983 were dashed when the Red Sox obtained veteran catcher Jeff Newman from Oakland in the offseason. Gedman and Gary Allenson had been splitting catching duties since Carlton Fisk had been lost to free agency after the 1980 season. Manager Houk basically carried only two catchers in 1981 and 1982, but decided to carry Newman as a third catcher in 1983. Sullivan was sent to Double-A New Britain (successor to Bristol), where he caught 43 games and also played 30 at first base. He got off to a great start and led the league in hitting after 30 games, but slumped to .229. His power numbers were good, though, with 15 doubles, 7 home runs, and a .772 OPS. He was moved to Triple-A Pawtucket at midseason, and was hitting only .186 in 27 games on August 15 when a foul tip fractured a fibula and sidelined him for the rest of the year.

Houk went with three catchers again in 1984, although Gedman became the undisputed number one—Allenson started only 27 games while Newman started 18. Sullivan spent the season at Pawtucket, where he hit .204, with 14 doubles, 1 triple, and 15 home runs in 383 at-bats. He played in two games at Boston as a September call-up.

Veteran manager John McNamara replaced the retiring Ralph Houk for the 1985 season. Gary Allenson had been granted free agency in November 1984 and it appeared that Sullivan had a good shot at making the squad as the number-three catcher. Newman, the presumed number two, was released on April 4, and McNamara decided to start the season with three catchers—Gedman, Sullivan, and Dave Sax, signed as a free agent from the Dodgers organization where he had hit a cumulative .307 in the last three years at Triple-A Albuquerque.

Boston's beat writers finally seemed to give credit to Sullivan. The *Globe's* Larry Whiteside wrote that he "made the squad on merit, not because he is the boss' son."[14] The *Boston Herald's* Joe Giuliotti wrote in *The Sporting News* that Sullivan "knows there have been, and probably always will be, those who whisper behind his back that he is in the big leagues because his father owns the club. But baseball people know that isn't true."[15] Sullivan felt he earned the spot by hitting .280 in the exhibition season and playing well defensively.

By the end of April, McNamara decided to carry only two catchers and sent Sax to Pawtucket. Sullivan hit his first home run in the majors on May 15, a solo shot off Seattle's Mark Langston. He made two appearances on the 15-day disabled list—on June 2 for a muscle tear in his left rib area, and on July 3 for a slightly fractured left wrist. Dave Sax was called back from Pawtucket in June and shared number-two catching duties with Sullivan for the rest of the season. Sullivan was hitting .240 before his first stint on the DL, but finished the season at .174. He started 23 games as a catcher, and played in a total of 32 games.

Despite his anemic hitting, Sullivan appeared to have the number-two catcher spot sewed up for 1986. Gedman had an All-Star year in 1985, hitting .295, compiling an .846 OPS, and starting 129 games. As a defensive specialist, Sullivan would be required only to spell Gedman once a week or so.

Sullivan had always taken advice on hitting from mentors inside and outside the organization, from Carl Yastrzemski, Ted Williams, Johnny Pesky, Sam

Mele, anyone. The *Boston Globe's* Leigh Montville described some intense sessions with Yaz in spring training. "The search continues. Head down. Head up. Closed stance. Swing. Swing again. … Hitting a thrown baseball is the toughest act to perform in American sport. Watch Wade Boggs hit the ball here and there and everywhere and you sometimes forget that fact. Watch Marc Sullivan and you remember."[16]

The Red Sox were 32–15 and in first place at the end of May, 2½ games ahead of the Yankees, and pennant fever began to strike New England. Sullivan started strong, too, and was hitting .306 (11-for-36) in 12 games through May 30, but went 12-for-83 the rest of the season to finish at .193. Fans got on him as his offensive futility grew. He was loudly booed when he struck out twice with runners on base in a game on August 31. Then he struck out his first three times at bat in his next game on September 3, bringing his average down to a season-low .168. Sullivan was placed on the 24-man postseason roster, but did not play in Boston's seven-game Championship Series victory over California or in their seven-game World Series loss to the New York Mets.

The Red Sox missed the deadline to sign free agent Rich Gedman on January 8, 1987, making him eligible to sign with other clubs and preventing Boston from re-signing him until May 1. Gedman's absence meant that Sullivan was the starting catcher when spring training started. He knew he was on the spot. "It's a good situation," Sullivan told *Boston Globe* writer Larry Whiteside. "I've got a chance to be No. 1 until May 1. … Don't get me wrong. I didn't go out and do handstands on Jan. 8. But I knew the situation with Geddy and I know what it means to me. I've even spoken with him about it."[17]

Many still doubted Sullivan's credentials. "Life isn't easy for the boss' kid when the boss' kid works in the boss' shop," wrote the *Globe's* Dan Shaughnessy. "Everyone assumes that you're only there because blood is thicker than pine tar. The paying public chuckles smugly and some of your coworkers think you're a snitch. … Sullivan has it tougher than most bosses' kids. He carries the weight of Rich Gedman's

contract dispute, Roger Clemens' walkout and his own anemic .200 career batting average. He knows a large percentage of the public believes the Sox failed to sign Gedman to Make Room For Sonny."[18] Sullivan was able to shake off some of the critics. "They keep calling me 'May 1,'" he said with a smile. "Then they ask me what I am going to be doing May 2 when (Rich) Gedman comes back."[19]

Johnny Marzano, an All-American with Temple in 1984, and the leading hitter on the US Olympic team in Los Angeles, was thought to be ready to challenge Sullivan for the starting position, but he hit only .194 in spring training and did not field very well. Sullivan solidified his position by hitting .350 in spring training. Manager McNamara went north with three catchers, Sullivan, Dave Sax, and Danny Sheaffer. The 25-year-old Sheaffer had been in the Boston organization since 1981 and hit .340 at Triple-A Pawtucket in 1986.

Sullivan got hits in his first three games to start the season, including a home run on the first pitch he saw in the home opener against Toronto. But he got only four hits in his next 11 games, and at the end of April, after starting 14 of the team's first 22 games, he was hitting .163. Sheaffer caught the other eight games, but his .179 was not much of an improvement.

Meanwhile, Gedman signed a two-year deal for a reported $883,000 per year, and played his first game on May 2, pinch-hitting for Sheaffer at Anaheim. Gedman's layoff appeared to have taken a toll—he never did display the batting stroke that earned him All-Star honors the previous two years. Gedman went on the disabled list in early July for a pulled groin muscle, and then on July 27 severely injured thumb ligaments on his left hand and was done for the season. He hit only .205, with one home run in 52 games.

Boston called Marzano up from Pawtucket to replace Gedman. At the time Sullivan was hitting only .171, while Sheaffer was at an anemic .107. They were having defensive problems, as well—Gedman and Sullivan had been charged with eight passed balls each. The team was 47–54 and going nowhere. It seemed like a good time to see what Marzano could do. "It makes no sense to let (Marzano) sit," manager McNamara told the *Herald's* Joe Giuliotti. "He's here. Let's find out about him."[20] Marzano caught 48 of the team's remaining games while Sullivan played in only 11 games the rest of the season.

Sullivan was a frequent target of boo-birds when he did play. It was especially vocal at a game on June 23, when he had a passed ball and struck out twice before being replaced by a pinch-hitter. The stoic catcher, who usually suffered his critics in silence, uncharacteristically lashed out at fans. "That's nothing new here," Sullivan told *Globe* reporter Kevin Paul Dupont. "That showed the kind of fans we've got here. They don't give a damn. That's all I've got to say. I try the best I can." Sullivan pointed out that Boston fans had once demeaned the Minnesota Twins' Jim Eisenreich when he was suffering with Tourette's syndrome.[21]

On July 26 the *Globe's* Jack Craig unloaded on Sullivan for striking out with the bases loaded in the July 21, 3–0 win over the Angels at Fenway Park. "The longer Sullivan plays, the more it appears he is on the team because his father, team co-owner Haywood Sullivan, wants Marc and his young family to enjoy the good life in the majors rather than the bad life in the minors. As [sports radio talk show host] Eddie Andelman repeatedly says on WHDH, he would do the same thing for his kid."[22]

At the close of the season Sullivan revealed he planned to try pitching in the Florida Instructional League. He told Joe Giuliotti that he actually began the process a month earlier when he started going to Fenway early and throwing to pitching coach Bill Fischer. "I'd throw for 10 to 14 minutes a day and once threw three days in a row so Fischer could see how my arm bounced back, and it responded well."[23] Sullivan had pitched a little in high school, and last pitched a few games in relief in the Cape Cod League in 1977 and 1978. But his plans were derailed when he injured his elbow before he had a chance to pitch in his first game.

Meanwhile, Red Sox general manager Lou Gorman was planning to trade Sullivan. He said he first talked to Haywood Sullivan about it near the end of the season. Haywood agreed. "His dad didn't interfere in the slightest," said Gorman. "But, like I said, it was delicate, trading a young man who happens to be the son of my boss. … What was tough for Marc was that he was under a lot of tremendous pressure here. The fans would get on him for his hitting or the fans would take out on him their frustrations with the team and Marc took a lot of guff for being the owner's son. But the thing is that Marc never opened his mouth about it, never complained, never said it was unfair."[24]

Sullivan was traded to the Houston Astros on December 14, 1987, for minor-league infielder Randy Randle. He seemed pleased. "The time is right for something like this to happen. Now maybe the focus can be on Marc Sullivan, the player, and not the owner's kid."[25]

Sullivan never made it back to the major leagues. A sore elbow limited his playing time, and Houston released him at the end of spring training. The Philadelphia Phillies signed him to a Triple-A contract to play for their Maine affiliate in the International League. Phillies catcher Darren Daulton broke his hand when he punched a locker-room wall after a game on August 27. Sullivan might have been called up to replace Daulton, but he had an injured left hand. The White Sox signed Sullivan to a Triple-A contract in 1989, and he played 84 games for Vancouver in the Pacific Coast League.

February 1990 found Sullivan working out during the major-league lockout at the Red Sox training camp in Winter Haven, waiting to be offered a minor-league contract. (He could legally use the locked-out facility because he was a nonroster player.) "The last two years, I've been a player-coach, even though I haven't had the title," he told the *Boston Globe's* Nick Cafardo. "I've been working with young pitchers and young players and I've really enjoyed it. I know now that I'd like to coach and manage in the minor leagues and someday make it to the majors."[26]

Sullivan eventually signed as a catching instructor in the Cleveland organization. He caught 12 games late in the season to fill a vacancy with Colorado Springs of the Pacific Coast League. That would be the end of his playing days. He was hired as an American League advance scout by the Texas Rangers in 1991. He was rumored to be a candidate for major-league coaching positions in the next several years, but none of them panned out. The Rangers dropped him in November 1994.

Sullivan has been involved in Fort Myers and southwest Florida real-estate development in his post-baseball career. As of 2015 he was president of Sullivan-Florida Group Inc., owner-operator of the Legacy Harbour Marina, Legacy Harbour Hotel & Suites, and Caloosahatchee Development & Realty Inc. He and his wife, Angela, have four children, Loreal (born in 1986), Brandon, Sierra, and Krystle.

Time seems to have removed any pain left over from Sullivan's difficult years in Boston. He has been involved in Red Sox fantasy camps for almost 20 years, as a member of pro-advisory staffs, as a camp director, and for a few years as the co-owner of New England Sports Franchises, the former owner of the franchise.

He returned to Fenway Park for a June 27, 2006, pregame ceremony at a game with—of course—the New York Mets, honoring the Red Sox' 1986 team. It was a heartwarming event … for fans as well as the old players. Bill Buckner, the '86 Series goat, said he couldn't attend because of a personal conflict, but his image on the video board was greeted with cheers. "That was really nice," [1986] second baseman Marty Barrett said of Buckner's reception. "I wish he were here to see that. It would have been fun. The fans here know. They got a win in 2004, and all of that was released, '46, '67, '75, '86, all of those guys feel like there's a weight lifted off their shoulders."

"You know what's interesting, and I really never thought about it," Barrett continued, "somebody told me the other day all these teams wanted to win it for the fans. But I heard the fans couldn't wait for a team to win it to help all of us who couldn't get it done. I thought that was pretty neat."[27]

Marc Sullivan had to feel the love as he jogged to his old position behind the plate.

SOURCES

In addition to the sources indicated in the notes, the author also consulted:

Baseball-reference.com, Retrosheet.org, and the University of Florida Athletics, gatorzone.com. He also accessed the Marc Sullivan player file at the National Baseball Hall of Fame Library, the 1975 Canton High School Yearbook, via archive.org, and corresponded by e-mail with

Bob Sherman, Chatham (Cape Cod Baseball League) vice president, on July 25, 2015, and with Judy Scarafile, Cape Cod Baseball League president, on July 28, 2015.

NOTES

1   Dan Shaughnessy, "2 Pitchers Demoted; More Cuts Today," *Boston Globe*, March 28, 1986.

2   Dan Shaughnessy, "One Giant Leap for a Franchise," *Boston Globe*, April 27, 1986.

3   "Another Sullivan for Florida," *St. Petersburg Times*, July 13, 1976: 3C.

4   Larry Whiteside, "In Dad's Footsteps; Marc Sullivan Finds Being the Boss' Son is Both Burden, Blessing," *Boston Globe*, February 28, 1982.

5   Peter Gammons, "Marc Sullivan Showing He's More Than Haywood's Son," *Boston Globe*, July 2, 1981.

6   Larry Whiteside, "Red Sox' No. 1 Draft Choice is the son of G.M. Sullivan," *The Sporting News*, June 23, 1979: 6.

7   Ibid.

8   Ibid.

9   Lou Pavlovich, "Slugger Wallach Leads Collegiate All-Star Choices," *The Sporting News*, August 11, 1979: 9.

10 Peter Gammons, "Ainge Won't Pass Up Deal With Blue Jays," *Boston Globe*, March 22, 1980.

11 Gammons, "Mark Sullivan Showing …," *Boston Globe*, July 2, 1981.

12 Ibid.

13 Peter Gammons, "Denman Stymies NY, 5-0," *Boston Globe*, October 3, 1982.

14 Larry Whiteside, "Trujillo Up, Brown Down; Sox Drop Newman, Retain Sax," *Boston Globe*, April 5, 1985.

15 Joe Giuliotti, "Work, Not Nepotism, Is Sullivan's Ticket," *The Sporting News*, April 29, 1985: 16.

16 Leigh Montville, "For Marc Sullivan, It's Strictly Hit or Miss," *Boston Globe*, March 24, 1986.

17 Larry Whiteside, "Sullivan Catches a Break," *Boston Globe*, February 22, 1987.

18 Dan Shaughnessy, "Sullivan a Rising Son in Rout," *Boston Globe*, March 8, 1987.

19 Larry Whiteside, "Pagliarulo Is Producing; New Papa Is Playing With Pride," *Boston Globe*, March 17, 1987.

20 Joe Giuliotti, "Something to Remember," *The Sporting News*, August 17, 1987: 23.

21 Kevin Paul Dupont, "No Big Move; Benzinger Sticking With His Old Home," *Boston Globe*, June 25, 1987.

22 Jack Craig, "Strategic Silence Coming From Sox' Booth?" *Boston Globe*, July 26, 1987: 57.

23 Joe Giuliotti, "Sullivan Makes a Pitch," *The Sporting News*, October 12, 1987: 24.

24 Michael Madden, "A Relatively Good Trade," *Boston Globe*, December 15, 1987.

25 "Notebook; N.L. West," *The Sporting News*, January 4, 1988: 58.

26 Nick Cafardo,"Staying in the Game: Sullivan Eyes Minors, Then the Front Office," *Boston Globe*, February 20, 1990.

27 Chris Snow, "'86ers Really Appreciate a Class Gesture," *Boston Globe*, June 28, 2006.

LA SCHELLE TARVER

By Mike Richard

OVER THE YEARS, THE RED SOX HAVE HAD players on their roster who were perhaps better known for the uniqueness of their name than for anything they did on the playing field.

You may recall Jennings Poindexter, Carmen Fanzone, Creighton Gubanich, Gar Finnvold, Izzy Alcantara, Win Remmerswaal, Osee Schrecongost, Hippolito Pichardo, and Arquimedez Pozo, to name a few.

You could add La Schelle Tarver to that list.

As a matter of fact, one night in Baltimore the P.A. announcer mistakenly introduced him as "Tarver La Schelle."

In a one-season major-league career that lasted only 13 games, Tarver was a .120 hitter (3-for-25), scoring three runs and driving in one during the summer of 1986 for the Red Sox. He did not produce an extra-base hit or steal a base although it was for his speed in the outfield and on the base paths that he was initially valued.

Tarver simply came on the scene at the wrong time –the Red Sox had proven veterans starting in their outfield that season.

Future Hall of Famer Jim Rice patrolled left field, Golden Glover Dwight Evans was in right, and former American League Player of the Year (*The Sporting News*, 1981) Tony Armas was their center fielder. In addition, Kevin Romine and Steve Lyons saw a good deal of reserve play that year before a late-season blockbuster deal brought playoff hero Dave Henderson on the scene.

La Schelle Tarver was born on January 30, 1959 in Modesto, California, the son of James Tarver and Mary L. Jackson. While he never met his father, he was the fourth of six sons born to his mother, who was

a nurse. He noted that he was the baby of the family for 11 years before his two younger brothers, Rodney and Ken Jackson, were born. His older brothers were Paul, Anthony, and Tyrone Brice.

Shortly after La Schelle was born, the family moved to Madera, California, where he grew up.

Born with a weak heart, Tarver was not allowed to play any organized sports when he was real young, but by the time he was 10 years old his mother acquiesced.

"I was always crying, because my friends would play baseball and football. My older brother Paul played Little League baseball and I wanted to be just like him," said Tarver.[1]

He was allowed to sign up for Little League baseball in 1968, but showed up for practice without a baseball glove.

"One of the coaches gave me a glove and it was the old kind, three fingers, a web and thumb," he recalled. "All the kids laughed, but it worked."

He was picked for the team Duncan and Shine and admitted he was not very good at first, but "by the time I was 12 I was on every all-star team and was always MVP of my team."

When he was 13, the varsity coach at Madera High School, Stan Bledsoe, coached the Babe Ruth all-star team. Tarver was later named the most valuable player of the all-star tournament.

"Coach Bledsoe would become my role model on the baseball field from that time on and was my coach all through high school," Tarver said. "He was a baseball guru and took me under his wing and worked with me to be fundamentally sound on the field."

The 5-foot-11, 165-pound outfielder, who batted and threw left-handed, was a Northern California All-American first baseman when he played at Madera High School. He was scouted by Fibber Harioma of the California Angels and after his 1977 high-school graduation was drafted by the Angels in the 42nd round of the major leagues' amateur draft. He opted instead to attend college.

Tarver played two years for Reedley (California) Junior College in 1978-79, then moved on to Cal State University-Sacramento in 1980.

"(Cal State) coach John Smith told me, 'I don't have a scholarship, but I have a big old pasture that you can roam out in center field,'" Tarver recalled. "He showed an interest in me, so I went there."

Cal State had produced several other major leaguers including infielder Mike Fischlin and pitcher Keith Brown.

"I never hit under .360 all through high school and college, and my speed was a big part of my game," Tarver said. "That was my separation from everybody else, I guess you could say."

After spending the summer of 1980 playing for the Humboldt Crabs in the Humboldt County baseball league for college players, Tarver was drafted by the New York Mets on August 18, 1980. He spent 1981 through 1985 in the Mets' minor-league system, where he hit .313 with 2 home runs, 174 RBIs, and 217 stolen bases in 599 games.

After a spring-training injury in 1981, Tarver spent his first minor-league season with the Shelby Mets of the South Atlantic League. The team also featured future major leaguers Lenny Dykstra, John Gibbons, Randy Milligan, and DeWayne Vaughn.

Tarver was the team MVP, leading Shelby in stolen bases with 57 while batting .314 and driving in 27 runs. He also played five games with the Lynchburg (Virginia) Mets of the Carolina League.

Tarver started the 1982 season with Lynchburg, where he was the one of the team's regular outfielders along with Herm Winningham and Milligan. Tarver hit .308 and stole 56 bases. He wound up the season with Double-A Jacksonville and Triple-A Tidewater.

"I started out (1982) in Lynchburg and was having a good season, and then there were injuries in certain places," Tarver said. "They didn't want to move some of their top draft picks like Darryl Strawberry and Billy Beane, so I guess I was doing well enough that they would send me up or down as they needed somebody."

Tarver made the jump full-time to the Double-A Jacksonville (Mississippi) Mets of the Texas League in 1983, joining an outfield that included Beane, Winningham, and John Christensen. There he batted .316 with 36 RBIs. At the end of the season he played in three games for Triple-A Tidewater Tides, managed by future Mets skipper Davey Johnson. That team featured several Mets players who would comprise the 1986 World Series championship team, including Wally Backman, Darryl Strawberry, Rick Anderson, and Ron Darling.

For the next two seasons, Tarver continued with Tidewater, batting .326 with 36 stolen bases in 1984 and .311 with 35 stolen bases in 1985. On November 13,

1985, the Mets sent Tarver, outfielder John Christensen, and pitchers Wes Gardner and Calvin Schiraldi to the Red Sox in exchange for pitchers Tom McCarthy, Bob Ojeda, and minor leaguers John Mitchell and Chris Bayer.

"I was playing winter ball in San Juan (Puerto Rico) and my agent at the time called me," Tarver recalled. "He said, 'I have some good news and some bad news.' He said, 'Well, you got traded,' so I asked what's the bad news was and he said, 'Well, it's not really bad news, you've been traded to the Red Sox.'"

Tarver looked it as an opportunity to perhaps play for a team that didn't put a lot of emphasis on speed, which had long been his calling card.

"When I got to Boston, speed wasn't something they were known for," he said, "but for me, it was just an opportunity to play and I felt I may have a chance. At the time, the Mets were stacked and they had Mookie Wilson in center, they had Dykstra coming up, they had Herm Winningham coming up, they had Terry Blocker coming up and all playing center field. So it was a good opportunity for me (in Boston) and I was excited."

In a rather auspicious debut in his first spring-training at-bat with the Red Sox, on March 7, 1986, against the Tigers, Tarver ended the game by lining into a triple play. It was reportedly the first triple play hit into by a Red Sox player in 21 years.[2]

With Mike Stenhouse and Mike Greenwell on first and second, respectively, with singles, Tarver pinch-hit for Mike Easler. His liner was caught by shortstop Doug Baker, who stepped on second to put Stenhouse out and threw out Greenwell before he could retreat to first.

Tarver began the 1986 season with Triple-A Pawtucket, spending time in the outfield with Boston prospects Mike Greenwell and Todd Benzinger.

"The Boston Herald and Globe sportswriters were always down in Pawtucket and they would come over and talk to me," Tarver said. "I was just tickled pink because

with the Mets I never had anybody from the New York sportswriters come and talk to me. It was just amazing to me."

Boston Globe writer Sean O'Sullivan wrote on June 29, 1986, that "Tarver, currently Pawtucket's starting right fielder, is one of those 'other guys' involved in the eight-man deal, but he hasn't been just any other guy on the field."[3]

At the time, Tarver was leading the International League in batting with a .359 average. He was in the midst of a stretch where he had hit in 16 of his last 17 games, going 31-for-70 (.443). He was also tops on the team in stolen bases with 20, despite having missed the first three weeks of the season with a groin pull.

When center fielder Tony Armas pulled a thigh muscle and went on the 15-day disabled list in mid-July, the Red Sox purchased Tarver's contract from Pawtucket. He became the eighth player at that point to make the jump from Triple-A to the parent club in 1986.

"I had no idea what Fenway even looked like. So I got in my car in Pawtucket and drove up (Route) 95 to Boston," Tarver recalled. "I got a block away from Fenway out on Yawkey Way and looking for the park. I guess I was looking for a stadium like Dodger Stadium or Candlestick."

"I called the office asking where the park was and whoever answered the phone said, in their Boston accent, 'You see that brick building that looks like a warehouse? Well, that's Fenway Park, just come to that gate,'" Tarver continued, with a laugh. "It was a heck of an experience for my first time in Boston."

In his major-league debut, on July 12, Tarver struck out against California's Mike Witt in his first at-bat and was somewhat taken aback by the loud ovation he received while trotting back to the bench after being retired on a 2-and-2 pitch.

"Perhaps Tarver was cheered because the 32,932 Fenway faithful were trying to be polite—after all, it was his first major league appearance," wrote the Boston Globe's Michael Vega. "Or maybe it was the manner in which

Tarver went down—he protected the plate and made Witt work for the out by tossing 11 pitches—that elicited the response."4

"I do remember an ovation, but you're just so tunneled in. I was disappointed I struck out, but I do remember it was a long at-bat," Tarver said. "What I also remember about Fenway and playing center field were the fans almost right on top of you. It was a warm welcome; they were really good to me."

The Red Sox embarked on a 13-game late-July Western road trip and Tarver played center field in his first three games. He didn't get his first hit until his third game, on July 19 in Seattle. He went 1-for-5, driving in a run and scoring a pair to help Roger Clemens to a 9-4 victory.

Armas rejoined the team on July 20 but was unable to come off the disabled list for another week. That evening Tarver picked up a hit in a 9-5 loss to Seattle and then had one more hit as the Red Sox fell in Oakland, 4-2, on July 22.

While the Red Sox were in Seattle, the *Globe* reported that trade talks were in the air but they apparently "fell apart after Seattle manager Dick Williams termed Boston's offer for outfielder Dave Henderson 'insulting.' The Red Sox were offering outfielder La Schelle Tarver and a minor league pitcher, probably Mike Brown."5

Once Armas returned to the lineup in early August, Tarver was sent back to Pawtucket, where he finished the season.

Henderson joined the Red Sox on August 19, 1986, along with shortstop Spike Owen, for pitcher Mike Trujillo and shortstop Rey Quinones. Henderson became the regular center fielder for the stretch run and the playoffs.

At the conclusion of the International League season, Tarver was called up along with pitchers Steve Crawford, Jeff Sellers, and Rob Woodward, first baseman Paul Dodson, and catcher Dave Sax as the rosters expanded for the end of the regular season.

In his first game back, on September 3, Tarver came on in the ninth inning in a game at Texas to pinch-run for Mike Greenwell. Spike Owen tried to move him to second on a bunt but struck out on three pitches. Rangers reliever Dale Mohorcic began working Wade Boggs low and away, but Boggs found a pitch to his liking and slashed it to the gap in left-center.

Tarver, off on the 3-and-2 pitch, never hesitated from first and came all the way around to score the eventual winning run in Boston's fifth straight victory.

"I was running with the pitch," Tarver told the *Globe*, "and I got a good jump. I was coming all the way after I saw the sign to go."6

For the remainder of the season, Tarver's role on the team seemed to be exclusively as either a pinch-runner or pinch-hitter, except in for a start in left field a September 30 loss to Baltimore, after Boston had clinched the American League East.

Tarver would not be with the team as it moved on to the playoffs, it had been announced on September 25 in the *Boston Globe*.

"Jeff Sellers, Rob Woodward, Dave Sax, La Schelle Tarver and Kevin Romine can participate in the clinch party, but none will be on Boston's postseason roster," it was noted.7

"They had set the roster and told us we weren't going to be part of the postseason," said Tarver. "I understood. and I wasn't surprised at that. But it would have been nice to play the Mets and all the players I came up with."

Tarver was named to the International League All-Star team in 1986, He hit .320 in 81 games with 19 doubles, 2 triples, 2 home runs, and 31 stolen bases.

When spring training in 1987 rolled around, Tarver was one of the young outfield candidates along with Benzinger, Greenwell, and Romine. However, the return of highly-touted Ellis Burks, who was coming back from shoulder surgery that caused him to miss the 1986 season, spelled the end for Tarver.

Early in the 1987 season at Pawtucket, Tarver made a sliding catch in left field and felt his right knee lock up. He had torn the cartilage in the knee. That game, his 13th of the season, was his last in Organized Baseball. "I had the surgery, but I didn't know it at the time it was a career-ending injury," he said. "No one told me at the time that there was a chance of me not playing again, but I never played another game after that."

Tarver began working with at-risk youth in poverty-stricken areas of Fresno, California, under a grant program for nearly a dozen years. He later went back to school for his business-administration degree and as of 2015 had worked for the sheriff's department for 15 years.

He returned to Boston for the 20th-anniversary reunion of the 1986 American League champions in 2006, and the 100th anniversary of Fenway Park in 2012.

As of 2015, Tarver had a 38-year-old daughter, Shontel Michelle Sumler, and four grandchildren, Kiah 18, Amira 17, Zarria 7, and newborn Suraya Sumler.

He was married for the first time on May 3, 2014. While he and his wife, Debra, were engaged, in 2012, she accompanied him to Boston for the Fenway Park 100th-anniversary celebration.

"It was great to see Fenway once again and share that experience with my daughter and wife," said Tarver. "Boston always does everything first-rate, the ownership and the people are just tremendous how they treat you when you do come back."

NOTES

1   All quotations from La Schelle Tarver come from interviews with the author on January 29 and February 5, 2015.

2   *Boston Globe*, March 8, 1986.

3   *Boston Globe*, June 29, 1986.

4   *Boston Globe*, July 13, 1986.

5   *Boston Globe*, July 22, 1986.

6   *Boston Globe*, September 4, 1986.

7   *Boston Globe*, September 25, 1986.

MIKE TRUJILLO

By Mike Richard

TO SAY THAT RIGHT-HANDED PITCHER MIKE Trujillo was a key member of the 1986 Boston Red Sox would be an over-exaggeration; he appeared in only three games that season. However, you can't dispute the fact that he was a key ingredient in the biggest trade the pennant winners made during their stretch run toward the American League pennant.

On August 22, 1986, the Red Sox completed the deal that very likely propelled them into the postseason when they sent Trujillo and shortstop Rey Quinones to Seattle for outfielder Dave Henderson and shortstop Spike Owen. Owen became the team's regular short-stop and Henderson hit one of the most important playoff home runs in Boston baseball history, while Trujillo went on to become simply a footnote in Red Sox lore. In five major-league seasons, parts of two of them spent with the Red Sox, he had a record of 12-12 with a 5.02 ERA and 96 strikeouts.

Michael Andrew Trujillo was born on January 12, 1960, in Denver, the son of Andy and Elaine Trujillo, and grew up in a small family with his only other sibling a sister, Julie. At the age of 6 he began playing in unorganized sandlot leagues in Denver, then moved up to a Bronco League team. (The Bronco League is a division of PONY Baseball.)

"When we were 12 our team traveled to Joliet (Illinois) for the regional championships and then moved on to St. Joseph, Missouri, for the Bronco League World Series," Trujillo recalled. "That was the first experience I had with a big-time format."[1]

At Mullen High School, Trujillo was a three-sport athlete, playing football, basketball, and baseball, and was offered athletic scholarships in all three sports. Proclaiming himself "a decent high-school player as a center fielder," he was named all-conference and all-state when Mullen captured the state championship during his senior season in 1978. "I was the number-two pitcher on the Mullen team behind Mike Deidel (brother of former major leaguer Jim), who was our number one (pitcher)," Trujillo said.

He was one of four players from his high school who went on to major-league baseball. Jim Deidel, Mark Holzemer, and Clint Zavaras were the others. "What people may not realize is how many major-league baseball players came out of the Colorado-Denver area," Trujillo said, rattling off the names of Goose Gossage, Tippy Martinez, Roy Halladay, Brian Fisher, Mark Knudson, and Danny Jackson.

Trujillo attended the University of Northern Colorado, where he pitched for the Bears from 1979 to 1982. "UNC was the best baseball program in the state," he said, noting that head coach Tom Petroff "was a father figure and mentor; next to my parents he was probably the most influential person through my college years. He was very knowledgeable about baseball."

"I was signed as an outfielder first and a pitcher second," Trujillo said. "I didn't throw real hard, even when I was in the big leagues, but I learned how to pitch well enough to be successful."

While in college Trujillo also played for the Boulder Collegians in a summer college league. He was drafted by the Chicago White Sox in the seventh round of the 1982 major-league draft.

It took Trujillo three years to reach the majors. After being drafted he joined the Niagara Falls Sox of the New York Penn League, where he posted a 5-4 record in 1982 with a 2.39 ERA and led the team in strikeouts with 100 in the 12 games he started. He moved on to Appleton (Wisconsin) of the Class-A Midwestern League in 1983, posting a 15-8 record and a 2.40 ERA. He led the team in starts (29) and complete games (11), and was second in strikeouts with 148. In 1984 he was promoted to Glens Falls (New York) of the Double-A Eastern League on a pitching staff that included future major leaguer Doug Drabek. Trujillo logged a team-best 13-3 record with a 2.37 ERA. He also pitched in eight games for the Denver Bears of the Triple-A American Association, with a 2-5 record and a 7.80 ERA.

The major leagues had beckoned early. "The first inkling that I may make it was when the White Sox called me up to start the Hall of Fame game against the New York Mets," Trujillo recalled. That game, played on August 2, 1982, resulted in a 4-4 tie that was ended in the eighth inning by rain.

On September 7, 1984, Trujillo was traded to the San Francisco Giants for third baseman Tom O'Malley. Then on December 3, he was selected from the Giants by the Red Sox in the Rule 5 draft. "For whatever reason, San Francisco traded for me but neglected to put me on their 40-man roster," Trujillo said. "I don't know if they were trying to sneak me through or if there was a clerical error on their part, but then Boston claimed me."

When the Red Sox brass saw the name Trujillo on the roster of the Phoenix Giants (Pacific Coast League), scout Ed Kenney recognized the hurler. Of all the pitchers in the White Sox system, Boston had rated Trujillo second only to Bruce Tanner. "There's got to be something wrong," Kenney told the gathering,

and they tried to find out if Trujillo had some dark secret in his past.[2]

"No skeletons," Trujillo said. "At the time I had faced New Britain [in the Eastern League] a number of times and did pretty well, so I'm sure (the Red Sox) would have watched me pitch quite a bit."

The 1985 Red Sox were looking for a fifth starter to go along with Roger Clemens, Oil Can Boyd, Bob Ojeda, and Bruce Hurst, since Al Nipper began the year on the disabled list. Among those looked to for the role were Bruce Kison, Mike Brown, and Trujillo.[3]

Manager John McNamara was unabashed in his praise for Trujillo after 1985 spring training, viewing him as a viable fifth starter. "I liked the way Trujillo pitched," said McNamara after the pitcher allowed two runs in a five-inning 8-7 exhibition victory over the White Sox. "With Nipper out, we have eight pitching spots set, two open. We also really have two starting spots open between Bruce Kison, Trujillo and Mike Brown."[4]

"I basically made it from Double-A to the big leagues. I probably could have used some more seasoning at the Triple-A level," Trujillo said. "Back in those days they had a pretty set schedule for guys to go through A, Double-A, and Triple-A ball, and I basically made it to the big leagues in 2½ years. Looking back, I probably could have used more seasoning, it was a big jump and I'm not sure I was ready."

Trujillo made his major-league debut against Chicago on April 14, 1985, in the fourth inning. He allowed six hits and four earned runs over three innings in an 11-6 loss to the White Sox. Despite the rocky start, Trujillo was inserted into the Red Sox starting rotation when Kison came down with a hamstring injury.

In his next start, against the White Sox on April 19, Trujillo lasted four innings and took the 8-1 loss. He made five more appearances before earning his first major-league win, on June 13 over Toronto. Trujillo relieved Bruce Kison in the fifth and pitched 2⅓ shutout innings, picking up the victory when the Red Sox scored four runs in the seventh for an 8-7 victory.

Trujillo spent the entire season with the Red Sox, making six more spot starts and doing a decent job out of the bullpen. On June 26 he threw 4⅓ innings of shutout relief of Al Nipper, but the Red Sox were blanked by Detroit, 3-0. He won his second game on July 12 in relief of Kison, pitching two innings in Seattle to keep the Red Sox close before some late-inning fireworks. Bill Buckner's two-run homer in the eighth and Rich Gedman's solo shot in the ninth led to a 5-4 Boston victory. Trujillo's third win came on August 22, when he worked eight innings, spacing eight hits and two runs on his way to an 8-4 win over the Texas Rangers.

As the season wound down, Trujillo began to show some of the promise the Red Sox had hoped to see from him. On September 1 he pitched a complete-game 10-3 win over Minnesota.

"While he is still in the fringe stage for 1986, and is mostly getting on-the-job training that he might have gotten in Triple-A this year, Trujillo is proving that the Red Sox were correct in their decision to keep him around, even if it meant sitting in the bullpen for over half a season," the *Boston Globe* wrote after that game.[5]

On September 15 Trujillo earned his only save of the season, pitching 2⅔ innings of one-hit, scoreless relief to help Boston to a 4-2 win over Milwaukee.

Trujillo pitched in five more games, getting a loss on October 4 against Milwaukee when he allowed a pair of 12th-inning runs. The loss evened his mark on the season at 4-4. He wound up his rookie year with an ERA of 4.82, recording 19 strikeouts in 84 innings pitched while allowing 23 walks and seven home runs.

"I had moderate success that first year, but I was used in a way where I was a spot starter, a long relief guy and I had a few chances for save opportunities," Trujillo said. "As a sinkerball pitcher, you needed to get regular work. It isn't an excuse, but I think if it was a situation where if I had been in a regular rotation or had a chance to pitch on a regular basis, there may have been a little more success."

After the season Trujillo, along with teammates Mike Rochfort, Tom McCarthy, and Mike Dodson, played winter ball for LaGuaira in Venezuela.

In February of 1986, the *Globe* forecast a promising season for the Red Sox right-hander: "When going over the Red Sox' pitchers, don't count out Mike Trujillo, who reportedly pitched very well in winter ball," the paper said.[6] However, when the season began, Trujillo found himself in Pawtucket, where he spent most of the season except for three relief appearances in late June after Sammy Stewart went on the disabled list.

"I pitched in Caracas and I was disappointed I didn't start the season with (the Red Sox)," Trujillo said. "I had a good spring training; I pitched well in Venezuela and was one of the top pitchers in winter ball. In 1985 the Red Sox had to keep me or offer me back to San Francisco, so I was basically going to stay in Boston regardless."

Following that brief call-up, Trujillo returned to Pawtucket and never made another appearance for the Red Sox. He was named the International League Fireman of the Year with a record of 8-9 and 12 saves. But he was no longer in the Red Sox system when the awards were announced.

On August 22 he was sent to the Seattle Mariners with shortstop Rey Quinones, pitcher Mike Brown, and minor-league outfielder John Christensen (named later) for Seattle outfielder Dave Henderson and shortstop Spike Owen.

Trujillo spent the remainder of the 1986 season with the Mariners, where he had the chance to finally pitch regularly on a staff that included Mark Langston, Mike Moore, Bill Swift, and Matt Young. "When I got to Seattle (manager) Dick Williams sat me down and said, 'You know, you're going to get the ball every four or five days and we just want you to go out and pitch, and relax, and see what you can do,'" Trujillo said.

Trujillo earned his first major-league shutout with a one-hitter on September 20 against the Kansas City Royals, 3-0, and nearly had a no-hitter. With two outs in the first inning, Lonnie Smith reached on an error by Mariners first baseman. "Jamie Quirk was the next guy up and he hit a soft line drive to left field for a single and that was it," Trujillo recalled. If nothing else, I can say I went 8⅓ innings of no-hit ball."

Trujillo finished the season with a 3-2 record. "I would have loved the opportunity to have played in the [1986] World Series, but being traded gave me the opportunity to pitch on a more regular basis with Seattle," he said. "It was decidedly different in going from a first-place team that was a World Series contender to a last-place team that was made up of a lot of guys in similar situation to my own in that we were two- or three-year players. I welcomed that opportunity and pitched well the remainder of the year. For the first time I thought I could go out, relax and be me, and pitch."

The 1987 season saw Trujillo appear in 28 games for Seattle, including 3-2 loss in a start against the Red Sox on May 12. Overall, he posted a 4-4 record and had a 6.17 ERA. The Mariners released Trujillo during spring training in 1988. "That came as a surprise because I had a really good spring training, but I was put in the bullpen. I think I was always better when I had the opportunity to pitch on a regular basis," Trujillo said.

The Detroit Tigers picked him up, and he spent most of the season in the minors with the Toledo Mud Hens, pitching only 12⅓ innings for the Tigers in a midseason call-up. "I had some success against the Tigers when I was with Seattle, but I think (Detroit) signed me more as an insurance policy. They had their rotation set, but in the event anybody got hurt they would have the ability to call somebody up that had some experience. That was my role."

In 1989, his final season in the major leagues, Trujillo pitched 25⅔ innings for the Tigers, allowing 35 hits. His last major-league game was on June 17, 1989, against the California Angels. He pitched the ninth inning, allowing one hit and striking out one batter.

On August 6, 1989, Trujillo was sold to the New York Mets. After two months pitching in 23 games for the Tidewater Tides, he was released, his baseball career brought to an end at the age of 29. "I got sold by the Tigers to the Mets with the plan to improve their bullpen for the playoff stretch," said Trujillo. "I was told I would go down, get some work and get the rust off. They were going to call me up for the playoffs, but it never happened."

Around this time, Trujillo began to develop some shoulder problems and he had surgery after the 1989 season. "I decided then to devote the rest of my time and energies to my wife and my daughter," Trujillo said.

He and his wife, Sandy, whom he had met while he was playing for the Tigers, were the parents of a daughter, Laura. Mike and Sandy later had a son, Drew.

Trujillo went into business for himself and in the mid-1990s became an agent for State Farm Insurance. As of 2015 he lived in Montrose, Colorado, about an hour away from the ski resort town of Telluride. "It's one of the most beautiful places in the world," he said. "You can ski in the morning and play golf in the afternoon."

Both of his children have had athletic careers of their own. Laura played basketball, golf, and softball, in which she was an exceptional catcher, and graduated from Wake Forest University. In 2015 she lived and worked in Chicago. Drew followed in his father's footsteps as a football, basketball, and baseball player and, like his sister, was a catcher. He had a golf scholarship to the University of Colorado.

Trujillo had the opportunity to return to Boston in 2012 for the 100th anniversary of Fenway Park and was impressed with the ceremony, which he called one of the greatest memories of his career. "What a class organization Boston is," he said of the commemoration. "What a great experience that was to come back, see all of the guys I played with and the other Red Sox greats. After (playing) baseball, it will be one of those things I'll never forget."

NOTES

1 All quotations from Mike Trujillo come from an interview with the author on April 16, 2015.

2 *Boston Globe*, March 28, 1985.

3 *Boston Globe*, March 27, 1985.

4 *Boston Globe*, March 30, 1985.

5 *Boston Globe*, September 2, 1985.

6 *Boston Globe*, February 23, 1986.

ROB WOODWARD

By Bob LeMoine

AT ONE END OF THE RED SOX DRESSING room stood a pitching master, a winner of 306 games and a future Hall of Famer with "flecks of gray in his hair," wrote Bill Parrillo of the *Providence Journal.*[1] His reputation preceded him. At the age of 41, Tom Seaver was in a Red Sox uniform for the first time and a sea of cameras and reporters engulfed him in that moment on June 30, 1986. Seaver had been acquired for his experience and leadership with the Red Sox contending for the pennant, in what the *Boston Globe's* Dan Shaughnessy called "a Fenway fantasy fulfilled."[2]

There was no fanfare at the other end of the dressing room, as a 23-year-old pitcher packed up his belongings, mindful that a living legend was taking his spot on the Red Sox roster. He shook a few hands and prepared for his drive down Interstate 95 to rejoin the Triple-A Pawtucket (Rhode Island) Red Sox. Rob Woodward attempted to speak with Seaver, but decided not to with the crowd, and instead, he quietly made his exit.

"The kid who was leaving," another player mentioned to Seaver, "I think he wanted to say hello. He's the guy you're replacing."

"Oh jeez, where is he?" Seaver asked. On his way to the field he stopped and chatted with Woodward at his locker. "Best of luck. You'll be back," the veteran reassured.[3]

Woodward would indeed be back, and spend parts of four seasons in Boston. While considered a top Red Sox pitching prospect at one point, he wound up pitching in only 24 major-league games, with a 4-4 record. Yet the kid from rural northern New Hampshire became a local legend and returned to his community roots, coaching and talking behind a microphone about the game he loved.

Robert John Woodward was born on September 28, 1962, in Hanover, New Hampshire, to Robert and Beverly Woodward. A 1992 directory listed Robert as working at Granite State Electric, and Beverly for Bond Optics, a manufacturer of optical products.[4] He starred in baseball, basketball, and football at Lebanon High School. He went 7-1 as a pitcher in his senior year, and batted .412 with seven home runs as a first baseman. Lebanon defeated Monadnock High School for the 1981 New Hampshire Class-I baseball championship. On a bases-loaded single in the fifth inning, Woodward, playing first base, cut off a throw from left field and picked off the runner, who had rounded first, ending the Monadnock rally as Lebanon won 7-3.[5]

The rural baseball team had a short schedule, so Woodward's coach, Ted Andress, sent out postcards to notify teams that he had a prospect to keep their eyes

on. Boston Red Sox scout Bill Enos took notice. "The word gets around. Scouts were watching me since my sophomore year of high school," Woodward recalled. "As a pitcher it's tough because you have fewer games and you have to take advantage of the time you have. Everything counts, you get maybe eight games and you can't afford to do poorly."[6]

"I think it's tougher for a person in New Hampshire to get noticed," said Woodward. "In New Hampshire, you only play 16 games in a season. You don't get the same amount of scouts as you would if you played in California."[7] Woodward was elated when he was drafted by Boston, the team he had been a fan of since his childhood. "I feel lucky to be able to play ball and just being drafted. Being from New Hampshire, I've always wanted to play for the Red Sox. I'm glad I got the chance."[8]

Woodward was selected by the Red Sox in the third round of the 1981 amateur draft. He pitched for Elmira of the short-season New York-Pennsylvania League, where he led the team with a 3.39 ERA with a 4-3 record in 11 starts, with three of the starts being complete games. Woodward also made the all-star team.[9] He struggled at Winter Haven of the Class-A Florida State League in 1982 with a 7-9 record and a 5.12 ERA. Woodward improved in 1983 with a 13-11 record and 4.14 ERA for Winston-Salem (North Carolina) of the Class-A Carolina League.

Woodward was invited to spring training with the Red Sox in 1984, and threw a scoreless inning with one strikeout against the New York Mets on March 12.[10] "I couldn't wait to throw it," Woodward said of throwing his first pitch for Boston. "I found out I'd see a little action today, and I was nervous in anticipation."[11] He had an impressive 1984 season, with a 10-12 log and a 3.96 ERA for New Britain of the Double-A Eastern League. Manager Rac Slider said Woodward had the best stuff of the pitching staff but needed another season at the Double-A level.[12]

Woodward worked an offseason job painting while other players had training regimens in preparation for the 1985 season. "You can't get outside for much running in New Hampshire in the winter," he said during spring training. "However, I wasn't very far behind anyone when I got here last week."[13] He began 1985 with New Britain, where he was 7-5 with a 3.54 ERA in 12 starts. In July he was promoted to Triple-A, Pawtucket of the International League, going 3-8 with a 4.46 ERA. Woodward won the "pitcher of the week" honors on July 15 as he went 2-0 with a 1.29 ERA, including a complete-game victory over Columbus.[14]

Woodward was called up to Boston on September 1. Very few fans saw his debut in the second game of a doubleheader against Cleveland on September 5 because it was actually September 6 by the time he got into the game at 1:42 A.M. The game had been delayed an hour and 25 minutes by rain. Woodward pitched before an estimated 200 fans, who were watching the Red Sox lose 9-5. "I think only my grandfather was up to watch me," he mused.[15] "It was a strange hour. The weather was miserable. We were losing (after winning the first game). But heck, I didn't care. It was the major leagues, a dream come true."[16] Woodward pitched two scoreless innings, and the game mercifully ended at 2:17 A.M. after the 8-hour 42-minute doubleheader.[17] Woodward followed this with one earned run in six innings of mop-up relief in Milwaukee on September 13.

Woodward made his first start in Detroit on September 29, and earned his first major-league victory, giving up four runs in eight innings. "I have to admit I was nervous early," he said, "and I was having trouble mainly because I was working slow... As the innings went on, I kept building up my quickness and was working faster toward the end of the game. Everything was falling into place. It's just exciting to be here and pitching."[18] His final start of the call-up was a no-decision against Milwaukee despite pitching nine innings with no earned runs allowed. Woodward's first stint in Boston was a success with a 1-0 record, 26⅔ innings pitched, and an ERA of 1.69.

Woodward began the 1986 season in Pawtucket. He had an 11-strikeout performance against Rochester, followed by a six-hit shutout over Tidewater, earning him the International League Pitcher of the Week honors.[19] He was recalled to Boston on May 21 when pitcher Al Nipper was placed on the disabled list.[20] At the time, Woodward was 3-2 with a 3.72 ERA at Pawtucket. "I feel I'm ready," he said. "I'm comfortable up here. With a little time, I might be able to fit right in. I don't know how I will be here. But the time I am up here, I want to go out and pitch the best that I'm capable of. That's all I can do at this point."[21]

Woodward started against the Rangers in Texas on May 24, pitching 7⅓ innings with no earned runs allowed, but the Red Sox bullpen surrendered the lead in a 3-2 loss. "I was very impressed with his location, the way he kept the ball down and the fact he didn't make mistakes to beat himself," John McNamara noted.[22] His next start was as an emergency replacement for Roger Clemens, giving up five runs in two innings at Minnesota. In a start against Cleveland on June 4, Woodward outpitched 47-year-old 300-game winner Phil Niekro with 6⅓ innings pitched, allowing three earned runs and earning his first victory of the season. "I don't even think about there being any pressure on me," he said.[23] The victory was the Red Sox' fifth straight, and they were in first place in the American League East, 4½ games ahead of New York.

Woodward's season unraveled from that point on. In New York he had a 7-2 lead but could not finish the fifth inning, throwing 69 pitches through four innings, including six three-ball counts.[24] On June 24 Woodward shut out the Yankees at Fenway Park through four innings, but fell apart in the fifth in an 8-1 loss. "I thought Woodward pitched very well," McNamara said. "You're talking about a man who was in Double-A ball last year. There were a couple of strange things that hurt him last night. But he kept us close until the sixth."[25]

The Red Sox were in first place in the standings, yet were hurting for pitching. With Bruce Hurst on the disabled list, Woodward, Jeff Sellers, and Mike Brown tried to fill in the gaps behind Roger Clemens and Oil Can Boyd. As Dan Shaughnessy of the *Globe* put it, the staff was "Clemens and Boyd and fill the void."[26] In need of pitching for a pennant run, they acquired 300-game winner Seaver from the Chicago White Sox.

To make room on the roster, Woodward was sent to Pawtucket on June 30. "I knew when I came up that it was because people were hurt. Now that people are starting to come back, I know I might have to go back to Pawtucket," he said. "Right now I'm caught up in the numbers game. The Red Sox are doing the best they can to win a pennant. I understand that. Maybe it's better to go down instead of to the bullpen, where I'll just get rusty and lose the things I've worked on."[27]

Woodward continued his dominance at Pawtucket, shutting out Richmond and Tidewater, and was named the International League Player of the Week in August.[28] He finished the season with eight complete games and four shutouts. On August 15 Woodward ran a consecutive scoreless innings streak to 27⅔, setting a Pawtucket record.[29]

Woodward was recalled by the Red Sox on September 1. The team's pennant drive reminded Woodward of his childhood when he watched the Red Sox 1975 pennant winners. "I loved those guys in '75. Now I'm here enjoying what they enjoyed then. It's quite a thing. I can't describe it. You really can't know what it's like to be part of this unless you're going through it. It's just so special," he said.[30]

While he did not pitch for Boston in September, Woodward made a different kind of appearance that is remembered in Boston sports history. On September 28 the Red Sox defeated Toronto 12-3 and clinched the American League East title. As the players sprayed champagne and celebrated in the clubhouse, WCVB television reporter Mike Dowling conducted an interview with Jim Rice and Don Baylor. A nude Woodward appeared on camera, on his way from the shower. As Jack Craig of the *Globe* wrote, "It was not a quickie scene. The camera lingered and so did Woodward as he dried himself with a towel. No one pulled the plug during the two minutes the naked athlete appeared intermittently in the background. It surely was the longest two minutes in Channel 5's generally distinguished existence."[31] Red Sox publicist Josh Spofford said Woodward didn't know he was on camera and was embarrassed by the incident.[32] WCVB sports anchor Mike Lynch apologized to viewers for the segment, but the station was flooded with calls from people complaining. Not everyone complained, however. One woman called and asked, "Are you going to show that again at 11?"[33]

Woodward finished the 1986 season pitching two games in relief in October, including a win over Baltimore after he had blown a save opportunity. He was not on the postseason roster, but after the Red Sox celebrated in the clubhouse when they defeated the California Angels and won the American League pennant, some players watched the television monitor and asked, "Where's Woody?"[34]

In spring training 1987, Woodward competed with Sellers, Nipper, and Bob Stanley for the fifth starter role. "I don't like to say that there's a little more pressure on me, because I went down last year. If anything, I know what to do now. I know what it's all about," Woodward said.[35] He made the team as a reliever and appeared in three games in April, pitching poorly with a 10.12 ERA in 5⅓ innings pitched. He was optioned to Pawtucket on May 2. "I'm happy with the way I'm progressing," Woodward said. "I haven't reached my peak as far as abilities go, but I keep learning."[36]

Woodward was recalled on July 27, and made his first start of the year in Texas on August 4. He left with a 5-4 lead in the seventh inning, but the Red Sox bullpen surrendered the lead. Still, it was encouraging for Woodward. "When they called me from Pawtucket, I really was only supposed to be here three days. So you know I was just happy to be here last night. … I just wanted to go out there. I didn't want to put any pressure on myself saying that I had to pitch good. I just knew that I wanted to pitch good, and I think I did."[37]

"I don't know what's in store for me after this," Woodward said. "You never know. I was just happy to get this chance to go out and throw the ball well."[38] Woodward didn't last through the second inning on August 9, and was sent back to Pawtucket on August 12. He finished the season with Boston in September. Woodward pitched seven innings against Baltimore on September 10 and left with a 3-1 lead which the

Red Sox bullpen surrendered. His only victory in 1987 came in Baltimore on September 18 in a 10-7 Red Sox win in the second game of a doubleheader. Woodward pitched in Yankee Stadium on his 25th birthday and deserved a win, but the Yankees scored six runs in the bottom of the ninth in the comeback victory. He finished 1-1 with a 7.05 ERA in 37 innings pitched with Boston and 12-8 with a 3.51 ERA in 136 innings pitched at Pawtucket.

Before the 1988 season, Woodward lost 30 pounds and suffered blurred vision as symptoms of juvenile diabetes.[39] "I was scared at first," he admitted. "I didn't know anything about it. I didn't know if I'd be able to play ball again. … So far, I've been able to do everything. I just have to eat at certain times and take (insulin) shots at certain times."[40] The reality was that Woodward was now in his fifth spring training with the Red Sox and was no longer considered a top prospect at age 25. "Consistency, that's the key," he acknowledged, knowing his career had been anything but consistent to that point.[41]

Woodward was again optioned to Pawtucket after spring training.[42] He was converted into a closer, and had 13 saves with a 1-4 record and a 3.86 ERA. But one last major-league appearance was still in his future. "I was out on the field in Pawtucket the other night, and all of a sudden they came out and said, 'You're going to Boston,'" Woodward said. "That's all I wanted to know. … I'm ready to pitch whenever they call upon me."[43] Woodward was needed for pitching help, as Sellers and Boyd were on the disabled list. On September 26 he pitched two-thirds of an inning of mop-up relief in an 11-1 loss to Toronto. It was his last major-league appearance. Woodward's Boston career finished at 4-4 with a 5.04 ERA in 24 games and 100 innings pitched.

Woodward spent the entire 1989 season at Pawtucket, as there was little room in the Red Sox bullpen with established players like Lee Smith, Bob Stanley, Mike Smithson, Dennis Lamp, and Rob Murphy as relievers. "I just have to be ready when an opportunity comes," a wistful Woodward remarked.[44]

Also in 1989, Woodward married Kathy Hurlburt, also a Lebanon High School graduate. Their son, Robert Edward Woodward, was born later that year.[45] To pay the bills, Woodward worked in construction over the winter. His career was at a crossroads. "I suppose I can go back to doing something like that again if it doesn't work out here," he said during spring training in 1990. "And I thought maybe I could help out with something as a coach at one of the high schools."[46] Woodward was released on April 2, after nine years in the Boston organization. "In that way, it's a relief," he said. "Now we can see if there's anything else out there."[47] He was seen two days later, in jeans and a T-shirt, playing catch with Steve Ellsworth, another pitcher who had been released, beside an orange grove at the Winter Haven, Florida, Holiday Inn.[48] "My agent's going to make some calls, find out from a few teams if there's any interest in me as a pitcher," Woodward said. "If there ain't, I'll go home."[49]

Woodward got another chance when he was signed by the Baltimore Orioles and assigned to Triple-A Rochester. He went 6-1 with a 3.00 ERA in 1990 and 7-7 with a 4.23 ERA in 1991. In a 1991 game, Rochester was short of players and Woodward was the designated hitter. Batting for the first time since high school, he went 0-for-3 with a strikeout.[50]

Woodward retired after the 1991 season and returned to New Hampshire to work in construction and carpentry.

Woodward coached the Lebanon Post 22 Senior American Legion baseball team for several years. "All we ask of them is stay committed to the team, and play hard and clean," he said.[51] One of his Legion players over the years was his son, Jake, whom he had coached from his T-ball days. "He taught me the mechanical things, keeping my balance point — things like that — and some of the more mental stuff, too," Jake Woodward said. "That getting ahead of batters makes a big difference in a game, and you can't fall behind. Pitch location — stuff like that."[52] Jake, a left-handed pitcher (his father was a righty), pitched for Lebanon High School, earned four letters in baseball and was the 2009 Class I baseball player of the year.

After high school he pitched for St. John's University and Southern New Hampshire University.[53]

In 2008 Rob Woodward signed on to co-host a Saturday-morning talk show on a Hanover radio station with Rich Parker, a New Hampshire golf coach. The two untrained co-hosts gave "shout-outs" to local businesses and athletes, a spelling-bee competition, lake reports, a joke of the week, and raised money for local causes. Woodward was known for his trademark "Who is it?" when a caller came on the air. A station commercial promoted the show with the tag, "You never know what they're going to say next."

The show was canceled in 2013 but the pair didn't stay off the air for long. A station in nearby Lebanon continued the show. "I never talked when I was a ballplayer," Woodward said of his radio experience. "One-word answers: 'Yes.' 'No.' … Now I just feel like I'm talking to friends. … So many people were disappointed when we were taken off the air. Now we'll have the opportunity to put a little happiness in their lives while they are going to the dump."[54]

NOTES

1 Bill Parrillo, "Season's Greetings, From the Red Sox," *Providence* (Rhode Island) *Journal*, quoted in *Miami News*, July 1, 1986: 4B.

2 Dan Shaughnessy, "A Fenway Fantasy Fulfilled; Tom Seaver Brings His 306 Career Pitching Victories to Boston," *Boston Globe*, June 30, 1986: 1.

3 "Season's Greetings, From the Red Sox."

4 Information provided by the library staff at the Lebanon (New Hampshire) Public Library, and the Lebanon Historical Society.

5 "Exeter Walks to Class L Crown," *Nashua* (New Hampshire) *Telegraph*, June 15, 1981: 21.

6 Nancy L. Marrapese, "Hometown Heroes: N.H. Players Make Their Mark in Big Leagues: Talent, Hard Work Required," *Boston Globe*, August 23, 1987, New Hampshire Week: 1.

7 "Hometown Heroes."

8 Larry Whiteside, "He Got The Call; Red Sox Beckon; Woodward Answers," *Boston Globe*, May 31, 1986: 21.

9 Peter Gammons, "On Baseball. Reds' Hopes for Cedeno Awfully High," *Boston Globe*, December 27, 1981: 1.

10 "Easler Wants to Blend in," *Nashua* (New Hampshire) *Telegraph*, March 13, 1984: 18.

11 Nick Cafardo, "Sox Camp Looking Brighter," *Quincy* (Massachusetts) *Patriot Ledger, reprinted in Lewiston* (Maine) *Daily Sun,* March 13, 1984: 15.

12 Peter Gammons, "On Baseball. Red Sox Farm System has Crop Still Growing," *Boston Globe,* September 8, 1984: 1.

13 "Woodward Seeks Spot With Sox," *Nashua* (New Hampshire) *Telegraph,* February 26, 1985: 14.

14 "Richmond's Estes Player of the Week," *Richmond* (Virginia) *Times-Dispatch,* July 16, 1985: C-3.

15 Nick Cafardo, "Woodward Wins First Start," *Nashua* (New Hampshire) *Telegraph, reprint from Quincy* (Massachusetts) *Patriot-Ledger,* September 30, 1985: 13.

16 Associated Press, "Woodward Hopes Dream Continues," *Lewiston* (Maine) *Daily Sun,* February 28, 1986: 23.

17 Bob Duffy, "Night and Day Fenway Split; 200 Insomniacs Stay For 2:17 A.M. Finish Friday; Sox Play Two Today," *Boston Globe,* September 7, 1985: 28.

18 Larry Whiteside, "Woodward Wounds Tigers," *Boston Globe,* September 30, 1985: 31.

19 "Woodward Paces Pawtucket," *Boston Herald,* April 28, 1986; 3; "IL Cites Pawsox' Woodward," *Boston Globe,* May 13, 1986: 4.

20 Larry Whiteside, "Armas Hopes Big Night Put Him Back in Swing," *Boston Globe,* May 22, 1986: 64.

21 "He Got The Call; Red Sox Beckon."

22 Joe Giulotti, "Nothing's Minor About Woodward," *Boston Herald,* May 26, 1986: 61.

23 Larry Whiteside, "Red Sox Keep Rolling, 6-4," *Boston Globe,* June 5, 1986: 53.

24 Larry Whiteside, "Red Sox Hold Off Yankees 7-6; NY Rally Falls Short," *Boston Globe,* June 18, 1986: 29.

25 Larry Whiteside, "Yankees Rattle Red Sox, 8-1; Defense, Woodward, Falter," *Boston Globe,* June 25, 1986: 49.

26 Dan Shaughnessy, "Memories are Made of This: Most Will Remember The 20-Strikeout Performance and the Marvelous 14-0 Start of Roger Clemens. Other Fans Will Gloat Ever So Slightly Over the Rise and Fall of the Red Sox' Opponents. There Will Be Pictures, Folded Stubs, Vignettes of the Red Sox' Championship; Season to Savor. Here's How the AL East Title Happened, From Start to Finish," *Boston Globe,* October 3, 1986: 31.

27 Jackie MacMullan, "Woodward Caught in a Numbers Game," *Boston Globe,* July 1, 1986: 66.

28 "Woodward Shuts Out Richmond," *Boston Herald,* July 31, 1986: 2; "DeCinces AL Player of the Week," *Boston Herald,* August 12, 1986: 5.

29 Joe Giuliotti, "Crawford Goes South," *Boston Herald,* August 16, 1986: 12.

30 Garry Brown, "Gorman Misses Party," *Springfield* (Massachusetts) *Union,* September 29, 1986: 23-24.

31 Jack Craig, "Dignity is Missing From Live Coverage," *Boston Globe,* September 30, 1986: 26.

32 Ibid.

33 Dan Shaughnessy, "A Day to Swap a Few Stories Around Camp," *Boston Globe,* April 3, 1990: 29.

34 Larry Whiteside, Michael Madden, and Dan Shaughnessy, "Hurst Ready For Series," *Boston Globe,* October 16, 1986: 48.

35 Charles Pierce, "Woodward Learns From a Master," *Boston Herald,* March 12, 1987: 83.

36 Nancy L. Marrapese, "Red Sox Pitcher Moved Up and Down in 1987," *Boston Globe,* August 23, 1987: 36.

37 Larry Whiteside, "Woodward Gets a Second Start," *Boston Globe,* August 6, 1987: 30.

38 Stephen Harris, "A Shot in the Arm for Sox," *Boston Herald,* August 5, 1987: 105.

39 Dan Shaughnessy, "Hurst Starts Working After Bout With Virus," *Boston Globe,* February, 19, 1988: 37; Tom Yantz, "Woodward Adjusting, Both on Field and Off," *Hartford Courant, reprinted in Schenectady* (New York) *Gazette,* May 19, 1988: 23.

40 David Cataneo, "Woodward Carries On," *Boston Herald,* February 20, 1988: 36.

41 Associated Press, "Woodward Seeks Steady Job With Red Sox," *Springfield* (Massachusetts) *Union-News,* February 29, 1988: 42.

42 Ron Borges, "Dodson, Four Others Sent to Minors," *Boston Globe,* March 29, 1988: 70.

43 Larry Whiteside, "Red Sox Stand-In Relieved," *Boston Globe,* September 2, 1988: 59.

44 Associated Press, "Woodward Awaits Next Chance," *Bangor* (Maine) *Daily News,* March 27, 1989: 21.

45 David Corriveau, "Red Sox Give Up on Woodward," *Valley News* (Lebanon, New Hampshire), April 2, 1990.

46 Ibid.

47 Ibid.

48 George Kimball, "Clemens By the Numbers," *Boston Herald,* April 8, 1990: B-24.

49 "Red Sox Give Up on Woodward."

50 Patti Singer, "Mussina Devours K's, Leaves No Room for Complete Games, *Baltimore Sun,* July 25, 1991. Retrieved January 24, 2015, from articles.baltimoresun.com/1991-07-25/sports/1991206081_1_kingwood-strikeouts-wings.

51 Poody Walsh, "Coming From Far and Wide," *Valley News* (Lebanon, New Hampshire), June 29, 2013. vnews.com/home/7216484-95/coming-from-far-and-wide.

52 Allen Lessels, "Lebanon's Jake Woodward Making His Own Name," *Manchester* (New Hampshire) *Union Leader,* July 3, 2011.

53 "Player of the Year Awards," New Hampshire High School Baseball Coaches Association. Retrieved January 27, 2015 nhhsbca.com/playeroftheyear.asp; "Jake Woodward," Baseball, St. John's University. Retrieved January 27, 2015. redstormsports.com/sports/m-basebl/mtt/woodward_jakeoo.html; "Season Preview: Baseball Looks to Defend East Region Crown,"

Southern New Hampshire University Penman Athletics. February 21, 2013. Retrieved January 27, 2015. snhupenmen.com/sports/bsb/2012-13/releases/20130221onaahl.

54 Don Mahler, "Back on the Air; Rich and Woody Return to Radio," *Valley News* (Lebanon, New Hampshire), January 31, 2014. Online edition. vnews.com/.../back-on-the-air-rich-and-woody-return-to-radio

JEAN R. YAWKEY

By Joan M Thomas

WHEN BOSTON RED SOX OWNER TOM Yawkey died in 1976, he left his entire baseball empire in the care of his wife Jean. At first it appeared that she had no interest in taking his place. However, circumstances arising from internal jockeying by others to take over the ballclub led to her emergence as one of three general partners in charge of the operation. Then, following disputes over management decisions and an agonizing legal battle, she gained majority control. Her passion for baseball outweighed her stoic reserve, and she spent the rest of her life in the quest of a World Series title. That ultimate prize remained as elusive to her as it had been to her husband. Nonetheless, she came to be known as the most powerful woman in baseball history.

Because she valued her privacy and avoided interviews, details of Jean Yawkey's early life remain somewhat vague. Much of what is known we owe to the journalistic efforts of Susan Trausch of the *Boston Globe*. In an enlightening piece titled "The Woman Who Owns The Red Sox Keeps Her Private Life Private," Trausch provides important biographical details.[1]

Born in Brooklyn, New York on January 24, 1909, Jean Remington Hollander was "raised in the village of Freeport, N.Y. on Long Island."[2] Although the identity of her parents remains uncertain, it is known the she had an older brother George. Jean graduated from Freeport High School in 1926. The editor of the school's paper, she once took honors in its annual public speaking contest. Following graduation, she married Charlie Hiller, the former star of Freeport's basketball team. The marriage was short-lived, ending either in divorce or when Hiller died. Then, for more than a decade, Jean made a living as a model and salesperson at New York City's exclusive women's clothing store, Jay Thorpe. A striking, statuesque brunette with dark brown eyes, her innate air of refinement served her well. Legend has it that she met Tom Yawkey at Jay

Thorpe when he was shopping there with his first wife Elise.[3]

Nowhere is it said that Jean Hollander broke up Tom Yawkey's first marriage. It is clear that that union was troubled. The two had been separated for three years before Elise filed for divorce in Reno in November 1944. The following month on Christmas Eve, Tom and Jean (then Jean Hiller) were married in a private ceremony in Georgetown, South Carolina where Tom owned a home and a large expanse of land. Trausch writes that at their wedding they were dressed in "their hunting clothes, casual pants and tops, much more like L.L. Bean than Jay Thorpe." This and other evidence points to Jean's persona as quite the opposite of that of Tom's first wife Elise, a socialite of the first order. Jean was more of an outdoors person, and gravitated toward a simpler way of life. Although Tom owned a mansion elsewhere in the Georgetown area, he and

Jean preferred to live in a relatively modest beach lodge on the South Island property during the offseason.

Born in Detroit in 1903, Tom Yawkey was raised by an uncle after his father died. Uncle Bill Yawkey once owned the Detroit Tigers. That no doubt contributed to Tom's lifelong love for the sport of baseball. In 1933, after his college years at Yale, and on attaining his 30th birthday, Tom seized the opportunity to use his substantial inheritance to purchase the Boston Red Sox. After he married Jean, it became obvious that she shared his baseball zeal. Compatible in other ways too, the couple did not gravitate toward the social set. During the baseball season they lived in a suite at Boston's Ritz-Carlton Hotel. Then their activities centered on the Red Sox. After a game at Fenway, they would immediately return to their hotel where they often entertained ballplayers and close associates.[4]

In time, Mrs. Jean Yawkey became a fixture at Boston's Fenway Park. She rarely missed a Red Sox home game. She and Tom sat in separate rooftop boxes because she disliked hearing him cuss with his pals. Her attention always on the game, she shared her box with trusted friends. Chain smoking and often sipping on a martini, her trusty binoculars on hand, she meticulously recorded each play of each inning in a specially-bound score book. Interestingly enough, her penchant for scorekeeping mirrors that of the first woman owner of a major-league team, Helene Britton, onetime owner of the St. Louis Cardinals. Moreover, Joan Payson, the original owner of the New York Mets devised her own complex method for game tallying.

Although a pall remained over the Red Sox organization owing to the fact that it was the last major-league team to integrate, Tom Yawkey was well liked by most who knew him. Many of the players looked on him as a father figure. He and Jean had no children of their own, so one could say the Red Sox became their family. Sadly, more than 30 years after they wed, Tom was diagnosed with leukemia. Boston fans and players alike were heartbroken when he died on July 9, 1976. He left his baseball holdings to a trust controlled by his widow. Tight lipped about her plans for the ballclub, Jean Yawkey finally issued a brief statement in April

of the following year. It simply said that offers to purchase the Red Sox would be accepted.

On September 29, 1977, it was announced that an agreement had been reached for an estimated $15 million. The group making the offer was headed by former Red Sox backup catcher Haywood Sullivan and the club's former trainer Buddy LeRoux. The plan placed Mrs. Yawkey in the background as a limited partner. But before the other American League owners could approve the proposition, she exerted her authority by firing the club's general manager Dick O'Connell and two of his aides. Haywood Sullivan was named as O'Connell's replacement.

O'Connell was undoubtedly more than competent in his job. Tom Yawkey hired him years earlier, and had every confidence in him. But, for whatever reason, Jean Yawkey did not like the man. Reports of the time reveal that she had not spoken to him for several years before Tom's death. O'Connell was probably not the first, and definitely was not the last person to be the target of Jean Yawkey's silent treatment. She replaced him with Haywood Sullivan, who had become somewhat of a surrogate son to her. Hired by O'Connell as director of player personnel in 1966, Sullivan eventually gained status as one of the few people invited to sit with Mrs. Yawkey in her rooftop box. So it seems that in addition to O'Connell's alienation of the deceased owner's wife, his dismissal may have also been fueled by something akin to nepotism.

Not long after the firings, the AL rejected the sale proposal. Then, when A-T-O Corporation of Ohio tried to force a sale with a bid of $18,750,000, Mrs. Yawkey stepped in and supplemented the Sullivan/LeRoux tender. Her contribution of Fenway Park upped it to $20.5 million. The value of the ballpark accounted for the increase. She also lent money to Sullivan and LeRoux so that they could avoid bank loans, which had been one of the league's main concerns. The final agreement named three general partners: Sullivan, LeRoux, and Mrs. Yawkey. Nine investors were limited partners, Mrs. Yawkey included. She was both a general and a limited partner. To manage her holdings, she formed the trust JRY Corporation, becoming its president and sole stockholder.

In May 1978, the AL owners approved the group's revamped bid. The new ownership retained Sullivan as general manager and named LeRoux vice-president, administration. Mrs. Yawkey served the role of team president. The three general partners wielded the power, but the limited partners were to collect a major share of the profits until their investment was returned with interest.

During the changes in management, the Red Sox continued playing over .500 as they had since 1967. But when they dropped to fifth in the AL East in 1980, Sullivan and LeRoux decided to fire manager Don Zimmer. Mrs. Yawkey vehemently opposed the move. This perhaps precipitated the distance that developed between her and Sullivan. The two continued to maintain something of a filial relationship, but they often butted heads in matters of hiring and firing. She apparently viewed his every disagreement as disloyalty. Another factor that came into play was her desire to continue operating the Red Sox in her husband's tradition. To her, building a winning club took priority over increasing revenue. Free agency had just come into being when Mrs. Yawkey took over, so that placed a new dimension on such a practice. It likely did not sit well with her when in 1981 the club lost its most popular player to the White Sox due to Sullivan's negligence. He mailed prized catcher Carlton Fisk's contract two days after the deadline.

Most of what is known about Jean Yawkey during her ownership years is based on observations by reporters, business associates, and Red Sox players and staff. She shunned interviews and public speaking. She even declined to speak at Cooperstown at her husband's induction into the Hall of Fame in 1980. That might lead to the belief that she was unapproachable and coolly detached. However, her acquaintances attributed that demeanor to shyness. Some said that she had a great sense of humor and a loud, hearty laugh. She was also known to engage in warm conversation with fans, ballplayers, and Red Sox staff members. But when approached by the media, she would clam up.

That's what made her willingly, if reluctantly, taking the spotlight during a nasty power struggle in 1983 so significant. At that time her indomitable strength of will prevailed.

A contentious relationship among the new owners existed from the start. LeRoux and Kentucky coal mine owner Rodgers Badgett, the limited partner with the largest investment, focused primarily on padding the profits. They even cut back on team and fan amenities. Because of her free-spending style, Mrs. Yawkey strongly disapproved of such tactics. Probably hoping to control an empire of his own, LeRoux made a failed attempt to buy the Cleveland Indians sometime early in 1982. Then, in May of the next year, Boston TV executive David Mugar made a substantial offer for LeRoux's and Badgett's shares in the Red Sox. Citing right of first refusal, Mrs. Yawkey and Sullivan prevented that deal from materializing. They had no quarrel with Mugar, but they wanted to purchase those shares at "fair market value" themselves. So they proposed eliciting an appraisal. By this time Mrs. Yawkey was no longer on speaking terms with LeRoux. The breaking point came when Badgett criticized her in a memo. Highly insulted, she blamed LeRoux. Finally, the former team trainer made a move that both bewildered and offended Red Sox nation.

On June 6, 1983, reporters gathered at Fenway anticipating the scheduled Tony Conigliaro Night, an event meant to benefit the former player hospitalized by a stroke. Taking advantage of the assembly, LeRoux called a press conference and made a startling announcement. He proclaimed that the majority stockholders were taking control of the Red Sox. That majority included himself, Badgett, and Boston attorney Al Curran. He rationalized that his investment as general partner coupled with Badgett's and Curran's limited partner shares outweighed all other interests. Naming himself managing general partner, he declared that the deposed Dick O'Connell would replace Sullivan as general manager. Choosing to engage in such histrionics just as Red Sox fans prepared to honor a fallen hero was tactless to say the least.

As the ballclub staff tried to make sense of the declaration, John L. Harrington, representing Mrs. Yawkey, and Sullivan took LeRoux's place at the conference table. Harrington declared that the majority of the three general partners ruled, and that there would be no change in command. Regardless of Sullivan's differences with Mrs. Yawkey, this was a situation that placed him solidly on her side. LeRoux's action was temporarily blocked by a court order, and the dispute went to trial.

In July, the case was heard by Judge James P. Lynch at the Suffolk County Courthouse. Although Harrington did most of the testifying on behalf of both Sullivan and JRY, on Wednesday, July 13, Mrs. Yawkey took the stand herself. *Boston Globe* reporter John Powers described her there for two hours "in her tinted glasses and simple checked pantsuit."[5] Though not at all comfortable in this fishbowl setting, she held her ground, responding to questioning with terse directness. She grew indignant when the defense counsel spoke with his back to her. "I do not understand you when you walk away from me," she charged. Few people realized before then that she suffered from a hearing problem. That physical deficiency undoubtedly contributed to her seeming reticence. And although she was subjected to some ridicule during the court ordeal, she ultimately won out.

In August, the court ruled the June 6 attempted takeover illegal, and "permanently enjoined and restrained" LeRoux from any future such attempted coup. It also held that if he wanted to sell his share, it must be offered to the other two general partners first. In one of her rare statements to the press, Mrs. Yawkey simply said "I'm very pleased," adding, "It hasn't been pleasant."[6] She went on to suggest that the partnership would continue as before. Nonetheless, she had gained new respect, refuting the notion that her shyness and hearing difficulty equated to weakness. The unpleasantness of the situation only served to toughen her, and she emerged as a person of note in the world of big-league baseball.

In 1984, Jean Yawkey was elected a member of the Board of the National Baseball Hall of Fame and Museum. She was the first woman to achieve that position. That same year, Lou Gorman came over from the Mets, replacing Sullivan as the Red Sox GM. The owners' squabble had arguably taken its toll on the Boston club. During the year of their court battle, the team's won/loss record dropped below .500 for the first time in nearly two decades. Gorman got it back on track, staying with the Red Sox for the remainder of Jean Yawkey's ownership years.

The enigmatic Mrs. Yawkey exhibited true class when in 1986 her beloved Sox came within a strike of capturing her's and Tom's long sought-after World Series title. When Buckner's error led to the club's devastating loss, though sorely disappointed she remained composed and almost philosophical. Several years later, Rico Picardi of Harry M Stevens, Inc, the Fenway Park concessionaire and a Red Sox limited partner recalled that at the time she was consoling everyone else. He said that with tears rolling down her face she said, "We got beat fair and square and there was nothing to be ashamed of."[7] The following year, she bought out LeRoux for an estimated $7 million, giving her two votes to Sullivan's one, effectively full control of the Red Sox. She also named Harrington, who by then had become her closest confidant, president of JRY Trust.

Against Sullivan's wishes, in 1988 Mrs. Yawkey fired manager John McNamara and gamely took the heat when criticized for the timing. Although Harrington was her chief spokesperson, he made it clear that Mrs. Yawkey was the one running the Red Sox. He once told *Boston Herald* reporter Tim Horgan that "…the buck stops with Jean."[8] By 1990, her relationship with Sullivan had deteriorated to the point that the two no longer spoke. Unlike those with others, her dispute with him was more akin to a family feud.

Although Boston won the division title in 1988, and again in 1990, Mrs. Yawkey didn't live to see her dream of a World Series title realized. On February 20, 1992, she suffered a stroke at her Four Seasons Hotel condo in Boston where she had lived alone since 1987. Found by a hotel employee who checked on her when she failed to come down for her morning paper, she was rushed to Massachusetts General Hospital. The 83-year-old baseball owner died there six days later. Her passing marked the conclusion of an era - the era of the Yawkey way.

Tributes to the departed Red Sox owner flooded the news. Such designations as Red Sox "grande dame" and "matriarch" conveyed the high regard held by New Englanders for Mrs. Yawkey. To some Boston residents she was "the soul of the city."[9] Unlike her female contemporaries, the bombastic, miserly Cincinnati Reds' Marge Schott and Padres figurehead Joan Kroc, Jean Yawkey was joined with her ballclub family till death. Having a generous nature, she paid and treated her employees well. Credited with keeping her "house" habitable, she prevented venerable Fenway Park from falling prey to the modern feeding frenzy that consumed so many of its counterparts.

In addition to her ballpark, the Baseball Hall of Fame in Cooperstown holds lasting evidence of Mrs. Yawkey's devotion to baseball. In 1990, she bequeathed a $1.5 million grant for the expansion and further development of its library. Five years earlier, she had commissioned sculptor Armand LaMontagne to do the remarkably lifelike basswood statue of Ted Williams for the museum. Also, her philanthropic endeavors are legendary. She particularly favored the Jimmy Fund of the Dana-Farber Cancer Institute, the official Red Sox charity.

A number of non-profit groups in New England and South Carolina received support from Mrs. Yawkey's JRY Trust. On May 15, 1988, she was honored "for her lifetime of community service" at Boston's Symphony Hall.[10] That night she graciously accepted a newly established award named for her, the Jean R. Yawkey Award. An organizer of the event observed that she was delighted with the big turnout, and later stayed and talked with people outside on the street.[11] Stories such as this counter her reputation as the Greta Garbo of sports.

The most telling tributes to Mrs. Yawkey were reactions to her death by active and retired Red Sox players. Revered slugger Ted Williams was said to be "hit hard by the loss of a friend."[12] Fellow HOFer Carl Yastrzemski, equally saddened by her death, told how much both the Yawkeys had meant to him. Then-current backup catcher John Marzano's statement to the *Boston Herald* reflected the feelings of many of his cohorts: "It's really sad—she was such a good person…everybody on the team will miss her."[13] He then reflected, "Here I am a guy who plays once a week, and every time she'd see me she'd say 'John, you're doing a great job, keep up the good work.' She was always nice to me."

On Friday, February 28, 1992, the ashes of Jean Remington Yawkey were ceremoniously spread over Winyah Bay at Georgetown, South Carolina Her husband Tom's had been distributed there near the Tom Yawkey Wildlife Center 16 years earlier. Years before that, the couple's initials, TAY and JRY, had been printed in white Morse code on the out-of-town scoreboard at Fenway Park. During the 1992 season, the Red Sox wore the initials JRY on their uniform sleeves in honor of Mrs. Yawkey. Three years later, she was inducted into the Boston Red Sox Hall of Fame.

Following Mrs. Yawkey's death, John Harrington controlled the Red Sox as president of JRY Trust. In 1993, the corporation bought out Sullivan's one-third share for $12 million. Eight years later, a group led by John W. Henry bought it all for $700 million with the proceeds going into a trust to benefit the numerous non-profit organizations that Jean Yawkey had favored. That truly marked the end of an era.

Stories about Jean Yawkey reveal that she enjoyed reading mystery novels.[14] Yet her life remains somewhat of a mystery. In the dozens of print tributes to her in 1992, none named any living relatives. Some seven years later, the news surfaced that her nieces had questioned the contents of her will. The two daughters of Jean Yawkey's brother George, who died in the 1970s, Patricia Hollander and Jane Esopa, believed that Harrington purposely left them out of the loop. The Long Island sisters, as well as Esopa's three daughters, each received a small sum from an insurance policy - but nothing more. They contended that not only did Harrington not inform them of Mrs. Yawkey's stroke (they heard about it on the news), but that he also failed to include them in the Georgetown memorial service. Harrington dismissed their charges with polite denials. Several news items suggest that the nieces' limited finances prevented them from pursuing the matter further. Why they did not benefit from their aunt's sizable fortune leaves room for all sorts of speculation. The truth may never be known.

There are those who believe that even during Jean Yawkey's years as owner, it was John Harrington who controlled the Bosox. Still, one only need note how her relationship with LeRoux, and then Sullivan soured. When they went up against her wishes, she shut them out. O'Connell too found himself a casualty of her ire, likely for similar reasons. So that would leave Harrington as either a master manipulator or simply one who followed orders without question. Perhaps the truth lies somewhere in between. All mysteries aside, Jean Yawkey's legacy remains intact. The Boston Red Sox and Fenway Park live on.

SOURCES

Bodley, Hal. "Very private Yawkey stuck by her Red Sox," *USA Today*, February 27, 1992.

Farmelant, Scott. "Boss Harrington," *Boston Magazine*, June 1996.

Gammons, Peter. "Court upholds Sullivan, Yawkey," *Boston Globe*, August 11, 1983.

Horgan, Sean. "End of a Red Sox era," *Hartford Courant*, February 27, 1992.

Horgan, Tim. "Make no mistake: Yawkey's in charge," *Boston Herald*, July 31, 1988.

Horgan, Tim. "Mrs. Yawkey Takes Over as Red Sox Angel," *Boston Herald*. March 18, 1978.

Krause, Steve. "Yawkeys ran Red Sox with class, integrity," New England Newsclip Agency, Inc. February 27, 1992.

Murphy, Joe. "Mrs. Yawkey, we'll miss you." New England Newsclip Agency, Inc., February 27, 1992.

Powers, John. "'Bosox' brouhaha brings Jean Yawkey to stand," *Boston Globe*, July 14, 1983.

Trausch, Susan. "The Woman Who Owns The Red Sox Keeps Her Private Life Private," *Boston Globe*, April 6, 1989.

Whitney, George. "Fans' Passion For Team Surpassed Only By Mrs. Jean Yawkey's," *Diehard*, March 1992.

"A night to honor Mrs. Yawkey," *Boston Herald*, May 22, 1988.

"Jean R. Yawkey Inducted Into The Boston Red Sox Hall Of Fame," Boston Red Sox press reelease, September 25, 1995.

"League Approves Sale of the Red Sox," *The New York Times*, May 24, 1978.

"Owners give approval to Sox sale," *North Adams Transcript*, May 24, 1978.

"Red Sox heirs in inheritance battle," *New York Post*, March 19, 1999.

"Yawkey Grant Of $1.5 million To Aid HOF Library Expansion," Hall of Fame News Release, Sept. 28, 1990.

Pacific Stars And Stripes, February 28, 1992.

Sports Illustrated

Syracuse Herald-Journal, July 13, 1999.

Berkshire Eagle, October 25, 1977.

Boston Globe

Middletown Press

The New York Times

The News (Frederick, Maryland)

Providence Journal-Bulletin

Albany Times-Union, New York

NOTES

1   Susan Trausch, *Boston Globe*, April 6, 1989.

2   Susan Trausch, *Boston Globe*, April 6, 1989.

3   *New York Times*, February 27, 1992.

4   Both the Susan Trausch article and one by David Cataneo in the *Boston Herald*. February 27, 1992 say that the Yawkeys sometimes entertained players there, but this is not something we have been able to verify.

5   *Boston Globe*, July 14, 1983.

6   "Court upholds Sullivan, Yawkey," Peter Gammons, *Boston Globe*, August 11, 1983.

7   "A night to honor Mrs. Yawkey," *Boston Herald*, May 22, 1988.

8   "Make no mistake: Yawkey's in charge," Tim Horgan, *Boston Herald*, July 31, 1988.

9   "Fans mourn loss of 'the soul of the city'" Kathryn Marchoki, *Boston Herald*, February 27, 1992.

10 Invitation to Jean Yawkey Night at the Pops, May 15, 1988. Note: The Colonel Daniel Marr Boys and Girls Club of Dorchester and The Massachusetts Association for Mental Health sponsored the event...The New England Council of Women Professionals established the award.

11 Susan Trausch, *Boston Globe*, April 6, 1989.

12 "Williams hit hard by loss of friend" Dan Shaughnessy, *Boston Globe*, February 27, 1992.

13 "Baseball world mourns death of Sox matriarch" Steven
    Solomon, *Boston Herald*, February 27, 1992.

14 Susan Trausch, *Boston Globe*, April 6, 1989 and "A night to honor
    Mrs. Yawkey," *Boston Herald*, May 22, 1988.

LOU GORMAN

By Dan Levitt

AT THE CONCLUSION OF THE BOSTON RED Sox' disappointing 1993 season, general manager Lou Gorman, manager Butch Hobson, and assistant general manager Mike Port met with a couple of the team's controlling partners, Haywood Sullivan and John Harrington, to talk about the status of the team and coaching staff. The quintet resolved to make a couple of changes to the coaching staff but, Gorman felt, left the employment status of pitching coach Rich Gale unresolved. Several days later Harrington called Gorman to ask if he had begun the process of considering Gale's replacement. When the general manager responded that he thought Gale could remain, Harrington quickly disabused him, telling him he thought that they all understood that the decision had been made to bring in a more senior pitching coach.

Gorman called Hobson to let him know he was going to have to sack Gale. "But that wasn't my understanding, was it yours?" demanded Hobson, who had just told Gale he was safe for another year. "How am I going to call him back now on the same day and tell him he's fired?" Gorman told Hobson to blame him, but also emphasized that Gale had to believe it was their decision, not ownership's. Quite understandably, Gale was furious and went public with his discontent, embarrassing the Red Sox as the rabid New England baseball press feasted on the debacle. Harrington fired Gorman a week or so later, and the latter believed that this was one of two incidents that directly led to his dismissal.[1]

Gorman was once described as "chubby, kinetic, rather trim … and affable and reasonable," and one of the most common words used to depict him was "optimist." Longtime baseball executive Joe McIlvaine said, "Lou's a builder. He's also the ultimate optimist. He never sees an empty glass, it's always half full."[2] Gorman turned these qualities into a relatively successful tenure with the Red Sox, but the Gale

episode encapsulates many of the difficulties at his two major-league GM stints, some inherent in the chaotic front-office structure he inherited and some due to his own limitations. For example, why was ownership getting involved in coaching decisions, and why for that matter wasn't Gorman letting his manager take the lead on finding replacements? Why wasn't Gorman aware that Hobson had rehired Gale when he clearly expected to be part of the process? Why didn't Gorman push back harder at his owners when they were doing something he strongly objected to within his sphere of operations? Unfortunately for Gorman, both of his GM opportunities occurred in organizations with muddled and overlapping lines of authority, and he never proved particularly adept at managing through and around the hierarchy.

James Gerald Gorman was born on February 18, 1929, in Providence, Rhode Island, to parents who had

come over from Ireland, originally with the last name of O'Gorman. Gorman's father was a firefighter in Providence, eventually rising to become deputy chief. The couple had seven children, and Gorman worked stocking shelves in a grocery store to help support the family. Mostly, though, as a youth Gorman loved sports. He saw his first game in Fenway Park with his father when he was 9.[3] By the time he was in high school at LaSalle Academy, Gorman had become one of the region's top athletes in football, basketball, and baseball. One of his prep highlights was playing quarterback for LaSalle in a game in the Sugar Bowl in New Orleans against Holy Cross Prep School.[4]

As a first baseman, Gorman earned the enduring nickname Lou because his play reminded some of Lou Gehrig. A relatively big kid, Gorman described his abilities: "I couldn't hit, but I was probably as good a fielding first baseman as you will see."[5] One of his favorite memories was meeting Ted Williams at a prep all-star game in Fenway Park in 1946. Williams told Gorman, "Son, that bat's too heavy for you," and picked out a more appropriate one.[6]

After high school Gorman gave professional baseball a try, playing one season in 1948 with his hometown Providence Grays in the Class-B New England League. Unfortunately, Gorman struggled at the plate, logging only one hit in 28 at-bats, which quickly ended his professional career. Instead, Gorman accepted a basketball scholarship to Stonehill College in Easton, Massachusetts, where he was also captain of the baseball team.[7] After graduation in 1953 Gorman joined the Navy. He had always loved boats and sailing, and the Navy seemed a natural spot for military service as the Korean War was winding down.

When Gorman left the Navy eight years later, he decided he wanted a job in baseball. He took a two-week course at the Mitchell Mick Baseball School, learning to run a minor-league baseball operation, and headed off for the December 1961 winter meetings. Toward the end of the meetings, a chance introduction in the hotel bar landed him the general manager's job for the Lakeland Giants, San Francisco's Class-D affiliate in 1962. The next year Gorman ad-

vanced up the minor-league chain, accepting a position as the GM for Kinston in the Class-B Carolina League in the Pirates system.

Gorman was slowly making a name for himself, and Orioles farm director Harry Dalton hired him to be his assistant for 1964. On its way to becoming baseball's model organization, Baltimore was a perfect spot to learn the business of building a major-league team. At the time the team was instituting the "Oriole Way," a blueprint to systematize scouting, training, and conduct throughout the organization. Gorman recognized the value of this approach, bringing the concept with him to next major-league stop, in Kansas City. Regrettably, Gorman could never establish an overall philosophical approach in his two stints as a major-league GM, partly because he never had full control over the front office.

A couple of years later when Dalton was promoted to Orioles GM, he elevated Gorman to farm director. In this role Gorman oversaw a number of well-respected future pennant-winning big-league managers in their minor-league apprenticeships, men like Earl Weaver, Darrell Johnson, Jim Frey, and Joe Altobelli. He also married Mary Louise Kelly, with whom he remained for the rest of his life; the couple had no children.

The four-team expansion for the 1969 season offered Gorman an opportunity for a new opportunity and a significant pay raise. Kansas City general manager Cedric Tallis brought Gorman in as director of minor league operations to be one his key lieutenants. In conjunction with scouting director Charlie Metro, Gorman put together the Kansas City Royals Instructional Manual to highlight how each defensive play should be executed. With his background in the highly successful Oriole Way, Gorman advocated consistent instruction throughout the Royals organization. Gorman also brought along a young assistant from Baltimore named John Schuerholz, just two years removed from teaching junior high school and destined to become one of baseball's greatest general managers.

With the Royals Gorman was part of a talented front office under Tallis. Nice-guy Gorman, traditionalist

Metro, and a free-thinking scout named Syd Thrift could not have been more different (and Metro didn't really respect either associate), but in sum they brought a broad and deep perspective to the task of building the team. As Schuerholz remembered, the disparate group worked very well together.[8] Gorman was a key contributor to this very successful team, remembered by Schuerholz as a man of "remarkable ability."[9]

Owner Ewing Kauffman also had Gorman oversee his pet project, the Kansas City Baseball Academy, after Thrift resigned. Although some in the organization felt the Academy was too independent and that it siphoned off too many resources from the regular minor-league organization, Gorman was sympathetic to the training: "The Academy staff developed some excellent methods of instruction and solid theories in teaching certain skills at all levels of the game. The players in the Academy program were all fundamentally sound and well drilled."[10] By 1973, however, while the Academy had produced several prospects, it had become too costly for its limited return and Kauffman reluctantly shut it down. For the next several years Gorman remained an important senior executive in the Royals front office, reporting to new general manager Joe Burke.

When the Seattle Mariners came calling in April 1976, offering Gorman the opportunity to build his own team, he jumped at the chance. Seattle had just been awarded an expansion franchise to short-circuit a lawsuit filed for allowing the previous expansion team to leave in early 1970 after just one season. With a new stadium, the Kingdome, in its preliminary stages, the area had made a commitment to baseball and demanded a franchise. Regrettably, in its haste to settle the lawsuit, the American League selected an undercapitalized ownership group. The partnership, led by comedian Danny Kaye, consisted of six men who put up just $30,000 each for the down payment and borrowed much of the $5.53 million purchase price from the league. With the advent of free agency that same year, deeper pockets would soon be required to adequately run a major-league franchise. Moreover, the scale of the partners' improvised approach to capital-izing the team can be inferred from their surprise when told they would have to shell out additional funds to fill out the standard complement of minor-league franchises after starting with just a Single-A and shared Triple-A team.

The owners technically bestowed the general manager title on Richard Vertlieb, who came over from the NBA's Golden State Warriors and effectively acted as the business manager. Vertlieb's title testified to the owners' baseball amateurishness but also to their emphasis on finances. In January 1977, three months before their first game, the team sent out a memo telling the other teams to "Please direct all future correspondence and inquiries for the general manager to: Dick Vertlieb, executive director-general manager."[11]

Despite this less-than-optimal environment, Gorman jumped in with enthusiasm and intelligence. Building a major-league organization from scratch is a huge undertaking. Gorman had thorough experience with the Royals in 1969 and had a good sense of the challenges he faced. Because of his owner's lack of capital, he had to both build for the future and also make sure the team played well enough to keep the fan base captivated. "We will build a solid foundation within our farm system as we did in Kansas City," Gorman told the press. "It will take time and patience, but I guarantee you that we'll get the job done. We'll do whatever we can through our expansion draft selections and through trades or signings to put a competitive team on the field in the early years. Our success, however, will be dependent upon the development of talent within our player development system."[12]

Calling on his Kansas City experience, Gorman put together a plan of action featuring five key elements.

First: Develop a scouting staff as soon as possible

Second: Hire a major-league manager

Third: Begin to look for cities to establish minor-league franchises

Fourth: Draw up a list of potential minor-league managers

Fifth: Develop an overall operating philosophy[13]

While one can quibble with the order—settling on an organizational philosophy might rightfully come before picking a manager—it shows a methodical and reasonable approach to the problem of building an expansion franchise.

True to his outline, Gorman hired a solid, relatively large scouting staff (including Jerry Krause, later to gain fame as the general manager for the Michael Jordan-era Chicago Bulls), bought in Bob Kennedy, most recently with the Cardinals, and landed Mel Didier from the Dodgers as his key lieutenant on personnel matters. He also named Darrell Johnson, whom he knew from his Orioles days and who had led the Red Sox to the 1975 American League pennant, as manager. The owners remained intimately involved, with Kaye, Gorman, and Johnson collectively deciding on Johnson's coaching staff. Gorman liked Kaye, a brilliant, unique individual, who demanded explanations from his baseball executive and learned the business quickly.

As the team prepared for the expansion draft, Gorman outlined his player philosophy for Kaye. "Probably the most important of many qualities, in my option, would be self-confidence and mental toughness," Gorman told him. "Next I think that commitment, drive, and toughness are important. If an athlete can combine these intrinsic characteristics with aggressiveness, enthusiasm, and leadership potential and extraordinary skill, we have a future Hall of Famer."[14] Unfortunately, not many of these would be available in the expansion draft.

Nevertheless, Gorman and his staff nabbed several players who could help the team. The first overall pick, center fielder Ruppert Jones, was only 22 years old, and first baseman Dan Meyer only 24. In Leroy Stanton and Bill Stein, he landed a couple of other useful regulars. He smartly went to work trading, buying, and signing players, assembling a surprisingly competitive team. In the inaugural 1977 season the team won 64 games, a strong showing for a first-year franchise, escaping the cellar by one-half game over the A's. The Kingdome played as an extreme hitter's park, which magnified the team's pitching weakness and exasperated Gorman, who believed that like the Orioles, "winning baseball clubs have always been built around pitching and defense," and that "good pitching will most consistently get out good hitting—not always, but enough times to win championships."[15]

Gorman continued to try to build an organization and stock it with capable players during the offseason. By early in the 1978 season, however, it became clear that all decisions were really being governed by their effect on the franchise's constricted finances. In May Vertlieb was forced out, and 30-year-old Kip Horsburgh, originally hired as director of sales and marketing, was put in charge of the organization. Gorman was finally given the general-manager title.

The six owners, none of whom had a controlling position, began to bicker and nudged Kaye out of his liaison role with Gorman. Meanwhile, Horsburgh immediately implemented a draconian austerity program, some of which was embarrassingly counterproductive. Didier recalled lambasting Horsburgh for taking worker's compensation out of minor-league player salaries at a time when many were making $195 every two weeks. This forced many to skimp on meals to make their rent payments, and "a lot of guys were losing weight."[16] The team also had an opportunity to sign two future major leaguers from Latin America, David Green and Candy Maldonado, but passed because the of the $30,000 pricetag. Other cost-cutting moves included gutting the scouting staff and dropping their Arizona Instructional League team.[17]

Gorman and his scouts wanted to draft future star Kirk Gibson with the sixth pick in the 1978 June amateur draft, but were overruled by an ownership that didn't want to meet his price. Instead the team selected outfielder Tito Nanni. Even here Didier needed to resort to financial subterfuge to increase the compensation necessary to sign Nanni. When Horsburgh uncovered the unreported additional guarantee he fired Didier. (Didier later wrote he had Gorman's acquiescence but protected him when their dodge was exposed.[18])

Nanni's eventual stagnation in the minors only further mocked this sorry organization.

In January 1979 Seattle again changed top executives with Dan O'Brien taking over for Horsburgh, further limiting Gorman's scope of authority. Gorman was now GM in little more than name only as O'Brien would essentially run baseball operations, even making road trips with the team. In fact, in 1980 Gorman's only journeys for the team were to spring training and the GM meetings. Moreover, he was not informed in advance when O'Brien fired Johnson or when he hired Maury Wills to replace him.[19] When Frank Cashen, recently named GM of the New York Mets, called Gorman to gauge his interest in becoming his key baseball lieutenant as VP of baseball operations, Gorman happily accepted the opportunity to rejoin his former Baltimore colleague.

Cashen was determined to build the Mets in the image of the Orioles from the 1960s: scouting, player development, young pitchers, power, and getting on base. With Gorman effectively acting as assistant general manager, Cashen turned the floundering Mets into one of the league's top teams of the late 1980s, winning 108 games and the World Series in 1986 and 100 games in 1988. But Gorman wouldn't be around for the payoff.

Gorman relished the challenge of turning around the Mets with Frank Cashen and believed he had been assured of the Mets GM job when Cashen eventually retired. Nevertheless, he was highly intrigued when his childhood favorite, the Boston Red Sox, approached him in December 1983. (At one time he even had a veteran vanity Massachusetts license plate with just the number "9" in recognition of childhood hero Ted Williams.[20]) After some soul-searching, he accepted the position of VP of baseball operations with the understanding that current GM and part-owner Haywood Sullivan would move up to an executive role within a year, naming Gorman GM. And in fact that is what happened. In June 1984, as part of an overall conclusion to a long-running takeover battle for control of the team, Sullivan was promoted to CEO and Gorman to GM. The team would now be overseen by the triumvirate of Sullivan, Harrington, and Jean Yawkey, widow of longtime owner Tom Yawkey and the source, through the Yawkey Trust, of most of the Red Sox capital.

The team Gorman inherited had just finished 78-84 but had a number of positives heading into 1984: a pitching staff led by young hurlers Bruce Hurst, Oil Can Boyd, and Bobby Ojeda, and about to welcome Roger Clemens; one of the American League's best players in Wade Boggs; and several still valuable veterans in Mike Easler, Jim Rice, and Dwight Evans. In his first significant move in May, Gorman swapped struggling veteran starter Dennis Eckersley (not yet the relief ace he was to become in Oakland) to the Cubs for veteran first baseman Bill Buckner, who provided a veteran presence for a few years.

For the most part during his first couple of years at the helm, Gorman only tinkered at the edges.

"I think the worst thing a new general manager can do," Gorman said, "is to start making changes without getting to know what he has and what he needs. The first year was a learning experience for me."[21] That the team jumped to 86-76 in 1984 also encouraged Gorman's inaction. When manager Ralph Houk retired after the season, Gorman named John McNamara to replace him.

After falling back to .500 in 1985, Gorman became more aggressive. His biggest deal sent a still-useful Ojeda among others to the Mets for several players, most notably hurler Calvin Schiraldi. More significantly, in August 1986 during the pennant chase, Gorman made one his best trades, surrendering little and landing two key contributors, shortstop Spike Owen and outfielder Dave Henderson.

In 1986, led by strong seasons from outfield stars Rice and Evans and one of the decade's best pitching seasons from Clemens, the Red Sox won the pennant. In the World Series against the Mets, a team he had helped build and still led by his old boss Cashen, Boston appeared to have won it before collapsing in Game Six in one baseball's most notorious late-inning breakdowns. The Mets' follow-up victory in Game Seven left Gorman and most of Boston sorely disappointed.

Not surprisingly, given that he was coming off a championship season and because of his seeming reluctance to make significant moves, Gorman left his team pretty much intact. Moreover, Sullivan had never really adjusted to player free agency and was generally loath to pay new-found market values, though the first several years of Gorman's tenure were during baseball's collusion years, limiting his scope of action for a time in any case. Had he been given the green light later in the decade, it remains unknowable how aggressive Gorman might have been, but in any case Sullivan's attitude left Gorman hamstrung in the pursuit of the best available free agents. Furthermore, Sullivan remained an active participant in the front office's internal deliberations at the winter meetings every year, further constraining Gorman's scope of action. Gorman was also hampered in that he had extremely small baseball operations staff. "I would liked to have added one or two of the scouts who I had previously worked with and whose judgment I was very familiar with," Gorman lamented, "to give me a couple extra trusted advisors when it came to trading and acquiring talent."[22]

The Red Sox ownership also remained closely involved in contract negotiations with the players. As opposed to some franchises in which the GM is given a target budget and allowed to build a team, Sullivan and Harrington wanted review all significant contract proposals in advance. This became particularly exasperating for Gorman when Clemens held out for a salary increase after the 1986 season. Gorman took much of the heat for the dispute, and in the end Sullivan formally took over the negotiations for Boston and even Commissioner Peter Ueberroth needed to get involved.

He also began to experience the intensity and volatility of the Boston press, which the folksy Gorman never really adjusted to. Years later he still harbored resentment over his treatment from the sportswriters. In just one example, he felt *Boston Globe* columnist Dan Shaughnessy made too much of his comment during the Clemens holdout that, "I'm certain that the sun will set tonight, and I'm also certain it will rise tomorrow morning and I'll have lunch tomorrow afternoon and we will get Roger Clemens signed."[23]

The team fell back in 1987, and with the club at 43-42 at the All-Star break in 1988, Jean Yawkey expressed her dissatisfaction over the performance of the team, telling Gorman to replace McNamara. During the offseason Gorman had added star closer Lee Smith, and a couple of good young outfielders developed in the Red Sox system, Mike Greenwell and Ellis Burks, were also now regulars. With Yawkey's sanction Gorman named coach Joe Morgan the new manager, technically on an interim basis. To further bolster the team, at the 1988 trading deadline Gorman sent young outfielder Brady Anderson and farmhand Curt Schilling to Baltimore for pitcher Mike Boddicker. Boddicker was a valuable contributor to the Red Sox in 1988 and for the next couple years, but it was a heavy price to pay—both Anderson and Schilling went on to stellar careers. Under Morgan the club rebounded to capture the AL East Division title before falling to the Oakland A's in the ALCS.

The team remained competitive over the next three years, including one more division title in 1990. Gorman smartly rode his nucleus while making a several lesser moves that benefited the team, such as the trade for Lee Smith and another for Nick Esasky. But once again ownership decided to change managers. In 1991 the team had been within a half-game of first in late September, but finished 3-11 down the stretch, and there had developed "the perception that the club had gotten away from [Morgan] and that there was dissention on the ballclub." And once again Gorman was not part of or in this instance even aware of the decision to replace the manager. While he knew of their general discontent, he was as surprised as Morgan when at a meeting with Gorman and Morgan, the owners told the manager he was out.[24]

By 1992 many of the naturally occurring holes—due to injuries and retirements—were filled by journeymen. Even the development of slugging young first baseman

Mo Vaughn could not offset this adverse trend. Nor could the loosening of the purse strings by ownership: Clemens was re-signed for a record contract, Gorman spent liberally to land hurlers Frank Viola, Danny Darwin, and Matt Young, and the team made a huge, albeit unsuccessful, offer to Twins free agent Kirby Puckett. The team also struggled to retain its stars in free agency: Hurst had left after the 1988 season, and Boston lost both Boggs and Burks after the 1992 season. In 1993 the team again finished below .500. Shortly after the Gale debacle, Harrington sacked Gorman, a firing Gorman also attributed to an earlier Shaughnessy article calling for his dismissal.[25]

Gorman had also hurt his cause by making another significant prospect-for-veteran trade (two years after the one for Boddicker), one that looked awful soon after he made it. During the 1990 pennant race, when Gorman felt he needed to strengthen his relief corps, he dealt minor leaguer Jeff Bagwell to the Astros to Larry Andersen. Gorman tried to live this trade down ever since, telling Bill Nowlin, "I had two scouts see him [Bagwell] and two managers see him plus we saw him in spring training, and no one plussed his power."[26] Nevertheless, at the time of the trade Bagwell had an .880 OPS as a 22-year-old in the Eastern League.

The team also failed to sign a couple of draft choices who could have helped the team. In the 1985 draft the team astutely selected Tino Martinez in the third round but couldn't sign him. With their first-round pick in 1986 the team drafted local multisport star Greg McMurtry. The team's scouts compared him to Willie Wilson and hoped to sign him away from attending the University of Michigan on a football scholarship. They offered a $172,000 bonus, well short of McMurtry's reported demand of $225,000, and lost him to football.[27]

Harrington kept Gorman with the Red Sox in an honorary role, one Gorman retained for many years, even after the team was sold to a consortium led by John Henry. Well respected for his generosity and integrity, he remained an ambassador for the organization. "Lou Gorman was first and foremost a gentleman," team executive Larry Lucchino recalled.

"He treated everyone with dignity and saw each person he encountered as a potential friend. I will deeply miss sitting and watching Red Sox home games with Lou, learning from his wisdom and character."[28] John Henry echoed these sentiments, "Above all else, Lou Gorman was a profoundly decent man who always had a kind word and an optimist's perspective."[29]

Gorman was genuinely excited in 2004 when the Red Sox finally won the World Series, 86 years after their last world championship, and he enjoyed his role with the Red Sox. "I was and still am a member of the Red Sox team," Gorman wrote in 2008. "And that was solace enough for me. ... I am still involved and still loving every moment of it."[30] Gorman died three years later, on April 1, 2011, at 82 of congestive heart failure.

During his first few years in Boston, Gorman's good natured optimism, baseball smarts, and overall team success made him well-liked around Boston despite some rough press over the team's various failures. When the team's fortunes took a turn for the worse, Gorman's folksy, open manner no longer seemed quite so endearing, and his interactions with the press became much more strained. He had successfully built a quality team around the nucleus that he inherited without surrendering any of his key performers. His farm system delivered enough replacements that the team won three division titles in five years even as some of his original nucleus aged out. The lack of comprehensive control over baseball operations coupled with the loss of several prospects and an ownership initially reluctant to spend in free agency made an already difficult task even more challenging.

At his two big-league GM stints Lou Gorman never really had the chance to bring the systematic, detailed approach to team building he had learned in Baltimore and was again part of in New York. How he would have succeeded with less intrusive ownership is unknowable, but Gorman succeeded reasonably well within the context he was given. Maybe just as importantly, he spent 50 years in and around professional baseball, knew just about everyone, and left baseball better for having been a part of it.

NOTES

1 Lou Gorman, *One Pitch From Glory: A Decade of Running the Red Sox* (Champaign, Illinois: Sports Publishing, 2005), 196, 201-206.

2 Joseph Durso, "Boston's Gorman Helped Build Mets" (syndicated from *New York Times*), unidentified newspaper article in Gorman Baseball Hall of Fame file.

3 Gerry Callahan, "Sox Serve Big Lou a Big Deal," *Boston Herald*, February 22, 1991.

4 Russ Conway, "Mr. Enthusiasm" (interview with Lou Gorman), *Eagle-Tribune* (Lawrence, Massachusetts), newspaper article in Gorman HOF file.

5 Ibid.

6 Ibid.

7 *New York Times*, December 27, 1982.

8 John Schuerholz, interview with author, March 11, 2013.

9 Schuerholz interview.

10 Lou Gorman, *High and Inside: My Life in the Front Offices of Baseball* (Jefferson, North Carolina: McFarland, 2008), 109.

11 Tracy Ringolsby, "Shipwrecked in Seattle," *Sport*, March 1984.

12 *High and Inside*, 141.

13 *High and Inside*, 142.

14 *High and Inside*, 149.

15 *High and Inside*, 162.

16 Mel Didier and T.R. Sullivan, *Podnuh Let Me Tell You a Story: A Baseball Life* (Baton Rouge: Gulf South Books, 2007), 107.

17 Tracy Ringolsby, "Shipwrecked in Seattle."

18 Didier and Sullivan, 107-108.

19 Tracy Ringolsby, "G.M. Gorman Leaves Mariners," *The Sporting News*, November 22, 1980; *High and Inside*, 178, 181.

20 Email from baseball historian Bill Nowlin, July 24, 2014.

21 Jim Vincent, "Here's the Deal: Gorman's Glad to Be Home," *New Bedford Standard-Times*, October 6, 1986.

22 *One Pitch From Glory*, 154.

23 *One Pitch From Glory*, 44.

24 *One Pitch From Glory*, 165-167.

25 *One Pitch From Glory*, 206.

26 Lou Gorman, interview with Bill Nowlin, September 5, 2006.

27 Allan Simpson, editor, *The Baseball Draft: The First 25 Years, 1966-1989* (Durham, North Carolina: American Sports Publishing, 1990), 267.

28 Amalie Benjamin and Chad Finn, "Lou Gorman; General Manager Built Contending Red Sox Teams," *Boston Globe*, April 2, 2011.

29 Gordon Edes, "Former Boston GM Lou Gorman Dies," ESPN.com, April 1, 2011.

30 *High and Inside*, 238.

JOHN McNAMARA

By Mark Armour

JOHN McNAMARA RAN A BIG-LEAGUE TEAM six times, plus another as an interim skipper. He kept getting hired because he was well respected by everyone in the game, including general managers and players. "Any player with an ounce of decency in him will play his heart out for John," said one of his San Diego players, Doug Rader.[1] Reggie Jackson credited him for his character in the face of bigotry. McNamara won a couple of division titles and a pennant, and managed a team that had the best record in baseball and still did not make the playoffs. But for all of that, McNamara is most famous for his role with the 1986 Red Sox, an extremely successful team by any measure, who lost a heartbreaking World Series that left many fans bitter toward the manager.

John Francis McNamara began his life on June 4, 1932, in Sacramento, California, the fourth of five children born to John and Josephine. The elder John was born in Ireland, immigrated to Boston as a young man, and made his way across the country by working on railroads. He died in 1944, leaving John to learn to play sports from his mother's two brothers, who played semipro ball and lived across the street. "I started school so I could learn to write my name so I could sign a baseball contract," he said.[2] Josephine went to work at the Department of Motor Vehicles to support the family.

McNamara starred in baseball (as a catcher) and basketball in Christian Brothers High School, earning all-city honors in each sport, before signing with the St. Louis Cardinals in 1951 for a $12,000 bonus. On the small side for a catcher, he spent 14 seasons in the minor leagues (taking two years out for a stint in the US Army) without getting close to the majors. He reached the Pacific Coast League with Sacramento in 1956, but hit just .171 in 76 games. "I could catch and I could throw," he recalled. "But I knew I wasn't going to make the big leagues. I was too small [5-feet-10,

175 pounds] and I couldn't hit. I was married and had four children to think about."[3] He began working toward an accounting degree at Sacramento State in his offseasons.

In 1958 McNamara was the regular catcher for Lewiston (Idaho), an unaffiliated team in the Northwest League, and impressed his bosses enough that they made the 27-year-old McNamara the player-manager the next year. "That was the turning point in my life," he said. "The next year the Kansas City A's took over the club. Hank Peters, who was running the A's farm system, asked me to stay. I owe everything to Hank."[4] He managed Lewiston through 1962 (winning a pennant in 1961), then spent a year each managing (and occasionally catching for) Binghamton (Eastern League), Dallas (Pacific Coast League), Birmingham (Southern League), Mobile (Southern League), and Birmingham again.

He won three minor-league pennants—in 1961 with Lewiston, in 1966 with Mobile, and 1967 with Birmingham. The Mobile club included Rick Monday, Sal Bando, John Odom, and Tony La Russa. "We were just a very good club, the kind that didn't lose a lot of games at a time," McNamara said. "There was no outstanding performer who carried us."[5] The next year he had Rollie Fingers, Dave Duncan, Joe Rudi, and Reggie Jackson. "Every man on this team has done something in the clutch," McNamara said after clinching the title.[6]

In his autobiography, Jackson writes of how McNamara helped the young player deal with the segregated South. "When we'd be on a road trip and we'd stop at a diner for hamburgers or something to eat, McNamara wouldn't compromise. It was simple for him: if they wouldn't serve me they weren't going to serve anybody. He'd just take the whole team out of the restaurant, we'd get into the bus and we'd keep driving."[7]

The 35-year-old McNamara, fresh off back-to-back titles with the A's best prospects, finally made the big leagues in 1968, as a coach with the relocated Oakland Athletics. Charlie Finley, the A's owner, changed managers constantly throughout his tenure, and McNamara was a candidate for the job that went to Bob Kennedy. After one season Kennedy was replaced by Hank Bauer, and the A's moved up to second in the AL West (88-74). Nonetheless, Bauer was fired in September and replaced by McNamara, who managed the last 13 games of the year and was invited back for 1970. The A's were a very young team, and McNamara had managed many of their best players in the minors. "Basically, we know what we have to do," he said in the offseason. "They've all polished the skills they showed in the minors, but we're making mistakes on fundamentals, mistakes in execution."[8] He pledged to work the club harder in spring training.

McNamara's A's finished 89-73, in second place, nine games behind the Minnesota Twins. Like most Finley teams, it was filled with owner-created drama. When star outfielder Reggie Jackson started slowly, Finley forced McNamara to platoon him and threatened to send him to the minor leagues. When Jackson hit a home run and gestured to the owner's box, Finley demanded that he apologize to the team, which Jackson did, in tears. At the end of the season, catcher Dave Duncan was asked about McNamara returning for 1971. "There's only one man who manages the club, Charlie Finley," said Duncan, "and we'll never win so long as he manages." Finley used Duncan's comments as a pretext to fire McNamara, reasoning that McNamara could not control his players.[9]

McNamara hooked on with the San Francisco Giants as third-base coach, and held that job for three years, through 1973. Just before spring training in 1974 he accepted a job managing the San Diego Padres, a terrible, near-bankrupt club that had just been rescued from relocation with their purchase by multimillionaire Ray Kroc. Team president Buzzy Bavasi selected McNamara over former Los Angeles Dodgers star Maury Wills, saying he wanted the more experienced hand.

McNamara lasted three full seasons in San Diego, finishing sixth (last), fourth, and fifth. He had some talent, particularly young star Dave Winfield, but was generally plagued by poor pitching. The club was 20-28 on May 28, 1977, when McNamara was fired and replaced by Alvin Dark. "I'm not sure we're doing the right thing," said Kroc, "but should we stand idly by and do nothing?"[10] McNamara's players were supportive. "Mac couldn't hit or pitch for us," said Gene Tenace, "it wasn't his fault." Rollie Fingers added: "Mac won't have any trouble finding another job."[11] McNamara spent the 1978 season as third-base coach for the California Angels.

In December 1978 he was hired to manage the Cincinnati Reds. After back-to-back World Series titles, the Reds had finished second the past two seasons and responded by firing manager Sparky Anderson in favor of McNamara. "Words can't describe how thrilled I was," McNamara told the press. "It took me a while to come down to earth."[12]

The 1979 Reds endured the loss to free agency of Pete Rose, finished 90-71, and eked out the National League West by 1½ games over the Houston Astros. In their manager's first trip to the postseason, the Reds lost the NLCS in three straight games to the Pittsburgh Pirates. The Reds fell off by just a single game in 1980 but finished third, and then fell victim the next year to the players' strike. Because the strike wiped out the middle third of the season, the owners decided that the division winners of the two "half-seasons" should meet in a series to determine the division champ. Though the Reds finished with the best record in all of baseball, they finished second in both "halves" of the season and missed the playoffs.

In 1982 the Reds, after losing starting outfielders George Foster, Dave Collins, and Ken Griffey, collapsed to last place, and McNamara was fired on July 20. "Sure, it hurts when it happens," he said. "It's a humiliating thing." He bore no ill will toward the man who fired him, GM Dick Wagner. "Things just didn't work out. But I still respect the man. He and his wife, Gloria, are good friends of mine."[13]

Once again, it did not take McNamara long to get another job. He next managed two years for the California Angels. The man who hired him, Buzzie Bavasi, had already hired him twice — to manage the Padres and then to coach the Angels. Gene Mauch had retired after winning the division in 1982, but McNamara's club received down years from Fred Lynn, Brian Downing, and Reggie Jackson and fell back to 70 wins. They got to .500 the next year as McNamara integrated Gary Pettis and Dick Schofield into what had been a very old team.

At the end of the 1984 season Red Sox manager Ralph Houk resigned and Haywood Sullivan, the team's GM, approached McNamara. The two were good friends, having each managed in the A's system 20 years earlier. Bavasi had retired from the Angels and McNamara's contract had expired, so he decided to step aside and move to Boston.

In Boston McNamara inherited a fair bit of hitting talent — Jim Rice, Wade Boggs, Dwight Evans — and a crop of young promising pitchers — Dennis Boyd, Bruce Hurst, Bob Ojeda, and the 22-year-old Roger Clemens. Clemens pitched very well in the first half but was felled by an arm injury and started just 15 games. The Red Sox hung around in the race for a few months (they were 7½ games out on July 26), but a rough stretch in August ended things and they finished 81-81, 18 games behind the Toronto Blue Jays.

Still, McNamara got good reviews in his debut in Boston. "He works players hard, strongly believes in discipline," said coach Rene Lachemann, who had played for McNamara in Oakland. "He speaks with a quiet voice, but he commands respect."[14] McNamara was also a strong delegator, allowing Bill Fischer to handle the pitching staff, Walt Hriniak the hitters, and Lachemann the defense. McNamara gave his coaches freedom, while leaving no doubt who was in charge.

The next year, 1986, is the year that history will most associate with John McNamara. The Red Sox were a good team and led the AL East nearly wire to wire. Clemens broke through with a magnificent 24-4 season, Boggs hit .357, and Jim Rice had his best season in years. And the team capped it off with two dramatic postseason series: a seven-game triumph over the Angels, and a seven-game tragedy at the hands of the Mets.

The regular season was not all a cakewalk. Most trying, for McNamara, was a trial associated with pitcher Dennis Boyd, who was so furious at KC manager Dick Howser for not choosing him for the AL All-Star team (he was 11-6) that he left the club. When he returned, the Red Sox suspended him and demanded that he seek psychiatric counseling. Years later Boyd admitted that he had been a heavy user of marijuana and crack cocaine that season. To McNamara, Boyd had "desecrated the uniform."[15] Boyd missed nearly a month in the middle of the pennant race. The Red Sox held on to win, with Boyd pitching well in September and pitching the division clincher against Toronto on September 28.

The postseason has become the stuff of legends. First, there was the ALCS, in which the Red Sox fell behind 3-1 in games before pulling of a dramatic come-from-behind win in Game Five in Anaheim, and then winning two more in Boston to close it out. Ordinarily, this would be a series everyone would remember in Boston. Sadly for Red Sox fans, it is not.

In the World Series, against the New York Mets, the Red Sox won the first two games at Shea Stadium, came back home to win one of three, then went back to Shea needing to win one of two games. They lost the sixth game in agonizing fashion, giving up a 3-2 lead in the eighth and then a 5-3 lead, and the ballgame, in the 10th. In Game Seven they held a 3-0 lead in the sixth but lost 8-5. Boston, New England, the Red Sox, and certainly John McNamara were devastated.

In the many heartbreaking disappointments the Red Sox suffered in their 86-year gap between championships, 1986 ranks near the top. And no one has been blamed more often than McNamara who (according to his critics): pulled Roger Clemens out of Game Six with the 3-2 lead; did not pinch-hit for Bill Buckner late in the game, allowing the gimpy first baseman to make a game-ending error; put the game in the hands of Calvin Schiraldi in the 10th inning; did not pitch Boyd in Game Seven while the game slipped away, etc.

McNamara has been asked to explain all of this and more for 30 years and counting. He adamantly says that Clemens asked out of Game Six, which Clemens has denied. McNamara protests that Buckner's bad knees did not affect the play—he got in front of the ball just fine, but it went through his legs. Schiraldi, the manager says, was his best relief pitcher—he had a 1.41 ERA for the season. As for Boyd, McNamara (and Fischer) later reported that he was too drunk. Boyd later admitted that when he found out he wasn't starting the game (the day before) he went straight to a crack house.[16] After the season, McNamara was named the AL Manager of the Year, an award he would have traded for one more victory.

The entire crew showed up again in 1987, which became a year of transition. Buckner, Don Baylor, and Dave Henderson gradually gave way to Mike Greenwell, Ellis Burks, and Todd Benzinger. Boyd got hurt, and several other players regressed. The club fell to 78-84, but the young players (and more to come, as Brady

Anderson, Jody Reed, Sam Horn, and John Marzano appeared ready) gave everyone optimism for 1988.

McNamara's grip on his job began to loosen early in the season when he lost the support of Jean Yawkey, who owned two-thirds of the team. When the Red Sox struggled again out of the gate, his job status became a daily distraction; things got only worse because of some off-field problems, especially a palimony suit filed against Boggs, and the stories that he had taken compromising photos of his teammates.

McNamara was fired at the All-Star break in 1988, just a few hours prior to the first game of the second half. The decision was made at a general partners meeting, with his old friend Sullivan dissenting. McNamara was reportedly angry at how it was handled, and it did not help his standing in Boston when the team (under new manager Joe Morgan) won their next 12 games and 19 of 20, and went on to win the AL East. "Let me say this in defense of John McNamara," said Dwight Evans. "A lot of things happened that you'll never hear about. He protected a lot of people. He took the blows for a lot of people."[17]

McNamara spent a year scouting for the Seattle Mariners before he got his sixth managerial chance when Cleveland hired him after the 1990 season. Hank Peters, another of his vast network of friends and admirers in the game, was his new boss. The Indians were in transition, and McNamara helped ease the way for youngsters Sandy Alomar Jr., Carlos Baerga, and Albert Belle, the early pieces in what would become a juggernaut. But McNamara would not stick around to see it, getting fired in July 1991, just his second year on the job. "I could sense it, especially in the last week," he said of his firing. "People started staying away from me like I had leprosy."[18] He spent the next five years in the Angels organization as a catching instructor, briefly returning to dugout as an interim manager in 1996.

During McNamara's long career in the game people often remarked on how focused he was on the game, how he talked and thought about baseball constantly. He did try to relax during his many hours of alone time. "I will have a book with me all the time whether at home or on the road and I'll read. What I read depends on my mood. Detective stories, cowboy stories, I'll read history. I really enjoy music, too, the Sinatra music, Tony Bennett, Barbra Streisand, Vic Damone. I think Damone is one of the best singers going. Nat 'King' Cole, I have a lot of tapes. I turn on a tape and read."[19]

John married Kathleen early in his pro career and they raised three daughters (Peggy, Maureen, and Susan) and one son (Mike). He later married Ellen Goode, a flight attendant, and the two have lived a quiet retirement in Nashville (Ellen's hometown) since leaving baseball.

NOTES

1   Phil Collier, "McNamara's philosophy: deal with others with your heart." *1979 Cincinnati Reds Yearbook*.

2   Ed Bridges, "Loves baseball, hates strikes," *Worcester Sunday Telegram*, August 4, 1985.

3   Bob Sudyk, "McNamara—Boston Adds Finishing Touch to a Major League Montage," *Hartford Courant*, undated (Spring 1984) clipping in McNamara's Hall of Fame file.

4   Sudyk, "McNamara—Boston Adds Finishing Touch."

5   Vincent Johnson, "Slow Start, Fast Pickup—That's Mobile Flag Story," *The Sporting News*, September 17, 1966: 39.

6   Frank McGowan, "A's Birmingham Farm Clinches Southern Crown," *The Sporting News*, September 9, 1967: 35.

7   Bridges, "Loves baseball, hates strikes."

8   Ron Bergman, "A's Boss is Bugged By One-Run Losses," *The Sporting News*, October 25, 1969: 14.

9   Ron Bergman, "Dick Williams on Finley's Firing Line; McNamara's Axing Blamed on Duncan," *The Sporting News*, October 17, 1970: 25.

10 "Padres Fire McNamara, Dark Appointed Manager," *The Sporting News*, June 11, 1977: 11.

11 Phil Collier, "Juggler Dark Quickly Shows Padres the Light," *The Sporting News*, June 18, 1977: 9.

12 Earl Lawson, "Reds Look to McNamara for Higher Standard," *The Sporting News*, December 16, 1978: 41.

13 Earl Lawson, "Reds' Fall Costs McNamara Job," *The Sporting News*, August 2, 1982: 34.

14 Sudyk, "McNamara—Boston Adds Finishing Touch."

15 Garry Brown, "McNamara was angry, because of what he's made of," *Springfield* (Massachusetts) *Republican*, July 13, 1986.

16 Dennis Boyd interview with Buster Olney, youtube.com/watch?v=CmmRvM2A-Hk.

17 Steve Fainaru, " 'Just a regular meeting' became turning point for Sox," *Hartford Courant*, October 4, 1988.

18 "McNamara says he saw scalp job coming," *New York Post*, July 10, 1991.

19 Bridges, "Loves baseball, hates strikes."

BILL FISCHER

By Bob LeMoine

"He describes himself as a very easy-going guy, but in the next breath he'll tell you he's a full-blooded German with a hot temper that sometimes explodes."

Earl Lawson, *The Sporting News*[1]

THE KANSAS CITY ROYALS GATHERED IN February 2008 at their spring facility in Surprise, Arizona. One coach, rumbling around on a golf cart, was ironically dubbed "Walking Wisdom" by players a quarter of his age. "Walking wisdom, eh?" said Bill Fischer, the Royals' senior pitching adviser. "Yeah, they should have been there that day when Ol' Walking Wisdom pitched for the Kansas City A's and decided to throw a bleeping fastball to Mickey Mantle. The Mick blasted it off of the bleeping right-field façade at Yankee Stadium. They called it 620 feet. They called it 734 feet. Whatever, it was bleeping far."[2]

"Grumpy. Crusty. Cantankerous. Gruff. Ornery," wrote Tim Pearrell, "all these things describe Bill Fischer, who will quickly engage you in a 15-minute session that's part argument, part debate."[3] Even when he was 29, Fischer was depicted by Bob Addie in *Baseball Digest* as a man who "looks more like one of those dads who have settled down to suburbia, roll the family jalopy out of the driveway at seven every morning and back again at 4:30 every night."[4]

A lifetime baseball man, Bill Fischer had a 20-year pitching career followed by 40-plus years as a scout, instructor, coach, and consultant. To nobody's surprise, he also spent two years instructing Marines. Fischer has been a wealth of wisdom about pitching and life, disseminated in a no-nonsense approach and style. Rick Bailey in the *Lexington* (Kentucky) *Herald* described Fischer as "heavyset with a weather-beaten face," who "stalks around the ballyard menacingly,

possesses a vise-like grip, and growls out his words. He loves baseball, especially his life in the major leagues."[5] He also practiced what he preached: He holds (as of 2015) the record for most innings pitched without walking a batter.

William Charles Fischer, the pitching coach of the Red Sox from 1986 to 1991, was born on October 11, 1930, in Wausau, Wisconsin, to William Constantine and Grace (Chizek) Fischer. William worked in steel, construction, and carpentry. Growing up during the Great Depression, the family "never had much fancy stuff," Bill Fischer recalled. "Food was very basic and the family had a big garden. My mother canned all kinds of food. We ate lots of potatoes as they were cheap and we lived in 'potato country.'"[6] At the time of the 1940 Census, the family was renting a home in Marathon, Wisconsin, near Wausau. Fischer had two brothers: Thomas, who played in the Chicago White Sox system from 1958 to 1960, and Gary, who played in the Los Angeles Dodgers and California Angels systems from 1964 to 1968. Neither brother made it to the major leagues. Fischer also had a younger sister, Rosemary.

At Marathon High School, Fischer played baseball and basketball.[7] Two weeks after graduation in June

1948, Charles "J.C." Gilman, the high-school principal and baseball coach, took him to a White Sox tryout camp at Wisconsin Rapids. White Sox farm director John Rigney, assistant Glenn Miller, and scout Red Ruffing watched Fischer throw for about 10 minutes. "Let's hide this kid in a hotel before someone else sees him," Rigney suggested.[8] "At the end of the tryout, they asked me if I'd like to play pro ball," Fischer remembered. "I was a minor at the time, so the next day I had to bring my dad down so I could sign."[9] Fischer signed a $150-a-month contract and was sent to the Wisconsin Rapids White Sox of the Class-D team Wisconsin State League. "No bonus, no nothing," Fischer said. "That's not a lot of bleeping money."[10]

The 17-year-old Fischer won his first 10 starts, the first three being a two-hitter, a three-hit shutout, and a two-hit shutout.[11] He had a streak of 26 scoreless innings,[12] and finished 14-3 with a 2.63 ERA.

Fischer went 16-15 with Hot Springs (Arkansas) of the Class-C Cotton States League in 1949, including an 11-strikeout performance.[13] In 1950 he was 11-7 for Waterloo of the Class-B Illinois-Indiana-Iowa League and 1-1 for Memphis of the Double-A Southern Association. His season included a 10-strikeout, four-hit performance for Waterloo.[14] In the offseason, Fischer worked for his father's construction business in Marathon and for a lumber company.[15] In his free time, he played on the local "Wee Willys" basketball team.[16]

Fischer was drafted into the US Marine Corps in 1951, at the height of the Korean War, and served as a drill sergeant. "I hated it, but I had a job to do," he said. "I was in charge of a platoon of 75 men. When I wanted my boots shined, I hollered for my personal shoeshine boy to do it, on the double. Everything was on the double. … I had those platoons sick of looking at me, I guess." Wryly, he recalled that "The only two-year contract I ever had in my life was when I was drafted into the Marines."[17] His baseball talents kept him in stateside while the war was waging. His San Diego team won the Marine Corps championship and played in Wichita, Kansas, at the National Baseball Congress Tournament.[18]

Fischer returned in 1954 and again pitched for Memphis, finishing 14-12 with a 3.86 ERA and throwing a one-hitter.[19] At Memphis again in 1955, he struggled, finishing 5-15 with a 4.85 ERA, but with 10 complete games.

Fischer was invited to spring training by the White Sox in 1956, and pitched well. "I never even saw a big-league game until I pitched in one in spring training in Tampa, Florida," he said in 1991.[20] He made the major-league roster, but failed to retire a batter in his first game, giving up four runs. After two more appearances, he was optioned on May 16 to Toronto of the Triple-A International League,[21] and in July was reassigned to Vancouver of the Pacific Coast League.[22]

Fischer made the White Sox roster again in 1957. His first major-league win came on May 12 at Detroit when he relieved Jeff Harshman in the second inning and finished with 7⅔ innings with four hits and one earned run in a 5-4 win. "It really was a wonderful Mother's Day present," Fischer said, "both for my own mother in Marathon as well as my wife at our home in Schofield, Wisconsin, which is nearby. Our baby daughter was also three months old on May 12. I'll never forget that day as long as I live."[23] The performance kept Fischer on the roster. "I realized that what I did out there probably would decide whether I spent the year in the majors or in the bushes," he said. "So I had to do the job."[24] Traveling secretary Bernie Snyderworth tore up Fischer's travel ticket, and he stayed the year in Chicago.[25]

Fischer won his first start, 6-2 over the Red Sox in Boston on May 19, pitching 6⅔ innings. Fischer's roommate, Paul La Palme, relieved him with Ted Williams at the plate representing the tying run. "I didn't want to let my roommate down," La Palme said. "Bill has been working awfully hard trying to make good up here. … I gave it everything to save the lead and the victory for him."[26] Williams flied out.

Fischer threw a complete-game victory on May 28 against Kansas City, allowing six hits and one earned run. He was 3-1 with a 1.76 ERA at the end of May, but slumped throughout June and July, losing his spot in the rotation. As an emergency starter, he threw his first major-league shutout on September 1 in Kansas City. On the 11th he pitched an 11-inning complete-game victory over the Red Sox, winning 4-1. Fischer finished the season 7-8 with a 3.48 ERA.

Fischer's 1958 season never got on track. In his first start, on April 20, he gave up two home runs, breaking his homerless streak at 101⅔ innings. His record through June 13 was 2-3 with a 6.69 ERA. But a highlight came at Fenway Park, when he was given two calves on Massachusetts Day, recognizing Fischer's work as a farmer in Schofield, Wisconsin.[27]

On June 15 Fischer was traded with outfielder Tito Francona to Detroit for infielder Ray Boone and pitcher Bob Shaw. He continued to struggle, going 2-4 with a 7.63 ERA. On September 11 Fischer was placed on waivers and was claimed by the Washington Senators for $20,000.[28] He started three games at the end of the season, going 0-3 with a 3.86 ERA.

Back with the Senators in 1959, Fischer pitched a classic against Whitey Ford of the New York Yankees on April 22. He shut out the Yankees for 10 innings but Washington lost 1-0 in the 14th. Ford pitched all 14 innings for the victory. Fischer said, "When I held the Yankees scoreless it did wonders for my confidence. You need a lot of luck in this game."[29] Fischer pitched a complete-game victory just four days later against Boston, allowing only an unearned run in the ninth inning. His next start was also masterful, a complete-game 9-1 six-hitter against Detroit. Fischer finished April 2-0 with a 1.06 ERA.[30]

Fischer credited Senators pitching coach Walter "Boom-Boom" Beck and manager Cookie Lavagetto with helping him find rhythm and relax. "I learned more about pitching in three weeks with Washington than I had learned in all my other years in baseball," he said at the time. "Cookie made me feel as if I belong."[31] Lavagetto said Fischer's new-found sinker and slider gave him confidence. "I felt all along he could help us because he has the heart," Lavagetto said.[32] However, Fischer struggled after being 8-3 on July 16, and didn't win again until September 18, finishing 9-11 with a 4.28

ERA. Besides farming, he spent time in the offseason driving a bus in Chicago.[33]

Fischer struggled with a 4.91 ERA for the Senators in 1960, and was traded to Detroit on July 22 for pitcher Tom Morgan. He improved his ERA to 3.44 with Detroit and finished 8-8, but slumped again in 1961, going 3-2 with a 5.01 ERA. He was traded to Kansas City with infielder Ozzie Virgil for infielder Reno Bertoia and pitcher Gerry Staley on August 2.[34] Fischer spent the early part of the 1962 season at Triple-A Portland (Pacific Coast League). He was recalled at the end of May and was used mostly out of the bullpen, going 1-0 with a 4.22 ERA at the end of July. Then the streak began.

On August 3 Fischer walked Cleveland third baseman Bubba Phillips leading off the bottom of the first inning. Fischer lost the game, 1-0. More significant is that Fischer did not walk another batter until the last game of the season, on September 30. His 84⅓ consecutive innings without allowing a walk shattered Christy Mathewson's record of 68 innings. "Nobody even noticed it until I pitched a game in Chicago," Fischer remarked decades later. "I got taken out of the game in the seventh inning and they put up on the scoreboard, 'Fischer has now gone 60 innings without a walk.' It was the first I knew of it. Then they started blowing it up a little bit."[35]

The record was broken against Baltimore, as Fischer got Brooks Robinson to ground into a force out at second. The streak ended when Fischer walked Detroit center fielder Bubba Morton, so the streak began and ended with two guys named Bubba. "There are only two reasons a guy is wild. He's got bad mechanics or he's afraid. I had pretty good mechanics, and I was too dumb to be afraid," Fischer remarked 50 years later.[36]

Kansas City owner Charlie O. Finley had promised Fischer a $1,000 bonus if he broke the record, and an extra $100 for every walkless inning thereafter. But Finley claimed he made a mistake with the offer. "You're going to pay me that bleeping money," Fischer insisted. Finley did pay, but months later took the amount out of Fischer's next contract.[37] Despite the record, Fischer was winless after August 17, one loss being to Jack Kralick's 1-0 no-hitter for Minnesota. Fischer finished 4-12 with a 3.95 ERA.

Fischer was an effective late-inning reliever in 1963, holding a 7-1 record with a 1.53 ERA at the end of May. "It's nice. It's great," Fischer said modestly. "But I'm just a …what is it they say? … a Humpty Dumpty. I'm 32. I'm not going to be a star. I'm just a mediocre pitcher. Thanks to Eddie Lopat [the Athletics' manager] I have come up with a new pitch, a slow curve. … He taught me his slow curve in five minutes."[38]

On May 22 the A's and Yankees were tied 7-7. In the 11th inning Fischer faced Mickey Mantle. Lopat fined any pitcher $200 for giving Mantle a good pitch to hit in a win-or-lose situation. "I got this one outside, but a little too high," Fischer recalled.[39] Mantle crushed the ball to right field and it nearly became the first fair ball hit out of Yankee Stadium. "The ball struck the façade on the right-field roof approximately 370 feet from home plate and 115 feet above field level," according to an article in a SABR publication.[40] Mantle said it was his hardest-hit ball ever. The Yankees bestowed on Fischer a picture of the moment, autographed by Mantle.[41]

Fischer finished 1963 with a 9-6 record and a 3.57 ERA. His ninth victory came over Boston on July 25 when he pitched six innings of shutout relief. It was his final major-league win; he was sent to Triple-A Portland at the end of the season, leaving him eligible for the Rule 5 Draft. Pat Friday, the A's general manager, told Fischer and said the club wanted to protect some young players and planned to bring him back after the draft. "Well, I was disappointed after the year I had," Fischer said a year later.[42] Meanwhile he was drafted by the Minnesota Twins, a move that reunited him with manager Sam Mele, who was on the Washington coaching staff when Fischer was on the team.

Fischer struggled in nine appearances out of the Twins bullpen in 1964, with a bulging 7.36 ERA. On May 22, 1964, exactly a year after the Mantle blast, Fischer threw his last major-league pitch for a walk-off home run by Baltimore's John Orsino. Fischer was returned to Kansas City and then placed on the retirement list.[43] Later in the season, the Twins hired Fischer as a scout, but then released him in early 1965.

Fischer contacted Glenn Miller, then the White Sox farm director, seeking a job as a coach or scout. Miller persuaded him to join Triple-A Indianapolis as a pitcher. On May 3 Fischer pitched a 1-0 two-hit shutout over San Diego, in which 70 of his 90 pitches were strikes. He blanked San Diego again on a three-hit shutout on July 20.[44] Fischer was 11-10 in 1965 and then 11-6 in 1966 with a league-leading 2.35 ERA.[45]

Fischer, now 36, went 12-4 with a 2.36 ERA in 1967, while also serving as a player-coach for Indianapolis.[46] "I want to pitch as long as my arm can help," he said. "The hitters will let me know when it's time to quit."[47] His 20th and final season was with the Triple-A Hawaii Islanders. He finished 8-9 with a 3.11 ERA.

From 1969 to 1974 Fischer was a Kansas City Royals scouting supervisor in Georgia, Alabama, and Florida[48] under Lou Gorman, the Royals' director of player development.[49] He was minor-league pitching instructor for the Royals from 1975 to 1977. In 1976 Fischer received the Ewing M. Kauffman Award for his outstanding contributions to the Kansas City organization.[50] Fischer worked with young pitchers Paul Splittorf, Dennis Leonard, and Dan Quisenberry.[51]

By this point, the Fischer family was living in Sarasota, Florida. He had three children with his first wife, Joan: Michael, Patti, and Mary Jo. Michael was a catcher on the Riverview High School baseball team in Sarasota. He was drafted by the Reds in the 43rd round of the 1979 amateur draft, but never made it to the major leagues.

In 1979 Fischer became the pitching coach of the Cincinnati Reds under new manager John McNamara. Fischer was elated, saying, "I never dreamed that I'd be back in the majors this year. And I really feel honored when the Reds offered me a job."[52]

The Reds had several challenges. "We had one starting pitcher—Tom Seaver," Fischer recalled. "We had to bring along the kids."[53] Fischer helped the Reds win the 1979 NL West title with an improved pitching staff. "Reds pitching was suddenly aroused from its backside," wrote Russell Manley of the *Tampa Times*, "nursed along by strong injections of young blood and some expert shuffling of veteran personnel when injuries gummed the works."[54]

Fischer found a breath of fresh air for his career. "This is my 31st year in pro baseball," he said, "and this one year has made my whole career worthwhile. … Shoot, last year at this time I was down in the Instructional League worrying about this kid pitcher or that guy. Now, I'm in a championship race."[55]

"I've worked with a lot of excellent pitching coaches in my time," McNamara said, "but Fischer has the best knowledge of mechanics I've seen. He's really helped youngsters like Frank Pastore and Charlie Leibrandt become 'pitchers' at very early stages of their careers."[56] Fischer also guided young pitchers Mike LaCoss, Joe Price, and Tom Hume.[57] Pastore joked that Fischer could connect well with pitchers, "from making so many mistakes in his career," but seriously added, "He's a mechanics fundamentalist and he has the ability to get his point across in simple language."[58] That "simple language" was, wrote Tim Sullivan of the *Cincinnati Enquirer*, "dominated by compound and profane adjectives. It is punctuated by spurts of tobacco juice which makes his uniform a constant headache for equipment manager Bernie Stowe."[59]

In 1980 the Reds finished 86-72 in third place. In 1981 Cincinnati had the best record in baseball, although the strike-shortened split season kept them out of the playoffs. Fischer was fired after back-to-back last-place finishes in 1982-1983. He returned to Kansas City in 1984, serving again as a minor-league pitching instructor, working with rookie pitchers Bret Saberhagen and Mark Gubicza.[60]

On November 24, 1984, Fischer married his second wife, Valeria.[61] Fischer's friend Mark Andrews introduced the couple at his bar, the Railway Inn, in Council Bluffs, Iowa, where the Fischers now lived. Andrews was Fischer's best man.[62]

In 1985 Lou Gorman, now the Red Sox general manager, hired Fischer as Boston's pitching coach, a position he held through 1991. He was reunited with manager John McNamara. "McNamara is very easy to work for," Fischer said. "He'll let you do your own thing. … McNamara is a pitcher's manager."[63] Fischer mentored Boston's young ace, Roger Clemens, and on a chilly night in April watched him strike out 20 batters, a major-league record. "I almost had tears in my eyes," Fischer commented. "It was the best game I ever saw pitched."[64]

Boston's 1986 pennant drive put two legendary pitchers under Fischer's care: the young Clemens and the veteran Seaver, who was reunited with Fischer. "We're all individuals, and he knows that," Clemens said. "Some pitching coaches will try to clone you and make you do the same things as other people. But we all have different capabilities, and he's got us all down."[65] "Our relationship is very comfortable," Seaver said. "Fisch might not be the most grammatically correct individual. But you have to listen to what he says, not how he says it."[66]

Fischer also worked with young Red Sox pitchers Bruce Hurst, Al Nipper, Calvin Schiraldi, and Wes Gardner. He saw Clemens win three Cy Young Awards, and the Red Sox reached the postseason in 1986, 1988, and 1990. Fischer emphasized the same strategy that brought him success on the mound: "I tell them there is no defense for bases on balls. If a pitcher doesn't see that, then he has to be pretty stupid."[67]

The BoSox Club, the official booster club of the Red Sox, named Fischer the Red Sox Man of the Year in 1988 for his contributions to the team and community, the first nonplayer to win the award. Fischer also coordinated youth clinics and participated in Boston Mayor Ray Flynn's drug education clinics.[68] Besides his playing days, Fischer said in 2015, his time coaching in Boston was "the best thing that ever happened to me."[69]

When McNamara was replaced by Joe Morgan in 1988, Fischer stayed on until both Morgan and he were fired after the 1991 season. "It's the only job in the world where you can't tell the truth," he commented. "If I could tell the truth people would be shocked. But I want to stay in baseball so I'm not saying anything."[70]

"I'm going to miss Bill Fischer," Clemens said. "I'm pretty loyal to a guy who I know has helped me. He deserves a great deal of credit for what he has done. I think I owe him just as much for the third [Cy Young Award] as I did for the other two."[71]

Fischer found a new job a month or so later, as the Atlanta Braves' minor-league pitching instructor. In 1994 he became the pitching coach for the Triple-A Richmond Braves under manager Grady Little.[72]

Fischer celebrated his 50th year in professional baseball in 1997. On August 3 he was honored by the Richmond Braves in a pregame ceremony. Tom Seaver praised Fischer at the gathering, saying, "My induction [into the Baseball Hall of Fame] in 1992 was one of the biggest thrills of my life and all that goes in part to your help and guidance. For that, I thank you very much."[73] In a recorded message, Clemens noted how he struck out 20 batters in a game twice without walking anyone and "that's especially a tribute to you, Fisch. Being a power pitcher, you always instilled in me the second part of that, being a pitcher. I thank you."[74] The Braves presented Fischer a silver bowl filled with 50 crystal baseballs, one for each year in the game. "That's enough about Bill Fischer. My day is over," Fischer gruffly remarked after the ceremony.[75]

In April of 2000 Fischer was offered the job of pitching coach of the Tampa Bay Devil Rays. Fischer accepted the position without even asking about a salary, and was on his way back to the major leagues.[76] "It's one more challenge for me. A last hurrah," he said.[77] Fischer stayed on through the 2001 season.[78] "Being around these young guys keeps you young. It's like a little medicine."[79] But manager Hal McRae, who had taken over during the season, wanted to make changes in the coaching staff. Fischer learned the morning of the last game of the season that he was being fired. In the spring of 2002, he found himself in the unfamiliar position of nowhere to go for spring training, even though Tampa was still paying him the $100,000 left

on his contract. The Atlanta Braves called, however, offering him a job as a part-time scout.

In 2004, Fischer became the Braves' minor-league pitching coordinator,[80] and in 2007 became the Kansas City Royals' senior pitching adviser. He still held that position in 2015, his 68th season in professional baseball.[81]

As "Walking Wisdom" continued zipping around on that golf cart in 2008, he mentioned one of his absolutes that he doesn't share often, one that extends beyond the pitcher's mound: "You've got to help somebody every day. It may just be a couple of words. It might be a kick in the butt. It might be grabbing them by the collar and saying, 'You're better than that.' But you gotta do it. You beat on them but you love them. That's what this game is about."[82]

While appreciating every pitching coach he ever had, Fischer said in 2015 that he had a special place for Gilman, his high-school principal, who took him to his first tryout in 1948.[83]

NOTES

1 Earl Lawson, "Tapes Help Fischer Spot Red Hurlers' Flaws," *The Sporting News*, March 10, 1979: 51.

2 Joe Posnanski, "Royals Pitching Advisor Fischer Shares Wisdom of 60 Years in Baseball," *Kansas City Star*, February 24, 2008: C1.

3 Tim Pearrell, "Golden Oldie; Fischer Carries Storied Career to 50-Year Mark," *Richmond* (Virginia) *Times Dispatch*, July 8, 1997: F1.

4 Bob Addie, "The Quiet Man Who's Loud on the Mound," *Baseball Digest*, August, 1959: 79-81.

5 Rick Bailey, "Reds' Pitching Would Draw Pessimism From Anyone but Fischer," *Lexington* (Kentucky) *Herald*, July 20, 1980: C2.

6 Bill Fischer, interview with the author on September 4, 2015.?

7 "Wausau Trims Indians, 13-6," *Janesville* (Wisconsin) *Gazette*, June 26, 1948: 11.

8 "Sox Story, 9 Years Old, May Become Best Seller," *Chicago Tribune*, May 15, 1957: 7.

9 Tom Martenson, "Bill Fischer: ML Record Holder to Begin 44th Year in Pro Ball," *Sports Collectors Digest*, November 29, 1991: 150.

10 Ibid.

11 "Rapids' Youth Hurls 2-Hitter," *Waukesha* (Wisconsin) *Freeman,* June 15, 1948: 9.

12 "Odd Homers Give Indians Win in 15th," *Janesville* (Wisconsin) *Gazette,* June 18, 1948: 8.

13 "Errors Costly As Bathers Even Set; Final Game Tonight," *Delta Democrat-Times* (Greenville, Mississippi), May 11, 1949: 6.

14 Bob Nesbit, "Plan Big Push to Win Pennant," *Terre Haute* (Indiana) *Tribune,* August 30, 1950: 8.

15 Martenson, 151.

16 "Odds 'N' Ends," *Rhinelander* (Wisconsin) *Daily News,* January 8, 1951: 6.

17 Burton Hawkins, "Griffs Cheered as Fischer Turns in Another Fine Job," *Washington Evening Star,* April 27, 1959: 21.

18 Martenson: 150.

19 Bill Ferguson, "Birmingham's Jack Urban Hurls Historic No-Decision No-Hitter," *Anniston* (Alabama) *Star,* August 23, 1954: 7.

20 Martenson: 151.

21 "Majors Cut Down to Player Limit," *Hagerstown* (Maryland) *Morning Herald,* May 17, 1956.

22 "White Sox Buy M'Donald," *Kansas City Times,* July 9, 1956.

23 Edgar Munzel, "Release Tag Ready, Fischer Lands Sox Job, Kinder Departs," *The Sporting News,* May 22, 1957: 9.

24 "Fischer Saves Job With ChiSox," *Milwaukee Sentinel,* May 14, 1957: 5.

25 Edgar Munzel, "Fischer, Latman Brighten Chisox''58 Hill Outlook," *The Sporting News,* September 25, 1957: 9.

26 Hy Hurwitz, "La Palme Pleased to Save His Roommate, Fischer," *Boston Globe,* May 20, 1957: 6.

27 "Massachusetts Day Planned By Red Sox," *North Adams* (Massachusetts) *Transcript,* May 29, 1958: 9; Joe Cashman, "Come From Behind Sox Make it 3 in a Row," *Boston Record American,* June 8, 1958: 33.

28 "Schofield Hurler Sold to Senators," *Rhinelander* (Wisconsin) *Daily News,* September 12, 1958: 8.

29 Burton Hawkins, "Griffs Cheered as Fischer Turns in Another Fine Job," *Washington Evening Star,* April 27, 1959: 21.

30 "Bill Fischer, Haddix Lead," *Sarasota Herald-Tribune,* May 6, 1959: 17.

31 Burton Hawkins, "A Feeling of Belonging," *Washington Evening Star,* June 19, 1959.

32 Bob Lassanske, "Senators' Fischer Finds New Life," *Milwaukee Sentinel,* May 4, 1959: 5.

33 Shirley Povich, "Hunch-Player Cal Comes Up With New One," *The Sporting News,* March 9, 1960: 15-16.

34 "Bertoia 'Key Man' in A's-Tigers Deal," *Boston American,* August 3, 1961: 50.

35 Pearrell, "Golden Oldie."

36 John O'Connor, "Control Master; R-Braves Pitching Coach Holds Record for Innings Without a Walk," *Richmond* (Virginia) *Times Dispatch,* August 22, 1998.

37 Ibid.

38 Jack Hand (Associated Press), "Modesty Is Becoming to A's Bill Fischer," *Free Lance-Star* (Fredericksburg, Virginia), May 21, 1963: 13.

39 "May 22 Means a Big Dose of Trouble for Bill Fischer," *The Sporting News,* June 6, 1964: 8.

40 William J. Jenkinson, "Long Distance Home Runs," in Bob McConnell and David Vincent, eds., *SABR Presents the Home Run Encyclopedia : The Who, What, and Where of Every Home Run Hit Since 1876* (New York: Macmillan, 1996). Retrieved from baseball-almanac.com/feats/art_hr.shtml August 12, 2015.; Jenkinson added, "Almost everyone in attendance believed that the ball was still rising when it was interrupted in midflight by the roof structure. Based upon that belief, this drive has commonly been estimated at about 620 feet if left unimpeded."

41 Martenson, 151; Fischer was berated by Lopat in the locker room after the game. "It was like he was screaming into the wind because everybody else was laughing," Fischer remembered. "It was so funny. Every time Ed would look at a guy, the guy would bust out laughing." Jane Leavy. *The Last Boy: Mickey Mantle and the End of America's Childhood* (New York: Harper Perennial, 2010), 257.

42 Bob Wolf, "Bill Fischer of Rothschild Found Minors Route to Better Opportunity," *Milwaukee Journal,* April 4, 1964: 19.

43 "Twins Bomb Angels in Slugfest," *Aberdeen* (South Dakota) *Daily News,* May 26, 1964; "Bill Fischer Placed on Retired List," *La Crosse* (Wisconsin) *Tribune,* May 27, 1964.

44 Johnny McDonald, "Padres' Streak Ends at 6, 2-0," *San Diego Union,* July 21, 1965.

45 "Fischer Snares Coast ERA title," *Eureka* (California) *Humboldt Standard,* September 9, 1966: 5.

46 "Beard Will Return as Indians' Coach," *Greensburg* (Indiana) *Daily News,* January 6, 1967: 1.

47 "Still Pitching," *Milwaukee-Journal Sentinel,* April 23, 1967.

48 "Fischer Inked as Scout by Royals," *San Antonio Express,* November 9, 1968: 19.

49 Paul O'Boynick, "Royals Reveal Wide Range of Group Benefits," *Kansas City Times,* January 7, 1969: 10.

50 From a biography in Fischer's file at the Baseball Hall of Fame.

51 Joe Giuliotti, "Sox Hire McNamara's Men to Coach: Lachemann, Fischer," *Boston Herald,* October 30, 1984: 49.

52 Earl Lawson, "Tapes Help Fischer Spot Red Hurlers' Flaws," *The Sporting News,* March 10, 1979: 51.

53 Peter Gammons, "Red Sox Add Lachemann," *Boston Globe,* October 30, 1984: 32.

54 Russell Manley, "Good-Natured Fischer Has Made Reds' Pitching Tough," *Tampa Times*, March 12, 1980.

55 "Fischer Says Season With Reds His Best," *Lexington (Kentucky) Herald*, September 20, 1979: C3.

56 Bill Conlin, "All-Star Team of Castoffs Reflects a Huge Turnover," *The Sporting News*, May 31, 1980: 22.

57 Earl Lawson, "Seaver, Pastore Big Wheels of Reds Staff," *The Sporting News*, March 15, 1980: 44.

58 Tim Sullivan, "Fischer Pitching Advice More Spit Than Polish," *Cincinnati Enquirer*, August 7, 1981.

59 Ibid.

60 "Sox Hire McNamara's Men."

61 John Brockman, "Sarasota's Fischer Named Reds' Coach," *Sarasota Herald-Tribune,* December 2, 1978: 3-D; Fischer interview.

62 Tim Pearrell, "Fischer Gets Call From Rays," *Richmond Times Dispatch*, April 13, 2000.

63 Larry Whiteside, "Fischer Is Having a Ball," *Boston Globe*, September 19, 1986: 69.

64 Joe Giuliotti, "A Record for the Rocket," *The Sporting News*, May 12, 1986: 19.

65 Ibid.

66 Ibid.

67 Michael Madden, "Fischer: Controlling Interest," *Boston Globe*, June 23, 1986: 27.

68 Joe Giuliotti, "Evans Swings to Bench With Hamstring Pull," *Boston Herald*, September 19, 1988: 102.

69 Fischer interview.

70 "Fischer Keeps His Mouth Shut," *Boston Herald*, October 13, 1991: B4.

71 Larry Whiteside, "Clemens Again a Young Man; Sox Ace Named Best AL Pitcher for 3d Time," *Boston Globe*, November 14, 1991: 65.

72 *The Sporting News*, December 27, 1993: 30.

73 "Pitching Mentor Marks 50th Year," *USA Today*, August 4, 1997.

74 Ibid.

75 Jon Solomon, "Ceremony Moves Fischer After Half-Century of Work," *Richmond (Virginia) Times Dispatch*, August 4, 1997.

76 Marc Topkin, "Rays Fire Williams, Hire Fischer to Take His Place," *St. Petersburg (Florida) Times,* April 13, 2000.

77 "Fischer Gets Call From Rays."

78 Marc Topkin, "McRae, Wanting His Own Staff, Fires Fischer," *St. Petersburg (Florida) Times*, October 8, 2001.

79 "Fischer Gets Call From Rays."

80 Bill Shanks, "Instructional League Report: Part One," published October 28, 2003, at scout.com/mlb/braves/story/194841-instructional-league-report-part-one.

81 "Royals Minor League Coaching Staffs Announced," published January 9, 2015, at wibwnewsnow.com/royals-minor-league-coaching-staffs-announced/.

82 "Royals Pitching Advisor Fischer Shares Wisdom of 60 Years in Baseball," *Kansas City Star*, February 24, 2008.

83 Fischer interview.

WALT HRINIAK

By David E. Skelton

THROUGHOUT HIS 12-YEAR PROFESSIONAL playing career, Walter John Hriniak (pronounced RIN-ee-ack) brought Gas House Gang-style intensity to the game. Typically wearing the filthiest uniform, he was dubbed "The Rat" for his tendency to "grovel around the dirt and grime and do anything to win a ballgame. 'I don't have the God-given ability of others, so I have to play like this,'" he modestly explained.[1] If Hriniak had been born 50 years earlier, he would have fit right in with the likes of Joe Medwick, Frankie Frisch, and other rough-and-tumble players of that era. But in 1968-1969 Hriniak's abilities got him a mere 99 major-league at-bats.

Instead Hriniak turned this same Gas House intensity to the study of hitting and became one of the most famous—and often derided—instructors in baseball. For though his techniques enhanced the career of many with the God-given talent he once lacked, Hriniak's methods—combined with a gruff, intense, no-nonsense style—afforded many detractors as well.

Hriniak was born on May 22, 1943, one of two children of Walter Edward and Ann Catherine (Gumaskas) Hriniak, in Natick, Massachusetts, 15 miles west of Boston. He was the grandson of Polish and Lithuanian immigrants. The Natick High School Redhawk was the All Bay State League Quarterback on the gridiron and the Bay State League Most Valuable Player on the hockey rink. But for the sandy-haired shortstop, baseball was where he particularly excelled:

First freshman to play Natick varsity baseball since 1920.

1961 team captain and most valuable player.

1961 Massachusetts Gridiron Club Memorial Outstanding Player.

In 1960 Hriniak was selected to play in the showcase Hearst Sandlot Classic in Boston, a popular venue for major-league scouts. A year later the high-school senior paced the Redhawks with a .461 average. He was pursued aggressively by the Boston Red Sox, Philadelphia Phillies, San Francisco Giants, Pittsburgh Pirates, and Milwaukee Braves. Shortly after graduation, Hriniak signed a contract with Braves scout Jeff Jones and received an $80,000 bonus.

Assigned to the Eau Claire (Wisconsin) Braves in the Northern League (Class C), Hriniak quickly wrestled shortstop from second-year prospect Demetri Alomar (the older brother of Sandy Alomar Sr.). Despite a mere 267 at-bats Hriniak, the team's youngest player, placed among the Braves leaders in RBIs (50), doubles (14), and batting average (.311). Significantly, he also placed among the leaders in walks, a practice he continued in subsequent campaigns. (This plate patience was one of the core principles Hriniak stressed as a coach years later.) In the Florida Instructional League

[271]

after the season, he caught the attention of Milwaukee manager Birdie Tebbetts, who said, "[The Braves] have a club policy of developing our own, and have especially high hopes for … infielder Walt Hriniak."[2] His debut success earned Hriniak a spot on Milwaukee's 40-man roster as the Braves' youngest position player.

Named to the Florida Instructional League's All-Star squad in 1962, Hriniak had less success with the Austin Senators in the Double-A Texas League the following spring. Unable to unseat shortstop Sandy Alomar, he settled in at second base. Though he was challenged at the advanced level—it was the first season Hriniak hit less than .300—there was no indication the Braves intended to give up on their 20-year-old prospect. But circumstances outside the baseball diamond would limit Hriniak to 175 at-bats with the Senators in 1964.

On the morning of May 22, Hriniak and teammate Jerry Hummitzsch were in a celebratory mood. Hriniak was observing his 21st birthday while Hummitzsch was basking in the wake of his 10-inning, three-hit, 1-0 win over the Fort Worth Cats. They set out for a predawn fishing excursion when, cruising along the winding roads west of Austin, Hummetzsch lost control of his sports car. The pitcher was killed when the vehicle overturned. Thrown through the windshield, Hriniak survived but his head and chest injuries kept him in the hospital more than two months. He recovered sufficiently to participate in the Florida Instructional League after the 1964 season. Years later Hriniak stoically recalled, "I never thought the accident had anything to do with my not making the big leagues. It happened, and I had to deal with it."[3]

Excluding a demotion to Class A in 1965, Hriniak remained with the Austin Senators into 1967. His middling offensive production slowed further promotion as he manned each infield position but first base. On April 21, 1967, Hriniak connected for a grand slam—his first homer in 134 games—in a 13-5 victory over the Albuquerque Dodgers. The blow rejuvenated his bat as the lineup's former eighth-place hitter placed among the Senators leaders in most offensive categories. Once again predating his coaching success, the 24-year-old studiously analyzed his approach:

"I choked up a lot and got right on top of the plate. My back foot wasn't but about six or seven inches from the plate and when you're that close, if you're not quick with the bat, they'll saw you off with that inside pitch."[4]

On July 13 Hriniak was pressed into service as an emergency catcher against the El Paso Sun Kings. He quickly proved his worth by gunning down three opposing baserunners, thereafter setting his course within the Braves organization. Promoted to the Triple-A Richmond Braves, Hriniak received as much play at catcher as he did the infield.

The 1968 season proved a watershed year for Hriniak. Reassigned to Shreveport, the Braves' new Texas League farm team, he sustained a split finger early in the season that hampered his play behind the plate. Refusing to sit, he was positioned at third base until the finger healed. Meanwhile Hriniak's batting stroke appeared fully restored when, after a 7-for-18 surge in August, he briefly led the league with a .313 average. The Topps Chewing Gum Company selected Hriniak as the Texas League's August Player of the Month and, at the end of the season, Double-A All-West All-Star catcher. Arguably his most productive season in professional baseball, Hriniak's successful campaign was carried out under the direction of manager Charlie Lau. The merger of the assiduous skipper and his hard-working disciple would prove profitable for years to come.

Lau was not the only person observing Hriniak's triumphant campaign. The Braves—since relocated to Atlanta—took notice and selected the catcher as one of the team's September call-ups. On September 10, 1968, Hriniak made his major-league debut, against the San Francisco Giants. The next day he collected his first two hits against Giants future Hall of Famer Juan Marichal while catching a four-hitter twirled by Braves righty Pat Jarvis. Atlanta manager Lum Harris offered lavish praise of the 25-year-old backstop, saying, "He called a good game. … Pat shook off very few pitches."[5] Harris's admiration continued that winter as he received reports of Hriniak's play in the Venezuelan League: "Our scouts say he is tearing up the winter league. … He is hitting well and throwing out everything that moves."[6] With the departure of Joe Torre in March, Hriniak appeared poised to take over the Braves' 1969 catching responsibilities.

But in March 1969, in a near-repeat of the preceding year, Hriniak asked to play at second base while a broken bone in his right thumb healed. Catching duties fell to Bob Didier by default while Hriniak was placed on the disabled list to start the season. Fully recovered, Hriniak got little play—one hit in seven at-bats through June 4—when he broke another finger and was placed on the disabled list a second time. Hriniak was still on the disabled list when, on June 13, he was traded to the San Diego Padres in a three-player swap for outfielder Tony Gonzalez. Hriniak came off the disabled list on June 27 and was promptly inserted into the starting lineup. Four days later he was relegated to pinch-hitting after reinjuring the finger sliding into second base. Hriniak returned behind the plate on June 27 and thereafter shared backup catching duties with two younger prospects. When Hriniak walked off the field on September 30, he had no way of knowing it was his final appearance as a major-league player.

On December 5, 1969, while Hriniak was again toiling in the Venezuelan League, the Padres acquired catcher Bob Barton from the Giants. Though the move cemented the backup role behind catcher Chris Cannizzaro, Hriniak's versatility made him a viable candidate as a utility player. He hung on until the next-to-last cut in spring training and was assigned to the Salt Lake City Bees in the Pacific Coast League. Moved to second base, with his gritty style of play he quickly captured the admiration of Bees manager Don Zimmer, who told sportswriters: "You are gonna love this guy. He battles every minute and will do anything in his power to help the club."[7] But 1970 proved to be Hriniak's last season as a full-time player. On April 3, 1971, he was traded back to the Braves organization and released that summer. Unsure where to turn, Hriniak received an unexpected call from an old acquaintance.

On August 24, 1971, Montreal Expos general manager Jim Fanning signed Hriniak as a free agent.[8] The Expos executive was very aware of Hriniak. He had been Hriniak's manager in Eau Claire and was well aware of the player's strong work ethic. In 1971 Hriniak played in a mere nine games for the Expos Triple-A affiliate at Winnipeg, but from the moment of signing, it appears, Fanning had another role in mind for the 28-year-old. In November Hriniak was signed as a player, coach, and manager, and his coaching career was launched. In 1972 he coached for the Double-A Quebec Carnavals until the New York-Pennsylvania League season began, when Hriniak took the managerial reins of the Jamestown Falcons. He continued in this capacity through 1973 while ushering in the careers of youngsters Larry Parrish and Gary Roenicke.[9]

Prior to the 1974 season Montreal announced Hriniak as manager of its West Palm Beach affiliate in the Florida State League (Class A). But when Larry Doby left the Expos, Hriniak was tapped to join the 1974 coaching staff. Serving as the team's first-base coach, he wasted little time "earning" a two-game suspension and a $200 fine. Hriniak was accused of bumping umpire Art Williams in a June 1 game against the Braves. Manager Gene Mauch was outraged because he—like many Montreal players—felt Williams had been the aggressor. In Hriniak, Mauch likely saw the same feisty approach that he brought to the game. Hriniak remained an Expos coach under Mauch. After the manager was fired in 1975, Hriniak became the hitting coach for the Double-A Denver Bears and then manager of the Rookie League Lethbridge (Alberta) Expos. While with Lethbridge, Hriniak served a five-day suspension in July 1976 for "spraying an umpire with saliva."[10]

At about the time Hriniak was serving his suspension, things were happening 2,500 miles to the east that would have a profound impact Hriniak's career. The reigning American League champion Red Sox were suffering through a dismal campaign. In July Boston fired Darrell Johnson, the manager, and named third-base coach Don Zimmer to replace him. Though Zimmer would be forced to seek another residence—he was renting Hriniak's Natick home—in

October Zimmer tapped Hriniak as his bullpen coach, launching Hriniak's 12-year term with the Red Sox.

Hriniak's untiring work ethic quickly earned him the nickname Iron Mike. Until he broke a shoulder in 1978, Hriniak threw batting practice, earning the respect of his Boston teammates. But Hriniak's lasting impact came through his work with the Red Sox batters. Though Johnny Pesky was Boston's hitting coach through much of Hriniak's 12-year stay, to many players Hriniak—under managers Zimmer, Ralph Houk, and John McNamara—was the de-facto hitting coach. Though afterwards one of Hriniak's sharpest critics, in 1978 Red Sox icon (and avid fisherman) Ted Williams remarked, "[Hriniak has] done well here with the club. … Good teachers [like him] are worth their weight in swordfish."[11]

Asked years later to explain his teaching methods, Hriniak bowed to his late mentor and manager Charlie Lau: "[I'm simply] carrying on the work of my friend, that's all. It's his stuff, I'm just teaching it." Stressing the need to create good habits by hitting to all fields, Hriniak painted the alternative: "[O]nce you start trying to pull everything, the pitchers and the defense all know what you are going to do. You have to commit yourself to pitches a lot sooner and get farther out in front and you are more wide open for breaking stuff. The percentages are against you."[12] Though this flew in the face of Williams's approach—an emphasis on a strong hip and torso rotation to whip the bat through the swing—Hriniak's methods drew many backers.

Carl Yastrzemski was one such adherent. When Hriniak joined the Red Sox in 1977, Yastrzemski was already at an age (37) when players were typically considering retirement. Yastrzemski credited Hriniak for the seven years of productivity added to his illustrious career. In 1979, upon reaching the twin thresholds of 400 home runs and 3,000 hits, Yastrzemski bought Hriniak a gold watch with the inscription:

To Walt. Thanks. I wouldn't have made 400 or 3,000 without your help.

"I mean that from the bottom of my heart," Yastrzemski said. "He helped me more than I can ever repay him for … throwing to me, helping me make adjustments in my stance. … I owe the man everything."[13] On September 13, 1979, Hriniak joined Yastrzemski and other guests in Washington when House Speaker Thomas "Tip" O'Neill saluted the slugger's long career at a luncheon in the speaker's Capitol office.

Dwight Evans proved another devotee. On July 4, 1980, the outfielder was struggling with a .189-5-22 batting line when he approached Hriniak for help. From July 1980 to August 1981, under the guidance of Hriniak's patient, hitting-up-the-middle approach, Evans struck at a .310 pace with an on-base percentage over .400. In the strike-shortened 1981 campaign Evans joined Babe Ruth, Ted Williams, Jimmie Foxx, and Mickey Mantle as the only American Leaguers to lead the league in both walks and total bases in a season. That same season another adherent, newly acquired third baseman Carney Lansford, led the league in hitting while dramatically reducing his strikeout totals. Three years later Tony Armas credited Hriniak for a 50-point boost to his average during the outfielder's Silver Slugger campaign. Throughout Hriniak's 12-year tenure, the Red Sox led the major leagues in team batting average six times.

Despite this success, the atmosphere surrounding Red Sox nation was far from idyllic. On the heels of the 1986 American League championship farm director Ed Kenney Sr. announced his retirement (later retracted), upset over his perception of Hriniak's meddling with the young hitters. The next year a country-club setting pervaded the clubhouse such that McNamara began contemplating banning golf clubs on road trips. The Red Sox finished in fifth place, largely due to the collapse of the pitching, but the finger-pointing did not stop there. Though the team's offense increased in 1987 to .278 with 174 home runs, the downward spiral of Jim Rice and catcher Rich Gedman focused unwarranted attention on the team's plate production in general and Hriniak in particular. A year later—after Boston rebound to division winner– Hriniak abruptly resigned from the Red Sox.

In October 1988 Hriniak signed a five-year, $500,000 contract with the Chicago White Sox, making him the highest paid coach in baseball.[14] Chicago had managed one winning season since capturing the AL West Division flag in 1983 (when Hriniak's mentor Charlie Lau was the hitting coach) and general manager Larry Himes saw in Hriniak an opportunity to improve upon "the worst [offense] in the American League since 1984."[15] Hired after Hriniak, manager Jeff Torborg had no say in the selection but that was of little concern to the new skipper. It was Hriniak whom Torborg had previously sought to assist his 21-year-old son Greg at Columbia University.[16] That winter, under Hriniak's guidance, many White Sox batters trekked to Boston to partake in what was dubbed the Larry Himes Scholarship Plan.

In February 1989 Harper Collins publishers issued *A Hitting Clinic: The Walt Hriniak Way.* Co-written with Henry Horenstein, Hriniak's 120-page book offered the basic theories behind the Lau-Hriniak hitting-up-the-middle approach so familiar to their many disciples: Head down ... "I start my swing by leading with my bottom hand and bring the bat on a downward plane to the ball." Then follow through on the swing, finishing with hands high and one hand on the bat for increased speed.

"[Hriniak] refreshed my memory of what Charlie Lau taught. He put my swing right,"[17] claimed Harold Baines during the left-handed hitter's only Silver Slugger campaign. Even more remarkable was Hriniak's work with catcher Ron Karkovice, whose average vaulted nearly 100 points over his 1988 output. Though the 1989 squad plummeted to a last-place finish, Chicago's batting average increased from .244 to .271 as the White Sox scored 62 more runs than in 1988. Hriniak's emphasis on line drives to all fields while cutting down on monster swings helped to push the White Sox into contention over the next five years—including a division title in 1993 and a first-place finish in the strike-shortened 1994 campaign. But underlying this success—the team's best run since 1967—lay marked turmoil. Himes was fired after the 1990 season. The rift that developed

between Torborg, the 1990 AL Manager of the Year, and new general manager Ron Schueler contributed to Torborg's departure a year later. Within months of Gene Lamont taking the managerial reins, reports emerged of a "growing sense that batting coach Walt Hriniak has worn out his welcome."[18]

The negative reports centered largely on Hriniak's handling of Frank Thomas. In 1992 the future Hall of Famer's home run output dipped from 32 to 24 and, in the midst of Chicago's disappointing third-place finish (and in a near-repeat of Hriniak's 1987 Boston experience), fingers were pointed toward Hriniak. His line-drives-to-all-fields focus—conducive to the cavernous environs of Comiskey Park—drew unwarranted criticism. "[W]hat [Hriniak's] doing to Thomas' stroke, well, it's almost criminal," commented an opposing AL manager. "[R]ight now [singles hitter] Len Dykstra has more power than Thomas."[19] Remarkably, few scribes sought out Thomas's opinion of the hitting coach as the right-handed slugger paced the league in doubles, walks, and on-base percentage.

Hriniak's influence with the White Sox seemingly came to an end 31 games into the 1995 season. Terry Bevington had replaced Lamont and the relationship between the new manager and his hitting coach appeared to have been rocky from the outset—Bevington feeling Hriniak's approach with the players was too hard-line, his style too old-school. Hriniak made it through the season and was fired in November, replaced by one of his Boston disciples, Bill Buckner. Hriniak retired to his native Massachusetts.

He settled northwest of Boston in Andover, Massachusetts, with his second wife,[20] Woburn, Massachusetts, native Karen Cogen. He continued conducting individual hitting instruction and coached high-school ball with a close friend while occasionally finding time to play golf. In 1998 Hriniak beamed when Mark McGwire cited his adoption of the Lau-Hriniak approach as contributing to his record-setting home-run season. Two years later, Frank Thomas called.

In 1998-1999 Thomas experienced two consecutive sluggish campaigns. Markedly, of the 44 homers struck over the two-year period, only three were to the opposite field. Beginning in January 2000, Hriniak began working with Thomas from his Massachusetts residence. When Chicago's spring camp opened a month later, the slugger flew Hriniak to the team's Tucson, Arizona, base for continued instruction. The White Sox management was not pleased. They let the instruction continue only after all other players had left the practice fields and clubhouse. But the intense workouts with Hriniak paid off when Thomas reached single-season highs with 43 homers and 143 RBIs in 2000. This success spawned at least one additional winter in Massachusetts for Thomas, added instruction from Hriniak in Tucson and (when Thomas moved on to Toronto) Dunedin, Florida.

In 2004 the Natick High School alum's name was added to the school's Wall of Achievement. Six years later Hriniak was among the first group of inductees in the Natick Athletic Hall of Fame. Over the years further accolades came at Cooperstown when at Hall of Fame induction ceremonies in 1989, 2000, 2005, and 2014, Yastrzemski, Carlton Fisk, Wade Boggs, and Frank Thomas each cited Hriniak's role in helping them gain admission to the shrine.

Hriniak ended his playing career with a scant 25 major-league base hits, nearly half (12) against Hall of Fame hurlers. But thousands more hits were credited to Hriniak as a coach. He was voted the best major-league hitting instructor in a players' poll conducted by the *Chicago Sun-Times* at the 1990 All-Star Game. Though he attracted many critics throughout his long career—including Hall of Famers Ted Williams and Ralph Kiner—no one could argue with the Gas House Gang-intensity Walter John Hriniak brought to his craft.

Acknowledgments:

The author wishes to thank Walt and Karen Hriniak for their review and input to ensure the accuracy of the narrative. Further thanks are extended to SABR members Mark Aubrey, Bill Deane, and Alan Cohen for their diligent research, and Carl Riechers for editorial and fact-checking assistance.

SOURCES:

Baseball-reference.com

ancestry.com

articles.latimes.com/1990-08-08/sports/sp-280_1_white-sox

articles.sun-sentinel.com/1990-08-06/sports/9002070593_1_walt-hriniak-swing-holy-war

boston.com/yourtown/natick/articles/2010/05/02/walt_hriniak_was_naticks_the_natural_now_hes_in_its_hall_of_fame/?page=1

sabr.org/research/hearst-sandlot-classic-more-doorway-big-leagues

sabr.org/bioproj/person/6af260fc

sabr.org/bioproj/person/fbfdf45f

sabr.org/bioproj/person/feaf120c

02df676.netsolhost.com/wordpress/walter-hriniak-2010-member/

Walt Hriniak, telephone interviews, February 21 and April 7, 2015

Hriniak, Walt, with Henry Horenstein. *A Hitting Clinic: The Walt Hriniak Way* (New York: Harpercollins, 1989).

Pietrusza, David (editor). *Baseball: A Biographical Encyclopedia* (New York: Total Sports Publishing, 2000).

NOTES

1   "Hriniak's 'Gashouse' Style Pleases Salt Lake's Zimmer," *The Sporting News,* May 23, 1970, 41.

2   "Baby Braves Earn A-Plus Rankings in Pilot Birdie's Book," *The Sporting News,* November 8, 1961, 26.

3   "He was Natick's 'The Natural,' now he's in its Hall of Fame," *Boston Globe,* May 2, 2010, 3.

4   "Garrett and Hriniak Shorten Swat Grip for Longer Wallops," *The Sporting News,* July 22, 1967, 43.

5   "Pappas Seems Set as Brave ... But Then Again," *The Sporting News,* September 28, 1968, 16.

6   "Braves' Brass Bursting With Optimism," *The Sporting News,* January 4, 1969, 50.

7   "Hriniak's 'Gashouse' Style."

8   Don Zimmer, then the Expos' third-base coach, likely played a role in recommending the signing.

9   Reunited in Denver three years later, Roenicke credited Hriniak for correcting flaws in his hitting approach.

10 "Rookie Leagues," *The Sporting News,* August 7, 1976, 42.

11 "Dinner With Ted a Rare Treat," *The Sporting News,* March 25, 1978, 62.

12 "No. 1 On The Hit Parade," *The Sporting News,* May 13, 1985, 3.

13 "Fenway Fans Roar Big Tribute to Yaz," *The Sporting News,* September 29, 1979, 14.

14 The Red Sox threatened to file tampering charges against Chicago but nothing came of this.

15 "A.L. West—White Sox," *The Sporting News,* November 7, 1988, 55.

16 Throughout his career Hriniak assisted many opposing players, including fellow New Englander Steve Lombardozzi, Cleveland outfielder Cory Snyder, Detroit's Tony Phillips, and Milwaukee's Rob Deer.

17 "A.L. West—White Sox," *The Sporting News,* August 14, 1989, 23.

18 "Can the White Sox save an unraveling season?" *The Sporting News,* August 10, 1992, 27. The circus-like atmosphere was further exacerbated in 1994 when Hriniak was assigned to work with Michael Jordan during the basketball great's brief foray in baseball.

19 "Caught On The Fly," *The Sporting News,* April 29, 1991, 3.

20 They married in 1990. A 1975 marriage to Patricia Ann Doherty had ended in divorce. The earlier union produced one child. This child—daughter Jill—provided Hriniak with two grandchildren.

RENE LACHEMANN

By Norm King

THERE HAVE BEEN MANY BROTHER COMBINA-tions in baseball, including the Nixons (Otis and Donell), the Fords (Gene and Russ), the Sherlocks (Monk and Vince), and the Moriartys (Bill and George). Rene Lachemann was part of a rare brother combination (with his brother Marcel) that both played and managed in the majors.[1]

Rene Lachemann was born on May 4, 1945, in Los Angeles, the son of Swiss immigrants William and Denise Lachemann. William was a chef at LA's legendary Biltmore Hotel and Denise was a homemaker. Rene was the youngest of four children who included, besides Marcel, brother Bill and sister Denise, the eldest.[2] All the Lachemann boys learned the value of hard work from their dad.

"[The brothers] worked alongside their father in the Biltmore kitchen during the summers," wrote Elliot Teaford in William's *Los Angeles Times* obituary. "They arrived at 6 a.m. and worked until 2 p.m. William drove the boys home, then returned to work at the hotel until midnight."[3]

As a youngster, Rene was friends with future Los Angeles Dodger Jim Lefebvre. The two started earning their baseball chops early, shagging flies for an American Legion team that was coached by Lefebvre's father, Ben, and included Rene's brother Bill and future Hall of Fame manager Sparky Anderson. That club won a national championship.

Lachemann was an all-city player at Susan Miller Dorsey High School, and was recruited by Dodgers scout Lefty Phillips not to play, but to serve as the Dodgers' batboy, soon to be joined by his buddy Jim. He also honed his receiving skills by catching batting practice and, being in Hollywood, got to hobnob with Hollywood stars.

"I was on the cover of *Confidential* magazine," Lachemann said. "It showed Doris Day looking over my shoulder into the Dodger dugout."[4]

Fortunately, Lachemann had more than a "que sera, sera" attitude about his baseball career, and was signed by the Kansas City Athletics in 1964 at age 19. He bypassed the lower levels of the minors and went right to Class A, with the Burlington (Iowa) Bees of the Midwest League. He batted .281 in 99 games, led in home runs with 24, and finished fourth in RBIs with 82.

Numbers like those will grab attention fast, as will a ringing endorsement from a coach who also happens to be a Hall of Famer. Legendary catcher Gabby Hartnett was the A's catching coach at spring training in 1965 and liked what he saw in Lachemann, both as a catcher and as an individual.

Rene Lacheman argues a call on behalf of Steve Lyons, 1985.

"That Lachemann, what an arm he has," Hartnett said. "He's a sweetheart."[5]

Hartnett's heartfelt assessment of Lachemann's ability, combined with the impressive numbers he put up in the Midwest League resulted in Rene's securing a roster spot when the team went north to begin the season.

The A's were laying the foundation of their 1970s Oakland dynasty. Future stalwarts Catfish Hunter, Blue Moon Odom, Bert Campaneris, and Dick Green all saw some playing time in Kansas City that year, but the A's were a terrible team, going 59-103. Lachemann got into 92 games, including 75 at catcher. His offensive numbers weren't spectacular, a .227 batting average with 9 home runs and 29 RBIs, but he received a backstop's ultimate compliment when the team's pitchers said they liked throwing to him.

"The catching of Rene Lachemann … has drawn praise from the [A's] pitching staff," wrote Joe McGuff. "Not only do the pitchers like to throw to Lachemann, they say he calls a good game."[6]

That praise didn't mean much when spring training convened in 1966. Veteran Bill Bryan was the number-one catcher in 1965, and the A's had acquired Phil Roof from Cleveland in the offseason. The assessment on Lachemann was that he had difficulty getting quick throws off and was unable to hit big-league pitching. He was sent to the Mobile A's of the Double-A Southern League and made only five plate appearances with Kansas City that year.

At Mobile Lachemann had respectable if not outstanding statistics, batting .256 with 15 home runs and 65 RBIs. But more importantly, one of his teammates was Tony La Russa, and the two would work together years later on another dynastic A's team.

Lachemann crossed the 49th Parallel in 1967 to play for the Vancouver Mounties of the Triple-A Pacific Coast League, where he hit .222 with 6 homers and 53 RBIs in 123 games. He got some extra work in after the PCL season ended, playing for the A's entry in the Arizona Fall League.[7] His manager on the AFL team was John McNamara, for whom Lachemann later coached on the 1986 American League champion Boston Red Sox.

Maybe the fact that he wasn't always getting his man at second base compelled the A's—now in Oakland—to return Lachemann to the Mounties for 1968. They called him up briefly in late April when injuries hit catchers Phil Roof and Jim Pagliaroni. Lachemann started 15 games, but he got only 9 hits in 60 at-bats for a .150 average with no home runs and 4 RBIs. He played his last game in the majors on June 8. He did somewhat better in Vancouver, hitting .249 in 62 games with 4 home runs and 14 RBIs.

The next four years were frustrating for Lachemann. From 1969 to 1972, he produced decent numbers with the A's new Triple-A affiliate, the Iowa Oaks of the American Association. In 1969 he hit 20 home runs and had 66 RBIs. After an off year in 1970 (5 homers, 20 RBIs), he hit 17 home runs and had 48 RBIs in 1971 and 11 homers with 37 RBIs in in 1972. Lachemann was also playing around the infield more often than he was behind the plate. In 1969 he played more games at first base (62) than he did at catcher (45). In 1970 he didn't catch at all, but saw time at first, second, and third. That's really terrific if you're out with your girlfriend but not so great if you want to be a major-league backstop. He wore the tools of ignorance only 21 times in 1971 and 1972. It was clear that in baseball terms Lachemann's biological clock was ticking. Then a job offer and some advice changed the course of his career.

As the 1972 season wound down, Oaks general manager John Claiborne approached Lachemann about a job managing in the A's system. Still hoping for a ticket to "The Show," Lachemann initially turned the offer down. That's when Iowa manager Sherm Lollar suggested that the give the opportunity a second thought.

"If I was you, Lollar supposedly said, I'd take a look around the clubhouse and reconsider," wrote Tracy Ringolsby.[8]

Lachemann looked around and saw that there were plenty of players in the clubhouse younger than he was. It was clear that he wouldn't return to the majors and that at 27 he was an old man. "I knew when the pink slips came out next spring, the older guys would get them," he said.⁹

Lachemann took Claiborne up on his offer and took the helm in Burlington in 1973 on his climb back up the minor-league ladder. He managed for three years at Class A, attaining only one winning season, when his Burlington Bees went 61-59 in 1974. He had his second, and last, winning season as a manager—at any level—in 1976 when he guided the Chattanooga Lookouts of the Double-A Southern League to a 70-68 mark, winning the league's Manager of the Year Award.¹⁰

That honor helped Lachemann garner a promotion for 1977 to Triple-A with the PCL's San Jose Missions, who that year were still affiliated with the A's. The Missions finished with a 64-80 record, but the Seattle Mariners chose to keep Lachemann as skipper when they took over the club in 1978. He stayed when the club switched its Triple-A affiliation to the Spokane Indians for 1979-80, having turned down an offer from A's owner Charlie Finley to manage the big-league club when Finley wouldn't give him sole authority over making out the daily lineup card.

The Mariners were entering their fifth season of existence when the 1981 season opened. They hadn't come anywhere close to the .500 mark in any of their previous four years, which is understandable in a new team, but they weren't getting any better. They went 59-103 in 1980, and had got off to an abysmal 6-18 start in 1981 under manager Maury Wills. Management decided that with this Wills there was no way, so they fired him on May 6 and brought in Lachemann. Lachemann was deemed an "interim" manager, but responded to a reporter's query that the title didn't bother him. "Interim?" he said. "I feel any manager in the big leagues is that way. If you don't do the job, you're gone."¹¹

The team initially responded well to the change, winning Lachemann's debut game 12-1 over Milwaukee, which started a modest four-game winning streak. They followed this up with a four-game losing skid on their way to a 44-65 combined record in the strike-shortened season. By Mariners standards that was pretty good, as was Lachemann's 38-47 mark. After the season, the team told him he could erase the "interim" from his business cards by signing him to a one-year contract for 1982 with options for two more years. Mariners players, who liked having him as their boss, welcomed the news.

"If you have a tough time playing for Lach, you'd have a tough time playing for anybody," said designated hitter Richie Zisk. "He's very up front as far as letting him know where he stands. "He gives them an honest answer to any question they ask."¹²

The Mariners had their first 70-plus-win season in 1982, going 76-86 and finishing fourth in the American League West. They still had offensive woes, finishing 12th out of 14 AL teams in runs scored, with 651. Their pitching buoyed them up with a 3.88 team ERA, fourth in the league. The team played very well before the All-Star break. On July 8 the Mariners had a 45-37 record, three games out of the division lead, but they plummeted in the second half. In a tirade the night before the team broke its record for victories in a season, pitcher Bill Caudill praised Lachemann and put the blame for the decline squarely on his team-mates' shoulders.

"That man [Lachemann] makes me want to go out and do well," Caudill said. "He and his coaches have done everything in the world to make us play. It's a shame some people just don't want to do more for him and themselves."¹³

Despite the team's slide, the Mariners kept Lachemann on for 1983. Well, for part of it, anyway. The poor play that plagued the team in the last half of 1982 continued; a 3-15 slump that included an eight-game losing streak, led to Lachemann's firing on June 25. Del Crandall replaced him, and Seattle limped to a 60-102 record and a last-place finish.

The unemployment checks didn't come for long. The Milwaukee Brewers, who went to the World Series in 1982, fired manager Harvey Kuenn after going 87-75 in 1983 and chose Lachemann to replace him for 1984. In fact, Brewers general manager Harry Dalton said that he hadn't considered anybody else.

Maybe he should have. The Brewers were a disaster that year, going 67-94 and finishing last in the American League East. Injuries were part of the problem; future Hall of Famer Paul Molitor blew out his right elbow and played in only 13 games. The offense as a whole was terrible, ranking last in the league in runs scored with 641. Cecil Cooper and Ted Simmons were both 100-RBI men in 1983, with Cooper having a team-leading 126. The two combined didn't reach that total in 1984 (Cooper had 67 and Simmons 52). The Brewers were mathematically eliminated from playoff contention on August 28. Lachemann was eliminated from his job on September 27 with three games left in the season. To his credit, he stayed on for the Brewers' last series of the year (in which they took two out of three from the Toronto Blue Jays).

The ink was barely dry on Lachemann's pink slip when one of the connections he made in his baseball travels came though with a job offer. John McNamara was named manager of the Red Sox for the 1985 season and hired Lachemann as his third-base coach. After two years in Boston, Lachemann decided he wanted to be closer to his home in Arizona and got a job as first-base coach with the up-and-coming A's under his old friend Tony La Russa. He finally reached the summit in 1989 when Oakland won the World Series, sweeping the San Francisco Giants.

Lachemann was rumored to be in the running for managerial positions with various teams while with Oakland. He was a finalist for the skipper's job with the White Sox in 1991 but Gene Lamont ultimately got the offer. Lachemann had to wait until the National League added two teams for the 1993 season for another managing opportunity, when the brand new Florida Marlins hired him to guide them through their inaugural season. General manager Dave Dombrowski thought of Lachemann as a very good baseball mind

who might have been too young and inexperienced for the job when he managed Seattle and Milwaukee.

"He was 36 when Seattle hired him," Dombrowski said. "I think he's learned from his managerial experiences, and I think it's been beneficial for him to be a coach for the Red Sox and for Tony La Russa in Oakland."[14]

One thing Lachemann probably didn't learn from La Russa was nepotism. He learned it somewhere because his first hire as manager was his brother Marcel as pitching coach. This was actually a legitimate choice because Marcel had held the job with the California Angels the previous 10 seasons.

Being the manager of an expansion team is a no-win situation. Well, very few wins anyway. The Marlins went 64-98 in their first year, which isn't bad by expansion-team standards when you consider that the 1962 Mets lost 120, the 1969 Expos and Padres each lost 110, and their expansion cousins, the Colorado Rockies, lost 95. Despite the record, Lachemann proved he was a winner when he and his wife, Laurie, whom he married in 1964, started the "Lach's Kid's" program. Lach's Kids gave inner-city youngsters the opportunity to attend a Marlins game, sit in the dugout, talk ball with Lachemann, scarf hot dogs, and take home souvenirs, all at his expense.

The club improved slowly but surely the next few seasons. It went 51-64 in the strike-shortened 1994 season and 67-76 in 1995. Unfortunately for Lachemann, the Rockies went 77-67 that year and made the playoffs as the wild card.

Clearly the Rockies were improving faster than the Marlins. The Marlins got off to a good start in 1996, and were at .500 (31-31) on June 10. Even on June 29, they were near the break-even point at 39-40, but then they lost seven in a row, leading to Lachemann's firing on July 7.

Lachemann had time to deposit a few unemployment checks this time, but wouldn't you know it? His old friend La Russa was now managing the Cardinals and needed a third-base coach. Lachemann was hired for the 1997 season. He stayed there until after the 1999 season, and then began a baseball odyssey of sorts. He served as bench coach with the Cubs (2000-2002), Mariners (2003-2004), and A's (2005-2007). In 2008 he moved back to the minors as hitting coach for the Colorado Springs Sky Sox, the Triple-A affiliate of the Rockies in the Pacific Coast League, and retained that position until 2012. He was called back up to the majors in 2013 with the Rockies to coach first base.

As of 2014 Lachemann was still in Denver as the catching and defensive positioning coach and living in Scottsdale, Arizona, with Laurie during the off-season. They have two sons, Jim and Britt, and three grandchildren.

SOURCES

Arizona Republic (Phoenix)

Baseball-almanac.com

Baseball-reference.com

Fort Lauderdale Sun-Sentinel

Galveston Daily News

Gettysburg (Pennsylvania) *Times*

Imdb.com

Indiana (Pennsylvania) *Gazette*

Kansas City Star

Kansas City Times

Los Angeles Times

San Bernardino County (California) *Sun*

Santa Cruz (California) *Sentinel*

Seattle Post-Intelligencer

Sports Illustrated

The Sporting News

Ukiah (California) *Daily Journal*

NOTES

1   Marcel managed the California Angels from 1994 to 1996.

2   Bill was a longtime manager in the San Francisco Giants and California/Anaheim Angels organizations.

3   Elliot Teaford, "William Lachemann Sill Providing Inspiration for Sons," *Los Angeles Times*, September 30, 1995.

4   Gordon Edes, "Rene Lachemann: This Is Your Life," *Fort Lauderdale Sun-Sentinel*, October 25, 1992.

5   Joe McGuff, "Gabby Hartnett Avoids Trademark of Catching Trade," *Kansas City Star*, March 9, 1965.

6   McGuff, "A's Hoping There's Still Magic In Veteran Mossi's Left Wing," *The Sporting News*, June 12, 1965.

7   In an October 18, 1967, article on the Arizona Fall League's A's squad, George Chrisman Jr., a writer for the *Arizona Republic*, said Lachemann was Canadian.

8   Tracy Ringoldsby, "Patient Lachemann Gets His Chance," *The Sporting News*, May 23, 1981.

9   Ibid.

10 In an effort to improve his managerial skills, Lachemann began managing in the Caribbean after the 1976 season, and continued doing so until 1981. He had his best year as a manager in 1978 when he guided Los Indios de Mayaguez of the Puerto Rican Winter League to the Caribbean Series championship, and earned the league's Manager of the Year Award.

11 United Press International, "Seattle Mariners Fire Maury Wills," *Ukiah Daily Journal*, May 7, 1981.

12 Ringoldsby, "Lachemann Led M's Turnaround," *The Sporting News*, October 24, 1981.

13 Ringoldsby, "Second-half Plunge Dims M's Record," *The Sporting News*, September 27, 1982.

14 Associated Press, "Lachemann making no predictions on Marlins," *Indiana* (Pennsylvania) *Gazette*, October 24, 1992.

JOE MORGAN

By Rory Costello

THERE HAVE BEEN TWO BIG LEAGUERS NAMED Joe Morgan — and it's not hard to tell them apart. Joseph Michael Morgan played fractions of four seasons in "The Show," finishing with three games for the 1964 Cardinals. He is white. Joe Leonard Morgan's Hall of Fame career ran from 1963 to 1984. He is black. Joe L., who became a broadcaster, talks more than much of his audience would like to hear. Joe M., who became a manager, does not. Harry Fanok, a minor-league teammate, said, "He didn't say a hell of a lot, but he was one tough dude!"[1]

But when Walpole Joe speaks, his Boston roots are audible. Despite nearly 40 years in pro ball, Joseph Michael Morgan is best remembered as manager of the Red Sox, whom he led from July 1988 through 1991. His teams won the American League East in 1988 and 1990, although the Oakland A's swept the playoffs both times. Yet even before the Red Sox finally wiped away 86 years of disappointment by winning the 2004 World Series, Morgan was a local blue-collar hero. He is also a classic salty raconteur with a well of stories; this brief career overview cannot do them justice.

Joe Morgan was born on November 19, 1930, in Walpole, about 18 miles southwest of Boston. This town has always been industrial; Joe's father, William Morgan, was an engineer for Kendall Mills. William and his wife, Mary Kennedy Morgan, had four other children: sons Billy and Jim, daughters Mary and Theresa.

Morgan was a two-sport star at Walpole High School and Boston College. Longtime Red Sox announcer Joe Castiglione called him one of the two best high-school hockey players in Boston area history, and he became an All-American center at BC.[2] In 2009 Morgan said, "If I was born in Canada, I would have played in the NHL for a long, long time. That's the

way I see it. I had the ability; all I needed was more ice time growing up."[3]

Instead, the shortstop went with Boston's other big-league baseball franchise back then, the Braves. In June 1952 Lucius "Jeff" Jones, the team's chief scout for New England, signed both Morgan and catcher Mike Roarke. Roarke, a fellow Boston College Eagle, later played and coached in the majors too (he also worked for Joe as pitching coach at Pawtucket, the Red Sox' top farm team).[4]

Jones no doubt also saw both men as they played in the Blackstone Valley League, a local semipro circuit. In 1988, Joe remembered his days as shortstop for Hopedale (1949-51). "It was a pretty good league, with a lot of guys who went on to Triple-A and some [like Walt Dropo] who played in the majors. I know I struggled to hit .270. The league folded after 1952 because of economics."[5]

John Henry called "the biggest story in New England since the Revolutionary War." Not wishing to contradict, Castiglione mused, "I think he understates." Unlike the LCS, Boston's 3-0 game edge let Joe anticipate Game Four's finish. This presumed a Series-ending victory, Boston leading, 3-0, in the fifth inning. That morning Castig decided the script must write itself: "I just hoped the final out would be definitive, no checked swing, did he or didn't he trap the ball?" In the seventh inning, he went to a restroom to change, expecting a postgame bath.

By the ninth, Trupiano was in the clubhouse, Joe alone, so focused "I wouldn't have heard a firecracker go off under me." Reliever Keith Foulke got Scott Rolen to fly out and Jim Edmonds to fan, Busch Stadium oozing Red Sox caps and shirts, non-ticket-holders admitted late by gracious ballpark brass. A lunar eclipse hung above the yard—a World Series first. Light bulbs resembled a phalanx of fireflies. Before now, Joe said, his greatest call "hasn't happened yet." It did Wednesday, October 27, at 10:40 P.M. Central Time. "Swing [by Edgar Renteria] and a groundball, stabbed by Foulke! He has it! He underhands to first! And the Red Sox have won baseball's world championship for the first time in 86 years! The Red Sox have won baseball's world championship! *Can you believe it?*" The question was rhetorical.

"The Boston Red Sox have forever put that 1918 chant to rest as this band of characters who showed great character all season have won the world championship for New England!" said Castiglione, who recited, "And there's pandemonium on the field!"—Martin's 1967 encomium—and Bart Giamatti's essay *Green Fields of the Mind*: Baseball "breaks your heart. It is designed to break your heart," except that now it sounded, as Fitzgerald wrote, "like a tuning-fork that had been struck upon a star." In 1975 a then-record 124 million people viewed all or part of the Red Sox-Reds World Series. Game Six of the 1986 Mets-Sox fall classic wooed 81 million, still baseball's most-watched-ever match. In our cable-fractured age, the 2004 Townies lured the highest Series audience since 1996. The *Boston Globe* swelled its daily press run from 500,000 to 1.2

million, selling out. In 1914 British Foreign Minister Sir Edward Grey lamented World War I: "The lamps are going out all over Europe; we shall not see them lit again in our lifetime." New England's lamps went *on* in late 2001, when new ownership bought the franchise.

The Saturday after the Series a rolling rally of 17 amphibious vehicles began at Fenway, turned onto Boylston Street, then Tremont Street and Storrow Drive, before entering the Charles River. It passed under the Harvard Bridge, a mass above and upon each bank—Boston's largest-ever event wooing three million of the devoted and crazed. Offseason the Red Sox took the Commissioner's World Series trophy to the far outposts of New England and beyond, Castiglione's signet now *Can you believe it?* In New Haven, Lucchino, the Yale Law alum, asked Joe to repeat it, rapture all around. For the first time since the tank and trench line, Charlie Brown ruled baseball's earth. By phone, mail, in person, and by Internet, the Nation hailed, as fife and drum had at Yorktown, "The World Turned Upside Down." At last Captain Ahab had caught Moby Dick, also hooking the 2007 and 2013 Series. Such a makeover is hard to find.

On Opening Day 2005 in the Fens—Sox 8, Yanks 1—Castiglione got a World Series ring, each Townie's presented by soldiers wounded in Iraq and Afghanistan. Watching was Joe's son Duke: a New York MY Fox 5 sports anchor and *Sports Extra* and WWOR MY 9 Yankees postgame host: formerly, WHDH Hub anchor, ESPN *SportsCenter* and *Around the Horn* guest host, and *Sunday Night Baseball*, World Baseball Classic, and WCBS New York reporter. (Joe's and wife Jean's other children were son Tom and daughter Kate.) The '05ers looked to Wakefield: Sox-best in wins, ERA, innings, complete games, and strikeouts. A year later, Schilling got his 200th victory and 3,000th K. "Unbelievable control," said Joe, "could be a prima donna, but ice cold under pressure." An old cigarette ad puffed, "I'd walk a mile for a Camel." Schilling would walk that long for a camera.

Boston won the 2005 wild card, losing the Division Series to Chicago. That offseason they obtained

Josh Beckett and Mike Lowell. Reliever Jonathan Papelbon had an 0.92 ERA in 2006. In September a Papi home run broke Jimmie Foxx's 1938 franchise-high 50. "There's a fly ball! Right-center field deep! Back by the bullpen!" said Joe. "And David Ortiz has set a Red Sox record," leading in homers (54) and RBIs (137). The Sox finished a worst-since-1997 third. In 2007, they swept the Division Series againstversus California, edged Cleveland in a taut seven-game LCS, and swept Colorado in the Series. To Joe, 2004 was "for dead relatives and friends who hadn't lived to see a title," many putting balls and caps and pennants on a gravesite, including his brother-in-law on Joe's late dad's. Signs at the rolling rally cited a college mate, Uncle Fred, "You won for my grandma"—catharsis. Ought-seven hailed success. "We were baseball's best team," said Castig, not certain in 2004. Beckett's 20-7 record topped the AL. Japanese pitcher Daisuke Matsuzaka—aka "Dice-K"—finished 15-12. Lowell led in RBIs (120), played a Fort Knox third base, and was a model citizen: to Castiglione, "maybe the most popular Red Sox since Yaz."

Papi had a fifth straight season of at least 31 homers (35) and 101 RBIs (117) or more. Dustin (.317) Pedroia had a dirty uniform by batting practice. The Series was as one-sided as 2004's. In Game Four, Boston's best fireman since Dick Radatz faced Seth Smith in the ninth. "Got him!" Joe said of Papelbon. "The Boston Red Sox become the first team in the [new] century to win two world championships!" The duck boat ride through downtown was as riveting as Boston's .333 Series average, trailing only 1960 New York's record .338. "We won. They lost," Lucchino reminded you—the rivalry still going yard. The Sox stole 96 bases in 120 tries. Jacoby Ellsbury, 23, stole nine in 33 games, hit .353, and was a teenage throb. "Some signs at our rolling rally proposed marriage [to him]," said Joe. Others would once have made mama wash her daughter's mouth out with soap.

Joe would win the Dick Young Award for excellence, enter the Italian-American Sports Hall of Fame, air New England College and Northeastern hoops, and have part of Franklin Pierce's ballpark named in his honor. The New Englander knew that objectivity was in a listener's ears. "We don't openly root, but we pull, for the Sox." The history major knew how they "are a historical team in a region filled with history." Joe knew, as Ronald Reagan said, that if a person hears 15 facts and one story "told well, it's the story he recalls." Daily, people met in Castig's "office"—Fenway—an usher, groundskeeper, vacationer from Canada; a "peanut vendor and a sausage guy across the street." Inside, "fans never see the passageways and shortcuts": grounds equipment behind the Monster, door behind the scoreboard, staircase leading to an interview room, batting cage, or pen. Joe felt Fenway ideal for hide-and-seek—as mysterious as Stephen King and unpredictable as Poe.

Persona helps fill baseball's dead air. A three-hour game may put the ball in play eight minutes. In 1960, another Joe, Garagiola, wrote the seminal *Baseball Is a Funny Game*. Boston's Joe especially liked to call gotcha on himself. One night 2007-partner Dave O'Brien addressed how Castig was no techie: retexting past messages, an accidental 3 A.M. phone call, a song about Joe somehow appearing on his iPod next to Marvin Gaye's. He liked high-definition TV—assuming he could turn it on. "I could really use a permanent Geek Squad," Joe confessed. "You need a personal assistant," Dave agreed. "That's going to be my Christmas gift for you. A full-time PA." Castiglione: "I'll take it." After commercial break, O'Brien praised his partner's "good-naturedness" about being technically challenged. Joe replied, "I know my limitations." No high-tech could save an especially slow game. "So we've played two really quick innings here," said Castig. Dave: "Yeah, moving right along." Joe: "You were clean shaven when this game began."

No one etched a ball Wallward like Joe, "never knowing if it might scrape the paint coming down." Want a drive to carry? "Pray the wind blows out." Want a fielder disrobed? "Hit to the Triangle."

Hope a bouncer over first becomes an inside-the-parker? "You've found the right place." The Wall's "nooks and crannies"—Fenway's "eccentric angularities," said Giamatti—became a sudden magic place when the Sox returned from the road in Sinatra's "wee small hours of the morning." It was empty as Joe "looked out on the field, which was almost mystical. Imagine: a fabled ballpark to yourself: You walk alone up a gangway, view the field lit only by the clock, see lights on Ted Williams Way, and watch Fenway just before dawn—well, it's breathtaking." No Voice equaled Castiglione as New England's personality of baseball in the flesh.

In 2011 Epstein built a "Dream Team" that by September 2 was fully nine games ahead of the Tampa Bay Rays in the American League East. Boston then braved an epochal 7-20 season-ending collapse: a fold worse than any Sox season, including 1978's 3-14 September apocalypse. The Townies blew a last regular-season night playoff spot, then finished last in the next year's 2012 train wreck. Worst to first: Stunningly, the poor-on-paper 2013ers won the franchise's third World Series in a decade. First to worst: The 2014 Sox went down the up staircase, placing last.

Worst to what? A rare 2015 certainty was that the Sox would fete Joe's record 33rd straight season on the air, passing the beloved Martin. Daily Sox co-flagships WEEI and WEEI FM "made sure," said Castig, "you can get us anywhere on the dial." Their eight-state radio network boasted 65 outlets, including 15 in New Hampshire and Massachusetts, 13 in Maine, Vermont 9, Connecticut 5, Rhode Island 1, and New York 6, including most deliciously three in my home of Rochester, Red Sox Nation's westernmost fort save Wyoming's one affiliate: a network among baseball's largest in states and outlets.

From time to time some wonder why the Townies so matter. Tell them to visit New England in the summer before the wind turns harsh and the leaves turn bare and a day matches night's jaw-dropping chill. Read the *Boston Globe* and *Herald*. At a diner, hear TV's Don Orsillo and Jerry Remy trade baseball patter. Listen to Joe and Dave O'Brien at an ice cream stand, in a bar, on the street, in a car. On the beach, hear the wireless, as ubiquitous as body oil, ferry a region's game. Have a clergyman ask, "How about those *Sawx*?" Due largely to Joe Castiglione, you will grasp what the religion of the Red Sox means.

SOURCES

I am indebted to several sources for the radio play-by-play and analysis contained herein: WEEI Radio executive sports producer Jon Albanese; noted major-league archivist John Miley; and Tom Shaer, former WITS Boston wireless reporter, now head, Tom Shaer Media in Chicago. Virtually all other material, including quotes, is derived from my books *America's Dizzy Dean* (St. Louis: The Bethany Press, 1978); *Voices of The Game: The Acclaimed Chronicle of Baseball Radio & Television Broadcasting—From 1921 to the Present* (New York: Simon & Schuster, 1992); *The Storytellers: From Mel Allen to Bob Costas: Sixty Years of Baseball Tales from the Broadcast Booth* (New York: Macmillan,1995); *Of Mikes and Men: From Ray Scott to Curt Gowdy: Broadcast Tales from the Pro Football Booth* (South Bend, Indiana: Diamond Communications, 1998); *Our House: A Tribute to Fenway Park* (Chicago: NTC/Contemporary, 1999); *Voices of Summer: Ranking Baseball's 101 All-Time Best Announcers* (New York: Carroll & Graf, 2005); *The Voice: Mel Allen's Untold Story* (Guilford, Connecticut: The Lyons Press, 2007); *A Talk in the Park: Nine Decades of Baseball Tales from the Broadcast Booth* (Washington D.C.: Potomac Books, 2011); and *Mercy! A Celebration of Fenway Park's Centennial Told Through Red Sox Radio and TV* (Potomac Books: Washington, D.C.: Potomac Books, 2012).

KEN COLEMAN

By Curt Smith

SOON AFTER THE 1967 WORLD SERIES ended, Fleetwood Recording Co. released a long-playing phonograph record, *The Impossible Dream*, a reprise of the Boston Red Sox magical same-year pennant. Narrating, Sox announcer Ken Coleman hailed "an affair twixt a town and a team," telling how the Boston American League Baseball Company used wonderwork to wave 1967's last-day flag. Pinching himself, Coleman still could not believe it. In a champagne-garbed clubhouse, he told the listener: "This is, if I may add a personal note, the greatest thrill of my life." It remained so till Coleman's death 36 years later.

Segue to another thrill, which might have surpassed even 1967's for Ken, had Dave Stapleton entered 1986 World Series Game Six to replace injured Bill Buckner and caught a routine ground ball that even most Little Leaguers nab. Stapleton didn't, since he was on the bench. Buckner didn't, since he misplayed the ball. For Coleman, 1967 and 1986 became baseball's both sides now, its Paradise and Lower Room, respectively. Each was sung by his silken and restrained voice, which never split an infinitive or dangled a participle—"a beautiful horn," said Boston Bruins mikeman Bob Wilson, "and, oh, Ken played it well." Despite that, Coleman could not listen to his call of Buckner's error until 1989.

Ken's score began shortly upon his April 22, 1925, birth in Quincy, a Boston suburb, 15 minutes from Fenway Park, his childhood icon Jimmie Foxx. At age 12, a BB accident cost an eye, Coleman trading heroes: Double X for the Red Sox and Boston Braves first daily Voice, ex-sportswriter Fred Hoey. From 1926-38, Hoey knit New England "giving the play-by-play of the home games of both Boston clubs," said *The Sporting News*. "He has one of the biggest daily followings of any announcer" due to the number of affiliates — a major-league then-high 22. In 1931, Ken, six, heard WNAC Boston hail "the first to work on a network [Yankee a.k.a. Colonial] covering the game," *TSN* said of Hoey "Day." By September, he had aired a record number of broadcast hours: 1,920, including that year's 320.

"Fred was known—this was something then — as 'The Man Who Does the Games'," said Ken, the 1954-63 Cleveland Indians and 1966-74 and 1979-89 Red Sox Man. Hoey found text ads easy. By contrast, *extempore* material "requires concentration on the subject … severe strain on the eyes [and] nerves." Fred tried to help the latter. In 1933, CBS Radio gave him a first network gig—the Pirates-Senators World Series. Grateful, he reached the booth before Game One, gassed. By the fourth inning, Hoey, incoherent, was yanked off the Classic. Unhorsed, Fred came home a conqueror. "In Boston, where people knew about his drinking, all was forgiven," said Ken. "He was The First, and as in love or anything else, the first, you don't forget."

Coleman wanted to be a *sans* spirits Hoey, "having to fight not to talk *like* him," Fred said. Coleman knew his region. He was also old-shoe, wearable. "His phrase was, 'He throws to first and gets his man,' which he said constantly," said Ken, "and I think I … picked it up because I'd listen to past tapes and *I've* said it." The Braves and Red Sox Voice was Boston's two-headed Janus, coining a style used by virtually every Hub baseball Voice: just the facts, ma'am, trumped a wild and crazy guy. He also knew how to vend—"Mention Fred," said Coleman, "and people remember Kentucky Club pipe tobacco and Mobil's Flying Red Horse"—and instill Euripidean concern. Boston's First couldn't believe he was gone, until he was.

In late 1938, Socony Oil and General Mills became each Hub club's sponsor, wanting *their* Voice, not a broadcaster identified with other goods. Fred paused a lot, lacking gloss. "Plus," said Coleman, "booze affected him over time." In 1939 Frank Frisch briefly succeeded him. Childless, unmarried, Hoey began a decade of last things and final bows. "On the air he *was* Boston baseball," Ken mused, "and it wasn't the same without him." In *Death of a Salesman*, Willie Loman says: "And that's the wonder of this country, that a man can end [up] with diamonds on the bases of being liked." Liked, Hoey ended up alone, dying in 1949.

By then, Coleman's father, William, a military man turned night watchman, had died, six years earlier, of a heart attack in Ken's high school senior year. His wife Frances was a housewife. After graduation their son, 18, joined the Army in 1943, served in Burma, and aired Indian rugby, cricket, and soccer on Armed Forces Radio, jibing, "*You* try performing with twelve thousand troops listening." Released, Ken took Oratory at Curry College, worked at a 250-watt Worcester affiliate, and then did golf, bowling, basketball, Boston University, Ohio State, and Harvard football, and Vermont's Northern Baseball League, still fighting the "urge to say, 'He throws to first and gets his man!'"

In *The Federalist*, Madison noted "leaders ambitiously contending for pre-eminence." In 1952, Coleman and

Lindsey Nelson contended for Cleveland Browns radio play-by-play until Nelson abruptly joined NBC TV. Ken inherited a 125-station four-State network. In the next 14 years, he aired seven champions, did eight network title games, and called each pro touchdown (126) by the greatest runner to ever touch a ball. Ken is the only man to see Jim Brown's every pro game (1957-65). "What stands out is how with minutes left, the Browns are up by seven, have the ball, and Jim runs out the clock," said Coleman. Raised in Cleveland, Jack Buck liked how Ken made time stand still: "People identify him with baseball, but he's the best football announcer I ever heard."

Each week at Cleveland Municipal Stadium, 80,000 filled the city's lakefront bowl, the Browns increasingly *en famille*. As a child, Ken's son Casey was a summer training camp water boy. Later, he became a Cleveland sportscaster: WTAM morning host; WJM four-time Emmy sports anchor; Indians host; and Browns play-by-play man. "The fifties were a time of football's growth, each year more people following it on regional, then network, TV," Coleman *fils* said. Virtually each Browns and Indians game telecast aired on WXEL, Channel 8, by Carling Brewing Co., at a time when "one company could afford to sponsor most, if not all, your coverage."

Carling's commercial signature was a belle named Mabel. Tribesmen of that generation can still sing "Mabel! Mabel! Black Label! Carling Black Label Beer!" In 1995, Ken said, "People come up, see me with my wife, and bellow, 'Hey, Mabel!'" (His then-wife's name was Ellen.) Coleman grasped baseball's episodic rhythm. He neither screamed nor patronized, believing in "not telling the audience what it already saw." A rookie should not be faulted for his club peaking too soon. Ken's first wed Mike Garcia, Early Wynn, and two Bobs, Feller and Lemon, going 78-29. Larry Doby had 32 homers and 126 runs batted in. In August, Cleveland won a league-record-tying 26 games, its 111-43 record topping Murderers Row's prior A.L.-best 110-44. "It seemed so easy," Coleman felt of '54. On September 12, a big-league record 86,563 jammed the

THERE WAS MORE THAN GAME SIX

oval, the Indians beating New York twice. *Each* year but 1954 the 1951-56ers placed second to the Yankees.

Improbably, Coleman aired the 1954-57ers with the post-Hoey play-by-playman of his youth, Jim Britt, voicing the 1940-42 and 1946-50 Red Sox and 1940-42 and 1946-52 Braves. "During the war both teams used fill-ins," said Ken. "Coming back, Britt seemed so erudite—the greatest command of language of any broadcaster I've heard"— commanding, but not hyperbolic." At 13, future *TSN* columnist Wells Twombly recalled "[Britt making] baseball sound better than red-haired girls with freckles." It seemed pitch-perfect: baseball's grammarian, in the Athens of America, each day signing off, "Remember, if you can't take part in a sport, be one anyway, will ya'?"

Britt telecast the 1954-57 Indians with Coleman by necessity, not necessarily choice. By 1950 Narragansett Beer—"the beer," ads said, "with the seedless hops"—had sponsored each Hub team on WHDH since 1945. Late that year, P. Ballantine & Sons Brewery inked a Braves-only pact on the Yankee Network, making Britt pick one club or the other. Jim chose the Braves over the Red Sox of Ted Williams, Johnny Pesky, and Bobby Doerr—to Coleman, "a terrible misjudgment as to the popularity of the teams." Sox owner Tom Yawkey countered by naming Curt Gowdy Britt's successor and — "He wanted to do it anyway," Ken said — making *all*, not just home, coverage *live*.

The Wyoming-born and -educated Gowdy spent 1949-50 as Mel Allen's Yankees aide. He became Voice of the Red Sox, then network TV sports' paradigm for a generation: 15 All-Star Games, 12 World Series, seven Olympics, and two decades of *The American Sportsman*. From 1966-75, Curt called virtually every network baseball game. To Ken, "Britt made the Sox opening—thus, Gowdy's rise — possible. He never recovered from what he'd done." In 1953, the Braves absconded for Milwaukee, deserting him. "When they left, there was nothing left for Britt. He stumbled around a year, then came to Cleveland," which Jim felt slumming after his reign on the Charles.

Indians second baseman Bobby Avila was a 1950s example of Britt refusing to go along to get along. Local dialect pronounced the All-Star's last name *Ah-VEE-la*. Britt preferred *AH-vee-la*. "We got every kind of calls and letters," said Coleman. "People didn't like it."

Carling Brewing's chairman said, "You know, Jim, in view of the local colloquialism, we should probably call him *Ah-VEE-la*, like most fans want."

The chairman's name was Ian Bowie, as in *row*. Britt said, "All right with me, Mr. Bowie," as in *boo*. In 1958, Britt returned to WHDH "haunted by the Red Sox' 'what if,'" said Boston broadcaster Leo Egan. Axed again, Britt moved to Detroit, St. Petersburg, and Sarasota, braving a divorce, unemployment, and arrests for drunkenness. He died in 1980, less tragic than forgotten, at home in Monterey, California. "In truth," *Globe* columnist Ray Fitzgerald wrote, "life had turned its back on him a long time ago."

Ken called himself "less mercurial, more serene" than Britt. "But we had this in common. Our first year we win 111 games, then afterward not much to tell." Reticence began with the 1954 World Series, originally thought a Cleveland cinch. Instead, in the one-out and -on eighth inning of the 2-all opener at the Polo Grounds, the Indians' Vic Wertz hit 460 feet to deep center field, whereupon Willie Mays made a catch with his back toward the plate, over his shoulder, to save a tie and become possibly baseball's all-time most replayed out. In the 10th, the Giants' Dusty Rhodes pinch-hit a fly 200 feet shorter than Wertz's down the right-field line for a homer: New York, 5-2. A day later Rhodes again homered: Giants, 3-1. In Cleveland, New York completed a 6-2 and 7-4 sweep. "In many ways," said Coleman, "the franchise was never quite the same."

To protect network exclusivity, baseball has banned local-team Series TV. Coleman watched 1954's on NBC. He felt the opener a metaphor for baseball's DNA — anticipation. "Anything can happen, and here did—a pee-wee homer, a long-distance out." Anticipation topped result for the rest of Ken's Cleveland stay. 1956: Herb Score won 20 games. Next

May Gil McDougald's liner careened off his right eye, wrecking Herb's career. 1959: Rocky Colavito slammed 42 homers, Ken having not yet coined "They usually show movies on a flight [long blast] like that." The Indians' second place marked their last contention till 1995. 1960: GM Frank Lane traded Colavito for Detroit's Harvey Kuenn. "I'm getting steak for hamburger," he bragged, having burned Cleveland's best filet since Lou Boudreau. In the 1960s, even anticipation died. The Tribe never drew a million people, missed the pennant by fewer than 15 games, or hinted that faith might last past June.

Hating the bogus, Coleman found humor in reverse. Once the now-Tiger Rocky retreated to the wall. "Back goes Wally against the rock," Ken said, "For those of you interested in statistics, that was my eleventh fluff of the year. It puts me in third place in the American League." Finally, tired of ghosts in the stands, Ken left to focus full-time on football, his timing still sure: In December 1964 the Browns won the N.F.L. title, jolting Baltimore, 27-0. His last Brownscast was Jim Brown's farewell on January 2, 1966, in another championship game: Green Bay 23, Cleveland 12. Straightaway Brown retired to make films. At his peak as an institution, Coleman revisited points of his past. Succeeding Gowdy, the new Voice of NBC TV's *Game of the Week*, the Red Sox chose the Quincy scion, who told himself, "you lucky stiff, going back to my roots, taking Britt's and Hoey's job."

In March 1966, Coleman was introduced as Boston's new Voice. Pain: no pitcher won more than 10 games for that year's ninth-place Red Sox. Progress: The Yawkeys drew 158,971 more than in 1965, ending the season 14 games nearer first. Jim Lonborg soon a/k/a *Gentleman Jim*, a future dentist, led in strikeouts and innings. Joe Foy, Mike Andrews, and George Scott debuted at third, second, and first base, respectively. Tony Conigliaro led in five team-high categories, including homers (28) and RBIs (93). Next year began with new manager Dick Williams vowing to: a) "have only one chief. All the rest are Indians"; and b) win more than he lost. The home opener drew 8,324. "In terms of interest," Ken said, "the bottom had fallen

out." Out of nowhere, 1967 reached the heart, unforgettably reviving baseball in the Fens. On April 14, a rookie began his bigs career at Yankee Stadium. "A kid pitcher from [Triple-A] Toronto," Ken said later, like liturgy. "That's where this story starts."

In a one-out ninth, "Billy Rohr [was] on the threshold," Ken said on WHDH TV. "Eight hits in the game—all of them belong to Boston ... Fly ball to left field! Yastrzemski is going hard — way back — way back! And he dives—and makes a tremendous catch! One of the greatest catches I've ever seen by Yastrzemski in left field! ... Everybody in Yankee Stadium on their feet roaring as Yastrzemski went back and came down with that ball!" Two batters later Elston Howard singled, Tony C. catching "it on the first hop. No chance." In late 1967, Fleetwood Recording repackaged WHDH's *The Impossible Dream*, from Broadway's *The Man from La Mancha*, as a must-Christmas gift. Coleman said of Rohr, "The fans began to sense it. This year was not quite the same."

That year riot seared nearly 130 cities. Protestors fought police. Viet Nam was a horror house. The Sox took a fractured time and briefly made it whole. Boston trailed by six games at the All-Star break. It preceded a 10-game road trip, the team returning to Logan Airport 10 and 0 to find 10,000 greeters. Said the pilot: "They seem happy with what you've done." As luminous were pilots from the Hub to Nova Scotia tracing a West Coast game by light in homes below. "It is late on a ... night in 1967," wrote the *Herald*'s Kevin Convey. "The house is dark except for the flashlight beside my bed. It is quiet except for my transistor. Ken Coleman didn't just call baseball games. He called my summers"—also spring and fall. Jose Tartabull lined a 15th-inning "base hit to right! Here comes Tony! Here comes George! And the Red Sox have won it, 1-0!" Another batter lashed a "line drive to Foy! Over to second! And on to first! A triple play!" When rookie Smith hit a scoreless 10th-inning triple, a listener "refused to enter the Sumner Tunnel until he heard the outcome." Hundreds of drivers backed up, hearing, too. By August 13, 2 1/2 games divided five teams. One Friday in late August Conigliaro hit against Jack Hamilton, whose pitch caused a wound around Tony's left eye, ending his year.

That Saturday *Game of the Week* visited the Fens, Gowdy wending from a "fine young lefthander [Ruth] known for hitting ability" via Williams' "moaning about the east wind that would blow off" the Charles to Mel Parnell, "a left-hander who [preferred] Fenway" to the road. Boston won on last-out ballet: "A chopper. Over the mound. May be tough," Martin said. "Charged by Petrocelli. Throws to first! The ball game is over! A clutch play by Rico Petrocelli ends it all … in a wild and woolly ball game in a twelve to eleven win by the Red Sox!" Next day they trailed the second game of a doubleheader, 8-0, leading Yaz to navigate the dugout. "'We're going to *win* this game!' he told each of us," said Rico. "Man, by now we *believed*!" In the eight-all eighth, a Boston infielder lofted a "fly ball deep into left-center field and it is … a *home run*!" Ken cried. "Jerry Adair has hit his second home run of the 1967 season and the Red Sox, who trailed, 8 to 0, are now leading in the eighth inning, *9 to 8*!" Adair's poke sired "a sound wave—one crescendo after another"—from 100,000 at Revere Beach, most listening to Sox radio. "Ken's attitude was beautiful," said Petrocelli. "To his death, he thought that reaction symbolized the year."

A week later Boston led, 4-3, in the ninth inning at Chicago, Duane Josephson batting. "Berry, a fast man on third," Martin said. "And there's a little looper to right field." TV's Coleman continued. "Caught by Tartabull! Runner tags! Here's the throw home! And he is *out* at home plate!" Before 1967, Jose would not have nabbed Aunt Maude. In September, you could throw a blanket over the Red and White Sox, Twins, and Tigers. Boston trailed, 5-4, in the ninth inning at Detroit. "There's a drive to deep right," blared Ken, "and it's tied up!"—Yaz again, five-all. Next inning reserve Dalton Jones went deep: Sox, 6-5. No. 8 won the 1967 Triple Crown [.326, 44 homers, 121 RBIs] with 23 hits in his last 44 at-bats. "One week left!" Coleman cried.

"Four teams within 1 and ½ games." By Thursday, the Twins led by a game with Saturday and Sunday left at Fenway. Stores closed. Churches opened. Boston must sweep to win or force a playoff. In Saturday's 2-all sixth inning, "Scott hits one deep into center field!" said Coleman. "This one is back! This one is gone!"—3-2. The bleachers soon were scene and actor: "Deep to right field! Number 44!"—Yaz's last regular-season homer: 6-2, Red Sox—final, 6-4. Seconds later Martin supplied a coda. "If you've just turned your radio on"—pause—"*it's happened again*. Yastrzemski's hit a three-run homer, and it's now 6-2, Red Sox"—final, 6-4.

On Sunday, Detroit had to twice beat California to tie the Sox or Twins. Minnesota led, 2-0, as Lonborg bunted safely to lead off the sixth. After two hits filled the sacks, Yaz "lines a base hit to center-field!" said Ken. "One run in, Adair's around third, he will score. Going to third is Jones. It's tied, 2-2!" Ken Harrelson hit to shortstop Zolio Versalles, who hesitated and was lost: "No chance at a throw to the plate. Safe! Jones scores! The Red Sox lead, 3-2!" Two more runs scored before "the Red Sox are out in the sixth," said Coleman. "But what a sixth inning it was!" Detroit won its home opener. Meantime, Minnesota's Bob Allison lined to the corner with two out in the eighth, Tony Oliva on first base, and Harmon Killebrew on second. Yaz threw to second base, nabbing Allison: Sox, 5-3. Next inning Rich Rollins batted with two out. "The pitch . . . is looped" toward shortstop," Martin said. "Petrocelli's back, he's got it! The Red Sox win!"—but what? No one knew: Detroit had to lose. "And there's pandemonium on the field!"– the most immortal line Ned ever spoke. "Listen!" As the ball settled in Rico's glove, students and workingmen and housewives became a wave, hundreds of bodies rocking. "I was terrified," said Lonborg: Petrocelli, too. "It's a miracle I'm even here," he said, in 2009 joining MLB Network radio, where '67 seldom wanders far away.

"[Afterward Sunday] the players came in from the field," Ken said, "some crying or yelling." A radio lit the background: "no ESPN, Ipod, or Internet, just [Detroit's] Ernie Harwell in the nightcap." The Angels led, 8-5, in a two-on and one-out ninth. The Tigers' Dick McAuliffe promptly hit into his second double play all year—uncorking Wakefield and Woonsocket and Brattleboro and Blue Hill. In the clubhouse, Rico saw tears in Yawkey's eyes: "spent so much money, all those near-misses, drinking champagne, more fan than owner." The next-day *Boston Record American* cover blared: "CHAMPS!" above a drawing of two red socks. It was crewel, not cruel. Coleman styled other upsets "child's play compared to 1967." It was unthinkable then to call a Series anticlimactic. This was. Through the mid-'70s local-team Voices did the Classic. In ideal symmetry, Gowdy and his Sox successor telecast each NBC Series game in Boston: Cards, in seven.

Save Yaz and Lonborg, Coleman became the person most affixed to 1967. It was *his*, even more than Britt's 1948, Martin's 1975, or Castiglione's 2004. A eulogy by the *Herald*'s Convey invoked the flashlight beside his bed. "There will be other summers. And I will listen to other announcers. But I will never stop hearing Ken Coleman."

In 1972, Coleman shifted exclusively to TV, tying caption to picture. In 1974, replacing WHDH as Sox video flagship, WBZ "told me they wanted a new cast." Next year Ken revisited Ohio to televise the Reds, his penny as lucky as the 1954 Indians and 1967 Townies. "Wherever Ken goes, fortune follows," Craig wrote. Cincinnati took the 1975-76 Series, Coleman bypassed as Reds Voice — radio's Marty Brennaman got the nod—on each Fall Classic. Then, in 1979, released from a last year in Cincy, Ken returned to Fenway, many expecting him to man Red Sox television, vacated when ball and striker Dick Stockton joined CBS. Instead, Coleman replaced Martin on radio, Ned strangely joining TV, where literacy was superfluous *v.* being radio's job one.

Back home, Coleman increasingly let his "kinder, gentler" side lighten a formal on-air presence. Befriending easily, Coleman urged 1980-82 wireless partner Jon Miller to develop his mimicry: "Ken said, 'You have something not many people have,

and you should do it on the air.' I'd just been goofing around, and soon I'm invited to banquets because of Ken. He was incredibly giving, saying be expressive, mimic." Then: "Ken's why I went to Boston." In the 1981 big-league split season, they called the end of professional baseball's longest game. It began April 18 at 8:25 p.m.: Triple-A Pawtucket's Bruce Hurst starts at home *v.* Rochester. Things adjourn 2-all at 4:07 a.m.—Easter—morning before *19* of an original 1,740 paid crowd. They resume June 23—"Dale Koza—line drive, base hit, left field, [Marty] Barrett scores, and Pawtucket wins it, 3 to 0, in *33* innings!" said Ken. Game time: *8:25*.

In 1979, Coleman called Yaz's three thousandth hit. "A ground ball base hit into right field! Just out of reach of Willie Randolph!" In 1983, No. 8 played his major-league record 3,308th and final last game. In the seventh inning, "The crowd is on its feet, everyone aware that very possibly this will be the last time he will ever step into that batting box," Ken mused. The din was insupportable. "Waving to them all, and they're all on their feet." Yastrzemski popped up, was replaced in the field, and "walked over to a little boy and tossed him his cap." Organist John Kiley played *auld lang syne*. As executive director of the Jimmy Fund, the Sox official charity, Ken spurred the Children's Cancer Research Foundation — now Dana-Farber Cancer Institute. Once he asked, "If you were paying your way today, who would you pay to see?" The Kid didn't hesitate. "Reggie!" Williams boomed. Ken informed the object of No. 9's respect. "'The man said that about *me*?' Jackson gaped. Later Reggie did a Jimmy Fund public service notice and gave "a considerable amount," Ken said. "'I know what the Jimmy Fund is about,' he said, 'and I want to put money where my money is.'"

Few people put money on the early-to-mid '80s Sox, noting that their last world title preceded by 61 days the original Armistice Day ending World War I. In 1983, Joe Castiglione succeeded Miller, off to Baltimore. At Fenway, the ex-Colgate University student disc jockey found Coleman pining for big band dance music a quarter of a century earlier. On the field, the Sox were more fox trot than rock 'n' roll; six place in 1983; little better in 1984-85. Once Cleveland scored twice in the eighth inning to lead, 3-2, Ken, almost asleep, saying, "Here comes the tying run and the winning run, and the Indians win!" Coleman then saw Bob Stanley pumping. "It was then that I realized that baseball is a nine-, not eight-, inning game."

Thirteen times the Olde Towne Team lost a pennant or World Series on the next-to-last or final day from 1946 through 2003. All disproved the Law of Averages (things even out) and upheld Murphy's Law (if things can go wrong, they will). Depending on your view, Johnny Pesky does or does not hold the ball. Luis Aparicio loses a division by falling down rounding third. Bucky Dent homers above the Monster. The worst was 1986's Grounder Under Bill Buckner's Glove. The *Globe*'s Peter Gammons had termed Yaz's farewell "a two-day Easter celebration." On Good Friday 1986, the parish team traded Mike "The Hit Man" Easler for 1979 A.L. Most Valuable Player Don Baylor—the first Sox-Yankees trade since reliever Sparky Lyle in 1972. "It was a great start to the season," said Castiglione. Who knew its end would be so antipodal?

On April 7, Dwight Evans banged the year's first pitch for a homer. Told no one had done it before, he jousted, "Big deal. We lost." On April 29, 1986, Boston's best mound prospect since World War II faced Seattle at home, setting a record for strikeouts in a game. "Strike three!" Ken gushed of Phil Bradley. "Roger Clemens has broken the major league record for strikeouts in one game! He has struck out twenty Mariners!" On May 15, the Sox took first place for good. Rocket began 14-0, not losing till July. Some baseball Voices don't speak on or off the air. At Wrigley Field, locking a colleague out of the booth, Harry Caray once kept him off TV. By contrast, Ken, Ned, and Joe avoided spite or strife.

The night of Rocket's launch, the Sox had just released their yearbook, listing players' musicians. Soon each Mr. C. was perusing it, Ken thinking, Joe said, that music ended in 1953. "This is interesting. Roger's favorite singer is Steve Nicks," said Coleman. Joe

paused, then said: "Ken, I believe that's Stevie Nicks." Ken was adamant: "Well, I know him well. I call him Steve." Castiglione: "Uh, Ken, Stevie is a girl." Next day Clemens sent a wall-sized Nicks poster to the booth. Till his death "Ken could break me up," said Joe, "by saying, 'Stevie is a girl.'" In 1967, Sox skipper Williams introduced Coleman and Martin to California's Crescent—aka "Hard Bellies"—Beach, surf up, seals sunning. Later the Voices acquainted Joe, going daily when the Sox visited Anaheim: Ken snorkeling, Castiglione swimming, and Ned diving and taking pictures. A clubhouse manager said: "There they go—two sixty-year-olds and a forty-year-old, playing in the sand."

On a flight, Ken read a biography, planned a Jimmy Fund event, or heard pre-Bill Haley and the Comets. Ned put his Walkman on, used a headset plug, and channeled the Chairman of the Board. "He loved Sinatra," said Joe. "Ken did, too, so he'd use the other plug—each listening to Ol' Blue Eyes and breaking into song." It was, he laughed, "not broadcast quality." The Sinatra ballad "Summer Wind" took a lofter toward the Wall. If "Luck Be a Lady," "Bewitched" was the Sox's card. "It Was a Very Good Year" could mean 1912; "Fly Me to the Moon," 1978. Liking "The Best Is Yet to Come," the booth couldn't know 1986's worst lay just ahead. "That's Life" was a favorite, the Sox having been a puppet, a pauper, a pirate, a poet, a pawn, but not since 1918 king.

On cue, the '86ers slumped in July, one journal asking, "Poised for another El Foldo?" Instead, the Sox won 11 straight, traded for outfielder Dave Henderson and shortstop Spike Owen, and rebuilt its lead. A Boston TV *Chronicle* special hailed "Pennant Fever Grips Hub": "Sox fans, knowing better, have put their skepticism on hold." Baylor clubbed 31 homers. Buckner had 102 RBIs—more irony: "fans," Owen said, "loving how he gutted it out"—ankles hurt, taped, and gouged again. Clemens started the All-Star Game. Dennis (Oil Can) Boyd and Bruce Hurst finished 16-10 and 13-8, respectively. On September 28, Boston took its first title since 1975. "A high pop-up! Buckner is there! It's all over! [Sox 12, Toronto 3]!" said Ned. The new divisional champion Townies hugged the man with the gimpy gait and high-topped shoes.

That fall, several friends in the Secret Service arranged lunch at the White House for a Red Sox party. "We're told no photos, above all, recordings," Joe smiled. "Someone forgot to tell Ken." Vice-President George H.W. Bush entered to recount his good-field, no-hit time at Yale — "I batted eighth," he said. "Second cleanup." President Reagan then entered "at his theatrical best," evoking the 1930s Cubs, re-creation, and film, especially 1952's *The Winning Team*. Reagan had played the great epilectic and alcoholic pitcher Grover Cleveland Alexander; Doris Day, his wife; Walter Brennan, a reporter. "Knowing the script by heart," said Castiglione, Coleman "had a recorder, determined to tape the Gipper." At lunch questions start, and "Ken's is a doozie."

In *The Winning Team*, Coleman noted, "[St. Louis's] Alex in relief strikes out the Yankees' Tony Lazzeri to save Game Seven" of the 1926 Series. "Right," says the President. Ken asked, "How did Doris Day take a cab all the way from mid-Manhattan to Yankee Stadium"—even then, a lengthy ride—"while Alex trudges from the pen?" "Well, ah," Reagan says. Next question. Lunch soon adjourns. "It was amazing," said Joe. "The Secret Service must have seen the recorder, but didn't say anything." That night the taped President guested on Ken's pre-game show. "With security, it could never happen today." What did astounds, even now.

The 1986 Red Sox, Angels, Mets, and Astros easily won their division, then began a month as the game had rarely been played before—"at its summit," *Newsweek*'s Pete Axthelm wrote. "It leaves you breathless." The now-best-of-seven L.C.S. began at Fenway, Clemens losing, 8-1. A day later Rice homered and Angels pitcher Kirk McCaskill lost a grounder in the sun: Sox, 9-2. Game Three: The Halos took a two-games-to-one playoff lead. Four: Clemens led by a 3-0 score—till Doug DeCinces homered and two batters singled to start the ninth inning. Reliever Calvin Schiraldi got a routine fly—till Rice lost it in the lights, another run scoring. Schiraldi went 1-2 to Brian Downing. Future

reference: One strike would win the game. Instead, the next pitch hit him, tying the score: Angels win, 4-3, in 11, lead three games to one. Enthused ABC's Al Michaels: "This series is getting interesting."

Next day Boston led, 2-1—until Bobby Grich drove to center field. Dave Henderson egressed, leapt, and knocked the ball over the wall for a two-run homer. In the ninth inning, despite Baylor's two-run dinger, one out would win Game Five, 5-4—and the Angels' first pennant. Manager Gene Mauch inserted reliever Gary Lucas, his last hit batter 1982. Lucas plunked Rich Gedman, yielding to Donnie Moore, who worked Henderson to a 2-2 count — Boston one strike from elimination. At "2:47 Pacific Coast time," said Coleman. Moore threw a forkball. "There's a fly ball to left field! Downing is going back … back … back! It's gone! It is gone! Dave Henderson has homered! And the Boston Red Sox have taken the lead! Boston has come up"—Ken's exact verbiage from 1967's last-day sixth-inning fivespot—"with four runs and has a 6 to 5 lead in the ninth!"

In *their* ninth, the Halos tied the score. After DeCinces and Grich failed with the bases full, Boston, reprieved, scored an eleventh-inning run. In the bottom half, "Schiraldi throws, and it's popped up down the first-base side!" said Ken. "[Dave] Stapleton in—he's got it! And the Red Sox have won it! One of the most incredible victories in the history of the Boston Red Sox, 7 to 6!" Pause: "Joseph [Castiglione], two days ago I became a grandfather [a girl]. This was her gift—truly an incredible baseball game." Back in Boston, the Townies took Game Six, 10-4, over and out behind Boyd. Next evening Clemens led, 4-0, when Rice homered deep to left. Boston won, 8-1: its first triumph in a winner-take-all game with a division title, pennant, or World Series at stake since 1912, and first seventh-game postseason victory since 1903.

The Sox were a 2 ½-to-1 underdog *v.* the 108-54 regular-season Mets, but won the first two Shuttle Series games, 1-0 and 9-3. Boston flew home "sitting pretty," said Joe. Games Three-Four were ugly: Mets, 7-1 and 6-2. Ted Williams first-pitched before Game Five. Hurst then won his second match, 4-2. Ahead:

a game that proved the proverb "If you want to make God laugh, tell Him your plans." At Shea Stadium, the Mets, behind, 2-0, in Game Six, tied on a single and double play. Barrett scored on a force attempt: 3-2. As omen, Rice was thrown out trying to score, a blister on Clemens' pitching hand made Schiraldi relieve, and Buckner stranded eight runners. In the eighth inning, Gary Carter's sacrifice fly retied the score. "Everything to decide," Ken said, "and nothing decided." Due to air the 10th, Joe deferred to his senior partner. At 11:59, Henderson's drive struck *Newsday*'s billboard. He reached the dugout as the clock struck midnight. Boston scored again: 5-3 insurance, having paid a 68-year premium. With two Mets out, the scoreboard read, "Congratulations Boston Red Sox." The Series trophy and 20 cases of Great Western champagne entered the visiting clubhouse. *Again* one out would win — the Classic.

All year Stapleton had replaced Buckner with Boston ahead. Inexplicably, skipper John McNamara kept Billy Bucks at first. After two singles, Ray Knight went to 0-2. A *strike* would end the famine. Knight singled, Gary Carter scored, and Kevin Mitchell took third: 5-4. "They're going to do it," a friend told Gammons. The Sox were going to lose in a way unimaginable for even them. *Sans* wild pitch all year, Stanley, relieving Schiraldi, threw six pitches to Mookie Wilson. "He throws the [seventh] pitch inside, it gets away from Gedman!" Coleman said: the inning's 13th pitch to win the Series. "And the tying run is home! The tying run scores! And down to second base goes Knight—55,078 fans go wild, as the Mets, with two outs and the bases empty, in the last of the tenth, have tied it up!" Wilson fouled off two more pitches. "Knight at second. Three and two," Ken resumed. "The pitch, ground ball to first base! Buckner—*it goes by him*! And here comes the winning run! The Mets have won it, 6 to 5, on a ground ball to Buckner that went through him!" At his Wellesley home, Martin rued the local-TV Series ban.

In one moment, Gammons wrote, "Forty-one years of Red Sox baseball flashed in front of my eyes." Speaker of the U.S. House of Representatives Thomas P. (Tip) O'Neill "didn't sleep for three months. I'd wake up every night seeing that ball go through Buckner's legs." The wild pitch completed Stanley's fall from 1970s comer to hard-luck oaf, a Hub driver trying to ram his car. Billy Bucks was threatened, Boston's Zakim Bunker Hill Bridge a/k/a "Buckner Bridge" because cars passed through its Y-shaped "legs." Released next year, Buckner said: "Things were good for me here until after the sixth game. After that, it just went down." Finally, he moved to Idaho. Game Seven was postponed to Sunday, the Nation sensing what lay ahead. Monday night the Red Sox again led, 3-0. In the sixth inning, Keith Hernandez singled with the bases loaded to plate two Mets runs. As New York tied the score, reliever Sid Fernandez gleamed, and Knight hit in the seventh, the Sox faced a fourth straight seven-game Series loss.

"The pitch!" said CBS Radio's Jack Buck. "Swing and a fly ball, left-center field, well-hit! May not be caught! It's gone! It's gone! Over the fence in left-center! A home run by Ray Knight to give the Mets their first lead of the evening, 4-3!" Final: 8-5. For the first time, the World Series final opposed ABC's *Monday Night Football*, routing it in audience share (55 to 14 percent) and Nielsen ratings (*38.9* to 8.8). In Los Angeles, New York, and Boston, the Series swaggered, 4-, 7-, and 19-to-1: "fourth-highest rating of all time for a World Series game," said NBC sports research's Greg Seamans, "and most-watched Series game of all time, with 34 million households." The Classic averaged a 28.6 rating—about 25 million households per minute.

The *Washington Post*'s Shirley Povich hailed "baseball as Americans know and love it—a throbbing, good-God-what's-next World Series." Some recalled the Classic differently, like a car crash or a storm. Next season Clemens left training camp when his salary was renewed at $400,000—half of Stanley's. G.M. Lou Gorman said, "The sun will rise, the sun will set, and I'll have lunch." A year later the '88ers took first place on Labor Day, lost six of the last seven, but won their second division or pennant in three years for the first time since World War I. Directly the L.C.S. went awry. Hurst dropped Game One, 2-1. Veteran *Globe* writer Clif Keane threw out next day's first ball. "They've got to do it soon," he said. "I'm running out of time." Boston was, too, swept by the A's. That offseason Ken had a heart attack, leaving Joe C. to do 1989 spring training radio alone. "Other teams' announcers did an inning or two," he said. "They got me through."

In Florida, a Sox-Dodgers exhibition lasted 15 innings. "Before [1997] interleague play, you'd only see the other league's guys at a Series or spring training," said Joe. "Today Vin Scully called a couple innings, no airs." Joe never forgot 1986's Game Six, "feeling Shea shake." Ken remembered, too. By 1989, he had founded the Bosox Club, was an eight-time Ohio Sportscaster of the Year and 12-time American Federation of Television and Radio Artists honoree, and hosted radio's *Ken's Corner* of poetry and inspiration. That year future Baseball Hall of Fame and Museum president Jeff Idelson was a Sox booth statistician intern. He left the Fens grasping why Voices become a beach bud, mountain messenger, and pillow pal: "A radio broadcaster has to remind you of sitting around a fire, hearing tales." Ken did.

In mid-1989, Coleman announced his retirement, Fenway's TV booth later named in his honor. He wrote variants of *Take Me Out to the Ballgame*, sung by Broadway's and the Yankees' Suzyn Waldman: "And if I can't actually be there, then give me the action by Curt, Ned, and Ken." He finished a fifth book — his favorite, *The Impossible Dream* — and again did Harvard football as he had 1968's last-quarter Crimson miracle — "This, of course," Coleman had marveled, "is *The* Play of *The* Game" — tying the score with seven seconds left. Half-an-hour later the student *Crimson* headlined: "Harvard Wins, 29 to 29." In 2000, he made the Red Sox Hall of Fame.

Among those mourning Ken's farewell was Pawtucket's radio Voice Don Orsillo: born Melrose, Massachusetts, raised on a Madison, New Hampshire farm, watched the Sox on "one of our four TV stations, coverage not wall-to-wall like now," and spent most nights by the kitchen radio, with Ken. "He was everywhere," said Don of "1967, Clemens' twenty-strikeout game, and Henderson's playoff blast." Growing up, Orsillo heard dad and mom insist he "reach for the stars." At 12, he

did, "vowing to air the Sox." Ultimately, Don attended Northeastern University, majored in Communication Studies, took a class from Castiglione, and as an intern like Idelson also became Fens booth statistician, then 2001- Sox TV Voice.

In the late 1990s, Ken took special interest in Fenway Park. In 1925, it had become a teenager the very month that he was born. Now many increasingly deemed it old-timey: too few luxury boxes and concession stands, too little parking, above all, too small. Rebuilding would be prohibitive, some said. Suites couldn't squeeze into a Wilsonian shoebox. The foundation was built to house one deck, not two. "Build a new park if you must. Get your new deck, loges, the better amenities," Coleman said. "But keep the outfield exactly as it is from one pole to another. That's how people know Fenway, what they see on the tube."

In 2002, a new ownership group headed by John Henry, Tom Werner, and Larry Lucchino began saving baseball's oldest park. The club kept the Green Monster, centerfield Triangle, and "field's distance, look, feel," said Coleman, exactly as they were. The real change came off the field, the Sox enlarging and renovating — staying put. Ken would have loved the decade-long preservation of "America's Most Beloved Ballpark" to make it capable of remaining the Sox arcade, it was said, until at least near the new mid-century. Soon Fenway became baseball's ATM machine.

On October 1, 1989, Coleman ended his final game behind the mike by thanking "the fans of New England for their support, their friendship, their patience and loyalty over the years" and for the Jimmy Fund, "which has been a most meaningful part of my professional life." He concluded: "This is Ken Coleman, rounding third and heading home." On August 21, 2003, Ken, 78, died, leaving sons Casey, since deceased, and William, daughters Kerry, Susan, and Kathleen, his wife Mary Sue, and former wife Ellen. He had long ago become "a most meaningful part" of Red Sox *Nation's* life — manifestly, even now.

SOURCES

I am indebted to several sources for the radio play-by-play and analysis contained herein: WEEI Radio executive sports producer Jon Albanese; noted major-league archivist John Miley; and Tom Shaer, former WITS Boston wireless reporter, now head, Tom Shaer Media in Chicago. Virtually all other material, including quotes, is derived from my books *Voices of The Game: The Acclaimed Chronicle of Baseball Radio & Television Broadcasting—From 1921 to the Present* (New York: Simon & Schuster, 1992); *The Storytellers: From Mel Allen to Bob Costas: Sixty Years of Baseball Tales from the Broadcast Booth* (New York: Macmillan, 1995); *Of Mikes and Men: From Rqy Scott to Curt Gowdy: Broadcast Tales from the Pro Football Booth* (South Bend, Indiana: Diamond Communications, 1998); *Our House: A Tribute to Fenway Park* (Chicago: NTC/Contemporary, 1999); *Voices of Summer: Ranking Baseball's 101 All-Time Best Announcers* (New York: Carroll & Graf, 2005); *The Voice: Mel Allen's Untold Story* (Guilford, Connecticut: The Lyons Press, 2007); *A Talk in the Park: Nine Decades of Baseball Tales from the Broadcast Booth* (Washington DC: Potomac Books, 2011); and *Mercy! A Celebration of Fenway Park's Centennial Told Through Red Sox Radio and TV* (Washington DC: Potomac Books, 2012).).

NED MARTIN

By Bob LeMoine

"Oh, Gertrude, when sorrows come they come not as single spies but in battalions."

Hamlet, Act 4, Scene 5, a favorite quote of Ned Martin when the Red Sox were having a particularly bad day

"WITH *THIS* BACK AND *THESE* KNEES? Mercy," Ned Martin asked rhetorically, using his trademark exclamation when asked if he was going to dance the jitterbug at his 50th high-school reunion. Still, he and his classmates of the Upper Merion High School in King of Prussia, Pennsylvania, Class of 1940, danced to the Big Band tunes of Artie Shaw, Benny Goodman, and Harry James. Martin also reflected on his English teacher and his "old country school." "Marie Wolfskill. Just an excellent English teacher in a little country school. ... What a major role that woman played in my life. ... it was largely because of her teaching I've been able to make my living through my use of the English language; it was because of her I developed a love for that language."[1]

Ned Martin could be called the Shakespeare of the broadcast booth, or baseball's Hemingway scholar-in-residence. He could inject a broadcast at the right moment with literary quotes, poems, or song lyrics, while his catchphrase of "Mercy!" summed up many moments of Red Sox history. Red Sox radio announcer Joe Castiglione called Martin "the most literate of all broadcasters ... a scholar of literature and a great Hemingway expert. He had a way of describing things very succinctly, honestly, and openly. He never interfered with an event."[2] Dave Weekley of the *Charleston* (West Virginia) *Gazette* recalled Martin's "low-key quiet confidence ... His delivery was easy on the ears and his renowned wit allowed him to refer to his beloved Shakespeare when the time was right."[3] Curt Gowdy called Martin "a highly intelligent guy with a great vocabulary and a good voice."[4]

A Red Sox announcer for 32 years, Martin also served his country in World War II, celebrating victory at Iwo Jima. But he was most at home behind the radio microphone, where his mastery of language painted pictures in the minds of his listeners. "Active verbs are really helpful. It isn't an awful thing to have a vocabulary and use it," Martin remarked.[5]

Those active verbs could be a ball "caroming" off the wall or "lofted" over it; a lead was "tenuous," and fans "vociferous." Home runs were "long gone and hard to find." The aging Gaylord Perry was called "sparsely thatched" on top. He would greet fans during a West Coast game with "Hello, wherever you may be at this ungodly hour," or sum up a poor Red Sox performance with "'It was death in the afternoon,' as Hemingway would have said." Martin's rich usage of literature gave us calls like "So the little children shall lead them as rookies Rice and Lynn have driven in all of the Red Sox runs,"[6] and it is often his descriptions Red Sox fans remember when reliving moments of Red Sox history from the 1960s through the early 1990s.

L to R: Ned Martin, Ken Coleman, Mel Parnell.

Edwin Martin III was born on August 9, 1923, in Wayne, Pennsylvania, one of two children of Edwin Martin Jr. and Doris Hatfield (Ramsey) Martin. Martin's father owned a hatchery in Florida where the family spent many winters.[7] Martin saw his first game at Shibe Park in Philadelphia at the age of 9. His father, a semipro pitcher, brought home a surprise gift for young Ned:

"One morning, when I was about 10, I got up and noticed two cocktail coasters my parents brought home the night before. I looked closer and saw that they'd been autographed by Johnny Marcum and Jimmie Foxx. Foxx! He was like God to me because the (Philadelphia) Athletics were my team. I've never forgotten what a thrill that was, or the thrill I later felt when I stood outside Shibe Park and collected the first one on my own from Skeeter Newsome."[8]

Martin enrolled at Duke University in 1941 and remembered a more innocent time. "The Depression was over and we were pretty much just concerned with growing up and enjoying ourselves. None of us had much interest in what was happening outside our own little worlds -but, man, we sure grew up in a hurry."

On December 7 Martin had taken his girlfriend to a movie and when he returned to the dorm he saw "everyone clustered around a radio. One guy turned to me and said, `Isn't it awful what the Japanese did? They bombed Pearl Harbor!"[9]

Martin responded, "'Pearl Harbor? That's in the Hawaiian islands, isn't it?' I figured it was a possession of ours, but what did it mean? I didn't know. We were just kids, away from home at a big university, with a football team on its way to the Rose Bowl, and the most important thing in the world was having a date for the Saturday night dance. I guess you could say we were kind of dumb."[10]

Martin enlisted in the US Marines in 1942, and later fought with the 4th Marine Division at the Battle of Iwo Jima in February 1945. "I'm not one of the guys you see raising the flag. I don't think we were there thirty

minutes before we came upon a shell-hole. I looked in and saw it filled with dead Marines; I mean blown-up Marines, with entrails and … oh God, I'd never seen anything like that before. Then I started looking around and pretty soon death got so common."[11]

On Day 26 of the campaign they rejoiced when word of US victory came. Martin rejoiced, "The flag was flying on Mount Suribachi—our flag! What a feeling!"[12]

Martin graduated from Duke in 1948 with a degree in English. He worked in advertising in New York City, but Madison Avenue was definitely not for him, and a stint at the Dell Publishing Company in Washington D.C.,[13] also unfulfilling.

Then Martin called old friend Bob Wolff, a former classmate at Duke who had helped him with his on-air delivery at the campus radio station.[14] Wolff was now the TV voice of the Washington Senators.

Wolf remembered Martin. "He told me that his present job was trying to get drug stores and supermarkets to carry paperback books, but what he really wanted to do was test himself in sportscasting. I had him read for me. He sounded pleasant, low key, smooth—good enough to get a start somewhere. I recommended he try WINX radio in Washington. … He could work on weekends, fill in on vacations, and be on call if a bigger position opened up."[15]

WINX, located in the Washington suburb of Rockville, Maryland, provided valuable broadcasting experience for Martin. "I went to Rockville and did it all on the ground floor—news, commercials, afternoon shows, playing hillbilly music."[16]

Martin then spent 2½ years announcing for WFRC radio in Athens, Georgia. "Nicest 2½ years I ever spent anywhere," he recalled. "Did all kinds of high school sports, women's sports. College baseball games. A young man named Francis Tarkenton was at Georgia then—quarterback on the football team, pitcher on the baseball team, point guard on the basketball team. I saw him strike out 20 guys in a baseball game once. I broadcast the game, in fact."[17]

In the late 1940s Martin met Barbara Rolley, and the two were married in 1951.[18]

In 1956 Martin became the play-by-play announcer on WCHS radio for the Charleston (West Virginia) Senators, a Triple-A affiliate of the Detroit Tigers in the American Association. Martin broadcast from a tiny booth at Watt Powell Park.[19] When Charleston was on the road, he announced play-by-play through wire re-creation. "Sometimes," he recalled, "the man who was at the park feeding back the information didn't have everything straight. … When a correction came through, I'd have to alleviate the situation as realistically as possible. One time, there was a man on first base when it came over the wire — correction, batter grounded out. Well, I already had the man safe on first, so I had to pick him off."[20]

Also the sports director at WCHS, Martin did play-by-play of the University of West Virginia football and basketball games. "I just believed in some vague way that I'd make it to the majors some day," he recalled. "I kept bothering people, sending tapes to the clubs in both major leagues, trying to show that I belonged."[21]

One of those tapes caught the ear of legendary Red Sox announcer Curt Gowdy. "He liked the tapes and the idea of having an announcer as his partner and not some ex-jock," Martin remembered. "I was lucky."[22]

Gowdy invited Martin to Baltimore to broadcast a Red Sox game against the Orioles in September of 1960. "We didn't call it an audition, but it was," Gowdy recalled.[23]

"I drove up from Charleston to Baltimore's Memorial Stadium and worked an inning and a half," Martin remembered fondly. "Now, there's a spot in my soul for that park, because that's the place I won the job."[24]

Gowdy was impressed and recommended Martin for the announcer position vacated by the departure of Bill Crowley.[25] Martin was hired by the Red Sox on December 21, 1960, and joined Gowdy and Art Gleeson in the booth for the combined WHDH radio and television.[26] This couldn't have come at a better time; Martin was fired as sports director at WCHS-TV

along with nine other employees in budget cuts.[27] He was now on his way to the major leagues.

"I'm not playing anymore, so I won't have to worry about you!" was Martin's greeting from Red Sox legend Ted Williams at the Red Sox spring-training site in Scottsdale, Arizona. Martin got to know Williams over the years as he would pop into the booth and talk fishing with his buddy Curt Gowdy.[28]

Martin's debut for the Red Sox was on a frigid Boston day, April 11, 1961, the same day rookie Carl Yastrzemski debuted in left field. Both had been in the American Association in 1960. Martin had interviewed Yastrzemski, then playing for the Minneapolis Millers, and asked him about the challenge of playing left field at Fenway Park, never imagining they would both be coming to Boston.[29]

Martin's broadcast rotation included innings 1 through 3 and 7 through 9 on radio and 4 through 6 on television.[30] His first year concluded with calling Roger Maris's 61st home run, breaking Babe Ruth's single-season record at the time. "This 37-year-old rookie broadcaster was glad I was there to do it," Martin recalled.[31] "What a climax for an amazing rookie year."[32] The call was not recorded, however, leaving the archives with only Phil Rizzuto's call of the historic home run.

Art Gleeson died after the 1964 season, and former Red Sox pitcher Mel Parnell joined Gowdy and Martin in the booth.[33] When Gowdy left the Red Sox in 1966 after 15 years to become the *NBC Game of the Week* announcer, Martin seemed like his natural replacement. He applied for Gowdy's job by sending a telegram to WHDH, but didn't get the job. "I'm just not a commercial person. I don't have the gift for gab," said a disappointed Martin.[34] The job was given to Ken Coleman, who had been a Cleveland Indians broadcaster. "It was a deep disappointment at the time. But Ken and I became good friends, and life went on."[35]

In 1965 Martin also did football play-by-play with Fred Cusick for the Boston Patriots.[36] From the 1960s to the early 1970s Martin was also the play-by-play announcer for Ivy League football teams: Dartmouth College (seven years), Harvard College (six years), and Yale University (two years).[37]

The 1967 Red Sox "impossible dream" team rejuvenated baseball in New England. Martin's voice guided fans along the journey to the World Series, and he was now receiving attention both locally and nationally for his broadcasting talents. A memorable Martin call was the final out in the Red Sox' pennant-clinching final game of the season as the Twins' Rich Rollins hit a popup:

"The pitch is looped toward shortstop. Petrocelli's back … he's got it! The Red Sox win! And there's pandemonium on the field! Listen!"[38]

Johnny Pesky replaced Mel Parnell and joined Martin and Coleman in the booth from 1969 through 1971. In 1971 Martin was nearly fired by WHDH for saying "bullshit" on an open microphone.[39] In 1972 WBZ-TV replaced WHDH as the flagship station for Red Sox television and shook up the broadcast teams. Martin finally became the Red Sox number-one radio announcer on WHDH, while Coleman became the number one TV announcer on WBZ. Martin was paired with John Maclean, who resigned because of illness and was replaced by Dave Martin (no relation).[40]

The 1974 season brought together what is considered one of the best broadcast teams of the era, as Martin was paired with Jim Woods. Woods had spent the previous 21 seasons as the number-two broadcaster supporting legends Mel Allen, Red Barber, Russ Hodges, Bob Prince, Jack Buck, and Monte Moore.[41] Clark Booth called Martin-Woods the "best play-by-play combination in the history of American sport."[42] Baseball Magazine named them the baseball broadcasting team of the 1970s.[43] Years later Martin fondly remembered Woods. "Jim was one of my closest friends and one of the best guys I ever worked with. He told me his five years in Boston were second only to his 12 in Pittsburgh. He really enjoyed his work and he was a throwback to the old days. I really enjoyed his company."[44]

As Red Sox fans listened to the 1975 Red Sox' pennant-winning season, they were again treated to many memorable Martin calls, including a catch by Fred Lynn on July 27:

"Swings, drive to left-center field. May be a gapper! Lynn is running, Lynn is going! He's got it in a great catch! A great catch by Freddie Lynn! Oh, mercy, what a catch by Lynn! He outran that ball in the alley in left-center and Red Sox fans are going ape out here. … This is World Series time!"[45]

On September 18, 1975, WMEX (which later became WITS) became the radio flagship station instead of WHDH, which had broadcast the Red Sox games continuously since 1945.[46] WMEX considered dumping Martin and Woods. A public outcry prevented the change. But WMEX jazzed up the broadcast with pregame and postgame shows, and ads were now read during innings. "It prostituted the product, hurt our rhythm, thus the game" Martin said.[47] For a man known for articulation, this watered-down writing was an insult and Martin once asked, after reading an ad, "Who the heck wrote the copy for this?"[48]

NBC's 1975 World Series coverage included a rotation of announcers for both radio and TV coverage, with Martin and Dick Stockton of the Red Sox and a Cincinnati Reds announcer, Marty Brennaman, joining NBC's Joe Garagiola, Curt Gowdy, and Tony Kubek. When Carlton Fisk hit the historic home run at Fenway Park in Game Six, it was Martin at the radio microphone:

"There have been numerous heroics tonight, both sides. One-o delivery to Fisk. He swings. Long drive, left field! If it stays fair it's gone! Home run! The Red Sox win! And the Series is tied, three games apiece!"[49]

Martin also did play-by-play with Ernie Harwell for the American League Championship Series from 1976 to 1978 for CBS Radio.

The Bucky Dent home run that ended the Red Sox' season in the one-game playoff against the Yankees in 1978 was summed up well by Martin: "Dent, a borrowed bat, and a little fly ball into the net, and the silence was deafening. Maybe Fenway's greatest silence ever—unless you were honoring someone who had passed away."[50]

The stunning playoff loss was also the final game for the Martin-Woods team and also Martin's last Red Sox radio broadcast. They were both fired by WITS, as general manager Joe Scallan said they needed better marketing exposure "for dealing with clients in the VIP lounge."[51] A disgusted Bob Ryan of the *Boston Globe* wrote, "The people who ruled over them and signed their paychecks had no idea how good and how special Martin and Woods were—none."[52] Woods went on to work for the USA cable network, while Martin became the new Red Sox play-by-play announcer on WSBK-TV, a vacancy that had opened up when Dick Stockton left for CBS. Martin was teamed with analyst Ken "Hawk" Harrelson from 1979 to 1981 and Bob Montgomery from 1982 to 1987.

Martin began his Red Sox career on the same day as left fielder Carl Yastrzemski, and in 1979 he called both Yaz's 3,000th hit and 400th home run. On October 1, 1983, he was master of ceremonies for Yaz Day, honoring Yastrzemski on his retirement.

In 1985 Martin and Montgomery also joined the New England Sports Network (NESN), and were now broadcasting all 162 Red Sox games between the two networks. It was on NESN, on April 29, 1986, that Martin called Roger Clemens' 20-strikeout performance against the Seattle Mariners, one of many highlights in that pennant-winning season:

"A new record! Clemens has set a major-league record for strikeouts in a game! Twenty!"[53]

On December 7, 1987, NESN and WSBK made changes. WSBK fired Martin and kept Montgomery, while NESN fired Montgomery and kept Martin. WSBK management felt Martin didn't draw out the strengths of Montgomery as an analyst and made repeated errors.[54] The station also wanted someone "with a little more pizzazz." Martin admitted, "Pizzazz. No, I'm afraid that just isn't me."[55]

Martin would be teamed on NESN with Jerry Remy, Montgomery with Sean McDonough on WSBK. Remy remembered Martin, as "the best possible guy to work with breaking in (to broadcasting) because he was so laid-back. He certainly helped me a lot."[56]

"Red Smith used to say he loved 'the music of the game.' What a great line," Martin once pondered. "There IS a music to it, whether it's the first crack of the bat at Winter Haven, a full house on Opening Day, the murmuration of a meaningless game in July, or the buzz you feel at a World Series. ... You can still see something in almost every game that you've never seen before. That's the beauty of baseball, I guess."[57]

Martin was told by NESN a day before the 1992 season ended that he was no longer in their plans. "I don't like to leave, and I don't like to leave this way," he said after his final broadcast. "I wasn't quite ready for it. They said I hadn't done anything wrong, but who knows what that means? I think they may be getting a more multi-purpose person in there ... and (someone who's) younger."[58]

Martin didn't feel he was through but, needing hip replacement surgery, decided to retire at age 69. After years of traveling city to city, he cherished the old farmhouse he bought with his wife, Barbara, in Clarksville, Virginia. He enjoyed walking his dogs, gardening, bicycling, and taking pictures on his 15 acres that included an old schoolhouse.[59] "This was his home. He felt really at peace here," daughter Caroline said.[60]

Martin returned to Boston in 2000 for an emotional induction into the Red Sox Hall of Fame. "The ovation wouldn't end. The place just exploded. Until then, I don't think he knew how much he was loved. He was a most modest guy," remembered Joe Castiglione.[61]

Martin participated in the Ted Williams public memorial service at Fenway Park on July 22, 2002. He reminisced with Carl Yastrzemski and Peter Gammons, saying Williams "said he didn't feel like a hero, but he was, along with Feller and Hank Greenberg. He was like an old John Wayne movie, but Wayne never played baseball."[62]

Sadly, the next day tributes would be spoken in memory of Martin. During his trip home from Boston he was riding a shuttle bus at the Raleigh-Durham Airport when he suffered a heart attack and died on July 23, 2002, at the age of 78. He was cremated. Martin left behind Barbara, his wife of 51 years; a son Edwin"Rolley" Martin; two daughters, Caroline Michnay and O'Hara Martin; and nine grandchildren.[63]

Martin was posthumously inducted into the West Virginia Broadcasters Hall of Fame in 2010 [64] and the Massachusetts Broadcasters Hall of Fame in 2011.[65]

SOURCES

In addition to the sources referenced in the text, the author was assisted by Ned Martin's file at the Baseball Hall of Fame, Cooperstown, New York.

NOTES

1   Joe Fitzgerald, "Martin Dances Down Memory Lane," *Boston Herald,* June 19, 1990, 72.

2   Gordon Edes and Chris Snow, "Sox Broadcaster Martin, 78, Dead," *Boston Globe,* July 24, 2002; D1.

3   Dave Weekley, "Martin Always Knew He Would Make It to the Majors," *Charleston* (West Virginia) *Gazette,* July 29, 2002, 3B.

4   Edes and Snow, "Sox Broadcaster Martin."

5   Jack Craig, "No Replacing 'The Natural' of Sox Radio," *Boston Globe,* October 9, 1992.

6   Craig, "No Replacing"; Robert D. Spurrier, "The Voices of the Red Sox," *Bennington* (Vermont) *Banner,* July 18, 1975.

7   Martin's widow, Barbara Martin, phone interview with the author, July 13, 2014.

8   Joe Fitzgerald, "Ned Martin Captured Moments and Made Them Into Memories," *Boston Herald,* July 21, 2003, 10.

9   Joe Fitzgerald, "Ned's Patriotism Will Never Flag," *Boston Herald,* December 6, 1991, 98.

10 Ibid.

11 Curt Smith, *Mercy! A Celebration of Fenway Park's Centennial Told Through Red Sox Radio and TV* (Washington, D.C.: Potomac, 2012), 71-72.

12 Ibid..

13 Craig; Curt Smith, *Voices of the Game: The First Full-Scale Overview of Baseball Broadcasting, 1921to the Present* (South Bend, Indiana: Diamond Communications, 1987), 382.

14 Smith, *Voices of the Game,* 382.

15 Bob Wolff, *Bob Wolff's Complete Guide to Sportscasting: How to Make It in Sportscasting With or Without Talent.* [Google Book preview] (New York: Skyhorse Pub, 2011).

16 Smith, *Voices of the game,* 382.

17 Bill Parrillo, "No Pizzazz, Just Professionalism by Ned Martin," *Providence Journal,* December 20, 1987, D-1. Some accounts have Tarkenton throwing a no-hitter in that game.

18 Martin's widow, Barbara Martin, phone interview with the author, July 13, 2014.

19 Weekley, "Martin Always Knew."

20 Chip Ainsworth, "The Voice of the Red Sox: The Advocate Talks to the Fast Talker," *Hartford Advocate,* May 24, 1978, 24.

21 Smith, *Voices of the Game,* 382.

22 Parrillo, "No Pizzazz."

23 Smith, *Mercy!* 72.

24 Ainswoth, "The Voice of the Red Sox."

25 Weekley, "Martin Always Knew."

26 "Ned Martin Joins Hub Team of Radio, Video Broadcasters," *The Sporting News,* December 28, 1960.

27 "A Good Job: You're Fired!" *Sunday Gazette-Mail,* Charleston, WestVirginia, November 27, 1960, 10A.

28 Jim Baker, "Tribute to Ted; Martin Rich in Storied Williams Lore," *Boston Herald,* July 23, 2002, 72.

29 Jack Craig, "Every Step of the Way Ned Martin Followed Yaz From Minors to World Series," *Boston Globe,* January 13, 1989.

30 Smith, *Mercy!,* 74.

31 Weekley, "Martin Always Knew."

32 Smith, *Mercy!,,,*75.

33 "No-Hit Hurler Parnell Joins Gowdy, Martin on Air Team," *The Sporting News,* January 23, 1965.

34 Smith, *Mercy!,* 82.

35 Craig, "Every Step of the Way."

36 Jeff Goldberg, "Martin, Voice of Sox, Dies; Legendary Red Sox Broadcaster Collapses at Airport," *Hartford Courant,* July 24, 2002; C1

37 Rich Thompson and Tony Massarotti, "Broadcaster Martin Dead," *Boston Herald,* July 24, 2002, 102.

38 Smith, *Voices of the game,* 395.

39 Smith, *Mercy!,* 8.

40 redsoxdiehard.com/players/broadcasters.html.

41 Smith, *Mercy!,* 20.

42 Smith, *Mercy!,* 110.

43 Peter Gammons, "Average Sox pay: $145, 692," *Boston Globe,* February 14, 1980.

44 Bob Monahan, "Jim Woods, Radio Broadcaster for Red Sox From 1974-1978; At 71," *Boston* Globe, February 22, 1988.

45 Smith, *Voices of the Game*, 405.

46 "Sox, WHDH End Longest Association," *Berkshire Eagle*, Pittsfield, Massachusetts, September 20, 1975, 22.

47 Ibid.

48 Spurrier, "The Voices of the Red Sox."

49 Smith, *Voices of the Game*, 408.

50 Smith, *Mercy!*, 123.

51 Smith, *Voices of the Game*, 392.

52 Smith, *Mercy!* 126.

53 Smith, *Voices of the Game*, 531.

54 Jack Craig, "Martin Out at Channel 38," *Boston Globe*, December 8, 1987.

55 Parrillo, "No Pizzazz."

56 Sean McAdam, "Ex-Red Sox Announcer Martin Dead at 78," *Providence Journal*, July 24, 2002, D-4.

57 Joe Fitzgerald, "Ned Martin Captured Moments."

58 Art Turgeon, "Fired Voice of the Sox Retired to Va. Farm," *Providence Journal-Bulletin*, October 29, 1995, B-2.

59 Ibid.

60 Smith, *Mercy!*, 163.

61 Smith, *Mercy!*, 164.

62 Baker, "Tribute to Ted."

63 *Richmond* (Virginia) *Times-Dispatch*, July 25, 2002, B6.

64 "Broadcasting Hall of Fame Announces 2010 Inductees," *Charleston Gazette*, November 24, 2010, 3.

65 Retrieved from massbroadcastershof.org/hof_martin_ned.htm, July 2, 2014.

BOB MONTGOMERY

by Bill Nowlin

NASHVILLE NATIVE AND RED SOX CATCHER Bob Montgomery was born Robert Edward Montgomery on April 16, 1944. He played his entire career with one major-league team—the Boston Red Sox—a career that encompassed the 1970s, from his debut on September 6, 1970, to his final game on September 9, 1979.

Monty took a while to make the majors, initially signing as an amateur free agent with the Red Sox on June 9, 1962. Baseball ran in the family. His father played sandlot ball and was apparently pretty good. Bob's younger brother, Gerald, was also in the Red Sox farm system for a while as a pitcher. Bob himself played several sports for Central High School in the Tennessee capital, and was all-state in three sports, but it was always baseball that held the greatest appeal. For Central, he pitched, played first base, and played outfield. It was only later that he made the move to set up behind the plate.

After high-school graduation, Red Sox scout George Digby got Bob Montgomery's signature on a contract and the 18-year-old was assigned to the Olean, New York, team in Boston's farm system. There he played outfield and third base and batted .273, earning him a step up in the system in 1963. The new year saw Montgomery playing in Waterloo, Iowa, under manager Len Okrie. Monty explained to author Herb Crehan that Okrie suggested he become a catcher. Okrie told him, "If you want to make it to the majors, you're going to have to make yourself into a catcher. You don't have the power to make it at the corner positions in the majors, but you could make it as a catcher." Monty got in a little backstop work late in '63, though Baseball-Reference.com shows him exclusively as a third baseman. The following year he served as the primary catcher for Waterloo and even made the league's All-Star team. He told Crehan that he'd found the transition a relatively easy one.

Although it was a long slog to make it to the majors, Monty said he never got discouraged. "I never thought about quitting. I had one goal in mind: to play baseball at the big-league level. I stayed focused on that goal and just moved a little closer every year." He continued to rise in the system, if slowly, and by 1969 was playing for Triple-A Louisville, the top club in Boston's system before Pawtucket assumed that honor. Montgomery played in over 100 games and batted a very strong .292. In 1970 Montgomery put in another year at Triple-A (hitting .324 in 131 games, and showing some power with 14 homers), and earned himself a call-up to the big-league club once Louisville's season was over.

Montgomery made his major-league debut, subbing for catcher Tom Satriano in a game the Sox were losing 6-1 to the Baltimore Orioles. He was called out on strikes in his first at-bat, but came up again in the Red Sox sixth with Dave McNally on the mound

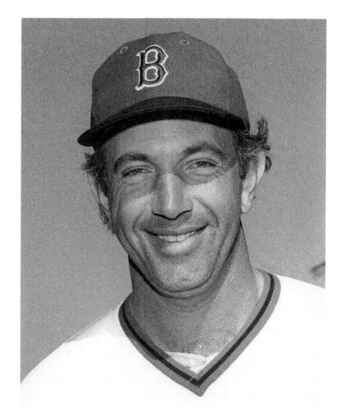

and runners on first and second and a run in. His single to right field moved up both Rico Petrocelli and Billy Conigliaro and loaded the bases. Two runs scored on a hit-by-pitch and a sacrifice fly, and the score was 6-4. The Red Sox went on to win the game in the bottom of the 11th when reliever Pete Richert loaded the bases and then threw a wild pitch as Billy Conigliaro stood in the batter's box and Montgomery waited in the on-deck circle. Monty took over as the regular catcher for the rest of the season.

The first of his 23 career home runs came a few days later, a September 11 solo homer in the fifth inning off future Hall of Famer Jim Palmer. Montgomery saw a lot of action in September, playing in 22 games and performing reasonably well (just three errors, while being credited with 143 putouts and 13 assists), though hitting a little anemically at .179. He threw out 47 percent of baserunners in stolen-base attempts. He enjoyed the winter months, with 14 major-league hits in the record books and what looked to be a steady job in the majors in 1971.

Duane Josephson was acquired over the winter to be the regular catcher, but a series of nagging injuries provided plenty of opportunities for a backup to play, so Montgomery shared catching duties in 1971. Josephson appeared in 91 games and hit .245 with 10 homers while Montgomery got into 67 games, hitting .239 with a couple of homers. Carlton Fisk was called up in September and made himself a catcher who would not be denied. His .313 batting average and great defense ensured that he would take center stage starting in 1972.

Montgomery understandably played the backup to Fisk, and appeared in just 24 games. He upped his average appreciably to .286, however, taking full advantage of the at-bats he had. The Red Sox missed winning the pennant by just a half a game in a season that opened late due to a player strike that was not resolved until several days into the regular season schedule.

Montgomery saw a little more action in 1973 — 34 games, 128 at-bats, and again a significantly improved batting average. He hit .320 in 1973. To work as a

backup catcher isn't the easiest of tasks, he told Herb Crehan. You have to be ready to step in and perform at any minute. "I focused on every single pitch, even if I hadn't played in a week." The attention to detail is key in a catcher, as reflected in Montgomery's climbing batting average, and probably served him well in his later career as a broadcaster with the Red Sox.

When Carlton Fisk suffered a season-ending injury on June 28, 1974, Montgomery stepped in and appeared in 88 games, with Tim Blackwell serving as his backup. Monty's average dropped to .252 but he filled in capably and the team continued to contend, remaining in first place until shortly after Labor Day.

Fisk was still unable to return as the 1975 season opened, due to a second injury — a broken arm suffered in spring training — and Montgomery was the main man strapping on the mask and chest protector and calling pitches for the 1975 team until Fisk was able to come back on June 23. Though his average slipped yet again, to .226, Monty played in 62 games and did his share to keep the Sox in the hunt. At the season's start, Montgomery was responsible for the game-winning RBI in four of the first 11 wins. Fisk hurt his finger in August and Monty got quite a bit of playing time in September. He also started a couple of games at first base, filling in there six times before season's end.

In postseason play, Montgomery saw no action at all in the three-game ALCS victory over Oakland, and almost missed out on any action in the World Series. He finally got his chance at almost the last possible moment, appearing as a pinch-hitter in the bottom of the ninth inning in Game Seven. Will McEnaney was in for Cincinnati to protect a slim 4-3 lead, and there was one out, after Juan Beniquez flied out to right. Monty could have become an instant hero with a home run over everything to left, tying the game and setting the stage for Yaz to come up with a winning back-to-back blow. Alas, it was not to be. Monty grounded out to the shortstop. Yastrzemski flied out to center field and the Series was over.

There was every hope that the Red Sox could come back and contend again in 1976, but they never got on track. Ownership even fired manager Darrell Johnson in the middle of the season, handing the reins to Don Zimmer. With Fisk healthy the full year, Monty got into only 31 games but did boost his average to a more respectable .247.

Montgomery got even less playing time in '77, but batted an even .300 in 40 at-bats, with a couple of homers in the mix.

The year 1978 was another exceptional Red Sox season. Fisk played in almost every game in 1977 and 1978, and Monty saw action in only 10 games; he hit .241 in 1978 on the strength of just seven hits in 29 at-bats — and more than half of those hits all came in one game, the second game of a May 21 doubleheader in Tiger Stadium. Montgomery was 4-for-5 that day, with an RBI triple in the ninth inning off Fernando Arroyo. The last game he was in, as the pennant drive was on in earnest, came against the Yankees on September 7 at Fenway, a 15-3 blowout for New York. He had two plate appearances, striking out the first time and drawing a walk the second.

The last year of the 1970s was the last year for Bob Montgomery as a major-league ballplayer. He went out with his head held high, appearing in 32 games and batting a career-best .349 in 86 at-bats. When he played his final game (September 9, 1979), he was 1-for-2 and scored a run, and also earned the distinction of being the last major leaguer to ever bat without a protective batting helmet on his head.

Though he tried to make the team in spring training in 1980, Montgomery just didn't have it any more. In April he turned 36 and the Sox were going with Fisk and Gary Allenson (Allenson had seen a lot of work in 1979, though with distinctly less production at the plate than Montgomery. He turned only 25, though, in 1980 and the Red Sox elected to look to him to

spell Fisk.) In 1980 and 1981, Monty worked a little in sports radio and did some Red Sox games on radio as a backup guy. For the 1982 season, WSBK, Channel 38, was looking to hire a new color commentator and interviewed Tony Conigliaro for the position. Tony's heart attack removed him from consideration and Montgomery was hired to do the color on Red Sox telecasts. Monty worked as Ned Martin's partner doing TV for the Red Sox for 17 years, right up through the 1995 season, when Channel 38's run with the Red Sox came to a close. He later worked as a color analyst for both the Pawtucket Red Sox and Portland Sea Dogs. He is credited with winning 11 Emmy Awards.

Montgomery began working in sales and marketing for Unison, a company based in Boston that specializes in signage work, and later for Adventures in Advertising, a marketing firm, involved in sale promotions and marketing premiums. He has also done work as a motivational speaker.

Bob Montgomery is a licensed pilot and an avid model railroader and golfer. He and his wife had one daughter.

Herb Crehan ends his *Red Sox Heroes of Yesteryear* profile of Bob Montgomery quoting Monty as saying of himself, "I was what they call a 50/50 player. I didn't help you an awful lot, but I didn't hurt you either." Crehan protests the modesty, terming Montgomery as "probably the premier backup catcher in the major leagues throughout the seventies."

SOURCES

Most of the information in this article, and all of Bob Montgomery's quotes, come from Herb Crehan's profile of Montgomery contained in his book *Red Sox Heroes of Yesteryear* (Cambridge, Massachusetts: Rounder Books, 2005). The always-helpful Retrosheet.org website provided a wealth of detail regarding Montgomery's year-by-year and even day-by-day play.

APRIL 29, 1986: BOSTON RED SOX 3, SEATTLE MARINERS 1, AT FENWAY PARK

THE FIRST 20-K GAME IN THE MAJORS

By Cecilia Tan and Bill Nowlin

ROGER CLEMENS MADE HIS MAJOR-LEAGUE debut in May 1984, but didn't really make his mark until after shoulder surgery cut short his 1985 season. The 23-year-old Texan came into 1986 determined to show he was as good as ever—or better—despite the surgery. He won his first three starts of the season, striking out 19 in 24⅓ innings. Clemens's ability to throw gas opened his teammates' eyes. Before he faced the Seattle Mariners on April 29, his fourth start, first baseman Bill Buckner told pitcher Al Nipper he thought Clemens would strike out 18 men. "The way he's been throwing and the way [the Mariners] have been striking out, 18 seemed like the number," Buckner later told the *Boston Globe*. Buckner's prediction came partly because of Clemens's prowess, and partly because the M's of '86 had proved to be particularly bad at making contact. In the season's first 19 games, they had racked up 166 K's, putting them on pace for some 1,400 total, 200 more than the previous worst (the 1968 Mets with 1,203). The past two games alone they had whiffed 20 times. The situation seemed primed for an assault on the record book.

On a chilly April night, Clemens took the hill at Fenway Park on six days' rest, thanks to a rainout and an offday. In the first inning, he faced Spike Owen, Phil Bradley, and Ken Phelps. He retired them on 21 pitches, striking out the side, despite going to a full count on all three men. All three went down swinging. The first man to hit a ball fair was Gorman Thomas, who led off the second, and lined to left. Then Jim Presley struck out, and Clemens caught Ivan Calderon looking. In the third, the M's could almost believe they were figuring Clemens out, as only Dave Henderson struck out, and leading off the fourth inning, Owen, facing Clemens for the second time on the day, singled, breaking up the possibility of a perfect game or a no-hitter.

But not the masterpiece. Clemens came back to strike out Bradley, Phelps, and Thomas. Thomas almost popped out, but first baseman Don Baylor dropped the ball, allowing Clemens to finish the batter off. Patrons at Fenway Park were already counting K's, and when Baylor fumbled the foul, there was an approving murmur because attentive fans realized this offered Clemens another chance for a strikeout. When he caught Thomas looking at a 3-and-2 pitch, The Rocket began a string of eight strikeouts in a row, knocking down some records along the way. At seven, Clemens surpassed Buck O'Brien and Ray Culp, two Red Sox pitchers who shared the team record for consecutive K's at six. When he got veteran catcher Steve Yeager on a 2-and-2 curveball, he tied Nolan Ryan and Ron Davis as the only American Leaguers to fan eight in a row. Fans began to put up red K signs on the back wall of the bleachers. "Where'd they come from?" Nipper asked in the next day's *Globe*. "Did those guys run out and get the cardboard and paint? Suddenly they were there."

Spike Owen, though, broke the string, ending the sixth with a fly to center—and some fans had been yelling, "Drop it!" wanting Roger to retire the side on a strikeout. Red Sox manager John McNamara checked with his ace to see how he was feeling. "I've been doing that every game this year, making sure his arm feels good," McNamara told the *Globe*. Clemens himself was fine, and he knew he was pitching as well as he ever had.

Boston's offense, meanwhile, had yet to come to life, and the game stood at 0-0. Clemens went out to pitch the seventh and struck out Bradley and Phelps again. Clemens then had Gorman Thomas down 1-and-2, and the crowd screaming for another K. But Thomas was looking for something in the strike zone, and he connected for a home run into the first row in the deep center-field bleachers. The Mariners had broken the scoreless tie and taken the lead. Clemens retired Presley on a grounder to first, but he was in a 1-0 hole, despite his mastery. McNamara checked with him again. This time Clemens admitted his legs were cramping a bit, but his arm was fine. McNamara had no intention of pulling his pitcher, who already had 16 strikeouts to his credit.

The Red Sox finally got to Mariners starter Mike Moore in the bottom of the seventh. With two outs, Steve Lyons singled and Glenn Hoffman walked. Dwight Evans promptly cashed them both in with a three-run shot. Now Clemens had a 3-1 lead, and he went out for the eighth still throwing heat, but unaware of the record numbers he was approaching. Two more men struck out in the eighth, bringing Clemens's total to 18. Clemens didn't know exactly how many men he had set down, only that it had been quite a few.

As he took the mound for the ninth inning, Nipper decided to tell him about the possibility that another record might fall. "Nipper told him he needed one to tie and two to set the record," reported Leigh Montville in the *Globe*. In Nipper's words, "Wouldn't it be a shame if a guy had a chance for something like that and didn't try for it? I wanted him to know. He's not the type of guy who would be affected by knowing."

Clemens was unfazed by the knowledge. He faced Spike Owen once more to lead off the inning. Could Owen make contact again? No, he went down swinging, and the record of 19 men in a nine-inning game was tied. Now Bradley, who already had three strikeouts, came up, and went down looking. It was strikeout number 20. Fenway's message board flashed the news that the single-game strikeout record had been broken. Wade Boggs came over from third base to shake Clemens's hand for breaking the record. But

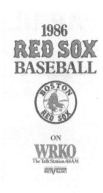

Courtesy of Bob Brady.

the game was not quite over. Ken Phelps' groundout was almost an afterthought, as in striking out 20 men Clemens had accomplished something that had never been done in 111 years of major-league baseball.

"When he has that kind of stuff, it's really not difficult to call the game," his catcher, Rich Gedman, told reporters after the game. "He just threw the ball to spots where they couldn't hit it." It took him 138 pitches (97 strikes) to finish the feat. Seattle put only 10 balls in play, only two of them pulled, as Clemens hit 97 on the radar gun repeatedly and did not go to a three-ball count on even one batter after the fourth inning.

"Watching the Mariners try to hit Clemens was like watching a stack of waste paper diving into a shredder," wrote Dan Shaughnessy in the *Globe*. Clemens's domination was, in some ways, superior to a no-hitter, or even a perfect game, because the record was singularly his. "If setting the major-league record for strikeouts in a game is any measure of a career," wrote the Associated Press, "[then] Roger Clemens is heading for the Hall of Fame." In fact, the Hall received Clemens's spikes, cap, and other mementos of the game.

Clemens's domination would continue all year, and he would finish the season at 24-4 and win both the Cy Young Award and the American League MVP Award, while helping Boston reach the World Series for the first time since 1975.

Extra Innings:

Rich Gedman, by virtue of catching all 20 strikeouts in the game, broke an American League record and tied a major-league record with 20 putouts by a catcher in a nine-inning game. Jerry Grote had previously been credited with 20 on April 22, 1970, while catching for the Mets, on the day when Tom Seaver struck out 19 Padres, including the final 10 in a row. Grote had also caught a foul pop for an out. The record would later be equaled by Dan Wilson on August 8, 1997, in the AL, and Sandy Martinez May 6, 1998, in the NL. Gedman would still hold the record for most putouts by a catcher on two consecutive days, though, with 36 over April 29 and 30, 1986.

A little more than 10 years later, Clemens later had another 20-K game, against the Tigers in Detroit on September 18, 1996. In 1998 Kerry Wood of the Chicago Cubs struck out 20 Astros on May 6.

The record for the most strikeouts in a big-league game belongs to Tom Cheney of the Washington Senators. He struck out 21 opponents, though it took him 16 innings to do so in the September 12, 1962, game against the Orioles. On May 8, 2001, Arizona's Randy Johnson struck out 20 Reds in nine innings; he was relieved after nine.

An earlier version of this article was published in *The 50 Greatest Red Sox Games* by Cecilia Tan and Bill Nowlin (Riverdale Avenue Books), and appears here by permission.

MAY 19, 1986: BOSTON RED SOX 8, MINNESOTA TWINS 7, AT FENWAY PARK

BOSTON WINS IN A WALK-OFF
FOR THE SECOND GAME IN A ROW

by Michael Huber

ON MONDAY NIGHT, MAY 19, 1986, THE Boston Red Sox hosted the Minnesota Twins at Fenway Park. The first-place Red Sox had defeated the Texas Rangers on Sunday in a stunning 10-inning finish. As Yogi Berra once said, it was déjà vu all over again on Monday, as Boston again rallied and won in walk-off fashion, beating the Twins 8-7.

The previous day, Boston had entered the bottom of the ninth trailing the Rangers 3-2. Leadoff doubles by Marty Barrett and Wade Boggs tied the score. In the top of the 10th the Rangers' Pete O'Brien scored on a walk, a single by Tom Paciorek, and an error by Red Sox catcher Rich Gedman to give Texas the lead again. Boston then created one of the more bizarre walk-offs in Boston history. With one out, Steve Lyons singled to center field. With Barrett batting, Rangers hurler Greg Harris appeared to have Lyons picked off but threw wild and Lyons scampered to second base. Barrett blooped a flare down the right-field line and the Rangers' George Wright dove to make a sensational catch. He gloved the liner, but the "ball came loose when Wright's glove hit the ground — one account said Wright trapped the ball — and then the fun started."[1] Lyons evidently thought the catch was going to be made, so he returned to second base and slid back into the bag just as Barrett came in standing up from the first base side. "I thought he caught the ball, so I decided to get my butt back to second. I knew I'd never see the field again if I got doubled off. The next thing I know, Marty was standing there, and he yelled, 'What are you doing here?' So I headed back to third because all of us can't be at second."[2] Right fielder Wright scooped up the ball and ran toward the infield.

As Lyons broke for third, Wright threw on the run, but the ball skipped past both third-baseman Steve Buechele and the pitcher, Harris, who was backing up the play. It went into the Texas dugout and both Lyons and Barrett were awarded two bases, giving Boston two runs and a walk-off 5-4 victory.

On Monday night, Boston took on the sixth-place Twins. Before a crowd of 18,428, Boston and Minnesota gave the fans their money's worth. John Butcher took the mound for the Twins, facing Boston's Mike Brown. Neither would get the decision. Brown gave up doubles to Roy Smalley and Kent Hrbek and a single to Mark Salas in the first inning. Boston answered in the bottom of the inning with a solo home run to right-center by Bill Buckner, cutting the Twins lead to 2-1. With one out in the bottom of the second, Boston's Don Baylor walked and moved to third on a double by Mike Stenhouse. Rey Quinones singled, driving in Baylor, and Steve Lyons followed with a line-drive double, scoring both Stenhouse and Quinones, and Boston had a 4-2 advantage.

In the first four innings, Boston batters put together seven hits in scoring four runs, but they also hit into four double plays[3] and had a runner thrown out at second to end an inning.

Kirby Puckett doubled and Hrbek and Tom Brunansky hit back-to-back homers off Brown in the top of the fifth, making it 5-4 in favor of the Twins. After Mark Salas singled, Boston manager John McNamara pulled Brown and brought in left-hander Tim Lollar. Lollar allowed a single to Gary Gaetti and a double to Mickey Hatcher that plated Salas and Gaetti, and

Minnesota had captured a 7-4 lead by batting around in the inning. Boston got a run on a walk and two singles in the bottom of the fifth, but then the innings ticked by and Minnesota still clung to its 7-5 lead.

Until the bottom of the eighth. Twins reliever Frank Pastore allowed a one-out single to Jim Rice. Rice moved to third on a single by Gedman. Don Baylor grounded to third, but it was deep enough for Rice to come home. At the end of eight innings, it was Minnesota 7, Boston 6.

One run down, Boston came to bat in the bottom of the ninth against closer Ron Davis. Quinones and Lyons quickly made two outs for the Red Sox. Barrett drew a walk on a 3-and-1 pitch. Boggs kept the inning alive with a double off the left-field wall, sending Barrett to third. Davis intentionally walked Bill Buckner, bringing Rice to the plate. Rice fouled off five 1-and-2 pitches and finally looked at ball four on the 11th pitch of the at-bat, drawing an RBI walk as Barrett scored the tying run.[4] Marc Sullivan, the backup catcher, who had come in after Gedman was lifted for a pinch-runner in the eighth, now faced Davis. Sullivan watched the first pitch cross the plate for strike one. The second pitch struck his left hip, forcing Boggs in with the winning run. The Red Sox had gained their second straight walk-off win. They extended their Eastern Division lead over the idle New York Yankees to one game. Boston had scored two runs on a double, three walks, and a hit batter, all with two outs in the bottom of the ninth.

The Twins' first four batters—Puckett, Smalley, Hrbek, and Brunansky—provided much of Minnesota's power, combining for four doubles, two home runs, and a single. Seven of the Twins' first 10 hits went for extra bases. Boston starter Mike Brown lasted 4⅓ innings and yielded six earned runs. Joe Sambito picked up the win for Boston, pitching a three-up, three-down top of the ninth. It was his first major-league victory since 1981.[5] Sullivan was playing in only his fifth game

of the season. (He was plunked by a Twins pitcher the next day, too.)

The Red Sox went on to build a six-game winning streak, and they won 10 of 11 from May 17 to May 28, with the only loss coming in a payback walk-off defeat to the Rangers in Texas on May 24.

Postscript

The author thanks Lisa Tuite of the *Boston Globe* for her assistance with obtaining sources.

SOURCES

Associated Press. "Red Sox Win in 9th on Pass, Hit Batter," in *New York Times*, May 20, 1986.

Dupont, Kevin Paul. "Sox Leave Twins on Short End, 8-7; Ninth-Inning Rally Beats Minnesota HRs," *Boston Globe*, May 20, 1986.

Shaughnessy, Dan. "Red Sox Get Second Wind; Rangers Miss Mark in 10th," *Boston Globe*, May 19, 1986.

"May 18, 1986 Texas Rangers at Boston Red Sox Play By Play and Box Score," baseball-reference.com/boxes/BOS/BOS198605180.shtml.

"May 19, 1986 Minnesota Twins at Boston Red Sox Play By Play and Box Score," baseball-reference.com/boxes/BOS/BOS198605190.shtml.

"Retrosheet Boxscore: Boston Red Sox 8, Minnesota Twins 7," retrosheet.org/boxesetc/1986/B05190BOS1986.htm.

"Weird, wild walkoffs," sports.espn.go.com/mlb/news/story?id=1610896.

NOTES

1   "Weird, wild walkoffs," sports.espn.go.com/mlb/news/story?id=1610896.

2   Dan Shaughnessy, "Red Sox Get Second Wind; Rangers Miss Mark in 10th," *Boston Globe*, May 19, 1986.

3   Kevin Paul Dupont, "Sox Leave Twins on Short End, 8-7; Ninth-Inning Rally Beats Minnesota HRs," *Boston Globe*, May 20, 1986.

4   The *Globe* reported Rice fouling off four pitches; the Associated Press reported five.

5   Associated Press, "Red Sox Win in 9th on Pass, Hit Batter," *New York Times*, May 20, 1986.

MAY 20, 1986: BOSTON RED SOX 17, MINNESOTA TWINS 7, AT FENWAY PARK, BOSTON

WADE BOGGS COLLECTS FIVE HITS FOR THE RED SOX

By Doug Skipper

WADE BOGGS REGISTERED THE FIRST of three five-hit performances during his Hall of Fame career on Tuesday, May 20, 1986, at Fenway Park, as he led the Boston Red Sox to a 17-7 victory over the Minnesota Twins.

Boston's 27-year-old third baseman slapped four singles and a double in six trips to the plate. The defending American League batting champion, Boggs reached on a bunt single in Boston's six-run first, singled in the second, doubled in the third, singled in the fifth, and reached on an error in the seventh.

Boggs' near-perfect performance helped Boston starter Roger Clemens boost his season record to 7-0 despite an imperfect performance. The Rocket, making his eighth start of the year, surrendered nine hits over seven innings and matched his 1986 season highs by giving up two home runs and five runs. He struck out just four, though he did not walk a hitter in coasting to the win.

"It was a tough battle for me tonight," said Clemens. "With the guys hitting like they did tonight, you can't complain."[1]

Clemens retired the Twins in the top of the first despite Kent Hrbek's two-out double, and then watched the Red Sox build a cushion.

Marty Barrett led off the Boston first with a ringing double and moved to third on Boggs' first hit of the game, a bunt single down the first-base line. Dave Stapleton drew a walk from Twins starter Frank Viola, and all three moved up on a Jim Rice single, with Barrett scoring the first run of the game. Don Baylor doubled to chase in Boggs and Stapleton and Tony Armas followed with a double to score Baylor, driving Viola from the game without having recorded an out. "After Marty hit that first ball off the wall, it just seemed like everyone wanted to jump on the train," said Clemens.[2] After relief pitcher Roy Lee Jackson retired Rey Quinones and Steve Lyons on fly balls to right, catcher Marc Sullivan singled to right to score Armas with Boston's sixth run of the inning, all charged to Viola. "I felt good when I was warming up," said Viola, "but I just couldn't keep it going into the game."[3]

The Rocket retired the Twins in order in the second and Boggs led off the bottom half with his second hit of the game, a single to left field. Stapleton doubled and one batter later, Boggs scored on Baylor fielder's choice to make it 7-0 at the end of two innings.

After a pair of singles and a wild pitch, Clemens surrendered a two-run single to Twins center fielder Kirby Puckett, but retired the next two hitters to escape the third inning.

The Red Sox matched the two-run outburst with a pair of their own in the bottom of the inning. Boggs collected his third hit, a double to right, to score Sullivan, and scored the ninth Red Sox run himself when Stapleton reached on a third-strike passed ball. Keith Atherton replaced Jackson and retired Rice on a force play, but Clemens returned to the mound for the fourth with a 9-2 cushion. He surrendered a run on Gary Gaetti's double and a single by Mark Salas, but got Puckett to hit into an inning-ending force out.

The Red Sox mustered only a single by Armas in the fourth, and Clemens coasted through the top of the fifth. In the bottom half of the inning, Boggs came to the plate for the fourth time, this time with two outs, and smacked his fourth hit, a single to center field, though he was stranded at first.

Gaetti homered in the top of the sixth to cut Boston's lead to 9-4, but Boston blew the game open in the bottom half of the inning. Baylor and Quinones drew walks, and with two outs Juan Agosto replaced Atherton. Lyons singled to score Baylor, and Sullivan singled to score Quinones. Barrett walked, and Boggs followed with his fifth hit in five tries, driving a single to center that scored Lyons and Sullivan and boosted the Boston lead to 13-4.

Clemens survived a home run by Greg Gagne in the top of the seventh, then watched as the Red Sox expanded the lead to 17-5. Rice, Baylor, and Armas all singled to start the bottom half of the frame, with Rice scoring on an error. Quinones plated Baylor with an RBI grounder, and one out later Agosto hit Sullivan with a pitch. Ron Davis replaced Agosto, and Barrett greeted the fifth Twins pitcher with a run-scoring single. Boggs came to the plate for the sixth time, and reached on an error by first baseman Mickey Hatcher that allowed Sullivan to score.

Boggs departed to an ovation from the Fenway crowd officially announced as 20,880, when Red Sox manager John McNamara inserted Ed Romero to pinch-run. After the inning, McNamara called on reliever Bob Stanley to replace Clemens, who departed with a 17-5 lead. Stanley surrendered a solo home run to Gaetti, his third hit and second homer of the game, a triple by Steve Lombardozzi, and a run-scoring sacrifice fly to Salas to trim the lead to 17-7, but closed the Twins out with a perfect ninth. "It didn't matter what we were going to do tonight," Gaetti said. "It was a horrible game. When you hit like (the Red Sox) were, you can't score enough runs to catch up."[4]

The win was the seventh straight for Clemens over eight outings. "I'm not surprised by my start," Clemens said. "I have high expectations for myself, and I just

hope it keeps going."[5] Clemens went on to win his next seven starts and run his record to 14-0 before finally absorbing a loss against Toronto on July 2. He finished the season 24-4 with a 2.48 earned-run average, and didn't surrender more than five earned runs in a game.

The Twins, who dropped to 14-25, losing for the ninth time in 10 games, finished with seven runs on 11 hits, but made five costly errors. Boggs collected five of Boston's 20 hits to raise his average to .383 and scored three of the 17 Red Sox runs. Armas (4), Sullivan (3), and Barrett, Rice, and Baylor (2 apiece) also collected multiple hits as the Red Sox raised their record to an AL-best 25-13.

"'I hope it keeps snowballing into something, and the team keeps rolling, too," Clemens said. "It's a nice feeling," Boggs said, "But it's like climbing Mount Everest: We have a long way to go."[6]

After serving up five hits to Boggs on May 20, Minnesota manager Ray Miller employed a "moving shift" the next night, and the Twins held Boggs hitless, though the Red Sox prevailed by a 3-2 score.

When the teams met later in the month, Minnesota shifted again when Boggs batted. "The shift was illegal," Boggs said. "The umpire told me that and said he was going to get them to stop it. Maybe he didn't correct it completely but he got the Twins to do it within the boundaries of the rules." Miller countered by saying, "I'm not saying it will work forever, but it's worth continuing until he solves it."[7]

Boggs solved the shift the next time the two teams met, collecting three hits in five at-bats on May 30 at the Metrodome, and the next night, after Miller scrapped the shift, Boggs slapped out five hits for the second time in 11 days. Again he collected four singles and a double, and raised his average to .402 for the season. He would finish the season at .357, winning his third of five AL batting titles.

He managed the feat just one more time, smacking five hits for the Red Sox at Fenway Park against Oakland on July 31, 1991.

SOURCES

In addition to the sources in the notes, the author also consulted:

Boston Globe, May 21, 1986.

Goodwin, Doris Kearns. "Batting Champ Wade Boggs Hits With a Cool Eye, a Hot Hand and a Resolve to Help His Sister Overcome Illness," *People*, June 16, 1986.

Madden, Michael. "Protected by His Cocoon, a Regimented Routine Helps Bosox Star Tune Out All Distractions," *The Sporting News*, July 14, 1986.

Minneapolis Star Tribune, May 21, 1986.

New York Times, May 21, 1986.

NOTES

1 Ed Burns, "American League Roundup," United Press International, May 21, 1986.

2 Ibid.

3 Ibid.

4 Ibid.

5 Ibid.

6 Ibid.

7 Pat Reusse, "It Was Shifty Business," *The Sporting News,* June 16, 1986: 16.

AUGUST 21, 1986:
BOSTON RED SOX 24, CLEVELAND INDIANS 5, AT CLEVELAND STADIUM

By Bill Nowlin

BASEBALL PURISTS CLAIM TO LOVE A 1-0 game settled in extra innings. Partisans of a particular team often take great pleasure in a true blowout—when it's their team that comes out on top.

Through the 2015 season the Red Sox have played in only four games in which they scored at least two dozen runs. The 29-4 game on June 8, 1950, ranks first. There was a 25-8 game in 2003, and then there were two 24-run games—one in 1940 and this game in 1986.

The Sox were in first place, 5½ games ahead of the Yankees, visiting the sixth-place Cleveland Indians, who still had a winning record at 62-59. The August 21 7:30 P.M. matchup pitted 21-year-old Indians southpaw starter Greg Swindell against Boston's Oil Can Boyd. It was Swindell's big-league debut. Though he won 123 games over 17 years, this was not one of them. He started well, though, inducing three infield grounders in the top of the first and then seeing Cleveland's leadoff batter, Tony Bernazard, homer into the right-field seats to give him an early lead.

It was in the top of the third that Swindell started to get in trouble, walking two batters and then seeing Jim Rice single in Spike Owen to tie the score. He walked the bases loaded then, and balked—bringing another run home. Dwight Evans singled in two more and it was 4-1, Red Sox.

A single, error, and two more singles saw the Sox up their lead to 6-1 in the fourth. The third single was off reliever Dickie Noles.

Boyd was pitching well, and it was still 6-1 after five. Then the Boston batters went to town. Most of the damage was done with two outs. The Sox scored once,

and had runners on first and second. Marty Barrett took third on Don Baylor's fly ball to center, the second out. Evans walked to load the bases. Then Bill Buckner walked, and Noles was excused, replaced by Jose Roman. The first batter Roman faced was Tony Armas, who "jumped on his second pitch and lined a cannon shot over the fence in left center."[1]

It was a large crowd—26,316—and they had come hoping to see a good game. Indeed, Bob Dolgan of the *Cleveland Plain Dealer* wrote, "The crowd, out for a good time, refused to be deterred. When the Red Sox pounded Swindell's successors for 12 runs in the sixth inning, to take a ridiculous 18-1 lead, the people, bless 'em, began cheering wildly for Boston to pour it on and score more runs."[2]

After Armas's grand slam, Roman promptly loaded the bases again with a walk, a single, and another walk. Enough, concluded Indians manager Pat Corrales, who called on Bryan Oelkers to take over from Roman. The hapless Roman had faced four batters and seen them all score, three on hits off Oelkers by Barrett and Rice. Oelkers loaded the bases again with a walk to Baylor, followed that with a pitch Evans smacked for two more runs, and then saw Buckner single in the 12th run of the frame. Tony Armas flied out to end the torture. Seventeen Boston batters had come to the plate. Eleven straight batters reached base, one short of the American League record, according to the *Boston Globe*. Eleven of the 12 runs in the inning had scored after two outs.

It was indeed 18-1. In the seventh, Spike Owen hit a solo home run to make it 19-1. Three singles off Oil Can in the bottom of the seventh narrowed the gap just a bit: It was 19-2 in Boston's favor.

Mike Greenwell and a couple of others were brought into the game; Greenie doubled to lead off the eighth. There were two outs made. Then Buckner singled Greenwell in. Then Tony Armas hit his second homer of the game, scoring Buckner ahead of him. Oelkers then hit Marc Sullivan, and Owen singled. Dave Stapleton pinch-hit for Wade Boggs (!) and singled in Sullivan. Ed Romero, who'd subbed in for Barrett, singled in Owen. Ten men had come to the plate, and five runs had scored—again, every one of them after there were two outs. Now the score was 24-2.

Bob Stanley pitched the eighth. Nothing happened of note. Joe Sambito pitched the bottom of the ninth, and he had some difficulty, giving up three runs on four hits—but there was a lot of room for a few runs. The Indians had scored first, and they had scored last, but the final score was Boston 24 to Cleveland 5. Boyd's record improved to 12-9, with a 3.94 ERA.

All but two of the Red Sox runs were earned; two of the six runs scored off Swindell were unearned.

Oddly, three Red Sox batters had gone hitless. Boggs was 0-for-5, though he scored one run. Baylor was 0-for-5, though he scored two runs. And Marc Sullivan was 0-for-4, and he scored two runs.

The number-nine batter, Spike Owen, scored six runs in the game. The only American Leaguer who had done so previously was another Red Sox player—Johnny Pesky, on May 8, 1946. It was only Owen's third game for the Red Sox. One of the runs he scored came on his homer, the first homer he'd hit in 424 at-bats. Owen hit 46 in the course of his career.

Tony Armas had six RBIs. The grand slam was the sixth of his career.

Larry Whiteside of the *Boston Globe* concluded, "Nothing on Shock Theater or the late night movie on HBO comes close to the havoc and devastation that was the sum total of Boston's 24-5 crushing of the Cleveland Indians last night."[3]

Master of understatement, Red Sox manager John McNamara said, "It was a good night." In the other clubhouse, Corrales was quoted: "Twenty-four to 5," he kept muttering after the game. "Twenty-four to 5."[4] To be fair to McNamara, he did add, "But I like to think some of the tough games we won on the last homestand after the West Coast trip had more impact than this one.

"The hitting was nice to see. And so was the pitching of Boyd. After the second inning, he showed us the way he is capable of pitching. I'm glad for the team and I'm glad for Oil Can. I hope this helps restore his confidence in himself."[5] It was Can's first win since July 8. And Boyd did go 4-1 for the rest of the regular season, lowering his earned run average to 3.78.

The Yankees were rained out, so the Red Sox gained a half-game in the standings. They had held first place since May 14 and never relinquished the lead.

NOTES

1   Joe Giuliotti, *Boston Herald*, August 22, 1986.

2   Bob Dolgan, *Cleveland Plain Dealer*, August 22, 1986.

3   Larry Whiteside, *Boston Globe*, August 22, 1986.

4   Ibid.

5   Ibid.

SEPTEMBER 4, 1986: NEW YORK METS 7, BOSTON RED SOX 3, AT FENWAY PARK

PRELUDE TO A CLASSIC
(CHARITY GAME FOR JIMMY FUND
OF DANA-FARBER CANCER INSTITUTE)

By Saul Wisnia

LOOKING BACK ON IT NOW, IT WAS SOMEthing akin to a 1972 moviegoer watching the final scene of *The Godfather* and immediately thinking, "I hope they make another one." Sequels were not commonplace then, but it seemed everyone wanted to see more of Michael Corleone and his trigger-happy family.

So it was with the September 4 exhibition game played between the first-place Mets of the National League East and the first-place Red Sox of the American League East. Billed as a possible World Series preview, the game captured the public's attention and drew a near-sellout crowd of 33,057 to Fenway Park despite having no bearing on the standings. In the days before interleague play, it was a chance for players and fans of both clubs to see each other up close, savor the moment, and dream of a Boston-vs.-New York showdown in October.[1]

This was a contest 19 months in the waiting. The Red Sox and Mets announced in February 1985 that they would play a pair of charity exhibition games the next two seasons, first at Fenway and then at Shea Stadium. The Boston game in '86 would benefit the Jimmy Fund of Dana-Farber Cancer Institute, which had been the Red Sox' official charity for more than 30 years; the Flushing Meadows contest in '87 would support amateur baseball in New York.

When the announcement was made, the Mets were a team on the rise and the Red Sox one in a rebuilding mode. By the time the 1986 game came to fruition, however, both clubs were genuine championship contenders.

New York was well on its way to a 100-win season, with a 20-game lead in its division and a star-studded lineup that included five-tool outfielder Darryl Strawberry, slick-fielding, clutch-hitting first-baseman Keith Hernandez, future Hall of Fame catcher Gary Carter, and 20-year-old pitching ace and reigning Cy Young Award winner Dwight Gooden. Boston had two future Hall of Famers in third baseman Wade Boggs (en route to his third batting title) and left fielder Jim Rice (homing in on his eighth 20-homer, 100-RBI campaign), as well as an ace pitcher in Roger Clemens (20-4 on the day of the game) who would win his first of seven Cy Young Awards that year. Complementing them were top veterans like Gold Glove right fielder Dwight Evans, gritty first baseman Bill Buckner, and DH Don Baylor (like Rice, a former AL MVP).[2]

Before the game the entire roster of players on both clubs were introduced to the crowd, as if it were a postseason game. Even the travel accommodations for the visitors had a playoff feel. The Mets had flown their entire team into Boston on a chartered plane that day, along with assorted wives, club executives, and staff members—nearly 100 people in all. Red Sox fans likely got a chuckle when they heard that the Mets players' bus broke down between Logan Airport and the Sumner Tunnel, and that 10 taxicabs and additional private cars were needed to get the New York squad to Fenway. In fact, the day's MVP might have been Mets equipment manager Charlie Samuels, who flagged down an airport limousine to transport the club's 70 bags of bats and other gear to the ballpark.

Once they finally got there, New York players expressed excitement at seeing the ballpark and taking a crack at the Green Monster left-field wall. "It's awesome," said Mets reliever Roger McDowell. He spent much of the pregame snapping photos of the Monster, and said later of the 37-foot-high fence, "It's the ninth wonder of the world. I stood out there and threw balls against the wall, as though I were Carl Yastrzemski waiting for the rebound."[3]

Red Sox rookie reliever Calvin Schiraldi, a former hotshot Mets prospect who failed to live up to his promise in New York and was traded to Boston the previous November, took the high road when asked his feelings about the game. "This is good for me," said Schiraldi, who had shined as Boston's closer since a midseason call-up. "I didn't perform to my ability with the Mets. I stunk it up with them. That's why I'm glad the Red Sox gave me a chance."[4]

Some Mets were also more than willing to state for the record that they hoped to be back at Fenway again soon in contests that counted. "I'm pulling for the Red Sox," said New York third baseman Ray Knight. "I'd love to be playing the big games here. In this atmosphere."[5] Mets manager Davey Johnson, one of the few on his team with a history against the Red Sox — having spent eight seasons battling them as an Orioles second baseman from 1965 to 1972 — hoped New York might have a psychological edge in the exhibition contest because its own regular-season race was all but over.

"There's been less griping about this game than any exhibition I can remember," Johnson told reporters. "First, it's against the Red Sox, the team with the best record in the American League. Second, we have a 20-game lead. A 20-game lead makes a lot of things easier. I'm sure we feel a lot better about this game than the Red Sox do."[6]

During batting practice the centers of attention had been Gooden and Clemens, as the two premier young pitchers in the game posed for cameramen behind the cage. Mets utilityman Howard Johnson fondly recalled hitting a home run off Clemens a couple years earlier while with the Tigers, but he wouldn't get a chance for a return act on this night. The starters were rookie Jeff Sellers for the Red Sox — just up from minor-league Pawtucket — and swingman Rick Aguilera for New York. The home club took a 2-0 lead in the third on singles by Tony Armas and Boggs, a walk to Marty Barrett, and a two-run hit by Buckner. This was nothing new, as the first baseman was one of Boston's top run producers all year and in the midst of a hot spell that would result in 8 homers and 22 RBIs during his last 26 regular-season games.

In the top of the fourth inning Buckner was involved in another play that while insignificant in an exhibition contest would prove an eerie foreshadowing of future events. After Wally Backman walked for New York, Lee Mazzilli hit a groundball that "Billy Buck" booted for an error.[7] Carter, serving as DH on this night, made Boston pay for the gaffe with a sacrifice fly to center that cut the lead to 2-1. The Red Sox went back up by two in the home half of the fourth on a walk to Evans and singles by Armas and Spike Owen.

The lead held until the eighth, when the Mets jumped on Boston reliever Joe Sambito. Tim Teufel and Mazzilli started it off with singles, Ray Knight had a pinch-hit double to make it 3-2, and then, after two outs, New York scored five more runs on an error by third baseman Ed Romero, an RBI single by John Gibbons, a walk to Kevin Elster, and a two-run hit by Kevin Mitchell. That was it for the scoring, as the Mets won 7-3.[8]

Afterward, as before the first pitch, nobody really wanted to dwell much on this game; the focus was on whether there would be four to seven *more* games between Boston and New York in October. *Boston Globe* columnist Leigh Montville called the night, coming near the end of a fantastic regular season by the Red Sox, "a chance to dream … a sneak preview of the dessert that possibly could follow this satisfying best of all possible main courses that is almost finished."[9]

And while Davey Johnson may have hoped that the one-game diversion would stall Boston's momentum, this wasn't the case. The Red Sox, whose AL East lead at the time was 4½ games over second-place Toronto entering the night, came into the exhibition with a five-game winning streak; after it, they won six more in a row to stretch their division advantage to 8½ games. As expected, the Red Sox and Mets each clinched their respective divisions by September's end.[10]

The stage was indeed being set for a return engagement.

SOURCES

In addition to the sources in the notes, the author also consulted:

Associated Press. "Red Sox and Mets Plan Charity Series," *New York Times*, February 17, 1985.

"In '86 Mets-Red Sox Exhibition, a Sign of Things to Come," *New York Times*, May 21, 2009.

NOTES

1   The Mets were the first National League team to play at Fenway Park since the Montreal Expos appeared in an exhibition game there in 1981. The Jimmy Fund charity aided by the Boston game was one with strong ties to the city's baseball history, as it was started with large help from the NL's Boston Braves in 1948, five years before they left the city for Milwaukee. Tommy Holmes, director of amateur baseball relations for the '86 Mets, had been a star outfielder on the '48 Braves and an early celebrity fund-raiser for the Jimmy Fund.
    Although the Red Sox and Boston Braves battled from 1901 to 1952 for the city's mythical baseball supremacy, they were part-ners in their support of the Jimmy Fund of Boston's renowned Dana-Farber Cancer Institute. Braves owner Louis Perini had made the Jimmy Fund his team's primary charity, and he, his staff, and players including Holmes helped raise more than $1 million in five years of appeals—an astronomical amount for the period. Then, when Perini moved his club west in the spring of 1953, he appealed to Red Sox owner Tom Yawkey to take over stewardship of the Jimmy Fund. Yawkey complied, and for many years the Braves returned to Boston for Jimmy Fund benefit games at Fenway. Today, more than 60 years later, the Red Sox-Jimmy Fund union is recognized as the longest-standing and most extensive team-charity relationship in all of profes-sional sports, and is responsible for millions raised for pediatric and adult patient care and cancer research at Dana-Farber. (A detailed look at this unique partnership can be found at jim-myfund.org/about-us/boston-red-sox/ and in *The Jimmy Fund of Dana-Farber Cancer Institute*, by Saul Wisnia.)

2   Nobody knew the makeup of both clubs better than Boston gen-eral manager Lou Gorman. A Rhode Island native and lifelong Red Sox fan, he had been director of baseball operations for the Mets in the early 1980s when the team was developing great young players like Strawberry, Gooden, left-handed pitcher Ron Darling, and outfielder Mookie Wilson. Then in 1984 he got his dream job in Boston and helped transform a last-place team into a pennant-winner in three years.

3   Joseph Durso, "Mets Beat Red Sox, 7-3, Just for the Fun of It All," *New York Times*, September 5, 1986.

4   Dan Shaughnessy, "This Time It's All in Fun; Sox Face Mets—For Charity, Not a World Series Championship," *Boston Globe*, September 5, 1986.

5   Leigh Montville, "Still Rolling Along," *Boston Globe*, September 5, 1986.

6   Ibid.

7   This was not the only eerie prologue to Buckner's infamous error in Game Six of the 1986 World Series. On October 6, after the Red Sox had entered the AL playoffs, Buckner was interviewed by reporter Don Shane of WBZ-TV in Boston and was quoted on air as saying, "The dreams are that you're gonna have a great series and win. The nightmares are that you're gonna let the win-ning run score on a groundball through your legs. Those things happen, you know. I think a lot of it is just fate." "Bill Buckner Talks Before 1986 World Series," WBZ-TV Boston interview, YouTube (youtube.com/watch?v=gb9ziUKRU3I), October 6, 1986. See also "What Bill Buckner Said 19 Days Before Game Six of the '86 World Series," mentalfloss.com, October 25, 2011.

8   Sambito's shellacking in the eighth may have resulted from his being such a familiar face. He had pitched against the Mets often during eight years as a reliever with the Houston Astros, and had even briefly been a Met himself in 1985 after coming back from Tommy John surgery. Released by New York that August, he had signed on with the Red Sox as a free agent in January of '86 and contributed a 2-0 record and 12 saves out of the Boston bullpen that year.

9   Montville, "Still Rolling Along."

10 The 1986 World Series was nearly a match-up of 100-win teams. The Mets finished 108-54; the Red Sox were 90-57 after beating Milwaukee on September 18, but went just 5-9 the rest of the season—including a four-game sweep at the hands of the Yankees to close out the campaign. Although Boston no doubt took its foot off the gas after clinching the AL East on September 28 with seven games to play, history would likely look back on the '86 fall classic as less of a David-vs.-Goliath duel had Boston been 100-62 instead of 95-65 in the regular season.

Even after their disastrous collapse at Shea Stadium in Games Six and Seven of the World Series, the Red Sox kept their com-mitment to play the second charity exhibition game against the Mets at this House of Horrors on May 7, 1987. The Mets won yet again, 2-0, before 32,347 fans, and the much-maligned Bill Buckner showed great humility and humor when he called out to Mookie Wilson—who had hit the grounder that skidded through his legs in Game Six, "Mookie, what do you say you hit me some groundballs?" See "A Hint of October on a Spring Night," *New York Times*, May 8, 1987.

SEPTEMBER 28, 1986: BOSTON RED SOX 12, TORONTO BLUE JAYS 3, AT FENWAY PARK, BOSTON

RED SOX CLINCH AMERICAN LEAGUE EASTERN DIVISION

By T.S. Flynn

A FEW HOURS BEFORE THE 154TH GAME of the 1986 Red Sox season, Dennis "Oil Can" Boyd and pitching coach Bill Fischer walked from the dugout to the Fenway Park bullpen. The Red Sox were in position to clinch the American League Eastern Division for the first time since 1975, and the early crowd cheered at the sight of the day's starting pitcher. "That let me know it's well appreciated," Boyd said after the game. "It gave me a burning desire."[1] Ironically, many of those fans had probably questioned Boyd's desire at various points during the 1986 season—his teammates, coaches, and Sox management certainly had.

Oil Can's turbulent season began when he reported to camp at an alarming 125 pounds. Late in spring training he met with Red Sox doctor (and limited partner) Arthur Pappas, who was concerned by the pitcher's slight appearance and yellow, bloodshot eyes. Pappas told the media that Boyd had contracted noncontagious viral hepatitis and he was sent to a hospital in Boston to recuperate. Boyd set the record straight in his autobiography: "I had the whole cover story about hepatitis, but it was flat-out me smoking crack every damn day."[2] When he returned to Winter Haven for the last week of spring training, Boyd also returned to his bad habits. The club fined him $2,150 for reporting more than an hour late for the final exhibition game. Boyd promised management and his teammates he was in control of his life. "I told them I'd get a handle on [my cocaine use], and for the most part I did. Throughout the '86 season I did pretty well. … In spurts it would get out of control."[3]

The Red Sox weren't favorites to compete for the postseason in 1986. The year before they finished 81-81, and Ben Walker of the Associated Press predicted that the '86 club "again may resemble a slow-pitch softball team—they will go as far as their bats carry them."[4] For the Red Sox to succeed, Boyd and the rest of the pitching staff needed to improve, and they did. Roger Clemens, who won the Cy Young Award that season, led a solid starting group that included Bruce Hurst, Al Nipper, Tom Seaver, and Boyd. The offense remained strong. Wade Boggs won the 1986 AL batting title and Jim Rice, Marty Barrett, Dwight Evans, and newcomer Don Baylor all produced at the plate.

On this day, the offense led the way. After a scoreless first inning, the Red Sox erupted in the second inning. Tony Armas led off with a single and advanced on a wild pitch by Duane Ward. Rich Gedman doubled him home. Spike Owen reached on a fielder's choice that resulted in no outs, and Wade Boggs walked to load the bases. Jays skipper Jimy Williams went to his bullpen, but Joe Johnson walked Marty Barrett and the Red Sox led 2-0. Bill Buckner knocked in Owen with another fielder's choice and, after Rice flied out, Baylor followed with a two-run single. Just like that, the Red Sox led 5-0 when Oil Can took the ball to start the third inning.

The Jays helped Boyd's cause in the early innings with a first-inning double-play grounder and two baserunners caught stealing in the second, but they went down quickly in the third on a lineout and a pair of strikeouts that negated a walk issued to Manny Lee. The Red Sox added another run before Boyd again toed the rubber. In the fourth, the Blue Jays offense finally broke through when Rance Mulliniks doubled and Lloyd Moseby homered to cut the Red Sox lead to 6-2.

The Red Sox responded, peppering Dennis Lamp (who had started the inning in relief of Johnson) and Jeff Musselman (who relieved Lamp with the bases loaded) to the tune of four unearned runs on an error, two singles, and a double by Evans. Red Sox 10, Blue Jays 2. Toronto scored a run in the top of the fifth when Moseby singled in Kelly Gruber, who had doubled, but with a 10-3 lead the rowdy Fenway crowd could be forgiven for thinking ahead to the playoffs.

After Jesse Barfield popped out for the Jays' first out of the sixth, Willie Upshaw singled and Whitt walked. Red Sox manager John McNamara appeared from the dugout and strolled to the mound for a word with Boyd. "I told him with a big lead to throw strikes," McNamara said. "All I was concerned about was that he stay involved and stay as intent as he was. I didn't want him taking anything for granted."[5] The 26-year-old pitcher had learned months earlier to take nothing for granted.

Leading up to the All-Star break, the Red Sox told Boyd that if he didn't voluntarily stop using cocaine, they'd put him in a rehabilitation clinic. He refused. Explaining his feelings at the time, Oil Can wrote, "I'm not living like I should, but I'm pitching like hell. ... I was concentrating and maintaining, because I knew I had to pitch well with me living like I was living."[6] His cocaine habit had become an open secret in baseball and, for the second time in as many years, Boyd was not selected to pitch in the All-Star Game despite his strong statistical case (11-6, 3.71 ERA). When reporters circled around his locker and asked for comments he reacted loudly and vehemently, tearing off his uniform and screaming. The clubhouse was cleared of reporters during the tirade. He refused Dr. Pappas's request to see him and left for home, where he locked the doors and refused to communicate with Red Sox representatives.[7] On July 13 the Associated Press reported that Boyd had been suspended three days for his outburst. "I should have been on [the All-Star team] and I should have been on it last year,"

he said. "I want my reward and I want it now. ... It was a heartbreaking situation. I just had to get home and get the hell away from the park. ... I'm an angry young man."[8]

On July 15, the day of the All-Star Game, Boyd's troubles worsened when he drove to a bodega in Chelsea, Massachusetts, to buy cocaine. Boyd claimed to have seen undercover narcotics officers, so he returned to his car without making any purchases. When he arrived back home, a police car pulled into the driveway behind him and Oil Can was apprehended after a scuffle. The police said Boyd told them he had a gun, Boyd said he only asked if he was under arrest.[9] A search for drugs and weapons came up empty, but he complained of a sore arm resulting from the police officers' rough treatment. On July 16, general manager Lou Gorman announced a new suspension that would remain in place until "certain issues are clarified to the satisfaction of the Red Sox organization." When asked if drugs were an issue, Gorman said, "There's nothing to indicate that's the problem right now. ... He feels he's being persecuted by [the police]."[10] A day later the club announced that Boyd had agreed to enter a hospital "for evaluation, including drug tests."[11] A few days into his stay, on a pass for dinner with his wife, Karen, Boyd was arrested for a three-year-old motor-vehicle violation when police stopped Karen for speeding. He paid the $25 fine. When the hospital released him after a weeklong stay, Oil Can reported that he'd passed his drug tests and was ready to pitch. According to the AP, a Red Sox official stated, "Boyd has to settle his finances before going back to the mound."[12] After catching up on delinquent mortgage and car payments and paying for the restoration of his home phone service, Oil Can finally rejoined the team on August 5. He'd weathered the worst month of his professional career and returned to form in August and September.

After McNamara's visit to the mound, the Jays loaded the bases on a Rick Leach infield single. But Boyd bounced back again, retiring the final 11 Toronto batters in order, and the Boston offense added two insurance runs in the bottom of the eighth. Oil Can won the 12-3 complete game, and the Red Sox won the American League Eastern Division title. In the clubhouse after the game a reporter asked Boyd about the irony of winning the biggest game of the year just months after it looked as if he might never be back with the team. "I got to block that out. My teammates don't want me to dwell on that. They say, 'Can you get back to business and we'll all get back to business.' My little adversity I went through—all that is now abolished. They said, 'You come back and we'll do something special,' and that's what we did today."[13]

NOTES

1   Dan Shaughnessy, "The Can Put a Lid on It All," *Boston Globe*, September 29, 1986.

2   Dennis "Oil Can" Boyd and Mike Shalin, *They Call Me Oil Can* (Chicago: Triumph Books: 2012), 66.

3   Boyd and Shalin, 68.

4   Ben Walker (Associated Press), "Tigers Expected to Reclaim Title from Jays," *Galveston* (Texas) *Daily News*, April 1, 1986.

5   *Boston Herald*, September 29, 1986.

6   Boyd and Shalin, 68.

7   Boyd and Shalin, 78.

8   Associated Press, "Boyd Explodes After Being Left Off Team," *Kerrville* (Texas) *Times*, July 13, 1986.

9   Boyd and Shalin, 81.

10 Associated Press. "Oil Can Slips Up With Law," *Kerrville Times*, July 17, 1986.

11 Associated Press. "Troubled Oil Can Enters Hospital," *Kerrville Times*, July 18, 1986.

12 Associated Press. "Oil Can Boyd tests negative for drugs," *New Braunfels* (Texas) *Herald-Zeitung*, July 25, 1986.

13 Shaughnessy.

OCTOBER 7, 1986: CALIFORNIA ANGELS 8, BOSTON RED SOX 1, AT FENWAY PARK

1986 AMERICAN LEAGUE CHAMPIONSHIP SERIES GAME ONE

By Allan Wood

THE 1986 BOSTON RED SOX WENT 95-66 during the regular season, their most wins in nearly a decade (99 in 1978), and won the American League East flag by 5½ games over the New York Yankees. It was their first postseason appearance in 11 years, since they lost the 1975 World Series to the Cincinnati Reds.

After second-place finishes in the AL West in 1984 and 1985, the California Angels came out on top with 92 wins, five games ahead of the Texas Rangers. The Angels and Red Sox played a best-of-seven American League Championship Series, only the second postseason since the ALCS had been extended from a best-of-five. The year before, the Kansas City Royals rallied to win the pennant over the Toronto Blue Jays after being down 1-3 in the inaugural best-of-seven series.

Red Sox fans were giddy with anticipation of the ALCS because of their ace: Roger Clemens, who won 24 games during the regular season, and led the AL with a 2.48 ERA and 0.97 WHIP. He ended up winning both the AL Cy Young and Most Valuable Player awards. Clemens was a hard-working ace who could potentially start three times in a best-of-seven series—a huge advantage. The fans' excitement was tempered with some caution, however, after Clemens was hit on the right (throwing) elbow by a line drive in his last regular-season start. However, Clemens brushed aside those concerns and pronounced himself ready for battle.

Like Boston manager John McNamara (who had managed the Angels in 1983 and 1984), California skipper Gene Mauch was able to set his rotation as he wished. He chose Mike Witt (18-10, 2.84) for Game One, at Fenway Park. Witt had been extremely durable and reliable, pitching into the seventh inning in 32 of his 34 starts. He threw 269 innings, only 2⅓ innings behind league leader Bert Blyleven of the Twins.

In the early innings against the Angels, Clemens was shaky—possibly because he had pitched only 1⅔ innings over the last 11 days. He struck out Ruppert Jones to start the game, but gave up a double to Wally Joyner and a two-out walk to Reggie Jackson. Clemens stranded both runners when Doug DeCinces flied out to deep center, with Tony Armas catching the fly ball two steps from the wall.

In the second inning, Clemens struck out the first two batters before his control deserted him and he began missing up and away. His fourth pitch to Bob Boone was perhaps the key to the entire inning. "At 2-and-1 he made a real tough pitch away that just missed," Boone said. "It was a slider or a cut fastball and I couldn't have done anything with it if it was a strike. I just had to watch it. It was real tough, real close."[1]

Home-plate umpire Larry Barnett called it ball three—thereby earning himself a little more enmity from Red Sox fans, who would never forget his refusal to call interference against the Cincinnati Reds on a 10th-inning bunt in Game Three of the 1975 World Series, a game won by the Reds three batters later.

Boone: "He missed and tried to hump up a little and then he missed again."[2] Boone walked. Clemens then walked Gary Pettis as well. "His fastball was rising and he may have been a little excited out there," Pettis said.[3] Clemens was annoyed at himself: "You can't walk the last two batters in the order. It's not characteristic of me."[4]

Jones lined a single to center and Boone scored. Joyner followed with his second double in as many innings, an opposite-field shot into the left-field corner, and Pettis scored. As Sammy Stewart began warming up in the Red Sox bullpen, Brian Downing lined a single to the base of the left-field wall for two more runs. The Angels led 4-0.

Clemens's 1-and-2 pitch to Downing was also very close. When Barnett called it a ball, Downing knew he had caught a break. "The 1-and-2 pitch was a pitch that, to be honest, was too tough to take," Downing said. "I took the same pitch the first time, and the umpire called it a ball. I figured he might call it a ball again."[5]

Clemens battled Reggie Jackson for nine pitches, finally striking him out and ending the inning. Clemens threw 45 pitches in the inning, 37 of them after he had two outs. "The velocity was there," Clemens said. "I was frustrated because I wasn't that far off [with my control]."[6] Boston catcher Rich Gedman maintained that Clemens "was right around the plate all the time," a dubious claim.[7]

In the third, a throwing error by Boston shortstop Spike Owen and singles from Boone and Pettis produced an unearned run for the Angels.

Mike Witt had not received much run support during his regular-season starts. He said his teammates' unexpected gift of a five-run lead "calmed me down a little to where I could gain control of myself and get into a nice little groove."[8]

Wade Boggs worked a nine-pitch walk to start the home half of the first, but Marty Barrett—after two bunt attempts—grounded into a double play. Witt set down the next 16 Boston batters without breaking a sweat. (The Red Sox lineup came into the game with a collective .178 batting average against the Angels' starter.) Witt walked Owen with two outs in the sixth. Boggs recorded the first Red Sox hit of the night on a high chopper to third; DeCinces made an excellent pick on the short hop, but couldn't get off a throw. Barrett followed with a single to right, scoring Owen. Bill Buckner ended the inning with a fly to short left.

Witt's 5⅔ no-hit innings were the second-longest no-hit stretch from the start of an LCS game, two outs shy of the 6⅓ innings posted by Baltimore's Mike Cuellar and Ross Grimsley in Game Four of the 1974 ALCS against Oakland.

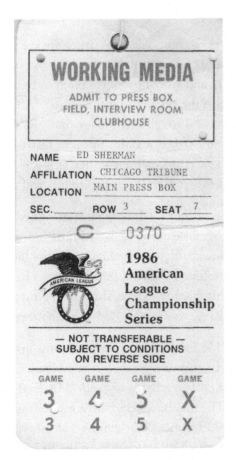

Ed Sherman's press pass, courtesy of Bob Brady.

Despite facing 19 batters (and throwing 84 pitches) in three innings and allowing five runs, Clemens stayed in the game. He had calmed down, retiring 14 of 15 Angels after Pettis's RBI single in the third. But the Angels battered him in the eighth—and, again, it was the bottom of the lineup that did the damage. (The last two spots in California's order reached base six times in eight appearances against Clemens.) Dick Schofield singled to right with one out. He stole second without a throw and scored on Boone's bloop single to right. After Pettis singled, McNamara went to his bullpen, calling on lefty Joe Sambito—who got a popup and issued a walk, loading the bases.

Bob Stanley came in and gave up a two-run single to Downing. California led 8-1.

Don Baylor doubled with one out in the Boston seventh, but was stranded there. Owen and Barrett singled in the eighth, but Witt retired Buckner on a fly to left. (Buckner's four at-bats ended the first, third, sixth, and eighth innings.) Witt set down the Red Sox in order in the bottom of the ninth, finishing his complete game on 116 pitches.

Clemens threw 143 pitches in 7⅓ innings and was charged with all eight runs. (His runs-allowed high during the regular season was only six.) He allowed 10 hits and walked three, and had five strikeouts.

The Angels were happy with their victory, but were adamant about not getting ahead of themselves. "We haven't forgotten our experience in Milwaukee in 1982," Downing said. "We were up in the [best-of-five] series, 2-0, and had to win only one of three in Milwaukee. We didn't."[9]

TV Note: Although ABC showed a pregame segment—"The Frustrations of the Red Sox in the '70s"—detailing the franchise's "agonies of the not-so-distant past," announcers Al Michaels and Jim Palmer made only one mention of Boston not having won a World Series title since 1918. That bit of information came from Michaels with two outs in the top of the ninth inning! In 1986, it had not yet become a media mantra.

California Angels - 041 000 030 - 8 11 0
Boston Red Sox - 000 00 000 - 1 5 1

NOTES

1   Michael Madden. "Clemens Walks on the Wild Side," *Boston Globe*, October 8, 1986: 81.

2   Ibid.

3   Ibid.

4   Leigh Montville. "Sure Bet Became Uncertain," *Boston Globe*, October 8, 1986: 1.

5   Larry Whiteside. "Roger—Down and Out, 8-1," *Boston Globe*, October 8, 1986: 81.

6   Leigh Montville.

7   Ibid.

8   Dan Shaughnessy. "Witt a Big Hit," *Boston Globe*, October 8, 1986: 81.

9   Larry Whiteside.

OCTOBER 7, 1986: BOSTON RED SOX 9, CALIFORNIA ANGELS 2, AT FENWAY PARK

1986 AMERICAN LEAGUE CHAMPIONSHIP SERIES GAME TWO

By Allan Wood

THE ANGELS WERE NO MATCH FOR BOSTON left-hander Bruce Hurst and an unforgiving afternoon sun as the Red Sox tied the series at one game apiece.

Boston right fielder Dwight Evans—a veteran of Fenway Park's sun and wind patterns since 1972—knew the day would be trouble before the game began at 3:00 P.M. "It's going to be rough. ... The sun is going to be in your eyes and the wind is going to make fly balls dance." Evans added: "It's going to be to our advantage."[1]

Angels manager Gene Mauch went with a different lineup against Hurst, with Rick Burleson leading off as the DH, George Hendrick in right field, and Bobby Grich at second base. The Red Sox used the same lineup as in Game One.

Boston began its revenge against the Angels for their Game One rout right away, scoring single runs in each of the first two innings off California starter Kirk McCaskill. Wade Boggs opened the first with a triple high off the wall in left-center. Gary Pettis misplayed the carom and Hendrick overthrew the cutoff man as Boggs slid safely into third.

Pettis said the ball took a "kangaroo bounce," adding, "What could I do? I thought I was in the right place. Strange."[2] Boggs: "The warning track is like concrete. I knew that ball was going to bounce if it hit the track."[3]

Marty Barrett worked a full count, then doubled down the right-field line. Boggs scored easily. After Bill Buckner lined to center, Jim Rice grounded to shortstop. Barrett was caught off the bag and tagged by Angels shortstop Dick Schofield. Don Baylor lined

a single off the scoreboard and Rice sprinted to third. Both runners were stranded when Dwight Evans flied to center for the third out.

Rich Gedman opened the second inning with a single to left-center. After Tony Armas struck out, Spike Owen reached first when his high chopper to shortstop took a bad hop over Schofield's head (it may have hit the spot where the infield grass meets the dirt). Boggs then chopped an 0-and-2 pitch to McCaskill, who misplayed the ball. It hit off his chest and dropped to the ground, and the Red Sox had the bases loaded.

"I've never lost a groundball in the sun before," McCaskill said. "It was unbelievable. I knew exactly where it was going to be. I went to make the play and then I lost it in the sun. I had to try and make a blind stab at it and I missed."[4]

Barrett lined a single to left, scoring Gedman. Buckner, who ended four different innings in Game One, ended this rally by grounding into a 3-6-1 double play.

The Angels tied the game against Hurst with single runs in the fourth and fifth. Leadoff singles from Brian Downing and Doug DeCinces and a one-out fielding error by Boggs loaded the bases for California in the fourth. Schofield grounded a pitch to the right of shortstop Spike Owen, who tried getting a force at third, but had trouble getting the ball out of his glove. His toss to Boggs was late, and Downing scored. Hurst rebounded, however, retiring Bob Boone on an infield popup and Gary Pettis on a liner to short center.

Wally Joyner homered to right-center with one down in the fifth, tying the game at 2-2. It was the first time a rookie had hit a home run in an ALCS.

Boston broke the tie in its half of the fifth. Buckner singled with one out and Baylor walked with two out. Dwight Evans was credited with a double on a popup that fell beyond Grich's reach in short right field. Buckner scored, giving Boston a 3-2 lead.

"I look up and the first thing I see is sun," Grich said. "So I'm blinded momentarily, I fire my glasses up, I look down momentarily and when I look up again, the ball is drifting back. So I went back on it, but by then the ball was in the wind, drifting back, and I could not get to it in time."[5]

Evans: "It was one of those balls that you don't know really where it was going to wind up. They played it right and waited until it came out of the sun. But the wind caught it. When I saw them look at each other, I knew it was trouble."[6]

In the sixth inning, the Angels stroked three straight singles off Hurst, but did not score. With Grich on second and Schofield on first and one out, Boone grounded a hard single into left. Jim Rice charged the ball. Grich rounded third and glanced at third-base coach Moose Stubing, who did not give a sign one way or the other. Grich instinctively put on the brakes and tried to scamper back to the base. Boggs leapt to cut off Rice's throw to the plate and tossed the ball quickly to Owen, who tagged out Grich. Grich was furious. He slammed his helmet to the ground and threw his arms up in the air. Grich continued yelling in the dugout as Hurst fanned Pettis for the third out. The misplay erased any momentum the Angels might have had. They would not threaten at all in the final three innings.

Grich: "I'm running as hard as I can and everything in my mind is to score a run. Now I've got to rely on my third-base coach. I didn't see his hands in the air, I took my three or four strides beyond third and then I realize he's telling me to hold up. So I tried to stop, lost my footing and I could not get back."[7]

Stubing took full responsibility for the play, admitting he "waited too long to commit."[8] Stubing said he did not see Boggs in position to cut off Rice's throw. "I

thought the throw was going all the way to home."[9] Stubing said he was yelling at Grich, but was late in putting up his arms to stop the runner.

Grich: "That's not the first time I've thrown my helmet. It was not a class act, it was just an emotional act, and I wasn't thinking. … I just snapped. … I didn't mean to show [Stubing] up, that's not professionalism. The first thing I said to him was, 'Moose, I'm sorry I showed you up, my man, but Moose, I've got to see some hands on that play.' "[10]

The Red Sox put the game away with three runs in both the seventh and eighth innings. Hurst went the distance, pitching what he described as a "nifty 11-hitter."[11] Hurst had missed nearly two months of the season with a groin pull, but returned in August in top form. He went 5-0 in September with two shutouts and a 1.07 ERA. On this afternoon, the *Globe* called Hurst "an island of sanity in a roiling whirlpool of silliness."[12]

Evans: "It was one of the toughest days I've ever seen here. … The sun was very bright and low. My sunglasses were so little help I took them off … after I lost Rick Burleson's pop fly in the seventh."[13]

Bob Boone said it was the toughest game he'd ever played in the sun.[14] "It seems like any time a team comes in here and isn't used to this place, miscommunications happen."[15]

| California Angels | - | 000 110 000 | - | 2 | 11 | 3 |
| Boston Red Sox | - | 110 010 33x | - | 9 | 13 | 2 |

NOTES

1   Leigh Montville, "Last Laugh in Comedy Of Errors," *Boston Globe*, October 9, 1986: 1.

2   Ibid.

3   Ibid.

4   George Kimball, "The Sunny Side of the Park," *Boston Herald*, October 9, 1986: 96.

5   Michael Madden, "For Grich and Angels, This Was a Lost Cause," *Boston Globe*, October 9, 1986: 49.

6   Larry Whiteside, "Hurst, Sun Shine for Sox; Lefty Stifles Angels; Misplays Do Rest, 9-2," *Boston Globe*, October 9, 1986: 49.

7   Michael Madden.

8   Charles Pierce, "Moose Stubs Toe At Third," *Boston Herald*, October 9, 1986: 98.

9   Michael Madden.

10 Ibid.

11 John Powers, "An Island in the Storm; Hurst's Composure Keeps Red Sox on an Even Keel," *Boston Globe*, October 9, 1986: 50.

12 Ibid.

13 Tim Horgan. "Wind and Sun Add Up to Wackiness," *Boston Herald*, October 9, 1986: 97.

14 Leigh Montville.

15 Lesley Visser. "Evans Shines on a Bright Day," *Boston Globe*, October 9, 1986: 55.

OCTOBER 10, 1986: CALIFORNIA ANGELS 5, BOSTON RED SOX 3, AT ANAHEIM STADIUM

1986 AMERICAN LEAGUE CHAMPIONSHIP SERIES GAME THREE

By Allan Wood

CALIFORNIA STARTER JOHN CANDALERIA pitched seven strong innings and the Angels got seventh-inning home runs from Dick Schofield and Gary Pettis and beat the Boston Red Sox, 5-3. The victory, which gave the Angels a 2-1 lead in the ALCS, provided some comfort to Angels manager Gene Mauch, who was ejected in the fourth inning after a lengthy argument about a play at the plate.

After going down in order in the first, the Red Sox took an early lead in the second. Jim Rice worked an eight-pitch walk and Don Baylor ripped a single past third baseman Doug DeCinces. While Dwight Evans was batting, Angels catcher Bob Boone picked Baylor off first base. Evans capped a 10-pitch at-bat with a hard single to left; Rice stopped at third. Rich Gedman grounded a single up the middle and Rice scored. Candaleria regrouped and retired the next two batters to hold Boston to one run.

Red Sox starter Dennis "Oil Can" Boyd — the subject of a pregame rumor broadcast by a Boston TV station that he had been in a car accident the night before[1] — looked superb in the early innings, facing the minimum number of batters through the first three innings. Boyd walked Pettis to open the first, but the speedy Angels outfielder was caught stealing.

In the bottom of the fourth, Wally Joyner and Brian Downing singled with one out. After Reggie Jackson popped up to shortstop, DeCinces squibbed the ball down the first-base line. The ball hugged the foul line and eventually hit the bag in fair territory. Both Boyd and first baseman Bill Buckner were watching the ball. Buckner grabbed it and fired it home. Joyner tried to score standing up and Gedman tagged him. Home-plate umpire Terry Cooney called Joyner safe, giving the Angels the game-tying run.

Gedman and Boyd were furious at the call and they argued vehemently. Cooney then asked the other umpires for help and third-base umpire Rich Garcia — who perhaps had the best view of the play — called Joyner out. And so the call was reversed, wiping the run off the board and ending the inning.

This time, it was Mauch's turn to rage at the umpires, which he did for close to 10 minutes. At one point, first-base umpire Nick Bremigan charged toward Mauch, but he was held back by another umpire. Bremigan ejected Mauch from the game.

ABC had 10 cameras at the game, but none of them captured a definitive look at the play. Additionally, it appeared as though all the ensuing fuss could have been avoided if Buckner — who was behind the first-base bag — grabbed the ball before it hit the base and either stepped on the base or tagged DeCinces.

Joyner: "I saw the ball getting away, so I came home. As I was approaching the plate, I saw Gedman reaching for the ball and so I figured I'd be out if I slid. I tried to step around him."[2]

Gedman: "I didn't have time to look to see what was happening. I didn't know if he was sliding or not but I thought he would be. … So I just caught the ball, whirled, and reached down with the tag. I got him … he stepped on my foot anyway. But I got him even before he stepped on me."[3]

Joyner: "Gedman did tag me. But I had landed on his foot and the plate before he did."

Gedman: "I went to Cooney—I couldn't believe he had called Joyner safe—and I was shouting at him, 'I got him! I tagged him out!' and that's when Cooney said to me, 'Wait a minute, wait a minute.' That's when he went to the third-base umpire [Garcia]."[4]

Cooney asked Garcia if Gedman had tagged Joyner. Garcia said yes. Garcia: "Cooney said that he felt if the runner had been tagged, he was out but that he had made the original call of safe because he did not see a tag."[5] Garcia then complicated the matter by adding, "I never said he was out at the plate; I only answered Cooney's question of whether a tag had been made."[6]

Joyner was playing in the game despite suffering the effects of an insect bite. "When I was playing in the second game, I thought someone must have stepped on me. ... I was sick all night with a 102-degree fever. I thought I had the flu."[7]

Boston—still leading 1-0—wasted a golden scoring opportunity in the fifth. Gedman looped a single into right-center and Tony Armas doubled off the wall in right. Right fielder Ruppert Jones appeared able to catch the ball, but he leapt at the wall too early and the ball caromed off the fence beside him. With runners at second and third and no outs, Boston did not hit the ball out of the infield. Owen grounded out to Joyner at first. Wade Boggs walked, loading the bases. Marty Barrett fouled out to first and Bill Buckner grounded to first.

The Angels tied the game in the sixth. Joyner walked with one out, took second on a failed fielder's choice attempt, and scored on Jackson's hard single through the infield into right. Boyd was furious as the game was tied 1-1 and manager John McNamara came out to the mound to calm him down. Boyd then got DeCinces to ground into an inning-ending double play.

California got to Boyd in the next inning. The Can retired the first two batters, but then Schofield connected with a hanging slider and homered to left. Bob Boone lined a single to center and Pettis hit a two-run homer to right, giving the Angels a 4-1 lead. Joe Sambito came out of the Red Sox pen to record the third out.

Boston came right back in the top of the eighth, scoring twice against Angels closer Donnie Moore. Marty Barrett singled and, one out later, Jim Rice doubled him to third. Moore balked Barrett home and, after a popup and a walk to Dwight Evans, Rich Gedman singled, scoring Rice and cutting the Angels' lead to 4-3.

The Angels grabbed an insurance run off Calvin Schiraldi in the eighth. Reggie Jackson walked with one out, went to third on an error by Wade Boggs, and scored on a sacrifice fly by Ruppert Jones.

With the Red Sox trailing by two runs, Mike Greenwell pinch-hit for Spike Owen to start the Red Sox ninth and flied out to center. Boggs also flied out to center, the ninth putout of the night for Pettis. Barrett lined a 2-and-1 pitch to right field for a single and Bill Buckner stood in as the potential tying run. But Buckner swung at Moore's first pitch and flied out to left.

It was announced before the game that Boston's Roger Clemens—who allowed a career-high eight runs in Game One—would start Game Four on three days of rest, something he had not yet done in his major-league career. Red Sox manager John McNamara's reasoning was simple: "You go with your best. If you're in a seven-game series, you go with your best pitcher three times."[8] McNamara was not concerned that Clemens had thrown 143 pitches in Game One. "I don't think that's high at all. He's a young kid."[9]

TV Note: When ABC showed replays of Pettis being thrown out trying to steal second in the first inning, it appeared as though Boston shortstop Spike Owen failed to tag the runner. This prompted a bizarre exchange in which analyst Jim Palmer maintained that if the catcher's throw beat the runner to the bag, it was not important whether the fielder tagged the runner; the mere "appearance" of a tag was enough. Al Michaels, ABC's play-by-play man, agreed, saying that as long as the fundamentals of the team in the field were sound, the out call was justified even if the runner was not tagged.

```
Boston Red Sox     -   010 000 020  -  3   9   1
California Angels  -   000 001 31x  -  5   8   0
```

NOTES

1   Jack Craig. "No Legwork, or Truth, in Report," *Boston Globe*, October 11, 1986: 31.

2   Michael Madden. "It Was Just Your Typical Safe/Out Call," *Boston Globe*, October 11, 1986: 25.

3   Ibid.

4   Ibid.

5   Ibid.

6   Ibid.

7   John Powers, Dan Shaughnessy, and Larry Whiteside. "They Seek a Throne," *Boston Globe*, October 11, 1986: 29.

8   Larry Whiteside. "McNamara Move Overshadows Game 3," *Boston Globe*, October 10, 1986: 51.

9   Leigh Montville. "They Decided to Gamble With Their Ace," *Boston Globe*, October 10, 1986: 51.

OCTOBER 10, 1986: CALIFORNIA ANGELS 4, BOSTON RED SOX 3 (11 INNINGS), AT ANAHEIM STADIUM

1986 AMERICAN LEAGUE CHAMPIONSHIP SERIES GAME FOUR

By Allan Wood

THE ANGELS RALLIED FOR THREE RUNS IN the bottom of the ninth inning against Roger Clemens and Calvin Schiraldi, and won the game, 4-3, in the 11th when Bobby Grich's one-out single scored Jerry Narron. California took a three-games-to-one lead in the best-of-seven ALCS, and put themselves one victory away from the franchise's first trip to the World Series.

For the Angels, it was yet another comeback in a season full of them. California led the American League with seven ninth-inning rallies in 1986, and became the first team to win an ALCS game in which it entered the ninth inning trailing by more than one run.

Before all that excitement, though, the game began as a pitchers' duel between Clemens and Don Sutton, California's 41-year-old starter. Clemens, who threw 143 pitches in Game One, was pitching on three days of rest for the first time. During the regular season, Clemens won 14 times after a Red Sox loss and his teammates needed him to come back strong after Boston lost Game Three. And although Clemens was somewhat erratic, giving up three hits and three walks in the first five innings, he kept the Angels off the scoreboard. Indeed, no Angels runner reached third base until the momentous ninth inning.

The Angels played without rookie first baseman Wally Joyner, who was hospitalized with a bacterial infection in his lower right leg. George Hendrick, usually an outfielder, took over at first.

The veteran Sutton, who overcame a rough start to the regular season and posted a 2.83 ERA after June

1, was superb through the first five innings, allowing only one baserunner: Wade Boggs's leadoff double in the fourth. In that frame, Marty Barrett bunted Boggs to third, but Sutton calmly worked out of the jam, getting Bill Buckner on a fly to short right and Jim Rice on a liner to shortstop.

California had its best scoring chance against Clemens in the bottom of the fourth. Brian Downing worked a nine-pitch walk to open the inning. Reggie Jackson flied to deep center. Doug DeCinces hit a grounder into the shortstop hole. Spike Owen ranged to his right and threw across his body to second base for the force, but his throw was low and got past Marty Barrett; it was Owen's third error of the series. The Angels had runners at first and second with one out. Hendrick hit a chopper up the middle and Owen was able to grab it, step on the bag and throw to first for an inning-ending double play.

Boston finally broke through against Sutton in the sixth. Tony Armas (1-for-12 in the series) lined a single to center and was bunted to second by Owen. Armas took third on Boggs's grounder to the right side and, after Barrett walked, he scored when Buckner ripped a double down the right-field line. Only a quick throw to the infield from right fielder Ruppert Jones held Barrett at third. Rice made the third out, but the Red Sox had a 1-0 lead.

Boston wasted a leadoff double from Don Baylor in the seventh, but struck for two runs in the eighth. It was an inning full of problems for the Angels, as it included two errors, a wild pitch, and a passed ball. Owen began with a groundball single off Vern

Ruhle. Boggs hit a grounder to second. Bobby Grich wanted to go to second and start a possible double play, but he bobbled the ball and had to take the sure out at first. Ruhle's wild pitch moved Barrett to third and he scored when Marty Barrett sliced a single to right-center, giving Boston a 2-0 lead. Chuck Finley relieved Ruhle. With Buckner batting, Boone's passed ball put Barrett at second. Buckner hit a hard shot to Grich, but the ball bounced off his glove into short right field. By the time Grich tracked it down, Barrett had scored. Doug Corbett was the next California pitcher. Jim Rice reached base when his groundball went through DeCinces' legs for an error. Don Baylor struck out and, after a walk to Evans that loaded the bases, Rich Gedman grounded into a fielder's choice.

The eight-batter Red Sox rally was time-consuming and Clemens may have been a bit rusty from sitting during the top half of the eighth. Jones smoked his first pitch of the inning into the right-field corner for a double and Bobby Grich battled for eight pitches before hitting a hard fly to center. Clemens struck out Brian Downing on a high full-count fastball and got Reggie Jackson on a grounder to second.

Boston manager John McNamara let Clemens, at 123 pitches, start the bottom of the ninth. During the regular season, the Red Sox were 83-1 in games in which they entered the ninth inning with a lead. Doug DeCinces blasted Clemens's 1-0 pitch over the fence in left center, giving the Angels their first run. Clemens got a groundout from George Hendrick, but gave up line-drive singles to Dick Schofield and Bob Boone. And finally, after 134 pitches, Clemens was lifted in favor of Calvin Schiraldi.

Gary Pettis looked at a ball, then drove the ball to deep left. Jim Rice took a couple of steps in, then tried to get back. He couldn't. The ball sailed over his head and one-hopped the wall. Schofield scored and Devon White (who was pinch-running for Boone) went to third. McNamara: "He just lost it. He said he lost the ball."[1]

After Jones was intentionally walked, loading the bases, Schiraldi fanned Grich for the second out.

Brian Downing took massive swings at Schiraldi's first two pitches, fouling one off, and falling behind 0-and-2. Schiraldi was one pitch away from nailing down a nailbiting 3-2 win, and tying the series at two games apiece, but his 1-and-2 offering slipped and hit Downing in the left thigh, forcing in the tying run. Schiraldi recovered to retire Jackson, but the game headed into extra innings.

"I had the situation in my hand," Schiraldi said. "And I bleeped it up. It was the first time that I didn't do my job in that situation. I wanted the game, I wanted that situation, and I blew it."[2]

Grich said afterward that Boone's single, Clemens's last batter, gave the team "a shot in the arm. That's when we really thought we could do it. Then there was Pettis's ball—Rice screwed it up in the lights or something—and we were on our way from that point on. The guys on the bench were just screaming and yelling."[3]

Angels reliever Doug Corbett had recorded the last two outs in the eighth inning—and he retired the Red Sox in order in the ninth, 10th, and 11th innings, allowing only two balls out of the infield.

Schiraldi breezed through the 10th on nine pitches, but surrendered a hard single to right field to backup catcher Jerry Narron in the bottom of the 11th. "I was looking for the fastball," Narron said, "something I could drive. I hooked it a bit, but it stayed fair."[4]

Pettis bunted Narron to second and Ruppert Jones was intentionally walked (his fourth walk of the night). Grich, who had seen 15 pitches in his last two plate appearances, wasted no time in this at-bat. He lined Schiraldi's first offering into left field. Rice grabbed the ball near the foul line and threw it in, but he had no chance to get Narron, who easily scored the winning run.

Thirty minutes after the game ended, Schiraldi was still in his uniform. "I screwed up. No question about it." He said the pitch to Pettis was "down and away, pretty much what I wanted to do with it," while the ball that plunked Downing and tied the game was the "worst pitch I ever made in my life."⁵

For Boston, lefty Bruce Hurst would pitch Game Five on three days of rest against Game One winner Mike Witt, as the Red Sox tried to keep their season alive.

```
Boston Red Sox    -  000 001 020 0  -  3   6 1
California Angels -  000 000 003 01-  4   112
```

NOTES

1   Leigh Montville. "Rice Lost the Ball and the Ballgame," *Boston Globe*, October 12, 1986: 29.

2   John Powers. "Sox on Top, Then Flop, 4-3; It Was a Disastrous Close for the Closer," *Boston Globe*, October 12, 1986: 29.

3   Ian Thomsen. "A Down-And-Up Ride for Grich," *Boston Globe*, October 12, 1986: 36.

4   Lesley Visser. "Corbett, Narron Surprised Heroes," *Boston Globe*, October 12, 1986: 36.

5   John Powers.

OCTOBER 12, 1986: BOSTON RED SOX 7, CALIFORNIA ANGELS 6 (11 INNINGS), AT ANAHEIM STADIUM

1986 AMERICAN LEAGUE CHAMPIONSHIP SERIES GAME FIVE

By Allan Wood

BEFORE THERE WAS DAVID ORTIZ, THERE was Dave Henderson. Before Big Papi thrilled Red Sox fans with his October heroics, the man they called Hendu brought Boston back from the dead in Game Five of the 1986 ALCS.

With the Angels one strike away from winning the pennant, Henderson—a backup outfielder obtained from the Seattle Mariners in mid-August—crushed a home run that gave Boston a 6-5 lead. Then, after the Angels tied the game in their half of the ninth, Henderson knocked in the game-winning run with a sacrifice fly in the 11th. The Red Sox' 7-6 victory sent the ALCS back to Fenway Park for Game Six (and, possibly, Game Seven). (Henderson also homered in the 10th inning of Game Six of the 1986 World Series; it would have been the Red Sox' World Series-winning run if not for the Mets' comeback.)

The California Angels led this series three games to one and fully expected to clinch the pennant in front of their own fans. Before the game, Red Sox players cited the Kansas City Royals, who came from being down 1-3 in both the ALCS (against Toronto) and World Series (against St. Louis) to capture a world championship.

With his team's backs to the wall, manager John McNamara gave the ball to Bruce Hurst, who had pitched a complete-game victory in Game Two. Like Roger Clemens in Game Four, Hurst would be starting on three days' rest. The Red Sox faced Mike Witt, who had gone the distance in California's Game One win.

Boston drew first blood in the second inning, when Jim Rice led off with a single and Rich Gedman lined a two-run homer into the right-field seats.

Hurst ended up pitching six innings, and left the game trailing 3-2. Bob Boone led off the third inning with a solo home run down by the left-field corner. With two outs in the sixth, Doug DeCinces ripped a double into the gap in right-center. Bobby Grich, who had struck out in his two earlier at-bats, drove a 1-and-2 pitch to deep left-center. Dave Henderson, who had taken over for Tony Armas in center field in the previous inning, raced toward the wall. Henderson timed his leap perfectly and the ball landed squarely in his glove. But his momentum carried him into the wall and his wrist struck the top of the fence. The collision jarred the ball loose and it fell over the fence. It was a two-run homer for Grich—and the Angels led 3-2.

"I thought I had it all the way," Henderson said. "But when my wrist hit the top of the fence it shook the ball loose and it was out of there. I was really disappointed, because I thought I should have caught it."[1]

California added two runs off reliever Bob Stanley in the seventh, and led 5-2.

Meanwhile, Witt was (again) having little trouble with the Boston hitters. After Gedman's blast in the second, Witt retired the next eight batters and 10 of the next 11. Gedman broke up Witt's string with a one-out double in the fifth, but Armas flied to left and Spike Owen grounded to second. Boston had men on base in the sixth, seventh, and eighth innings, but could not get anyone past first base.

The Anaheim Stadium crowd was roaring as Witt faced the heart of the Red Sox order in the ninth inning. Three more outs—and the Angels would clinch their first-ever pennant. Bill Buckner grounded a single up the middle, and was replaced by pinch-runner Dave Stapleton. Jim Rice fouled off two pitches, then looked at strike three on the outside edge.

Don Baylor worked the count to 2-and-2 and took a very close pitch that was inside and called a ball. Witt's full-count pitch was outside, but Baylor reached out and hooked it, pulling it to deep left. The ball carried and carried, sailing over the fence for a two-run homer. The crowd was quieter, but they knew their Angels still held a 5-4 lead—and when Dwight Evans fouled to third for the second out, they began loudly cheering again.

One out away—and Gene Mauch came out of the dugout to make a pitching change. He wanted left-hander Gary Lucas to face Gedman, who had singled, doubled, and homered against Witt. Gedman had faced Lucas only twice before—July 27, 1986, and in Game Four of this ALCS—and he had struck out both times.

Witt, who had thrown 123 pitches, said he was not tired. "I felt like I was pitching from the seventh inning on, on adrenaline mostly. But I was getting people out. … I called Boone out. We were going to discuss how we were going to handle [Gedman]. But … we never got to discuss it."[2]

Lucas threw only one pitch—and it sailed up and in and hit Gedman on the right hand. As the Boston catcher trotted to first base, Mauch made another change, bringing in closer Donnie Moore to face Dave Henderson. Henderson took a ball low, then a strike that was a little higher. When he swung and missed on a pitch low and away, Moore and the Angels were one strike away.

Dave Stapleton: "I looked across the field and I could see everyone in the Angels dugout getting ready to celebrate. … They had those nice little smiles that you get before you start hugging everyone."[3]

Moore threw ball two in the dirt, and Henderson fouled off two pitches. Moore's 2-and-2 pitch—the seventh pitch of the at-bat—came in a little low. Henderson swung and as soon as he hit it, he knew. The ball sailed far over the fence in left for a two-run home run—a shot that gave the Red Sox a 6-5 lead. Henderson took three steps out of the batter's box, watching the flight of the ball. As it cleared the fence, he jumped and spun around. And then he began a fast trot around the bases.[4]

Henderson: "The pitch I fouled off was a fastball I should have hit. I had to step out of the batter's box and gather myself, think about what I had to do. With two strikes I had to protect the plate. I really just wanted to reach down and make sure I at least put the ball in play."[5]

Moore: "I'd been throwing him fastballs, and he was fouling them off, fouling them off. Then I threw him an offspeed pitch and I shouldn't have thrown it. I should have stayed with the hard stuff. The kind of bat speed he has is offspeed. That pitch was right in his swing."[6]

Stanley began the bottom of the ninth—his third inning of work—by giving up a single to Boone. Ruppert Jones pinch-ran, and Gary Pettis bunted him to second. Lefty Joe Sambito came out of the bullpen. Rob Wilfong knocked Sambito's first pitch into right field. Dwight Evans charged the ball and made an accurate throw home, but Jones was too speedy and he slid in ahead of the tag. The game was tied: 6-6.

McNamara vowed before the game to stay away from Calvin Schiraldi, who had pitched in Games Three and Four, so he went with Steve Crawford, essentially the last man on the staff. Schofield lined a single to right, sending Wilfong (carrying the AL pennant in his back pocket) to third base. The Red Sox intentionally walked Brian Downing, setting up a force at any base. With both the infield and outfield playing in, DeCinces flied out to short right field, too shallow for Wilfong to tag up. Bobby Grich then lined a pitch right back to the mound, which Crawford speared easily in his follow-through. Game Five went to extra innings.

The Angels nearly won the game in the bottom of the 10th, when Gary Pettis hit a drive to deep left field. Rice, with his back to the wall, caught the ball over his head for the third out.

Moore hit Don Baylor to begin the Red Sox 11th. Evans singled to center. Gedman popped up a bunt attempt to third. DeCinces barehanded the ball on a bounce, but his throw was off target, and the bases were loaded. Henderson swung at Moore's first pitch and flied to center—scoring Baylor and giving Boston a 7-6 lead.

Schiraldi ended up pitching in the game after all, coming in to face the top of the California order in the bottom of the 11th. He struck out Wilfong and Schofield, and ended the game when Downing fouled to first. "I was awake all night wondering if I'd ever get a chance to redeem myself," Schiraldi said, referring to his poor performance in Game Four. "This has to be the biggest game of my life."[7]

Boston Red Sox	020	000	004	01	-	7	12	0
California Angels	001	002	201	00	-	6	13	0

NOTES

1 George Kimball, "Henderson's Unlikely Hero," *Boston Herald*, October 13, 1986: 96.

2 Ian Thomsen, "Angels' Party Gets Crashed," *Boston Globe*, October 13, 1986: 46.

3 Leigh Montville, "It Ain't Over Till It's Over," *Boston Globe*, October 13, 1986: 1.

4 In the major leagues' first 648 postseason games, no team had ever taken a lead of two or more runs into the ninth inning and lost. And then it happened *twice* within 24 hours. In ALCS Game Four, on October 11, Boston held a 3-0 lead before the Angels tied it and won in 11 innings. The following day the Red Sox scored four times in the top of the ninth in Game Five, and eventually won in 11 innings. It happened *a third time*, on October 15, when the Astros blew a 3-0 lead in Game Six of the National League Championship Series, as the Mets came back to win the game (and the pennant), 7-6 in 16 innings.

5 George Kimball.

6 Ian Thomsen.

7 Joe Giuliotti, "Schiraldi Gets Redemption," *Boston Herald*, October 13, 1986: 74.

OCTOBER 14, 1986: BOSTON RED SOX 10, CALIFORNIA ANGELS 4, AT FENWAY PARK

1986 AMERICAN LEAGUE CHAMPIONSHIP SERIES GAME SIX

By Allan Wood

TWO DAYS AND 3,000 MILES AWAY FROM ITS improbable 11th-inning victory in Game Five of the American League Championship Series, the Boston Red Sox continued their march toward the AL pennant with another elimination-game victory. Back home in Fenway Park, the Red Sox batted around in the third inning, scoring five times off Angels starter Kirk McCaskill, and won Game Six easily.

The day before the game, Red Sox starter Dennis "Oil Can" Boyd called his assignment "the biggest game I've ever pitched. … I have to pitch the best game I've ever pitched."[1]

Boston second baseman Marty Barrett said his teammates were feeling no pressure, despite trailing in the series, three games to two: "I was running in the outfield before the game and I said to myself, 'This is almost like a dream.' There was no pressure. None. We all felt we shouldn't even be playing this game. … The fifth game was our seventh game."[2]

Barrett hoped the Red Sox could get out to a quick lead. "We've got to jump on them for a change. … I'd like to see us get five or six runs in the first three innings."[3]

Boyd, pitching on short (three days) rest, had a rough beginning, throwing 44 pitches in the first inning and giving up two runs, the runs scoring on consecutive doubles by Reggie Jackson and Doug DeCinces. With two outs and the bases full of Angels, Red Sox reliever Al Nipper was warming up in the bullpen and Boyd was likely one more hit away from being taken out of the game. Boyd battled Rob Wilfong for 11 pitches—Wilfong fouled off eight straight of-

ferings—and got him to pop up to first for the third out. (While it's hard to label a play in the top of the first inning as the turning point in the game, retiring Wilfong was a critical out for the Red Sox. Barrett: "I don't think people realize how big that [out] was."[4])

"I really wanted Oil Can to get out of that jam because, ideally, we were hoping he'd give us seven innings," Red Sox manager John MacNamara said. "He was throwing the ball well, but I couldn't let him stay out there if he got us into a hole."[5]

"I went out there with the right idea," Boyd said, "but then I started rushing a little bit. The balls were feeling big in my hand. … I only yielded two runs. … I just have to leave that inning where it was."[6]

Boyd was instantly let off the hook as his teammates tied the score in the bottom half of the first, although they did not record a hit. Wade Boggs and Marty Barrett both walked; Boggs scored on a passed ball and Barrett scored on Jim Rice's groundout to second. Boyd: "The runs picked me up. … I knew a job had to be done and my guys had come to play."[7]

The Red Sox would not get their first hit until the third inning, when Spike Owen lined a single to center. Boggs followed with a single to right. Barrett, who led the American League in 1986 with 18 sacrifice bunts, tried to put one down, but failed. He then lined a 1-and-2 pitch into the left-center-field gap, scoring Owen. (Barrett was now 7-for-8 with runners in scoring position in the ALCS.) Bill Buckner followed with an RBI single to center and Boston led 4-2. After a visit to the mound, McCaskill got Rice to ground to third. DeCinces threw home and Barrett was caught in a rundown and eventually tagged out.

Don Baylor singled to right-center. Buckner hobbled to third on his bad ankles and did not try to score. However, Rice seemingly expected Buckner would be waved home; he rounded second and Baylor took a big turn at first. As the ball came in from the outfield, Rice scrambled to get back to second. Angels first baseman Bobby Grich cut the ball off on the third-base side of the mound. "I saw what I thought to be Rob Wilfong at first in a ready position," Grich said. "But when I let the throw go, I realized it was their first-base coach [Walt Hriniak]."[8] Grich's throw was wild. Buckner limped home and Rice was also awarded the plate. Baylor advanced to third and Boston led 6-2. Dwight Evans's short fly dropped into center field for a hit, bringing Baylor home. That was the end of McCaskill's night. The six hits he allowed in the inning tied an ALCS record. Left-handed reliever Gary Lucas struck out Rich Gedman and got Dave Henderson on a popup. Boston led 7-2.

Meanwhile, Boyd had settled down after his troubles in the opening inning. Oil Can stranded a man in scoring position in the second, and struck out two Angels in the third. Grich and Wilfong began the fourth inning with singles, but Boyd fanned Bob Boone and Gary Pettis, and retired Ruppert Jones on a fly ball into the right-field corner. A California single in the fifth was erased on a double play.

Boston added a run against Angels reliever Doug Corbett in the fifth inning. Baylor was hit by a pitch, and Evans and Gedman followed with singles, loading the bases. Henderson's hard smash to third hit off DeCinces' glove. He did recover in time to force Evans at third, but Baylor scored easily, making it 8-2.

Boston finished its scoring in the bottom of the seventh. Gedman singled, Henderson walked, and both came home on Spike Owen's triple into the triangle in center. Owen's fourth error of the series (which set an ALCS record) gave the Angels a run in the eighth, to complete the scoring.

Barrett's sixth-inning single was his 11th hit of the series, tying an ALCS record set by Chris Chambliss of the Yankees in 1976 and Fred Lynn of the Angels in 1982. However, both Chambliss and Lynn collected their hits when the ALCS was a best-of-five series.

Reggie Jackson set two ALCS batting records. His first-inning RBI was the 20th ALCS run batted in of his career, breaking George Brett's record. Jackson also broke Brett's record of 36 ALCS hits when he singled in the fifth inning.

California's rookie first baseman Wally Joyner remained back on the West Coast sidelined by a bacterial infection. According to an Angels spokesman, Joyner "had his shin lanced twice, but the swelling came back. Hopefully, he'll join us for Game Seven."[9]

Angels reliever Donnie Moore received two cortisone injections after Game Five — one for his arm and one for his rib cage. Moore: "The changeup is what really hurts. My arm doesn't hurt as much when I'm throwing a fastball or a slider. But you'd like to have command of all of your pitches."[10]

After the Game Six win, Roger Clemens — Boston's expected starter in a winner-take-all Game Seven — told reporters he was suffering from an allergic reaction that felt like a head cold or the flu. "I had a problem with people smoking on the charter flight home from California," Clemens said. "I'm allergic to smoke to a certain point. ... When it happens it breaks me out into a cold sweat. ... I started to feel it on the plane. I had some ice put on my face. ... Because of that, I couldn't do as much running as I normally would have done yesterday, the day before I pitch. ... My whole body feels weak. ... All I'm hoping is that this doesn't make my legs weak. ... I don't think it will affect my arm at all."[11]

```
California Angels  -  200 000 110 -  4 11 1
Boston Red Sox     -  205 010 20x - 10 16 1
```

NOTES

1   Joe Giuliotti, "Sox Hope It's in the Can," *Boston Herald*, October 15, 1986: 96.

2   Leigh Montville, "There's Only One Game That Matters Now," *Boston Globe*, October 15, 1986: 1.

3   Joe Giuliotti.

4   Lesley Visser, "Subtly, Barrett Makes His Mark," *Boston Globe*, October 15, 1986: 50.

5   Tim Horgan, "Straight-A Students," *Boston Herald*, October 15, 1986: 133.

6   Michael Madden, "New ID for Can," *Boston Globe*, October 15, 1986: 49.

7   Larry Whiteside, "Sox Take It to the Limit, 10-4; Blitzing of Angels Forces Showdown," *Boston Globe*, October 15, 1986: 49.

8   Joe Giuliotti.

9   Lesley Visser, "Joyner Still Hospitalized," *Boston Globe*, October 15, 1986: 51.

10 John Powers, Jackie MacMullan, Lesley Visser, Ian Thomsen, "Moore Gets Cortisone," *Boston Globe*, October 15, 1986: 54.

11 Roger Clemens, "Roger: I'll Be Ready," *Boston Herald*, October 15, 1986: 137.

OCTOBER 15, 1986: BOSTON RED SOX 8, CALIFORNIA ANGELS 1, AT FENWAY PARK

1986 AMERICAN LEAGUE CHAMPIONSHIP SERIES GAME SEVEN

By Allan Wood

THE BOSTON RED SOX CLINCHED THEIR 10TH American League pennant by winning their third straight elimination game — overcoming a one-game-to-three deficit and advancing to the World Series for the first time in 11 years. Roger Clemens, working on short rest for the second time in the series, pitched seven innings, allowing only one run and four hits. Red Sox second baseman Marty Barrett tied an American League Championship Series record with 11 hits and was named the series' Most Valuable Player.

There was little doubt about the outcome of this game. The Red Sox led 3-0 before the California Angels collected their first hit and they drove Angels starter John Candelaria from the mound with four runs in the fourth inning. (However, all seven runs charged to Candelaria were unearned.)

"The Red Sox ascended to what was thought to be an unreachable height last April," wrote Joe Giuliotti in the *Boston Herald*. "The victory by the team that was supposed to finish fifth, climaxed a long, uphill struggle that saw them turn back every challenge during the regular season and again in the playoffs."[1]

Tim Horgan of the *Herald* called Game Seven "a mere formality" and said the Red Sox have "become so coldly proficient that the pennant-clinching game was curiously devoid of suspense and emotion. ... Even the Red Sox' victory celebration was as orderly and decorous as the game itself. There's a professionalism bordering on ruthlessness in this ballclub that's tough to describe, but heartening."[2]

Boston DH Don Baylor believed that the Red Sox' remarkable comeback in the ninth inning of Game Five, when the Angels were one strike away from winning the pennant, "broke their morale. I really don't think they ever recovered from it. ... I think they were pressing, really trying to convince *themselves* that 1982 wasn't on their minds."[3] In the ALCS that season (a best-of-five), the Angels lost the pennant when they dropped three straight games to Milwaukee after winning the first two. (Baylor was a member of the Angels that season.)

Marty Barrett: "Since we came back from the grave Sunday, the pressure has been on the Angels. ... We've been playing with the house's money."[4] Barrett called the Red Sox' performance in the ALCS "the greatest comeback ever. We were dead in Anaheim, absolutely dead. I think that's why we played so loose."[5]

Dwight Evans, who homered in the seventh, said: "Before the game I said we had to go out and kick, grab, bite, scratch, punch, and do whatever we had to do to get there. And we did."[6]

Jim Rice began the second inning by reaching second base on a throwing error by California shortstop Dick Schofield. Don Baylor — the only Red Sox batter to hit safely in all seven games — singled to left and Rice held at third. Evans worked an eight-pitch walk to load the bases. Rice scored on Rich Gedman's grounder to second. Candelaria fell behind Dave Henderson, 3-and-1, then put him on intentionally. After Spike Owen popped up for the second out, Wade Boggs singled up the middle, scoring two more runs.

Boston stranded runners at second and third in the third inning, then put the game away in the fourth. Henderson reached third when his fly to deep center was dropped by Gary Pettis. He then scored on Owen's single to right, a sinking line drive that Ruppert Jones could not catch. Candelaria struck out Boggs and got Barrett to fly to center, but he walked Dave Stapleton (who had pinch-run for Bill Buckner in the previous inning). Jim Rice then blasted a three-run home run off the left-field light tower, giving the Red Sox a 7-0 lead and ending Candelaria's outing. Rice scored eight runs in the series, an ALCS record.

Clemens allowed only three hits, one walk, and two hit batsmen through seven innings, and the Angels managed to get only two runners past first base in that time. When Clemens allowed a leadoff single to Ruppert Jones in the eighth, Boston manager John McNamara went to the bullpen. Calvin Schiraldi gave up a single to Rick Burleson on his first pitch. He struck out Brian Downing and Reggie Jackson — with the Fenway Park fans roaring on every strike — before allowing a two-out hit to Doug DeCinces that brought home California's only run of the game.

Schiraldi struck out the side in the ninth — mowing down Gary Pettis and two pinch-hitters, Jack Howell and Jerry Narron — putting an exclamation point on the Red Sox' victory. "The adrenaline was flowing like it never has before. I was just throwing strikes, and they weren't swinging at them."[7] Schiraldi added that in the final inning, he had "to stop every now and then to catch [my] breath."[8]

The Fenway Park crowd of 33,001 had been celebrating since the sixth inning. When Evans hit a solo home run in the seventh, giving Boston an 8-0 lead, loud chants of "We want the Mets!" broke out. (The Mets had clinched the National League pennant with a 16-inning victory over the Astros earlier in the day.)

After seeing the Angels' fans signs in Game Four (e.g., "Another Boston Choke"), Red Sox fans countered with their own, using the initials of the station broadcasting the series: "Angels Bats Choke," "Atta Boy Clemens," "Anaheim Bus — Catch It."

"Coming back home meant a lot to the ballclub," Jim Rice said. "We consider our 34,000 just as strong as their 64,000. Playing in your own backyard gives you a lift."[9]

Red Sox manager John McNamara said that Clemens was "under the weather" and he spoke to his starting pitcher after every inning, beginning in the fifth. "After the seventh he said he was getting a little wobbly. He said he could give me one more inning but I wasn't going to let him stay out there if he retired Jones. We were just waiting for Schiraldi to get ready."[10]

Clemens: "In the fifth inning I knew I wasn't going to be able to finish. I could feel myself getting dizzy. … I felt weak and knew I needed good pitches to get the maximum out of my legs to get those innings in. I had to really drive."[11] Clemens ended up throwing 93 pitches in his third start of the series.

The Angels, who had been one pitch away from their first-ever pennant, were crushed. "I don't have a hell of a lot to say," manager Gene Mauch said. "Except that I hurt like hell for those players. They laid their hearts out there and it got stepped on. Eight months of hard work."[12]

The Angels played the final four games without Wally Joyner, their outstanding rookie first baseman, who batted .445 in the first three games but suffered a bacterial infection in his lower right leg.

Donnie Moore, the losing pitcher in Boston's epic Game Five win, retired the Red Sox in order in a meaningless eighth inning. "I accept the fact that I am the goat of the series," Moore said. "It's just going to have to be something I live with."[13]

Marty Barrett believed that the Angels' spirits were broken when they lost Game Five. "They were in their dugouts with the security guards, the way we were tonight. I heard their batboys already had the champagne uncorked. They had it. They had it dangling in front of them."[14]

"We've had so much magic this year," Wade Boggs said. "Look at the ways we've won. Something weird's always happened when we needed it. Always."[15]

The front page of the *Boston Herald* said it best: "Bring On The Mets!"

```
California Angels  -  000 000 010 -  1  6  2
Boston Red Sox     -  030 400 10x -  8  8  1
```

NOTES

1   Joe Giuliotti, "Champions!," *Boston Herald*, October 16, 1986: 104.

2   Tim Horgan, "Welcome to the End of an Era," *Boston Herald*, October 16, 1986: 95.

3   George Kimball, "Dignity, Destiny," *Boston Herald*, October 16, 1986: 91.

4   Tim Horgan.

5   Lesley Visser, "Barrett's Game Second to None," *Boston Globe*, October 16, 1986: 46.

6   Joe Giuliotti, "Sox Rout Angels," *Boston Herald*, October 16, 1986: 90.

7   Charles Pierce, "Fenway Showdown Becomes a Carnival," *Boston Herald*, October 16, 1986: 93.

8   Leigh Montville, "It's a Flag for Fenway; Next, a New York-Boston World Series," *Boston Globe*, October 16, 1986: 1.

9   Dan Shaughnessy, "Finally, Rice Has Spotlight," *Boston Globe*, October 16, 1986: 45.

10 Joe Giuliotti, "Sox Rout Angels."

11 Roger Clemens, "Clemens Credits Team Support for His Success," *Boston Herald*, October 16, 1986: 92.

12 John Powers, "Another Bitter Pill for Mauch," *Boston Globe*, October 16, 1986: 49.

13 Charles Pierce, "No Party for Fallen Angels," *Boston Herald*, October 16, 1986: 94.

14 David Cataneo. "Barrett Proves He's Valuable Property," *Boston Herald*, October 16, 1986: 96.

15 Leigh Montville.

WHY WAS BILL BUCKNER STILL ON THE FIELD AT THE END OF GAME SIX?

MANY SOX FANS ARE STILL UPSET THAT manager John McNamara did not put Dave Stapleton into Game Six of the 1986 World Series as a late-inning defensive replacement for Bill Buckner, as he so often did during the season itself. Stapleton played his entire major-league career with the Red Sox (1980-1986).[1]

Pity that John McNamara did not employ "our" Dave Stapleton as he usually did. It may have saved the day (and helped Boston win the World Series) had our guy been at first base. It would probably have been a routine play and no one would remember it today—there likely wouldn't have even been a controversy regarding ownership of the baseball. Many fans probably wouldn't even recall Stapleton, even though he did get two hits in three American League Championship Series at-bats. Stapleton is more remembered for the play he never got the chance to make.

During the 1986 regular season, Stapleton appeared in 39 ballgames, twice exclusively as a pinch-hitter. He started eight games. The other 29 times he was inserted into the game as a late-inning defensive replacement, sometimes first as a pinch-runner and sometimes first as a pinch-hitter. Twice he was inserted before the eighth, but the rest of the time it was in the eighth inning or later. He played first base most of the time, six times subbing for Don Baylor but mostly for Bill Buckner. He also played second base six times and third base twice. It wasn't for his average (he batted .128). It was for his defense; he handled 101 chances in 118 innings and never once made an error.

In the ALCS, Dave Stapleton appeared in four games:

Game Two—Came in to play the ninth, taking Buckner's place at first.

Game Five—After Buckner singled to lead off the ninth, Stapleton came in to run for him—and scored the first run of the four-run rally that gave the Red Sox the lead. The game went into extra innings, and he played the three final innings. He singled in his one at-bat.

Game Six—After Buckner singled in the sixth, Stapleton came in to run for him. He played the final three innings. He was 1-for-1 in his only at-bat.

Game Seven—After Buckner singled in the third, Stapleton came in to run for him. He played the final six innings. He was 0-for-1 in his only at-bat, but he walked in the fourth and scored.

In the ALCS, then, Stapleton played 13 innings on defense, replacing Buckner each and every time. He was 2-for-3 at the plate, walked once, and scored two runs. He had 13 chances on defense, and did not commit an error.

In the World Series, Stapleton appeared in three games.

Game One—He came in for defense and played first base for the final two innings of the game.

Game Two—After Buckner singled to lead off the eighth, Stapleton came in to run for him. He flied out in the ninth, and was 0-for-1 at the plate.

Game Five—He came in for defense and played first base for the ninth inning.

All in all, Stapleton played five innings on defense, with five chances, and did not commit an error.

Come Game Six, one might have expected Red Sox skipper McNamara to follow the pattern he himself had set in the regular season and in seven prior playoff games. He did not. Buckner flied out to end the top of the eighth. All the Red Sox needed was to get six

Courtesy of Bob Brady.

more outs, and Buckner was unlikely to come up to bat in the ninth. McNamara left Buckner at first base. Things happened.

The understanding is that McNamara left Buckner in the game, rather than replace him, out of sentiment—that he thought Buckner deserved the opportunity to be on the field to fully enjoy the moment the Red Sox won the world championship. Oil Can Boyd had a different take. In a 2015 interview, Boyd first noted all that Buckner had done for the team and how, almost all season long, he'd been banged up: "Everything that could be hurt on a ballplayer was hurt on him. Every game they had to cut him out of the [bandages he was wrapped in] and get him out of the ice pool. He got more than 600 at-bats that year." Baseball is a nine-on-nine game, Boyd said, and it was

disappointing to him to see how the media outside of Boston "turned the fans against a particular ballplayer for losing a ballgame. We know the game doesn't work like that. He was the best hitter we had on the ball team." In reviewing video of the play, he thinks there's a good chance Mookie Wilson was beating the pitcher to the bag and it wouldn't have mattered if Buckner had gloved the ball.

As far as McNamara's sentiment clouding his better judgment, Boyd doesn't feel that way. He understood how you'd give a guy like Buckner a break during the regular season, but, he said, "This is the World Series. I'm going to keep the most important players that got me here, they're going to be on the field until the ballgame ends. Dave Stapleton could have missed the same ball. You just don't take a guy out of a ballgame in the World Series and say I'm putting in my best defense. Bill Buckner stays on the ballfield until it's over with. You can't take Bill Buckner out of the lineup."[2]

SOURCES

This article is adapted from Bill Nowlin and Jim Prime's *The Red Sox World Series Encyclopedia [No Longer the Word's Shortest Book]* (Burlington, Massachusetts: Rounder Books, 2008), 218, 219.

NOTES

1   Oddly, there was another Dave Stapleton who played in 1987 and 1988, but he was a left-handed pitcher from Miami, Arizona, who appeared in 10 games for the Brewers. (He never made an error.) There is also another Bill Buckner, a right-handed pitcher who first broke into the major leagues in 2007. He was 3 years old at the time of the 1986 World Series.

2   Author interview with Dennis "Oil Can" Boyd, January 6, 2015.

THE REVENGE OF 1912

By David Kaiser

TWO OUTSTANDING TEAMS FROM THE LEADING baseball towns of the Northeast — New York and Boston — meet in an exciting World Series. Their rosters are loaded with future Hall of Famers, and their fans are probably the most raucous and devoted in the league. After a seesaw battle filled with close games, the deciding contest ends in the ninth inning with the teams in a tie. In the top of the 10th, the visitors push the lead run across the plate, and victory seems close at hand. But in the bottom of the inning, two catastrophic blunders by the visitors allow the home team first to tie the game on a base hit, and then to win it on a walk-off sacrifice fly. Not for 74 years will a team lose the World Series after coming so close to winning it — and that World Series, in 1986, will involve the same two cities, New York and Boston. The 1986 World Series was not simply the latest of a series of disastrous Red Sox near-misses, but rather a classic example of how what goes around, comes around.

The 1912 New York Giants and Boston Red Sox were super teams, each part of a long-running dynasty. Led by two Hall of Fame pitchers, Christy Mathewson and Rube Marquard, John McGraw's Giants won their second consecutive pennant with a record of 103 wins and 48 losses, slightly superior to the 108-54 record of the 1986 Mets. The 1912 Red Sox, one of the most dominant teams of all time, did even better with the help of their legendary outfield of Tris Speaker, Harry Hooper, and Duffy Lewis, going 105-47 with additional help from pitcher Smoky Joe Wood, who posted an extraordinary record of 34-5. While McGraw's team had been at least contenders for the pennant for about a decade, the Boston club had returned to the top for the first time since 1904 — when the Giants had refused to meet the champions of the upstart American League in what would have been the second modern World Series. The 1912 teams played one of the most exciting World Series of all time.

The Series opened in New York on October 8, and the Red Sox, behind Wood, survived a Giants rally in the bottom of the ninth to win, 4-3. The two teams (and an army of writers) took the five-hour train ride between New York and Boston every day, alternating games without one day off. In the second game, held at Fenway, Mathewson — whom McGraw had decided not to pitch against Wood — lasted the entire game, which was called for darkness at the end of 11 innings, tied 6-6. Matty pitched well but was badly hurt by five errors. In Game Three the Giants evened the Series behind Marquard, surviving a Red Sox rally in the bottom of the ninth at Fenway to win, 2-1. Joe Wood pitched Game Four on two days' rest and the Red Sox emerged victorious, 3-1. The Red Sox took a commanding 3-1 lead in Game Five, when Hugh Bedient outdueled Mathewson 2-1 back at Fenway. The Red Sox needed just one more game.

Undaunted, the Giants jumped off to a 5-0 lead in the bottom of the first in Game Six at the Polo Grounds, and the lead held up for a 5-2 victory. They faced Wood for the third time in Game Seven at Fenway, but showed him no respect whatsoever, scoring six runs in the top of the first and driving him off the mound in the second on the way to an 11-4 blowout. With the schedule extended to an eighth and deciding game, the National Commission decreed a coin toss to determine the home-field advantage. The Red Sox won, sparing the teams a seventh consecutive train ride, and Mathewson, on two days' rest, faced Hugh Bedient.

The Giants pushed the first run of the game across in the third inning on a walk and a double. In the fifth, Red Sox right fielder Harry Hooper leapt into the temporary seats in right field to steal a home run from Larry Doyle that would have doubled the Giants' lead. And in the seventh inning the Red Sox tied the game on a lucky Texas League double to left and a hit that bounced off the third-base bag. Olaf Henriksen, pinch-hitting for Bedient, had driven in the tying run, and Smoky Joe Wood took the mound yet again in the top of the eighth.

The tension became unbearable as both teams failed to score either in the eighth inning or the ninth. This was only the second time in the first nine years of the modern World Series that the fall classic had gone to a deciding game, and the first time that game had gone into extra innings. With one out in the top of the 10th, Giants left fielder Red Murray doubled, and first baseman Fred Merkle—whose baserunning blunder had cost the Giants a pennant in 1908—singled him home to take the lead. Wood got the next two batters, and the Red Sox came to bat for what turned out to be the wildest, most controversial inning in the history of the World Series—until 1986. Five of its key participants—Fred Snodgrass and Chief Meyers of the Giants, and Wood, Tris Speaker, and Harry Hooper of the Red Sox—told the story of that inning years later in two oral-history compilations, *My Greatest Day in Baseball* and *The Glory of Their Times.*

Mathewson appeared to be off to a good start when Clyde Engle, pinch-hitting for Wood, lifted a high fly ball to straightaway center field. The Giants' center fielder, Fred Snodgrass, settled under the ball, got it into his glove—and dropped it. Engle, hustling all the way, reached second base with the tying run, and the Boston crowd came to life. "I dropped the darn thing," Snodgrass told Lawrence Ritter in the early 1960s.[1] Harry Hooper came to the plate, and the Red Sox expected him to try to bunt the runner to third. Snodgrass moved closer to second base, ready to back up a pickoff throw that Mathewson might try to hold him there. Hooper did foul off two bunts—just as Vic Wertz did in 1954, when he came to bat in the eighth inning of the first game of the World Series against the Giants with two men on and the score tied, 2–2. But then Hooper, like Wertz, swung away, and, like Wertz, drove a drive deep over the center fielder's head. In both cases, the center fielder—Snodgrass in 1912, Willie Mays in 1954—took off for deepest center, and both men made the catch. According to Snodgrass, he nearly doubled Engle up returning to second base. In any event, the Giants needed just two more outs.

The Giants had turned 123 double plays during 1912, and Mathewson may have been hoping for another when he walked Steve Yerkes to put men on first and third. But the batter now was Tris Speaker, a .383 hitter who so far had eight hits in the Series. Mathewson's prayers seemed to be answered when he fooled Speaker and the Red Sox center fielder lifted a foul popup down the first-base line. "I was going to yell for [Giants catcher] Meyers to make the catch for I didn't think he could," Speaker recalled, "but before I could open my mouth I heard Matty calling, 'Meyers, Meyers.'" That was how Hooper remembered the play too, but Meyers himself blamed the Red Sox bench.[2] In any event, first baseman Merkle—who was closer to the ball—held back, and Meyers could not reach it. It fell safely in foul ground.

Returning to the batter's box, Speaker called out to his fellow immortal on the mound. "Well, you just called for the wrong man," he said. "It's going to cost you this ball game."[3] And he lined the next pitch for a single to right that tied the game, with Yerkes going to third base and Speaker advancing to second when the throw came in to the plate. Mathewson purposely walked Duffy Lewis in another attempt to set up an inning-ending double play, but Larry Gardner flied to right, and Yerkes scored the winning run when Josh Devore's throw was wide. The Red Sox had won the World Series. The next morning's *New York Times* blasted Snodgrass as the villain—a burden he carried for the rest of his life.

Sitting in front of my television set in Pittsburgh in 1986, I watched the Mets, down 3–2 in games, battle back twice to tie Game Six at 2–2 in the fifth inning and 3–3 in the eighth. I saw the Red Sox take a 5–3 lead in the top of the 10th on Dave Henderson's homer, Wade Boggs's double and Marty Barrett's single. I saw Calvin Schiraldi get the first two outs in the bottom of the 10th, whereupon the Mets got three straight singles to draw within a run, with men on first and third. And then I felt my insides fall out when Bob Stanley threw a wild pitch and the Mets scored the tying run. That, I was sure, was the end of my hopes as a Red Sox fan yet again. Buckner's error was, for me, nothing but a painfully appropriate anticlimax. Two nights later, Game Seven made it official.

It was a day or two after that that my thoughts turned to an earlier World Series, and I suddenly hit upon the uncanny similarities in the bottom of those two 10th innings of Game Eight in 1912 and Game Six in 1986. In both cases, the visiting team needed just three outs to win. In both cases, not one, but *two* disastrous misplays kept them from getting them: Snodgrass's muff and Mathewson's call for Meyers in 1912, and Stanley's wild pitch and Buckner's error in 1986. Moreover, I could already see that Stanley's

more serious mistake (in the context of the game) was being forgotten, while Buckner, like Snodgrass in 1912, was taking all the heat from the fans and the media. And, of course, the same two cities were involved. I suddenly realized the fateful significance of what I had just lived through. It was the revenge of 1912.

NOTES

1   Lawrence S. Ritter, *The Glory of Their Times* (enlarged edition, New York: Harper, 1984), 110.

2   John P. Carmichael, *My Greatest Day in Baseball* (New York: A.S. Barnes, 1945), 67; Ritter, *Glory*, 150.

3   Ritter, *Glory*, 150.

A PARADE FOR THE FALLEN

By Bob Brady

HAVING HONORED THE BOSTON CELTICS IN June with a huge downtown parade and City Hall rally to celebrate the team's 16th NBA championship, Ray Flynn, Boston's mayor, had hoped for the opportunity to do likewise in the autumn for a championship Red Sox ballclub. Generation upon generation of Bosox fans had longed to be part of such a celebration. However, once again the team fell short of its fall classic goal — this time by the heartbreaking failure to secure just one more strike from an opposing Mets batter.

Nevertheless, going against the long-standing sports tradition of honoring only the victorious, the Hub's top official felt that the ballclub and its fans deserved a post-World Series public commemoration. In addition to paying tribute to a team that had greatly exceeded expectations all year, the event would provide a cathartic effect on the championship-starved Red Sox fan base. For those of advancing years, this might prove to be their once-in-a-lifetime opportunity to experience a semblance of what the future would hold in store if their beloved ballclub ever reached the pinnacle of baseball supremacy.

A tentative commitment to the mayor for a post-Series parade had been made by the Red Sox in advance of the Game Six debacle and the anticlimactic seventh-game loss. Given those crushing blows, general manager Lou Gorman doubted that the team would be receptive toward participating in the scheduled commemoration. However, upon arriving back in Boston from New York in the early-morning hours of October 28, the ballclub was met at Logan Airport and Fenway Park by a sizable contingent of cheering, emotional fans. Thus energized, Gorman did his best to convince his depressed ballplayers that Boston wanted and would turn out for a parade and rally the following day.

After a brief one-day respite, the general manager, skipper John McNamara, and about half of the players,

including some family members, gathered the following morning at Fenway Park to board flatbed trucks to navigate the streets of Boston.[1] Mayor Flynn declared Wednesday, October 29, as Red Sox Appreciation Day. The event kicked off at 11 A.M. with a parade that started at Copley Square, near the finish line of the annual Boston Marathon, past Boston Common, and onto City Hall Plaza. As often happens when considerable crowds gather, estimates of its size varied wildly. In this instance, reports ranged from a low of 250,000 to upward of 750,000 people lining the city streets and attending the rally. Included in the throng was the author of this piece, who took an unauthorized "extended lunch hour" from work to be part of the assemblage and capture some of the day's magic in photographs.

Any trepidation among the players choosing to participate that they would not be well received was quickly dissipated. The crooked streets of Beantown were lined with well-wishers, many of whom held handcrafted banners and signs thanking the team for a great season. Along the route, office workers hung out of windows and showered the streets below with confetti.

City Hall Plaza was packed with fans anticipating the arrival of the team. The crowd swelled further as those who had followed the parade joined the populace. A giant pair of 45-foot inflated Red Sox hung from City Hall. An elevated platform in front of the municipal building served as a gathering point for officials and the day's honorees. In addition to Mayor Flynn, Massachusetts Governor Mike Dukakis greeted the conquered heroes.

From the makeshift stage, Lou Gorman spoke on behalf of the Red Sox organization, thanking the fans for their tremendous support and pledging to bring a world championship to the city. Joe Castiglione, the team's radio broadcaster, introduced the attending players. Roger Clemens, Jim Rice, Bill Buckner, and

Ballplayers, staff, and families arrive at City Hall Plaza for the parade. Photograph courtesy of Bob Brady.

Bruce Hurst received long ovations and each chose to offer a few brief remarks of gratitude and encouragement to the crowd. Buckner's presence drew lasting cheers and he summed up the sentiment of the team when he said, "Thanks. We needed this."[2]

And so too did their fans!

NOTES

1   For an inside view of Gorman's efforts, see Lou Gorman, *One Pitch From Glory: A Decade Of Running The Red Sox* (Champaign, Illinois: Sports Publishing LLC), 27-35.

2   Gorman, 34.

Huge inflated red socks hang from the front of Boston's City Hall. Photograph courtesy of Bob Brady.

THE 1986 WORLD SERIES

By Matthew Silverman

T HAD BEEN A HALF-GENERATION SINCE EITHER franchise had seen the World Series. And each team was somewhat haunted by failures late in its seven-game losses, resulting in grueling "what if?" scenarios due to obscure left-handers. For the New York Mets it was George Stone, having a career year in 1973 but bypassed for the Game Six start in Oakland with the Mets needing to win just one game. Mets manager Yogi Berra opted for ace Tom Seaver and his ailing shoulder on short rest. New York's seven-game loss to the Swingin' A's, though bitter, paled in comparison to Boston's Game Seven loss in 1975. Coming one night after the epic Game Six win on Carlton Fisk's 12th-inning home run, the '75 Red Sox let a 3-0 lead get away in Game Seven, but they were still tied with the Reds when manager Darrell Johnson brought in left-handed Jim Burton to pitch the ninth. Burton was victimized by a bloop single by Joe Morgan that gave the Reds the game and the world championship, 4-3.

No Met remained in 1986 from the 1973 pennant winner, though '73 shortstop Bud Harrelson had become the third-base coach and ace Tom Seaver was in a Red Sox uniform, but unable to pitch because of a bad knee. Two-thirds of the Red Sox outfield had been on the team in 1975: Dwight Evans and Jim Rice. Though Evans put his talents on display in 1975 with a game-tying home run in the ninth inning of Game Three and a tremendous game-saving catch (and throw) in the 11th inning of Game Six, Rice—who placed second in Rookie of the Year voting and third in MVP balloting to teammate Fred Lynn—sat out the 1975 postseason after a pitch broke his left hand. Now, 11 Octobers later, the future Hall of Famer finally got his first taste of the World Series.

It would be a momentous World Series, the first Series meeting between New York and Boston since the 1912 World Series, and the first meeting since 1960 by two Northeastern teams (taking into account teams from New England to Pennsylvania). It was not Yankees-Red Sox, one of baseball's fiercest rivalries, but it was a new and exciting twist coming after both the Mets and Red Sox endured palpitating League Championship Series: The Red Sox claimed the pennant by rallying from being down three games to one and trailing by three runs in the ninth inning of Game Five, while the Mets beat the Astros three times in their last at-bat, culminating in a 16-inning epic Game Six at the Astrodome that was the longest postseason game played to that time.

It was riveting television, even if it took a while for the Series to go from ho-hum to humdinger. The 28.6 rating for the 1986 World Series was almost as high as Boston's epic seven-game 1975 World Series loss. The 1986 Series was watched by more people than Mets World Series in 1969 and 1973, in a pre-cable era with

Ed Sherman's press pass, courtesy of Bob Brady.

a lot less competition on TV. The 1986 World Series was seen by an average of 36.37 million viewers per night. A 46 ratings share for the '86 Series remains untouched as of 2015.[1]

No matter which side you rooted for, the 1986 World Series was something you couldn't look away from. While it represented a bitter chapter in the annals of Boston, which has enjoyed multiple world championships since then, it has remained a touchstone for Mets fans. Their dominant team that won more than any major-league club from 1984 to 1990 did not reach another World Series during that span, and in the intervening years went to the Series just twice more, falling in five games to the Yankees in

2000 and the Royals in 2015. Losing to the Yankees in the World Series is something the Red Sox can't even claim. But the Red Sox would endure one of their bitterest moments in the final week of October 1986. For the Mets, as announcer Bob Murphy said moments after the final, "The dream has come true."[2]

NOTES

1   "World Series Television Ratings." baseball-almanac.com/ws/wstv.shtml.

2   "Murphy's Classic Calls." MLB.com, August 4, 2004. newyork.mets.mlb.com/content/printer_friendly/nym/y2004/m08/d04/c818742.jsp.

OCTOBER 18, 1986: BOSTON RED SOX 1, NEW YORK METS 0, AT SHEA STADIUM

GAME ONE / 1986 WORLD SERIES

By Matthew Silverman

F THE LAST WORD ON THE 1986 WORLD SERIES was "unforgettable," the first word was "freezing." The heaters were on full blast in both dugouts at Shea Stadium, pitchers were allowed to blow on their hands, and bats were wrapped in towels. The fall classic felt like winter, but both teams would rather be in frigid New York than warm at home in front of the television.

"If you ever wondered what happened to Johnny Unitas's old cleats, Bill Buckner is wearing them," Vin Scully told the NBC audience early in the Series opener.[1] The announcers and many in the press treated Buckner playing on his painful ankles as heroic, or at least admirable. "When your requirement for a hotel room, the most important thing is to be near the ice machine to ice down your leg, that tells you the determination of that fellow," Scully's partner, Joe Garagiola, chimed in about Buckner.[2]

But from his first at-bat, when he bounced into a double play in the first inning, it was clear that Buckner's mobility was severely compromised, even though he said his new high-top shoes made a difference. Sitting and watching from the dugout was perfectly healthy Don Baylor, who had started at first base 13 times in '86 while committing just one error. But without the designated hitter in the National League park, Baylor was stapled to the Boston bench at Shea Stadium. The DH had been used in both the AL and NL park in the World Series in even years from 1976 through 1985, until the rule was changed by Commissioner Peter Ueberroth late in the 1986 season to follow the rule of the home park starting with the '86 World Series.[3] So Baylor, a former MVP with

31 home runs in 1986, who had waited 15 years as an everyday player—plus four losing American League Championship Series—to finally reach the World Series, would have to wait a couple of days longer.

A future manager, Baylor had plenty of time on the bench to think about how the recent rule change could affect the Series. "The advantage will probably be to the Mets because they can get a hitter four or five swings," Baylor said. "But if I have to sit and watch, that takes away a regular from us."[4] He was forced to watch Bruce Hurst bat for the first time in the majors, striking out all three times. But no one was talking about Hurst's hitting.

With the wind off Flushing Bay pushing the temperature down into the 40s, Hurst handcuffed the Mets from the outset. He struck out the first two Mets, Mookie Wilson and Lenny Dykstra, and fanned four his first time through the lineup. The second time through, however, Wilson and Dykstra each reached base and Hurst had to navigate Keith Hernandez and Gary Carter to get out of the third inning. It was the last time the Mets had multiple runners on base all night.

Ron Darling wasn't bad, either. After a single by Marty Barrett in the first, he retired the next nine batters before Buckner singled with two outs in the fourth. Darling wild-pitched him to second and then walked Jim Rice, but Dwight Evans, whom Darling had watched from the Fenway Park bleachers growing up in Worcester, Massachusetts, flied out to end the inning. Someone Darling had played against in high school in Worcester in the 1970s would hit the ball that proved the difference in the 1986 World Series opener.

"We went to different schools, rival schools," Gedman recalled three decades later as hitting coach for the Red Sox Double-A affiliate in Portland, Maine. "He's a couple of years younger than I am. But still it's nice to see somebody from the area make it to the major leagues—not only make it to the major leagues, but have an opportunity to win a world championship. It's a shame that both can't win, but I was happy for him."[5]

Gedman's routine grounder in the seventh inning went through Mets second baseman Tim Teufel's legs and brought home Jim Rice with the game's only run.

Seeing that the Red Sox had a chance to take the opener on the road from the brash 108-win Mets, the overwhelming World Series favorites among Las Vegas oddsmakers at 2½ to 1, Boston manager John McNamara pulled out all the stops. And he pulled his starting pitcher—not to mention his first baseman.

Calvin Schiraldi, the key player the Red Sox got from the Mets the previous offseason in the eight-player deal that sent Bob Ojeda to New York, came on to pitch the ninth inning after Hurst had limited the Mets to

four hits and four walks. (Ron Darling, on the short side for the Mets, allowed just three hits and three walks in seven innings.) McNamara sent up Mike Greenwell to bat for Hurst with two outs in the top of the ninth after left fielder Kevin Mitchell threw out Dwight Evans at the plate on Dave Henderson's single. Boston never got that insurance run, but the Red Sox did have defensive insurance. As McNamara had done in all four wins in the ALCS, Dave Stapleton came on to play first base for the hobbled Buckner with Boston leading.

After Schiraldi walked Strawberry to open the bottom of the ninth, Stapleton fielded Ray Knight's bunt and got the lead runner at second. Schiraldi retired former teammates Wally Backman and Danny Heep and the Red Sox had Game One. The Mets, who hit just .189 in the NLCS in Houston but hit the jackpot three times in their last at-bat, looked more anemic than unlucky against Boston in the Series opener. The Mets had not been shut out at Shea Stadium since September 1985, but the second postseason series in as many weeks began with a 1-0 Mets loss. For the Red Sox, facing Dwight Gooden the next evening

Shortstop Rafael Santana (#3) being introduced and greeting his teammates before one of the games.

with their own ace, Roger Clemens, on the mound, winning Game One was just what the doctor ordered. Well, maybe not Doc Gooden.

NOTES

1   New York Mets 1986 World Series Collector's Edition, Game One. MLB Official DVD, A&E Home Video, 2006.

2   Ibid.

3   G. Richard McKelvey, *All Bat No Glove: A History of the Designated Hitter* (Jefferson, North Carolina: McFarland & Co., 2003), 86, 92.

4   George Vecsey, "The Designated Hitter Rule Is Unfair to Don Baylor," *New York Times*, October 19, 1986.

5   Author interview with Rich Gedman, August 14, 2014.

OCTOBER 19, 1986: BOSTON RED SOX 9, NEW YORK METS 3, AT SHEA STADIUM

GAME TWO / 1986 WORLD SERIES

By Matthew Silverman

FOR EVERY GREAT WORLD SERIES PITCHER'S duel, there are a dozen duds that don't live up to the hype. Game Two certainly fell into the latter category; the hype belonged in a class by itself. The game's starting pitchers had each put together 24-4 seasons by age 24—Dwight Gooden pulled off the feat in 1985 at age 20 and the elder Roger Clemens did it in 1986, starting the year by winning his first 14 decisions and setting a major-league record by fanning 20 in an April game. Game Two of the World Series also featured the same starters from that year's All-Star Game. The only other time it happened was in 1939 between Red Ruffing of the Yankees and Cincinnati's Paul Derringer.1 That World Series game had been a pitcher's duel pulled out by New York in its final at-bat. This time … not so much.

Gooden's 1986 had not been a 24-4, Triple Crown season like his 1985, but his 17-6 mark, 2.84 ERA, and 200 strikeouts all stood in the top five in the NL—along with his 250 innings, .739 winning percentage, 12 complete games, and 1.108 WHIP. Toss in 17 innings with just two runs allowed in the NLCS against Houston. But New York writers had spent much of the year postulating after almost every bad inning, "What's wrong with Doc?" That thinking was on the mark in Game Two.

Gooden got through the first two innings allowing only one baserunner but four hard-hit outs. His luck ran out in the third. After Gooden walked Spike Owen to lead off—despite being ahead 1-2—Roger Clemens came up for his first major-league at-bat. It was a tough assignment, with Keith Hernandez charging in full tilt as he'd done for years against National Leaguers,

collecting every Gold Glove since 1978 (and winning 11 straight Gold Gloves eventually). Hernandez got to the bunt quickly enough, but he hurried unnecessarily and bounced the throw to second. Everybody was safe. The next three hitters each drove in runs with hits, including what would be Bill Buckner's only RBI of the World Series. Boston held a 3-0 lead on the night of the full harvest moon. "So far at least it's been the Red Sox doing the harvesting," offered Vin Scully on NBC.2

The Mets finally scored in their 12th inning at the plate in the World Series, and even then they were frustrated by two superb plays by Wade Boggs to rob the Mets of hits—and runs. With Boston up 4-2 and two Mets aboard and two outs in the fourth, Davey Johnson let Gooden bat. Bill Buckner made a nice play on Gooden's grounder and threw to Clemens covering to end the threat. Letting a Cy Young winner hit in the fourth inning of a two-run game didn't seem too controversial a decision … until the top of the fifth. Then, after Jim Rice singled, Dwight Evans launched a ball on the roof of the tent over the picnic area in left field. Gooden trudged off the mound, struggling through the fifth, his night clearly done. Who would have thought he'd outlast Clemens?

Having a four-run lead and needing two outs to qualify for the win, Clemens was removed at the end of a long talk with John McNamara with two Mets on base. The eventual Cy Young winner and AL MVP gave way to middle reliever Steve Crawford. He allowed a single to his first batter, Gary Carter, to make it a 6-3 game, and then Crawford retired both Darryl Strawberry and Danny Heep. Heep in left field and Howard Johnson at third base were shake-up-the-lineup moves by Davey

Johnson that didn't work. At least on this night. That pair replaced Ray Knight and Mookie Wilson, who'd had big hits late in the marathon NLCS Game Six in Houston, and would have some magic left in them yet in October. But Heep and HoJo could have gone 6-for-6 between them in Game Two and the Mets would still have been far off the Boston hit parade. The Red Sox outhit the Mets, 18-8, including five straight singles in the eighth.

The Red Sox were looking to turn back the clock many decades. The year 1918, the season Boston won its last world championship, was brought up repeatedly in the press and on the air. Boston's odds-defying five-game winning streak since they'd stared defeat in the face in Anaheim seemed to be gaining momentum, especially as the Series shifted to Fenway Park. The Red Sox had beaten both Darling and Gooden and now they had to face a pitcher they knew so well they'd shipped him out of town the previous winter.

NOTES

1   Associated Press, "Scherzer Outduels Harvey in Battle of All-Stars." Yes Network. web.yesnetwork.com/news/article.jsp?ymd=20130824&content_id=58228382&oid=0&print=true.

2   *New York Mets 1986 World Series Collector's Edition*, Game Two. MLB Official DVD, A&E Home Video, 2006.

OCTOBER 21, 1986: NEW YORK METS 7, BOSTON RED SOX 1, AT FENWAY PARK

GAME THREE / 1986 WORD SERIES

By Matthew Silverman

BOB OJEDA HAD NO LOVE LOST FOR THE Red Sox, and the feeling was mutual. The free-thinking and independent southpaw had not always fit in when Fenway was his home park, and his hard-line pro-union stance leading up to the previous year's two-day strike had not endeared him to all of the team's veterans. He got a fresh start in New York. Lou Gorman, Frank Cashen's assistant in New York, had returned to his native New England to take over as Boston's GM in 1985, and his big move in terms of pitching was to send Ojeda to New York in an eight-man deal that netted Calvin Schiraldi, who eventually became Boston's closer. Ojeda had to work his way into New York's rotation from the bullpen. That probably cost him 20 wins, but his 18-5 mark produced the best winning percentage (.783) of any pitcher in the National League—in fact, the top four pitchers in winning percentage were all Mets, including the Mets' other lefty starter, Sid Fernandez. After the beating the Mets took in Game Two, Davey Johnson re-worked his rotation on the fly and moved Fernandez, an All-Star with 16 wins and 200 strikeouts, to the bullpen. And then he gave the Mets all of Monday off, telling his players to stay at the Sheraton while he went to Fenway Park and took the heat. The Mets had played at Fenway in a charity exhibition game six weeks earlier. They'd already *ooh-ed* and *ah-ed* at the fabled Green Monster and taken their practice swings at the big wall. Now it was for real.

Lefty-swinging Lenny Dykstra wasn't aiming at the left-field wall, but he was thinking home run. And the Mets leadoff hitter, with just eight homers all year—plus a game-winning blast in the NLCS—pulled Oil Can Boyd's third pitch inside the foul pole in right. The mood on the Mets bench changed completely and the next three batters all hit the ball hard and reached base. Gary Carter's double made it 2-0 and put runners on second and third. Yet when Darryl Strawberry fanned for the 17th time in 29 postseason at-bats, it looked as if Boston might avoid a big inning when Ray Knight hit a grounder to third.

Keith Hernandez should have been out dead to rights, but he stopped and headed back to third. Catcher Rich Gedman threw to Boggs in the baseline instead of Spike Owen at the base and the runner was safe. But Carter was just a few steps from third and now he was in a rundown. When Hernandez faked home, Marty Barrett shifted his full attention as if the Mets first baseman had transformed into Rickey Henderson, but Barrett's fleeting glance back was all it took and Carter dove back into second. The bases were loaded.

While Red Sox fans still had their hands on their head wondering what happened, Danny Heep—the first designated hitter in Mets history—lined a single to score both Hernandez and Carter. The slow-footed but quick-minded baserunners had helped the Mets score as many runs in one inning as they had in the first two games.

The Mets had just one baserunner over the next six innings against Oil Can Boyd, but it all came apart for the Can in the seventh. Rafael Santana and Dykstra singled—his third of four hits in the game —and with two outs Boyd walked Keith Hernandez on four pitches to bring up Gary Carter. Boyd got ahead 0-and-2. Carter pulled a single into left and tried to take second on the throw but was caught in a rundown. This time the Red Sox tagged him out. Too late to do any good.

Dennis "Oil Can" Boyd pitching for Boston in Game Three of the World Series.

Bob Ojeda, who stood between his old team taking complete control of the World Series and his new team getting back into it, did not look like the pitcher who came into the night with a lifetime 4.39 ERA at Fenway Park. A free spirit who spoke his mind, he was not quite Bill Lee rebelling against Red Sox management a few years earlier, but Ojeda was motivated to beat his old team. He played it more diplomatically, though far from dully, in an interview NBC broadcast during the game: He told NBC, "Part of me is still here, beyond a doubt because I left some blood here and some tears here, as dramatic as that sounds, and I grew up here. But I belong somewhere else now, but I enjoyed my time here."[1]

Ojeda buzzed through Boston with his assortment of off-speed pitches and his well-placed fastball. "The left-hander changed speeds like an Indy 500 driver," *New York Daily News* columnist Phil Pepe wrote of Ojeda's Game Three start.[2]

The Red Sox reached base eight times against Ojeda, just two times fewerthan the Mets did against Boyd, but the Mets got the big hits with men on base. The Red Sox went 1-for-7. When three Red Sox reached base in the third inning and scored their lone run—on a Marty Barrett single—Ojeda was visited by manager Davey Johnson, as opposed to pitching coach Mel Stottlemyre. Ojeda responded by fanning Bill Buckner on four pitches and getting Jim Rice, representing the tying run, to ground out on the first pitch. On his 114th and final pitch of the night, in the seventh, he retired another future Hall of Famer, Wade Boggs. This time the game wasn't on the line, it was in his back pocket.

Roger McDowell retired all six batters he faced to finish the 7-1 victory. Davey Johnson's decision to give the Mets Monday off and not make them come to Fenway and be prodded by the hungry media looked brilliant. After the game Johnson said, "It's my job to sense things on the ballclub and to do things that will stimulate them. I felt they needed their rest."[3] Three decades later, Johnson was more pragmatic. "I couldn't get away with that today," he said. "If I did that today I'd probably be fined $250,000, I don't know. But I just felt like we needed a break, you know?"[4]

NOTES

1   *New York Mets 1986 World Series Collector's Edition*, Game Three. MLB Official DVD, A&E Home Video, 2006.

2   Phil Pepe, "Wall Falls to Ojeda," *New York Daily News*, October 22, 1986.

3   Ibid.

4   Author interview with Davey Johnson, March 31, 2015.

OCTOBER 22, 1986: NEW YORK METS 6, BOSTON RED SOX 2, AT FENWAY PARK

GAME FOUR / 1986 WORLD SERIES

By Matthew Silverman

F BOBBY OJEDA TANTALIZED THE TEAM HE ONCE played for in Game Three of the 1986 World Series, Ron Darling tortured the team he grew up rooting for in Game Four. A night after Ojeda got the Mets on the board for the first win of the Series by holding Boston to 1-for-7 with runners in scoring position, Darling allowed 10 Red Sox to reach base. None of them scored.

Darling was just 7 years old when the 1967 Red Sox won the Impossible Dream pennant and took the Cardinals to Game Seven of the World Series. At 15, he was in the bleachers for fabled Game Six of the 1975 World Series at Fenway Park as a high-school student. He attended Yale and performed well enough to be a first-round pick by Texas before winding up with the Mets system in a trade a year later.

Hawaiian-born, Ivy-educated, a *GQ* cover boy, and second in the Mets rotation only to phenom Dwight Gooden, Darling had something for everybody. George Vecsey of the *New York Times* described Darling that week as "a walking display for the polyglot beauty of Hawaii: the looks of his French father and Chinese mother making him strikingly handsome even among his healthy young colleagues. Yale University certainly claims him, even if he doesn't have his degree yet. And in the crush of the 1-0 loss on Saturday night, which included a painful collision with Dave Henderson near home plate, Darling found time to be extra gracious to a reporter from Worcester, Mass., his home town since the age of 7."[1]

But all that experience and awareness didn't mean he wasn't nervous heading into his first-ever game at the ballpark he thought of as home. His pregame warmup had not been good and ended early, but his nervousness began to pass after he spotted Ron Darling Sr. on the field in uniform for the National Anthem with the Air Force Reserve. Ron Jr. went and stood by his dad during the anthem at Fenway. "In my head, at least, I was transformed," Darling later wrote. "I went from someone who couldn't throw a strike to someone would not be denied, all in the space of a pregame ritual."[2]

The Red Sox loaded the bases in the bottom of the first, with Darling issuing back-to-back two-out walks to Jim Rice and Don Baylor to face Dwight Evans, who had made a spectacular, game-saving catch in front of Darling in the Fenway bleachers in Game Six of the 1975 World Series. Now Darling saved himself, inducing Evans to ground out and stranding three. He allowed a leadoff double in the second to another familiar face, Worcester high-school rival turned Red Sox catcher Rich Gedman. Gedman went to third on a grounder but stayed there when Darling retired Wade Boggs to end the threat.

When the Red Sox took a two-games-to-none lead in the World Series, John McNamara opted to stay with the four-man rotation, while his counterpart, Davey Johnson, felt compelled to cut down to a three-man rotation. And while Darling—pitching on short rest—labored the first time through the Boston order, Al Nipper, who had last appeared in a game 17 days earlier, pitched to just one Met over the minimum with eight groundouts and a strikeout to go with one measly single. Then Wally Backman led off the fourth with a single through the middle. McNamara called for a pitchout, but Keith Hernandez threw his bat at the ball and hit a grounder to shortstop. Though Hernandez was out, Backman moved up a base. And

Excited Fenway Park crowd before one of their home games in the World Series.

Nipper soon wished he had been more careful against Gary Carter with a base open.

Carter crushed Nipper's first-pitch fastball into the net over the Green Monster. Suddenly Nipper looked rusty. Darryl Strawberry doubled and Ray Knight singled him home to make it 3-0 Mets.

Darling retired 10 straight until he walked Spike Owen in the fifth. Owen failed to take second when Carter could not locate a pitch in the dirt, and that cost Boston when Marty Barrett's single moved Owen two bases. As he did all night, Darling was unhittable with runners in scoring position and he got Bill Buckner to pop up to end the threat.

The Mets failed to add top their lead when Gary Carter was thrown out by Jim Rice trying to tag up to end the top of the sixth, but an even more crucial—and unexpected—outfield assist ended the bottom of the sixth. With Dwight Evans on first, Rich Gedman hit a wall ball against Darling. But the Mets had an ace up their sleeve: the former manager of the Red Sox. Darrell Johnson, who managed the 1975 Red Sox to the pennant, was now a scout for the Mets

and gave a detailed report on Boston's tendencies. Keith Hernandez recalled years later how the Mets prepared for one bit of intel. "They hit flyballs off the Monster and Darrell Johnson and Davey [Johnson] told them how when you get a ball off the Monster, you think it's a double, but you've got a chance to throw the runner out," Hernandez said. "The runner on first is not going to score on that double, but you have a chance to throw that runner out at second base if you field the ball off the wall cleanly because it's so close … and Mookie fielded it cleanly and threw it in to second base. Right to second base."[3] Gedman was out and the inning was over. Both the crowd and the Boston bench remained frustrated.

The Mets roughed up Nipper's replacement, Steve Crawford. Lenny Dykstra's drive in the seventh inning glanced off Dwight Evans's eight-time Gold Glove and landed in the visiting bullpen for a home run. Gary Carter hit a no-doubter in the eighth, his second homer of the night clearing the Green Monster as well as the screen and disappearing under a van across Lansdowne Street.

As a final bit of torment, Darling walked two batters in his final inning, but his 115th pitch was popped up by Bill Buckner. Roger McDowell ran into trouble in relief in the eighth, allowing two runs on three hits and a walk, but Jesse Orosco came in and got Wade Boggs to ground out and strand two more baserunners. The Red Sox left 11 men on base. They left their World Series lead behind as well.

NOTES

1 George Vecsey, "Ron Darling in the Fourth," *New York Times*, October 20, 1986.

2 Ron Darling, and Daniel Paisner, *The Complete Game: Reflections on Baseball, Pitching, and Life on the Mound* (New York: Alfred A. Knopf, 2009), 72.

3 Author interview with Keith Hernandez, December 22, 2014.

OCTOBER 23, 1986: BOSTON RED SOX 4, NEW YORK METS 2, AT FENWAY PARK

GAME FIVE / 1986 WORLD SERIES

By Matthew Silverman

AFTER GAME FOUR, REPORTERS ASKED Red Sox manager John McNamara about his slumping hitters, notably former batting champion Bill Buckner and reigning batting champ Wade Boggs, who against the Mets were hitting a combined .171 (6-for-35), effectively neutering the advantage provided by their hottest hitter, Marty Barrett, who batted between the lefties in the lineup and was hitting .412 (7-for-17). "Sure I'm concerned," the manager replied, "but what am I going to do about it."[1] Starting Bruce Hurst would help a great deal.

Buckner and Boggs were not the heroes in Game Five, but they each hit safely against Dwight Gooden. The Red Sox hammered Dr. K again, waiting him out as he tried to beat them with his curveball. On a night when his fastball did not have its usual movement, half of his 82 pitches were curves. *Boston Globe* reporter Dan Shaughnessy likened that idea to "a *Playboy* centerfold trying to impress her date in the kitchen."[2] Gooden's strategy cooked up trouble. He reached two strikes a dozen times, but fanned just three while allowing seven singles and two triples. Boston also coaxed two walks from Gooden and took advantage of a key infield error.

With Boston leading 1-0 on a Spike Owen sacrifice fly, Bill Buckner hit a grounder that shortstop Rafael Santana mishandled. Jim Rice walked and Don Baylor struck out, bringing up Dwight Evans with two outs. Two days in a row Evans had been retired with the bases loaded to end the first inning; now up with two men on in the third, he lined a Gooden fastball into right-center field with Buckner hobbling home and bellyflopping across the plate as the throw sailed wide. "He's got the Red Badge of Courage on his chest," NBC's Vin Scully said as Buckner scraped his battered body off the ground for congratulations in the Boston dugout.[3]

Bruce Hurst, pitching on four days' rest, was not as sharp as he'd been in Game One, but he was just as effective. He stranded two Mets in both the third and fifth, striking out Lenny Dykstra and retiring Tim Teufel after the Mets put runners on second and third with one out. Boston doubled its lead in the home fifth as the first three Red Sox hit safely to start the inning. Davey Johnson handed the ball to Sid Fernandez.

Fernandez, an All-Star, 16-game winner, and 200-strikeout pitcher in 1986, had been banished to the pen when the Mets manager cut his four-man rotation to three after his team's Shea debacle to start the World Series. Asked to stem the tide in Game Five, Fernandez allowed a run-scoring double to Dave Henderson to make it 4-0, which was no crime given that Hendu's average stood at .471 as he stood on second base. But Fernandez got out of the jam and allowed just two other hits, walked none, and fanned five while pitching the final four innings. It may have been too late to save the game, but just giving a night's rest to weary Mets relievers Roger McDowell and Jesse Orosco was a positive.

Hurst didn't need any relievers, though John McNamara had the bullpen warming up as the game neared its conclusion. The Mets finally scored on Hurst after 15⅓ innings of frustration when Tim Teufel hit an opposite-field home run on an 0-and-2 pitch in the eighth. McNamara had batted for Hurst in the ninth inning of Game One with a one-run lead, but at Fenway Park, with the designated hitter preclud-

Boston Red Sox left fielder Mike Greenwell batting; Wade Boggs on deck. Gary Carter is catching.

ing Hurst from batting, McNamara stayed with the southpaw. He did send in a new first baseman, however. As he'd done in Boston's six previous postseason wins in October 1986, Dave Stapleton came in for defense. He made the first two putouts of the ninth. The third out did not come as easily.

Mookie Wilson doubled to left and Rafael Santana singled to score Wilson and bring the tying run to the plate. Up came Lenny Dykstra, who'd homered the past two nights and won a game in New York with a homer in the ninth inning in the NLCS. This time

he chased a high fastball for strike three and Boston led the Series once more, breaking the visiting team's mojo to boot. Finally, a home team won a game in the 1986 World Series. It would not be the last time.

NOTES

1   *New York Daily News Scrapbook History of the N.Y. Mets 1986 Season* (New York: New York News, 1987), 235.

2   Dan Shaughnessy, *One Pitch Away* (New York: Beaufort Books Publishers, 1987), 247.

3   *New York Mets 1986 World Series Collector's Edition*, Game Five. MLB Official DVD, A&E Home Video, 2006.

OCTOBER 25, 1986: NEW YORK METS 6, BOSTON RED SOX 5 (10 INNINGS), AT SHEA STADIUM

GAME SIX / 1986 WORLD SERIES

By Matthew Silverman

RIGHT FROM THE FIRST INNING IT WAS obvious this was not going to be a typical game. Even by World Series Game Six standards, this one was out of this world. And that is where Mike Sergio came from, drifting down onto the Shea Stadium infield in a parachute with a modest "Go Mets" sign hanging off it. A veteran skydiver and a middling actor, he made the jump because he was incensed by a balloon-festooned banner at Fenway Park that he had seen on TV. He would serve jail time the following summer for his breach of airspace and flouting of an untold number of laws. But he was quickly hustled off the field in Game Six and the first pitch by Bob Ojeda was thrown less than a minute after he landed. The game was what mattered. And what a game.

After being so rudely interrupted from above, the Red Sox scored in the first on a double by Dwight Evans and added another in the second on Marty Barrett's RBI single. That seemed as though it could go a long way with Roger Clemens on full rest pitching full bore and no-hitting the Mets through four innings, but the Mets were making Clemens work. He threw 72 pitches (49 strikes) to get that far and the crowd was working him, too. Chants of "Ro-ger! Ro-ger" were payback for the derisive catcalls by the Fenway faithful of "Dar-ryl! Dar-ryl!" Strawberry started the home fifth with his second walk of the night and—just as he'd done in the second inning—he stole second. On the next pitch Ray Knight singled through the middle and Strawberry crossed the plate to cut Boston's lead in half. Mookie Wilson singled to right field and Knight took third with no one out when Evans bobbled the

ball. That proved key since Danny Heep, batting for Rafael Santana, bounced into a double play that tied the game. It marked the first time, other than 0-0, that a 1986 World Series game was tied.

Given a reprieve, Bobby Ojeda batted for himself (he grounded out) and threw another inning. Going six innings was quite a feat for Ojeda since Boston had runners on base in all but one inning yet left eight on base against Ojeda. The Red Sox took advantage of shoddy defense by the Mets in the seventh against Roger McDowell, with Knight's errant throw pulling Keith Hernandez off first to put runners on the corners. Boston, without a steal attempt in the Series, tried the hit-and-run several times and usually sent runners on 3-and-2, as the Red Sox did Jim Rice in the seventh. His jump enabled him to beat a throw to second on what looked like a double-play ball. The Mets got Dwight Evans at first, but because Rice was safe at second, Marty Barrett crossed home plate for a 3-2 Boston lead. When Rich Gedman followed with a single it looked as if Boston would double its lead, but for the second time in the Series, Mookie Wilson, who had a notoriously weak arm and had undergone shoulder surgery the previous winter, threw to Gary Carter on the fly and the catcher rode Rice away from the plate for the third out. Rice's speed, or lack thereof, had kept him from scoring on Evans's rattling ball in the gap in the first inning, and it haunted Boston again, but not nearly as much as much as a decision by John McNamara that would stay with Red Sox fans for years to come.

A blister on Roger Clemens' pitching hand kept him from being effective with his breaking pitches and he logged 134 pitches through seven innings, but it was a time when the number of pitches was often ignored and Clemens had thrown 10 complete games during the season while logging 155⅔ more innings than the previous year (not even counting his five postseason starts covering an additional 34 innings). But with a runner on first and no one out in the eighth inning against McDowell, McNamara had Spike Owen bunt, and then he batted for Clemens with Mike Greenwell—highlight on "green" for the 23-year-old outfielder who had yet to even play enough to qualify as a rookie. He fanned on three pitches.

With Clemens done, ex-Met Calvin Schiraldi came in in the Mets eighth to try to finish off the first Red Sox title in 68 years. He gave up a hit to the first batter he faced, Lee Mazzilli, batting for Jesse Orosco, who had thrown one pitch to finish the Red Sox eighth. Lenny Dykstra followed with a bunt and Schiraldi bounced the throw to second. The Mets wound up tying the game on Gary Carter's sacrifice fly. The tension trebled.

The bottom of the ninth seemed like a carbon copy of the eighth, with the Red Sox messing up the force play on a bunt. This time it was Rich Gedman who made a bad throw. The difference was that Davey Johnson, never a fan of the sacrifice, bunted twice in a row in the eighth and the Mets scored; in the ninth, pinch-hitter Howard Johnson looked bad trying to bunt the first pitch, swung away on the next, and fanned on the third pitch. The Mets did not score and the game moved to the 10th.

The second-guessers took a front-row seat when Dave Henderson homered just above the "a" in the *Newsday* sign. Many scribes started moving toward the visiting clubhouse, where champagne—loaned to the Red Sox by the Mets—was now being iced. The championship indeed looked for all the world to be on ice when Boston scored a second run off Rick Aguilera on Marty Barrett's single.

With two outs in the bottom of the 10th, with the baseball world wondering how the Mets hadn't bunted a second time in the ninth, with writers—depending

Mets catcher Gary Carter being interviewed.

on where they hailed from—either spouting lyrically about the end of an epic New England baseball drought or New York's failure to get down a bunt, and with frustrated Keith Hernandez sitting in his manager's office drinking a beer, the game changed. Gary Carter singled. Pinch-hitter Kevin Mitchell singled. Ray Knight, down 0-and-2, singled to center to score Carter and send Mitchell to third. John McNamara came out, took the ball, and handed it to Bob Stanley.

Stanley, who led Boston with 16 saves—Schiraldi, not called up from the minors until late July, was third on the club with nine—faced Mookie Wilson, whom he'd faced three times, retired twice, and struck out once in the Series. With the count 2-and-2, Wilson jackknifed out of the way of a slider that, in the words of the man who called it, Rich Gedman, "ran inside a little bit and I didn't get it."[1] The ball went to the backstop, Kevin Mitchell scored, and the game was tied. With Shea Stadium shaking, the Mets dugout ecstatic, Keith Hernandez superstitiously refusing to leave the manager's office during the rally, and Mookie Wilson still at the plate, the game hurtled toward its implausible climax.

On the 10th pitch from Stanley, Wilson hit a "little roller up along first," as Vin Scully said of almost every such groundball in the Series, but this was no routine grounder. The ball skipped through Bill Buckner's legs and Ray Knight scored. "Behind the bag! It gets through Buckner! Here comes Knight and the Mets win it!"[2]

No words were spoken on NBC for three minutes as announcer and network let the reactions on camera and the screaming by the fans say it all. Sometimes words just can't adequately capture a moment. When Marv Albert put microphones in front of Wilson and Knight, they didn't have much luck, either. There wasn't much left to say, or give. "I'm just exhausted right now," Knight admitted. "I'm happy, but I've never been more tired than I am right now."[3] Boston was sick and tired, especially given that Dave Stapleton had replaced the

ailing Buckner at first base for defense every time Boston held the lead in the final inning during the postseason. With one unforgettable exception.

NOTES

1   Author interview with Rich Gedman, August 14, 2014.

2   *New York Mets 1986 World Series Collector's Edition*, Game Six. MLB Official DVD, A&E Home Video, 2006.

3   Ibid.

OCTOBER 27, 1986: NEW YORK METS 8, BOSTON RED SOX 5, AT SHEA STADIUM

GAME SEVEN / 1986 WORLD SERIES

By Matthew Silverman

IN THE YEARS THAT FOLLOWED, IT WAS SIMPLE to say that victory in Game Seven was preordained after their miraculous escape from Game Six, but triumph in the deciding game was far from assured. As in the 1975 World Series, the Red Sox—after their own legendary '75 Game Six win on Carlton Fisk's home run—took a 3-0 lead in Game Seven. Both 1975 and 1986 ended with Game Sevens Boston wished it could it forget but could not; those with longer memories recalled Game Sevens from 1946 and 1967.

First, all parties had to wait an extra day in 1986. After the Mets' dramatic Saturday-night victory, Sunday was a washout and the teams convened again on Monday night. The two baseball teams did not only have to contest each other, but the game also went up against Giants-Redskins from the Meadowlands on *Monday Night Football*. The competition was a total rout in terms of ratings, with baseball on NBC garnering a 38.9 rating and 34 million viewers, the largest audience ever for a World Series contest, while the football game had just an 8.8 rating, ABC's lowest since *MNF* debuted in 1970. In addition, the reactions from the crowd at Giants Stadium were such that they confused the football players on the field who were not following the goings-on at Shea Stadium.[1] What a game they missed.

Dwight Evans and Rich Gedman hit back-to-back home runs for the Red Sox in the second inning, with Gedman's ball bouncing off irate Darryl Strawberry's glove on its way over the fence. Then Wade Boggs singled home Dave Henderson and it was 3-0. Two innings later, with a man on second and two outs, Mets starter Ron Darling was replaced by Sid Fernandez,

an All-Star who had been bounced from the rotation when the Mets fell behind two games to none. Now he played as important a role as any Met in 1986. Standing between the Mets and oblivion, El Sid walked his first batter, batting champion Wade Boggs, to bring up Marty Barrett, who had already tied a World Series record with 13 hits. Fernandez got him to fly to right to end the inning and start a stretch of seven straight batters retired to take the Mets through the top of the sixth.

Like Ron Darling, Boston's Bruce Hurst was making his third start of the World Series. The rainout bumped Oil Can Boyd from the rotation, and Hurst, pitching on three days' rest, was brilliant. He retired 16 of the first 17 batters with Rafael Santana grounding out to start the home sixth. And just like that, everything changed.

Lee Mazzilli, batting for Fernandez, singled to left. Another switch-hitter, Mookie Wilson, followed with a single. The tying run came to the plate for the first time in the game, yet Hurst could have gotten out of the jam by getting Tim Teufel to hit into a double play. He pitched carefully to Teufel, who had hit him better than any other Met in the Series, going 4-for-9 and breaking up Hurst's string of 15⅓ innings of shutout ball in the Series with a home run in Game Five. In Game Seven, Teufel walked on five pitches to load the bases.

That brought up a left-handed batter against the southpaw, but lefty vs. lefty was secondary as Keith Hernandez stepped to the plate. He was as qualified for the job as any player in Mets history. To that point he had the franchise's highest career average by 22 points (Hernandez at .309 topped Steve Henderson's

Darryl Strawberry hit a solo home run in the eighth inning of Game Seven to help the Mets beat Boston.

.287 for best average in at least 1,000 at-bats by a Met through 1986) and he had led the juggernaut '86 Mets in batting average, runs, hits, and doubles.[2] And Hernandez as a St. Louis Cardinal had come through in almost this exact same spot in the 1982 World Series against the Milwaukee Brewers, following a walk by a lefty (Bob McClure) to a right-handed batter (Gene Tenace). Back then Hernandez cracked a game-tying two-run single off McClure and the Cards went on to beat the Brewers.

"I was like, 'You've got to be kidding me,'" Hernandez said of the similarities between his sixth-inning World Series at-bats in Game Seven in '82 and '86. "It was the same situation basically, which I thought was kind of ironic."[3]

And he came through again. Hernandez's two-run single got the Mets on the board. And while Hernandez didn't tie the game as he had in the 1982 World Series, Gary Carter followed by knocking in the tying run.

Hurst got through the inning, but when Tony Armas pinch-hit for him the following inning, it became a battle of bullpens—and that played to the Mets' strength. Roger McDowell, who had won 14 games and saved 22 during the season, fanned Armas while setting down the Red Sox in order in the seventh. In the bottom of the inning Calvin Schiraldi returned to the scene of New England's nightmare two nights earlier. Ray Knight, who scored the winning run on Bill Buckner's fateful error in Game Six, scored the tiebreaking run again, this time under his own power. He drilled Schiraldi's fastball over the wall in left-center as the Mets took a 4-3 lead. Schiraldi allowed a hit to Lenny Dykstra, a wild pitch, and an RBI single to Rafael Santana. After McDowell's sacrifice, John McNamara replaced Schiraldi with Joe Sambito, who walked two batters (one intentionally) and permitted an insurance run when Hernandez drove home another run home against a lefty. Bob Stanley ended the rally by retiring Gary Carter.

Boston came ever so close to tying the score in the eighth inning. In his 82nd appearance and 142nd inning of relief (postseason included), McDowell was done. The first three Red Sox got hits off him, with Dwight Evans' two-run double making it a 6-5 game. Jesse Orosco, who had saved 21 games during the year, plus three wins and a save in October, came in with the tying run on second and no one out. Rich Gedman hit a bullet that was snagged by Wally Backman, brought in for defense. Orosco fanned Dave Henderson, and Don Baylor, in his only at-bat of the Series in the NL park, grounded out to end the threat.

The Mets opened up the lead when Darryl Strawberry homered and Jesse Orosco — in the old "butcher boy play" — pulled back a bunt attempt and singled through the vacated hole to take an 8-5 lead into the ninth. With two down, nobody on, and New York preparing to explode, Marty Barrett swung through the fastball. Orosco's glove went airborne, and the Mets were world champions.

What had been a rather ho-hum World Series for five games turned into an all-time classic thanks to the comebacks in the final two games. Parachutists dropping in, balls going through infielders' legs, balls bouncing off gloves into the stands for home runs, teams skipping workouts, botched bunt plays, muffed rundowns, designated hitters, pitching changes that were made, pitching changes that weren't, and curses unleashed by long-dead sluggers — it wasn't a work of art, but the images produced in the 1986 World Series were indelible marks on the baseball landscape. The pain stayed with Red Sox fans for 18 years, until they finally won their next World Series, and the memory of '86 glory would have to last as Mets fans endured decades without a title and their own brand of demons.

NOTES

1   Michael Goodwin, "NBC Scored in Game 7, Too," *New York Times*, October 29, 1986.

2   *1987 Mets Information Guide*: 216.

3   Author interview with Keith Hernandez, December 22, 2014.

BY THE NUMBERS

By Dan Fields

1986 BOSTON RED SOX

1st

Major-league pitcher to strike out 20 batters in a nine-inning game: Roger Clemens, on April 29 against the Seattle Mariners. He had eight consecutive strikeouts (fourth inning to sixth inning) to tie the AL record. He didn't walk a batter and gave up only three hits. The Red Sox won 3-1.

1st

Starting pitcher since 1971 to win an MVP Award: Roger Clemens. He was the unanimous selection for the AL Cy Young Award. Clemens led the majors in wins (24, the most by a Red Sox pitcher since 1949) and winning percentage (.857) and led the AL in ERA (2.48), WHIP (0.969, the lowest by a Red Sox pitcher since 1914), and hits per nine innings pitched (6.3). He finished second in the AL in strikeouts (238). Clemens was also the MVP of the 1986 All-Star Game on July 15 in Houston; he was the AL's starting pitcher and threw three perfect innings.

1.89

Walks per nine innings pitched by Oil Can Boyd, second best in the AL.

2

Grand slams by Jim Rice in a three-game series against the Minnesota Twins on September 5 through 7. During the series, he had seven hits in 12 at-bats and drove in 10 runs.

2.18

Ratio of strikeouts to walks by Boston pitchers, best in the AL.

2.99

ERA of Bruce Hurst, fourth lowest in the AL.

4

Shutouts by Bruce Hurst, tied for second in the AL.

8.62

Strikeouts per nine innings pitched by Bruce Hurst, second best in the AL. Roger Clemens was third in the league, with 8.43 strikeouts.

11

Consecutive games won by the Red Sox from August 30 to September 10.

14

Consecutive wins by Roger Clemens to start the season. His first loss was on July 2 against the Toronto Blue Jays.

18

Sacrifice hits by Marty Barrett, most in the AL and tied (with Robby Thompson of the San Francisco Giants) for most in the majors.

20

Consecutive games in which Wade Boggs had a base hit, from August 29 to September 18. During the streak, he hit nine doubles and batted .405.

20th

Consecutive year in which Tom Seaver started at least 20 games. In his final season, Seaver started 12 games for the Chicago White Sox and 16 games for the Red Sox. He finished his career with a record of 311-205, an ERA of 2.86, and 3,640 strikeouts.

21-7

Record of the Red Sox during May.

24-5

Score by which the Red Sox beat the Cleveland Indians on August 21. Spike Owen (batting ninth) scored six runs to tie a twentieth-century major-league record, Tony Armas hit two home runs (including a grand slam) and drove in six runs, Bill Buckner had five hits (all singles), and Marty Barrett and Dwight Evans each drove in four runs.

24-10

Record of the Red Sox in one-run games. The .706 winning percentage was best in the majors.

25

Double plays grounded into by Bill Buckner, second most in the majors.

25.2

At-bats per strikeout by Bill Buckner, the highest ratio in the majors. Marty Barrett had 20.2 at-bats per strikeout and finished second in the majors.

31

Home runs by Don Baylor, tied for sixth in the AL. He hit 22 homers on the road, second most in the majors.

35

Times that Don Baylor was hit by a pitch, an AL record (through 2014). He was hit by two pitches in three games (on May 1, May 17, and June 30).

36

Complete games by Boston pitchers, second most in the majors. The Twins had 39 complete games.

41

Stolen bases by the Red Sox, fewest in the majors. The team with next fewest steals, the Baltimore Orioles, had 64.

47

Doubles by Wade Boggs, second in the majors. This was the most by a Red Sox player since 1938, when Joe Cronin hit 51. Marty Barrett, Bill Buckner, and Jim Rice each had 39 doubles in 1986 and tied for third in the AL.

54

Base runners caught stealing as catcher by Rich Gedman, most in the AL.

66

Games played by Bob Stanley, tied for fifth in the AL.

95

Wins by the 1986 Red Sox, against 66 losses. The Sox won the AL East by 5 1/2 games over the New York Yankees.

105

Walks drawn by Wade Boggs, most in the majors. He had at least 200 hits and 100 walks in four consecutive seasons (1986 through 1989). Dwight Evans drew 97 walks in 1986, second in the majors. In a 12-inning game against the California Angels on July 10, Evans drew four walks.

107

Runs scored by Wade Boggs, tied for fifth in the majors.

110

RBIs by Jim Rice, fourth in the AL. He had two five-RBI games, on May 28 and September 5. Bill Bucker had 102 RBIs and finished 10th in the AL.

207

Hits by Wade Boggs, fourth in the AL. He had two five-hit games in a 12-day span (May 20 and May 31). Jim Rice had 200 hits, tied for fifth in the league.

.298, .345, and .542

Batting average, on-base percentage, and slugging average of Rich Gedman on the road. His numbers at Fenway Park were .214, .284, and .299. He hit 14 home runs on the road, two at home.

312

Times on base by Wade Boggs, most in the majors. Jim Rice got on base 266 times and finished third in the AL.

320

Doubles by the Red Sox, most in the majors and a franchise record at the time.

334

Putouts as a left fielder by Jim Rice, most in the majors.

.346

On-base percentage of the Red Sox, second highest in the majors. The Yankees had an OBP of .347.

.357

Batting average of Wade Boggs, highest in the majors. He was consistent, hitting .357 at home and .356 on the road and going .359 against right-handed pitchers and .352 against left-handed pitchers. Jim Rice had a .324 average in 1986 and finished fifth in the AL.

.367

Batting average of Marty Barrett (11 for 30) in the AL Championship Series against the Angels. He had four multi-hit games, with three hits each in Game Two and Game Six. The Red Sox eliminated the Angels in seven games, and Barrett was chosen the MVP.

.453

On-base percentage of Wade Boggs, highest in the majors.

474

Walks allowed by the Red Sox, fewest in the majors.

707

Strikeouts by Boston batters, fewest in the majors. The team with the next fewest strikeouts, the Blue Jays, had 848.

713

Plate appearances by Marty Barrett, fourth in the majors.

.939

OPS of Wade Boggs, second best in the majors.

1986 NEW YORK METS

1-2-3-4

Rank in winning percentage in the NL by Bob Ojeda (.783), Dwight Gooden (.739), Sid Fernandez (.727), and Ron Darling (.714).

1.090 and 1.108

WHIP of Bob Ojeda and Dwight Gooden, who finished third and fourth in the NL.

2.57, 2.81, and 2.84

ERA of Bob Ojeda, Ron Darling, and Dwight Gooden, who finished second, third, and fifth in the NL.

3.11

ERA of the Mets, lowest in the majors.

4

Mets players who started at the 1986 All-Star Game. At the age of 21 years, 7 months, and 30 days, Dwight Gooden was the youngest pitcher to start an All-Star Game. Batting third, fourth, and fifth for the NL were first baseman Keith Hernandez, catcher Gary Carter, and right fielder Darryl Strawberry. Gooden gave up two runs in three innings and took the loss.

5

Hits by Darryl Strawberry on April 30 and Mookie Wilson on May 23.

7

RBIs by Gary Carter on July 11 against the Atlanta Braves. He hit a three-run homer in the first inning and a grand slam in the second inning, both off David Palmer.

8.8

Strikeouts per nine innings pitched by Sid Fernandez, third in the NL.

9th

Consecutive Gold Glove Award at first base won by Keith Hernandez. He also won in 1987 and 1988 to run the streak to 11.

12

Complete games by Dwight Gooden, tied for second in the NL.

14

Strikeouts by Sid Fernandez in seven innings on September 1 against the Giants.

14

Games won in relief by Roger McDowell, including his first seven decisions of the year.

15

Sacrifice flies by Gary Carter, most in the majors.

17.6

At-bats per home run by Darryl Strawberry, third in the NL. Gary Carter had 20.4 at-bats per home run and finished seventh.

18, 17, 16, and 15

Wins by starting pitchers Bob Ojeda, Dwight Gooden, Sid Fernandez, and Ron Darling, respectively. All finished in the top 10 in the NL.

20-4

Record of the Mets through May 10. The team won 11 consecutive games from April 18 through April 30.

After losing to the Braves on May 1, the Mets won seven straight.

21

Double plays grounded into by Gary Carter, tied (with Tony Pena and Johnny Ray, both of the Pittsburgh Pirates) for most in the NL.

21 1/2

Games by which the Mets won the NL East over the Philadelphia Phillies.

22 and 21

Saves by Roger McDowell and Jesse Orosco. The 1986 Mets were the third team in major-league history with two pitchers who had at least 20 saves in a season.

27

Home runs by Darryl Strawberry, tied for fifth in the NL. Gary Carter had 24 home runs and finished ninth.

75

Games played by Roger McDowell, second among NL pitchers.

94

Walks drawn by Keith Hernandez, most in the NL.

94

Runs scored by Keith Hernandez, tied for fifth in the NL.

103

Home runs allowed by the Mets, fewest in the majors.

105

RBIs by Gary Carter, third in the NL. Darryl Strawberry had 93 RBIs and finished seventh.

108

Wins by the 1986 Mets, the most in the majors since the Cincinnati Reds won as many in 1975.

141

Strikeouts by Darryl Strawberry, tied for second in the NL.

.189

Batting average of the Mets in the NL Championship Series against the Houston Astros, who batted .218. The Mets won the series in six games, and the final game (16 innings) was the longest in postseason history until 2005. Jesse Orosco had three wins, all in relief. Mike Scott of the Astros, who threw a shutout in Game One and allowed one run in a complete-game win in Game Four, was named the MVP.

200

Strikeouts thrown each by Sid Fernandez and Dwight Gooden, tied for fourth in the NL.

250

Innings pitched by Dwight Gooden, fifth in the NL.

.263

Batting average of the Mets, highest in the NL.

269

Times on base by Keith Hernandez, third in the NL.

.310

Batting average of Keith Hernandez, fifth in the NL.

.339, .401, .and .740

On-base percentage, slugging average, and OPS of the Mets, all best in the NL.

.379

Batting average of Ray Knight against left-handed pitchers, best in the majors. He hit .243 against right-handed pitchers.

.4126

On-base percentage of Keith Hernandez, second in the NL. He was edged by Tim Raines, who had an OBP of .4133.

.507

Slugging percentage of Darryl Strawberry, second in the NL.

631

Walks drawn by the Mets, most in the NL.

783

Runs scored by the Mets, most in the NL.

.865

OPS of Darryl Strawberry, fourth in the NL. Keith Hernandez had an OPS of .859 and finished seventh in the league.

.9963

Fielding percentage as first baseman by Keith Hernandez, best in the majors. He edged Don Mattingly of Yankees, who had a .9960 fielding percentage.

1,083

Strikeouts by New York pitchers, second most in the majors.

2,767,601

Attendance of the 1986 Mets at Shea Stadium, a franchise record at the time.

1986 WORLD SERIES

0

Stolen bases by the Red Sox during the Series. The Mets had seven steals, including three each by Darrly Strawberry and Mookie Wilson and one by Wally Backman.

0-2

Record of Boston reliever Calvin Schiraldi, who took the loss in both Game Six and Game Seven, and New York starter Dwight Gooden, who lost Game Two and Game Five.

2-0

Record of Bruce Hurst, who won Game One and Game Five. He also started Game Seven. Hurst had an ERA of 1.96 in 23 innings during the Series.

6

Runs scored each by Dave Henderson and Jim Rice during the Series.

9

RBIs each by Gary Carter and Dwight Evans during the Series.

.391

Batting average of Ray Knight (9 for 23). With two outs in the bottom of the 10th inning of Game Six and the Mets trailing by two runs, Knight singled to drove in Gary Carter and advance Kevin Mitchell to third. Mitchell then scored on Bob Stanley's wild pitch, and Knight advanced to second. Knight scored the winning run after Mookie Wilson's grounder went through the legs of Bill Buckner. Knight also hit the tie-breaking home run in the seventh inning of Game Seven. He was voted MVP of the World Series.

.433

Batting average of Marty Barrett (13 for 30). Dave Henderson hit .400 (10 for 35). Barrett's total of 24 hits in the ALCS and World Series were a single-season postseason record at the time.

AROUND THE MAJORS IN 1986

1

Hit allowed by Jimmy Jones of the San Diego Padres in his first major-league game, a 5-0 shutout of the Astros on September 21. He threw only two more shutouts in his eight-year career.

1st

Game at shortstop by Barry Larkin of the Reds, on August 17 against the Padres. He would play 2,075 games at short, winning nine Silver Slugger Awards and three Gold Glove Awards.

1st

Pitcher to clinch a playoff spot with a no-hitter: Mike Scott. He struck out 13 and walked two while no-hitting the Giants on September 25 to clinch the NL West title for the Astros. Scott led the majors in ERA (2.22), strikeouts (306), innings pitched (275⅓), WHIP (0.923), hits per nine innings pitched (5.95), strikeouts per nine innings pitched (10.0), and ratio of strikeouts to walks (4.25), and he tied with teammate Bob Knepper for most shutouts in the NL (five). He was the winner of the NL Cy Young Award.

1st

Year in which every major-league team had a home attendance of at least 1 million. The Pirates topped the mark in its last home game (September 28), finishing with 1,000,917.

1st

Major-league pitch faced by Jay Bell of the Indians, which he hit a home run off Bert Blyleven of the Twins on September 29. In 1986, two other players hit a home run in their first major-league at-bat: Will Clark of the Giants (April 8, off Nolan Ryan of the Astros) and Terry Steinbach of the Oakland A's (September 12, off Gregg Swindell of the Indians).

2

Grand slams by Larry Sheets and Jim Dwyer of the Orioles in the fourth inning on August 6 against the Rangers. Toby Harrah of the Texas Rangers hit a grand slam in the second inning. It was the first game in major-league history with three grand slams. The Rangers won 13-11.

2

Inside-the-park home runs by Greg Gagne of the Twins on October 4, both off Floyd Bannister of the White Sox. He also hit a triple in the game.

2

Players who hit for the cycle in 1986: Tony Phillips of the A's on May 16 and Kirby Puckett of the Twins on August 1.

2

Players with at least 25 home runs and 80 stolen bases: Eric Davis of the Reds (27 home runs and 80 stolen bases) and Rickey Henderson of the Yankees (28 home runs and 87 stolen bases). They are the only players in major-league history to achieve this feat in a season (through 2014).

2

Players with at least 200 hits, 20 home runs, and 20 stolen bases: Joe Carter of the Indians (200 hits, 29 home runs, and 29 stolen bases) and Kirby Puckett (223 hits, 31 home runs, and 20 stolen bases). They were the first players in AL history to accomplish the feat.

3

Home runs by designated hitter Juan Beniquez of the Orioles, on June 12 against the Yankees. In 112 other games in 1986, Beniquez hit a total of three home runs.

3

Home runs by Reggie Jackson of the Angels, on September 18 against the Kansas City Royals. He joined Stan Musial and Babe Ruth as the only players aged 40 or older to hit three home runs in a game.

3

Batters hit by Mitch Williams of the Rangers in 1⅓ innings on July 30 against the Orioles.

3

Hits by Russ Morman of the White Sox in his first three at-bats in the major leagues, on August 3 against the Detroit Tigers. In the second inning, he hit a single off Randy O'Neal. In the fourth inning, he hit a solo home run off O'Neal and a run-scoring single off Jim Slaton,

3

Wild pitches thrown by Mark Clear of the Milwaukee Brewers in ⅓ of an inning on September 16 in the second game of a doubleheader against the Red Sox.

3

Players with 500+ home runs who hit their first in 1986: Barry Bonds of the Pirates (June 4), Mark McGwire of the A's (August 25), and Rafael Palmeiro of the

Chicago Cubs (September 9). All later faced allegations of using performance-enhancing drugs.

3rd

NL MVP Award won by Mike Schmidt. He joined Roy Campanella and Stan Musial as the only three-time winners in the senior circuit. Schmidt led the NL in home runs (37), RBIs (119), slugging average (.547), OPS (.937), and at-bats per home run (14.9), and he tied with teammate Von Hayes for most extra-base hits (67). He also led the majors in intentional bases on balls (25), and he won his 10th and last Gold Glove Award at third base.

4

Home runs allowed by Mario Soto of the Reds in the fourth inning on April 29 against the Montreal Expos.

4

Doubles by Rafael Ramirez of the Braves on May 21 (13 innings) and Damaso Garcia of the Blue Jays on June 27.

4

Times that Robby Thompson of the Giants was caught stealing (in four attempts to steal second base) on June 27 against the Reds. He was thrown out by Bo Diaz in the fourth, sixth, ninth, and 11th innings.

4

Home runs by Bob Horner of the Braves on July 6 against the Expos. He hit three solo homers and a three-run homer. Despite Horner's efforts, the Braves lost 11-8.

4

Errors by third baseman Bob Brenly of the Giants during the fourth inning on September 14 against the Braves. He did better at the plate, hitting a solo home run in the fifth, a two-run single in the seventh, and a walk-off solo homer in the bottom of the ninth as the Giants won 7-6.

4:16

Duration of a nine-inning game between the Orioles and Yankees on June 8, setting an AL record. The Orioles won 18-9.

5

Consecutive batters struck out by Fernando Valenzuela of the Los Angeles Dodgers at the 1986 All-Star Game, equaling Carl Hubbell's 1934 feat. Valenzuela struck out Don Mattingly, Cal Ripken, and Jesse Barfield in the fourth and Lou Whitaker and Teddy Higuera in the fifth.

5

Triples hit by the Phillies on August 2 against the Cubs. They also had seven doubles. Gary Redus hit two triples and a double, and Juan Samuel hit two doubles and a triple.

5

Stolen bases by Tony Gwynn of the Padres on September 20 against the Astros. He stole both second base and third base in the first and sixth innings and stole third base in the eighth inning.

6

Shutouts by Jack Morris of the Tigers, most in the majors.

7

Walks thrown by Joe Cowley of the White Sox in a no-hit game on September 19 against the Angels. He allowed one earned run. Cowley never won another major-league game, losing his last two decisions in 1986 and going 0-4 with the Phillies in 1987.

8

RBIs by Alvin Davis of the Mariners on May 9 against the Blue Jays. He hit a three-run home run in the first inning, a run-scoring single in the second inning, and a grand slam in the seventh inning.

8

Consecutive batters struck out by Jim Deshaies of the Astros to start the game on September 23 against the Dodgers — a twentieth-century record.

9

Leadoff home runs by Rickey Henderson, a single-season record at the time.

10th

Career game with five hits by Pete Rose of the Reds, on August 11 against the Giants. In his 24th and final season as a player, the player/manager batted .219 in 72 games. Rose retired with 4,256 hits in 3,562 games, both major-league records (through 2014).

11

Players on the Angels in 1986 who were at least 35 years old: catcher Bob Boone, second-baseman Bobby Grich, third-baseman Doug DeCinces, left-fielder Brian Downing, right-fielder George Hendrick, designated hitter Reggie Jackson, utility infielder Rick Burleson, and pitchers Ken Forsch, Vern Ruhle, Jim Slaton, and Don Sutton.

12

Losses in relief by Ken Howell of the Dodgers.

13

Consecutive games played by pitcher Dale Mohorcic of the Rangers between August 6 and August 20. During the streak, he had two saves, two blown saves, and one loss.

14

Triples by Brett Butler of the Indians, most in the majors. Mitch Webster of the Expos led the NL with 13 triples.

14.1

At-bats per home run by Rob Deer of the Brewers, best in the majors.

15

Consecutive road losses by the A's from May 24 to June 23.

17

Years as teammates by Tony Perez and Pete Rose (1964 to 1976 with the Reds, 1983 with the Phillies, and 1984 to 1986 with the Reds).

18

Innings played by the Astros and the Cubs in a September 2 game at Wrigley Field that was suspended for darkness in the 15th inning and completed on September 3. A total of 53 players appeared in the game, including Greg Maddux of the Cubs in his major-league debut (as a pinch-runner in the 17th inning). The Astros won 8-7.

18

Losses by Rick Mahler of the Braves, most in the majors. Richard Dotson of the White Sox and Mike Morgan of the Mariners led the AL with 17 losses.

19.0

At-bats per strikeout by Ozzie Smith of the St. Louis Cardinals, best in the NL.

20

Complete games by Fernando Valenzuela, most in the majors. Tom Candiotti of the Indians led the AL with 17 complete games.

21

Wins by Fernando Valenzuela, most in the NL.

22

Wild pitches by Bobby Witt of the Rangers, most in the majors. In his second major-league game, he threw four wild pitches and eight walks in five no-hit innings on April 17 against the Brewers. Nolan Ryan led the NL with 15 wild pitches.

23

Age in years of Jamie Moyer of the Cubs made his major-league debut, on June 16. He faced off against 41-year-old Steve Carlton of the Phillies and got the win. Moyer was 49 years old when he played in his final game on May 27, 2012.

25

Consecutive games with a base hit by Steve Sax of the Dodgers, from September 1 to September 27. During the streak, he hit 10 doubles and batted .406.

28

Double plays grounded into by Julio Franco of the Indians, most in the majors.

30

Strikeouts in a nine-inning game between the Mariners (18 strikeouts) and A's (12 strikeouts) on April 19 to set a modern-day record.

30 ⅔

Consecutive innings in which the Blue Jays did not score a run, from July 25 to July 28.

31 ⅔

Consecutive innings in which the White Sox did not allow a run, from August 31 to September 3.

32

Consecutive innings in which Jack Morris did not allow a run, from July 4 to July 23.

35

Home runs by Dave Kingman of the A's, setting a record for most homers by a player in his final season.

36

Saves by Todd Worrell of the Cardinals, most in the NL. He was named the league's Rookie of the Year.

39

Games started by Tom Browning of the Reds and Rick Mahler of the Braves, most in the majors. Mike Moore of the Mariners and Frank Viola of the Twins led the AL with 37 starts.

40

Home runs by Jesse Barfield of the Blue Jays, most in the majors.

43 and 41

Age in years of Tommy John and Niekro, starting pitchers for the Yankees in a doubleheader on August 30 against the Mariners. They were the first pair of 40-plus teammates to start a doubleheader since 1933.

46

Saves by Dave Righetti of the Yankees, a major-league record at the time. He broke the former record of 45 by saving both games of a doubleheader against the Red Sox on the last day of the season.

50

Home runs allowed by Bert Blyleven, a major-league record (through 2014). He allowed five home runs in 5⅓ innings on September 13 against the Rangers. Kevin Gross of the Phillies led the NL with 28 home runs allowed.

53

Doubles by Don Mattingly of the Yankees, most in the majors. He also hit 31 home runs, becoming the first AL player since Hank Greenberg in 1940 to have at least 50 doubles and 30 home runs in a season. Von Hayes led the NL with 46 doubles.

83

Games played by Craig Lefferts of the Padres, the most by any pitcher in the majors. Mitch Williams led the AL with 80 games, a league record by a rookie pitcher at the time.

86

Extra-base hits by Don Mattingly, most in the majors.

107

Stolen bases by Vince Coleman of the Cardinals, most in the majors. It was the second of three consecutive years in which he stole at least 100 bases. Rickey Henderson led the AL with 87 steals.

117

RBIs by AL Rookie of the Year Jose Canseco of the A's, the most by a rookie since Walt Dropo had 144 in 1950. Canseco became the first player in major-league history to drive in at least 110 runs with a batting average of .240 or lower.

121

RBIs by Joe Carter, most in the majors.

130

Runs scored by Rickey Henderson, most in the majors. Tony Gwynn and Von Hayes led the NL with 107 runs.

143

Walks allowed by Bobby Witt, most in the majors, in only 157⅔ innings. Floyd Youmans of the Expos led the NL with 118 walks.

163

Games played by Tony Fernandez of the Blue Jays, most in the majors.

185

Strikeouts by Pete Incaviglia of the Rangers, most in the majors and an AL record at the time. Juan Samuel led the NL with 142 strikeouts.

238

Hits by Don Mattingly, most in the majors and a new Yankees record. Tony Gwynn led the NL with 211 hits.

241

Wins by Steve Carlton with the Phillies between 1972 and 1986.

245

Strikeouts thrown by Mark Langston of the Mariners, most in the AL. He also led the league in strikeouts per nine innings pitched, with 9.2.

.256

Batting average of Willie McGee of the Cardinals, down almost 100 points from his league-leading average of .353 in 1985.

271 ⅔

Innings pitched by Bert Blyleven, most in the AL.

300th

Career win by Don Sutton of the Angels, on June 18 against the Rangers. He became the 19th pitcher to reach the mark. On June 28, he and 47-year-old Phil Niekro of the Indians became the first 300-win pitchers to face each other since 1892. On July 27, Sutton and Tom Seaver faced off as 300-game winners.

.334

Batting average of Tim Raines of the Expos, best in the NL.

388

Total bases by Don Mattingly, most in the majors. Dave Parker of the Reds led the NL with 304.

.433

Batting average of Randy Bush of the Twins as a pinch-hitter (13 for 30). Candy Maldonado of the Giants had a .425 average as pinch-hitter (17 for 40, including four home runs).

475

Estimated length in feet of the first major-league homer by Bo Jackson of the Royals, on September 14 off Mike Moore of the Mariners. Jackson was the 1985 Heisman Trophy winner and the first overall pick in the 1986 NFL draft, but he chose to play with the defending World Series champions instead. Jackson played in the majors until 1994 and also played with the Los Angeles Raiders from 1987 to 1990.

.573

Slugging average of Don Mattingly, best in the majors.

600

At-bats without a home run by Vince Coleman.

687

At-bats by Tony Fernandez, most in the majors. Tony Gwynn led the NL with 642 at-bats.

742

Plate appearances of Don Mattingly, most in the majors. Steve Sax led the NL with 704.

.967

OPS of Don Mattingly, best in the majors.

1,015

RBIs by Eddie Murray in his first 10 seasons (1977 to 1986), all with the Orioles.

1,148

Strikeouts by Seattle batters, an AL record at the time.

1,480

Games won by Earl Weaver in 17 years as Baltimore's manager (1968 to 1982 plus 1985 and 1986).

2,181

Games played during 18 seasons with the Dodgers by Bill Russell, who retired after the 1986 season.

2,000th

Career hit by Robin Yount of the Brewers, on September 6. He was 10 days shy of his 31st birthday. Only six other players had reached the mark at a younger age.

3,000th

Career strikeout by Bert Blyleven, on August 1 against Mike Davis of the A's. He became the 10th pitcher to achieve the milestone.

4,000th

Career strikeout by Steve Carlton of the Giants, on August 5 against Eric Davis of the Reds. He became the second pitcher (after Nolan Ryan) to accomplish the feat.

SOURCES

Nemec, David, ed. The Baseball Chronicle: Year-by-Year History of Major League Baseball (Lincolnwood, Illinois: Publications International, 2003).

Society for American Baseball Research. The SABR Baseball List and Record Book (New York: Scribner, 2007).

Solomon, Burt. The Baseball Timeline (New York: DK Publishing, 2001).

Sugar, Burt Randolph, ed. The Baseball Maniac's Almanac (third edition) (New York: Skyhorse Publishing, 2012).

baseball-almanac.com

baseballlibrary.com/chronology

baseball-reference.com

retrosheet.org

thisgreatgame.com/1986-baseball-history.html

HOW THE 1986 RED SOX WERE BUILT

By Rod Nelson

Name	Salary	Acquired	POS	SCOUTING DIR	SCOUT1	SCOUT2	ORG	SIGN YR	SIGN DATE	Type	Rnd	Num
Marty Barrett	$435,000	Amateur Draft	2B	Kasko, Eddie	Boone, Ray		BOS A	1979		Sec	1	1
Wade Boggs*	$1,350,000	Amateur Draft	3B	Mahoney, Neil	Digby, George		BOS A	1976	06/10/1976	Reg	7	166
Oil Can Boyd	$375,000	Amateur Draft	P	Kasko, Eddie	Scott, Ed		BOS A	1980		Reg	16	414
Mike Brown	$80,000	Amateur Draft	P	Kasko, Eddie	Britton, Wayne		BOS A	1980		Reg	2	48
Roger Clemens	$340,000	Amateur Draft	P	Kasko, Eddie	Doyle, Danny		BOS A	1983	06/21/1983	Reg	1	19
Pat Dodson*	$1,017,757	Amateur Draft	1B	Kasko, Eddie	Stephenson, Joe		BOS A	1980		Reg	6	154
Dwight Evans		Amateur Draft	OF	Mahoney, Neil	Stephenson, Joe		BOS A	1969		Reg	5	107
Mike Greenwell*	$60,000	Amateur Draft	OF	Kasko, Eddie	Digby, George		BOS A	1982	06/09/1982	Reg	3	72
Bruce Hurst*	$495,000	Amateur Draft	P	Mahoney, Neil	Lee, Don		BOS A	1976		Reg	1	22
Steve Lyons*		Amateur Draft	OF	Kasko, Eddie	Johnson, Earl		BOS A	1981		Reg	1	19
Al Nipper	$265,000	Amateur Draft	P	Kasko, Eddie	Lenhardt, Don		BOS A	1980		Reg	8	206
Jim Rice	$1,984,423	Amateur Draft	OF	Mahoney, Neil	Brown, Mace	Hopkins, Paul	BOS A	1971		Reg	1	15
Kevin Romine		Amateur Draft	OF	Kasko, Eddie	Boone, Ray		BOS A	1982		Reg	2	42
Jeff Sellers		Amateur Draft	P	Kasko, Eddie	Stephenson, Joe		BOS A	1982		Reg	8	202
Bob Stanley	$1,060,000	Amateur Draft	P	Mahoney, Neil	Sczesny, Matt		BOS A	1974		Sec	1	7
Dave Stapleton	$300,000	Amateur Draft	1B	Mahoney, Neil	Bolling, Milt		BOS A	1975		Reg	10	231
Marc Sullivan	$110,000	Amateur Draft	C	Kasko, Eddie	Digby, George	Enos, Bill	BOS A	1979		Reg	2	52
Rob Woodward		Amateur Draft	P	Kasko, Eddie	Enos, Bill		BOS A	1981	06/14/1981	Reg	3	70
Steve Crawford	$330,000	Amateur Free Agent	P	Kasko, Eddie	Doyle, Danny		BOS A	1978	05/06/1978	FA	ND	-
Rich Gedman*	$650,000	Amateur Free Agent	C	Mahoney, Neil	Enos, Bill		BOS A	1977	08/05/1977	FA	ND	-
Rey Quinones	$60,000	Amateur Free Agent	SS	Kasko, Eddie	Maldonado, Felix		BOS A	1982	07/08/1982	FA	ND	-
Glenn Hoffman	$350,000	Free Agency	SS	Mahoney, Neil	Stephenson, Joe		BOS A	1976		Reg	2	46
Joe Sambito*	$500,000	Free Agency	P	Stallings, Lynwood	Rapp, Earl		HOU N	1973		Reg	17	404
Dave Sax		Free Agency	C	Wade, Ben	King, Ron		LA N	1978	06/16/1978	FA	ND	-
Mike Trujillo	$85,000	Rule 5 Draft	P	Winkles, Bobby	Monroe, Larry		CHI A	1982		Reg	7	172
Tony Armas	$1,000,000	Traded	OF	Peterson, Harding	Haak, Howie		PIT N	1971	01/18/1971	Fa	x	
Don Baylor	$660,696	Traded	DH	Shannon, Walter	Mattick, Bobby	Phillips, Dee	BAL A	1967		Reg	2	39
Bill Buckner*	$785,000	Traded	1B	Campanis, Al	Brenzel, Bill		LA N	1968		Reg	2	25

Name	Salary	Acquired	POS	SCOUTING DIR	SCOUT1	SCOUT2	ORG	SIGN YR	SIGN DATE	Type	Rnd	Num
Wes Gardner	$70,000	Traded	P	McIlvaine, Joe	Mason, Joe		NYM N	1982		Reg	22	550
Dave Henderson	$412,000	Traded	OF	Didier, Mel	Harrison, Bob	Laspina, Tom	SEA A	1977		Reg	1	26
Tim Lollar*	$541,250	Traded	P	Bergesch, Bill	Walker, Jerry		NYY A	1978		Reg	4	104
Spike Owen#	$255,000	Traded	SS	Keller, Hal	Chalk, Dave	Harrison, Bob	SEA A	1982		Reg	1	6
Ed Romero	$375,000	Traded	SS	Widmar, Al	Delgado, Felix		MIL A	1975	11/14/1975	FA	ND	-
Calvin Schiraldi	$75,000	Traded	P	McIlvaine, Joe	Terrell, Jim		NYM N	1983	1983	Reg	1	27
Tom Seaver		Traded	P	Burbrink, Nelson*	Minor, Harry	Moore, Johnny	MIL N	1965	06/08/1965	Fa	x	
Mike Stenhouse*		Traded	OF	Menendez, Danny	Harper, Al		MON N	1980		Sec	1	4
Sammy Stewart	$381,113	Traded	P	Ritterpusch, David	Tutor, Rip		BAL A	1975	06/15/1975	FA	ND	-
La Schelle Tarver*		Traded	OF	Gebrian, Pete	Partee, Roy		NYM N	1980	08/18/1980	FA	ND	-

NOTE: Tom Seaver received a $50,000 signing bonus. Wade Boggs received one of $7,500.

CONTRIBUTORS

NIALL ADLER has been paid to watch sports (and sometimes theatre) since 1998. Everything from diving to swimming, water polo, Aussie Rules, horse racing, hockey, futbol and gridiron, and... baseball on four continents and at two of the top collegiate programs, Long Beach State and Stanford. He's even judged a demolition derby. Educated at the University of San Francisco and farther South in Melbourne, Australia, he's worked some larger events like BCS Bowl Games, the Australian Open, Pan American Games and the Melbourne Cup.

MALCOLM ALLEN, a loyal Baltimore-born Orioles fan and former Memorial Stadium usher, worked distributing vintage Jamaican music all over the world for much of his adult life. Raising two daughters, Ruth and Martina, he is also working on a full-length biography of Joaquin Andjuar.

WILL ANDERSON, who died in March 2015, wrote nine books on beer but is noted in baseball circles as a 2002 inductee into the Maine Baseball Hall of Fame and member of the committee to bring the Portland Seadogs to Maine. He also wrote about roadside architecture, baseball, and 1950s Rock and roll, and was honored with the Maine Historic Preservation Award for his "diligent and dedicated service in support of Maine's historic and cultural heritage." He authored the 1992 book which was a precursor of SABR's "team books"— *Was Baseball Really Invented in Maine?* He followed that work with *The Lost New England Nine (2003),* by which time the Tom Simon-edited *Green Mountain Boys of Summer* (2000) had also been published.

AUDREY LEVI APFEL is a leading research analyst for Gartner, Inc., advising organizations worldwide and publishing research on technology trends and projects. Her contribution to this book represents the first time she has written about her lifelong passion and interest in all things baseball—particularly New York baseball. She was raised in Queens, in the shadow of Shea Stadium. Audrey resides in the strong baseball outpost of Stamford, Connecticut - where Bobby Valentine and Brian Cashman have been known to rappel off of a 22-story building together at Christmastime dressed as elves.

MARK ARMOUR, the director of the Baseball Biography Project and the co-author of the 2015 book *In Pursuit of Pennants* (Nebraska) writes baseball from his home in Corvallis, Oregon. Some say that the recent Red Sox championships have wiped out the pain of 1986. They are wrong.

ERIC ARON has been a SABR member since 2002. In addition to his writing for SABR, he has contributed to other websites and magazines, including Throughthefencebaseball.com, NewEnglandFilm.com, and *Imagine Magazine*. He lives in Boston and holds a Master's degree in Public History & Museum Studies. He enjoys documentaries, playing hoops, and laughter Yoga. When he was 13 growing up in Rye, New York, he watched Game Six on television with his father. After the Mets won, his father, a lifelong Brooklyn Dodgers fan, kept shaking his head over and over, repeating "I don't believe it...I don't believe it!"

TYLER ASH graduated Elon University ('15) with a Bachelor of Arts Degree in Communication, concentrating in print journalism and minoring in business administration. He wrote for rantsports.com, covering the New England Patriots. He interned at the *Revere Journal* in the sports department and was a contributor to the *Pendulum*, Elon University's news outlet. Tyler is a member of SABR who has written SABR BioProject biographies, and maintains a personal blog—tylerashsportsblog.com. He was a featured radio personality on *One on One Sports* for WSOE 89.3, Elon's student radio home for weekly sports talk.

A lifelong Blue Jays fan who was born and raised in Toronto, Thomas Ayers has earned degrees from the University of Toronto, the London School of Economics and Queen's University. Currently practicing labour and employment law, he has contributed several other biographies to the SABR Baseball Biography Project. He attended Game Five of the 2015 ALDS between the Texas Rangers and Toronto Blue Jays, which was certainly the most memorable game he's ever seen.

RICHARD BOGOVICH is the author of *Kid Nichols: A Biography of the Hall of Fame Pitcher* and *The Who: A Who's Who*, both published by McFarland & Co. Most recently he wrote a chapter on Jorge Comellas of the Cubs for *Who's on First: Replacement Players in World War II*, after having contributed to *Inventing Baseball: The 100 Greatest Games of the Nineteenth Century*. He resides in Rochester, Minnesota.

BOB BRADY joined SABR in 1991 and is the current president of the Boston Braves Historical Association. As the editor of the Association's quarterly newsletter since 1992, he's had the privilege of memorializing the passings of the "Greatest Generation" members of the Braves Family. He owns a small piece of the Norwich, Connecticut-based Connecticut Tigers of the New York-Penn League, a Class-A short-season affiliate of the Detroit Tigers. Bob has contributed biographies and supporting pieces to a number of SABR publications as well as occasionally lending a hand in the editing process.

FREDERICK C. (RICK) BUSH, his wife Michelle, and their three sons Michael, Andrew, and Daniel live in northwest Houston. He has taught both English and German and is currently an English professor at Wharton County Junior College in Sugar Land. Though he is an avid fan of the hometown Astros, his youth has left him with an abiding affinity for the Texas Rangers and Pittsburgh Pirates as well. He has contributed articles to SABR's BioProject and Games Project sites and, in addition to his contribution to this volume, he has written articles for SABR books about the 1979 Pittsburgh Pirates, 1972 Texas Rangers, Milwaukee's County Stadium, the Montreal Expos, and baseball's winter meetings. Currently he is also serving as an associate editor, photo editor, and contributing author for a SABR book about the Houston Astrodome.

AUGUSTO CÁRDENAS lives in Maracaibo, Venezuela, and is the author of *My Story: Luis Aparicio*, the authorized biography of the only Venezuelan inducted into the Hall of Fame, and also the baseball beat writer of *Diario Panorama*, a local newspaper with 100 years of experience. He has covered the Venezuelan Winter League since 2000, and has been the special correspondent for his newspaper to cover Major League Baseball games, MLB Spring Trainings, All-Star Games, the World Baseball Classic, the Nippon Professional Baseball and the Caribbean Series. Cárdenas is a SABR member who loves to write about the Venezuelan players who saw playing when he was a just a kid.

RALPH CARHART is a theatrical production manager and director by trade. He is also an amateur baseball historian with a particular interest in the origins of the game. He received the 2015 Chairman's Award from the SABR 19th Century Committee and is a member of the 19th Century Baseball Grave Marker Project, spearheading the effort to place stones at the unmarked graves of forgotten pioneers. For the last five years he has been working on a project he calls "The Hall Ball," in which he is attempting to take a photograph of a single baseball with every member of the Hall of Fame, living and deceased. The ball is pictured in either the hands of the living baseball great, or at the grave of those who are no longer alive. As of this writing he has photographed 264 of the 310 members. To see the photos he's taken so far, visit www.thehallball.sportspalooza.com.

ALAN COHEN has been a member of SABR since 2011, and is vice president/treasurer of the Connecticut Smoky Joe Wood Chapter. He has written more than 25 biographies for SABR's BioProject, and has contributed to several SABR books. His first game story about Baseball's Longest Day—May 31, 1964 (Mets vs. Giants) has been followed by several other game stories.

His research into the *Hearst Sandlot Classic (1946-1965)*, an annual youth All-Star game which launched the careers of 88 major-league players, including 1986 Mets manager Davey Johnson and 1986 Mets announcer Fran Healy, first appeared in the Fall, 2013 edition of the *Baseball Research Journal*, and has been followed with a poster presentation at the SABR Convention in Chicago. He is currently expanding his research and is looking forward to having a book published. He serves as the datacaster (stringer) for the Hartford Yard Goats, the Colorado Rockies affiliate in the Class-AA Eastern League. Born in the shadow of Shea Stadium, he grew up on Long Island and graduated from Franklin and Marshall College in Lancaster, PA with a degree in history. He has four grown children and six grandchildren and now resides in West Hartford, Connecticut with his wife Frances, two cats and two dogs.

WARREN CORBETT is the author of *The Wizard of Waxahachie: Paul Richards and the End of Baseball as We Knew It*, and a contributor to SABR's Baseball Biography Project. He lives in Bethesda, Maryland.

RORY COSTELLO, a lifelong Mets fan, was at Shea Stadium for Games Three and Four of the 1986 NL Championship Series. The first World Series game he attended was none other than Game Six in 1986. He remembers seeing the premature congratulations to the Red Sox flashing on the Diamond Vision screen and feeling Shea rock on its foundation with the energy of the crowd. Rory lives in Brooklyn, New York with his wife Noriko and son Kai.

JOHN DIFONZO grew up in Somerville, Massachusetts where he was the Sports Editor for his high school newspaper. He is a lifelong Red Sox fan and season-ticket holder since 2004 currently living in Beacon Hill with his wife, Gabriella. John is a graduate of Tufts University and holds a Master of Science in Finance from Bentley University and is a CFA chartholder.

ALEX EDELMAN is a 2012 graduate of New York University, where he majored in English literature and wrote a thesis on the concept of landlessness in *Moby Dick*. This is the seventh BioProject collection he has appeared in. His second effort, on 1967 Red Sox pitcher Billy Rohr, received a Jack R. Kavanaugh Award. A native of Boston who spent several years working in PR departments at the Red Sox, Dodgers, and Brewers, Edelman is also an acclaimed professional stand-up comedian. In 2014, he won the Foster's Edinburgh Comedy Award for Best Newcomer, the first American to do so since 1997. He enjoys Italian food and the work of David Foster Wallace.

JEFF ENGLISH is a graduate of Florida State University and resides in Tallahassee, Florida with his wife Allison and twin sons, Elliott and Oscar. He is a lifelong Cubs fan and serves as secretary of the North Florida/Buck O'Neil SABR chapter. He has contributed to multiple SABR projects.

GREG ERION is retired from the railroad industry and currently teaches history part-time at Skyline Community College in San Bruno, California. He has written several biographies for SABR's BioProject and is currently working on a book about the 1959 season. Greg is one of the leaders of SABR's Baseball Games Project. He and his wife Barbara live in South San Francisco, California.

DAN FIELDS is a manuscript editor at the *New England Journal of Medicine*. He loves baseball trivia, and he attends Boston Red Sox and Pawtucket (Rhode Island) Red Sox games with this teenage son whenever he can. Dan lives in Framingham, Massachusetts, and can be reached at dfields820@gmail.com.

T.S. FLYNN is an educator and writer in Minneapolis who has published short fiction, essays, reviews, and articles. His blog, *It's a long season*, is a hobby and habit, and he is currently working on his first book-length project, an excavation of the 65-year baseball career of Tom Sheehan.

JAMES FORR is a past winner of the McFarland-SABR Baseball Research Award, and co-author (with David Proctor) of *Pie Traynor: A Baseball Biography*. He lives in Columbia, Missouri and is one of the leaders of SABR's Games Project.

DAVID FORRESTER recalls his brother breaking an antique piece of furniture during the seventh game of the 1986 ALCS. Or it might have been himself. David is a nonprofit executive and lifelong Red Sox fan now living in exile with the Seattle Mariners. He joined SABR over a decade ago when his historical research uncovered Allie Moulton, the first person of African American ancestry known to have played in the segregated major leagues.

IRV GOLDFARB has been a member of SABR since 1999 and has written numerous bios and articles for various SABR publications. He is a member of the Black Sox, Deadball, Origins, and Negro League committees. Irv works at the ABC Television network and lives in Union City, New Jersey with his wife Mercedes and their cat, Consuelo. They are all New York Met fans and would rather not talk anymore about the 2015 World Series.

JOHN GREGORY is a retired software developer. He has been a SABR member since 1984, and was one of the founders of the SABR-L mailing list in 1995. John currently lives in the Boston area, but maintains an abiding love for the Minnesota Twins.

GENE GUMBS worked in higher education for 25 years as a director of athletic communications. He also had stints as a sports editor for newspapers, a college and high school assistant basketball coach, and six years as a television color commentator for minor-league hockey and college football, basketball, and ice hockey. He currently works as a manuscript editor for a publishing company, and does stat work and broadcasting for local colleges and universities. He also maintains a personal blog and podcast — thesportsmicroscope.com. A lifelong Red Sox fan, Gene holds a degree in English from Franklin Pierce University in New Hampshire. He contributed a chapter to *Spahn, Sain, and Teddy Ballgame: Boston's (almost) Perfect Baseball Summer of 1948*, a SABR publication (Rounder Books, 2009).

DONNA L. HALPER is an Associate Professor of Communication at Lesley University, Cambridge Massachusetts. A media historian who specializes in the history of broadcasting, Dr. Halper is the author of six books and many articles. She is also a former broadcaster and print journalist.

LESLIE HEAPHY, a lifelong Mets fan, is a history professor at Kent State University at Stark. She is a member of the SABR Board of Directors and is the editor of the national journal, *Black Ball*. She has published numerous articles and books on the Negro Leagues and women's baseball.

PAUL HENSLER is a longtime Angels fan who witnessed Dave Henderson's derring-do in Game Five of the 1986 ALCS. The author of *The American League in Transition, 1965-1975: How Competition Thrived When the Yankees Didn't,* Paul has contributed to SABR's *Baseball Research Journal* and *NINE: A Journal of Baseball History and Culture.* He also has presented at the Cooperstown Symposium on Baseball and American Culture.

SABR member **MICHAEL HUBER** is Dean of Academic Life and Professor of Mathematics at Muhlenberg College in Allentown, Pennsylvania, where he teaches an undergraduate course titled "Reasoning with Sabermetrics." He has published his sabermetrics research in several books and journals, including *The Baseball Research Journal, Chance, Base Ball, Annals of Applied Statistics,* and *The Journal of Statistics Education,* and he frequently contributes to SABR's Baseball Games Project.

JOANNE HULBERT, co-chair of the Boston Chapter and the SABR Arts Committee, cherishes the art and poetry of baseball, must still avert her eyes when watching the 1986 film clip of the ball skittering through Buckner's legs, yet has found a modicum of relief from anguish while researching her portion of the Red Sox - Mets World Series history and is able now to at least watch until the ball approaches that pivotal moment and may soon be able to visually endure the ball passing through that inverted "V" that portended a lost victory.

DAVID KAISER, a historian, is the author of *Epic Season: the 1948 American League Pennant Race,* as well as six other books on diplomacy and international politics. He is a frequent contributor to the SABR-L list and has given two presentations at national SABR conventions. A former faculty member at Harvard University, Carnegie Mellon, the Naval War College, and Williams College, he lives in Watertown, Massachusetts.

MARK KANTER grew up in Bristol, Pennsylvania, where he became a life-long Philadelphia Phillies fan. He got the itch while watching the last few outs of Jim Bunning's perfect game on Father's Day in 1964. He graduated from the Pennsylvania State University attaining a bachelor's degree in Psychology with a minor in Middle Eastern History. He attended the University of Maryland studying Sports Studies. He received a master's degree in Industrial Engineering from the University of Massachusetts. He has written several articles for SABR's *Baseball Research Journal* and was the editor for Boston SABR 2002 convention publication. He has been a member of 10 SABR Team Trivia Championships since 1997, inclusive. He decided to take on the challenge of writing the Marty Barrett biography because one of his best friends is a friend of Marty's cousin. He and his wife, Lynne, who is also a great baseball fan in her own right, live in the idyllic seaside community of Portsmouth, Rhode Island.

MAXWELL KATES is a chartered accountant who lives and works in Toronto. He recently stepped down after 12 years as Director of Marketing for the Hanlan's Point Chapter. His feature article on Tom Seaver has previously appeared in *The Miracle Has Landed*, along with biographies of Tom Terrific's 1969 Mets teammates Ron Taylor and Rod Gaspar. Years before, he worked in sports radio for News Talk 610 CKTB in St. Catharines, Ontario. Years before that, in true New York Mets fashion, he submitted a banner for a summer camp ecology project which read "Save Water - Don't Send Mets Pitchers to the Showers!" The banner was rejected; the camp director was a Mets fan.

JIMMY KEENAN has been a SABR member since 2001. His grandfather, Jimmy Lyston, and four other family members were all professional baseball players.

A frequent contributor to SABR publications, Keenan is the author of *The Lystons: A Story of One Baltimore Family* and *Our National Pastime*. He is a 2010 inductee into the Oldtimers Baseball Association of Maryland's Hall of Fame and a 2012 inductee into Baltimore's Boys of Summer Hall of Fame.

NORM KING lives in Ottawa, Ontario, and has been a SABR member since 2010. He has contributed to a number of SABR books, including, *"That's Joy in Braveland": The 1957 Milwaukee Braves* (2014), *Winning on the North Side. The 1929 Chicago Cubs* (2015), and *A Pennant for the Twins Cities: The 1965 Minnesota Twins* (2015). He thought he was crazy to miss his beloved Expos after all these years until he met people from Brooklyn.

LEE KLUCK of Stevens Point, Wisconsin worked as a processor in Transportation Operations Support for Sentry Insurance. A Sentry transportation motto circa 1988 is: "The Speed of the Leader Determines the Rate of the Pack."

RUSS LAKE lives in Champaign, Illinois, and is a retired Professor Emeritus. He was born in Belleville, Illinois, on the "other side of the river" from downtown St. Louis. The 1964 Cardinals remain his favorite team, and he was grateful to go to 28 games at Sportsman's Park (aka Busch Stadium I) before it was demolished in late 1966. His wife, Carol, deserves an MVP award for watching all of a 14-inning ballgame in Cincinnati with Russ in 1971—during their honeymoon. He joined SABR in 1994 and, later in that same year, was an editor for David Halberstam's *October 1964*.

BOB LEMOINE grew up in South Portland, Maine, and watched the 1986 World Series on a black-and-white TV with rabbit ears. His mom didn't sleep very well during the series with all the yelling coming from downstairs. While Bob's own high school years were scarred with the Red Sox losing the World Series, he recovered and now works as a high school librarian in New Hampshire, surrounded by students who have never heard of rabbit ears. Bob joined SABR in 2013 and has contributed to several publications. He is a co-editor with Bill Nowlin on an upcoming

SABR book, *Boston's First Nine: the 1871-75 Boston Red Stockings.* He's glad to have seen the Red Sox win three world titles in color.

LEN LEVIN attended Game Three of the 1986 World Series. The Red Sox lost, but happily, he has seen the Olde Towne Team win many other games. A retired editor at the *Providence Journal* and the *Quincy Patriot Ledger,* Len copyedits many of SABR's publications, including this one, and also edits the written decisions of the Rhode Island Supreme Court.

DAN LEVITT is the author (with Mark Armour) of *In Pursuit of Pennants: Baseball Operations from Deadball to Moneyball,* published in 2015 by the University of Nebraska Press. He is also the author of several other notable baseball books including *The Battle that Forged Modern Baseball: The Federal League Challenge and Its Legacy* and *Ed Barrow: The Bulldog Who Built the Yankees' First Dynasty.* In 2015, Dan received the Bob Davids Award.

MICHAEL MARTELL is currently a student at Kent State University, majoring in business management. Michael is a diehard Cleveland sports fan. He attended his first Cleveland Indians baseball game at two months of age, and his love of baseball continues to this day. He can often be found at Progressive Field, located on the corner of Carnegie Avenue and Ontario Street. That location is where he eagerly awaits to see the Indians first World Series championship in over 60 years.

SHAWN MORRIS is a newer member to SABR. As a doctoral candidate in the history program at Kent State University, he aims to focus his dissertation upon how sports has, and continues to, successfully break down social and cultural barriers. He has also authored articles regarding the historiography of Negro League Baseball in Cleveland, and the city's first professional black baseball team, the Tate Stars.

ROD NELSON (SABRscouts@gmail.com) is the former Research Services Manager for the Society for American Baseball Research. He is Chairman of the SABR Scouts Committee and project leader

for the Who-Signed-Whom database and Scouts Register which has been integrated into the *Diamond Mines* exhibit at the National Baseball Museum in Cooperstown, accessible at http://scouts.baseballhall.org. Nelson launched the Baseball Necrology online forum which has stimulated activity in this important area of baseball research.

SKIP NIPPER is the author of *Baseball in Nashville* (Arcadia Publishing, 2007) and shares his love of Nashville's famous ballpark, Sulphur Dell, through www.sulphurdell.com. A 1972 graduate of Memphis State University, Nipper is a retired sporting goods sales representative. He was a co-founder of the Grantland Rice-Fred Russell Nashville chapter of SABR, and currently serves as secretary for the Old Timers Baseball Association of Nashville. He also has contributed to *Sweet 60: The 1960 Pittsburgh Pirates,* and *The Team That Time Won't Forget: The 1951 New York Giants.* His wife Sheila calls baseball his "other woman," which allows him to research and write about his favorite subject without trepidation. The Nippers reside in Mt. Juliet, Tennessee.

BILL NOWLIN, for better or worse, still vividly remembers the elation of Hendu's homer that spared the Sox from losing the ALCS and the deflation that followed the ball skittering through Buckner's legs, and all that fell apart from that point forward. There was, after all, Game Seven, when the Red Sox led 3-0 through five innings. Like most Red Sox fans, he wallowed in loserdom until 2004. Then things got better. A veteran of more than 45 years in the record business, Bill spends most of his time writing or editing books about baseball.

ARMAND PETERSON is a retired engineer and manager, living in Maple Grove, Minnesota. He's been hooked on baseball since he saw some cousins play a town team game on a hardscrabble field in eastern South Dakota when he was nine years old. He was Yankees and Mickey Mantle fan in his youth—thanks to indoctrination by his baseball-playing older cousins—but switched his allegiance to the Minnesota Twins when the Senators moved to Minnesota in 1961. Since retirement he has co-authored Town Ball: The Glory Days of Minnesota Amateur Baseball, and has contributed to several other SABR biographies.

RICHARD J. PUERZER is an associate professor and chairperson of the Department of Engineering at Hofstra University in Hempstead, New York. His previous research and writings on baseball have appeared in *Nine: A Journal of Baseball History and Culture*, *Black Ball*, *The National Pastime*, *The Cooperstown Symposium on Baseball and American Culture* proceedings, and *Spitball*. He was co-director of The 50th Anniversary of the New York Mets Conference, held at Hofstra University in April, 2012.

DAVID RAGLIN has been a member of SABR for 30 years, and serves as the Vice President of the Bob Davids (Mid Atlantic) Chapter of SABR. He is the co-author of three books on the Detroit Tigers, has served as an editor, fact-checker, and writer for two SABR BioProject books (*Go Get 'Em Tigers* on the 1968 Tigers, and *What a Start! What a Finish* on the 1984 Tigers). He also wrote a biography for the BioProject book on the 1934 Tigers. Dave and Barb met at a SABR event in 2001 and have been married for 13 years.

ALAN RAYLESBERG is an attorney in New York City. He is a lifelong baseball fan who enjoys baseball history and roots for the Yankees and the Mets. Alan also has a strong interest in baseball analytics and is a devotee of baseball simulation games, participating both in draft leagues and historical replays.

MIKE RICHARD is a lifelong Red Sox fan who still counts the Impossible Dream season as his greatest all-time baseball thrill. However, 1986 rates high in his memory because that was the year he took his son Casey (then three) to his first Red Sox game. He retired as a guidance counselor from Gardner (Massachusetts) High School and is a sports columnist for the *Worcester Telegram & Gazette*. A Massachusetts high school sports historian, he has authored two high school football books: *Glory to Gardner: 100 Years of Football in the Chair City*, and *Super Saturdays: The Complete History of the Massachusetts High School Super Bowl*. He has also documented the playoff history (sectional and state championships) of all high school sports in Massachusetts. He lives in Gardner and also owns a home in Sandwich on Cape Cod with his wife Peggy. They are the parents of a son Casey, a daughter Lindsey, and have a grandson Theo.

CARL RIECHERS retired from United Parcel Service in 2012 after 35 years of service. With more free time, he became a SABR member that same year. Born and raised in the suburbs of St. Louis, he became a big fan of the Cardinals. He and his wife Janet have three children and he is the proud grandpa of two.

JOEL RIPPEL is the author or co-author of nine books on Minnesota sports history. He has contributed to several SABR publications including *The National Pastime*, *The Emerald Guide to Baseball* and *A Pennant for the Twin Cities: The 1965 Minnesota Twins*.

MATTHEW SILVERMAN has written numerous books on baseball, including the recently released book from Lyons Press on the 1986 Mets, *One-Year Dynasty*. He also authored *Swinging '73*, and *100 Things Mets Fans Should Know and Do Before They Die*. An alum of Ted Williams Baseball Camp, he has written on the Olde Towne team many times, including *Red Sox by the Numbers* with Bill Nowlin, which has recently been updated and released, along with uniform number books he co-authored on the Mets and Cubs. He flew from college in Virginia to New York to attend Games One and Two of the 1986 World Series, but those aren't exactly the games at Shea that everyone remembers.

MARK SIMON works for ESPN Stats and Information, editing their blog and helping run the @ESPNStatsInfo Twitter feed. He also writes regularly about baseball for ESPN.com. In his spare time he has written a book on Yankees history (published by Triumph Books in June 2016) and obsessively studied every aspect of Game Six of the 1986 World Series.

DAVID E. SKELTON developed a passion for baseball as a child when the lights from Philadelphia's Connie Mack Stadium shone through his bedroom window. Long since removed from Philly, he graduated from the

University of Texas at Tyler with a Bachelor in Business Administration. He now resides with his family in central Texas but remains passionate about the sport that evokes many childhood memories. Employed for over 30 years in the oil and gas industry, he became a SABR member in early 2012 after a chance holiday encounter with a Rogers Hornsby Chapter member.

DOUG SKIPPER has contributed to a number of SABR publications, presented research at national and regional conventions, and profiled more than a dozen players, managers, and game profiles for the SABR Baseball Biographical Project. A SABR member since 1982, he served as president of the Halsey Hall (Minneapolis) Chapter in 2014-2015, and a member of the Deadball Era Committee and the Lawrence Ritter Award Committee, and is interested in the history of Connie Mack's Philadelphia Athletics, the Boston Red Sox, the Minnesota Twins, and old ballparks. A market research consultant residing in Apple Valley, Minnesota, Doug is also a veteran of father-daughter dancing. Doug and his wife have two daughters, MacKenzie and Shannon.

CURT SMITH shows that "writing can be art," said *USA Today*, which calls him "the voice of authority on baseball broadcasting." His 16 books include the classic *Voices of The Game, Pull Up a Chair: The Vin Scully Story, A Talk in the Park: Nine Decades of Baseball Tales from the Broadcast Booth*, and his newest, *George H. W. Bush: Character at the Core*. In 1989-93, Smith wrote more speeches than anyone else for President George H.W. Bush, *The New York Times* terming his work "the high point of Bush familial eloquence." Smith is a GateHouse Media columnist, Associated Press award-winning radio commentator, and senior lecturer of English at the University of Rochester. He has hosted or keynoted the Great Fenway Park Writers series, numerous Smithsonian Institution series, and the Cooperstown Symposium on Baseball and American Culture. The former Gannett reporter and *The Saturday Evening Post* senior editor has written ESPN TV's *Voices of The Game* documentary, created the Franklin Roosevelt Award in Political Communication at the

National Radio Hall of Fame, and been named to the prestigious Judson Welliver Society of former Presidential speechwriters.

While laid up with a ruptured Achilles tendon in 1998, **JON SPRINGER** began a research project to chronicle every uniform number in Mets history. That project became the acclaimed Mets By The Numbers website (mbtn.net), and book of the same name. A graduate of the University of Delaware, Jon is an editor at a business publication in New York and a former daily newspaper sports writer. He lives in Brooklyn with his family.

MARK S. STERNMAN serves as Director of Marketing and Communications for MassDevelopment, the quasi-governmental economic-development authority of Massachusetts. In October 1986, he had just started his freshman year at Dartmouth College. Returning from a frat party in the late stages of Game Six, he saw the fateful final frame in the company of a fellow freshman from Boston's Chinatown who cried silently as the game ended. A fan of the Expos and the Yankees, Sternman liked and likes neither the Mets nor the Sox, but did root for Mike Stenhouse thanks to his Montreal ties.

ANDY STURGILL lives in suburban Philadelphia where he grew up rooting for Lenny Dykstra and the Macho Row Phillies. He enjoys reading and visiting ballparks with his wife, Carrie.

CECILIA TAN has been writing about baseball since her fourth grade book reports on the biographies of Willie Mays and Reggie Jackson. She is the author of *The 50 Greatest Yankees Games*, and her work has appeared in *Yankees Magazine, Gotham Baseball, Baseball Ink*, and *Baseball Prospectus*. She has served as SABR's Publications Director since 2011.

JOAN M. THOMAS is a freelance writer and long-time SABR member. Her published books on baseball include *St. Louis' Big League Ballparks* and *Baseball's First Lady*. She has also written a dozen biographies for SABR's BioProject web site. Following the St. Louis Cardinals while living in that city for decades, she moved back to her native Iowa in 2014. She is now engrossed in the research of baseball in that state.

CINDY THOMSON is a freelance writer and co-author of *Three Finger, The Mordecai Brown Story*, the biography of a Cubs Hall of Fame pitcher. She is also the author of a historical fiction series. The final novel, *Sofia's Tune*, released in 2015. She has written for SABR's BioProject, and contributed to several SABR publications including *Deadball Stars of the American League*, *Detroit Tigers 1984*, *New Century, New Team: The 1901 Boston Americans*, and *The Great Eight: The 1975 Cincinnati Reds*. A life-long Reds fan, she writes full time from her home in Central Ohio where she and her husband Tom raised three sons to root for Cincinnati. She also mentors writers and is a member of the American Christian Fiction Writers and the Historical Novel Society. Visit her online at: http://www.cindyswriting.com.

CLAYTON TRUTOR is a PhD candidate in US History at Boston College. His dissertation examines the politics and the cultural response to the arrival of professional sports in Atlanta. He teaches US History at Northeastern University in the College of Professional Studies. He has contributed to several SABR biographical projects and writes about college football for several blogs on SB Nation. You can follow him on twitter @ClaytonTrutor.

ALFONSO TUSA is a writer who was born in Cumaná, Venezuela and now writes a lot about baseball from Los Teques, Venezuela. He's the author *Una Temporada Mágica* (A magical season), *El Látigo del Beisbol. Una biografía de Isaías Látigo Chávez.* (The Whip of Baseball. An Isaías Látigo Chávez biography), *Pensando en ti Venezuela. Una biografía de Dámaso Blanco.* (Thinking about you Venezuela. A Dámaso Blanco biography) and *Voces de Beisbol y Ecología* (Voices of Baseball and Ecology). He contributes in some websites, books and newspapers. He shares many moments with his boy Miguelin.

NICK WADDELL is a graduate of Wayne State University and DePaul University College of Law. He's a lifelong Tigers fan, and previously wrote the biography on Al Kaline for *Sock It To 'Em Tigers*. He thinks a good baseball game involves peanuts, keeping score, and trying to decode the other team's signs.

JOSEPH WANCHO lives in Westlake, Ohio, and is a lifelong Cleveland Indians fan. He has been a SABR member since 2005. He serves as the chair of SABR's Minor Leagues Research Committee. He was the editor of the book *Pitching to the Pennant: The 1954 Cleveland Indians* (University of Nebraska Press, 2014).

STEVE WEST is a math nerd, a history nerd, and a wannabe writer. Combine these with his love of baseball and the SABR BioProject is right in his wheelhouse. Steve works as a data analyst in the energy industry, messing around with computers and numbers all day long, and comes home and does the same with baseball stats while watching Rangers games at night. Steve (a SABR member since 2006), his wife Marian and son Joshua are die-hard Rangers fans, which is one reason why Steve is now editor of a BioProject book on the 1972 Texas Rangers.

DAVE WILLIAMS is a lifelong Mets fan. He is currently a Territory Manager with Wilson Sporting Goods in Glastonbury, Connecticut where he resides with his wife and daughter. They do not understand how he can agonize over the Mets' lack of offense year after year.

SAUL WISNIA still recalls being chased to his Syracuse dorm room by taunting Mets fans after Game Seven of the 1986 World Series, and then waking up to a door plastered with jubilant *Daily News* headlines. He recovered to write numerous books on Boston baseball, including *Fenway Park: The Centennial, Miracle at Fenway*, and *For the Love of the Boston Red Sox*. He's also been a sports and news correspondent at the *Washington Post*, a feature writer for the *Boston Herald*, and a contributor to numerous SABR publications, the *Boston Globe*, and *Sports Illustrated*. Since 1999, he has chronicled the Red Sox-Jimmy Fund relationship as senior publications editor-writer at Dana-Farber Cancer Institute, where his office sits 300 yards from Fenway Park.

A lifelong Pirates fan, **GREGORY H. WOLF** was born in Pittsburgh, but now resides in the Chicagoland area with his wife, Margaret, and daughter, Gabriela. A Professor of German Studies and holder of the Dennis and Jean Bauman Endowed Chair in the Humanities at North Central College in Naperville, Illinois, he edited the SABR books *"Thar's Joy in Braveland." The 1957 Milwaukee Braves* (2014), *Winning on the North Side. The 1929 Chicago Cubs* (2015), and *A Pennant for the Twins Cities: The 1965 Minnesota Twins* (2015). He is currently working on a project about the Houston Astrodome and co-editing a book with Bill Nowlin on the 1979 Pittsburgh Pirates.

ALLAN WOOD has written about sports, music, and politics for numerous magazines and newspapers for 35 years. He is the author of *Babe Ruth and the 1918 Red Sox* and the co-author of *Don't Let Us Win Tonight: An Oral History of the 2004 Boston Red Sox's Impossible Playoff Run.* He has also written The Joy of Sox blog since 2003, and has contributed—as a writer or editor—to five books published by SABR. He lives in Mississauga, Ontario, Canada.

JACK ZERBY grew up following the Pirates. Writing about the Mets' late-season visit to Three Rivers Stadium in 1986 brought back memories of Fan Appreciation Day at old Forbes Field. Jack joined SABR in 1994 and co-founded the Seymour-Mills Chapter in southwest Florida. Now retired from law practice and work as a trusts/estates administrator, he lives in Brevard, North Carolina, with his wife Diana, a professional violinist.

THE SABR DIGITAL LIBRARY

The Society for American Baseball Research, the top baseball research organization in the world, disseminates some of the best in baseball history, analysis, and biography through our publishing programs. The SABR Digital Library contains a mix of books old and new, and focuses on a tandem program of paperback and ebook publication, making these materials widely available for both on digital devices and as traditional printed books.

GREATEST GAMES BOOKS

BRAVES FIELD:
MEMORABLE MOMENTS AT BOSTON'S LOST DIAMOND
From its opening on August 18, 1915, to the sudden departure of the Boston Braves to Milwaukee before the 1953 baseball season, Braves Field was home to Boston's National League baseball club and also hosted many other events: from NFL football to championship boxing. The most memorable moments to occur in Braves Field history are portrayed here.
Edited by Bill Nowlin and Bob Brady
$19.95 paperback (ISBN 978-1-933599-93-9)
$9.99 ebook (ISBN 978-1-933599-92-2)
8.5"X11", 282 pages, 182 photos

INVENTING BASEBALL: THE 100 GREATEST
GAMES OF THE NINETEENTH CENTURY
SABR's Nineteenth Century Committee brings to life the greatest games from the game's early years. From the "prisoner of war" game that took place among captive Union soldiers during the Civil War (immortalized in a famous lithograph), to the first intercollegiate game (Amherst versus Williams), to the first professional no-hitter, the games in this volume span 1833–1900 and detail the athletic exploits of such players as Cap Anson, Moses "Fleetwood" Walker, Charlie Comiskey, and Mike "King" Kelly.
Edited by Bill Felber
$19.95 paperback (ISBN 978-1-933599-42-7)
$9.99 ebook (ISBN 978-1-933599-43-4)
8"x10", 302 pages, 200 photos

BIOPROJECT BOOKS

WHO'S ON FIRST:
REPLACEMENT PLAYERS IN WORLD WAR II
During World War II, 533 players made the major league debuts. More than 60% of the players in the 1941 Opening Day lineups departed for the service and were replaced by first-times and oldsters. Hod Lisenbee was 46. POW Bert Shepard had an artificial leg, and Pete Gray had only one arm. The 1944 St. Louis Browns had 13 players classified 4-F. These are their stories.
Edited by Marc Z Aaron and Bill Nowlin
$19.95 paperback (ISBN 978-1-933599-91-5)
$9.99 ebook (ISBN 978-1-933599-90-8)
8.5"X11", 422 pages, 67 photos

VAN LINGLE MUNGO:
THE MAN, THE SONG, THE PLAYERS
Although the Red Sox spent most of the 1950s far out of contention, the team was filled with fascinating players who captured the heart of their fans. In *Red Sox Baseball*, members of SABR present 46 biographies on players such as Ted Williams and Pumpsie Green as well as season-by-season recaps.
Edited by Bill Nowlin
$19.95 paperback (ISBN 978-1-933599-76-2)
$9.99 ebook (ISBN 978-1-933599-77-9)
8.5"X11", 278 pages, 46 photos

ORIGINAL SABR RESEARCH

CALLING THE GAME:
BASEBALL BROADCASTING FROM 1920 TO THE PRESENT
An exhaustive, meticulously researched history of bringing the national pastime out of the ballparks and into living rooms via the airwaves. Every play-by-play announcer, color commentator, and ex-ballplayer, every broadcast deal, radio station, and TV network. Plus a foreword by "Voice of the Chicago Cubs" Pat Hughes, and an afterword by Jacques Doucet, the "Voice of the Montreal Expos" 1972-2004.
by Stuart Shea
$24.95 paperback (ISBN 978-1-933599-40-3)
$9.99 ebook (ISBN 978-1-933599-41-0)
7"X10", 712 pages, 40 photos

BASEBALL IN THE SPACE AGE:
HOUSTON SINCE 1961
Here we have a special issue of *The National Pastime* centered almost entirely on the Houston Astros (né Colt .45s) and their two influential and iconic homes, short-lived Colt Stadium and the Astrodome. If you weren't able to attend the SABR convention in Houston, please enjoy this virtual trip tour of baseball in "Space City" through 18 articles.
Edited by Cecilia M. Tan
$14.95 paperback (ISBN 978-1-933599-65-6)
$9.99 ebook (ISBN 978-1-933599-66-3)
8.5"x11", 96 pages, 49 photos

NORTH SIDE, SOUTH SIDE, ALL AROUND
THE TOWN:BASEBALL IN CHICAGO
The National Pastime provides in-depth articles focused on the geographic region where the national SABR convention is taking place annually. The SABR 45 convention took place in Chicago, and here are 45 articles on baseball in and around the bat-and-ball crazed Windy City: 25 that appeared in the souvenir book of the convention plus another 20 articles available in ebook only.
Edited by Stuart Shea
$14.95 paperback (ISBN 978-1-933599-87-8)
$9.99 ebook (ISBN 978-1-933599-86-1)
8.5"X11", 282 pages, 47 photos

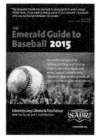

THE EMERALD GUIDE TO BASEBALL: 2015
The Emerald Guide to Baseball fills the gap in the historical record created by the demise of *The Sporting News Baseball Guide*. First published in 1942, *The Sporting News* Guide was truly the annual book of record for our National Pastime. The 2015 edition of the *Emerald Guide* runs more than 600 pages and covers the 2014 season; it also includes a 2015 directory of every franchise, rosters, minor league affiliates, and career leaders for all teams.
Edited by Gary Gillette and Pete Palmer
$24.95 paperback (ISBN 978-0-9817929-8-9)
8.5"X11", 610 pages

SABR Members can purchase each book at a significant discount (often 50% off) and receive the ebook edtions free as a member benefit. Each book is available in a trade paperback edition as well as ebooks suitable for reading on a home computer or Nook, Kindle, or iPad/tablet.
To learn more about becoming a member of SABR, visit the website: sabr.org/join

SABR BioProject Books

In 2002, the Society for American Baseball Research launched an effort to write and publish biographies of every player, manager, and individual who has made a contribution to baseball. Over the past decade, the BioProject Committee has produced over 3,400 biographical articles. Many have been part of efforts to create theme- or team-oriented books, spearheaded by chapters or other committees of SABR.

A PENNANT FOR THE TWIN CITIES:
THE 1965 MINNESOTA TWINS
This volume celebrates the 1965 Minnesota Twins, who captured the American League pennant in just their fifth season in the Twin Cities. Led by an All-Star cast, from Harmon Killebrew, Tony Oliva, Zoilo Versalles, and Mudcat Grant to Bob Allison, Jim Kaat, Earl Battey, and Jim Perry, the Twins won 102 games, but bowed to the Los Angeles Dodgers and Sandy Koufax in Game Seven
Edited by Gregory H. Wolf
$19.95 paperback (ISBN 978-1-943816-09-5)
$9.99 ebook (ISBN 978-1-943816-08-8)
8.5"X11", 405 pages, over 80 photos

MUSTACHES AND MAYHEM: CHARLIE O'S THREE TIME CHAMPIONS:
THE OAKLAND ATHLETICS: 1972-74
The Oakland Athletics captured major league baseball's crown each year from 1972 through 1974. Led by future Hall of Famers Reggie Jackson, Catfish Hunter and Rollie Fingers, the Athletics were a largely homegrown group who came of age together. Biographies of every player, coach, manager, and broadcaster (and mascot) from 1972 through 1974 are included, along with season recaps.
Edited by Chip Greene
$29.95 paperback (ISBN 978-1-943816-07-1)
$9.99 ebook (ISBN 978-1-943816-06-4)
8.5"X11", 600 pages, almost 100 photos

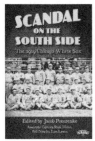

SCANDAL ON THE SOUTH SIDE:
THE 1919 CHICAGO WHITE SOX
The Black Sox Scandal isn't the only story worth telling about the 1919 Chicago White Sox. The team roster included three future Hall of Famers, a 20-year-old spitballer who would win 300 games in the minors, and even a batboy who later became a celebrity with the "Murderers' Row" New York Yankees. All of their stories are included in Scandal on the South Side with a timeline of the 1919 season.
Edited by Jacob Pomrenke
$19.95 paperback (ISBN 978-1-933599-95-3)
$9.99 ebook (ISBN 978-1-933599-94-6)
8.5"x11", 324 pages, 55 historic photos

WINNING ON THE NORTH SIDE
THE 1929 CHICAGO CUBS
Celebrate the 1929 Chicago Cubs, one of the most exciting teams in baseball history. Future Hall of Famers Hack Wilson, '29 NL MVP Rogers Hornsby, and Kiki Cuyler, along with Riggs Stephenson formed one of the most potent quartets in baseball history. The magical season came to an ignominious end in the World Series and helped craft the future "lovable loser" image of the team.
Edited by Gregory H. Wolf
$19.95 paperback (ISBN 978-1-933599-89-2)
$9.99 ebook (ISBN 978-1-933599-88-5)
8.5"x11", 314 pages, 59 photos

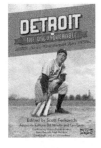

DETROIT THE UNCONQUERABLE:
THE 1935 WORLD CHAMPION TIGERS
Biographies of every player, coach, and broadcaster involved with the 1935 World Champion Detroit Tigers baseball team, written by members of the Society for American Baseball Research. Also includes a season in review and other articles about the 1935 team. Hank Greenberg, Mickey Cochrane, Charlie Gehringer, Schoolboy Rowe, and more.
Edited by Scott Ferkovich
$19.95 paperback (ISBN 9978-1-933599-78-6)
$9.99 ebook (ISBN 978-1-933599-79-3)
8.5"X11", 230 pages, 52 photos

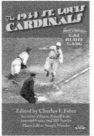

THE 1934 ST. LOUIS CARDINALS:
THE WORLD CHAMPION GAS HOUSE GANG
The 1934 St. Louis Cardinals were one of the most colorful crews ever to play the National Pastime. Some of were aging stars, past their prime, and others were youngsters, on their way up, but together they comprised a championship ball club. Pepper Martin, Dizzy and Paul Dean, Joe Medwick, Frankie Frisch and more are all included here.
Edited by Charles F. Faber
$19.95 paperback (ISBN 978-1-933599-73-1)
$9.99 ebook (ISBN 978-1-933599-74-8)
8.5"X11", 282 pages, 47 photos

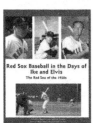

RED SOX BASEBALL IN THE DAYS OF IKE AND ELVIS: THE RED SOX OF THE 1950S
Although the Red Sox spent most of the 1950s far out of contention, the team was filled with fascinating players who captured the heart of their fans. In *Red Sox Baseball*, members of SABR present 46 biographies on players such as Ted Williams and Pumpsie Green as well as season-by-season recaps.
Edited by Mark Armour and Bill Nowlin
$19.95 paperback (ISBN 978-1-933599-24-3)
$9.99 ebook (ISBN 978-1-933599-34-2)
8.5"X11", 372 pages, over 100 photos

THE MIRACLE BRAVES OF 1914
BOSTON'S ORIGINAL WORST-TO-FIRST CHAMPIONS
Long before the Red Sox "Impossible Dream" season, Boston's now nearly forgotten "other" team, the 1914 Boston Braves, performed a baseball "miracle" that resounds to this very day. The "Miracle Braves" were Boston's first "worst-to-first" winners of the World Series. Includes biographies of every player, coach, and owner, a season recap, and other great stories from the 1914 season.
Edited by Bill Nowlin
$19.95 paperback (ISBN 978-1-933599-69-4)
$9.99 ebook (ISBN 978-1-933599-70-0)
8.5"X11", 392 pages, over 100 photos

SABR Members can purchase each book at a significant discount (often 50% off) and receive the ebook edtions free as a member benefit. Each book is available in a trade paperback edition as well as ebooks suitable for reading on a home computer or Nook, Kindle, or iPad/tablet.
To learn more about becoming a member of SABR, visit the website: sabr.org/join

Society for American Baseball Research

Cronkite School at ASU
555 N. Central Ave. #416, Phoenix, AZ 85004
602.496.1460 (phone)
SABR.org

Become a SABR member today!

If you're interested in baseball — writing about it, reading about it, talking about it — there's a place for you in the Society for American Baseball Research. Our members include everyone from academics to professional sportswriters to amateur historians and statisticians to students and casual fans who enjoy reading about baseball and occasionally gathering with other members to talk baseball. What unites all SABR members is an interest in the game and joy in learning more about it.

SABR membership is open to any baseball fan; we offer 1-year and 3-year memberships. Here's a list of some of the key benefits you'll receive as a SABR member:

- Receive two editions (spring and fall) of the *Baseball Research Journal*, our flagship publication
- Receive expanded e-book edition of *The National Pastime*, our annual convention journal
- 8-10 new e-books published by the SABR Digital Library, all FREE to members
- "This Week in SABR" e-newsletter, sent to members every Friday
- Join dozens of research committees, from Statistical Analysis to Women in Baseball.
- Join one of 70 regional chapters in the U.S., Canada, Latin America, and abroad
- Participate in online discussion groups
- Ask and answer baseball research questions on the SABR-L e-mail listserv
- Complete archives of *The Sporting News* dating back to 1886 and other research resources
- Promote your research in "This Week in SABR"
- Diamond Dollars Case Competition
- Yoseloff Scholarships

- Discounts on SABR national conferences, including the SABR National Convention, the SABR Analytics Conference, Jerry Malloy Negro League Conference, Frederick Ivor-Campbell 19th Century Conference
- Publish your research in peer-reviewed SABR journals
- Collaborate with SABR researchers and experts
- Contribute to Baseball Biography Project or the SABR Games Project
- List your new book in the SABR Bookshelf
- Lead a SABR research committee or chapter
- Networking opportunities at SABR Analytics Conference
- Meet baseball authors and historians at SABR events and chapter meetings
- 50% discounts on paperback versions of SABR e-books
- 20% discount on MLB.TV and MiLB.TV subscriptions
- Discounts with other partners in the baseball community
- SABR research awards

We hope you'll join the most passionate international community of baseball fans at SABR! Check us out online at SABR.org/join.

SABR MEMBERSHIP FORM

	Annual	3-year	Senior	3-yr Sr.	Under 30
U.S.:	❑ $65	❑ $175	❑ $45	❑ $129	❑ $45
Canada/Mexico:	❑ $75	❑ $205	❑ $55	❑ $159	❑ $55
Overseas:	❑ $84	❑ $232	❑ $64	❑ $186	❑ $55

Add a Family Member: $15 each family member at same address (list names on back)

Senior: 65 or older before 12/31 of the current year

All dues amounts in U.S. dollars or equivalent

Participate in Our Donor Program!

Support the preservation of baseball research. Designate your gift toward:
❑ General Fund ❑ Endowment Fund ❑ Research Resources ❑ _____
❑ I want to maximize the impact of my gift; do not send any donor premiums
❑ I would like this gift to remain anonymous.

Note: Any donation not designated will be placed in the General Fund.
SABR is a 501 (c) (3) not-for-profit organization & donations are tax-deductible to the extent allowed by law.

Name _____

E-mail* _____

Address _____

City _____ ST_____ ZIP_____

Phone _____ Birthday _____

* Your e-mail address on file ensures you will receive the most recent SABR news.

Dues $_____

Donation $_____

Amount Enclosed $_____

Do you work for a matching grant corporation? Call (602) 496-1460 for details.

If you wish to pay by credit card, please contact the SABR office at (602) 496-1460 or visit the SABR Store online at SABR.org/join. We accept Visa, Mastercard & Discover.

Do you wish to receive the *Baseball Research Journal* electronically?: ❑ Yes ❑ No

Our e-books are available in PDF, Kindle, or EPUB (iBooks, iPad, Nook) formats.

Mail to: SABR, Cronkite School at ASU, 555 N. Central Ave. #416, Phoenix, AZ 85004

Made in the USA
Middletown, DE
14 July 2021